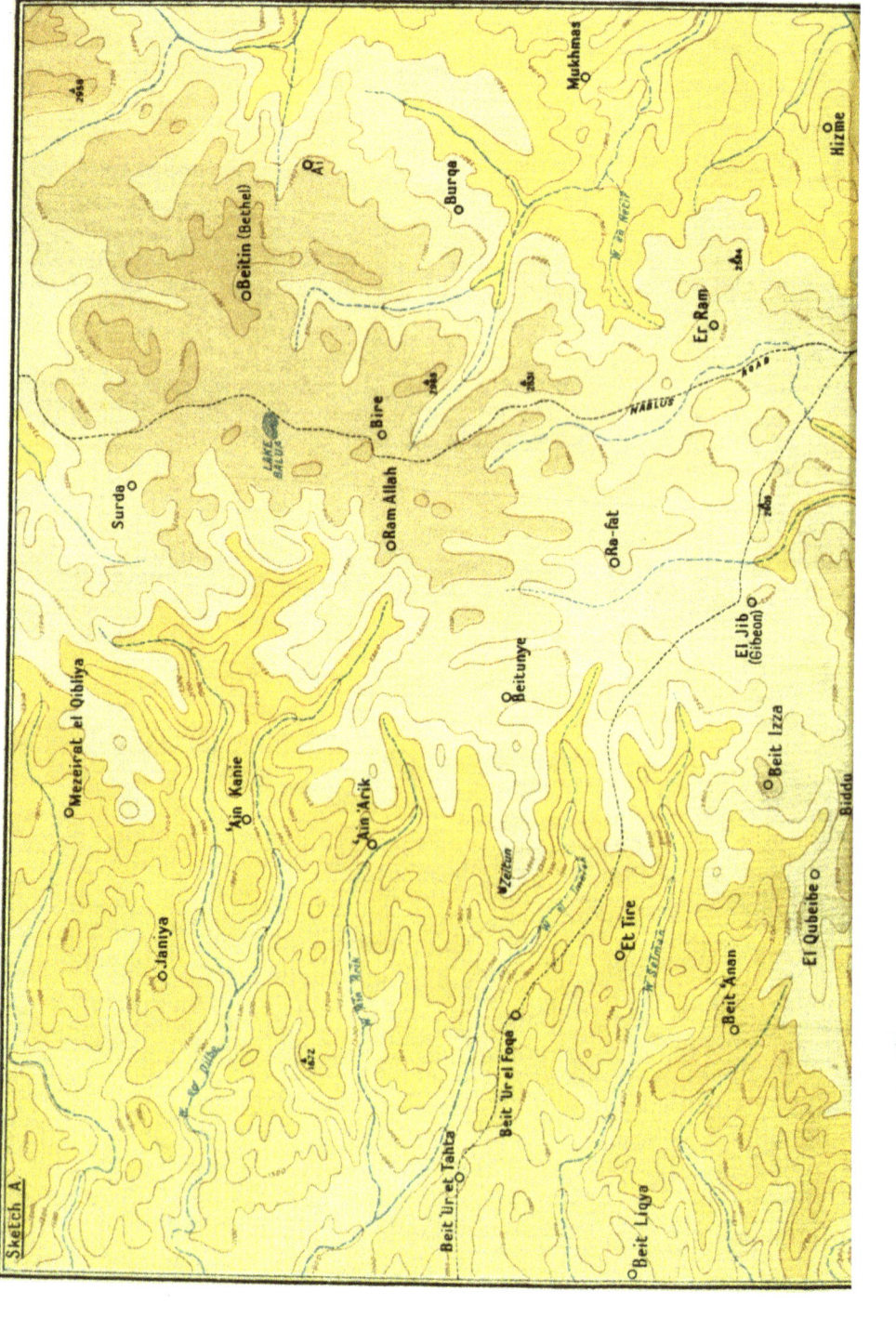

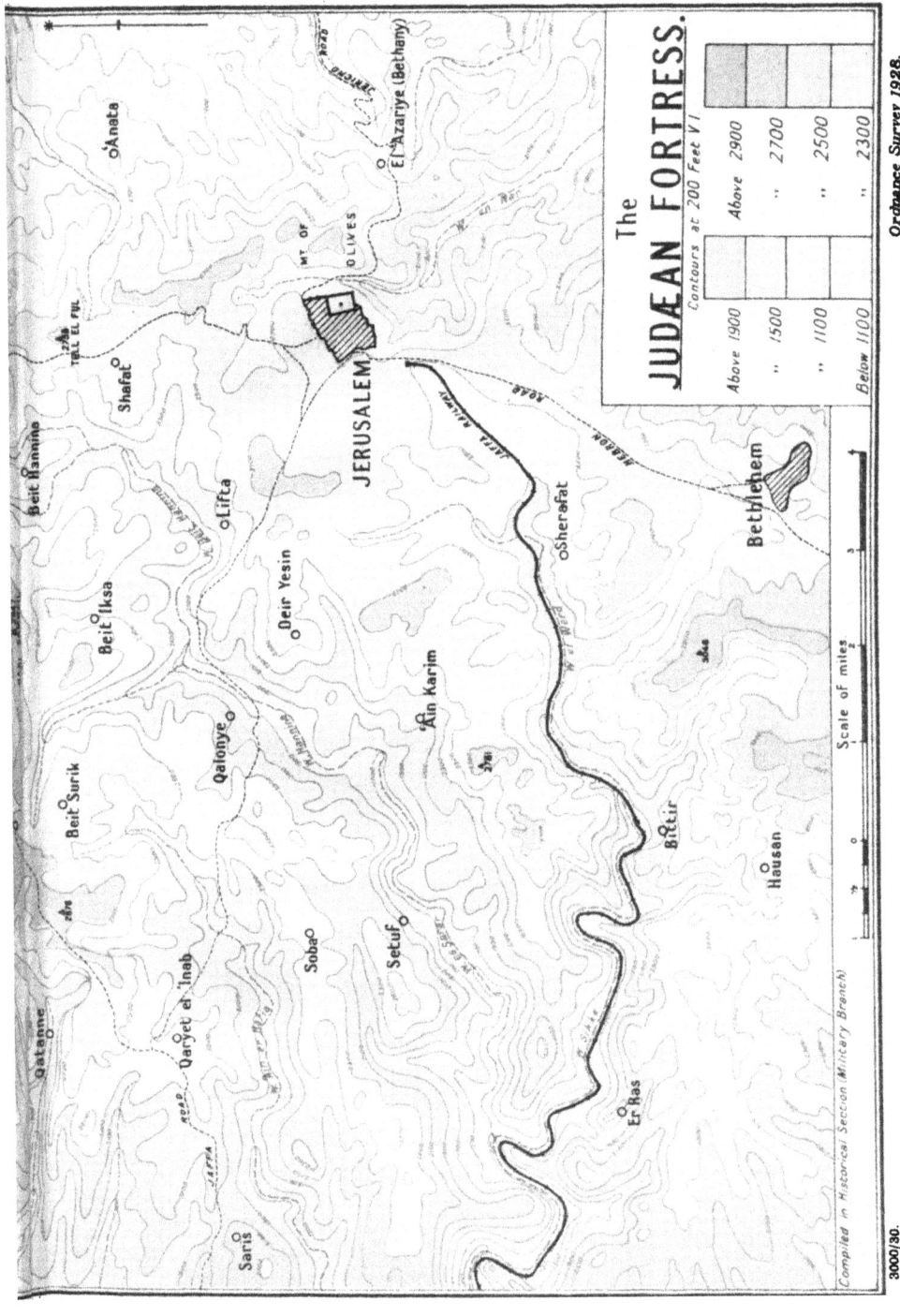

History of the Great War.

MILITARY OPERATIONS.

[*Crown Copyright Reserved*]

# HISTORY OF THE GREAT WAR
BASED ON OFFICIAL DOCUMENTS
BY DIRECTION OF THE HISTORICAL SECTION OF THE
COMMITTEE OF IMPERIAL DEFENCE

# MILITARY OPERATIONS EGYPT & PALESTINE

FROM JUNE 1917 TO THE
END OF THE WAR

Part I

COMPILED BY
Captain CYRIL FALLS
LATE R. INNIS. FUS. AND GENERAL STAFF

MAPS COMPILED BY
Major A. F. BECKE
R.A. (RETIRED), HON. M.A. (OXON.)

The Naval & Military Press Ltd

Published by
**The Naval & Military Press Ltd**
5 Riverside, Brambleside, Bellbrook
Industrial Estate, Uckfield, East Sussex,
TN22 1QQ England
Tel: +44 (0) 1825 749494
Fax: +44 (0) 1825 765701
www.naval-military-press.com
www.military-genealogy.com
www.militarymaproom.com

*In reprinting in facsimile from the original, any imperfections are inevitably reproduced and the quality may fall short of modern type and cartographic standards.*

# PREFACE.

The narrative of the British operations in Egypt, Palestine, and Syria is here completed. The first volume carried the record to June 1917, when General Sir Edmund Allenby was appointed to the command of the Egyptian Expeditionary Force; this brings it to the conclusion of the Armistice with Turkey, and also contains a very brief account of measures taken to enforce the terms of the Armistice and a few words upon the administration of the country occupied as a result of the campaign.

Once it had been laid down that the history was to be completed in two volumes, the limits of each were obvious and almost inevitable : the " Maxwell " period of defence and the " Murray " period of the reconquest of Sinai and the establishment of the Army within the Palestine frontier belonged naturally to the first volume; the " Allenby " period of the conquest of Palestine and Syria to the second. This demarcation had, however, the inconvenience that the second volume had to bear the burden of all the continuous large-scale operations. The offensive at Gaza and Beersheba and the subsequent battles in the Judæan Hills for the capture and in defence of Jerusalem lasted from the end of October to the end of December 1917, without a breathing-space. In February 1918 began the operations in the Jordan Valley, first the capture of Jericho, then the two raids into Trans-Jordan, with important engagements between them, lasting until the 4th May. Here there is for the first time a real break; for the summer was occupied in reorganization, and except for one action in the Jordan Valley in July the front was quiet until the final offensive, which began on the 19th September and lasted until the 30th October, the date of the Armistice. As a result, whereas in the first volume there were many months out of the three years covered which could be dismissed in a few lines or a paragraph, the events of this period have in great part to be described from day to day.

The rigid compression thus made necessary was found all the more difficult because of the interesting character of the operations and of the country. Here is a campaign fought almost entirely by the troops of Great Britain and of the Empire—and in which almost all the Empire but Canada had part—in a theatre large enough, in proportion to the number of troops engaged, for manœuvre; filled with spectacular episodes which were absent from the battlefields of France, and resulting in brilliant and overwhelming victory. The country is not only sacred ground, but from the point of view of early political and military history the most important in the world, with the most ancient records, which have been analysed by the greatest and most diverse scholarship. The coast plain of Palestine was for thousands of years the military highway between Egypt on the one hand, Asia and Europe on the other. Up and down it in the course of their endless wars and invasions swept Egyptians, Babylonians Assyrians, Philistines, Persians, Phœnicians, Greeks, Romans, Arabs, Crusaders, Turks—unconscious potters whose clay was mankind, the thumpings of whose bloody hands may still be traced in our destinies. Among the predecessors of Lord Allenby and General von Falkenhayn in Palestine and Syria are Thothmes III, Rameses II, Ashurbanipal, Alexander, Titus, Saladin and Richard of England, Baibars, Tamerlane, Selim, and Napoleon. They are perhaps the most celebrated of the warriors, but a page could be filled with the names of others of no mean fame.

The compiler of this volume was urged by a number of military friends and correspondents to concentrate upon, (a) an accurate and detailed account of the tactical operations; (b) a careful record of supply and transport, which was, according to his advisers of this school of thought, the most important feature of the campaign; (c) the more personal and individual side, the " human interest," which undoubtedly was to be found in abundance if there were space to record it; (d) the historical and spiritual associations of Palestine. He made an effort to content them all, without much hope that this was possible. But he had to bear in mind that the first aspect, and the second in only slightly lesser degree, were what he had been officially set to bring out. They could not be neglected. For the others

## PREFACE

he did what he could and, in particular, made notes of the footprints of the Crusaders when he came upon them. The Crusaders' castles, also, have been shown on a number of maps and sketches. How hard it is to please all is proved by letters from two critics on the same chapters. One declares that these chapters gave him the impression of " great technical accuracy with distinct lack of atmosphere," while the other suggests cutting out the " verbiage " about people and events so that a fuller account of operations may take its place. It is to be feared that only the most severely conscientious students will sympathize with the second critic. As for the first, the writer has every sympathy with him, but was too often unable to comply with his wishes owing to being cribbed within the bars of his allotted space. Yet in the end those bars had to be broken. It had to be recognized that the British official histories are a compromise between the needs of the Staff College student and those of the general public, that both must be treated as fairly as possible, and that if this were done the volume would be far larger than the average. It was therefore eventually decided to publish it in two parts in order not to produce a clumsy-looking and unwieldy book.

With regard to the material, the British records are generally good. This is particularly true of the final offensive, those of the cavalry being especially excellent, and the brigade narratives of the 4th Cavalry Division, illustrated by photographs and wash drawings as well as maps, the best that the writer has ever had the fortune to see. The records of the French infantry brigade for the short period in which it is concerned were so full that no application to Paris was necessary, but for the cavalry regiment the Historical Section of the French War Office has been good enough to supply a copy of the war diary for September 1918. A few war diaries were lost when ships which were carrying them home were sunk by submarines in the Mediterranean, but these have as a rule been adequately replaced by narratives written by the brigade commanders. A far greater difficulty has been that of plotting the positions of units, due to the lack of detail on the maps in use during the greater proportion of the campaign. After the front had become fixed a contoured survey, on a scale of 1/40,000, was carried out up to the line held in the summer of 1918, and for some miles north of this maps were printed, on the same scale, based on aeroplane photographs and the old Conder-Kitchener survey.[1] The new survey has been used for the maps and larger-scale sketches in this volume, but the reader must remember that it was not available during the earlier operations. The maps of Trans-Jordan were very poor. The labour and skill of Major A. F. Becke, who has made use of aeroplane photographs, of plans and sketches in travellers' books, and of the originals in Conder's "Survey of Palestine"—which are superior to the reproductions—have been particularly valuable here. The layered map of Trans-Jordan (Map 16) is from the topographical point of view by far the best ever published of the Jordan Valley just north of the Dead Sea and the country eastward as far as 'Amman. Sketches of actions during the pursuit to Damascus and Aleppo, such as the capture of Samakh and the Affair of Haritan, have been taken from sketches in the records, made at the time by engineers attached to the formations concerned.

Chapters in draft have been circulated to over five hundred officers who took part in the campaign. The compiler is deeply indebted to many of them for criticisms and suggestions, and can only regret that he has not been able to use to an even greater extent the material which they have supplied. "A Brief Record of the Advance of "the Egyptian Expeditionary Force," an official work first published in Egypt just after the Armistice and reprinted in 1919 by H.M. Stationery Office, has been constantly consulted. Volume VII of the official Australian history, by Mr. H. S. Gullett, has also proved of great value.

From the enemy's side the records are fair. By far the best is the semi-official Turkish work "*Yilderim*,"[2] by Lieut.-Colonel Hussein Husni Amir, which has a large

---

[1] These maps are all the more reliable because Conder's trigonometrical heights may be considered absolutely accurate, while the numerous heights which he took with an aneroid are correct within about 20 feet. It must be added that complaints of the Conder survey came mainly from the younger officers, brought up upon the luxury of contoured maps which their seniors scarcely knew.

[2] This is in Turkish, and there is no published translation. There is a less important German work of the same name, of which some use has been made. They are referred to as Turkish and German "*Yilderim*" respectively.

number of maps. Soon after the capture of Jerusalem his detailed narrative ends, but is continued by that of General Liman von Sanders, which, though much briefer and almost unprovided with maps, is also useful. The volumes of " Zwischen Kaukasus und Sinai " (referred to as " Sinai ") have again been consulted. Of the mass of documents captured at Turkish G.H.Q. on the 20th September 1918, some of the most important were printed by the British Intelligence and have been preserved. The replies made by the Historical Section of the Turkish War Office to a questionaire addressed to it just after the war have been useful. By the courtesy of General Freiherr Mertz von Quirheim, Director of the German *Reichsarchiv*, the compiler has been provided with copies of the most significant wireless reports sent to Germany by Generals von Falkenhayn and Liman von Sanders, of the complete war diary of the German *703rd Battalion* during the First Trans-Jordan Raid, and of the diaries of *Yilderim* and the *Asia Corps* during the final British offensive.

A tabular record of the battles and actions of the campaign has been included among the appendices, as in the previous volume. The numbers of the troops engaged on either side are only approximate, and often it has been as hard to ascertain those of the British as those of the enemy. It is, in fact, a strange result of the complication of modern warfare and its wastefulness of man-power that we find it easier in many cases to record the number of men who took part in battles of the Napoleonic Wars than it is to do so for the wars of our own time. In some cases during the Palestine campaigns the rifle strength of a division was telegraphed home as being about 9,000 at a time when its battalions were only 400 strong in action.

The parts played by the Navy and Royal Air Force have been recorded in detail sufficient only to explain their influence upon military operations. Their own official histories have appeared or are in course of publication. Histories of the Medical and Veterinary Services have also appeared, and have been drawn upon when necessary.

As in all the volumes issued by the Branch, two sets of maps have been prepared. Those of one series, described as " sketches," are bound in the volume ; the larger " maps " are issued separately. The sketches, again, are of two sorts : strategical or situation sketches, which are on a small scale, and tactical, which illustrate actions decided upon a limited area of ground. Owing to the length of the operations, many days of important fighting have not been indicated on the maps. Often where there was a struggle lasting several days but with little movement, as in the operations north of Beersheba and the Battle of Nabi Samweil, the maps have been marked to show the situation at an early stage only. This has seemed preferable to the system often employed by Continental historians of covering the maps with a bewildering succession of arrows indicating successive attacks, counter-attacks, and retirements. To make the general reader more or less independent of the map volume, a general map of Palestine as far north as Nablus and Tul Karm (Map 2) has been placed in a pocket at the end of the first part of the text. Since, however, this is a campaign wherein the last blow (at Haritan) was struck 370 miles away from the first (at Beersheba) [1] and active operations were in progress for over eight months, he cannot expect to find all the names mentioned in the text unless he purchases also the map volume. All the maps and sketches, with the exception of three reprints from official publications (Maps 2, 2A, and 3), have been compiled under the supervision of Major A. F. Becke, and drawn by Mr. J. S. Fenton, late R.E., the principal draughtsman attached to the Branch. The excellence of the reproduction is due to the careful and thorough methods of the Ordnance Survey at Southampton.

Thomas Hardy's poem, " Jezreel," which appears in Chapter XXIV, was when published in *The Times* marked " No copyright," the author evidently desiring that it should be reproduced by any one desiring to do so ; and Mrs. Hardy has expressed her pleasure that it should be reprinted in this book. It is included in " Late Lyrics and " Earlier " and the " Collected Poems."

Acknowledgment must be made to the Air Ministry for having specially taken a series of photographs of the ground about Et Tafila on which the sketch of the Arab action there is based, and to an officer whose name is un-

---

[1] If we consider the Arab operations outlined in the volume, the Wadi Hamdh bridges near Medina, attacked in May 1918, are some 750 miles from Muslimiya Station, occupied on the 29th October.

## PREFACE

known to the writer for the drawing of the Maghar position, made on a recent staff tour. The photographs reproduced, other than those marked as the copyright of the Imperial War Museum, the Royal Air Force, and the Australian War Museum,[1] and that of the Wadi el Far'a, which was sent by an officer of the South African Defence Force, were taken by the writer himself.

The writer has worked entirely without an assistant in reading, analysing, and co-ordinating the vast quantity of material available for this volume, so has no acknowledgment to make on that score, while the blame for errors and imperfections must fall upon his head alone. He is, however, indebted to Major Becke in respect of several historical allusions; also to Mr. W. B. Wood, M.A., late of Worcester College, and Mr. C. T. Atkinson, of Exeter College, for their painstaking revision of the final text.

*July* 1930.  C. B. F.

## NOTES.

THE convention commonly observed in the British Army regarding the distinguishing numbers of Armies, Corps, Divisions, etc., is here followed. That is to say, they are written in full for Armies, in Roman figures for Corps, in Arabic figures for smaller formations and units. The customary Roman figures are employed for Artillery Brigades and Heavy Artillery Groups for numbers up to one hundred, Arabic figures being used for higher numbers. We have thus XX Corps, 60th Division, 4th Cavalry Division, 180th Infantry Brigade (in which the word "Infantry" is always omitted unless the context demands that the formation shall be distinguished from a cavalry brigade), 10th Cavalry Brigade, LXVII Brigade R.F.A.; but 301st Brigade R.F.A.

Turkish and German formations and units, to distinguish them from British, are printed in italic characters, thus: *Seventh Army, XX Corps, Asia Corps, 7th Division, 21st Regiment.*

Abbreviations of regimental names are employed: for example, " 4/K.O.S.B." for 1st/4th Battalion the King's Own Scottish Borderers. With Indian Regiments, where the number forms part of the title and does not merely indicate the number of the battalion, this convention is not used, and we have therefore " 53rd Sikhs," " 1/8th Gurkha " Rifles " or " 1/8th Gurkhas." Second-line Territorial battalion titles are written thus: " 2/4th Queen's." The titles of the Australian Light Horse Brigades are abbreviated to " L.H. Brigade," and those of the Australian Light Horse Regiments to " A.L.H." ; that of the New Zealand Mounted Rifles Brigade to " N.Z.M.R. Brigade " or " New Zealand " Brigade." G.H.Q. for General Headquarters and E.E.F. for Egyptian Expeditionary Force hardly require explanation.

The spelling of Arabic, Hebrew, and Turkish place-names has been taken from the lists compiled for Palestine,

Syria, and Trans-Jordan by the " Permanent Committee " on Geographical Names for British Official Use," so far as these apply. The optional long accent (-) has been omitted from the long vowels, but the inverted comma ('), representing the Arabic letter ع and the Hebrew ע, has been retained. Some officers who have read the chapters in typescript have strongly criticized this method of spelling and complained that the place-names have an unfamiliar appearance. It is hard to believe, to take half a dozen instances at random, that El Buggar will prove unrecognizable as El Baqqar, Beitunia as Beitunye, Arak el Menshiyeh as 'Iraq el Menshiye, Mejdel as Majdal, Kalkilie has Qalqilye, or even Esdud as Sdud. The " Army " spellings might have stood had they been consistent ; as they were not, it has seemed best to follow the most scientific system of transliteration throughout. In the very rare cases where there may be difficulty in distinguishing a well-known name, an explanatory footnote has been added. It must be remembered that some of the conventional forms are due merely to the fact that most people do not pronounce an " r " before a consonant in the same syllable. The official form Tul Karm is spelt as a Scotsman—perhaps a stage Scotsman—would pronounce it ; the conventional Tul Keram must have been devised to help the weaker Southron.

It having been pointed out to the compiler that the forms " Djemal," " Djevad " of the well-known Turkish proper names, which were used in the previous volume, represented merely French attempts to pronounce the equivalent of an English hard " J," and were contrary to modern English usage, they have been abandoned in this volume in favour of " Jemal " and " Jevad."

A list of place-name meanings with a glossary of words found in place-name components is placed at the end of the first part. These lists were compiled by Major A. F. Becke and Mr. J. S. Fenton, and checked by the Director-General of the Survey of Egypt, to whom the compiler is deeply indebted.

CONTENTS.

PART I.

CHAPTER I.

THE SITUATION OF THE COMBATANTS IN THE SUMMER OF 1917.

|  | PAGE |
|---|---|
| Indecision of the Turks | 1 |
| Sir Philip Chetwode's Appreciation | 7 |
| Sir Edmund Allenby's Requirements | 12 |
| Transport and Water Supply | 17 |
| *Note*: Turkish Reinforcements in Palestine | 25 |

CHAPTER II.

THE EVE OF THE OFFENSIVE.

| The Plan of Attack | 25 |
| Beersheba: the Turkish Dispositions and Strength | 33 |
| The Concentration: the Attack on the Yeomanry Mounted Division | 36 |
| *Note*: Falkenhayn's Intentions | 42 |

CHAPTER III.

THE CAPTURE OF BEERSHEBA.

| The Approach March of the XX Corps | 44 |
| The Attack of the XX Corps | 48 |
| The Approach March of the Desert Mounted Corps | 52 |
| The Attack of the Desert Mounted Corps | 55 |
| *Note*: Kress and Ismet Bey | 61 |

CHAPTER IV.

THE ATTACK ON THE GAZA DEFENCES.

| The Plan of Attack and Preliminary Bombardment | 63 |
| The Attack | 69 |
| *Note*: The Battle from German and Turkish Sources | 76 |

CHAPTER V.

THE CAPTURE OF THE SHERIA POSITION.

| The Operations North of Beersheba, 1st–2nd November | 68 |
| The Operations North of Beersheba, 3rd–5th November | 84 |

xv

# CONTENTS

|  | PAGE |
|---|---|
| The Plan of Attack on the Turkish Left | 92 |
| The Capture of the Sheria Position | 95 |
| The Operations North of Beersheba, 6th November | 101 |
| *Note*: The Turkish Movements from the 1st to the 6th November | 105 |

### CHAPTER VI.

**THE BREAK-UP OF THE TURKISH FRONT AND THE PURSUIT, 7TH–9TH NOVEMBER.**

|  |  |
|---|---|
| The XX Corps on the 7th November | 107 |
| The Desert Mounted Corps on the 7th November | 111 |
| The Desert Mounted Corps on the 8th November. The Affair of Huj | 117 |
| The Desert Mounted Corps on the 9th November. The Advance to the Mediterranean Shore | 124 |
| The Capture of the Wadi el Hesi Defences by the XXI Corps, 7th–8th November | 129 |
| *Note*: The Turkish Movements from the 7th to the 9th November | 140 |

### CHAPTER VII.

**PREPARATIONS FOR THE ATTACK ON JUNCTION STATION.**

|  |  |
|---|---|
| The Operations of the 10th November | 142 |
| The 11th and 12th November—The Turkish Counter-Attack at Barqusya and the Capture of Burqa | 146 |
| *Note*: The Turkish Movements from the 10th to the 12th November | 154 |

### CHAPTER VIII.

**THE CAPTURE OF JUNCTION STATION.**

|  |  |
|---|---|
| The Plan of Attack | 156 |
| The Action of El Maghar and Occupation of Junction Station | 158 |
| Operations from the 14th to the 16th November | 175 |
| *Note*: The Turkish Movements from the 13th to the 15th November | 182 |

### CHAPTER IX.

**THE ADVANCE INTO THE JUDÆAN HILLS AND BATTLE OF NABI SAMWEIL.**

|  |  |
|---|---|
| The Plans and the Country | 184 |
| The First Stage of the Advance, 19th–20th November | 189 |
| The Capture of Nabi Samweil, 21st–22nd November | 197 |
| The Attacks on El Jib, 23rd–24th November | 205 |
| Contemporary Events in the Plain, 19th–20th November | 213 |
| *Note*: The Turkish Movements from the 16th to the 25th November | 217 |

# CONTENTS

### CHAPTER X.

**THE TURKISH COUNTER-ATTACKS IN DEFENCE OF JERUSALEM.**

|  | PAGE |
|---|---|
| The Attacks of the 27th November | 218 |
| The Attacks of the 28th November | 223 |
| The Fighting from the 29th November to the 3rd December | 229 |
| *Note :* The Battle from the Turkish Side | 236 |

### CHAPTER XI.

**THE CAPTURE OF JERUSALEM.**

| | |
|---|---|
| The Plan of Attack and Advance of Mott's Detachment | 237 |
| The Capture of Jerusalem. The Operations of the 8th December | 243 |
| The Surrender of Jerusalem | 252 |
| The Advance of the 9th December | 256 |
| Sir Edmund Allenby's Entry into Jerusalem | 259 |

### CHAPTER XII.

**THE BATTLE OF JAFFA AND THE DEFENCE OF JERUSALEM.**

| | |
|---|---|
| The Passage of the Nahr El 'Auja | 265 |
| Preparations of the XX Corps | 275 |
| The Turkish Attack | 279 |
| The "Left Attack" of the XX Corps | 282 |
| The General Attack of the XX Corps | 286 |
| *Note :* The Battle from the Turkish Side | 291 |

### CHAPTER XIII.

**PROBLEMS OF THE FUTURE.**

| | |
|---|---|
| Transport and Policy | 292 |
| Administrative and Political Problems | 299 |

### CHAPTER XIV.

**THE CAPTURE OF JERICHO AND ACTIONS OF TELL 'ASUR.**

| | |
|---|---|
| The Capture of Jericho | 302 |
| The Action of Tell 'Asur—Operations of the XX Corps | 310 |
| The Operations of the XXI Corps | 323 |
| *Note :* The Turkish Side | 327 |

### CHAPTER XV.

**THE PASSAGE OF THE JORDAN AND THE RAID ON 'AMMAN.**

| | |
|---|---|
| The Passage of the Jordan | 328 |
| The Capture of Es Salt and First Attacks on 'Amman | 335 |
| The Last Attack and the Withdrawal | 343 |
| *Note :* The Battle from German and Turkish Sources | 348 |

CONTENTS

### Chapter XVI.

Operations between the First and Second Trans-Jordan Raids.

| | PAGE |
|---|---|
| The Action of Berukin | 350 |
| The Turkish Attack on the Jordan Bridgeheads | 358 |
| A Demonstration over Jordan | 361 |
| Note: The Actions of Berukin and the Bridgeheads from German and Turkish Sources | 362 |

### Chapter XVII.

The Second Raid into Trans-Jordan.

| | |
|---|---|
| Preparations for the Raid | 364 |
| The Second Action of Es Salt—30th April | 367 |
| The Turkish Counter-Attack in the Valley—1st May | 374 |
| Deadlock and Withdrawal—2nd–4th May | 380 |
| Note: The Battle from German and Turkish Sources | 392 |

### PLACE-NAMES. Palestine and Syria.

1. Meanings of some place-names in Palestine and Syria .. i
2. Glossary of some terms found in components of place-names (Arab and Hebrew) on the maps of Egypt, Sinai, Palestine, and Syria .. vi
3. Some of the more important dates in the history of the Holy Land .. xii
4. Comparative sizes .. xiv

## PART II.

### Chapter XVIII.

The Arab Campaign.

| | |
|---|---|
| The Last Half of 1917 | 395 |
| The First Eight Months of 1918 | 402 |

### Chapter XIX.

The Reorganization of the Force .. 411

### Chapter XX.

The Hot Weather of 1918.

| | |
|---|---|
| Summer Conditions on the Front | 422 |
| The Affair of Abu Tulul | 429 |
| The Opposing Forces | 438 |

# CONTENTS

## CHAPTER XXI.

### THE EVE OF MEGIDDO.

|   |   |
|---|---|
| The Projected Offensive | 447 |
| The Plan of Attack | 455 |
| The Concentration | 461 |

## CHAPTER XXII.

### THE BATTLES OF MEGIDDO: THE 19TH SEPTEMBER.

|   |   |
|---|---|
| The Infantry Plan of Attack | 468 |
| The Battle of Sharon | 472 |
| The Battle of Nablus | 488 |
| *Note*: The Action of the Enemy on the 19th September | 494 |

## CHAPTER XXIII.

### THE BATTLES OF MEGIDDO (*continued*).

|   |   |
|---|---|
| The Final Operations of the XX Corps | 496 |
| The Final Operations of the XXI Corps | 504 |
| *Note*: The Action of the Enemy on the 20th and 21st September | 511 |

## CHAPTER XXIV.

### THE INRUPTION OF THE DESERT MOUNTED CORPS.

|   |   |
|---|---|
| The 4th Cavalry Division | 513 |
| The 5th Cavalry Division | 522 |
| The Australian Mounted Division | 529 |
| The Capture of Haifa and the Actions at the Jordan Fords | 532 |
| The Capture of Samakh and Tiberias | 542 |
| *Note*: The Action of the Enemy from the 22nd to the 25th September | 545 |

## CHAPTER XXV.

### THE OPERATIONS OF CHAYTOR'S FORCE.

|   |   |
|---|---|
| The Capture of the Jordan Crossings | 547 |
| The Capture of 'Amman and Interception of the Ma'an Garrison | 552 |

## CHAPTER XXVI.

### THE PURSUIT THROUGH SYRIA AND CAPTURE OF DAMASCUS.

|   |   |
|---|---|
| Orders for a New Advance | 560 |
| The Arab Northern Army | 563 |
| The Advance on Damascus | 567 |
| The Capture of Damascus | 586 |
| *Note*: The Action of the Enemy from the 26th September to the 1st October | 594 |

## CONTENTS.

### Chapter XXVII.
### The End of the Campaign.

| | PAGE |
|---|---|
| The Occupation of Riyaq and Beirut | 596 |
| The Occupation of Homs and Tripoli | 604 |
| The Capture of Aleppo and the Affair of Haritan | 609 |
| The Armistice with Turkey | 618 |
| The Occupation of Northern Syria | 622 |
| *Note:* The Terms of the Armistice with Turkey | 625 |

### Chapter XXVIII.
### Epilogue.

| | |
|---|---|
| The Policy of the Campaign | 628 |
| The Strategy of the Campaign | 634 |
| The Tactics of the Campaign | 642 |

### TABLE OF APPENDICES.

| | | |
|---|---|---|
| 1. | Tabular Record of Operations | 650 |
| 2. | Order of Battle of the Egyptian Expeditionary Force, October 1917 | 660 |
| 3. | Order of Battle of the Egyptian Expeditionary Force, September 1918 | 666 |
| 4. | Order of Battle of *Yilderim*, October 1917 | 673 |
| 5. | Order of Battle of *Yilderim*, September 1918 | 674 |
| 6. | German Formations with *Yilderim* | 675 |
| 7. | Force Order No. 54 | 676 |
| 8. | XX Corps Instruction | 680 |
| 9. | XX Corps Order No. 12 | 685 |
| 10. | Desert Mounted Corps Operation Order No. 2 | 686 |
| 11. | XXI Corps Order No. 11 | 689 |
| 12. | XX Corps Order No. 13 | 691 |
| 13. | Telegraphic Orders by Desert Mounted Corps | 693 |
| 14. | XXI Corps Order No. 12 | 693 |
| 15. | Desert Mounted Corps Operation Order No 7 | 695 |
| 16. | XXI Corps Order No. 14 | 696 |
| 17. | XX Corps Order No. 17 | 698 |
| 18. | 60th Division Order No. 60 | 700 |
| 19. | 52nd Divisional Section Order No. 3 | 702 |
| 20. | To General Officer Commanding 60th Division | 705 |
| 21. | Operations of XXI Corps | 707 |
| 22. | Desert Mounted Corps Operation Order No. 16 | 710 |
| 23. | Force Order No. 68 | 713 |
| 24. | XXI Corps Order No. 42 | 715 |
| 25. | XX Corps Operation Order No. 42 | 718 |
| 26. | Desert Mounted Corps Operation Order No. 21 | 720 |
| 27. | Telegraphic Order by Desert Mounted Corps | 723 |

## SKETCHES, MAPS AND ILLUSTRATIONS.

### SKETCHES.

*(Bound in Volume.)*

#### PART I.

| | | | |
|---|---|---|---|
| Sketch A. | The Judæan Fortress | *At beginning* | |
| ,, 1. | Third Gaza, 6 p.m. 28th October 1917 | *Facing p.* | 37 |
| ,, 2. | Third Gaza, 6 p.m. 31st October 1917 | ,, | 45 |
| ,, 3. | Capture of Beersheba, 31st October 1917 | ,, | 51 |
| ,, 4. | Third Gaza, 6 p.m. 1st November 1917 | ,, | 63 |
| ,, 5. | Third Gaza, 6 p.m. 3rd November 1917 | ,, | 69 |
| ,, 6. | Third Gaza, 6 p.m. 6th November 1917 | ,, | 75 |
| ,, 7. | Affair of Huj, 8th November 1917 | ,, | 119 |
| ,, 8. | Wadi el Hesi, 8th November 1917 | ,, | 131 |
| ,, 9. | Third Gaza, 6 p.m. 10th November 1917 | ,, | 139 |
| ,, 10. | Capture of Junction Station, 13th–14th November 1917 | ,, | 155 |
| ,, 11. | Action of El Maghar, 13th November 1917 | ,, | 165 |
| ,, 12. | Jerusalem Operations, 6 p.m. 19th November 1917 | ,, | 189 |
| ,, 13. | Battle of Nabi Samweil, 6 p.m. 21st November 1917 | ,, | 207 |
| ,, 14. | Turkish Counter-offensive, 6 p.m. 28th November 1917 | ,, | 217 |
| ,, 15. | Wilhelma, 27th November 1917 | ,, | 221 |
| ,, 16. | Turkish Attack, 28th November 1917 | ,, | 223 |
| ,, 17. | Attack on Beit 'Ur el Foqa, 29th–30th November 1917 | ,, | 231 |
| ,, 18. | Capture of Jerusalem, 6 p.m. 7th December 1917 | ,, | 233 |
| ,, 18A. | Jerusalem | ,, | 239 |
| ,, 19. | Capture of Jerusalem, 8th–9th December 1917 | ,, | 243 |
| ,, 20. | Passage of Nahr el 'Auja, 20th–21st December 1917 | ,, | 276 |
| ,, 21. | Defence of Jerusalem, 6 p.m. 30th December 1917 | ,, | 283 |

## SKETCHES AND MAPS

| | | |
|---|---|---|
| Sketch 22. | Capture of Jericho, 19th–21st February 1918 | *Facing p.* 303 |
| ,, 23. | Tell 'Asur, 230th Brigade, 8th–10th March 1918 | ,, 315 |
| ,, 24. | Theatre of Operations in Trans-Jordan | ,, 327 |
| ,, 25. | 'Amman, 30th March 1918 | ,, 343 |
| ,, 26. | Turkish Attack on Jordan Bridgeheads, 11th April 1918 | ,, 357 |
| Diagram I. | Palestine : the Lie of the Land | ,, 185 |
| ,, II. | Outline of Ground around the Holy City | ,, 253 |

### PART II.

| | | |
|---|---|---|
| Sketch 27. | Et Tafila, 25th January 1918 | ,, 399 |
| ,, 28. | Affair of Abu Tulul, 14th July 1918 | ,, 429 |
| ,, 29. | Abu Tulul, Cavalry Operations, 14th July 1918 | ,, 433 |
| ,, 30. | Megiddo, Zero Hour 19th September 1918 | ,, 463 |
| ,, 31. | Megiddo, Midnight 19th–20th September 1918 | ,, 487 |
| ,, 32. | Megiddo, 9 p.m. 20th September 1918 | ,, 497 |
| ,, 33. | Megiddo, 9 p.m. 21st September 1918 | ,, 501 |
| ,, 34. | Capture of Haifa, 23rd September 1918 | ,, 533 |
| ,, 35. | Megiddo, 9 p.m. 24th September 1918 | ,, 537 |
| ,, 36. | Action at Makhadet el Mas'udi, 24th September 1918 | ,, 539 |
| ,, 37. | Capture of Samakh, 25th September 1918 | ,, 543 |
| ,, 38. | Arab Raids and 4th Cav. Division, 16th–17th September 1918 | ,, 563 |
| ,, 39. | Advance to Damascus, 29th–30th September 1918 | ,, 569 |
| ,, 40. | Attack on Irbid, 26th September 1918 | ,, 577 |
| ,, 41. | Pursuit from Damascus to Aleppo, 1st–28th October 1918 | ,, 597 |
| ,, 42. | Administration of Occupied Territory | ,, 607 |
| ,, 43. | Affair of Haritan, 26th October, 1918 | ,, 613 |

### MAPS.

*(In Separate Case.)*

| | | |
|---|---|---|
| Map | 1. | Palestine (layered). |
| ,, | 2. | Palestine 1/250,000 (Southern Section).[1] |
| ,, | 2A. | Palestine 1/250,000 (Northern Section). |

---

[1] In pocket at end of Part I. of text volume.

# MAPS AND ILLUSTRATIONS xxiii

| | | |
|---|---|---|
| Map | 3. | Syria 1/250,000, Beirut Sheet. |
| ,, | 4. | Gaza–Beersheba Line, October 1917. |
| ,, | 5. | Capture of Beersheba, 31st October 1917. |
| ,, | 6. | Operations of XXI Corps, 1st–2nd November 1917. |
| ,, | 7. | Operations North of Beersheba. |
| ,, | 8. | Capture of Sheria Position, 6th November 1917. |
| ,, | 9. | Capture of Junction Station, 13th–14th November 1917. |
| ,, | 10. | Battle of Nabi Samweil. |
| ,, | 11. | Capture of Jerusalem, 8th–9th December 1917. |
| ,, | 12. | Passage of the Nahr el 'Auja, 21st–22nd December 1917. |
| ,, | 13. | Defence of Jerusalem, 27th–30th December 1917. |
| ,, | 14. | Actions of Tell 'Asur, 9th–12th March 1918. |
| ,, | 15. | Operations of XXI Corps, 12th March 1918. |
| ,, | 16. | Raid on 'Amman, 21st March–2nd April 1918. |
| ,, | 17. | Action of Berukin, 9th April 1918. |
| ,, | 18. | Second Raid into Trans-Jordan. |
| ,, | 19. | Megiddo 1918 (layered map with Turkish Dispositions 19th September 1918). |
| ,, | 20. | Megiddo 1918 (contoured map with British Attack 19th–21st September 1918). |
| ,, | 21. | Envelopment of Turkish Armies by Desert Mounted Corps, 19th–25th September 1918. |
| ,, | 22. | Operations of Chaytor's Force, 20th–29th September 1918. |
| ,, | 23. | Railway Map of Near East, 1914–1919. |

ILLUSTRATIONS.

PART I.

| | | |
|---|---|---|
| Qatra–Maghar Position | *Facing p.* | 168 |
| Jaffa–Jerusalem Road | ,, | 194 |
| Looking westward from Ram Allah | ,, | 200 |
| Pontoon Bridge over Jordan | ,, | 334 |
| 'Amman from the south-west | ,, | 338 |

PART II.

| | | |
|---|---|---|
| Et Tafila : looking east at the Battlefield | *Facing p.* | 402 |
| Wrecked Turkish Transport in Wadi el Far'a | ,, | 504 |
| Wadi 'Ara : Entrance to the Musmus Pass | ,, | 516 |
| Valley of Jezreel from Zir'in | ,, | 520 |
| Scene in the Barada Gorge | ,, | 572 |

# CHAPTER I.

### THE SITUATION OF THE COMBATANTS IN THE SUMMER OF 1917.

#### (Maps 1, 2, 4.)

#### INDECISION OF THE TURKS.

WHEN General Sir Edmund Allenby arrived in Cairo on Maps 1, 2. the 27th June 1917 the British Government had already decided upon their policy with regard to the campaign in Palestine. His coming marked the opening of a fresh phase, which those who sent him desired should be characterized by strong and unceasing aggression. The new Commander-in-Chief had to make his appreciation, to decide and report what additional means he required to enable him to pass to the offensive. The plan of campaign had to be drawn up, the objectives of the first battle to be chosen. But the defeat of the enemy and the eventual destruction of his forces, the capture of Jerusalem, and the expulsion of the Turks from Palestine were fixed as the final goals to endeavour.

So, though the questions of resources needful and methods most effective remained to be discussed, the British knew what they wanted. Very different was the enemy's case. On the Turkish side the advocates of two widely different schemes were in the throes of a quarrel. The balance inclined now to one side, now to the other, with resultant waste of effort and confusion. And when at last the sounder plan prevailed it was too late. The blow fell and caught them half prepared. To discover the real nature of the alternatives which perplexed Turkish counsels it is necessary to glance at a factor in Turkish political life which had first appeared about ten years earlier, though it did not become of great importance until the outbreak of war. It bears not only upon the situation now under discussion but upon the Turkish attitude to the campaign in Palestine from this time forward, and its significance will be found to be even greater in the summer and autumn of 1918.

Before the revolution of 1908 the average Turk had little consciousness of race. Islam represented to him an idea greater than Ottoman nationality, and religious fanaticism was aroused in his breast more easily than patriotism. He was therefore a supporter of pan-Islamism before ever that word came into fashion. Pan-Islamism was, in brief, the recognition of a bond, political as well as religious, between all Moslems. Its chief exponent was the Sultan Abdul Hamid, and its decline began with his fall, though it still had many powerful adherents. The pan-Turanian movement, which succeeded it, had its origin—actually outside Turkey—in somewhat vague and mystical propaganda for the unity of the "Turanian"[1] races. Its effect in Turkey may be likened to that of the writings of Nietzsche, Treitschke, and others in Germany. The doctrines of the philosopher and historian were taken over by the politician and trimmed to suit his purposes. Pan-Turanianism speedily became pan-Turkism when adopted by the leaders of the Young Turks who came to power after the revolution. Some of these men were Jews, others lax Moslems. Upon them and their disciples the bond of Islam lay more lightly than upon the old-fashioned Turk, and their ideals were nationalist rather than religious. They were ready to play Islam false in pursuit of their aims, though careful to conceal this intention by a parade of pan-Islamic sentiments. They were more interested in effecting union with the Turkish peoples of Trans- and Cis-Caucasia, Persian Azerbaijan, and Turkestan—the birthplace of the Turkish race—than in the retention of Arabia and Syria, though they had no desire to abandon these provinces. Instead of ridding themselves of them, they began to subject their inhabitants to rigid "Turkification"; that is to say, they attempted to gain the minor object of pan-Turkism—the strengthening of Turkish nationalism within the Empire—because for the time being there was no opportunity of reaching the major object—the linking

---

[1] The term is, strictly speaking, philological, and was coined to express the element of kinship between certain non-Aryan languages, such as Turkish, Magyar, and Finnish. "Turan" is a Persian word applied in Persian medieval literature to the steppes of Central Asia.

up of Ottoman Turks with other Turkish races. They also played, though perhaps less eagerly before the outbreak of war than after it, with the cult of the pagan Turanian warriors, such as Jenghis Khan, in a manner reminiscent of some aspects of the Nietzschean philosophy in Germany.

Until the beginning of the war that was all they could do to make realities of their dreams. But when that moment came it brought its opportunities. It is interesting to note how strongly pan-Turkish aims influenced their early operations. The threat to the Suez Canal was perhaps the most valuable contribution they could have made to the cause of their Allies. But it was in no sense pan-Turkish policy, and consequently it was made half-heartedly. The march through the desert was a fine feat, but the attack on the Canal was never really pressed. On the other hand, the offensive in Trans-Caucasia, of no particular value to Germany except that it contained a certain number of Russian troops, was their main effort. In this an army more than six times as great as that which crossed Sinai in January 1915 was broken and dispersed. Yet all through the two years which followed, even when the Allies at Gallipoli were threatening the Empire's capital, the Turks never gave up their Caucasian projects.

The whole aspect of the war in the Near and Middle East changed with the collapse of Russia. Britain was now Turkey's only serious opponent. In Mesopotamia and in Palestine the two were at grips. In both theatres the British had carried out offensives; in the former their efforts had been successful and had been richly rewarded by the capture of Baghdad; in the latter they had failed and had ended in deadlock before Gaza. The loss of Baghdad was a serious blow to pan-Turkish aspirations. The city stood upon the main route to Persia, which was to be to Turkey what Bavaria was to Prussia. And here German interests coincided with their own, for Germany had not abandoned those eastern ambitions from which had emerged the idea of the Baghdad Railway. Germany now came forward as the friend in need to assist in the recovery of Baghdad. She offered one of her most distinguished soldiers with a large staff and a detachment of highly trained troops. She would supply lavishly ammunition and other materials of war, with abundant gold, the most needed of them. Great columns of mechanical transport should file through the Cilician Gates; launches should be set afloat on the Euphrates. The picked Turkish divisions serving in European theatres—two in Galicia, two with the Bulgarians on the Struma, three in Rumania—should be released. This was an infusion of fresh blood to stir the weary body of Turkey to new life. The recapture of Baghdad would further the aims of the inner group which directed Turkish policy; it would also provide a resounding triumph for Moslem arms to arouse enthusiasm among the ignorant masses. The project was decidedly attractive.

But what meanwhile was to happen in Palestine? Would the British sit down before Gaza and accept defeat, or return to the attack with forces no stronger than those which had been defeated? Neither policy accorded well with their traditions. Both the Turkish army commander, Ahmed Jemal Pasha, and the German commander at the front, Kress von Kressenstein, gave warning that the force in Palestine must be strengthened. And if their fears for the safety of Jerusalem did not greatly affect the pan-Turks, they still had one unanswerable argument. What would be the fate of the expeditionary force in Mesopotamia if the British invaded Syria and got astride its communications at Aleppo and the foot of the Amanus?

Of the triumvirate which brought Turkey into the war two men, Enver, Minister of War and Vice-Generalissimo, Talaat, formerly Minister of the Interior and lately become Grand Vizier, were pan-Turks of extreme type. The third, Jemal, Minister of Marine and commander of the *Fourth Army*, did not belong to that faction. He had been sent to Syria because it was desired to have him out of the way, but his championship of Islam had at times been inconvenient, and was never more so than now, when he set himself to oppose the Baghdad scheme. This was already in train, two divisions from Galicia and Macedonia having begun their move eastward in June 1917, while a number of others were under orders. General (Marshal in the Turkish Army) Erich von Falkenhayn, formerly, in succession, Prussian Minister of War, Chief of the Staff of the German Field Armies, and commander of the *Ninth Army* in Rumania, had been appointed to the command of

*Army Group F.*, or *Yilderim* (Thunderbolt or Lightning),[1] 1917. as the Turks called it, which was to carry out the enterprise. June. A new army, the *Seventh*, was to be formed for service under *Yilderim*, while the *Sixth Army*, already in Mesopotamia, was to be completely re-equipped and was also to come under its orders. Considerable preparations had already been made. At Neuhammer, in the forests of Silesia, was assembling and training the German force, the rôle of which was already planned to the smallest detail, through all the stages of its approach in 400 motor-lorries to the point, south of Ramadi, where it was to strike the British left flank, 2,500 miles away. Well might a Turkish staff officer, after the lecture illustrated by diagrams on a blackboard to which he listened at Neuhammer, compare his feelings to those aroused by a Jules Verne romance.[2]

This German *Asia Corps*, better known as *Pasha II*, the title given to it by the Turks, was a detachment of all arms. It had only three battalions of infantry, but was particularly strong in artillery, machine guns, trench mortars, aircraft, wireless equipment, and mechanical transport. The German authorities had evidently given considerable thought to the formation of this expeditionary force, making it formidable in equipment, and so designed that each battalion, with, if necessary, a machine-gun company, a trench-mortar detachment, its " infantry-artillery platoon," and a troop of cavalry, was self-sufficing for an independent mission. It was an excellent device for stiffening an ill-trained army. Strength numerically Germany could not spare, but the troops were all picked men, of perfect physique, and thoroughly fit for tropical service.[3]

While Sir Edmund Allenby was on his way out to Egypt, on the 20th June, Enver Pasha held a conference at Aleppo, where he had temporarily fixed his headquarters. It was attended by Izzet, commanding the *Caucasus Group of Armies;* Mustapha Kemal, commanding the *Second Army* in the Lake Van area; Jemal, commanding the *Fourth*

---

[1] *Yilderim* was the nickname of Sultan Bayazid I, earned by his rapidity when he destroyed the troops of " the Last Crusade " at Nicopolis in 1396. It was also applied to Napoleon in Egypt.

[2] Turkish " *Yilderim*," Part 1, Chapter III.

[3] An order of battle of the German formations attached to *Yilderim* is given in Appendix 6.

*Army* in Syria; and Halil, commanding the *Sixth Army* in Mesopotamia. Enver was accompanied by the German General Bronsart von Schellendorff, C.G.S. at Constantinople, and by the Under-Secretary to the Ministry of War. The rôle of *Yilderim* was the subject of discussion. The *Seventh Army* was to concentrate at Aleppo and to move along the Euphrates to the neighbourhood of Hit, 90 miles W.N.W. of Baghdad and approximately 450 miles by march route from Aleppo. Jemal proposed that one of its divisions should be sent down to Riyaq, north of Damascus and at the end of the broad-gauge railway, as a reserve to the Palestine front. Enver refused to consider this suggestion, but Jemal's representation of the weakness of his position in Southern Palestine may be said to have struck the first blow against the Baghdad scheme.[1]

It is unnecessary to follow the controversy through all its tortuous channels of intrigue. It need only be said that Falkenhayn speedily came to the conclusion that the Palestine front was of vital importance and threatened by a British offensive. He now desired to transport thither the *Seventh Army* and to carry out an offensive against the right flank and rear of the British, with the object of driving them back into the desert. Jemal wanted reinforcements, but he did not want *Yilderim*, and still less Falkenhayn, in the territory which he ruled as absolute Viceroy. Mustapha Kemal, ablest and most vigorous of Turkish soldiers, who had been appointed to the command of the *Seventh Army* in place of the *Second*, refused to serve under Germans. Finally Falkenhayn, after a visit to Southern Palestine and a reconnaissance of the front from the high ground north of Kharm on the 10th September, which convinced him of the possibilities of a Turkish offensive, gained his point. He obtained permission from Enver for the immediate transfer of the *Seventh Army*, then assembling at Aleppo, to the Palestine front. The *Fourth Army*, Jemal's command, was broken up, though he was to remain Commander-in-Chief of Syria, north of the *Sanjak* of Jerusalem, and of the Turkish forces in Arabia. *Yilderim* was also to direct the operations in Mesopotamia. Seven divisions were concentrated at Aleppo or under orders to

---

[1] Turkish " *Yilderim*," Part 1, Chapter II.

move there.[1] *Pasha II* was ordered to move from Neu- 1917. hammer to Constantinople, where it would have to await Sept. transport. Large sums of money were provided for the purchase of grain east of the Jordan to supplement the supplies to be carried by rail and road from the north. One heavy blow fell upon *Yilderim*, however; for forty-eight hours after Falkenhayn had quitted Haidar Pasha Station, on the Asiatic side of the Bosporus, on the 6th September, there was a great explosion, followed by a fire, in the station, and vast quantities of ammunition and warlike stores were destroyed.

Falkenhayn had won his first battle—against his allies —and a victory over Jemal upon his own ground was no mean achievement. Yet it was not without disadvantages from another point of view. Kress, the one German commander able to work in harmony with Jemal, and the other German officers at the front saw the danger more clearly than the rest of their countrymen, though Liman von Sanders in Constantinople was also aware of it. *Yilderim's* coming, they feared, marked the end of close co-operation with the Turkish authorities. Kress knew that Jemal was no soldier, but he knew also that he was an able man, the only man with the power and the will fully to exploit the resources of the country. In any case the struggle against prejudice and personal ambitions had lasted too long. The troops which might have rendered the Gaza-Beersheba front secure could not now arrive in time.

### Sir Philip Chetwode's Appreciation.

Sir Edmund Allenby assumed command of the E.E.F. Maps 2, 4. at midnight on the 28th June, and shortly afterwards took train to Eastern Force headquarters at Deir el Balah. His arrival was a strong stimulus to the troops. To study the ground he visited every part of the front, and the vigour of his personality impressed itself on officers and men. Rumour flies fast in an army, especially when it is not engaged in active operations, and now through the trenches and from camp to camp word sped that the new commander

---

[1] The Turkish reinforcements sent to the Palestine front are given in Note at end of Chapter.

had come with a new policy, and that he was assured of the means to carry it out. Spirits rose at the prospect of an offensive which would make an end of the period of trench warfare, and, with good fortune, of the campaign itself.

General Chetwode and his chief General Staff Officer, Br.-General G. P. Dawnay, had prepared an elaborate appreciation of the situation, which had been forwarded to meet the Commander-in-Chief on his arrival in Egypt. It was upon this appreciation and the scheme contained in it that Sir Edmund Allenby, as he has stated in his Despatches, based his subsequent plan of operations.

This document began with the statement that the enemy had definitely decided to hold the Gaza–Beersheba line, whatever might have been his intentions when he first took it up. This position was strong by nature and was rendered still stronger by lack of water in front of it, which made it impossible for the British, unless they made the most elaborate preparations, "to get within half-arm distance "except in the left sector." In an attack upon it, forces approximately equal in numbers, with only a small superiority in artillery, would not command success.

It was possible that the enemy might attempt to throw the British back to the frontier at Rafah, but no more considerable offensive was probable in any circumstances. His defensive power depended upon how far the increasing Russian inactivity in the Caucasus relieved him of anxiety in that quarter, upon what new operations he attempted in Mesopotamia, and, above all, upon the capacity of his single narrow-gauge railway. He had already accomplished so much in overcoming the difficulties of transportation that it was possible that he might be able to maintain in future sixty or seventy battalions at the front.

Merely to drive the enemy from the Gaza–Beersheba line would be of no great value. He had behind him selected and partially prepared positions, while every mile he retired would lessen his difficulties regarding supply and particularly water. On the other hand, the British had not, as in Mesopotamia, a great river to facilitate the transport of supplies in an advance. They had instead the sea, but supply by sea upon an open beach was precarious and unreliable, particularly in winter. In the coast belt there were no roads suitable for mechanical transport,

# SIR PHILIP CHETWODE'S APPRECIATION

and the best rate of progress to be hoped for from the railway, under the most favourable circumstances, was not more than three-quarters of a mile a day.[1] Careful preliminary arrangements and reorganization of land transport, with the fullest possible use of transport by sea, might enable them to allow the enemy less breathing-space than then appeared possible, but no hope could be cherished of attaining a rate of pursuit such as had been achieved in Mesopotamia.

1917.
June.

"It would be fatal, in my opinion," General Chetwode continued, "to make a half-bite at the cherry and to "attempt an offensive with forces which might permit us to "attack and occupy the enemy's present line, but which "would be insufficient to inflict on him a really severe blow "and to follow up that blow with fresh troops pressing "closely on his heels. Nothing less than seven divisions "at full strength and our three cavalry divisions will be "sufficient for this purpose, and they will be none too many. "Divisions of such poor rifle strength as the 52nd, 53rd, and "54th, and with no drafts to keep them up, will disappear "in three weeks' fighting."

General Chetwode then turned to consider the enemy's position from the tactical point of view. It ran from the sea at Gaza, roughly along the Gaza–Beersheba road for thirty miles, and was held by about fifty battalions. The Turks were therefore widely dispersed, but their lateral communications were fairly good. Gaza had been made into a strong modern fortress, well entrenched and wired, with good observation and a glacis on its southern and south-eastern face across which attacking infantry could not move by day with any fair prospect of success. The remainder of the position consisted of a series of field-works, mutually supporting as regards artillery fire, if not always as regards that of machine guns and rifles. These works were on an average 1,500 to 2,000 yards apart, except that the Beersheba defences were four miles from the left flank of the main position.

The British line was also extended. From the sea to Sheikh Abbas it varied in distance from 400 to 2,500 yards from the enemy's line. From Sheikh Abbas it ran south

---

[1] Br.-General Sir G. Macauley has pointed out that the main line could have advanced faster than this, but that its rate of construction was affected by the necessity of constructing branches.

to Tell el Jemmi in a series of strong points, and thence along the Wadi Ghazze to Qamle. The southern portion diverged from the line of the enemy's position owing to the absence of water to the east. In front of it lay an absolutely flat plain in the form of a triangle, with the apex at Bir Ifteis on the Wadi Imleih, 15 miles south-east of Gaza, while north of the Wadi esh Sheria the ground rose gradually to the Gaza–Beersheba road. The approaches to the enemy's centre between Khirbet [1] Sihan and Hureira were therefore in full view of the Turkish position, and an attack in this direction would be seriously exposed and could not be adequately supported by artillery. East of the triangle the ground rose gradually towards Beersheba, and, though intersected by wadis and in parts stony, was suitable to the operations of all arms. But the only point not within the enemy's defences where there was water was Bir el Esani, on the Wadi Ghazze, 7 miles south-east of Qamle.

It appeared that the enemy regarded his defences at Hureira as a possible pivot; that if attacked at Gaza he would be prepared to abandon Beersheba and withdraw his flank into the rough hills above it; and that if driven out of Gaza he would pivot on his left at Hureira and occupy a position between that point and Deir Sneid, $6\frac{1}{2}$ miles north-east of Gaza, which had been partially prepared.

An attack on Gaza would be an attack on the enemy at his strongest point. The defences would have to be reduced by sheer weight of artillery. Success would probably only be local, and the enemy would be prepared to stand again between Hureira and Deir Sneid.

An attack on the enemy's centre about Atawine would likewise be carried out under heavy disadvantages: lack of artillery observation and of cover, great difficulties as regards water. Nor would it be possible, if such an attack were successful, to widen the gap by means of mounted troops unless either Hureira or Gaza were also taken. An attack on the Hureira group of works from the west involved the same difficulties in respect of lack of water and unfavourable ground.

There remained, then, the possibility of attacking the enemy's "nerve centre and pivot" at Hureira and Tell

---

[1] Khirbet, ruin, shortened hereafter to "Kh." as in Vol. I.

esh Sheria from the south and south-east. By rapid 1917. extension eastward of the railway from Qamle or Shellal[1] June. it would be possible to place a force on the high ground west of Beersheba and south of Bir Abu Irqaiyiq, where the Turkish railway crossed the Wadi Imleih, which would either compel the evacuation of Beersheba or afford a favourable position for an attack upon it, while holding off any enemy force attempting to move to its relief down the Gaza-Beersheba road.

"Once established on the high ground between Beer-
"sheba and Hureira, and with Beersheba in our possession,
"we can attack north and north-westward, always from
"higher ground, always with observation, with water at Beer-
"sheba, with water at Esani, with water at Shellal, Fara, and
"Qamle, with rail-borne water east of Shellal, and with the
"only prospect, which no alternative course affords, of find-
"ing a flank on which we can use our great preponderance in
"mounted troops; not an ideal flank, for east of Tuweiyil
"Abu Jerwal (6 miles N.N.E. of Beersheba) the country
"becomes mountainous and rocky, but still a flank which
"should afford us great opportunities; with water at Tell
"en Nejile, 14 miles to the north, and the possibility of
"cutting the enemy's railway behind him; with water at
"Sheria and Hureira—a little salt, but good enough for
"animals; and with a strong pivot on our left flank from
"Abbas to the sea, on which to swing our right forward
"towards Nejile and to force the enemy by manœuvre to
"abandon Gaza."

The chief factor in success on this flank would be rapidity of action. The enemy must be made to believe until the last moment that a renewed offensive on the Gaza front was contemplated, and subsidiary operations on this front would actually, it appeared, be necessary. There might seem to be some risk in thus weakening the British centre, but, in fact, a hostile counter-stroke between the British defences at Sheikh Abbas and the force established about Beersheba would be a very risky venture for the Turks. It might, indeed, be hoped that they would attempt it, and thus find themselves between the jaws of pincers.

Detailed proposals for the operations were not set

---

[1] Mention is made later in this Chapter of the branch line to Shellal.

forth in the appreciation, though they were under consideration. But there was one essential condition. The proposition was based on a minimum of seven infantry and three mounted divisions, all up to strength and fully equipped—which the infantry then south of Gaza was not—and with first reinforcements in the country, which should amount if possible to 20 per cent. for the infantry, and should in no case fall below 10 per cent.

### SIR EDMUND ALLENBY'S REQUIREMENTS.

The Commander-in-Chief spent five days in reconnaissance of the front, in discussion of the situation with General Chetwode, and in inspection of the troops. On the 12th July, after his return to Cairo, he telegraphed to the War Office his views and requirements. Both, it will be seen, were strongly influenced by General Chetwode's appreciation.

He began by stating that, in his opinion, the Turks had realized that the loss of Jerusalem, following upon the fall of Baghdad, would have disastrous consequences, and that they had therefore determined to oppose upon the Gaza–Beersheba line a further advance of the British. After describing that position and the difficulties of attacking it, he stated that, on a first impression, its most vulnerable portion appeared to be between Hureira and Irqaiyiq, where the works were less strongly organized than those to the north-west and the Turkish system was dominated by the higher ground between Irqaiyiq and Beersheba.

The enemy's force in Southern Palestine was estimated to be five divisions and one cavalry division in front line, with at least one additional division in reserve south of Jerusalem. This represented, with unattached units, about 46,000 rifles, 2,800 sabres, 250 machine guns and 200 guns.[1]

---

[1] The British Intelligence at the War Office and in Palestine had as yet no adequate conception either of the heavy wastage caused by sickness among the Turkish troops at the front, or of the extent to which the more recently arrived divisions had been depleted by desertion en route. The rifle strength given above was greatly in excess of the real figure, perhaps nearly double it. The sabre strength was nearly three times the real figure. The *3rd Cavalry Division* consisted of three regiments only, totalling 1,500 sabres, and one of them had been sent into Trans-Jordan at this date. A detailed estimate of Turkish strength prior to the launching of the British attack will be found in Chapter II.

Reinforcements consisting of the *26th Division* and another 1917. regiment were reported to be moving south. Against July. this force the British had four infantry and three cavalry divisions, exclusive of the 60th Division, then in process of equipment, and the 75th Division, which would be for some months unable to take the field. Units were below establishment, and over 5,000 reinforcements were required to complete them.

It appeared that the enemy was contemplating an offensive, but had not yet decided whether to carry it out against Baghdad or on the Palestine front. At present it seemed likely that the decision would be in favour of Baghdad and that in Palestine he would remain on the defensive.[1]

The railway across Sinai was now capable of supplying seven divisions, three cavalry divisions, and the necessary proportion of army troops. With a force of this strength Sir Edmund Allenby was prepared to take the offensive, with good prospect of being able to capture Gaza and Beersheba and a reasonable possibility of being able to reach Jerusalem. But for any operation beyond the Jerusalem–Jaffa line, and perhaps even to maintain that line, he would require a considerable increase of strength. This would necessitate the doubling of the railway from Qantara to Rafah, which should be begun at once, as it would take six months, and a double track would certainly be needed eventually. The doubling of the railway would involve the doubling of the pipe-line. He did not include the 75th Division among the seven divisions required, because it had as yet no artillery, only nine battalions of infantry, and would probably not be fit to take the field before December.

Sir Edmund Allenby had at once made up his mind that in the forthcoming operations he would command in person his troops in the field. This decision made it necessary to divide General Headquarters, hitherto in Cairo, into two echelons, as in France. The major part, consisting of the General Staff, the Adjutant-General's and Quartermaster-General's branches, and in most cases the Directors

---

[1] Sir Edmund Allenby was undoubtedly right in his view that this was the enemy's intention at the moment. See p. 5.

## 14 SIR EDMUND ALLENBY'S REQUIREMENTS

of Administrative Services, was to follow the Commander-in-Chief to Palestine and to be established near Khan Yunis. Representatives of the administrative services and departments, and those portions of the staff required to deal with the control of Egypt under martial law were to remain in Cairo. The decision also involved the abolition of the Eastern Frontier Force and the formation of two corps and a cavalry corps directly under G.H.Q.

His full requirements were two divisions (making eight with the 75th), each with thirty-six 18-pdrs. and twelve 4·5-inch howitzers; additional field artillery to bring that of the divisions in the country up to the same strength;[1] heavy artillery totalling eight 60-pdrs., thirty-eight 6-inch howitzers, twelve 8-inch howitzers, and four 6-inch Mark VII guns;[2] thirteen anti-aircraft sections of two guns apiece; three additional squadrons of aircraft, and one flight to replace that serving in the Hejaz; with considerable increase in signal services, Royal Engineers (Army Troops companies for work on roads, railways, water supply, and hutments), and medical services.

The demands of the main theatre of war, where the Third Battle of Ypres was in progress, and still more the shortage of shipping, made it impossible to comply fully with these requests. The problem of the Force's maintenance was becoming more and more difficult, since it already numbered over 200,000 men, without counting 60,000 labourers and followers. Sir William Robertson therefore induced the Commander-in-Chief to include the 75th Division in the seven divisions required, provided that three Territorial battalions were sent from India to bring it up to strength. Its artillery was already on the way.[3] With regard to the other reinforcements, the Government were unable to give a definite reply for some time, both because their despatch depended upon the shipping that

---

[1] An additional total of thirty 18-pdrs. and thirty-two 4·5-inch howitzers.

[2] The heavy and siege artillery in the country or already promised, to which the above was to be additional, consisted of twenty-six 6-inch and four 8-inch howitzers, twenty-four 60-pdrs. The demand was based on the calculation that four 60-pdrs. and eight 6-inch howitzers were required for each division, including the 75th.

[3] Included in it was the 1st South African Field Artillery Brigade, a new representative of the Empire in the Force, which distinguished itself by brilliant work.

## THE WAR CABINET'S INSTRUCTIONS

1917.
July.

could be made available and because they desired to take the bulk of them from Salonika, whence they were unable to withdraw troops without the consent of their Allies. The doubling of the railway to Rafah was, however, authorized on the 21st July. Finally, on the 10th August, the Commander-in-Chief was informed that an Allied conference [1] had agreed to the transfer of a division from Salonika to Egypt. His other demands were generally met, with the important exception of artillery. Of the thirty-two field howitzers for which he had asked (to bring batteries to six-gun strength) none were available, but the sixteen 3·7-inch mountain howitzers promised instead were to prove no bad exchange. All his divisional artilleries were to be brought up to the strength in 18-pdrs. which he had laid down, with the exception of the division from Salonika, which was two six-gun batteries short. His demands for heavy artillery were also cut down, but not seriously.[2] Generally speaking he had not been stinted. But he learnt that by no possibility could these reinforcements arrive in time for operations in September.

On the same date he was informed of the War Cabinet's general instructions. During the coming autumn and winter it was of the highest importance to " strike the Turks " as hard as possible." A big victory in Palestine would tend to strengthen the confidence and staying power of the people at a season when a like success in Europe was improbable. It would also have the effect of increasing the war-weariness of Turkey and her dissatisfaction with her German mentors. No geographical objective could be set as a goal to the Force, because it was uncertain how far the situation in Russia would permit the enemy to divert troops from the Caucasus. Sir Edmund Allenby was simply enjoined to defeat the Turks opposed to him, to follow up his success vigorously, and to continue to press them to the limit of his resources.

---

[1] This conference was held at Paris on the 26th and 27th July.

[2] He was to have a total of twenty-eight 60-pdrs. to give him four per division, which was what he had asked for, but, as has been stated, his original demand for eight divisions had been cut down to seven. Instead of the sixty-four 6-inch howitzers which he had at first considered necessary, he was to have a total of forty-six, but this was only ten short of the eight per division which he had asked for. His demand for 8-inch howitzers was cut down by two, and that for 6-inch guns was for the time being halved.

# 16 SIR EDMUND ALLENBY'S REQUIREMENTS

The division promised from Salonika proved to be the 10th (Irish) Division, which had previously seen service in Gallipoli. It was well trained and had had few battle casualties during the period of upwards of two years spent in the Macedonian theatre, but it had suffered very severely from malaria. Its arrival began in the last days of August.

On the 12th August three corps were formed: the XX Corps, commanded by Lieut.-General Sir P. W. Chetwode, hitherto in command of Eastern Force; the XXI Corps, commanded by Lieut.-General E. S. Bulfin, who had come from Salonika in command of the 60th Division; and the Desert Mounted Corps, commanded by Lieut.-General Sir H. G. Chauvel, previously in command of the Desert Column. The distribution of the troops between the three corps was as follows:—

DESERT MOUNTED CORPS.
    A. & N. Z. Mounted Division.
    Australian Mounted Division.
    Yeomanry Mounted Division.
    Imperial Camel Corps Brigade.

XX CORPS.
    10th Division (nominally G.H.Q. Troops).
    53rd Division.
    60th Division.
    74th Division.
    Four Brigades Heavy Artillery.

XXI CORPS.
    52nd Division.
    54th Division.
    75th Division.
    Three Brigades Heavy Artillery.

The 7th Mounted Brigade, of two regiments only, was retained as Army Troops. In the first week of September was formed the "Composite Force" from the Imperial Service Indian troops, the 1st Battalion British West Indies Regiment, and detachments from the French and Italian Contingents. It had about 3,000 rifles and six squadrons, but was without artillery or second-line transport.

Virtually no changes were made in the senior personnel of G.H.Q., except that Major-General L. J. Bols, who had been Sir Edmund Allenby's chief General Staff Officer in France, succeeded Major-General A. L. Lynden-Bell as C.G.S. in September, and that Br.-General G. P. Dawnay, formerly chief General Staff Officer Eastern Frontier Force, was brought in as Deputy C.G.S.

1917.
Aug.

## Transport and Water Supply.

Sir Edmund Allenby was not long in deciding upon the general outline of his plan of attack. This will be considered in detail a little later, but it is convenient here to summarize the instructions issued to corps commanders on the 15th August before dealing with the questions of transport and water supply.

The Commander-in-Chief announced his intention of taking the offensive as soon as he had seven divisions ready for action and his other arrangements were complete. The main offensive would be made against the enemy's left flank, while vigorous operations would be undertaken simultaneously against his right centre and right. The main attack on the enemy's left would be carried out by the XX Corps and the Desert Mounted Corps, the other operations by the XXI Corps. If it were found necessary to take the offensive before the seventh division arrived, the XXI Corps would be left with only two divisions, but in that case its share would be limited to a demonstration to cause the enemy to apprehend that the main attack would be delivered against his right centre and right.

After the initial operations of the XXI Corps an advance on Beersheba would be made by the XX Corps and a portion of the Desert Mounted Corps to capture the place and, if possible, annihilate its garrison. The XX Corps, with sufficient mounted forces to protect its right, would then advance north and north-west against the left flank of the enemy, and drive him from his positions at Tell esh Sheria and Hureira. While these operations were in progress a portion of the Desert Mounted Corps would be retained at Shellal, in the gap between the XX and XXI Corps, in case enemy forces should move against the left flank of the former.

If the wells at Beersheba were to be secured, it was necessary that the place should be captured in the course of a single day. The date of the advance against Sheria and Hureira would then depend upon the amount of transport needed and the date when it would be available ; and the XX and Desert Mounted Corps were instructed to submit their own estimates of their requirements. As soon as the XX Corps began this attack upon the left of the main Turkish position, the Desert Mounted Corps would pass behind the infantry and, joined by that portion of the mounted troops left at Shellal, would advance on Tell en Nejile, on the railway 18 miles north of Beersheba, to complete the rout of the enemy's left, threaten his line of retreat, and possibly effect large captures.

The further course of operations could not yet be predicted. The XX Corps might be called upon to continue the advance from Hureira towards Gaza, rolling up the enemy's line. But in the event of a sweeping success that corps might well find itself so far from railhead or so crippled by casualties as to be unable to pursue. It would then be necessary for the XXI Corps to take over a large proportion of the other's transport and to confirm the success by capturing Gaza and advancing up the coast. The corps commanders now knew what was to be demanded of them and could at once begin to frame their plans and make their preparations.

At the moment the Commander-in-Chief still thought it possible that he might launch his offensive in September. But he speedily decided that, in order to complete the vast preliminary work necessary, and to allow his reinforcements time to learn something of the ground and become used to the conditions, he would have to postpone it until the end of October. He would then run a considerable risk of his operations being hindered by the rainy season, which generally begins about mid-November, and a minor risk of being himself attacked before he was ready, if the enemy strongly reinforced his front meanwhile. Those risks he would have to accept. In any case the time was none too long.

The machinery of supply which this offensive involved differed very much from that of the other theatres in which British Armies were fighting. On the Western Front immense preparations had to be made before an offensive for the provision of water, the collection of supplies, stores, and ammunition. Material and lorries to carry it forward had to be ready for the construction of temporary roads to replace those destroyed in the course of the battles or intentionally damaged by the enemy, and to make permanent roads as soon as possible. Even in France there were times when the difficulties became for the moment insuperable. When the Germans retreated to the Hindenburg Line in March of 1917, the devastation of the country, the mining and barricading of roads, and the very unwieldiness of the forces engaged prevented a close pursuit. In the last few weeks of the war the problem was even more serious, when the Allies outran their railheads, and railway lines were blown up behind them by means of mines with delayed action days or even weeks after the enemy had passed by. But, broadly speaking, no choice of objectives was influenced by considerations of supply, except when winter conditions made ground impassable. A good network of railways and roads enabled preparations to be made anywhere.

1917. Aug.

In Palestine the case was different. General Allenby had not the great material resources available in France, and though he was in command of an army which was of considerable size judged by any standard except that of the Great War, he was fighting in an undeveloped and partly desert country, in many districts almost waterless and with roads which would not merit the name in France —fighting, in short, in what may be described as " smallwar" conditions. In the coming battle, as in others that were to follow, the attackers had no alternative, if they failed to capture from the enemy an exiguous water supply, but to retire to their starting-point. Time after time in the days to come the Desert Mounted Corps was faced by the problem of whether to allow a beaten enemy to withdraw and recoup or to founder invaluable horses by continuing the advance without water. The only metalled road running northward was that from Beersheba to Jerusalem through Hebron, up the spine of the Judæan Hills, and it was in many places a mere mass of loose stone lying upon the bed of an ancient bridle-path. In the coast district the country was at least flat, and the tracks might be expected to be fairly serviceable until the coming of the rains; but it was doubtful whether they would stand the weight of heavy mechanical transport, and it was proposed to use none in the preliminary operations, with the exception of Holt caterpillar tractors and trucks for the heavy artillery and its ammunition. This left supply beyond railhead largely dependent upon camel transport—a cumbrous and expensive method, which made very high demands upon those responsible for its effective organization.

The preliminary arrangements for the supply of the force with food, water, and ammunition were therefore of paramount importance. It is necessary to describe in turn (i) the railways, (ii) the organization of mechanical and camel transport, and (iii) the arrangements in respect of water.

(i) The main single-track railway from Qantara had, as related in the previous volume, reached Deir el Balah at the date of Sir Edmund Allenby's arrival. It just sufficed, independently of sea transport, to maintain the force before Gaza.[1] As soon as he received instructions to double this line the work was put in hand by Br.-General Sir G. Macauley, Director of Railway Transport, and it advanced very quickly. By the end of August eight miles from Qantara had been doubled, while bank work and the laying out of sleepers and rails had been completed for approximately another ten miles. Qantara Station was enlarged. By the end of September the double line was in use beyond Qatiya, a distance of over 30 miles as the track lay. At the end of October, on the eve of the offensive, it was in use up to Bir el Mazar, a distance of 70 miles; a mile a day having thus been laid throughout the last two months.

It was also recorded in Vol. I that early in May Sir A. Murray had decided to construct a branch from the main line at Rafah to the Wadi Ghazze to enable operations to be carried out upon a broader front. This line reached Bir Qamle about the date of Sir Edmund Allenby's arrival, and a short loop to Shellal from a point 4 miles north-west of Qamle was soon afterwards constructed. The latter branch it was decided to continue eastward to the neighbourhood of Kharm, 6 miles east of the Wadi Ghazze, to

---

[1] In Vol. I, p. 358 *et seq.*, the measures already taken to increase the carrying power of the line are mentioned.

facilitate the supply of the force attacking Beersheba and the Turkish left wing. This work would, however, have to be done at the last moment and very rapidly; otherwise it would be for the enemy a pretty plain pointer to British intentions. Two or three miles of light-railway track were subsequently to be laid eastward from Kharm and another branch from Qamle. General Allenby also decided to extend the main line across the Wadi Ghazze and construct a dummy station on the right bank. This would have the effect of making the enemy believe that the main attack was to come against Gaza, but the extension would be of real value shortly afterwards, if it was in fact found necessary to transfer the weight of the attack to the left flank, a possibility foreshadowed in the instructions already quoted.

For the supply of the front during the period of trench warfare there was already a network of light lines, totalling over 12 miles in length, in the area between Deir el Balah and the Wadi Ghazze. These would obviously be of great value for the secondary operations against the Gaza defences, during which, as will be explained, the XXI Corps was to be denuded of transport to make the XX and Desert Mounted Corps mobile.

(ii) With regard to mechanical transport there were only four M.T. Companies totalling 180 lorries, and these were all at Cairo, nor had there been any provision for their use in the original transport scheme, because it was not thought possible to employ them. Before the advance to Beersheba began it was found by reconnaissance that they could be employed, not only on the Tell el Fara–Beersheba track, but actually across country to bring up ammunition to the heavy battery positions. Three companies were therefore entrained to Kharm at the end of October, and proved of great value. There were also available 134 Holt tractors, chiefly required for the transport of ammunition, though 24, with trailer trucks, were handed over to the Desert Mounted Corps for rations and R.E. stores.

With the exception of the XXI Corps' ammunition tractors, practically the whole of the transport available was handed over to the XX and Desert Mounted Corps. The former was allotted two companies and two sections of " light burden " camels, and also the horsed wagons of two of the XXI Corps' divisional trains. With the horsed divisional trains of the 10th, 53rd, 60th and 74th Divisions the corps had now three echelons of supply for three of its divisions and two for the fourth division; that is to say, three days' mobile rations for three divisions, and two days' for one division were to be ready, loaded up, when the advance began. The Desert Mounted Corps was allotted, together with the tractors and trucks above mentioned, one company and three sections of " light burden " camels, giving it also three days' rations. Four " heavy burden " camel companies (about 7,000 camels) were organized as a water convoy, to be allotted as circumstances demanded, under the orders of G.H.Q. This left the XXI Corps immobilized from the 8th October, on which date its divisional trains were withdrawn to rest in view of their coming exertions, and dependent for supplies upon the light railway system from Deir el Balah. But large dumps of seven days' rations on a mobile scale were also formed close to the front line in readiness for the operations.[1]

(iii) The provision of 7,000 camels as a special water convoy has been mentioned. At Shellal, where springs yielded great quantities of slightly saline water, and a rock basin had been dammed to store half a million gallons, arrangements were made by Br.-General E. Evans, D.A. & Q.M.G. of the XX Corps, for the filling of 2,000 camel *fanatis* (25,000 gallons) per hour. The other preparations undertaken by the Chief Engineer, Major-General H. B. H. Wright, were of two natures: the extension of piping and the development of local supplies. The main pipe-line was extended from Rafah to Shellal, and pipes stacked ready to begin carrying it eastward after the attack. Troops at Shellal were therefore drinking Nile water 140 miles from its source. Small-gauge pipes were also laid to the British positions south of Gaza from wells at Deir el Balah and in

---

[1] These dumps were formed at Sheikh Ajlin near the beach, on the Rafah–Gaza road, at Mansura, etc., and contained, in round figures, 300,000 rations for British troops, 14,000 for Indians, 40,000 for Egyptians, and also large quantities for camels, horses and mules. Their original purpose was in part a provision against the flooding of the Wadi Ghazze, of which the natives gave warning, but by the forethought of General Bulfin they were established as far forward as possible for use in case of an advance and carefully camouflaged.

the bed of the Wadi Ghazze. With regard to the second 1917. source of supply, there were springs, or water not far below Aug. the surface, at various points along the Wadi Ghazze, the upper reaches of which have been given various names by the Arabs—Wadi Shanag, Wadi Imalaga, Wadi Khelasa, Wadi Asluj. This country was once far more thickly inhabited and far more fertile than it is now. The desert and its people were subdued and civilized colonies planted here and there, but the people of the desert have swept back again—as in great tracts of Northern Africa, as in Trans-Jordan—and all that remains of the colonies are large mounds, below which lie their ruins. It was already known that there was water at Esani, within easy distance for reconnaissance from Qamle. It was discovered from the records of the Palestine Exploration Society that Khelasa, 13 miles south-west of Beersheba, was the site of the Greek city of Eleusa, said to have contained 60,000 inhabitants, and that Asluj, 16 miles south of Beersheba, had also been a considerable town. Starting with these clues, Lieut.-Colonel R. E. M. Russell, C.R.E. of the Desert Mounted Corps, examined a number of natives, who informed him that there was a large water supply at these sites. It was arranged that directly these places were occupied the field companies R.E. of the XXI Corps should set about the development of wells at Esani, while the field squadrons of the two Australian divisions and the field troop of the Camel Brigade did the same work at Maalaga, Abu Ghalyun, Khelasa, and Asluj. Pumps and canvas troughs for watering horses were prepared in great quantities.

These preparations, which came within the sphere of Major-General Walter Campbell, the Deputy Quartermaster-General, were the most important and difficult; but the Deputy Adjutant-General, Major-General J. Adye, had also some problems hard enough to solve. To him it fell to decide upon the position of field hospitals and dressing stations, and to make all arrangements for the collection, reception, and treatment of casualties. This had to be done at the last possible moment; for the appearance of new hospitals and clearing stations near the front is one of the surest guides to an enemy's intelligence service of an impending offensive.

The object of recording these arrangements at length —though even then without entering into a tithe of their detail—is that they occupied the minds of commanders and staffs more than the actual operations to be undertaken. If the troops allotted to the enterprise could be placed in position east and west of Beersheba, Beersheba would fall. If the XX Corps could then be maintained in that area, the rolling up of the enemy's left at Tell esh Sheria was a comparatively simple and a remarkably promising scheme. But could it be maintained there? It will be shown that, even with all this forethought, unexpected difficulties arose, and that the operation did not proceed quite in accordance with the original plan.

NOTE.

TURKISH REINFORCEMENTS IN PALESTINE.

The seven divisions which it was originally designed to put under the command of *Yilderim*, in addition to the troops already in Palestine and Mesopotamia, were the *19th* and *20th* from Galicia, the *24th* and *42nd* from the Dardanelles, the *48th* from the Caucasus, the *50th* from Macedonia, and the *59th* from Adana in the Gulf of Iskanderun. Of these the *19th* and *24th* were the only ones to arrive before the opening of the Third Battle of Gaza (see Chapter II). The *20th Division* arrived in time to take part in the Jerusalem operations, and the *48th* soon afterwards. The *42nd* does not appear to have reached Syria till the summer of 1918. The other two, the *50th* and *59th*, were broken up, probably at Aleppo, and the troops divided between the Palestine and Mesopotamia fronts.

It was afterwards decided to transfer two more divisions to Palestine from the Caucasus, the *1st* coming into action in the attempt to retake Jerusalem at the end of December, and the *11th* appearing in March 1918.

## CHAPTER II.

#### THE EVE OF THE OFFENSIVE.

(Maps 1, 2, 4; Sketch 1.)

### THE PLAN OF ATTACK.

THERE were no operations of importance during the period of the great summer heat, while the preparations mentioned in the last chapter were in progress.[1] In the plain east of the Wadi Ghazze on the British right flank numerous small actions took place, each side seeking opportunities to lay ambushes for the other. The Turkish patrols, aided by Bedouin whose sole military virtues were displayed in affairs of this sort, were enterprising enough, and kept the British mounted troops thoroughly alert. In the neighbourhood of Gaza trench raids were carried out on both sides, the most important being one by the 162nd Brigade (54th Division) on the 20th July, against Umbrella Hill, south-west of Gaza. The Turkish garrison of the hill was completely demoralized, left 101 dead in the trenches, and lost 17 prisoners, a trench mortar and a machine gun. The British losses in the actual raid were trifling, but, as so often happened on the Western Front in these enterprises, the heavy bombardment of their trenches which followed did much to square the account, there being over one hundred casualties from this cause. On the 5th August a German airman made a bold attempt to damage the pipe-line, landing beside it near Salmana and blowing in a couple of lengths of piping before he was driven off by the fire of a patrol. On the 16th August a squadron of the 7th A.L.H. attempted to pass through the Turkish outposts in the gap between Beersheba and the main position, in order to blow up a section of the railway near Abu Irqaiyiq. Unfortunately a small Turkish patrol came upon the scene while the explosives were being placed in position; though

1917.
July-Aug.
Maps 2, 4.

---

[1] There is a good description of the summer conditions in "The Fifty-second (Lowland) Division," by Lieut.-Colonel R. R. Thompson.

it was annihilated, the alarm was given, and the Australian squadron had to retire before the engineers with it could fire the charge.

Bold enterprises of this type and constant patrolling made the mounted troops intimately acquainted with the ground from the Wadi Ghazze to the neighbourhood of the Beersheba defences. The Commander-in-Chief and Generals Chetwode and Chauvel themselves carried out numerous reconnaissances, covered by large bodies of mounted troops. These movements were on some occasions construed and reported by the enemy as attacks.[1] They undoubtedly contributed to lull him to a sense of security when the real concentration took place. The British aircraft took many hundreds of photographs, from which accurate maps of the Turkish defences were produced by the Field Survey Company of the Royal Engineers. Meanwhile the work went forward without interruption, as the blazing heat of August gave way to the milder though still trying autumn weather —hot by day and cold by night—and the Force made ready for the great offensive.

On the Turkish side also there was activity, though mainly with defence in view. The positions along the Gaza –Beersheba road, mere skeletons at the time of the Second Battle of Gaza, were immeasurably strengthened, though owing to the shortage of barbed wire in the country and the difficulties of transporting it from Europe there was little for the left of the line. The railway branch from Et Tine, of which mention was made in the first volume, was completed to Beit Hanun, $4\frac{1}{2}$ miles north-east of Gaza, to supply the right flank, and a short spur taken off from Deir Sneid, a little higher up, to Huj, to supply the centre.

In early October there was a discussion regarding policy between Sir Edmund Allenby and the C.I.G.S., historically curious because it illustrates vividly the impossibility of correctly estimating Turkish resources and intentions in this theatre. It will be recalled that there had been no mention of a definite territorial objective in the Government's instructions to the Commander-in-Chief. Now, on the 5th October,

---

[1] See "My War Memories," by General Ludendorff, p. 504 (English translation). "At the end of August large masses of English cavalry "advanced on Beersheba so as to work round the left flank of the Gaza "front and reach the water-supply of Jerusalem. This enterprise failed."

## THE WAR CABINET AND PALESTINE 27

Sir William Robertson telegraphed that the War Cabinet had again discussed affairs in Palestine, and had insisted upon the desirability of eliminating Turkey from the war at a blow. It was thought that her general condition was now such that a heavy defeat, followed by the occupation of the Jaffa–Jerusalem line, might induce her to break with her Allies. General Allenby was asked to estimate his requirements for such an operation, bearing in mind that two German divisions were reported to be preparing for the East.[1] He was subsequently informed that fresh British divisions could be sent to him at the rate of one every sixteen days.

1917.
Oct.

Sir Edmund Allenby estimated that a total of twenty divisions, including the two German, might be brought against him, and that to drive back this force and occupy the line in question he would require the same number, that is, an addition of thirteen divisions. Probably the enemy would not be able to employ more than twelve divisions on the front, but he could replace them as required. Similarly, even when the British railway to Rafah was doubled, he himself would not be able to employ more than fourteen, but six would be concentrated on the Canal ready to replace those in need of rest. Not until after the launching of the offensive was the Commander-in-Chief informed of the improbability of his force being increased in any degree, still less nearly trebled. In the event, the Jerusalem–Jaffa line was to be occupied securely within two months of the opening of the British offensive. Its capture, after a heavy Turkish defeat, did not have the effect desired by the Government, but, on the other hand, it did not lead to any notable increase of Turkish strength. It was at about this period also that the Government again discussed the possibility of a landing at Alexandretta. The project would have required at least six divisions and a million tons of shipping, at a moment when Great Britain was going hungry for lack of the flour and meat from abroad on which she was so gravely dependent, and when thousands of American troops were unable to cross the Atlantic for lack of transport. It is therefore not surprising that the scheme was quickly abandoned.

---

[1] The report was, in fact, an exaggerated account of the preparations of the *Asia Corps*. (See p. 5.)

Meanwhile Sir Edmund Allenby was preparing his plans, based strictly upon the means actually at his disposal. On the 22nd October his orders for the attack were issued.[1] His intention was to take the offensive against the enemy at Gaza and at Beersheba, and, after capturing Beersheba to make an enveloping attack on the left flank of the enemy's main position in the direction of Sheria and Hureira. On a date to be notified later, the XX Corps and the Desert Mounted Corps (less one mounted division) would attack Beersheba with the object of gaining it by nightfall.

As soon as Beersheba was in British hands and arrangements had been made for the restoration of its water supply, the XX and Desert Mounted Corps were to move rapidly forward to attack the left of the enemy's main position. The XX Corps would capture first the group of trenches between the railway and the Wadi esh Sheria, then cross the wadi and take the Hureira trenches. The Desert Mounted Corps, picking up its detached division, hitherto filling the gap between the XX and XXI Corps, would then advance north to capture Tell en Nejile and operate vigorously against the enemy's left flank, should he throw it back to oppose the advance of the XX Corps.

Four days before the attack on Beersheba the XXI Corps with powerful naval co-operation was to open a systematic bombardment of the Gaza defences, gradually increasing in intensity. On a date subsequently to be determined, but probably after the occupation of Beersheba and before the attack on the left of the main Turkish line, the XXI Corps was to attack the south-western defences of Gaza, with the object of capturing the enemy's front line system from Umbrella Hill, on the Rafah–Gaza road, to Sheikh Hasan, on the beach 3 miles north-west of the town.

In order to carry out the attack on Beersheba the XX Corps was to move into position facing the defences south of the Wadi es Sabe on the previous night. For the attack two divisions were to be employed, while a third covered the left flank. The objective of the corps was the enemy's works west and south-west of Beersheba to the Beersheba–Khelasa track. The Desert Mounted Corps was also to move from its area of concentration at Khelasa and Asluj

---

[1] Appendix 7.

## THE PLAN OF ATTACK

on the same night, so as to be ready to co-operate with the XX Corps by attacking Beersheba from the east and north-east. Its objective was the enemy's defences from south-east to north-east of Beersheba and the town itself, but the main weight of the attack was to be directed from the east and north-east in order to break down resistance as quickly as possible. The corps was then to act with all possible vigour to prevent the escape of the garrison, or at least drive it well beyond the high ground immediately overlooking the town from the north. It was also of great importance to push troops rapidly into Beersheba to protect wells and pumping plant from destruction. Not till the situation as regards water at Beersheba had become clear, so that the movement of the XX and Desert Mounted Corps against the Sheria defences could be arranged, would the G.O.C. XXI Corps receive orders to carry out his attack on the defences south-west of Gaza. The Yeomanry Mounted Division, the rôle of which was to fill the gap between the XX and XXI Corps, was to be under the orders of the XX Corps till the morning of the attack on Beersheba, and then to come directly under G.H.Q.

1917. Oct.

The main operation, then, depended upon the speedy capture of Beersheba with its water supply, and all subsequent moves hinged upon the success of this first. On the 23rd October, the day after the issue of the operation order, the Commander-in-Chief sent supplementary instructions to General Chauvel, commanding the Desert Mounted Corps. He pointed out first of all that the attack of the XX Corps could probably not be launched before 10 a.m., and that the Desert Mounted Corps should aim at being in position east of Beersheba in time to move forward against the mound Tell es Sabe, 3 miles east of the town, before the enemy had time to realize that he was also being attacked, and in greater strength, from the south-west. Vigorous and rapid action against enemy advanced posts or patrols met with during the approach march would therefore be necessary.

If the Turkish commander at Beersheba had early information of the movement of large mounted forces against his left rear, he might withdraw. Should he attempt to rejoin the main force by moving north-west, his retreat was to be harried. He might, on the other hand, attempt to withdraw north-east, up the Hebron road, but unless he began his retreat early during the night before "Zero" day, the mounted troops ought to be able to inflict serious loss upon his detachment. If he fell back fighting to the hills north of Beersheba he must be driven off them as quickly as possible, in order that the town should not be commanded by his artillery, by envelopment of his left flank, while the XX Corps would be instructed to co-operate by attacking him from the south and south-west. After he had been driven back the Desert Mounted Corps would be required to secure this high ground north of Beersheba until relieved by other troops.

Above all, General Chauvel was to bear in mind that a great strain would be thrown upon his troops and horses when, after the capture of Beersheba, the main operation against the enemy's left began. It was of vital importance that the horses should be kept fresh for the second and principal phase of the attack, in so far as this was permitted by the necessity of taking Beersheba as early as possible.

Several ruses were employed to deceive the enemy. One, which may be described as strategic, was an endeavour to make the Turks believe that a landing on the northern coast of Syria, probably in the Gulf of Iskanderun, would be attempted from Cyprus. Sites for camps were laid out on the island, and as much stir as possible made by garrison troops. Bogus messages were despatched by wireless, and inquiries made of contractors regarding the provision of rations on a considerable scale. Docks and wharves were labelled for the embarkation and disembarkation of troops and stores, and reports circulated that it was proposed to form a base on the island.

This ruse does not appear to have had any success.[1] But another, of a very much simpler nature, was to have an extraordinary effect, an effect, indeed, hardly to be matched in the annals of modern war. An officer on the staff at

---

[1] "On the 17th October an aerial reconnaissance over Cyprus established the fact that no preparations were being made there." Turkish "*Yilderim*," Part 2, Chap. III.

The plans mentioned above had been approved by a telegram to Cyprus from G.H.Q. on the 6th October, and it is to be presumed that the work had not made sufficient progress by the 17th to give the appearance of a new base from the air. There is no evidence that the rumours which were intended to be carried to the Turks by their agents reached them, at any rate before the Third Battle of Gaza.

# A SUCCESSFUL RUSE

G.H.Q. rode out into No Man's Land on the 10th October, 1917. accompanied by a small escort, as if on reconnaissance. Near El Girheir, on the bank of the Wadi Hanafish, he was fired on by a Turkish cavalry patrol, which then gave chase. He pretended to be wounded, rolled about in the saddle, and finally dropped field-glasses and other articles, including a bundle of papers in a haversack, which he had previously stained with fresh blood from his horse. Having ascertained that a Turkish trooper had picked up the papers, he made his escape. The most important papers in the portfolio were mock agenda for a conference at G.H.Q., indicating that the main attack would be carried out against Gaza, accompanied by a landing on the coast north of the town, with subsidiary operations by mounted troops against Beersheba, more or less as a feint; together with G.H.Q. instructions for the above attack. There were also a few rough notes on a cipher, sufficient to enable an expert in cipher work to decode any dummy messages it might be desirable to send out by wireless later on. Other private documents were so cleverly faked that they greatly heightened the effect of the principal ones.[1]

After the capture of Gaza an order was found, signed by Colonel Ali Fuad Bey, commanding the Turkish *XX Corps*, stating that he had rewarded the N.C.O. in charge of the patrol which had obtained such valuable information, and warning his own officers against carrying papers when they were on reconnaissance. But before that happened the effect of the ruse was seen. Work on trenches immediately decreased on the enemy's left and was greatly increased on

---

[1] Twenty pounds in notes were included to give the impression that the loss was not intentional. There were personal letters from home of a type which it might be expected the recipient would not willingly lose. There was a private letter from an imaginary staff officer indicating that the main attack would be on Gaza and frankly criticising the obtuseness of G.H.Q. in not operating against the other flank. There was also the copy of a telegram from G.H.Q to Desert Mounted Corps stating that a staff officer was going out on patrol towards El Girheir. A few days later a notice was inserted in Desert Corps orders that a note-book had been lost and that the finder was to return it to G.H.Q. A party was sent out to search for it, and the officer in command threw away some sandwiches wrapped up in a copy of the orders on the approach of the enemy.

The officer who planned and carried out this ruse has requested that his name should not be made public, and though it is well known not only in the British Army but to the Turks, it has seemed reasonable to comply with his desire.

his right. The enemy was deceived, and the deception had a very important effect upon his plans.[1]

It may be stated here that there were some senior officers, of what may be called the " Gaza School," who disagreed with General Chetwode's appreciation, upon which this plan was based. To them it appeared that the failure of the Second Battle of Gaza in no way proved an attack on the enemy's right to be faulty strategy; for (in their eyes) the tactical dispositions for that attack had been faulty. An assault on the defences between Gaza and the sea, carried out in much greater strength than that which actually took place on the 2nd November, would, they thought, have broken through. Arguing after the event, they point out how much four brigades accomplished here—subsequently to the capture of Beersheba, be it noted, however—and suggest that with another division the front could have been completely ruptured. If that be granted, the advantages of this strategy are patent. Mounted troops concentrated south-west of Gaza would have started fresh. They would have advanced straight on Junction Station, following a course upon which they could be supplied with comparative ease and on which water could always be obtained, at the worst by sinking wells near the shore. Those who uphold this strategy also point out that the essence of the Beersheba-Tell esh Sheria plan was that the Desert Mounted Corps should envelop the retreating Turks, and that, owing to the preliminary exertions of its horses and the shortage of water on the route followed, it failed in large measure to accomplish this object and was very weary by the time it had caught up the marching infantry.

In discussing the plan adopted by Sir Edmund Allenby there must be a great difference in our attitude according as we consider it in the light of what actually happened or in the uncertainty prevailing before the attack. The invaluable ruse which has been described would not have worked the other way. The Turks could be *confirmed* in their belief that Gaza was the objective; they could not have been *dissuaded* from this belief by any faked plan of attack on Beersheba. Then, it must have appeared likely that the

---

[1] Evidence on this subject will be found in Note at end of Chapter, in which the Turkish conception of British intentions is discussed.

break-through would be a slow and costly operation, and 1917. even that the risk of complete failure was not small. Had Oct. all gone well, the corridor opened for the pursuit would have been most uncomfortably narrow and exposed to artillery fire, being limited by the gardens of Gaza and the long ridge east of the town. Finally, the advance up the coast would have been conducted with an unbroken enemy retiring on the high ground to the south-east instead of the beaten troops whose threats the British were able virtually to disregard. Even if we take into account our present knowledge, we shall have to admit that there were accidents in the pursuit by the mounted troops from Tell esh Sheria which could hardly have been anticipated, quite apart from the water shortage. There is no real analogy between the offensive of September 1918 and that of October 1917, because in the Battles of Megiddo the British were able to pin down the whole Turkish front while they broke the right flank; whereas if they had attempted to break the right flank at Gaza they would not have been in a position to pin down the Turkish forces on the whole Gaza–Beersheba line. The military student may, however, find a problem or war game of great interest in working out an imaginary attack in accordance with the scheme of the " Gaza School."

BEERSHEBA: THE TURKISH DISPOSITIONS AND STRENGTH.

Beersheba (Hebrew, Be-er Sheva; Arabic, Bir es Sabe) Maps 1, 2, 4. was, for all its fame, at the beginning of the war a poor Sketch 1. little Arab town. The new Turkish railway made of it a considerable base; good store-buildings were put up at the station, and a square of pretentious houses followed, containing even a German "beer garden." The town lies at the foot of the Judæan Hills, in a valley through which the Wadi es Sabe runs to join the Wadi Ghazze at Bir el Esani. North of the valley the ground rises somewhat sharply, Tuweiyil Abu Jerwal, 6 miles to the N.N.E., being 1,558 feet high, that is, overlooking the town by 700 feet. The town is also commanded from the east and south, though to a lesser extent, while it is approached on the south-east by a spur of the bleak plateau of Edom. Beersheba is well supplied with water, as students of Genesis will recall—Bir es Sabe probably means " The Seven Wells "—but within a circle of some six miles from its centre there is little or none, except when the rains set running the tributary wadis of the Ghazze. It has always been of some importance as a trading centre, and tracks of varying quality radiate from it. Northeast, generally following the bed of the Wadi el Khalil, a tributary of the Wadi es Sabe, runs the road through Edh Dhahriye, Hebron, and Bethlehem to Jerusalem, frequently winding its way through steep gorges; north-west is the road across the open plain to Gaza, 26 miles away in a direct line;[1] west is the track through Tell el Fara on the Ghazze to Rafah; south-west a road, metalled by the Turks early in the war, through Kossaima and Bir el Hassana, with a camel track from Kossaima to Nekhl and Suez; south a track through Asluj, with branches to the Wadi 'Araba and the sea at 'Aqaba; due east a track to the Dead Sea at Zuweira.

On the north-west, west, and south it was defended by a semi-circle of well-constructed trenches, protected by some wire, though little by the standard of the Western Front or even that of the Gaza defences. It was, however, virtually an isolated fortress, for between the north-western point of its defences and the main Turkish line, which crossed the railway 8 miles to the north-west, there were only half a dozen small works. Moreover, from the east it was scarcely defended at all, a few narrow, unwired trenches being the only artificial obstacles on that side,[2] though the Wadi es Sabe itself afforded a good fire position from which to sweep the flats to the south.

Beersheba was known to be the headquarters of the Turkish *III Corps* (Ismet Bey), which had under its command the *27th Division*, an Arab formation of two regiments only, and the *3rd Cavalry Division*. A regiment of the *53rd Division*, which was on the Gaza flank, had also been stationed at Beersheba till after mid-October. Then Kress

---

[1] The distance from Beersheba to Gaza is thus approximately that from Westminster to Guildford or to East Grinstead.

[2] No record of these last-named trenches has been found after considerable search among aeroplane photographs. It is possible that they were dug at the last moment. They are therefore not shown on Map 4, "The Gaza–Beersheba Line." On Map 5, "The Capture of Beersheba," they have been sketched from a Turkish map, on which they are shown more or less conventionally. They can therefore only be regarded as approximate, though all the other trenches are accurately reproduced from aeroplane photographs.

obtained permission to replace this regiment by the *48th* of 1917. the *16th Division* from Tell esh Sheria, thus strengthening his Oct. right at the expense of his left-centre : a disastrous policy, as it turned out, and one mainly due to the ruse already described. Finally, on the 28th October, the *2nd Regiment (24th Division)* was moved up from reserve into the town. The total strength of the garrison was approximately 5,000 rifles and sabres, 60 machine guns, and 28 guns.

The main Turkish position from the shore west of Gaza to south-east of Tell esh Sheria was held by the *XXII Corps* (Refet Bey) on the right and the *XX Corps* (Ali Fuad Bey) on the left. The dispositions, at least as regards the troops in front line, were known to the British Intelligence. They were as follows, from right to left :—

> *XXII Corps* (holding Gaza defences, headquarters Jebaliye) : *53rd* and *3rd Divisions ; 7th Division* in *Eighth Army* reserve about Deir Sneid ;
>
> *XX Corps* (headquarters Huj) : *54th, 26th,* and *16th Divisions ; 24th Division* [1] in reserve about Kh. Jemmame, east of Huj ;
>
> *Yilderim Reserve : 19th Division* at 'Iraq el Menshiye, on the railway, 25 miles north of Beersheba and 19 north-east of Gaza.

The estimated strength of the Turkish force in line and in reserve was 40,000 rifles. It actually appears to have been about 33,000 rifles, 1,400 sabres and 260 guns. This includes the *19th Division* at 'Iraq el Menshiye, though it was a long day's march from the front,[2] and the *12th Depot Regiment* which apparently moved from Jerusalem to Hebron just before the battle. The British preponderance in infantry was therefore about two to one ; in mounted troops eight to one [3] ; in guns about three to two. But, once again, hard

---

[1] This division had been moved hastily south, and its machine-gun companies did not arrive till after the battle.
[2] See Note at end of Chapter.
[3] The official rifle strength of the E.E.F. on the 28th October 1917 was : Infantry Divisions and Camel Brigade 80,000, Cavalry 15,000. These figures include, however, large numbers employed in special duties and not available with battalions and regiments. The actual strengths may be taken as about 60,000 and 12,000 respectively. An army on the defensive can employ a considerably higher proportion of its rifle strength than one which is attacking.

as the Turkish soldier might be expected to fight, strong as was the position which he held, it was the country which was the greatest obstacle and caused most anxiety as the day of battle approached.

The headquarters of the *Eighth Army* (Kress von Kressenstein) was at Huleikat, north of Huj. Falkenhayn and his staff were known to be in Syria, but it was believed that they had not come down to Southern Palestine. *Yilderim* headquarters was in fact at Aleppo until after the opening of the attack.

### The Concentration: The Attack on the Yeomanry Mounted Division.

The concentration of the XX and Desert Mounted Corps for the attack on Beersheba involved a march across the enemy's front, a manœuvre always attended by risk even when, as here, it is carried out under cover of a line of posts in a strong position. The date of the attack had been fixed for the 31st October. It had originally been intended to complete the concentration within seven days, but it was decided eventually, in order to give the Desert Mounted Corps more time for the development of wells and storage of water at Khelasa and Asluj, to begin it three days earlier. These preliminary moves were the most anxious of all, not by reason of danger from the enemy, for they were beyond reach of his arm, but because they supplied the clue, if the Turks could read it aright, to the whole programme.

On the 21st October the two corps held the Wadi Ghazze, the Australian Mounted Division at Qamle with one brigade on outpost duty, the 60th Division from Qamle to Shellal, with the 158th Brigade of the 53rd Division on its left, in touch with the troops of the XXI Corps. The remainder of the XX and Desert Mounted Corps lay in bivouac between Deir el Balah and Rafah. That night the 179th Brigade of the 60th Division and the 2nd L.H. Brigade of the A. & N.Z. Mounted Division moved up the wadi to Esani, where work on the water supply was at once begun. The Camel Brigade marched to Abu Ghalyun, south-east of Esani on the Wadi Imalaga, and on the night of the 23rd

Sketch 1.

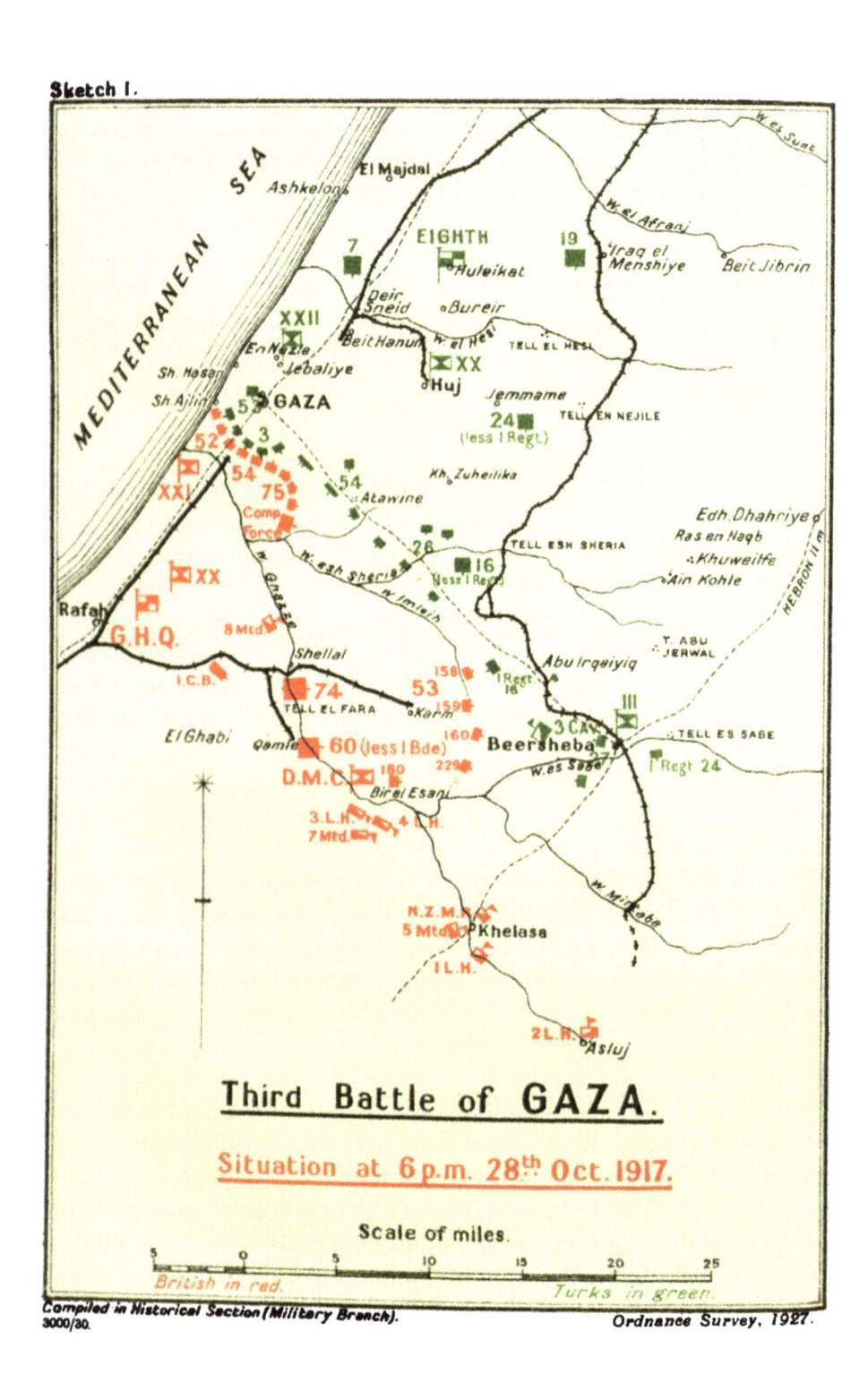

# Third Battle of GAZA.

Situation at 6 p.m. 28th Oct. 1917.

Scale of miles.

British in red.   Turks in green.

Compiled in Historical Section (Military Branch).   Ordnance Survey, 1927.

moved on to Khelasa, where it cleared a number of deep wells blown in by the Turks and fixed up pumps.

1917.
Oct.

These places were, as has been stated, a considerable distance from the enemy's position. Now came the first moves along a line of approach to Beersheba more direct and much more seriously exposed to attack. On the morning of the 23rd October the 5th Mounted Brigade, Australian Mounted Division, moved across the Ghazze to take up a line of observation south of the Wadi Imleih and west of its tributary the Wadi Hanafish, with its right on the Tell el Fara–Beersheba track at El Baqqar. In the dim light of dawn the leading troop of the Gloucester Yeomanry on the right was attacked and driven back upon its squadron by a squadron of Turkish cavalry, which rode in shouting loudly. The Turks were dislodged from El Baqqar at 6 a.m., and fell back eastward. The whole position was shortly afterwards occupied, but the Turks on several occasions attempted to charge and were only beaten back by the quick action of the Hotchkiss guns. It was the first occasion on which the Turkish cavalry had shown itself aggressive, but the advance had apparently not unduly alarmed the enemy, who made no further attempt to dislodge the British for four days.

On the night of the 24th the 2nd L.H. Brigade advanced from Esani to Asluj, the N.Z.M.R. Brigade replacing it at Esani. Until the engineers of the A. & N.Z. Mounted Division, who accompanied the 2nd L.H. Brigade, had developed the supply, there was serious shortage of water at Asluj, all the more so because it was necessary to allow Bedouin passing through on a trek southward to draw enough to take them to the next wells. The chief cause of delay was that the wells were choked with mud which was practically impervious and so prevented any inflow. In some cases horses had to be sent back ten miles to Khelasa to water. On the same evening the 53rd Division closed up to the Wadi Ghazze between Hisea and Shellal, and on the night of the 25th the 158th Brigade advanced across the wadi and took up a line through El Imara, with right on the Tell el Fara–Beersheba road, in order to cover work on the railway extension to Kharm.

On the night of the 26th the 8th Mounted Brigade, temporarily under the orders of the 53rd Division, took over from the Australian Mounted Division a long outpost line from El Baqqar on the right, along the Wadis Hanafish and esh Sheria, to a point south of El Mendur. The Hants Battery R.H.A. accompanied the brigade and was disposed to cover its right flank. Orders had been received that the right of the line from El Baqqar to a point 3 miles west of Bir Ifteis was to be held at all costs. The rest was merely to be occupied by a line of standing patrols, because, as has previously been explained, a brigade of the 53rd Division was entrenched behind it. The line was occupied by the Middlesex (1/County of London) Yeomanry on the right, the 3/County of London Yeomanry on the left, and the City of London Yeomanry in reserve, north-west of Kh. Khasif.

After a quiet night, a post west of Bir el Girheir, where a troop of the Middlesex Yeomanry under Captain A. McDougall was dug in, was suddenly attacked in great strength at 4.10 a.m. on the morning of the 27th. Two troops of the Middlesex from support were sent forward to work round to the right of the post. In face of heavy fire they advanced to within view of it, to find that it was almost surrounded by the enemy. A squadron of the City of London Yeomanry from reserve, under Major L. P. Stedall, succeeded in reaching a very slight hummock 200 yards south of the hill occupied by the post. It was here under very heavy machine-gun fire which—so small was the cover—just grazed the horses' saddles after the men had dismounted, and was pinned to the ground. Yet though it could not reach the post, it prevented the enemy from surrounding it completely. The Middlesex troop itself made a magnificent defence all day in a support trench, until late in the afternoon the advance of infantry of the 53rd Division induced the enemy to withdraw.

The right-hand post of two troops north of El Baqqar had less good fortune. It also was attacked by several squadrons, which, sweeping round its right, forced the guns of the Hants Battery near Kh. Khasif to withdraw. Here, too, relieving troops failed to reach the position, though they prevented the enemy from making further progress. The last message from Major A. M. Lafone, in command of the post, contained the words, "I shall hold on to the last." A little later a mass of Turkish cavalry was seen to surge

right over the position. It had then held out for just seven 1917.
hours.¹  29 Oct.

The total losses of the 8th Mounted Brigade in this very gallant action were 10 officers and 69 other ranks, mostly belonging to the two posts of the Middlesex Yeomanry. The resistance of these posts in face of overwhelming odds had prevented the enemy from taking full advantage of this reconnaissance in force—carried out by an infantry regiment and the *3rd Cavalry Division* ²—and perhaps from digging himself in upon the position. Had he done so, he could have rendered work on the railway impossible, and would have been extremely difficult to dislodge. On the approach of the British infantry and the 3rd L.H. Brigade the Turks withdrew all along the line, and the position was occupied by the 53rd Division.

Now the advance began to quicken, the water preparations having been nearly completed. By the morning of the 29th the A. & N.Z. Mounted Division was at Khelasa, with its leading brigade still at Asluj; the Australian Mounted Division had its head at Khelasa and its tail west of Esani; the 74th Division had moved forward a brigade to the right of the 53rd, which was holding open the line of advance at El Baqqar; the head of the 60th Division was about Maalaga, and its rear had closed up to Esani. Thus, while the left flank of the advance was covered by the 53rd Division, the 60th and 74th each provided protection to its own front. The Yeomanry Mounted Division had moved from the shore to the Ghazze between Shellal and Tell el Fara; and the 10th Division, previously stationed at Rafah, was also on the move forward.

The advance was a monument to staff work and skill in the memorizing of almost featureless country by guides—junior officers for the most part—who carried out hasty reconnaissances. From first to last it was conducted without a hitch.

---

[1] There were only three survivors of the garrison of this post. They related that it was heavily and persistently shelled by the enemy in the intervals between mounted attacks. One charge was brought to a halt almost on the lip of the trench, 15 dead being counted within 20 yards of it. Finally the garrison was reduced to five, who withdrew to a trench just behind the original line. Major Lafone sprang out into the open to meet the last charge, and was ridden down. He received the posthumous award of the Victoria Cross.

[2] See Note at end of Chapter.

The columns moved almost entirely by night. Elaborate precautions were taken to prevent the enemy guessing how large was the concentration, though it was, of course, impossible that he should not discover that a general movement eastward was in progress. Camps were left in position with fires lit in them at night, and the troops by day concealed themselves in the beds of the wadis. By day the plain appeared almost deserted. When the warning whistle signalled enemy aircraft in sight the troops, though already in the cover of the gullies, threw themselves down on their faces and remained motionless till the danger was over. In fact, however, owing to the activity of the patrols of the 40th Wing R.F.C., only a single German machine succeeded in taking photographs of the area covered by the flanking movement, and it was brought down near Khelasa, the occupants being captured. Hardly had dusk screened the land from view when the whole area swarmed into life like a stirred ant-hill. From Shellal the labourers hastened along the railway east of the Ghazze, stripped off the brown camouflage which screened their uncompleted work, set about plate-laying and the screwing up of the pipe-line. Regiment after regiment of Australians, New Zealanders, and Yeomanry rode south-eastward, till by the 30th October there were 12,000 men and as many horses at Asluj and Khelasa. Closer to the enemy's front advanced the infantry divisions. Huge columns of camels, having picked up the loads stacked ready for them in long rows, filed out across the Ghazze almost in silence, to disappear in the dust raised by their own feet. The supply tractors ground their way forward; the lorry columns, railed up from Cairo, were now also at work; half a dozen wheeled divisional trains marched with their burdens. Each column had its allotted route, not necessarily on an existing track; for movement across country was not much more difficult in the light of a moon nearly full. The transport column of the Desert Mounted Corps alone from Tell el Fara on the night of the 28th was six miles long. By midnight vast clouds of dust hung over the teeming plain. But by dawn all was still once more.

It was, however, impossible to prevent all observation, and the Turks had numerous Bedouin agents in their pay. There is evidence that they were fairly accurately informed of the British dispositions. Their maps correctly show, on the evening of the 26th, a brigade of mounted troops at Asluj, 1917. the Camel Brigade at Khelasa, a brigade of infantry and more Oct. cavalry about Esani. *Yilderim's* report to Constantinople on this evening that the movements against Beersheba were probably feints to divert attention from Gaza is comprehensible. But by the 28th the enemy had discovered that the camps at Khan Yunis and Rafah were empty, and that there were three brigades of infantry—there were in fact four—in the neighbourhood of El Baqqar and Kharm. Next day he had marked down the British dispositions with notable accuracy: three infantry divisions east of the Ghazze, the 10th Division approaching the wadi, and actually more cavalry at Asluj and Khelasa than were there. Why then did he persist in the belief that the main attack would be against Gaza ? It seems clear that the main reason was that this theory had been ineradicably fixed in his mind by the ruse which has been described, the effect of which was heightened when the bombardment of the Gaza defences began on the 27th. But in justice to the enemy commander it must be added that the British superiority in numbers was so great that, despite this dispersion, they were still strong enough on their left to have made their principal effort on that flank.

By the morning of the 30th the concentration was 30 Oct. complete, though the mounted troops, and especially the Australian Mounted Division, had long marches to make before they could launch their attack on Beersheba. The A. & N.Z. Mounted Division was all at Asluj, where General Chauvel and the staff of the Desert Mounted Corps joined it during the day. The Australian Mounted Division was at Khelasa. The 60th Division had not been required to move, and its brigades were upon the triangle Abu Ghalyun –Bir el Esani–Rashid Bek. The 74th Division had moved up to Kh. Khasif on the Tell el Fara–Beersheba track. The 53rd Division was now dug in along the Wadi Hanafish. The Camel Brigade, after assisting in the development of water supply, had been withdrawn to the Ghazze. Kharm Station had been finished on the 28th, that is, two days earlier than its allotted date. On the Gaza front the bombardment had increased, ships of the British and French Navies joining in on the 29th.

At 5.30 p.m. the troops of the A. & N.Z. Mounted

Division began to take their places for the final march, the 7th A.L.H. having already moved out as advanced guard; and by 8 p.m. the whole great column was clear of the dismantled station of Asluj. Hardly had the rattle and thud of hooves died away to the north-east when the camp guard and details heard the sound anew from the north-west. It was the head of the Australian Mounted Division, approaching from Khelasa.

NOTE.

The Turkish dispositions and strength before the Third Battle of Gaza have already been given. The latter is mainly compiled from the figures given in Turkish "*Yilderim,*" by far the best authority available. The infantry rifle strengths on 30th September are given as follows:—

| | | |
|---|---|---|
| *3rd Division* | 3,698 | |
| *7th Division* | 2,886 | |
| *16th Division* | 3,789 | |
| *24th Division* | 3,200 | |
| *26th Division* | 2,901 | |
| *27th Division* | 2,408 | (76% Arabs). |
| *53rd Division* | 3,100 | |
| *54th Division* | 2,738 | |
| *12th Depot Regiment* | 2,336 | (97% Arabs). |
| *136th Regiment* | not known | |
| | 27,056 | |

If we take the strength of the *136th Regiment* as 1,011, a figure given elsewhere, we reach a total of 28,067. Then there is the *19th Division*, which had not arrived at the above date. It was stronger than most of the others, and had a "Storm Battalion" six hundred strong; so it may be put at 4,000. The total is now 32,067. There were also, it appears, a few camelry. The calculation of 33,000 rifles is certainly not far from the mark. The *3rd Cavalry Division*, not counting one regiment which was over Jordan, had about 1,100 sabres; with a few weak divisional cavalry squadrons we have 1,400 sabres at most. The artillery strength of the *Eighth Army* on the 1st October is given as 268 guns; the artillery of the *19th Division* appears to have been still on the move. There were no other formations of any size which could possibly intervene in the battle; for the head of the next division, the *20th*, did not reach Ramle till about mid-November.

The machinery of command was being reorganized at the moment of the launching of the British offensive. As has previously been stated, the *Seventh Army* headquarters had come to Syria, accompanied by two corps headquarters, which had originally been intended for the offensive against Baghdad. The headquarters of the *XV Corps* was left in Aleppo to fulfil a function somewhat similar to that of a British headquarters Lines of Communication. The headquarters of the *III Corps* had recently moved down to Beersheba and taken over the detachment holding that town. That of the *Seventh Army* (Fevzi Pasha) had arrived at Hebron, but was being given a few days to reconnoitre the line. Orders had been issued that at midnight on the 31st October it would take over command of the *III Corps* at Beersheba and also of the *16th* and *24th Divisions* of the *XX Corps*. It appears, however, that Fevzi exercised no control during the early stages of the battle, the command of the whole front remaining in practice in the hands of Kress.

*Yilderim* itself was caught in a still more awkward predicament. Its first echelon had arrived at Jerusalem from Aleppo on the 29th, and Falkenhayn with the rest of his staff—or such officers as were on their feet ; for many of the Germans seem to have succumbed to the unhealthiness of Aleppo—intended to begin his journey down by motor on the 31st. When the British attacked he appears to have been at first afraid to commit himself to a run of considerably over four hundred miles, on indifferent roads, which would have taken two days, during which time he would have been in telegraphic communication with Jerusalem and the front only at rare intervals.

The success of the ruse to deceive the Turks as to the point of attack has been mentioned. It appears that the documents were examined with great care by Kress, and that, while not overlooking the possibility that they were faked, he inclined strongly to believe in their authenticity. At any rate, even after the attack on Beersheba had begun, he refused to believe the reports of the commander of the *III Corps* as to the British strength, ordered Beersheba to be held, and sent no reinforcements. Falkenhayn had suggested holding the only general reserve, the *19th Division*, either at Beersheba or in the hills north of it, but this measure Kress strongly opposed, and the Marshal gave way to the commander whose knowledge of the front was so much more intimate than his own.

Though they expected the main British attack to be directed against Gaza, the enemy commanders were to some extent concerned by the isolated position of Beersheba. Kress had urged during the summer that the detachment holding the town should be withdrawn into the Judæan Hills to the north, where it would have been virtually unassailable ("Sinai," i, p. 36). This measure was at that time opposed by the Turkish authorities not only on sentimental but also on economic grounds, since it would have involved the abandonment of considerable corn-lands. At a later stage Falkenhayn forbade it. Had the British offensive been postponed another two months, or been repulsed, the Marshal would have had at his disposal three or four more Turkish divisions, and above all the German *Asia Corps*. Though he would have still been inferior in numbers, it is certain that he would at once have passed to the offensive. For this purpose Beersheba, a fortress on the flank of the British position, with railhead, good water supply and a large accumulation of stores, would have been of vital importance. He could not bring himself to abandon it even when he saw the storm gathering.

The reconnaissance in force on the morning of the 27th was made by the *125th Regiment*, *16th* Division, from Tell esh Sheria, and by troops of the *3rd Cavalry Division* from Beersheba. It was carried out on an order from Falkenhayn at Aleppo. Falkenhayn also ordered the *Eighth Army* to carry out an attack southwards from Hureira on the morning of the 31st (Turkish " *Yilderim*," Part 2, Chap. III). This was forestalled by the British attack on Beersheba. Nothing is said as to its projected strength, and Kress himself does not mention the order.

## CHAPTER III.

### THE CAPTURE OF BEERSHEBA.

(Maps 1, 2, 5; Sketches 2, 3.)

#### THE APPROACH MARCH OF THE XX CORPS.

Maps 2, 5.   Now was come the moment for which the Force had been preparing since the arrival of its new Commander-in-Chief, four months earlier. The most serious difficulties which the capture of Beersheba involved were, as a fact, already mastered. The vast and complicated arrangements for the supply of the attacking troops had been completed; the infantry to attack from the west, the mounted troops to attack from the east, had been concentrated within a march of the positions on which they were to deploy. Greatly superior strength had been massed against the weakest portion of the enemy's line, and it was as certain as are any human consequences that Beersheba would fall. But there was cause for anxiety still as to how quickly and in what manner its capture would take place; for if the enemy were given time to destroy its wells and pumping machinery the value of the prize would be sadly diminished.

In accordance with General Chetwode's orders and preliminary instructions,[1] the 60th Division (Major-General J. S. M. Shea) on the right and the 74th Division (Major-General E. S. Girdwood) on the left were to attack the defences between the Beersheba–Khelasa track and the Wadi es Sabe. On the immediate left of the 74th Division, and under its orders, a temporary formation known as "Smith's Group," under the command of the G.O.C. Imperial Camel Brigade, Br.-General C. L. Smith, and consisting of that brigade and the 158th Brigade of the 53rd Division (less two battalions), was to hold a line from the Wadi es Sabe to just north of the Beersheba–Tell el Fara

---

[1] XX Corps' Instructions (G.O. 14/9) are given in Appendix 8.  XX Corps' Order No. 12 is given in Appendix 9.

Sketch 2.

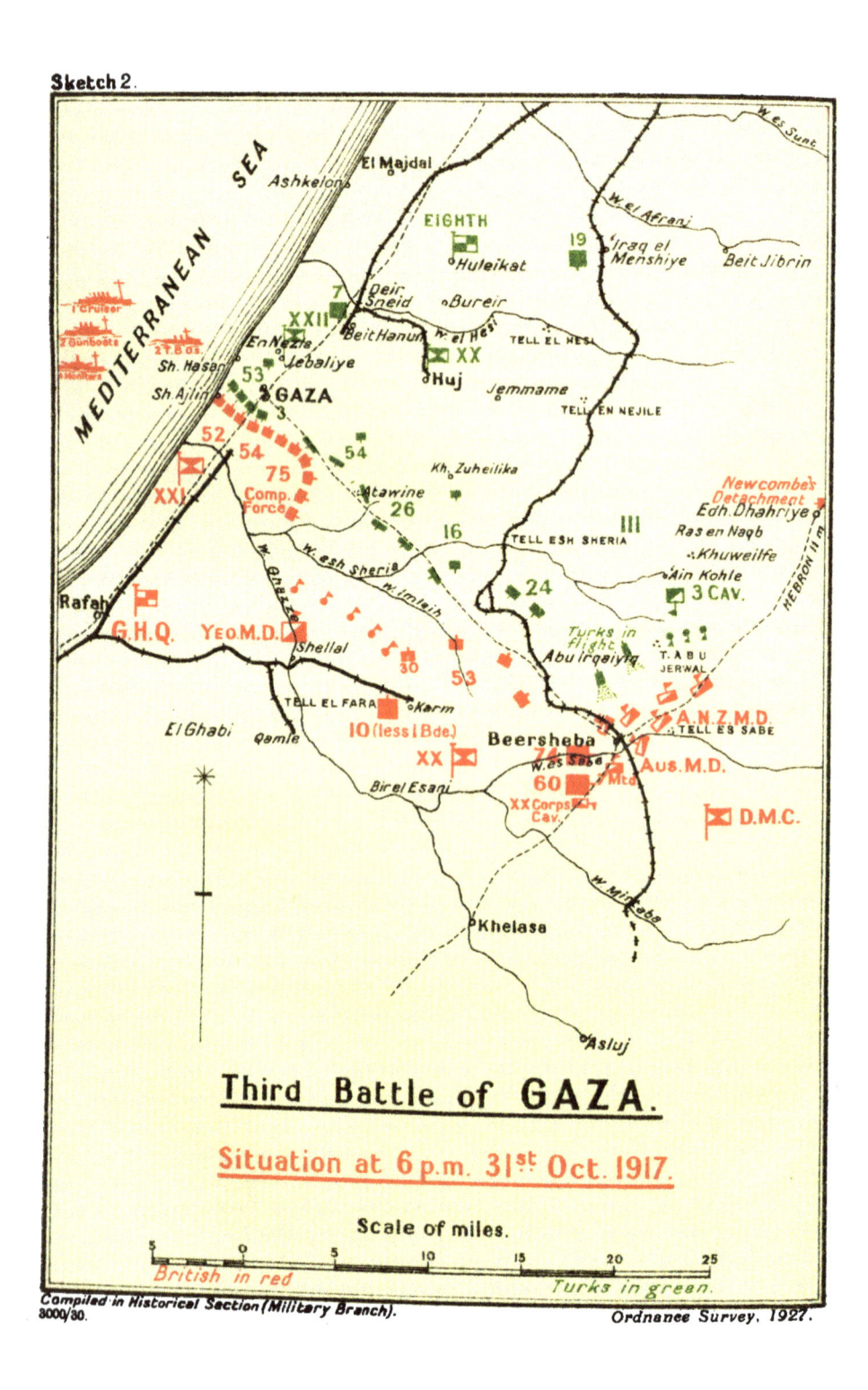

# Third Battle of GAZA.

## Situation at 6 p.m. 31st Oct. 1917.

Scale of miles.

British in red.    Turks in green.

Compiled in Historical Section (Military Branch).    Ordnance Survey, 1927.

## THE PLAN OF ATTACK

track. Smith's Group was therefore to face the northern section of the main defences of Beersheba, but no attack was to be made on the trenches north of the Wadi es Sabe until those south of it had been captured, nor even then without an order from the XX Corps. The 53rd Division, with a brigade of the 10th Division attached, was to hold a line of hastily entrenched posts from the left of Smith's Group to about a mile north of Kharm Station—a front of over seven miles—in order to secure the left flank of the corps against a counter-attack from the northward. This division was to be prepared to attack the Beersheba garrison if it retreated along the Gaza road. The 10th Division, less one brigade, was to be in corps reserve east of the Wadi Ghazze at Shellal. Here also was to be stationed the Yeomanry Mounted Division, G.H.Q. reserve, which would have out a line of posts connecting the left flank of the XX Corps with the right of the XXI about El Mendur.

1917.
30 Oct.

The attack was to be carried out in two stages, the first against some strong outlying works on the right centre at Point 1069,[1] by the left of the 60th Division. It was to be preceded by a bombardment and launched on the order of the G.O.C. 60th Division, when he considered that the artillery preparation had been sufficient. The main attack was to begin when the commanders of the two divisions were satisfied that the wire was adequately cut, again on the order of Major-General Shea, whose division was to direct. Its objective was the remainder of the trenches defending Beersheba and the Turkish batteries behind them. No troops were to advance beyond the line of the final objective, which was about a mile and a half behind the enemy's wire, except to capture Turkish guns, without the permission of the corps commander. The capture of Beersheba itself was the task of the Desert Mounted Corps, which required the water in the town for its horses.

Counter-battery was to be carried out by the XCVI Heavy Artillery Group, consisting for this occasion of five batteries (one 4·5-inch howitzer, two 60-pdr., and two 6-inch howitzer). The divisional artilleries of the 60th and 74th Divisions were to be reinforced, the former by one 18-pdr.

---

[1] Known as Point 1070 at the time of the attack. The alteration is due to the later survey.

battery of the Yeomanry Mounted Division and one 3·7-inch howitzer battery; the latter by one field artillery brigade detached from the 53rd Division. This division was to have at its disposal its own divisional artillery, less the brigade mentioned above, a field artillery brigade of the 10th Division [1] and one 60-pdr. battery. Its right brigade was to bombard the trenches north of the Wadi es Sabe, in order to deceive the enemy as to the frontage of the attack, and afterwards to endeavour to keep down flanking fire from them during the advance of the 74th Division. Omitting the artillery of the 10th Division in reserve, and also one field artillery brigade and one heavy battery attached to the 53rd Division, which were not directly engaged against the Beersheba defences, there were eight 6-inch howitzers, eight 60-pdrs., thirty-two 4·5-inch howitzers, four 3·7-inch howitzers, ninety-six 18-pdrs. available. The allotment of ammunition was about 200 rounds per gun.

The approach march was as well organized as had been all the preliminary moves. The 60th Division began its advance at 5.30 p.m. on the 30th in three brigade groups. Careful preliminary reconnaissances had been carried out, and two men had been placed in the mouth of each gulley where there was a risk of the troops taking a wrong turning. On the right the 179th Brigade (Br.-General Fitz-J. M. Edwards) struck out across country from Abu Ghalyun to the Khelasa–Beersheba road. Some difficulty was found in moving guns and transport until this track was reached, but little thereafter. The 2/13th London, acting as advanced guard, was fired on by outlying snipers during its advance to the Wadi Halgon. The 180th Brigade (Br.-General C. F. Watson) which was to form the divisional reserve, moved straight across country from Esani and took up a position in a sharp bend of the Wadi Mirtaba in rear of the 179th. The 181st Brigade (Br.-General E. C. Da Costa) on the left followed two routes, artillery and wheeled transport north of the Wadi es Sabe, infantry and pack south of

---

[1] Lest it appear a needless complication to take away one artillery brigade from the 53rd Division and give it another from the 10th, it must be recalled that the 53rd Division had one infantry brigade of the 10th Division under its orders. This brigade (the 30th) moved up on the left of the 53rd Division as a fully equipped brigade group, with an artillery brigade, a field company Royal Engineers, etc.

## APPROACH MARCH OF XX CORPS 47

it. Small enemy patrols opened fire, but were not permitted to impede the advance. The 522nd Field Company R.E. rapidly improved the route for the two field artillery brigades, so that they were in position by 1.30 a.m. The divisional artillery was divided into two groups, one to support each of the two attacking brigades.[1] The Corps Cavalry Regiment (Westminster Dragoons) which had been holding a line of observation to cover the division during the night, now concentrated south-east of its right flank. Its mission was to link up the right of the XX Corps with the troops of the Desert Mounted Corps south of Beersheba.

1917.
31 Oct.

The whole of the 74th Division—the head of which, it will be recalled, was at Kh. Khasif—followed the Tell el Fara–Beersheba track. The 229th Brigade led, the other two marching in mass, one north, the other south, of the track. The march discipline was extremely good, and each of the rear brigades presented, in the words of an eye-witness, " a wonderful sight, a solid square of troops moving in the " bright moonlight with a ripple of dust in front like the " bow-wave of a ship, rising into a great cloud through " which the moon shone redly in the rear." Changes in direction, necessary twice, were made by marching the directing flank on to a lantern already set up, halting, and lighting another lantern on the outer flank; so that the brigade faced on the required bearing.

About Taweil el Habari, 6 miles west of Beersheba, the division turned south-east and crossed the Wadi es Sabe. This movement was covered by an advanced guard of two battalions of the 229th Brigade (Br.-General R. Hoare). The artillery moved last, straight across country from El Baqqar, and was in position along the Wadi Abushar by 3.15 a.m.[2] In this division also it was divided into two groups, one to support each brigade in the attack.[3]

The four brigades destined to carry out the assault had

---

[1] Right Group, to support 179th Brigade: 303rd Brigade R.F.A., 10th Mountain Battery, Berks Battery R.H.A. Left Group, to support 181st Brigade: 301st and 302nd Brigades R.F.A.

[2] The exact lines of advance of the division, as well as those of the 60th, are difficult to describe owing to the absence of names on the map. They can, however, easily be followed by the arrows on Map 5.

[3] Right Group, to support 231st Brigade: XLIV and 268th Brigades R.F.A. Left Group, to support 230th Brigade: 117th and 266th Brigades R.F.A.

ample cover in the Wadi Halgon and its tributaries, in the
"London Wadi," a tributary of the Wadi Mirtaba, and in a
number of little wadis running north-westward to the Wadi
es Sabe, to the most important of which the names "Queen's
"Wadi," "Surrey Wadi," "Sussex Wadi," and "Y Wadi"
were given. The 181st Brigade found it possible to
establish Stokes mortars in some of these gullies, and they
did good service in the bombardment of the outer works at
Point 1069.

General Chetwode's advanced headquarters opened at
El Baqqar at 5 p.m. on the 30th October.

### The Attack of the XX Corps.

It was a cold, still night, precursor of a hot and breathless day. Over the troops' left shoulders the bombardment of Gaza, more than twenty miles away, was rumbling, and the horizon flickered with gun-flashes till breaking day concealed them. From the Turkish trenches in front there came not a sound. Then, at 5.55 a.m., the XX Corps' own artillery set about its work. The ground, after the scorching heat of summer, was dry as powder and bare of vegetation; there was no breath of wind; so that after an hour's bombardment the Turkish defences were screened in a dense cloud of dust. At 7 the bombardment was stopped for three-quarters of an hour to permit the murk to clear a little and the observers to locate their targets. Visibility did not much improve during the pause, but from what could be seen of the wire it was by no means all cut. Br.-General Da Costa decided that further delay would prove more costly in the long run than an immediate assault, and got Major-General Shea's permission to carry it out after a final intense bombardment of ten minutes, beginning at 8.20. At this hour the 2/22nd London advanced against Point 1069 itself and the 2/24th against the works just north of it. The wire-cutting parties cut the necessary gaps while the barrage was still upon the Turkish trenches 30 yards ahead, and within a few minutes the works were captured with 90 prisoners, the brigade having so far suffered about one hundred casualties.

While this attack was in progress the leading brigades of the 74th Division advanced in conformity with the 181st Brigade, coming as they topped the successive low cliffs under accurate shrapnel fire, which inflicted heavy loss upon the 231st Brigade on the right. Direction was hard to keep upon ground which, though extraordinarily rough and broken, had few easily distinguishable features. The 231st Brigade (Br.-General C. E. Heathcote) edged off slightly to its right, forcing the 230th (Br.-General A. J. M'Neill) on the left to fill the gap with two supporting companies of its right battalion, the 10/Buffs. As the troops neared the enemy's entrenchments machine-gun fire slowed down the advance, but by 10.40 the 231st Brigade was within 500 yards of the front line, and the 230th, the left of which was slightly refused, about 400 yards further off. Batteries now moved forward to positions from which the wire covering the main defences could be cut.

The sun was well up when the new bombardment began; the stones which bestrewed the ground were already burning to the touch, and the hillsides radiated heat. At 11.40 Major-General Shea told Major-General Girdwood that the wire on his division's front appeared to be cut and asked how soon he would be prepared to attack. Major-General Girdwood replied that he could not see whether or not the wire on his front was cut, but that the 74th Division would go forward when the 60th was ready. General Chetwode then ordered the assault on the main line to be launched at 12.15 p.m., at which hour the bombardment was to increase in intensity.

The four brigades, 179th, 181st, 231st, and 230th, advanced swiftly, to a great extent screened by the dust and smoke of the bombardment. In every case but that of the 181st Brigade their attack was carried out by two battalions in first line. The 181st Brigade had three battalions in line, the 2/22nd London remaining in the captured position at Point 1069. Dispositions varied slightly, but those of the 2/14th London, which are recorded in detail, may be taken as typical. It had two of its four companies in first line, each on a front of two platoons, the companies in two " waves," each of two lines—50 yards between lines and 100 yards between waves. Where the troops were attacking salients in the enemy's position there were two further waves in similar formation 300 yards in rear, formed from the remaining companies. The troops advancing against re-entrants were not thus supported and were echeloned slightly in rear.

During the period of waiting several parties of Turks had been seen withdrawing, and when the assault reached the trenches resistance on the 60th Division's front was never very determined. The loss of Point 1069 had without doubt demoralized the enemy here. The 2/15th London, right battalion of the 179th Brigade, suffered somewhat severely from the fire of a machine gun, but when that was captured all resistance was over  The 2/13th London of this brigade then passed through the other two battalions, and its leading company attacked two field-guns beyond the final objective with Lewis-gun fire, drove off the detachments, and captured the guns. All the 60th Division's objectives were in its hands before 1 p.m.

The 74th Division had a less easy task. Major-General Girdwood had ordered the artillery to lengthen range very slightly and thus turned the dust, which had prevented observation of fire, to advantage ; for it formed a screen behind which the infantry was enabled to cut the wire. The two Welch Fusilier battalions of the 231st Brigade met with stout resistance. In one post which fought to the last Corporal John Collins of the 25th bayoneted fifteen Turks.[1] These two battalions suffered nearly two-thirds of the casualties of the whole corps and took three-quarters of its prisoners. All objectives were captured within a few minutes of those of the 60th Division.

It was now uncertain whether or not the works north of the Wadi es Sabe were held. To the 230th Brigade there appeared to be little or no movement in them, but there was some long-range fire from that flank, and patrols of Smith's Group were also shot at when they approached the wire. Major-General Girdwood obtained permission from General Chetwode to attack these trenches from the south with the 230th Brigade while the 5th and 6th R.W.F. of Smith's Group attacked them from the west. The operation was first ordered to take place at 6 p.m. and then postponed till 7 p.m., but even then Smith's Group reported that the two

---

[1] This N.C.O. had displayed remarkable gallantry and leadership during the period when the battalion was lying under heavy fire, and had repeatedly carried wounded men back to cover. After the incident recorded he advanced with a Lewis-gun section beyond the objective and covered the consolidation of the captured position. He was awarded the Victoria Cross.

Sketch 3

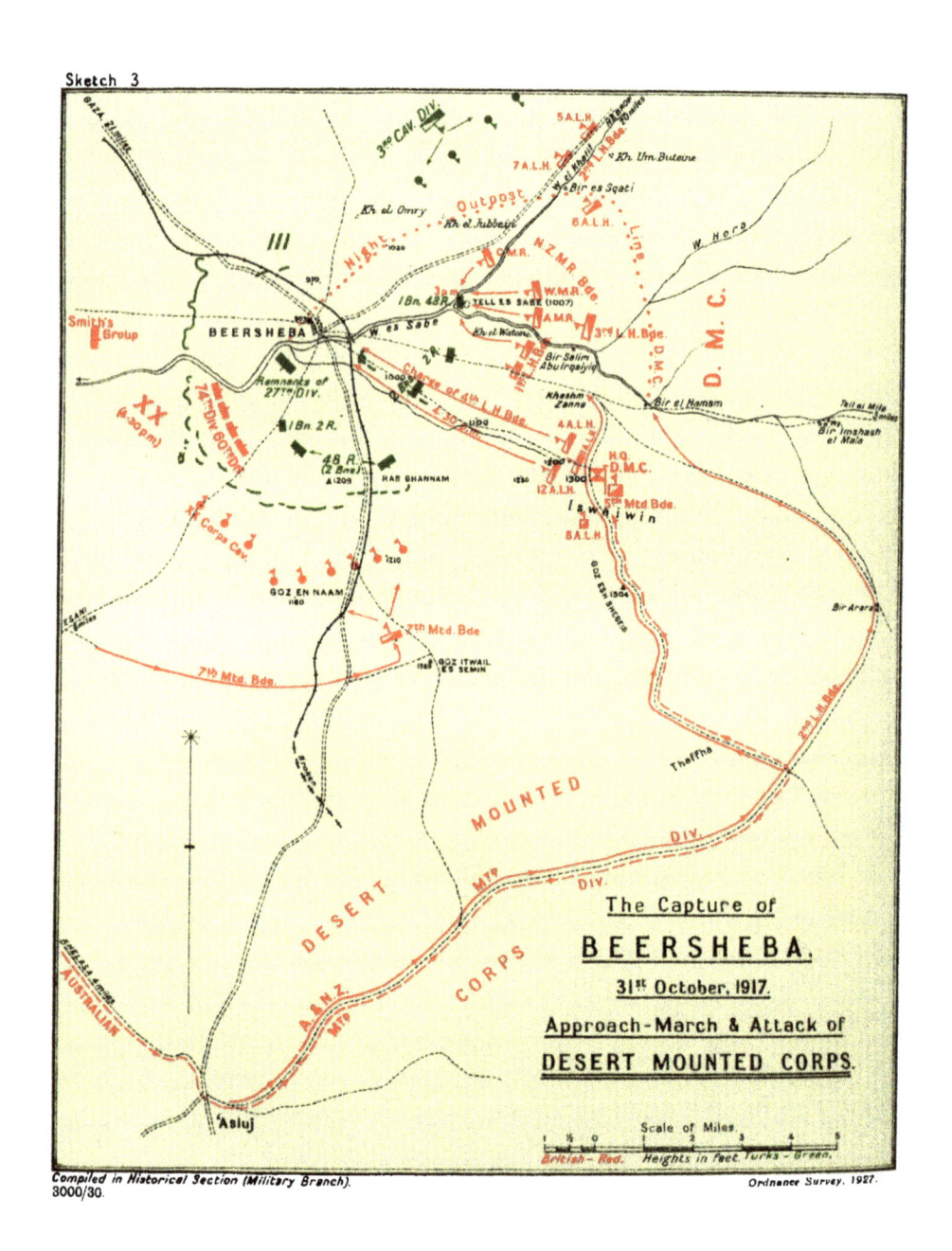

The Capture of
**BEERSHEBA.**
31st October, 1917.
Approach-March & Attack of
DESERT MOUNTED CORPS.

battalions under its orders could not get into position by that hour. Br.-General M'Neill was therefore instructed by Major-General Girdwood to carry out the attack alone, so as to avoid altering the artillery programme already arranged. The 16/Sussex advanced at the appointed time and occupied all the enemy's trenches up to the Beersheba–Tell el Fara road with little difficulty. The works had, in fact, been evacuated, and the only resistance was from a handful of snipers. An abandoned battery was captured by the Sussex.

1917.
31 Oct.

Beersheba itself had by this time fallen to the Desert Mounted Corps, so that the XX Corps had no further task. The 60th and 74th Divisions bivouacked on the battlefield behind a line of outposts. The 53rd Division, to which the battalions in Smith's Group had been returned, remained to cover the flank in the positions which it had occupied during the action, still with the 30th Brigade under its orders. The remainder of the 10th Division, which had moved up to Goz el Basal during the afternoon, bivouacked there.

In the course of the day 419 prisoners, 6 guns, numerous machine guns, and a quantity of material of all sorts had been captured by the XX Corps. The Turkish defences were excellently sited and deeply dug. With good wire they would have been formidable, but, lacking a strong obstacle in front, the garrison was too weak and too little resolute to make a serious resistance, except at isolated points. Nor was the weak Turkish artillery able to give it much assistance—though it punished the 231st Brigade severely early in the day—for the British heavy guns, well served by their observers during the preliminary bombardment, kept down its fire and destroyed its observation posts.[1] The British casualties had been suffered chiefly from shrapnel and machine-gun fire during the preliminary bombardment

---

[1] The attack afforded one interesting testimony to the importance of concealing work while actually in progress. Early aeroplane photographs of the defences showed a large hole dug on the top of Point 1069, with open cable-trenches radiating from it. The next photographs showed the hole covered, and the trenches filled in but still clearly visible. The final ones showed that the observation post had been carefully, but uselessly, camouflaged. Orders were given that particular attention should be paid to this observation post and the trenches, which were still visible, during the bombardment. After the battle it was found to be a dugout with a steel roof and trap door at the top. A headless Austrian artillery officer was lying inside.

and while the troops were closing to within assaulting distance of the trenches They amounted to 136 killed, 1,010 wounded—including a high percentage of walking cases—and 5 missing.

### The Approach March of the Desert Mounted Corps.

Map 5.
Sketches 2, 3.

The two tasks of the Desert Mounted Corps were, to " attack Beersheba from the east so as to envelop the " enemy's left rear," and to " seize as much water supply as " possible in order to form a base for future operations " northwards." The first objective of the leading division (the A. & N.Z. Mounted Division from Asluj) was a line through Bir el Hamam and Bir Salim Abu Irqaiyiq, on the road running eastward to Tell el Mila and the Dead Sea at Qasr Zuweira. Next it was to swing up its right and advance to the Hebron road between Bir es Sqati and Tell es Sabe, a fortified hillock at the confluence of the Wadi el Khalil and Wadi es Sabe. Finally it was to hold a line north-east of Beersheba, with its left on the town mosque. The division, leaving Asluj at 6 p.m. on the 30th October, was to march by way of Thaffha, 11 miles south-east of Beersheba, and Iswaiwin, except for the 2nd L.H. Brigade, which was to take a wider sweep through Bir 'Arara. The Australian Mounted Division was to follow by the former route, to be concentrated at Iswaiwin at 9.30 a.m., and to be prepared to advance either directly westward on Beersheba or northward to assist the A. & N.Z. Mounted Division. The 7th Mounted Brigade was to move eastwards from Esani through Goz Itwail es Semin, 7 miles E.S.E. of Beersheba, and establish a line of posts astride the Asluj road. Its mission was to observe the enemy's defences at Ras Ghannam, to follow the Turks if they retired, and to be ready to co-operate either with the remainder of the Desert Mounted Corps or with the XX Corps on its left.[1]

The marches before the mounted troops were therefore long. That of the A. & N.Z. Mounted Division from Asluj to Bir el Hamam was 24 miles, that of the Australian Mounted Division from Khelasa through Asluj to Iswaiwin

---

[1] Desert Mounted Corps Order No. 2 is given in Appendix 10.

## APPROACH MARCH OF CAVALRY

30 miles, that of the 7th Mounted Brigade about 17 miles. Moreover, each man carried two days' rations for himself, one day's forage, and a two days' emergency ration of grain in a sand-bag. Seeing that Australians, New Zealanders and the Midland Yeomen of the 5th and 7th Mounted Brigades were big men, there must have been about twenty stone on every horse's back. But the horses of the whole corps were, if a little fine drawn, hard and fit, already inured to long marches and long periods without water, while horsemastership learned in the hard school of Sinai had reached a level so high that sore backs were seldom seen.[1]

1917. 31 Oct.

The head of the A. & N.Z. Mounted Division reached the cross roads east of Thaffha at 12.20 a.m. and halted while reconnaissances were carried out. Then the column split and pursued its march, the 2nd L.H. Brigade moving by the Bir 'Arara track, the remainder of the division turning left-handed and marching on Iswaiwin, with the Wellington Regiment as advanced guard. It had been reported that there was a Turkish post at Goz esh Shegeib on this road; a little further north there was an encounter with a small body of the enemy, but the march was not checked. By 8.30 a.m. the troops were in position, the 2nd L.H. Brigade on the right north of Bir el Hamam, in touch with the N.Z.M.R. Brigade at Bir Salim Abu Irqaiyiq, the 1st L.H. Brigade in rear of the New Zealanders. One regiment of the Australian Mounted Division, the 8th A.L.H. (3rd L.H. Brigade), had marched in rear of the A. & N.Z. Mounted Division and turned off north of Iswaiwin on the track running into Beersheba. It had orders to reconnoitre the enemy's works about Ras Ghannam, and cover the concentration of its own division at Iswaiwin.

The head of the Australian Mounted Division reached Asluj at 8.30 p.m. on the 30th and remained there three and a half hours to water its transport, the 8th A.L.H., as previously stated, moving off with the A. & N.Z. Mounted Division. The division reached its area of concentration without incident, and advanced a short distance from Iswaiwin towards Ras Ghannam, the 5th Mounted Brigade remaining

---

[1] The marching-out state of the N.Z.M.R. Brigade has been preserved: 95 officers, 1,763 other ranks, 1,727 riding horses, 144 packs, 243 draughts, 27 mules, 35 camels, 36 Hotchkiss guns, 12 (Vickers) machine guns. This was probably the strongest brigade.

at Iswaiwin in corps reserve. The 7th Mounted Brigade reached Goz Itwail es Semin at 5 a.m. on the 31st. The South Notts Hussars then took up without opposition a line from a mile and a half south of Ras Ghannam to Goz en Na'am. Patrols pushed forward towards Ras Ghannam found the trenches strongly held. Between 8 and 9 a.m. the brigade got touch with the 4th L.H. Brigade on its right and the XX Corps Cavalry on its left.

Thus the great march had been successfully accomplished, and the troops were in position for the next move. The enemy may have been aware of the concentrations at Asluj and Khelasa, but he was completely surprised by the appearance of two cavalry divisions to the east, not having contemplated that the British mounted troops would move, at any rate in such numbers, so far from water. The bombardment of the XX Corps had already alarmed him as to his western defences. Now there was observed a bustle about Beersheba as the few troops available took up positions to the east. But Ismet Bey was already in a hopeless situation unless the reinforcements which he demanded arrived speedily. They were refused, and he was bidden not to evacuate Beersheba. Perhaps Kress recalled the British withdrawal from Gaza seven months before, when the garrison had been in even worse straits than it was here. But in war fortune seldom bestows such favours twice.

Mention must be made of one small independent force also on the move in the early morning of the 31st, which was to have an effect altogether disproportionate to its size. It was commanded by Lieut.-Colonel S. F. Newcombe, R.E., and consisted of 70 British camelry and a few Arab scouts, with ten machine guns, a number of Lewis guns, a supply of explosives, and three days' rations. Colonel Newcombe was, it will be recalled, the first head of the British Mission to the King of the Hejaz.[1] Being in Cairo in September, he proposed to Sir Edmund Allenby that he should take a small party through the desert east of Beersheba—country which he had surveyed before the war and in which he knew some of the inhabitants [2]—to raise the Bedouin against the Turks

---

[1] Vol. I, p. 235.
[2] The survey had been carried out only as far north as the Wadi es Sabe, but Captain Newcombe (as he then was) had acquired a good knowledge of the country north and north-east of Beersheba.

at the moment of the British attack, carry out raids, and block the Hebron road after Beersheba had been captured. Sir Edmund Allenby gave permission for this bold enterprise to be attempted. Colonel Newcombe's detachment left Asluj on the 30th, and after an extremely rapid march through the hills reached Es Semua, 20 miles north-east of Beersheba. On the evening of the 31st he moved down to the Hebron road, captured a few prisoners, and cut the telegraph to Jerusalem. He heard that night from the Bedouin of the capture of Beersheba, and determined to hold the Hebron road, so as to cut off the enemy's retreat to the north, hoping for a speedy advance by the British cavalry. His further adventures will be recorded when we come to the British operations in the hills north of Beersheba.

### THE ATTACK OF THE DESERT MOUNTED CORPS.

At 9.10 a.m. the N.Z.M.R. Brigade (Br.-General W. Meldrum) began its advance on Tell es Sabe, Canterbury Regiment on the right, Auckland on the left, each with four machine guns. The mound of Tell es Sabe was the best defensive position on the eastern side of Beersheba. Though low, it commanded all the ground to the east and also that south of the Wadi es Sabe. It was flat-topped with steep flanks, strewn with boulders, and upwards of 20 acres in extent. Several machine guns on its top raked all the plain.[1] On the right of the New Zealanders the 2nd L.H. Brigade (Br.-General G. de L. Ryrie) was ordered to advance on Bir es Sqati, establish itself astride the Hebron road, and thus protect them from counter-attack from the north. The advance began swiftly, in full view of Major-General Chaytor, who had established his headquarters near Khashim Zanna. From this point of vantage he could see, within an hour of the opening of the attack, the 2nd L. H. Brigade 2 miles north of Bir el Hamam, with patrols beyond the Wadi Hora, and the New Zealanders across the Wadi es Sabe.

The 7th A.L.H., the leading regiment of the 2nd L.H. Brigade, advancing from Bir el Hamam at a gallop, speedily gained the Hebron road at Bir es Sqati, the pace of its

---

[1] The tell was held by one battalion (300 strong or a little more) and one machine-gun company. See Note at end of Chapter.

advance rendering the shrapnel fire from the hills above Beersheba innocuous. Just beyond the road, however, it was held up in a small wadi by the enemy on the heights and was unable to make further progress. The Turkish commander had withdrawn his *3rd Cavalry Division* (only 1,100 strong) into the hills to prevent the envelopment of Beersheba, and it fulfilled its task. Despite the criticisms directed against him by Kress, it is difficult to see how he could better have employed this force, and it is probable that had he kept the division in the Beersheba defences the place would have fallen earlier and the garrison been annihilated.[1]

Welcome news was received from Br.-General Ryrie that there was water in the little wadi which enters the Wadi es Sabe at Bir el Hamam, and in the Wadi Hora. These pools were the result of a recent rain-storm and had already been reported from the air.

The task of the New Zealanders was a stiff one, and the advance of the brigade, from the moment when the Auckland Regiment was within 800 yards of Tell es Sabe, was slow. The Somerset Battery was in action at a range of 3,000 yards, but could do little to keep down the fire of the machine guns upon the mound. At 10 a.m. Major-General Chaytor ordered the 1st L.H. Brigade (Br.-General C. F. Cox) to despatch a regiment to cover the left flank of the N.Z.M.R Brigade. The 3rd A.L.H. moved up to Kh. el Watan on the Wadi es Sabe and obtained touch with the New Zealanders. Br.-General Meldrum arranged that the regiment should advance south of the wadi and swing in upon the mound from the south while his own brigade pressed the attack from the east. A little later the 2nd A.L.H. was ordered up on the left of the 3rd to stiffen the attack, which was making slow progress. At 11 a.m. the Inverness Battery came into action against Tell es Sabe, and, covered by its fire, the Somerset Battery boldly moved up to within 1,300 yards and opened fire with increased effect. Enemy aircraft were now circling above the battlefield and dropping bombs, which caused a good many casualties to horses.

At 1.30 p.m. General Chauvel ordered the Australian Mounted Division to place the 3rd L.H. Brigade (Br.-General

---

[1] See Note at end of Chapter.

L. C. Wilson)[1] at Major-General Chaytor's disposal. Its regiment on the outpost line astride the Iswaiwin–Beersheba track had not yet been relieved by one from the 4th L.H. Brigade. The 3rd Brigade crossed the Wadi es Sabe, followed by " B " Battery H.A.C., with orders to move upon the right of the N.Z.M.R. Brigade. But its support was not required. The diversion of the 1st L.H. Brigade across the wadi had already begun to make its weight felt. Moreover the Canterbury Regiment had crossed the Wadi el Khalil, and, though galled by fire from the hills, was threatening Tell es Sabe from the north. Soon after 2 p.m. the Auckland Regiment began its assault, advancing by a series of short rushes from cover to cover. At 2.40 a small outlying hummock east of the tell was captured with 60 prisoners and two machine guns, which were turned against the main position. At 3 o'clock the Aucklands made their final dash and within a few minutes Tell es Sabe was in their hands. Another 70 prisoners and two more machine guns were captured. At once the Turkish artillery began to shell the mound, while several aeroplanes swooped down upon it and dropped bombs. Major-General Chaytor then ordered the 1st L.H. Brigade to advance on the final objective, from Point 1020, north-east of Beersheba, to the mosque.

The attack had so far been successful, but the natural strength of Tell es Sabe and the stubborn resistance of its small garrison had seriously delayed the Desert Mounted Corps, and even now the New Zealand Brigade was unable to advance beyond this point. West of Beersheba the XX Corps had all its objectives, and could without doubt have captured Beersheba itself before the mounted troops. The objective, had, however, been allotted to the Desert Mounted Corps, and Sir Edmund Allenby, who had come up to General Chetwode's headquarters at El Baqqar, ordered General Chauvel to capture it before nightfall. General Chauvel, who had already realized that he was behind his programme, ordered Major-General Hodgson to direct the 4th L.H. Brigade (Br.-General W. Grant) to attempt to enter the town from the east. General Chauvel had hesitated for a moment whether to employ the 5th Mounted Brigade, which was in

---

[1] Br.-General J. R. Royston, who was a South African, had been invalided home in October.

reserve and was armed with the sword unlike the Australians, but as the 4th L.H. Brigade was closer in he decided that it should attack. "Put Grant straight at it!" was his order to Major-General Hodgson.[1]

The 4th L.H. Brigade had the 11th A.L.H. holding a long line of posts astride the Iswaiwin–Beersheba track, in touch with the 7th Mounted Brigade. The 4th and 12th Regiments were east of Iswaiwin. Horses had been fed and rested, though not watered, after their long march the previous night. Squadrons were dispersed to escape the bombs of the German aeroplanes, so that it was after 4.30 p.m. when Br.-General Grant had them ready, and the sun went down just after the attack was launched. The 4th A.L.H. deployed north of the Iswaiwin–Beersheba track, the 12th south of it. The 11th A.L.H. was ordered to concentrate and follow the other two regiments as a reserve. Similar orders were sent by General Chauvel to the 7th Mounted Brigade on the left; and the 5th Mounted Brigade, hitherto in corps reserve, was ordered to advance on Beersheba in rear of the attacking troops.

The 4th and 12th A.L.H. then advanced at a trot, but soon quickened pace to a gallop, each on a frontage of one squadron. The men, having no swords, carried bayonets in their hands. The 4th A.L.H. had all three squadrons in the charge, but one squadron of the 12th had been directed to co-operate with the machine-gun squadron (less one subsection following each regiment) which was to move along a wadi on the left of the track and protect the left of the advance against attack from the neighbourhood of Ras Ghannam, where the enemy could be seen in some strength in his trenches.

As the charging squadrons swept down the gentle slope towards Beersheba, enveloped in a cloud of dust, the 12th A.L.H. came under machine-gun fire from these trenches.

---

[1] "Australian Official History," p. 393. The records are lacking in information here. At 3.30 p.m. General Chauvel sent a message to the Australian Mounted Division ordering it to attack Beersheba with one brigade, but without mention of mounted action. It is General Chauvel's recollection that he gave no orders personally to Br.-General Grant, but spoke only to Major-General Hodgson. Br.-General Grant, however, states that Major-General Hodgson took him to the corps commander, who directed him to "take the town before dark," without giving him instructions as to how the attack was to be carried out, and that he himself was therefore solely responsible for the mounted charge.

The Notts Battery, which had unlimbered at the point of deployment, found the range with its second shot and quickly drove the enemy from the position. The principal Turkish trenches on the front of the charge faced south, and there was only one shallow trench facing east, across which the 4th A.L.H. swept without checking. At the next group of trenches there was a short fight. Two squadrons of the 12th A.L.H. swept straight on into Beersheba, but the remainder of the attacking force dismounted after passing through the trenches and attacked with the bayonet. The Turks fought grimly, and a considerable number were killed. Meanwhile the leading squadrons had reached the town, capturing prisoners and guns en route. When the 11th A.L.H. reached Beersheba, Br.-General Grant ordered it to push through the town and hold it against attack from the north, west, and south-west. On its way through the regiment captured about 400 prisoners who were retreating from the south-west. The 4th A.L.H. took up a line from the Wadi es Sabe to the mosque, the 11th A.L.H. from the mosque to the Khelasa road, while the 12th A.L.H. remained in reserve near the railway viaduct.

Finding the enemy evacuating his trenches at Ras Ghannam, the 7th Mounted Brigade had also advanced, and reached Beersheba by 6.30 p.m. On the right the A. & N.Z. Mounted Division with the 3rd L.H. Brigade attached had also reached its final objective, and by 6 p.m. was holding a line of outposts through Bir el Hamam, Bir es Sqati, Point 1020, and to within a hundred yards of the mosque. Though the haste with which the Turks in Beersheba retreated up the Gaza road and to the north prevented them from carrying out a tithe of the destruction they had planned, yet the water supply in the town would not itself have sufficed for the needs of all the horses. The pools discovered by the 2nd L.H. Brigade, and others in the Wadi es Sabe, were therefore exceedingly valuable. But this supply was not to last for long.

The total captures by the Desert Mounted Corps in the day's fighting were 70 officers and 1,458 other ranks. Of these over a thousand were captured by the 4th L.H. Brigade, either in the course of the charge, or from the troops who retired from the southern front and were intercepted by the 11th A.L.H. Nine field guns were also captured. The brigade's own casualties were very small, owing to the enemy having been driven out of that part of the Wadi es Sabe immediately west of Tell es Sabe before the charge : 2 officers and 29 other ranks killed, 4 officers and 28 other ranks wounded, and one missing. The high proportion of killed to wounded in this small total was, Br.-General Grant reported, due to the close fighting round the Turkish trenches. The total casualties of the corps were extraordinarily light, being under two hundred.[1]

That Beersheba fell before the day was out was almost certainly the result of the brilliant charge by the 4th L.H. Brigade, even though, as we now know, Ismet Bey had already issued orders for withdrawal to the north and the formation of a rear guard upon the line of the Wadi es Sabe. Even supposing that this rear guard could have been dispersed during the night, which is not probable, the charge was none the less important. Beersheba without its wells would not have been a valuable possession, and it was the 4th L.H. Brigade which was entirely responsible for their preservation. Nor would the losses of the Turks have been nearly so heavy had they been allowed to carry out an orderly retirement. As it was, more than half the dismounted troops in the town were captured or killed, while out of 28 guns 9 fell into the hands of the Desert Mounted Corps and 6 into those of the XX Corps. Only the *3rd Cavalry Division* withdrew without loss. The corps commander himself narrowly escaped capture.

Yet another result was the effect on Turkish morale, an effect greatly increased by the charges of the Yeomanry—

---

|  | Killed. | Wounded. |
|---|---|---|
| [1] Officers . . . . | 6 | 15 |
| Other Ranks . . . | 47 | 129 |

It must be understood that the Light Horse and Mounted Rifles when acting dismounted did not attempt to push home an attack against strong opposition. The "Australian Official History" (p. 235) thus defines their tactics :—

"The extreme caution displayed at most stages of these dismounted "attacks, and the relatively light casualties usually suffered, may be "somewhat puzzling to those who have served only with infantry. But "the explanation is simple. A light horse line is a slender striking force, "and leaders dare not commit it to a decisive charge unless the odds of "battle are strongly in its favour. A premature assault against a strongly "placed enemy . . . might in a few minutes have ended in the complete "destruction of the attacking regiments."

pushed home with the sword in their case—which will be 1917. recorded in the accounts of the next fortnight's fighting. 31 Oct. Till now the Turks had looked upon the British mounted troops as chiefly valuable for reconnaissance, or raids in superior numbers on isolated posts, as at Rafah, and had considered that the Turkish infantry had little to fear from them. Nor perhaps had it much to fear even now, unless the men lost their nerve, but that is precisely what was to happen at Maghar, at Abu Shushe, and on several other occasions. The commanders of the British mounted troops first learnt from this incident their own strength, and that in this theatre there was likely to be brilliant opportunity for the cavalry arm even in frontal attack, whereas mounted infantry tactics were never likely to achieve decisive success. A page had been turned in the annals of the campaign.

### NOTE.

Of no action in the course of the campaign have we a fuller account from the Turkish side than of the capture of Beersheba. Several chapters of Turkish "*Yilderim*" are devoted to the battle and its lessons, and the subsequent reports of Kress and of Ismet Bey, commanding the *III Corps*, are included. The *27th Division* consisted of two regiments, the *67th* and *81st*, which defended Beersheba from the west, the former south of the Wadi es Sabe, the latter north of it. From the Khelasa road to Ras Ghannam was the *48th Regiment*, *16th Division*. In reserve was the *3rd Cavalry Division* (*6th* and *8th Regiments*), and the *2nd Regiment* of the *24th Division*. This division had moved south from Tell en Nejile, and another regiment, the *143rd*, was in the hills about 6 miles N.N.W. of Beersheba, but it was under the orders of the *XX Corps* and took no part in the action.

When Ismet Bey perceived that he had to face an attack by the mounted troops from the east he placed one battalion of the *48th Regiment* and a machine gun company at Tell es Sabe, first one and then apparently a second battalion of the *2nd Regiment* south-east of the town, and moved the *3rd Cavalry Division* into the high ground to the north-east, to guard the Hebron road and prevent Beersheba from being surrounded from the north. At noon he had reports from Essad Bey, commanding the *3rd Cavalry Division*, and also from the air that there were "two to three "cavalry divisions to east and south," and so informed the commander of the *Eighth Army*. According to the Turkish version Kress replied : "No, "they are only two cavalry brigades." A little later, in response to a more detailed report and a demand for instructions, Kress is stated to have telegraphed : " Beersheba will be held. The battle will be continued."

Ismet Bey, learning of the loss of the *67th Regiment's* position and the virtual annihilation of two of its battalions, next despatched the third battalion of the *2nd Regiment* to the south-west. He had now used up all his reserves, except for two companies of the *81st Regiment*, north of Wadi es Sabe, which he withdrew to Beersheba. All that stood between the British 60th and 74th Divisions and the town was the reserve battalion of the *67th Regiment* and one battalion of the *2nd*.

At 3 p.m., despite "the courageous and obstinate defence to the last "man" of Tell es Sabe, the hill was captured. At 4 p.m. the corps commander ordered a general retirement to " north of the town," and directed the engineer company attached to the *27th Division* to destroy the water supply. The *48th Regiment* was to retire first and take up a rear-guard position on the Wadi es Sabe. Then came the charge of the 4th L.H. Brigade, which entered the town when headquarters was on the point of leaving. Ismet Bey escaped on foot, gathered a score of men about him, beat off the attacks of some Australian troopers, and reached the headquarters of the *143rd Regiment*. Thence he sent a message to Essad Bey to keep touch with the enemy, hold the high ground, and guard the Hebron road as well as the track to Tell esh Sheria through Kh. el Omry. The remnants of the infantry were reorganized as well as possible near Bir Abu Irqaiyiq Station, and reached Tell esh Sheria on the following morning. It is added that the destruction of the wells was not carried out, partly owing to damage done to " preparations " by the British artillery, but mainly owing to the Australian charge.

Kress (" Sinai," i, p. 43), complains that Ismet Bey had employed his reserves too soon and particularly criticizes the withdrawal of the mobile reserve, the *3rd Cavalry Division*, to the hills. The only reflection on the action of the corps commander in the Turkish account is that he remained at the telephone in Beersheba, which was overlooked from all sides, and therefore could see nothing of the battle. He should, Colonel Hussein Husni suggests, have been at an observation post on the high ground to the north. For the rest the Turks put the blame on Kress and quote the following passage from his report :—

" It was not possible to send reinforcements to Beersheba on the first
" day of the battle, to take up a more extensive position. Secondly, I
" had no idea that Beersheba would fall so rapidly, and did not see the
" necessity for these reinforcements. In addition, it was considered that
" the enemy's main attack would be against Gaza, and that the attack on
" Beersheba was a feint. Besides, a possible disembarkation on the coast
" had to be watched. Finally, lack of water precluded all idea of locating
" the *Yilderim* reserves north of and near Beersheba."

Regarding this last point, the Turkish report remarks that there was at Tell esh Sheria a well with a motor pump and a large reservoir, and that the wells at Kh. Abu Khuff and Bir Khuweilfe, 10 and 11 miles N.N.E. of Beersheba, contained more than enough water for an infantry division. The truth of this statement is proved by the fact that all the troops engaged in the hill fighting during the next week watered from these wells. But that is a minor question. The gist of the Turkish criticism lies in the following passage :—

" The battle of Beersheba should have been fought on different lines.
" The group should have retained its mobility in preference to holding the
" front. It was unnecessary to accept a decisive combat against heavy
" odds at Beersheba. The army commander should have given the *III*
" *Corps* commander a ' directive,' some time before, and . . . everything
" should have been so organized that the group could not be surrounded at
" once, and so that it could retire, in case of necessity, before superior
" forces to the Dhahriye–Abu Khuff line without loss."

Certain criticisms of Falkenhayn seem to show that he also believed the *Eighth Army* commander to have been at fault, and it was apparently for this cause that Kress, undoubtedly one of the greatest masters of desert warfare the war produced, was relieved of his command when the front had been stabilized, after the British capture of Jerusalem. Hussein Husni's summing up of Kress's action in the battle is contained in the sentence :
" He relied on ——'s pocket book."

Sketch 4.

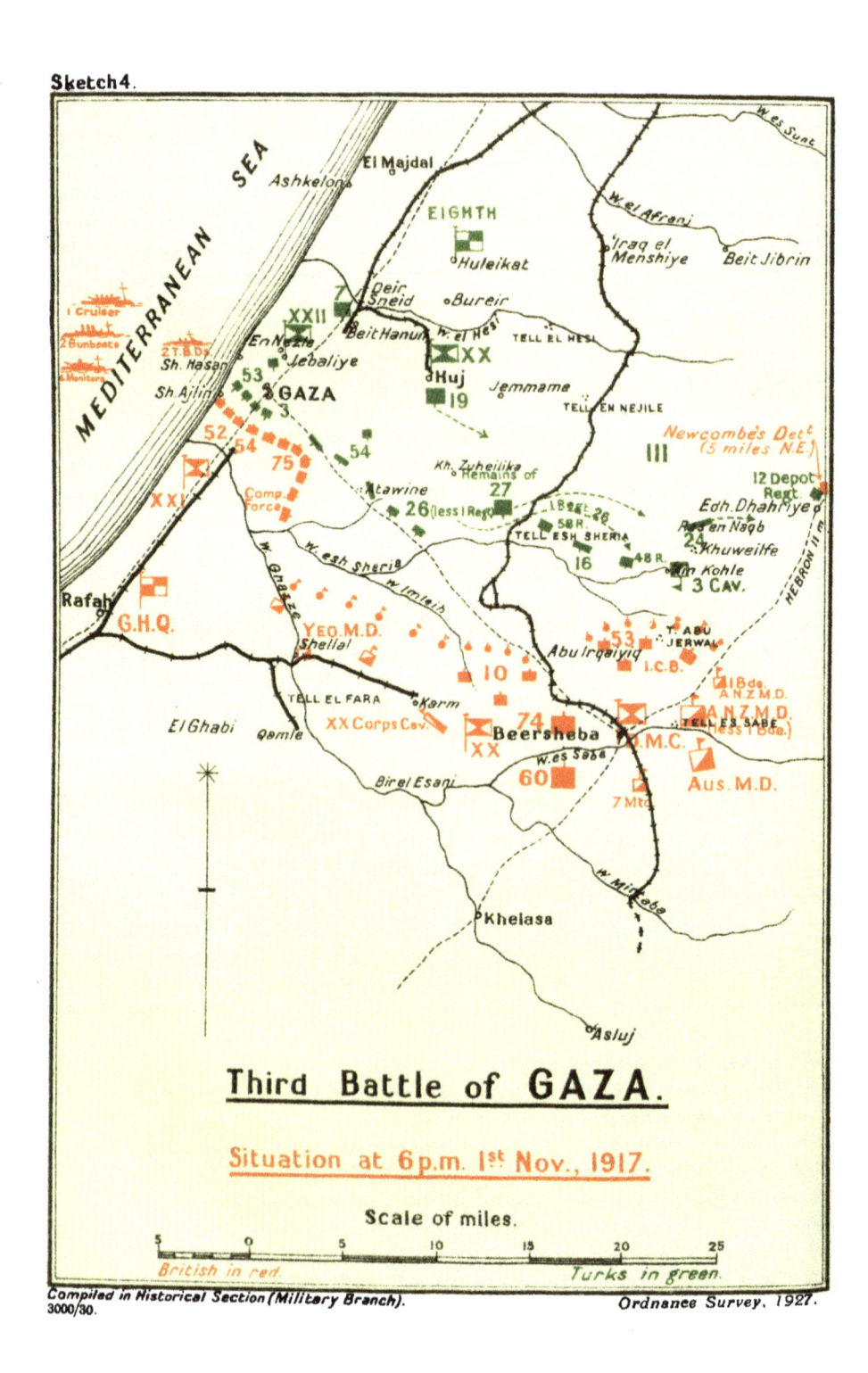

# Third Battle of GAZA.

Situation at 6 p.m. 1st Nov., 1917.

Scale of miles.

British in red.   Turks in green.

Compiled in Historical Section (Military Branch).
3000/30.                                Ordnance Survey, 1927.

## CHAPTER IV.

### THE ATTACK ON THE GAZA DEFENCES.

(Maps 1, 2, 4, 6; Sketches 4, 5, 6.)

THE PLAN OF ATTACK AND PRELIMINARY BOMBARDMENT.

THE capture of Beersheba, though a necessary preliminary to the attack on the left of the main Turkish line, was in itself a complete operation. The fighting in the hills which followed it may be considered as part and parcel of the attack on the Sheria position by the XX Corps, and will be described with it in the next chapter. We turn now, therefore, to the operations of the XXI Corps on the other flank at Gaza, which were to follow the Beersheba attack and precede that at Sheria. *Maps 2, 4, 6. Sketch 4.*

The date of the assault on the Gaza defences was not fixed until the results of the fighting at Beersheba were known. Sir Edmund Allenby hoped that the Gaza operation would attract the Turkish reserves, thus easing the task of the XX Corps; he therefore intended to begin it from twenty-four to forty-eight hours before the Sheria attack was launched. If the Turks did reinforce their right at the expense of their left, the capture of the Sheria position would be so much the easier, and the mass of the British mounted troops, passing behind the enemy's flank, would have the opportunity of making a vast haul of prisoners and guns, perhaps of virtually destroying the opposing force. But the Commander-in-Chief was not in the grip of any fixed idea such as that with which the Turks reproach his opponent, Kress von Kressenstein. He waited on events, to exploit them. Though his original attack at Gaza was primarily a feint, he was prepared, if his cavalry failed to envelop the enemy's left completely, to transfer his weight to the coast, where advancing troops could be supplied more easily. What actually happened was rather outside his calculations, but he was quick to profit by it. The Turks, who had been so much concerned for the safety of Gaza and had massed their greatest strength on that flank, now, after the capture of Beersheba, became anxious regarding the Hebron road. Their anxiety was increased by the bold conduct of Lieut.-Colonel Newcombe's little detachment, which seemed to presage a general advance up the road. They did not, indeed, weaken the Gaza front—where their reserve division was at once drawn into the battle—to secure the road, but they moved considerable forces eastward from Sheria. Thus they depleted the Sheria position quite as much as if they had reinforced Gaza, and locked up nearly half their force in the Judæan Hills, where it took no part in the fighting for a week after the capture of Sheria. Then Sir Edmund Allenby transferred his attention to that portion of the enemy's force remaining in the coast plain, which was so weakened that two infantry divisions and the mounted troops—all that could at first be fed—sufficed to defeat and pursue it, and hustled it northward to Jaffa.

The first reports from Beersheba were optimistic with regard to the water supply there captured, and led Sir Edmund Allenby to hope that he would be able to attack the Sheria position on the 3rd or 4th November. He therefore ordered the Gaza attack to be carried out on the 2nd. But during the 1st it became apparent that the wells at Beersheba were not so good as they had seemed, and that longer preparations would be necessary. The Commander-in-Chief decided, none the less, not to postpone the Gaza operations.

The land bombardment had begun on the 27th October, the naval on the 29th. The heavy artillery at the disposal of General Bulfin consisted of 68 medium or heavy guns and howitzers, and was divided into three groups, known as "Right Counter-battery Group," "Left Counter-battery Group" and "Bombardment Group."[1] But the whole of

---

[1] Each counter-battery group consisted of four 60-pdrs., eight 6-inch howitzers, four 8-inch howitzers; the bombardment group of eight 60-pdrs., twenty-two 6-inch howitzers, four 8-inch howitzers, two 6-inch Mark VII guns.

There were at this date no heavy artillery brigades with definite establishments in the Force. Instead there were a number of group headquarters, to which a varying number of heavy batteries were attached. Nor was there, until the following December, a brigadier-general commanding heavy artillery either in the XX or XXI Corps. During the Gaza operations Colonel O. C. Williamson Oswald, commanding the LXI Heavy Artillery Group, acted in this capacity, having no batteries directly attached to his group headquarters.

## THE NAVAL ASSISTANCE

the heavy artillery was available for the neutralization of Turkish batteries, and this was laid down as its chief mission during the assault. The main task of the two 6-inch guns was the surprise bombardment of the Turkish railhead at Beit Hanun, which was carried out at a range of about 9 miles with balloon observation.[1] There was no shortage of ammunition, as is shown by the fact that 300 rounds from a 6-inch howitzer (or 180 from a 6-inch and 80 from an 8-inch) were allotted for the destruction of each hostile battery located, and by the record that about 15,000 rounds were fired by the heavy artillery prior to the day of the attack. With the divisional artilleries of the 52nd, 54th and 75th Divisions, the bombardment was the heaviest carried out in the course of the war outside the European theatres.[2] The fire of the field artillery was to be concentrated upon the more important points, the barrage covering less than half the total frontage. Bombardments of enemy batteries with gas shell were carried out on the 29th, 30th and 31st October, but appear to have had little or no effect.[3]

The naval assistance, provided by Rear-Admiral T. Jackson, was given by the cruiser *Grafton*, the French coastguard ship *Requin*, the monitors *Raglan* (14-inch), *M.15* (9·2-inch), *M.29*, *M.31*, and *M.32*, the British destroyers *Staunch* and *Comet*, and the French *Arbalète*, *Voltigeur*, *Coutelas*, *Fauconneau* and *Hache*; the river gunboats *Ladybird* and *Aphis*; three seaplane carriers, and a number

---

[1] Two balloons were available, of which one was shot down by Turkish shrapnel.

[2] While the bombardment itself was from Outpost Hill to the sea, a distance of 6,000 yards, the frontage of the attack was little over 4,000 yards. It is of interest to note that 68 heavy guns to 4,000 yards, or one to every 60 yards, is exactly the proportion employed by the British on the first day of the Battle of the Somme (1st July 1916). The weight of artillery, it need hardly be said, increased greatly in subsequent operations on the Western Front—*e.g.* one heavy gun to 28 yards in the Battle of Arras, one to 27 on the 8th August 1918. But when we take into account the naval artillery and the enormous weight of its projectiles—one monitor had a 14-inch gun, *Requin* two 27·4-cm. (10·8-inch), *Grafton* and another monitor each two 9·2-inch, without counting the secondary armaments of the big ships or the large number of guns of 4-inch and over carried by the small—this bombardment must be reckoned a very heavy one by any standard. Figures as to naval ammunition expended are not available, save that two 6-inch monitors fired 192 rounds on the 30th October alone, and that *Requin* sailed for Port Said on the 2nd November, having used all her supply.

[3] See Note at end of Chapter.

of trawlers, drifters, and motor launches. All this considerable flotilla was not present at any one moment,[1] as detachments had to return to Port Said for coal and ammunition, or, in the case of the smaller vessels, when there was bad weather. Attacks by hostile aircraft were beaten off without difficulty, and the only loss was caused by a direct hit on the *Requin*, a shell from a land battery bursting on her mess-deck and resulting in 38 casualties. It must, however, be added that after the Gaza operations were over, on the night of the 11th November, a submarine succeeded in finding the passage through the nets, and sunk both *Staunch* and *M.15*.

To keep alive the enemy's anxiety as to a landing on the coast behind his right flank, Rear-Admiral Jackson organized a feint embarkation on the 1st November, the day before the infantry attack. Motor launches, trawlers, and tugs arrived and anchored off Deir el Balah in the morning, and at 4.30 p.m. began the embarkation of men of the Egyptian Labour Corps, who were marched down to the beach in fours in view of the enemy. By the time some hundreds had been embarked it became too dark for the enemy to observe any longer what was happening. The men were then landed, but surf boats continued to pull about, showing occasional lights, to give the impression that embarkation was still going on. At 11 p.m. the flotilla left for Port Said, but two trawlers were sent to appear the following morning off the mouth of the Wadi el Hesi.

The attack of the XXI Corps was to be against the enemy's works from El Arish Redoubt, half a mile west of the Rafah–Gaza road, to Sheikh Hasan on the shore. Owing to the distance between the British and Turkish trenches, General Bulfin had suggested to Sir Edmund Allenby that it should be made by night. It appeared that the risk of loss of direction and of disorganization in the darkness was less serious than that of exposing the troops to machine-gun fire in daylight during their crossing of the heavy sand of No Man's Land. On the right flank the final objective was only 500 yards behind the Turkish front line, but on the left it was 2,500. The whole attack was to be carried out

---

[1] The ships shown on Map 6 and on Sketches 2, 3, 4 and 5, may be taken as approximately the number in action at one time.

under the orders of Major-General S. W. Hare, commanding  1917.
the 54th Division, at whose disposal were put, in addition  26 Oct.
to his own division, the artillery, the 412th Field Company
R.E., and the 156th Brigade (Br.-General A. H. Leggett) of
the 52nd Division. The capture of "Umbrella Hill," a
dune just west of the Rafah–Gaza road which overlooked
the main objective, was to be a distinct operation, carried
out some hours before the main attack. Certain earlier
subsidiary operations were to be carried out on the right
of the 54th Division by the 75th, which was to advance its
line in the Happy Valley between the Es Sire and Burjabye
ridges and was to raid Outpost Hill. On the night of the
main operation the Composite Force, which had taken over
the front on the right of the 75th Division, was to advance
the line in the direction of Atawine Redoubt on the Gaza–
Beersheba road. On the following night the 75th Division
was again to raid Outpost Hill.[1]

The advance of the line in the Happy Valley from the
track known as "Watling Street" to Lee's Hill was successfully accomplished by the 75th Division during the night
of the 26th, before the general bombardment began. The
raid on Outpost Hill was made by the 3/3rd Gurkhas of the
233rd Brigade, 75th Division, at 3 a.m. on the 1st November.
It was large enough to induce the Turks to believe, when the
attack on Umbrella Hill was launched the following night,
that this was but another raid of the same nature. After a
short but intense bombardment, a party consisting of two
British and three Gurkha officers and 220 riflemen, under
the command of Captain W. G. Bagot-Chester, entered the
enemy's defences on the hill. The garrison was overwhelmed, a number refusing to quit their dug-outs, in which
they were bombed. Twenty-six were killed with bayonet
or *kukri* and 16 prisoners brought in. The losses of the
Gurkhas were 2 killed and 23 wounded.

The attack on the Gaza defences by the troops under the
command of Major-General Hare was divided into four
phases, the first or preliminary, against Umbrella Hill, having
it own "Zero" hour, at which an intense bombardment was
to open. Ten minutes later the artillery was to lift, maintaining fire at reduced rate on the approaches to Umbrella

---

[1] XXI Corps Order No. 11 is given in Appendix 11.

Hill, and the 7/Scottish Rifles, with one company 8/Scottish Rifles, 156th Brigade, was to assault the position. The second phase was the capture of the enemy's front line from El Arish Redoubt to Sea Post on the shore. This attack was to be carried out by the left of the 156th Brigade (4/Royal Scots and one company 8/Scottish Rifles), the 163rd Brigade (Br.-General T. Ward), and the 161st Brigade (Br.-General W. Marriott-Dodington) less one battalion in divisional reserve. In the third phase the attack, by the 163rd and 161st Brigades, was to force its way deeply into the south-western defences of Gaza. The fourth and final phase, beginning 90 minutes after Zero, was to be made along the shore and carried out by the 162nd Brigade (Br.-General A. Mudge). Its objectives were " Gun Hill " and Sheikh Hasan, the latter over 3,500 yards from the British front line at Sheikh Ajlin.

The Palestine Tank Detachment had at this date eight tanks, of which two were to be held in reserve during the operations. None were to be employed in the first phase against Umbrella Hill. In the second two tanks were to support the infantry against El Arish Redoubt, with further objectives north of it. The other four were to attack with the 163rd and 161st Brigades, and after assisting in the capture of the trenches on their front, and in some cases flattening out wire, were to advance to Sheikh Hasan carrying R.E. stores.

The greater part of the ground over which the attack was to be made consisted of sand of the seashore, which here extends a considerable distance inland. It differs from the desert sand of Northern Sinai, which also appears in places south of Gaza, in that it supports no vegetation except an occasional tuft of grass. It was extremely tiring to the feet, which sank at each step to the ankles, but it was, on the other hand, of little value from the point of view of cover, as no revetment would hold it up under bombardment. The enemy's trenches, even where built up with sand-bags, which was generally the case only in the redoubts were blown in by the British artillery, and in many cases almost disappeared. The Royal Engineers of the 52nd and 54th Divisions laid a number of wire tracks across the sand prior to the attack, in addition to working for several weeks on water supply to the front line. The wire tracks were

Sketch 5.

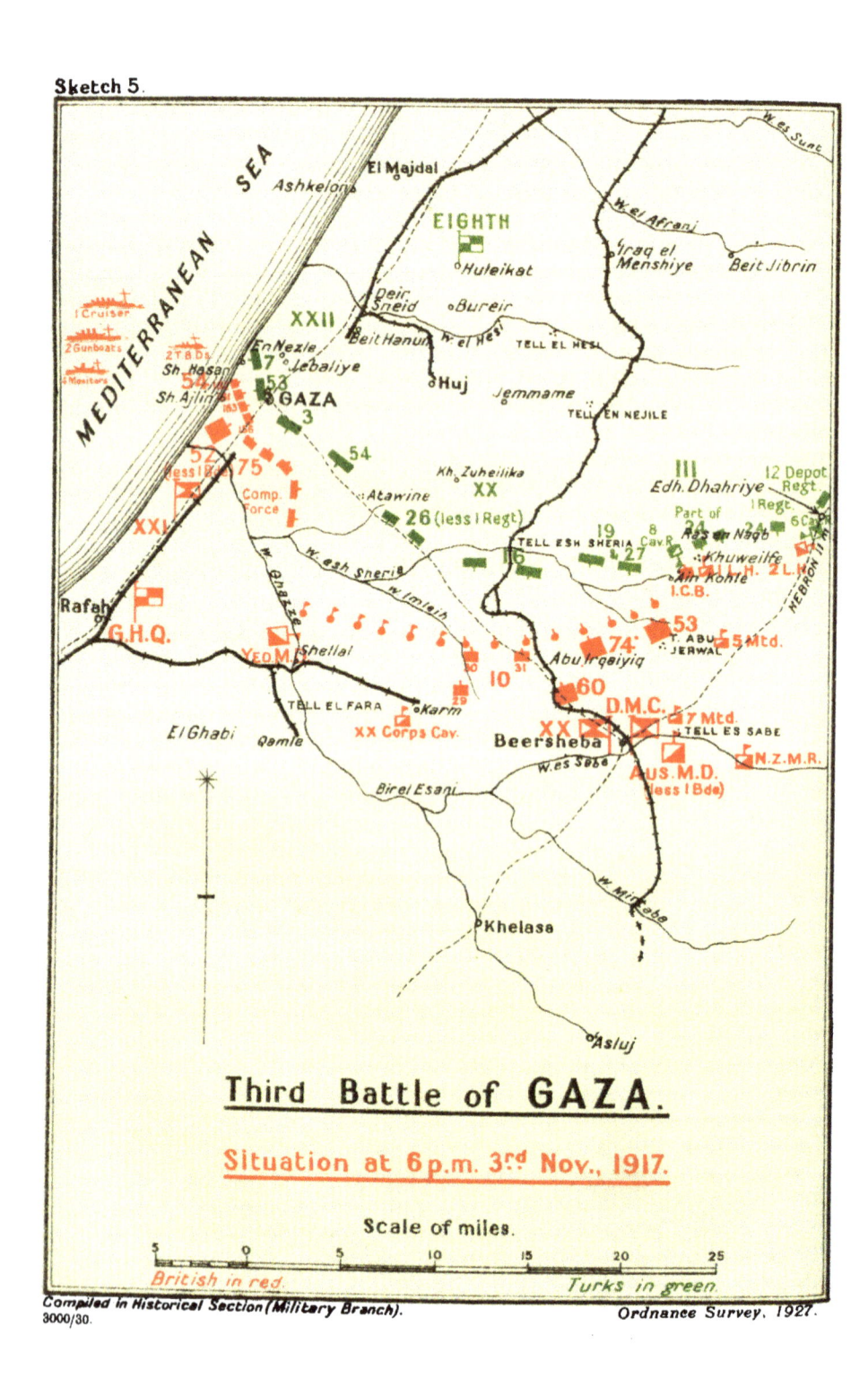

# Third Battle of GAZA.

## Situation at 6 p.m. 3rd Nov., 1917.

Scale of miles.

British in red.     Turks in green.

Compiled in Historical Section (Military Branch).     Ordnance Survey, 1927.
3000/30.

# ATTACK ON UMBRELLA HILL

required chiefly for the evacuation of wounded, supplies being brought up by camels and by a tramway which ran through the dunes.

1917.
1 Nov.

The wire covering the Turkish front line was fairly strong, but there was comparatively little further back, though some of the switch lines were wired. The defences of Gaza were held by the two divisions, the *53rd* from the shore to the eastern face of the town, then the *3rd*.[1] The *7th Division*, *Eighth Army* reserve, was close at hand, and might be expected to reinforce the front promptly. The artillery of the *XXII Corps* consisted of 116 guns, including the divisional artillery of the *7th Division*. Six large naval guns had been located by the British artillery observers, as well as several batteries of 150-mm. howitzers. Though the activity of the Turkish batteries was apparently diminished by the 1st November as a result of the British neutralizing fire, the frontal attack to which Major-General Hare's force was committed was a formidable undertaking if the defenders were sufficiently resolute.

### THE ATTACK.

Umbrella Hill, just west of the Rafah–Gaza road and on the fringe of the sand-dunes, was defended by a network of trenches, and was an advanced work in the enemy's system, connected by three long communication trenches with the main line in rear. It was known to be held by a battalion of the *138th Regiment*, about 350 strong. The wire round it had been thoroughly cut by the British artillery during the preceding days.

Map 5.
Sketches 4, 5.

The 7/Scottish Rifles (Lieut.-Colonel J. G. P. Romanes), with a company of the 8th Battalion of that regiment attached and a second acting as carriers, assembled before 10 p.m. on the 1st November in rear of the British front line. At 10.50 a covering party advanced into No Man's Land, but was unfortunately observed by a Turkish outpost which, despite the fire of Stokes mortars, had remained in Fisher's Orchard, south of the work. The alarm was given

---

[1] Each division had all three regiments in line and a divisional reserve of one battalion from each regiment.

70   ATTACK ON THE GAZA DEFENCES

and brisk machine-gun and musketry fire opened from the trenches on Umbrella Hill. The intense British bombardment began at 11, causing the Turkish fire to slacken and enabling a tape to be laid whereon the troops formed up. Rocket signals sent up by the enemy brought down a Turkish barrage, which did not, however, cause serious loss.

At 11.10 the assault was launched. The troops, who had to be restrained by their officers from attacking through the British barrage, advanced with great dash, and quickly captured the hill. Casualties were light, partly owing to the fact that the Turkish high-explosive shell was smothered in the sand; but it was another matter when the consolidation of the position, with the assistance of the 412th Field Company R.E., was begun. Most of the surface of the hill was soft sand, and the communication trenches, which the Turks had not revetted owing to lack of material, had become so shallow as a result of the bombardment that they gave little cover. The Turks shelled their lost trenches heavily, and the casualties of the 7/Scottish Rifles, very few in the actual assault, amounted to 103 within twenty-four hours,[1] while the two companies of the 8th Battalion also suffered. On the Turkish side 3 officers and 55 other ranks, 3 Lewis guns, and large quantities of bombs were captured, and a considerable number killed.

1917.
2 Nov.

Zero for the second series of operations was 3 a.m. on the 2nd November, by which time the Turkish artillery activity that had followed the capture of Umbrella Hill had, as anticipated, died down. On the right, at El Arish Redoubt, the 156th Brigade's section of the attack carried out by the 4/Royal Scots was completely successful, after fierce fighting. As the waves moved through the Turkish trenches, six defensive mines were exploded in the redoubt, causing some loss to the attackers but only temporary confusion. Several small local counter-attacks were beaten off. At 6.30 a.m. came a really heavy one, which drove back the leading company of the Royal Scots, after all its officers and senior non-commissioned officers had become casualties. One platoon from another company was rushed up, the troops were rallied, and the Turks driven back. Reinforcements

|                | Killed. | Wounded. | Missing. |
|----------------|---------|----------|----------|
| [1] Officers . | 1       | 4        | —        |
| Other Ranks .  | 20      | 57       | 21       |

from the 7/Royal Scots and 8/Scottish Rifles were sent up, 1917. and the position was finally consolidated, with the exception 2 Nov. of a very small area which appeared to be untenable and was therefore evacuated.

The assault of the 163rd and 161st Brigades was less successful. The tanks carried out their part well, the two directed on El Arish Redoubt both passing through it, though one was ditched and the other hit soon afterwards. A third passed along the front line from Sea Post to Beach Post, rolling out the wire all the way. The partial failure of the infantry was mainly due to mistakes in direction on the part of battalions of both brigades, though the troops had been carefully trained over trenches as nearly as possible replicas of those now being attacked. It had been hoped that the moon, which was full on the 30th October, would have assisted the maintenance of direction, but the night was both cloudy and hazy. The heavy Turkish barrage, which caused considerable loss and smothered the position in dust, contributed to the confusion.

On the the right of the 163rd Brigade the 5/Suffolk entered the western half of El Arish Redoubt at the same moment as the Royal Scots entered the eastern. Keeping close to an accurate barrage, it over-ran the whole objective with little loss, but was withdrawn from the third line owing to its exposed situation, and proceeded to consolidate the second. The 8/Hampshire split into two bodies, one of which swung right-handed into Triangle Trench, outside its objective. The other captured Burj Trench. The 4th and 5th Norfolk in second line lost direction also, in part owing to their companies being misled by the mistake of the Hampshire in front. On ground spouting dust and smoke and covered by a maze of shallow trenches, some confusion followed, and only small bodies reached Gibraltar and Crested Rock, to fall back when they found themselves isolated. Similar loss of direction occurred in the 161st Brigade. The right company of the 5/Essex, which should have captured Zowaiid Trench, swung across the front of its battalion and attacked Rafah Redoubt. The other companies, seeing troops in front assaulting what should have been their objective, thought that these must be the 6/Essex at Beach Post and that they themselves were too far to the left. They therefore wheeled right-handed and entered

Zowaiid Trench,[1] apparently supposing it to be the front line of Rafah Redoubt. On the the left the 6/Essex, which made no mistake, captured Beach and Sea Posts with slight casualties. The battalions passing through to the objectives of the third phase suffered from these mishaps, and became involved in heavy and confused fighting in Rafah Redoubt and Rafah Trench. Eventually Cricket Redoubt was captured with the aid of the tank from Beach Post.

Cricket Redoubt having been taken, the other misadventures had fortunately no serious effect upon the progress of the fourth phase, the attack of the 162nd Brigade, except on the extreme right, where the 10/London had to turn the enemy out of Rafah Redoubt, which had only been partially penetrated. This battalion lost touch with the barrage and suffered heavy loss. The brigade was also deprived of the assistance of the few tanks allotted to its support, which had been put out of action in the previous phases. The attack was, however, completely successful. There was a sharp struggle for Gun Hill, which was taken with the bayonet. By 6 a.m. the brigade was ready to assault Sheikh Hasan, and went forward after a quarter of an hour's bombardment, capturing this place without much difficulty and taking 182 prisoners. The tank at Cricket Redoubt, which had been disabled, was now repaired sufficiently to bring up a load of engineers' stores to Sheikh Hasan, but was again put out of action soon afterwards.

The tanks had contributed to the success of the attack, but their casualty list was high, and in the opinion of some observers they prematurely alarmed the Turks at the beginning of the second phase, which might otherwise have taken them completely by surprise. The two reserve tanks which were ordered forward at 4 a.m. to support the infantry north of Rafah Redoubt, were unfortunately loaded on top with sand-bags as well as other R.E. material. In both cases the sand-bags were set afire and the tanks temporarily put out of action. It had nevertheless been, generally speaking, a notable achievement on the part of the tanks,

---

[1] This is one version of the affair. The other is that the officers realized what had happened and that Zowaiid Trench was not being attacked, and therefore decided to attack it themselves. Owing to the heavy casualties sustained by them it was not possible to clear up this point. In any case considerable delay was caused.

## TURKISH COUNTER-ATTACKS

which were, with three exceptions, worn and obsolete Mark 1917. I machines, survivors of the Second Battle of Gaza. This 2 Nov. was the detachment's last employment.

It had been intended that if possible the Imperial Service Cavalry Brigade should exploit the success. To clear a way for the cavalry a company of the 4/Northamptonshire was ordered to capture Lion Trench, three-quarters of a mile north-east of the shrine at Sheikh Hasan. The task was carried out by 7.30 a.m. and the wire cleared from the beach. Twenty minutes later, however, the enemy in considerable numbers attempted to surround Lion Trench, and the company, which was so far forward that little artillery support could be given to it, was forced to withdraw. Large bodies of the enemy were now seen advancing in open order on Sheikh Hasan from the north and north-east, and at 8.57 a.m. a barrage was put down by the whole of the Corps Heavy Artillery on a line 3,000 yards long, running north and south, about two miles east of that point. This barrage, which had been prepared and registered with aerial observation by Br.-General H. A. D. Simpson Baikie, B.G.R.A., in case the enemy's reserve division about Deir Sneid advanced to counter-attack, scattered the Turks in all directions and caused heavy casualties. After the counter-attack had broken down a new attack on Lion Trench was ordered, but later cancelled by Major-General Hare, and the 4/Northamptonshire, which had been assembled to make it, was employed instead in the afternoon in an attack on Yunis Trench. .The battalion reached its objective, but was driven back by another Turkish counter-attack. Turkish troops in large numbers moving across the ridge in the direction of Sheikh Hasan were apparently screened from the British ground artillery observers by the smoke, but were caught by the fire of the monitors and destroyers and suffered terrible loss.

The enemy's heavy batteries shelled Sheikh Hasan throughout the day, but as a result of the British fire and the infantry advance all his artillery, with the exception of a few mobile guns, was withdrawn by night to northeast of Gaza. The British consolidated their position during the night, and the Turks were heard working hard to strengthen Turtle Hill. The weather, as the result of a *Khamsin*, became extremely hot and dusty on the 3rd, and 3 Nov.

(103)

74                ATTACK ON THE GAZA DEFENCES

the troops suffered severely. A new attack on Yunis trench at 4.30 a.m. by the 4/Essex was momentarily successful, but the battalion, which was not disposed in sufficient depth, was ejected by a counter-attack and lost heavily during its withdrawal. On the night of the 3rd the enemy made two bold demonstrations on the front of the 75th Division at Sheikh Abbas, but was on each occasion driven off by machine-gun and musketry fire. The Composite Force had been ordered to cancel the projected advancement of the line towards the Atawine Redoubt, and the 75th Division's raid on Outpost Hill was postponed, but both formations kept up active patrolling.

The attack on the western defences of Gaza had not reached all its objectives, but had fulfilled the Commander-in-Chief's object. Severe losses had been inflicted on the enemy, of whom upwards of a thousand were subsequently buried in the captured trenches, while 28 officers and 418 other ranks, 29 machine guns and 7 trench mortars, had been captured. The reserves on the immediate front had been pinned down ; for two regiments of the *7th Division* were identified between Gaza and the sea. But the cost had been serious. The losses had been increased by the attacking battalions' failure to keep direction, and by the fact that too many men were crowded into the captured trenches,.the shallowness of which had not been fully realised. The total casualties from the beginning of the operation to the evening of the 4th November were 2,696.[1]

Maps 4, 6.
Sketch 6.

On the 6th November the XX Corps captured the Sheria position. On the morning of the 7th the mounted troops were to break through from Tell esh Sheria and attempt to cut off the enemy between that point and the sea. Now was the moment, therefore, for General Bulfin to renew his effort at Gaza. The 75th Division's postponed raid on Outpost Hill was expanded into a strong attack, with Middlesex Hill also as an objective, to be carried out on the night of the 6th. The 54th Division was ordered to make another assault on Turtle Hill, and Yunis and Balah Trenches, at 4.50 a.m. on the 7th. The Corps Heavy Artillery had filled up to a

|  | Killed. | Wounded. | Missing. |
|---|---|---|---|
| [1] Officers . . . | 30 | 94 | 10 |
| Other Ranks . . | 331 | 1869 | 362 |

Sketch 6.

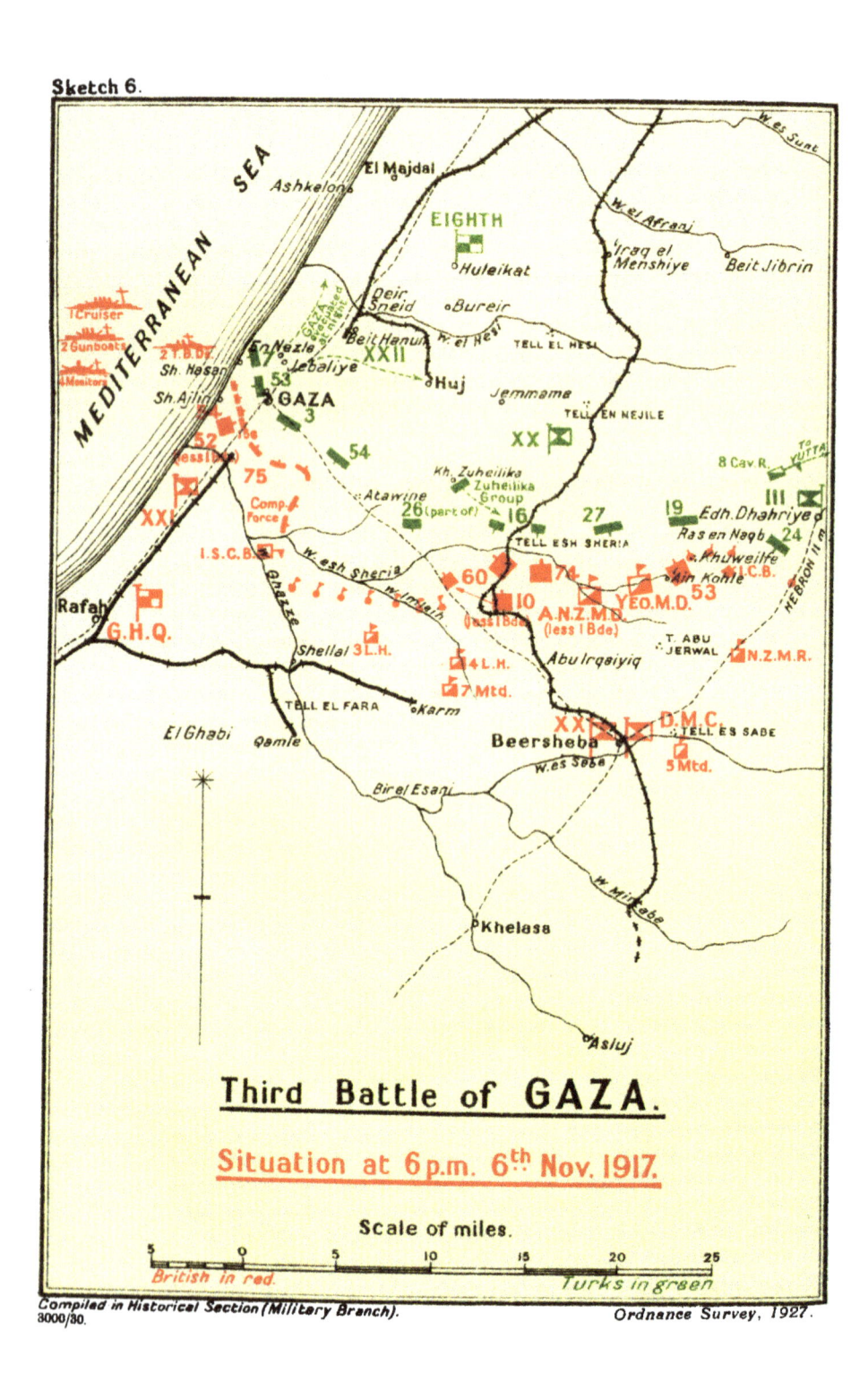

# Third Battle of GAZA.

Situation at 6 p.m. 6th Nov. 1917.

Scale of miles.

British in red.     Turks in green.

Compiled in Historical Section (Military Branch).
3000/30.
Ordnance Survey, 1927.

thousand rounds per gun immediately after the bombardment of the 2nd November, and was still prepared to give strong support to the attack, which was to be carried out by two battalions from each of the 161st and 162nd Brigades.

1917.
7 Nov.

But the enemy had slipped away. The trenches immediately in front of Umbrella Hill were found empty as early as 9.30 p.m. Outpost Hill was occupied at 1 a.m. on the 7th by the 233rd Brigade, which was then ordered to make good Green Hill and the Labyrinth. This was accomplished by 5 a.m., after some slight opposition by individual riflemen. By 7, patrols were on Ali Muntar, last in British hands on the morning of the 27th March, five months before. The 234th Brigade on the right found, however, that the enemy's works east of the Wadi Mukaddeme—Beer Trenches and Road Redoubt—were still held in some strength, with numerous machine guns. The last of these to be held by the Turks, the notorious Tank Redoubt, scene of some of the bloodiest fighting of the Second Battle of Gaza, was occupied by the brigade that night.

The 54th Division had speedily guessed from the silence on its own front that the enemy was gone there also, and had pushed out patrols. Lion and Tiger Trenches and Sheikh Redwan were occupied by 4.35 a.m., a quarter of an hour before the assault was to have been launched, and the 162nd Brigade advanced through the gardens and fields to the main road northward. Patrols entered Gaza and found not a living soul in its streets. It was, indeed, the ghost of a city. Viewed from a short distance it appeared comparatively little damaged. But the houses were mere shells; there was hardly one of them that had not been hit by the British artillery, and they had been gutted by the Turks, who had torn up every scrap of cloth to make sand-bags and had removed most of the wood-work for the revetment of their trenches. The gateway of Palestine had fallen once again and had been left a complete wreck.

The 54th Division was ordered by the XXI Corps to take up a line from the Jaffa road north of Sheikh Redwan to the sea. But fresh troops were required for the pursuit, and the all-important task of preventing the enemy from establishing himself upon the line of the Wadi el Hesi, which was naturally strong and partially fortified. This task was allotted to the 157th Brigade, 52nd Division, hitherto in corps reserve, which was ordered to move north along the shore, its head reaching Sheikh Hasan at 12.15 p.m. The turning of the line of the Wadi el Hesi must be left to a later chapter.

The fighting here had been of a nature entirely different to that at Beersheba. At Gaza, in the first assaults, four brigades of infantry, numbering about 10,000 rifles, attacked four Turkish regiments numbering 4,500 rifles. In the later stages of the battle the whole of the Turkish *7th Division* was drawn in, and also the reserve of the *3rd Division*, only the right of which was on the front of the attack, so that from first to last over 8,000 Turkish rifles were employed. These were not long odds in favour of the attackers, when the great strength of the position is taken into account. Moreover, if the Turkish machine gunners to some extent failed to take advantage of their opportunities, the infantry fought furiously, and their counter-attacks were made with the greatest gallantry. The British attack had achieved all that could have been hoped for ; it had inflicted very heavy loss on the enemy, drawn in his reserves north of Gaza, as intended. But it had accomplished far more than this. It had, in conjunction with the operations of the XX Corps, brought about the evacuation of a very strong fortress, and opened a gateway for the swift advance which was to prevent the enemy from consolidating himself in his second line of defence.

NOTE.

THE BATTLE FROM GERMAN AND TURKISH SOURCES.

Kress ("Sinai," i, pp. 44–5) states that the preliminary bombardment of Gaza had little material effect, but severely tried the nerves of the garrison. The commander of the *Eighth Army* had no knowledge of the objectives set by General Bulfin to his troops, and describes the attack as ending in a repulse. Refet Bey, commanding the *XXII Corps*, contrived to plug the breach on the morning of the 2nd November, but sent an urgent demand for reinforcements, whereupon the *20th* and *21st Regiments* of the *7th Division* were despatched to his assistance. This division, Kress definitely states, had been kept near Deir Sneid in case of a British landing.

After the first attack the continual pounding of the British guns began to tell very seriously on the troops of the *XXII Corps*, and finally—probably on the 4th November—the third regiment of the *7th Division*, the last reserve of the Army, was given to Refet Bey. Kress then obtained from Falkenhayn permission to evacuate Gaza, hoping to be able to make a new stand upon the line of the Wadi el Hesi. The withdrawal was begun on the night of the 5th and finished early the following night. Kress pays Refet Bey what is probably the highest tribute he bestows on any Turkish

## GERMAN AND TURKISH ACCOUNTS

commander in the course of his record. He describes the evacuation as extraordinarily clever, and states that the commander of the *XXII Corps* gave on this occasion " fresh proof of his wonderful skill, energy, and " personal bravery." Only a few worn-out guns were left behind. British officers report that though the captured trenches were in a state of chaos, the camps and bivouacs had been methodically evacuated and no litter left.

It is to be noted that the British gas shell at Gaza had so little effect that the Turks were not even sure whether or not it had been employed. On this subject Colonel Hussein Husni (Turkish " *Yilderim*," Part 3, Chap. II) writes :—

" It was reported towards evening (*i.e.* on the 31st October, actually " the third day on which gas shell was used) that the enemy were using gas " shell. We had no defensive arrangements whatever. . . . In spite of " the information from the front of the employment of gas in the bombard- " ment, it is worthy of note that no casualties from this cause were reported. " Probably the yellow smoke emitted by certain shells on explosion was " mistaken for gas."

# CHAPTER V.

### THE CAPTURE OF THE SHERIA POSITION.

(Maps 1, 7, 8; Sketches, 5, 6.)

### THE OPERATIONS NORTH OF BEERSHEBA, 1ST–2ND NOVEMBER.

**Maps 1, 7, 8. Sketch 5.** AFTER the capture of Beersheba the next move of the XX Corps, by Sir Edmund Allenby's programme, was the attack on the left of the enemy's main line of defence. But this line, after crossing the railway south of Tell esh Sheria, came to an end in the hills—petering out into a few small isolated works—some eight miles N.N.W. of Beersheba. It was therefore necessary for the XX Corps to make a considerable advance into the hills before it could roll up the enemy's flank, and it was ordered to do so next morning, the 1st November. In this movement the Desert Mounted Corps was to cover the right flank, the dividing line between the two corps being from Beersheba, through Kh. el Omry, to Tuweiyil Abu Jerwal, 6 miles N.N.E. of the town.

The situation of Beersheba, in a shallow valley at the southern foot of the Judæan Hills, has already been described. The country north and north-east of it is marked by no striking features, and may be described as stone desert, as contrasted with the sand desert of which the Force had seen so much. Here and there were small patches of cultivation, but nowhere was there much earth above the rock, while jagged outcrops, as well as loose boulders, made progress difficult enough for men on foot, and yet more so for cavalry or pack animals. The watershed for some miles north is a sharply defined ridge, on either side of which are innumerable little gullies, the creation of the winter rains. At this period, however, there was little water between Beersheba and some wells and cisterns at Bir Khuweilfe, 10 miles north of the town.

To cover the right of the XX Corps General Chauvel 1917. employed the A. & N.Z. Mounted Division, withdrawing 1 Nov. the Australian Mounted Division into reserve. The 2nd L.H. Brigade was ordered to advance along the Hebron road three miles beyond Bir es Sqati, the furthest point hitherto occupied; while the N.Z.M.R. Brigade was to push a regiment up each of the bridle-paths leading from that road to Kh. er Ras and Kh. el Leqiye, thus establishing strong posts between the road and the right of the XX Corps at Tuweiyil Abu Jerwal. These brigades reached the positions to which they were directed, but in each case came into contact with bodies of Turks well supplied with machine guns. The Canterbury and Wellington Regiments in particular had some brisk fighting. By the day's end 179 prisoners and 4 machine guns had been taken.

On the front of the XX Corps General Chetwode had ordered the 53rd Division with the Camel Brigade attached to move north and seize a line from Tuweiyil Abu Jerwal to Kh. el Muweile, 3 miles west of it. The division marched through Beersheba at 6.30 a.m., and by 3 p.m. the whole of the line was taken up without opposition. The transport had remained in Beersheba to water, and was at night sent up to the troops with water and rations. The Camel Brigade came under the orders of the A. & N.Z. Mounted Division at night, one battalion remaining under the 53rd Division.

So far, so good, but future prospects did not appear to be very bright. The pools in the Wadi el Hora were shrinking as a result of leakage when the mud had been disturbed; the supply of water in Beersheba only just sufficed for the needs of the troops actually in the town; the few wells found to the north and north-east had little water in them, and that at great depth. It was therefore decided to send the New Zealand Brigade next morning to Bir Imshash el Male, 12 miles east of Beersheba, where there were reported to be good wells. It must be added that there was no grazing in the area in which the A. & N.Z. Mounted Division was operating, to supplement the small ration of pure grain for the horses.

Water could be found only by a further advance, and the 7th Mounted Brigade with a regiment of the 3rd L.H. Brigade attached was ordered to move out on the morrow under the command of the A. & N.Z. Mounted Division and occupy the area Tell Khuweilfe, Bir Khuweilfe, Bir Abu Khuff, and 'Ain Kohle. The 2nd L.H. Brigade, at the disposal of which were put the 1st Light Car Patrol and the 11th Light Armoured Motor Battery, was ordered to push strong patrols along the Hebron road and endeavour to occupy the village of Dhahriye, 15 miles north-east of Beersheba. The two motor units had the special mission of reconnoitring tracks and searching for water, on both of which they were to report direct to corps headquarters.

1917.
2 Nov.

The 2nd L.H. Brigade on beginning its advance came under the fire of a body of the enemy established at Deir Saide, west of the road. The Turkish guns, which could be clearly seen, were silenced, temporarily at least, by the fire of the Ayrshire Battery, and the brigade pushed slowly forward. The 6th A.L.H. was left near Deir Saide to hold this enemy force, while the remainder of the brigade attempted to outflank it. The 5th A.L.H. moved north along the track from Kh. Salanta, parallel to and east of the Hebron road, while the 7th A.L.H. moved up that road itself. The country was more difficult than that encountered the previous day, the hills being steep and rocky, the valleys deep, the sides of the wadis cliff-like: all doubtless child's play by comparison with what had to be surmounted before November was out, but troublesome enough to a force which had spent three years on desert flats. The advance was very slow, and the turning movement was not completed when darkness fell.

The 7th Mounted Brigade (Br.-General J. T. Wigan) had marched up the Khuweilfe track which leaves the Hebron road near Kh. el Jubbein, picking up at this point the 8th A.L.H. It reached the fork in the track a mile north-west of Kh. er Ras without difficulty, and then began its real task. On the right the South Notts Hussars was ordered to seize the dominating height known as Ras en Naqb; the Sherwood Rangers was to work up the left track and occupy the high ground at Kh. Abu Khuff. The Essex Battery was ordered to support from the fork both regiments, which would be nearly four miles apart if they reached their objectives.

By 1.40 p.m. the South Notts Hussars had covered

half the distance  By 3, after driving back the small 1917.
bodies of the enemy which opposed its advance, it occupied 2 Nov.
Ras en Naqb, capturing 11 prisoners and 2 guns.

On the other flank, however, the Sherwood Rangers was held up astride the Wadi Kohle, considerably short of its objective. There had been here an exciting race between the Turks moving eastwards and the British moving northward, the Turks just winning. Lieut.-Colonel H. Thorpe, commanding the Sherwoods, believes that had the advance been made a couple of hours earlier the whole watershed could have been secured. In that case the subsequent course of events might have been very different; but it must be added that, had the regiment reached Kh. Abu Khuff and the hills to the east, it would have had a desperate struggle to maintain itself. It was considered unsafe to leave the South Notts in its isolated position at Ras en Naqb during the night, and the regiment was withdrawn after dark, with orders to reoccupy the position in the morning. The captured guns were tipped into deep gullies. The 8th A.L.H. had been directed soon after 2 p.m. to advance between the two Yeomanry regiments against Tell Khuweilfe. The enemy was found too strongly established upon this dominating position to be ejected by a force of this strength, and the regiment remained at night about a mile south-east of the tell. The 7th Mounted Brigade had found absolutely no water for its animals all day, less fortunate in this than the 2nd L.H. Brigade, which had discovered some pools near the Hebron road.

There had been no fighting on the fronts of the Camel Brigade and 53rd Division, but some anxiety. At 10 a.m. General Chetwode arrived at divisional headquarters north of Beersheba with Major-Generals Shea and Girdwood, for a conference with Major-General Mott, bringing information that, according to the reports of the R.F.C., the enemy was rapidly moving troops eastward. The division was therefore to dig in at once. Its left brigade (the 160th) would be relieved that night by a brigade of the 74th Division at Kh. el Muweile.

British commentators on the battle have generally taken it for granted that the Turkish movement eastward was offensive, or at least designed to draw the British into the hills north of Beersheba. All the evidence goes to show that it was, in fact, dictated by the enemy's anxiety for his left flank and for the Hebron road. This will, indeed, appear obvious enough if an attempt is made to appreciate the situation after the fall of Beersheba from his point of view. Beersheba had fallen unexpectedly soon; to guard the road there was only the weak *3rd Cavalry Division* in the hills on a wide front, and the *12th Depot Regiment*, strong in numbers but composed entirely of Arab recruits and without machine guns. Two British cavalry brigades had moved north on the heels of the retreating Turks; one infantry division (the 53rd) had been observed marching on Tuweiyil Abu Jerwal, apparently to exploit the success. Might not the British march straight on Jerusalem by the one good road north, which was virtually undefended? Even now Turkish critics—scarcely comprehending the requirements of British stomachs as compared with those of their own people—are of opinion that they should have done so.

Fully to appreciate the Turkish sentiments in this matter one must turn again to Lieut.-Colonel Newcombe's detachment, which was left holding the Hebron road north of Dhahriye. Its commander had hoped that the Arabs of the hills would join him, but, though they were friendly enough and provided him with guides, they could not screw up their courage so far. However, he still expected that the British cavalry would move north, and determined to do what damage he could meanwhile. On the 1st November he was attacked by about a hundred Turks, but dispersed them with considerable loss. By the morning of the 2nd he had blocked all communication between Hebron and Dhahriye for forty hours. But his time was up. Lorries with a hundred German transport men from Hebron and Bethlehem moved south to attack him, and from Dhahriye two companies of the *143rd Regiment* advanced northward.

The Turkish companies, commanded by a German officer, succeeded in reaching positions from which they could have destroyed his detachment in a few minutes. He had already had twenty men killed and most of his machine guns disabled. As no other force depended upon him, he decided to surrender. He learned from his captors that considerable numbers of troops were on the move against him, and that the alarm caused by his advance 1917. had spread far and wide, because the enemy feared a 2 Nov. general Arab rising.[1]

By the 2nd November, then, the Turks were thoroughly alarmed for their left flank. Communication between the headquarters of the *Seventh Army* at Hebron and the troops at Kh. Abu Khuff had been cut by the exploit of the South Notts Hussars in capturing Ras en Naqb. The consequent confusion and lack of information were very dangerous to an army already defeated and in retreat. The Turks seem to have deduced from the fact that Newcombe's detachment had advanced far to the east of the Hebron road that other troops were likely to follow from this direction; for they moved the *6th Cavalry Regiment* out to Yutta, 4 miles east of the road north of Dhahriye. At Dhahriye itself were the *143rd Regiment*, and part of the *2nd Regiment*, with 600 men of the *12th Depot Regiment* and nine guns, all under the command of the *24th Division* headquarters, which had moved there from the neighbourhood of Tell esh Sheria.

In the hills west of the road were the remnants of the *Beersheba Group*, consisting of the *27th Division* (1,350 strong), including the *48th Regiment*, with 7 guns and 27 machine guns; also the *8th Cavalry Regiment*. That is to say, by the evening of the 2nd November there were perhaps 4,000 rifles and sabres from Yutta to the left of the *16th Division* in the original defences south of Tell esh Sheria.

---

[1] The following account of affairs in Hebron is given by Obergeneralarzt Steuber, who visited the town just afterwards (German "*Yilderim*," p. 114): "The place was like a disturbed ants' nest; the "staff of Army headquarters was standing beside its horses saddled for "hasty retreat. What had actually happened was that a hostile patrol "of camelry, about seventy strong, had approached the town from the "direction of the Dead Sea, and had been cut off. The riding camels, "splendid animals specially trained by the Bedouin for long-distance work, "lay exhausted in an open space. Their riders, half dark sons of the "desert, half white Englishmen, well fed but wild-looking and unkempt "in appearance from their existence in the desert, were taken away in "motor-lorries. Mounted Turkish gendarmes dashed through the excited "populace. The main body of the English was said to be only a few "kilometres off. As in all panics of this sort, rumour had grossly "exaggerated the facts. A whimsical touch was given to the affair by "an old Arab procuress, who in the midst of the universal terror was "calmly preparing to meet the enemy with a band of scantily clad dancing- "girls wearing coloured transparent veils. The Orient once again pro- "vided a strange scene, which would have been incredible in other theatres "of war."

It is true the Turks did contemplate a counter-attack on the morning of the 3rd November with the aid of the *19th Division*, then moving towards Kh. Abu Khuff, but this was to have been launched from the west and was designed to check the British advance up the Hebron road. There was no thought of bluff in the Turkish movements, which merely represented a desperate endeavour to close the Hebron road and to prevent their left from being outflanked.

From the British point of view the situation was unsatisfactory. G.H.Q. still hoped that it might be possible to launch the XX Corps against the left of the Turkish line by the 4th, but Generals Chetwode and Chauvel were becoming more and more concerned by the difficulty of completing their preparations. A *Khamsin* which began to blow on the 2nd added greatly to the demands for water and to suffering when they could not be met. Washing and shaving had to be forbidden altogether, so that, in the words of an eye-witness, a conference of field officers looked like a Nihilist meeting. But more than traditional smartness and self-respect was thus threatened; for dirt and its accompaniments soon lower the efficiency of the soldier—at any rate of the cleanly British soldier. The administrative staffs of the two corps were hard at work reorganizing water transport,[1] and the engineers improving the wells in Beersheba, but the whole machine was strained to the uttermost to keep the troops at a distance from the town supplied.

### The Operations North of Beersheba, 3rd–5th November.

General Chetwode ordered the 53rd Division to advance on the 3rd November with the object of establishing itself upon the track running through 'Ain Kohle towards Tell esh Sheria. The advance was made in two main columns.

---

[1] Br.-General E. F. Trew, D.A. and Q.M.G. of the Desert Mounted Corps, had tanks fitted on to lorries which he sent to railhead for water. This was to supply the horses of his corps, but on learning from the XX Corps that its men were as badly off as his horses, he handed over the water for their use. In the XX Corps tickets corresponding to the numbers of their horses and mules were issued to units, and each animal, on the ticket being presented at the troughs, was given five gallons.

## ADVANCE OF 53RD DIVISION

On the right the 160th Brigade (Br.-General V. L. N. Pearson) moved up the slight valley running from south to north, east of the Abu Jerwal peak. One battery only accompanied the brigade, as Major-General Mott did not wish to take more horses than necessary out of reach of the water at Beersheba, and it succeeded in reaching a position within range of the Khuweilfe heights. The left column consisted of the 159th Brigade (Br.-General N. E. Money) and the 265th Brigade R.F.A. It followed the rather better track leading to Kh. Abu Khuff. A third column, consisting of the 266th Brigade R.F.A., escorted by the 5/R. Welch Fusiliers, moved further east, where there was comparatively flat ground, on the track leading through Kh. el Leqiye towards Kh. Khuweilfe. The 158th Brigade, less 5/R. Welch Fusiliers, remained in the original position as divisional reserve, but sent back its animals to water and feed in Beersheba. Major-General Mott accompanied the right infantry column, which was to direct, the two brigades communicating by helio.

The day was hot, and the troops, labouring over the rough and broken ground, suffered greatly from thirst. By 12.30 p.m. the right column had come up with the mounted troops, which, as will be recorded, had now closed up to Tell Khuweilfe. Major-General Mott ordered the 160th Brigade to push on its advanced guards and if possible occupy the hills in front, but it was quickly found that the enemy was in strength and prepared to fight hard for the position. No further progress was made that evening, though after sunset a patrol of the 4/Sussex, with an interpreter as guide, succeeded in working its way right round the Turkish position and approaching the wells behind it.[1] The patrol, though fired on by a few Turks at the wells, was able to return to the British lines. But the longed-for water remained in the hands of the enemy, and the exhausted troops, who had finished the contents of the two water-bottles which each man carried, were issued with only about a quarter of a pint apiece. The 159th Brigade on the left, moving on 'Ain Kohle, had several sharp little actions with detachments of the enemy, who handled their machine

---

[1] Probably either at Bir Khuweilfe or Bir el Bestan, but it is impossible to say which.

guns skilfully. The brigade had orders not to advance beyond the Wadi Kohle till the high ground to the northeast had been captured, and therefore took up a line south of the wadi, in close touch with the enemy. It had suffered severely in the course of the day, chiefly from shell fire, and had nearly 400 casualties.

To co-operate with the 53rd Division Major-General Chaytor's orders for the 3rd November were that the 2nd L.H. Brigade should continue the movement against Dhahriye, that the 7th Mounted Brigade should reoccupy Ras en Naqb as early as possible, and that the 1st L.H. Brigade should move up from Beersheba, relieve the 7th at Ras en Naqb, and attack the ridges west of Tell Khuweilfe. The 1st L.H. Brigade left its bivouacs at midnight. The stillness which had fallen upon the battlefield, the moon shining on the white buildings of Beersheba through the haze of dust raised by a hot east wind, the charnel smell tainting the air, made it seem to the troops that they were quitting a ravished and ghostly sepulchre.

Before dawn the South Notts Hussars moved on Ras en Naqb and reoccupied it without difficulty. The enemy was not here in strength, but at Tell Khuweilfe, $2\frac{1}{2}$ miles to the south-west, the case was very different. The 1st L.H. Brigade and Inverness Battery advanced with the object of occupying a line between these two points at 7 a.m., and an hour later the 1st A.L.H. was within 350 yards of the enemy's position on the left. No further advance was possible, and the attack of the infantry was awaited, the fire of the regiment's Hotchkiss guns and four attached machine guns checking the attempts of the Turks to attack its left flank. A squadron of the 2nd A.L.H. reached Ras en Naqb soon after 10 a.m. to relieve the South Notts Hussars, but owing to threatening movements by the enemy in front of the position the Yeomen remained on the ground till the afternoon. A squadron of the 3rd A.L.H. was also moved up to Ras en Naqb, and an attack by a couple of Turkish companies was beaten off without difficulty. Neither the 1st nor the 7th Brigade could water its horses, and Major-General Chaytor decided to relieve them both by the 5th Mounted Brigade, Australian Mounted Division, which had been put at his disposal by General Chauvel. The relief was carried out in the course of the afternoon, and first the 7th Mounted Brigade, then 1917. the 1st L.H. Brigade withdrew to Beersheba. The relief 3 Nov. of Ras en Naqb was a difficult affair. Behind the hill there was ample cover, but to reach it an advance had to be made under heavy machine-gun fire from the enemy, who had pressed in close to the position. The Yeomanry rode in across the rough ground at a gallop, and reached shelter with few casualties.

Meanwhile on the extreme right the 2nd L.H. Brigade had acted boldly. Patrols working round the enemy's flank reached a point within less than a mile of the Hebron road two miles north of Dhahriye. A general advance began at 10.15 a.m., but it was obvious that so small a force on a front of several miles could carry out no serious attack, and General Chauvel decided that it should not be pressed. This brigade was the only one engaged which had found itself water, but the supply in its area was insufficient for more than another two days at most, possibly one day only, if evaporation were quick.

The positions held at night by the British were as follows: the 2nd L.H. Brigade from a short distance north of Kh. Salanta across the Hebron road to El Jabry, a front of about 3 miles; the 5th Mounted Brigade on a line from thence to Ras en Naqb, now strongly held. The Warwick Yeomanry protected the left flank, not in touch with the 53rd Division and far in advance of it. On the front of the 53rd Division the 5/Welch Fusiliers (originally intended, it will be remembered, as escort to the artillery, but ordered by Major-General Mott to support his attack on the Khuweilfe heights) was about Kh. Umm er Rumanim, facing Tell Khuweilfe; next came the 160th Brigade, facing the ridge of which Hill 1706 is the chief feature. The 2nd battalion of the Camel Brigade, which had been put at Major-General Mott's disposal, connected the 160th with the 159th Brigade, which was south of the Wadi Kohle. The 229th Brigade of the 74th Division, echeloned to the left rear of the 159th, protected the left flank.

The reason for the strong resistance of the enemy on this date was that his line had been reinforced by portions of the *19th Division*, and that its commander, arriving at Tell esh Sheria after four days' travelling and finding there hopeless confusion, obeyed the classic maxim and marched to the sound of the guns. The task in front of the British 53rd Division was now more difficult than ever.[1]

Before noon on the 3rd the Commander-in-Chief had telegraphed to Generals Chetwode and Chauvel that their corps were to advance and attack the enemy's left flank next day, concluding his message with the words: "The "Commander-in-Chief expects Sheria and Nejile to be "reached to-morrow." General Chetwode had come to the conclusion that a general attack on the 4th was an impossibility, and his B.G.G.S. Br.-General W. H. Bartholomew, had a conversation on the telephone with Major-General L. J. Bols, the C.G.S. at G.H.Q., in which it was agreed that the attack should be postponed at least until the 5th. Br.-General Bartholomew stated that a conference, attended by the divisional commanders, would take place at 9 a.m. on the 4th at Beersheba, and that after it was over he would be able to inform G.H.Q. what was the minimum time required for the completion of preparations. Late at night Major-General Bols telegraphed that though the Commander-in-Chief was loath to postpone the operation beyond the 5th, he did not wish to hurry his lieutenants if they thought postponement absolutely necessary to their preparations. But he bade them bear in mind how great was the importance of taking advantage of the success at Beersheba, and the value of the position which they had gained on the enemy's flank. He added, as a spur to endeavour, that there was as yet no sign of weakening on the part of the Turks at Gaza.

After the conference was over, at 10.15 a.m. on the 4th, General Chetwode telegraphed his final decision :—

"General Chauvel and myself, after closest consul-"tation, have decided with great reluctance that, owing to "water difficulties and thirst of men, postponement till "6th November is inevitable.

"G.O.C. 53rd Division thinks he will not be able to "take Khuweilfe till to-night, November 4th."

In the afternoon Sir Edmund Allenby drove over to Beersheba from Khan Yunis for a conference with Generals Chetwode and Chauvel, and after hearing their views agreed to the postponement being made.

The rôle of the mounted troops on the 4th November

---
[1] See Note at end of Chapter.

was mainly defensive, though the 2nd L.H. Brigade con- 1917.
tinued its threats against Dhahriye. The New Zealand 4 Nov.
Brigade had been ordered at midnight to return from Bir
Imshash el Male and relieve the 5th Mounted Brigade
between El Jabry and Ras en Naqb. Unfortunately the
brigade was unable to quit its bivouac till the afternoon.
The wells from which much had been hoped had proved to
be mere water-holes which were now drying up altogether,
so that when the brigade did move off watering had not
been completed. Meanwhile a heavy attack was launched
on the 5th Mounted Brigade. Cavalry advanced on both
flanks, but the main attack came against Ras en Naqb.
Here the Gloucester Hussars had just been relieved by the
Worcester Yeomanry, and had moved back to its horses.
Being urgently summoned to support the position, a
squadron mounted and returned at the gallop, and the
horses kept their footing on ground over which the men
when dismounted had had difficulty in picking their way.
A squadron of the Warwick Yeomanry also arrived in the
nick of time. The Turks pushed on with great resolution
—their attack was carried out by order of Falkenhayn
himself—and in some places got within a hundred yards of
the Yeomanry line. But they could advance no further,
against cool, steady shooting, and after dusk desisted from
their attempt and drew off. The 5th Mounted Brigade
was then relieved by the New Zealanders. It had over
fifty casualties in the day's fighting, and great difficulty
was experienced in carrying the wounded back from this
exposed position, over rough ground, to the sand-carts in
the valley behind.

Meanwhile the 53rd Division had renewed its attack
on the Khuweilfe position, an attack which Major-General
Mott saw launched before hurrying down to Beersheba to
attend General Chetwode's conference. This day's operations were to be the least successful of all the confused
fighting which took place in the hills.

Major-General Mott had over night ordered the 158th
Brigade to concentrate at 3 a.m. north of Kh. er Ras, with
the intention of renewing the attack with a fresh brigade.
On hearing of this, Br.-General Pearson, commanding the
160th, requested that his troops should be allowed to
finish the task which they had begun, and the divisional

commander assented—as it proved, unfortunately. For the convoys bringing up food and water from Beersheba lost their way, and the brigade had to begin the attack on empty stomachs. The artillery bombardment began at 5 a.m. and the infantry advance a quarter of an hour later. Some progress was made, and the lower slopes of Hill 1706 were occupied, but soon afterwards the C.R.A. reported that his ammunition convoy from the wagon lines some eight miles in rear had also failed to appear and that he was short of shell to support a serious attack. At 8.25, therefore, the 160th Brigade was ordered to hold its ground. Men and animals suffered terribly from thirst in the course of another day of blazing sun, and the lot of the wounded was heartbreaking. The administrative staff of the XX Corps had arranged for a special motor-lorry column with water to be sent up as far forward as the ration dump on the Kh. el Jubbein track, where troughs and small tanks had been put up by the 437th Field Company of the 53rd Division. This was accomplished during the afternoon after great exertions on the part of the drivers, and helped to ease the difficulty. But the division's own camel convoy with water did not arrive till 4.30 a.m. on the 5th. Even the 158th Brigade, in divisional reserve, suffered severely, though in its case it had been possible to send the animals back to Beersheba for water. The mules of one battalion went 53 hours without a drink.

Later in the day the 158th Brigade, less the 5/Welch Fusiliers, was ordered by Major-General Mott to concentrate and move up behind the 160th. It was his intention to employ it in another attack on the heights before the next dawn, but a message was received from General Chetwode that this operation was not to take place without his direct order. It was eventually postponed until the morning of the 6th, to be carried out then in conjunction with the main attack of the XX Corps. The revision of plans was fortunate for the 158th Brigade, as it had been forced to leave its machine-gun company behind, the mules not having returned from Beersheba.

The 5th November was marked by another strong attack on Ras en Naqb, which was beaten off by the Canterbury Regiment of the New Zealand Brigade. The brigade was to have been relieved that night by the Camel Brigade, but

## RESULTS OF THE HILL FIGHTING

in the tortuous valleys the 4th Battalion of this brigade lost its way, and touch was not made with it till after dawn on the 6th. Br.-General Meldrum was therefore obliged to send back almost all his horses to Beersheba to water. Fortunately the next morning was dark and foggy, thus saving loss during the relief, which was not complete till 10.45 a.m. The New Zealanders suffered severely enough, however, having 87 casualties to men and 119 to horses. They marched back on foot to bivouac on the Hebron road about four miles north-east of Beersheba.

1917.
5 Nov.

On the Hebron road the 2nd L.H. Brigade, which had not been relieved, as it had plenty of water and some grazing for its horses, continued its activity. A patrol of one troop reached Es Semua, 7 miles due east of Edh Dhahriye. In view of the rôle the mounted troops were to play in the coming operations the brigade was ordered to hold its advanced position till the moon rose, then to fall back to Tuweil el Mahdi, east of Bir es Sqati. This withdrawal was completed at 6.30 a.m. on the 6th. The 2nd Battalion of the Camel Brigade now held the right of the British line, facing almost east at Qurnet Ghuzale, with the 4th Battalion at Ras en Naqb. The 2nd L.H. Brigade moved back to Beersheba during the day, leaving, however, a squadron of the 7th A.L.H. and the greater part of its machine-gun squadron attached to the Camel Brigade.

In the course of the morning the Australian Mounted Division, with the 7th Mounted Brigade attached, instead of the 5th, which was not ready to move, relieved the Yeomanry Mounted Division in G.H.Q. reserve, and took over the line of observation connecting the XX and XXI Corps. The Yeomanry Division was ordered to march at night to fill the gap on the right of the 74th Division which would be caused by the development of the attack on the Sheria position, to be launched on the 6th.

The fighting in the hills from the 1st to the 5th November had resulted tactically in a drawn battle, satisfactory to neither side. There had been some confusion, due mainly to the inaccuracy of the maps,[1] and also perhaps

---

[1] One error persistently made was the confusion of Tell Khuweilfe with Hill 1700, which is 1,100 yards south-west of it. This was due to the position of the actual word "Tell Khuweilfe" on the Palestine Exploration Fund Map in use. The reader must be reminded that the contoured 1/40,000 survey, from which Map 7 is drawn, had not at this period been carried out.

to the fact that the forces were operating under the command of two separate corps. Yet strategically the British were to have no cause to complain of the result. They had established themselves in a position of vantage from which to roll up the enemy's flank, and all his efforts had not been able to dislodge them, though they themselves had not won all they desired. They had drawn in his reserve, the *19th Division*, which would otherwise have gone to Tell esh Sheria. All the ground lent itself admirably to defence, as is proved by the fact that in the whole course of the fighting neither side can be said to have made a single successful attack, with the exception of the capture of Ras en Naqb. The only other aspect of the operations deserving note is the extraordinary difficulty of keeping the troops supplied with water, though the outposts of the infantry were never more than ten miles from Beersheba. This was due, even more than to the nature of the routes, to the fact that the arrangements for water supply in the town had not yet been set in order.

THE PLAN OF ATTACK ON THE TURKISH LEFT.

Map 8.
Sketches
5, 6.

The problem before the staffs of the XX and Desert Mounted Corps and of the Royal Engineer units at their disposal may be set out in very simple terms, without entering into detail. It was so to organize the water supply at Beersheba that the whole force based upon the town could march out with a day's supply for the troops and every animal having drunk its fill. It was the impossibility of effecting this by the morning of the 4th, or even of the 5th, which had compelled the postponement of the general attack. The Turks, it has been stated, had done little serious damage to the wells. But the engines working the pumps and the pumps themselves had been put out of action, while several wells in gardens were not found until the 3rd or 4th November. These pumps had to be put into working order, and new pumping plant which had been carried by a train of eight caterpillar tractors brought into use. All the plant used at Asluj was also dismantled by the Desert Mounted Corps and brought in, but it did not reach the town till the afternoon of the 3rd. In one case a *saqqia* was kept in operation, and this ancient mechanism

## PREPARATION FOR THE MAIN ATTACK 93

proved as efficient as the pump, since it drew as much water 1917. —about 1,500 gallons an hour—as the well would produce.[1] 5 Nov. By the morning of the 5th November, the output had reached its maximum, little under 400,000 gallons a day, and the problem was solved.

With regard to ammunition, the main dump had been established north-west of Beersheba, but for the attack on the Sheria position a small dump of about 7,000 rounds 18-pdr., 1,500 rounds 4·5-inch howitzer shell, and a million and a quarter rounds of small arms ammunition was formed with some difficulty by the 74th Divisional Ammunition Column near Muweile. With the ammunition carried by the batteries themselves, this supply was adequate, but no more than adequate. The tracks, and especially that from Tell el Fara to Beersheba, had been greatly improved by the Egyptian Labour Corps under the orders of Br.-General R. L. Waller, Chief Engineer of the XX Corps.

The objectives of the XX Corps' attack were the enemy's trenches which ran for approximately eight miles eastward from the Wadi esh Sheria at Hureira, and also the water supply at Tell esh Sheria, 2 miles north of their centre. This trench system, known as the Qawuqa System, from Kh. Qawuqa at its centre, was cut into two halves by the Beersheba railway. East of the railway, it consisted of a series of strong points, in some cases as much as 400 yards apart, facing due south. There were also several isolated works to the east and south. West of the railway there was a continuous trench, and an almost continuous second line connected with it by numerous communication trenches. This part of the system was in the form of a half-moon, facing south-east, south and south-west. East of the railway there was no wire, west of it the wire was not thick, nor even continuous; but all the works and trenches were well sited and constructed. The system extended to the foot of the hills, and was dug across an arid, dusty plain, bare

---

[1] A *saqqia* consists of a cumbrous wooden pinion on a vertical shaft, rotated by a mule at the end of a lever; the pinion gears into a large wooden wheel, on the axis of which is a smaller one which works an endless chain with buckets on it. The machine is mechanically correct in design, but its materials and the design of its parts cause a great deal of friction.

An interesting account of the Beersheba water supply, with diagrams and illustrations, is given in the R.E. Manual " Palestine Water Supply," pp. 34–36, and in Appendix V to that volume.

of cover except for a number of wadis. It was held by only one division, the *16th*, with only two regiments actually in the trenches, yet, even so, a frontal attack upon it would have been a matter of considerable difficulty. But it was to be taken in flank. The situation of the XX Corps may be likened to that of a man who desires to demolish a wall, working along it from one end, but who, before he can obtain room to swing his hammer, must clear away obstructions at that end. He has cut away the obstructions so far as he can, but not so far as he desires, and has just room to swing his hammer, but only just. The wall is the entrenched Turkish line; the obstructions are the Turkish forces in the hills, which had been pushed back just sufficiently far to permit of that line being enfiladed and rolled up, but still held positions inconveniently close to the flank of the British attack. To ensure that these forces should not interfere with the advance, the 53rd Division was to maintain its pressure and endeavour to " occupy the "general line Khuweilfe–Rujm edh Dhib " [1] as the attack progressed. It was to pass to the command of the Desert Mounted Corps on the morning of the 6th. Meanwhile it was to extend its left in order to set free a brigade of the 74th Division. The Yeomanry Mounted Division was to concentrate near 'Ain Kohle for the purpose of filling the gap which would appear between the 74th and 53rd Divisions when the 74th advanced westward.

Major-General Mott considered that in order to occupy the left of the line mentioned above he would be forced to move a dangerously large proportion of his troops down from the heights on which they were now installed and thus leave his right flank open to the risk of an attack from the Khuweilfe hills, where the enemy appeared to be in greatest strength. He could best fulfil his mission, he argued, by attacking these hills, the most dominating position on the whole battle front. If he did so, his left would not, indeed, be in a position to advance, but he would most effectually pin the enemy to his ground; for it seemed certain that the Turks would put in every man they could spare to hold

---

[1] This name, " Cairn of the Wolf," stood for a group of mounds, but in the orders its significance was the spot where it was written on the map. This was north of the Wadi Khuweilfe and 5 miles W.N.W. of Tell Khuweilfe.

Khuweilfe. Sir Edmund Allenby, after the interview on the 4th with General Chetwode which has been recorded, went on with General Chauvel to see Major-General Mott, heard his arguments, and authorized him to attack the Khuweilfe position at the same time as the operation of the XX Corps began, without seeking to press forward on his left.

1917.
5 Nov.

The troops taking part in the main attack were to be in their positions of assembly by dawn on the 6th November: the 74th Division deployed as close as possible to the flank of the enemy's line of works east of the railway; the 60th facing some isolated works north of Bir Abu Irqaiyiq; the 10th echeloned to the left front of the 60th, with one brigade ready to attack on its left. The 74th Division, which was to direct, had as objective the line of the works east of the railway, after which it was to cover the right of the 60th Division, seize the high ground north of Tell esh Sheria, and protect the water supply. The 60th Division and one brigade of the 10th were then to cross the railway and capture the trenches west of it to a depth of two miles. The two remaining brigades of the 10th division were to be held in corps reserve. The heavy artillery consisted of the 15th and 181st Heavy Batteries, the 378th, 383rd and 440th Siege Batteries, under the orders of Br.-General A. H. Short, G.O.C. R.A. XX Corps.[1]

THE CAPTURE OF THE SHERIA POSITION.

It had taken six days of fighting to prepare the way for Sir Edmund Allenby's great coup, the rolling up of the left of the main Turkish line, yet the delay had had no serious effect, and the attack was now about to be carried out in the most favourable circumstances. The operations in the hills had drawn in more and more Turkish troops, and above all the first-class troops of the *19th Division*, till now there were at least seven infantry regiments between the Hebron road and the left of the defensive line, and only two regiments in this line up to the Wadi esh Sheria, a distance of 6½ miles.

The 74th Division had a difficult and hurried task in reaching its jumping-off line. Preliminary instructions

---
[1] XX Corps Order No. 13 is given in Appendix 12.

had been issued by Major-General Girdwood for the brigades to concentrate about 3,000 yards north-west of the position which they were subsequently directed to take up in XX Corps Order No. 13, and revised verbal instructions were not issued to the battalion commanders till dusk was falling.¹ However, the new positions were for the most part reached by 3.30 a.m. on the 6th. But there was not time to rush the advanced Turkish work V.46 before dawn, as the 230th Brigade had been instructed to do. This was perhaps not altogether a disadvantage, since the Turks were not put on the *qui vive* until the general advance began.

The attack was carried out by the 229th Brigade on the left with the 230th slightly echeloned to its right rear. The 231st Brigade, further echeloned behind the right of the 230th, was to occupy the high ground south of the Wadi esh Sheria. The artillery, to which the 10th Mountain Battery was attached, was under the orders of the C.R.A., Br.-General L. J. Hext, the 268th Brigade R.F.A. being detailed to support the 230th Brigade and the XLIV and 117th Brigades R.F.A. the 229th.

1917.
6 Nov.

The attack was launched without preliminary bombardment or barrage. The ground was burnt-up grass-land or tilth, less broken and stony than that of the Beersheba fighting, but veined by steep-sided wadis. The 16/Sussex, which advanced on the left bank of the Wadi Union, began moving forward at 4 a.m., and an hour later carried V.46. A circular work beyond, hitherto unlocated, made a much

---

¹ The corps order was issued at 8.30 a.m. on the 5th. There is no record of the hour at which it reached the 74th Division, but Major-General Girdwood states that he was first informed of the alteration by General Chetwode, whom he was summoned to meet for a reconnaissance during the morning.

The following extract from the diary of Br.-General A. J. M'Neill, 230th Brigade, is quoted in " The 74th (Yeomanry) Division in Syria and France," by Major C. H. Dudley Ward, p. 194 :—

" 5th November.—Did reconnaissance in morning, and C.Os. went
" out to do ditto, according to the plan of attack to-morrow. But a wire
" at 3 ordering all brigadiers to headquarters, and plan all changed.
" Very hurried verbal orders given, and I rushed back to get it out to
" C.Os. before dark. Poor devils had no chance of reconnaissance of new
" ground, but all swore they understood the rough idea, and off they went
" to get things moving, as we calculated it would take all night getting
" into position. . . . Finally at 3.30 a.m. all were reported in position,
" and I then rode forward to my first battalion headquarters, under a cliff
" at the bend of a wadi [the Wadi Union], not far from the enemy advanced
" work called V.46."

## LAUNCH OF THE ATTACK

stouter resistance. The senior company commander, Captain G. H. Powell-Edwards, detached a platoon of his own and one of another company to deal with it, while he led the remainder of the battalion forward. After a fierce struggle the straight shooting and dash of the Sussex platoons triumphed over superior numbers, and the work was taken by a bayonet charge. Seventy Turks surrendered and 30 dead were found in the trenches. V.47 on the front of the 231st Brigade also made a brave fight and was not captured by the 24/Welch till 7 a.m.

1917. 6 Nov.

The advance was now carried out at an extraordinary speed. By 6 a.m. the 230th Brigade had possession of the three works, V.38, 39, and 45; and soon afterwards the large redoubt, of which the trenches were numbered V.29, 35, 36, and 37, was in the hands of the 229th. Close support of the infantry by the artillery had so far been impossible owing to bad visibility, but now batteries were moved up to positions close to the line reached by the foremost troops. The 231st Brigade, the last battalion of which had not been relieved by the Yeomanry Mounted Division till 5 a.m., had followed the attack and driven a screen of Turkish skirmishers off the high ground on the right. Here the 24/Welch beat off several counter-attacks in the course of the day.

Next the 229th Brigade attacked the strong system of works V.26–28. Serious resistance was met here, especially from behind some cactus hedges in V.26, but all the trenches were in the hands of the attackers by 8.30 a.m. A company of the 16/Sussex, seeing a Turkish battery north of the Wadi Uxbridge firing at the troops of the 229th Brigade, attacked it with one Lewis gun and two rifle sections. With such skill was this party handled that after one drum had been fired at short range the battery, with a personnel of 3 officers and 25 men, surrendered. The enemy launched two counter-attacks on the 16/Sussex, and very nearly retook his lost battery, to withdraw which he brought up teams of oxen. When the second was at its most threatening the forward observing officer of the 268th Brigade R.F.A. came up just in time to range his batteries on the advancing Turks. Their line, assailed by the shrapnel, wavered, halted, and finally reeled back in disorder—a serious threat to the attack being thus averted.

There was now a short pause, during which battalions, which had become somewhat intermixed, were reorganized. Then the 229th Brigade again moved westward along the line of the enemy works, meeting with less opposition, though harassed by enfilading artillery fire from north of the Wadi esh Sheria. At about 1.15 p.m. it reached the railway, its final objective, where the 14/Black Watch captured another field battery, in the act of limbering up to escape the advance of the 60th Division.

The attack of the 60th and 10th Divisions did not begin until that of the 74th had reached its objective, but the three brigades which were to make it, the 180th, 179th, and 31st (Br.-General E. M. Morris) began their advance soon after 8 a.m. so as to be ready to assault the trenches west of the railway as soon as the 74th Division had reached it. By 10.30 the artillery—the whole divisional artillery of the 10th Division being employed in addition to that of the 60th—had reached positions from which it could bring fire to bear on the enemy's trenches. Wire-cutting was continued till 12.15 p.m., by which time each 18-pdr. battery had cut two ten-yard gaps in the wire immediately east of the railway. The field artillery then began a bombardment of the trench west of the railway. The XCVI Heavy Artillery Group, under the orders of the XX Corps, had also advanced sufficiently far to bombard the trenches about Kh. Qawuqa.

At 12.35 p.m. Br.-General Edwards rode up to the leading battalions of the 179th Brigade, which were then waiting for the 180th to draw level. Seeing a number of Turks retiring, he ordered the assault to be launched at once As the infantry went forward, it came under fairly heavy artillery and machine-gun fire, the 179th Brigade suffering most, as the 180th was some distance in rear. Each brigade had two battalions (2/18th and 2/19th London on the front of the 180th Brigade; 2/13th and 2/16th London on that of the 179th) in line, with one in close support. The attack was a fine example of the methods of pre-war training: a steady advance until the leading troops were held up by fire; then the building-up of a strong firing line; and finally the assault. As the battalions swept through the enemy's trenches the field artillery lifted to the works in second line.

## ADVANCE ON TELL ESH SHERIA

Br.-General Morris, commanding the 31st Brigade, having himself gone well forward, saw the troops of the 179th Brigade advancing and ordered his own brigade to attack at 1 p.m., without awaiting a direct order from the 10th Division. His battalions went forward in artillery formation, the 5/R. Irish Fusiliers echeloned to the left rear of the 179th Brigade, the 2/R. Irish Fusiliers slightly echeloned behind that battalion. The railway was crossed without casualties, owing to the earlier attack of the 60th Division, and the first objective taken with ease. There was a brief fire fight for the works S.58 and 59, just short of the final objective, but by 2.30 p.m. this was in the hands of the attackers. The enemy was then seen to fall back towards the strong Hureira Redoubt beyond the Wadi esh Sheria. Patrols of the 179th Brigade pushed rapidly forward on his heels and took possession of the whole system east of the wadi.

1917.
6 Nov.

Before he had learned of the complete success of the attack, General Chetwode had, at 3.5 p.m., warned the divisional commanders that the 31st Brigade would be required to hold the line of the final objective, the remainder of the 10th Division concentrating on the railway east of Kh. Qawuqa, while the 60th Division would concentrate in readiness to move north against Tell esh Sheria. A little later he also ordered the 74th Division to be ready to advance on the right of the 60th. At 4.30 p.m. he issued orders for the advance to begin as early as possible, the 60th Division to secure a strong bridgehead north of Tell esh Sheria and protect the water supply there, the 74th taking up a line facing north-east, from the most easterly works, V.38, 39, and 45, to Kh. Barrata.

The 181st Brigade, which had already concentrated north of the Wadi Samarra, was ordered to advance at once on Tell esh Sheria, but did not receive the message until shortly before darkness fell. Meanwhile a company of the 2/20th London, 180th Brigade, under Captain A. Reynolds, which had been in support to the original attack and had occupied the high ground on its brigade's right, had pressed forward alone towards the station. By 5 p.m. it had established itself within 500 yards of the sidings. Captain Reynolds sent back a message giving his position and suggesting that a strong attack should be launched at once, before the enemy had time to organize a new line of defence. Br.-General Watson ordered the 2/17th and the remainder of the 2/20th to move to his support and capture the viaduct across the Wadi esh Sheria. But as these battalions and also the head of the 181st Brigade moved up they were met by very heavy machine-gun fire, and it appeared that further progress against a position which had not been reconnoitred by daylight was impossible. It was decided to renew the advance towards the wadi at 3.30 a.m., by which time the moon would have been up long enough to allow some reconnaissance to be carried out. To complicate affairs, an ammunition dump near the station to which the enemy had contrived to set light, began to blow up with a series of terrific explosions. Tents and stores flamed up fiercely, so that troops in the neighbourhood were brilliantly illuminated and presented ideal targets to the Turkish machine gunners, who were themselves hidden. Meanwhile the 74th Division had taken up its position as ordered, except that Br.-General M'Neill had wisely instructed the left battalion of the 230th Brigade not to cross the Wadi esh Sheria and extend to Kh. Barrata until touch had been obtained with the 60th Division. Touch was not obtained during the night, owing to the inability of the 60th Division to cross the wadi.

The crossing of the Wadi esh Sheria may properly be considered a part of the pursuit, especially as the 60th Division, which was to effect it, came under the orders of the Desert Mounted Corps on the morning of the 7th November. It will therefore be left to the next chapter, which describes the break-up of the Turkish front and the retreat. The capture of the Qawuqa defences had been brilliantly executed and completely successful. Nor was the cost very high in country which gave little cover. The casualties were approximately 1,300, the captures upwards of six hundred,[1] together with twelve guns, a number of machine guns, great quantities of small arm and artillery

---

[1] Neither casualties nor captures can be given exactly, because the 60th Division, heavily engaged the following day, includes the whole fighting in its returns ; but it does not appear that this division had more than 300 casualties on the 6th. The 74th Division suffered much more severely, having just a thousand casualties, two-thirds of this number in the 229th Brigade.

## OPERATIONS NORTH OF BEERSHEBA 101

ammunition. It may be argued that it was a general's **1917.**
rather than a soldier's battle, because the greatest difficulty **6 Nov.**
that had to be faced was that of placing the attacking troops
on the enemy's flank, and because, when that was accomplished, the overwhelmingly superior numbers of the
British made the result of the battle inevitable. This is
true, but not all the truth. The whole success of the
attack depended upon the resolution of the 74th Division
in the early stages, and the Yeomen did not fall short of the
expectations formed of them. Their advance began in
darkness, over unknown ground, with indifferent maps, so
that they had no artillery support in the first stage of their
attack. In these circumstances the skill with which the
machine-gun companies and Lewis-gun sections supported
the infantry was a big factor in the success, but the biggest
was the infantry's own determination to close swiftly with
the enemy.

THE OPERATIONS NORTH OF BEERSHEBA,
6TH NOVEMBER.

In the early morning of the 6th November the forces **Maps 7, 8.**
in the hills were disposed as follows : on the right the Camel **Sketch 6.**
Brigade with its centre on Ras en Naqb and its right covered
by patrols of the 2nd L.H. Brigade ;[1] in the centre the
53rd Division, which was to come under the orders of the
Desert Mounted Corps at 6 a.m. that day, with its right
south-west of Tell Khuweilfe ; on the left the Yeomanry
Mounted Division, engaged in relieving the right of the
74th Division to free it for the main attack on the Qawuqa
trenches. The rest of the Desert Mounted Corps was widely
scattered : the Australian Mounted Division, with the 7th
instead of the 5th Mounted Brigade, connecting the XX
and XXI Corps, its brigades based for water on Kharm and
Shellal ; the 1st L.H., 5th Mounted, and New Zealand
Brigades north-east and east of Beersheba, watering and
resting their horses for the work before them.

The attack was to be carried out by the 158th Brigade
(Br.-General H. A. Vernon) with the 4/R. Sussex of the 160th

---
[1] The greater part of the 2nd L.H. Machine-Gun Squadron, with a squadron of the 7th A.L.H. as escort, was also attached to the Camel Brigade.

attached, and was to be supported by the whole of the 53rd Divisional Artillery with the exception of one battery, and by the 91st Heavy Battery, which had been brought up with some difficulty. The 3rd Battalion Camel Brigade, under the orders of the 53rd Division, was to protect the right of the 158th Brigade. The objective was Tell Khuweilfe itself and the three peaks south-west of it, the highest feature for several miles. After the capture of this ridge it was intended to establish a line beyond the Wadi Khuweilfe to the north. An intense bombardment of the ridge, beginning at 4 a.m., was to be carried out for twenty minutes before the launching of the assault; and all sixteen guns of the machine-gun company had been so placed that they could put a barrage first on the near face of the ridge and afterwards, as the infantry went forward, on the reverse slopes.

The assembly close up to the position was an affair of great difficulty. On the right was the 1/Hereford, the right of which was directed on Tell Khuweilfe; next came the 6/R. Welch Fusiliers; then the 7/R. Welch Fusiliers; and on the left the 4/R. Sussex. The 5/R. Welch Fusiliers was in reserve. The 3rd Battalion Camel Brigade was to follow the Hereford, take over Tell el Khuweilfe after its capture, and establish itself upon that commanding feature in order to fulfil its rôle of protecting the right flank.

The darkness in which the action began was followed by a dense mist; units in some cases were scattered in the fierce and confused fighting; and all the reports were written with reference to a faulty map. It is therefore no easy task to reconstruct the events of the early morning. It appears that the 6/R. Welch Fusiliers was a little late in starting and that the Hereford, feeling for touch on its left, swung slightly left-handed. The result was that its right company, closing towards its left, wheeled across the front of Tell Khuweilfe instead of straddling it and was raked with fearful effect by Turkish machine guns atop of it. Except at this point, however, there were few casualties as the infantry moved forward behind an excellent barrage. In the centre the left company of the Hereford and the 6/R. Welch Fusiliers carried their objectives with the bayonet; then pressing forward down the slope beyond, surprised and captured nine field guns with their detachments. But the companies which had made this advance were now far ahead of the troops on either flank, and, suddenly counter-attacked from three directions, were compelled to abandon the guns and withdraw to higher ground. To crown their misfortune they were mistaken in the mist for Turks and fired on by the British artillery, so that they fell back once more, portions of their line in some confusion. The Turks followed up quickly and captured some prisoners at this point before the troops were rallied and had taken up a new line, on which a company of the 5/R. Welch Fusiliers was moved up to support them. On the left the 7/R. Welch Fusiliers and 4/R. Sussex both captured their objectives, Hill 1706 and the spur to the west.

1917.
6 Nov.

As day broke the 3rd Battalion Camel Brigade found itself in front of Tell Khuweilfe, but too far off to have a chance of carrying it with a rush now that the barrage had lifted, and completely exposed on the flat ground south of the hill. Lieut.-Colonel N. B. de Lancey Forth, finding that he had lost touch with the Hereford, had run forward, letting slip through his hand the telephone line which that battalion had unreeled in its advance, and found to his dismay that the wire turned left-handed, almost at right angles to the true direction of the attack. Realizing what had happened, he swiftly moved his own men behind the cover of a low spur faintly visible on his left—only just in time, for a moment later the ground over which they had been advancing was swept by a blast of machine-gun fire which would have annihilated them. Then began an extraordinary struggle. The spur proved to be the northern flank of a little valley running from west to east, and the commanding officer placed the bulk of his force on the northern ridge, with a strong detachment on the southern. Hardly had these dispositions been made when an attack was launched by the enemy against the eastern end of the northern ridge. It was beaten off, but immediately afterwards the enemy attacked from the north, across the low ground between the ridge and Tell el Khuweilfe. This attack also was held, though with great difficulty. Then came the most critical moment of all. The enemy suddenly appeared moving along the ridge from the west, driving before him a party of the Hereford which had lost all its officers.  One of the Camel Corps officers, Lieutenant E. W. Dixon, rushed out in front of his men, waving his hat and urging them forward.  The infantry turned with the advancing Camel Corps and drove the enemy back along the spur, though the Turks maintained themselves at the head of the valley, which they swept with machine-gun fire.

The action was full of extraordinary incidents, since neither side quite knew the other's position or whence to expect an attack.  For example, Lieut.-Colonel de Lancey Forth, galloping across the valley from his southern post, had actually ridden through a line of Turks during their first attack from the east in the misty half-light.  Even after the morning had cleared the fighting was at very close quarters.  But one of the most notable events of the day was yet to come.  The 2nd Australian Machine-Gun Squadron under Captain J. R. Cain, which had been in action to the south-east, came on the scene at 10 a.m. to support the Camel Corps.  Galloping straight up the valley under heavy machine-gun fire, it endeavoured to seize the Turkish position at the head.  In this it failed, suffering serious loss and only escaping annihilation by getting into dead ground below the Turks.  Yet its presence ensured the left flank and the magnificent gallantry of its dash into action was an inspiration to the hard-pressed Camel Corps.

On the right, then, there was a deadlock all day, and so close were the opponents that it was difficult for any man to move a yard without drawing upon himself a shower of bullets.  On the left the 7/R. Welch Fusiliers and 4/Sussex were established on the high ground.  Br.-General Vernon, considering that it was out of the question to attempt the capture of Tell Khuweilfe by daylight and still more to advance beyond the Wadi Khuweilfe, ordered his troops to hold what they had gained.

This was no easy matter.  The Turks launched one counter-attack after another upon the two battalions on the left, and at last succeeded in driving the 7/R. Welch Fusiliers from its position.  After a short bombardment the battalion regained the ground by a bayonet charge.  At 9.30 a.m. Major-General Mott had put the 2/10th Middlesex at the disposal of Br.-General Vernon, who placed it in reserve behind his centre.  The last Turkish counter-attack was launched at 3.30 p.m. and was repulsed with heavy loss.

## FINAL SITUATION AT KHUWEILFE

The 159th Brigade on the left had been ordered in the morning to make an attempt to ease the pressure on the 158th by advancing on 'Ain Kohle, but, with only a single battery at its disposal, found it impossible to get forward. Major-General Mott also made several urgent requests for a mounted brigade, or even a regiment, to be handed over to him as a mobile reserve, but the Desert Mounted Corps was unable to spare him this reinforcement.

1917.
6 Nov.

So the situation remained all night and a great part of the following day, when the enemy began to draw off. Once again the attack at Khuweilfe had fallen short of complete success. The Turkish *19th Division* had fought with the resolution which this crack formation from the European battlefields was to display later on in the Judæan Hills. When the Hereford and 6/R. Welch Fusiliers broke their line, the regiments on either flank closed in, and at the same time a battalion from reserve attacked from the north. Yet on this hard-fought day the troops under Major-General Mott's command had finely fulfilled their mission and rendered invaluable service to the British divisions in the plain below. Costly though their frontal attack was,[1] it prevented the enemy from withdrawing a man or a gun from the hills to support the cracking front at Tell esh Sheria, still less to make a diversion by attacking the right flank of the XX Corps in its advance.

NOTE.

THE TURKISH MOVEMENTS FROM THE 1st TO THE 6th NOVEMBER.

On the morning of the 1st November the headquarters of the *III Corps*, which had fled to Tell esh Sheria, moved to Dhahriye on the Hebron road, whither it was followed by the *143rd Regiment* of the *24th Division*. The remains of the former *Beersheba Group*, now numbering only about

---

[1] The casualties of the 158th Brigade (less those of the attached Sussex, Middlesex, and Camel Corps) on the 6th and 7th November were reported by Br.-General Vernon to be 620. The 3rd Battalion Camel Brigade had 76 casualties, the 2nd Australian Machine-Gun Squadron 27, and the Middlesex 14. The losses of the Sussex are not known. The Turks claim to have captured 200 prisoners, but the 158th Brigade reports only 42 missing. It is possible that a proportion of the 207 reported killed were actually captured by the enemy. The Turks left between three and four hundred dead on the field, of whom some had probably fallen in the earlier engagements.

1,500 rifles [1] was reorganized at Tell esh Sheria and moved up to the hills about Tell Khuweilfe in the evening.

On the following day the *125th Regiment* of the *16th Division* was also moved into the hills, coming temporarily under the orders of the *27th Division*. The *6th Cavalry Regiment* was moved far out on the left flank to Yutta. Falkenhayn had ordered a counter-attack to be carried out in a south-easterly direction on the morning of the 3rd November, with the object of driving the British off the Hebron road and preventing them from outflanking the Turkish left. For this purpose the *19th Division* was to be put at the disposal of Ali Fuad, commanding the *XX Corps*, who also proposed to employ part of the *16th Division*, while the *3rd Cavalry Division* operated on his left flank. This operation was prevented by the British advance that morning, and also by the fact that the *19th Division*, delayed and split up by anxiety as to the right flank, did not begin to arrive on the Khuweilfe heights till the afternoon.

Early on the morning of the 4th Falkenhayn, still at Aleppo, ordered the recapture of Ras en Naqb. This attack carried out by the *8th Cavalry Regiment*, and the *77th Regiment, 19th Division*, was, as we know, repulsed owing to the staunchness of the 5th Mounted Brigade.[2] The Marshal arrived at Damascus on this evening and remained there for the night. On the evening of the 5th he reached Jerusalem and established his headquarters in the German Hospice on the Mount of Olives. His first act was to give Kress, the commander of the *Eighth Army*, permission to withdraw his heavy artillery at Gaza and east of the town to north of the Wadi el Hesi. Owing to the shortage of horses for the guns a proportion of them were moved by rail. Part of the *26th Division*, holding the front between Kh. Sihan and Abu Hureira which had not yet been attacked, was also withdrawn during the night to Kh. Zuheilika, 5 miles N.N.E. of Abu Hureira, to form a new reserve. It was with these troops, known as the *Zuheilika Group*, that Colonel Ali Fuad held the Wadi esh Sheria on the evening of the 6th and prevented the 60th Division from crossing.

---

[1] The *67th Regiment* of the *27th Division* arrived at Tell esh Sheria at a strength of 1 officer and 27 men (Turkish " Yilderim," Part 3, Chap. III).

[2] It is of interest to record that the guns captured by the South Notts and thrown into gullies by them on their retirement from the Ras en Naqb (p. 81) were recovered by the enemy during this attack (Turkish " Yilderim," Part 3, Chap. III).

## CHAPTER VI.

### THE BREAK-UP OF THE TURKISH FRONT AND THE PURSUIT, 7TH–9TH NOVEMBER.

(Maps 2, 4, 8; Sketches 7, 8, 9.)

### THE XX CORPS ON THE 7TH NOVEMBER.

As soon as he heard of the capture of the Qawuqa system on the evening of the 6th, Sir Edmund Allenby, anticipating that the Wadi esh Sheria would be crossed that night, issued orders to General Chauvel for the launching of the Desert Mounted Corps through the enemy's broken centre. The Yeomanry Mounted Division, the 53rd Division, and the Camel Brigade, all under the command of Major-General G. de S. Barrow, were to hold the position already attained in the hills north of Beersheba, but the Australian Mounted Division was to be returned from G.H.Q. reserve to the Desert Mounted Corps. General Chauvel was ordered to advance rapidly on Jemmame and Huj in order to secure the water supply and thus enable the mounted troops to operate westward from those points and cut off the Turkish troops between the Wadi esh Sheria and the sea.[1]

1917.
7 Nov.
Maps 2, 8.

But, in fact, the expected breach at Tell esh Sheria had

---

[1] 8.10 p.m. 6th Nov. 1917.
G.O.C. Descorps will at once collect all available mounted troops except Yeomanry Division and will push through to Jemmame and Huj. Australian Division is transferred from general reserve to Descorps and has been ordered to send staff officer to report to Descorps to explain situation of division and take instructions. 3rd Light Horse Brigade is being ordered from Shellal at 7 a.m. to-morrow, by Imleih and Irqaiyiq, where Descorps will send instructions to meet them, but the advance will not be delayed to wait for this brigade, which must follow on. Object of Descorps will be to secure the water at Jemmame and Huj with a view to operating rapidly from those places so as to cut off or pursue the Gaza garrison. Chief expects the enemy to be pressed with the utmost vigour.
G.O.C. Yeomanry Division will take command of right flank, with 53rd Division and Camel Brigade attached to his command, and will form a defensive flank on approximately the line he holds at present, taking every opportunity that may offer of punishing the enemy.

not yet been fully opened, and while the mounted troops were moving up it was necessary for the 60th Division to complete this operation. The ground in the vicinity of the Wadi esh Sheria had been reconnoitred as well as possible during the night, and the flames at the station had gradually died down. Major-General Shea ordered an attack to be carried out at 3.30 a.m. on the 7th by the 181st Brigade on the right and the 180th on the left to secure the railway viaduct and establish a bridgehead north of the wadi. The leading battalions of each brigade began to move forward soon after this hour, but, feeling its way cautiously over the broken ground, the 2/22nd London of the 181st Brigade, which had the furthest to go, did not reach the wadi till nearly 5.30 a.m., about an hour before sunrise. No artillery was employed until it was light enough to distinguish the Turkish position.

The enemy had, as we have seen, brought up the *Zuheilika Group*, probably small in numbers but fresh, to support the remnants of the *16th Division*, and had a strong position beyond the Wadi esh Sheria. Directly he was aware of the advance, he swept the bed with machine-gun and rifle fire from the higher ground on the right bank. The shooting in the dim light was wild and ineffective, but when attacked at close quarters he fought grimly with bomb and bayonet. The Londoners would take no denial. On the right, east of Tell esh Sheria itself, the 2/22nd London charged up the slope and flung the Turks back from it. Lieut.-Colonel A. D. Borton, who had personally reorganized the leading waves when they were checked by heavy machine-gun fire, walking up and down his line with supreme contempt for danger, now led a party of volunteers against a Turkish battery firing at point-blank range, capturing the guns and the detachments.[1] The battalion then crossed the railway (which bent sharply eastward north of Tell esh Sheria), and established itself about a thousand yards beyond it. Nearly a hundred prisoners were taken. The 2/23rd London, which had followed in close support, extended the line to the right, and further troops of the brigade were brought up later to extend to the left of the 74th Division at Kh. Barrata. On the left the 180th Brigade was equally successful. The

---

[1] Lieut.-Colonel Borton was awarded the Victoria Cross.

## THE WADI ESH SHERIA CROSSED 109

2/17th and 2/20th London charged in silence across the wadi. After hand-to-hand fighting the 2/20th stormed Tell esh Sheria, taking 74 prisoners, including a regimental commander, while the 2/17th rushed four machine guns in action on a mound a little west of it. The two battalions then advanced to a position about 1,500 yards beyond Tell esh Sheria and in touch with the 181st Brigade. Several small counter-attacks were made by the enemy, but were beaten off without great difficulty. It was a brilliant piece of work, and casualties were not, in the circumstances, high.[1]

1917. 7 Nov.

During the night orders had been received from G.H.Q. that one infantry division would follow the troops of the Desert Mounted Corps, which was marching on Huj on the morning of the 7th, and would come temporarily under the orders of General Chauvel. General Chetwode selected the 60th Division for this task and ordered the 10th to take its place when it advanced and guard the invaluable water supplies captured at Tell esh Sheria.

There was only one more task for the XX Corps: to capture the Hureira Redoubt on the Gaza–Beersheba road beyond the Wadi esh Sheria, and thus widen the breach in the enemy's line. This the 31st Brigade of the 10th Division was ordered to carry out, and was allotted the LXVIII Brigade R.F.A. and one extra howitzer battery, C/268.[2]

The attack was launched at 7 a.m. The heavy artillery had previously bombarded the redoubt, but owing to lack of communication could not support the actual attack. This was made over open ground in full view of the enemy.

---

[1] It is impossible to give separate casualties for this operation, as they are not recorded, but they can be deduced with fair accuracy. The total casualties of the 181st Brigade for the 6th and 7th were as follows:—

|  | Killed. | Wounded. | Missing. |
|---|---|---|---|
| Officers | 3 | 6 | — |
| Other Ranks | 32 | 203 | 10 |

A total of 254. Now this brigade was in support to the original attack on the Turkish trenches at Qawaqa and had few if any casualties till after nightfall. The 180th Brigade had 279 casualties in the two days, certainly more than half of them in the attack on Tell esh Sheria. The losses for this assault must have been close on four hundred, though it was made on a frontage of three battalions only. The Turks also lost fairly heavily, however, and it was estimated that the dead left on the field outnumbered the prisoners taken—nearly two hundred.

[2] It may be mentioned that this battery was brought into action by pack-mules of the 5/R. Irish Fusiliers, its horses being miles away watering.

The Turkish shells fell for the most part behind the attacking troops, and there were few casualties until they were within 1,200 yards of the redoubt. Thenceforward the advance continued in face of heavy machine-gun fire. The 2/R. Irish Fusiliers, to which were attached two companies of the 5th Battalion, moved directly on the redoubt, its left flank on the long trench running up from the Rushdi system to the Wadi esh Sheria. The 6/R. Inniskilling Fusiliers with four machine guns followed behind its right flank, with orders to capture the detached works north-east of the redoubt. Three hundred yards short of the position the 2/R. Irish Fusiliers was brought to a halt, but the supporting company at once began to work its way round the southern face of the redoubt along the wadi, while the Inniskillings on the right captured the hairpin-shaped work north of the wadi. At this threat of encirclement the bulk of the garrison evacuated the redoubt, which was then assaulted by the Irish Fusiliers and taken, with 28 prisoners and four large trench mortars. The Inniskillings subsequently captured two 150-mm. howitzers in position north of the wadi, after the Turkish gunners had got rid of as much ammunition as possible by firing on Major-General Longley as he rode back from Hureira after congratulating his troops. The redoubt was found to be extraordinarily strong, with two lines of deep trenches and many machine-gun emplacements. It dominated the surrounding country, but its prominence made it an easy target; and Lieut.-Colonel H. B. H. Orpen-Palmer, commanding the 2/R. Irish Fusiliers, was of opinion that, had time been allowed for a thorough artillery preparation, it could have been taken with little loss. Prisoners stated that its garrison had consisted of 200 men with 30 machine guns. Patrols were quickly pushed forward and occupied without resistance the Labbi and Mustapha trenches to the north-west and north. The 2/R. Irish Fusiliers, which had borne the brunt of this difficult attack, had 122 casualties [1] out of the 276 incurred in it.

The capture of the Hureira Redoubt and the trenches beyond it concluded the operations of the XX Corps in the Third Battle of Gaza, except that on the morning of the

---

|  | Killed. | Wounded. |
|---|---|---|
| [1] Officers | 2 | 5 |
| Other Ranks | 21 | 94 |

## THE CAVALRY ON THE 7TH NOV.

8th the 10th Division moved a detachment along the Gaza–Beersheba road until touch was made about Atawine with the Composite Force of the XXI Corps. The XX Corps was now to hand back to the XXI the transport which it had borrowed, making it impossible to supply the troops under its orders in advance of their present positions. Its captures from the 31st October to the end of the operations (including abandoned guns found by the 10th Division on the 8th when it moved up the Gaza–Beersheba road) were 2,177 prisoners, 45 guns, 7 trench mortars, 50 machine guns. Its casualties numbered nearly 5,500, and as the Turkish defence had been chiefly dependent on the machine gun, the proportion of killed to wounded was low.[1]

1917.
8 Nov.

### THE DESERT MOUNTED CORPS ON THE 7TH NOVEMBER.

The Desert Mounted Corps' great moment was come; the moment for exploitation of success, for which the mounted troops had been maintained at a strength far higher in proportion to that of the infantry than in any other theatre of war, was in sight. But the numbers available for the operation were small by comparison with the Commander-in-Chief's original expectations. He had hoped to employ the whole of the Desert Mounted Corps, but now it had been necessary to leave the Yeomanry Mounted Division in the hills. Nor did the A. & N.Z. Mounted Division march complete, for it left behind the N.Z.M.R. Brigade in support to the 53rd Division, two squadrons and machine guns, and the greater part of its Field Squadron Australian Engineers, which was still at work on the Beersheba wells. The 11th and 12th Light Armoured Car Batteries, which would have been very useful, were also left on the Hebron road. No. 1 Light Car Patrol followed the division, but was obliged to halt some distance south of Tell esh Sheria and await daylight. There were therefore only four brigades immediately available (the 1st and 2nd of the A. & N.Z. Mounted Division; 4th and the attached 7th Mounted Brigade of the Australian Mounted Division), and though the 3rd L.H. and 5th Mounted

7 Nov.

|  | Killed. | Wounded. | Missing. |
|---|---|---|---|
| [1] Officers . . . | 63 | 198 | — |
| Other Ranks . | 869 | 4,246 | 108 |

Brigades were on the move to rejoin,[1] that only made six out of a total of ten mounted brigades. Nor were these troops and their horses by any means as fresh as might have been desired, the 2nd L.H. and 5th Mounted Brigades having been particularly hard worked within the past three days. Several horses of the 5th had actually died of exhaustion at the Beersheba troughs.

General Chauvel issued orders before midnight on the 6th for the two divisions to advance on the Wadi esh Sheria, the A. & N.Z. Division to pass through the infantry west of Kh. Umm el Bakr at 5 a.m., as advanced guard to the corps, and seize a line from Ameidat Station, 5 miles north-east of Tell esh Sheria, to Kh. Shuteiwy el Oseibi, 4½ miles west of the station. He also instructed the 3rd L.H. and 5th Mounted Brigades to rejoin the Australian Mounted Division at Tell esh Sheria.[2]

**Maps 2, 4.** During the night the two brigades of the A. & N.Z. Mounted Division had moved up from Beersheba, their position at 4 a.m. being as follows :—1st L.H. Brigade on a line south of the 'Ain Kohle–Tell esh Sheria track (on which it had relieved the 6th Mounted Brigade), with its left 4 miles east of Tell esh Sheria ; 2nd L.H. Brigade about 4 miles south-east of Tell esh Sheria. Major-General Chaytor and his staff had also moved westward during the evening ; his wires had been disconnected at 10 p.m. ; and in consequence he did not receive his orders till 4.10 a.m. on the 7th. This fact and difficulties in moving over the rough ground in darkness resulted in the 1st Brigade not reaching the Wadi esh Sheria just north of Kh. Umm el Bakr till 7.15. Even then it was without its battery of artillery, for it was impossible to move the guns till daylight. It was not until 8.50—nearly four hours late—that the 2nd A.L.H. moved out, followed by the 1st and 3rd Regiments in echelon on its right. Only then was it apparent how admirably chosen was the point upon which the brigade had been directed. The result of the British attacks on the

---

[1] The 3rd L.H. Brigade was holding the long outpost line connecting the XX and XXI Corps, and it was the necessity of relieving it that caused delay in its advance. The 5th Mounted Brigade, it will be recalled, had been left behind near Beersheba when the Australian Mounted Division marched west to relieve the Yeomanry Mounted Division in general reserve, and now had a long night march to rejoin.

[2] Desert Mounted Corps G.A. 208 is given in Appendix 13.

previous day and that morning had been to cause the Turkish troops to close in towards Tell esh Sheria on the one hand and the Khuweilfe heights on the other. Now the gap had been found. There was no opposition whatever in front, while for the first couple of miles the left flank was covered by the troops of the 60th Division. Some shelling from the right flank there was, but the Australians quickened speed from a trot to a gallop, and suffered little loss. Ameidat Station, 4½ miles from the starting point of Kh. Umm el Bakr, was captured within two hours. The light horsemen swept down upon it, shook out to surround it, and the Turkish troops guarding it were apparently too astounded by the break-through to make any resistance worthy of the name. There was a big haul of prisoners and booty: 31 officers and 365 other ranks, large dumps and 27 trucks loaded with ammunition, ordnance stores such as arms and saddlery, a quantity of forage, and a complete field hospital. The Australians had only two men killed.

1917.
7 Nov.

At noon patrols of a squadron each were sent out towards Tell en Nejile, 4 miles further up the railway, and Kh. Jemmame, on the wadi of the same name, 4 miles to the north-west. Both were held up by bodies of the enemy, the latter especially; for it found the slight ridge of Tell Abu Dilakh, half-way to its objective, occupied in some strength. News of the fall of Gaza arrived at 12.30 p.m. and with it Major-General Chaytor received a message urging him to push on to Jemmame with all speed to attempt to cut off the Turkish garrison. But there was no sign of the Australian Mounted Division on his left, and the Turks, having got over their first panic, were resisting in more determined fashion.

The 2nd L.H. Brigade came up on the left of the 1st at 3 p.m. and the 1st was then moved east of the railway, where it held an outpost line from north of Ameidat Station to a mile and a half south-east of it. The 2nd Brigade was then ordered to attack the enemy's position at Tell Abu Dilakh. The 5th A.L.H., supported by a squadron of the 6th, made an advance of over a mile, the enemy shelling wildly and fruitlessly all the time. But once it was within effective machine-gun range the situation changed completely. Little further progress was made, and when dusk brought the operation to an end the Turks were still securely established upon the ridge.

There seems little reason to doubt that, had the Auslian Mounted Division followed the Anzacs through the breach at Kh. Umm el Bakr, thus at once establishing four instead of two brigades on parallel lines to the enemy's retreat, something like disaster would have befallen the Turks. The haul of prisoners might not have been so great as G.H.Q. still anticipated, because, unknown to the British, the enemy had during the night of the 6th withdrawn the bulk of the *54th Division*, holding the line between the Wadi Mukaddeme and Kh. Sihan, as well as the *26th*—it was actually part of the *54th* which was now making what Kress describes as a brilliant defence at Tell Abu Dilakh.[1] But the mounted troops would have gained twenty-four hours and infinitely greater opportunities of breaking up the Turkish rear guards and capturing the guns and transport which the wretched, half-starved teams were painfully dragging northward.

General Chauvel had himself come up to Tell esh Sheria soon after its capture by the 60th Division. At 8.5 a.m —three-quarters of an hour before the A. & N.Z. Mounted Division advanced—he issued orders to the Australian Mounted Division to move up to the Wadi esh Sheria just east of the railway, and send officers to report to him for orders. It should be noted, in view of what follows, that it was not yet committed to launching its attack at any particular point. The division (consisting for the moment of the 4th L.H. and 7th Mounted Brigades) had moved off from the Wadi Hanafish at 2.45 a.m. and was concentrated 3 miles S.S.W. of Tell esh Sheria at 7.30 for a hasty meal. While here it was rejoined by the 5th Mounted Brigade ; the 7th then returned to the command of the Desert Mounted Corps and was ordered to develop the water supply in the Wadi esh Sheria. To General Chauvel it appeared that a sudden attack through the troops of the 60th Division would probably disperse the enemy and afford the Australian Division the opportunity of finding touch with the Anzacs in the shortest possible time, thus making up for the delay which had already occurred. At 10.15 he ordered Major-

---

[1] " Sinai " (Kress) i, p. 49.

General Hodgson to " move with centre on Kh. Buteiha 1917.
" [3,000 yards W.N.W. of Tell esh Sheria] *via* G. 23 central 7 Nov.
" [on the railway 1,000 yards north of the wadi] : object,
" (*a*) to drive enemy from front of 60th Division in order to
" enable it to concentrate, and (*b*) to gain touch with A. &
" N.Z. Mounted Division."

Major-General Hodgson had therefore his exact line of advance laid down for him, and it proved to be against a very hard section of the Turkish front. He gave verbal orders to Br.-General Grant, commanding the 4th L.H. Brigade, to carry out the attack. It was nearly 11 a.m. (the hour at which General Chauvel learnt of the capture of Ameidat Station)[1] when the leading squadrons reached the wadi, and there, having been long without water, they halted for a few minutes to let their horses drink. Then the 12th A.L.H. on the right, 11th A.L.H. on the left, attempted to advance and pass through the front of the 60th Division. It was at once apparent that a mounted attack was out of the question, so heavy was the fire of the enemy. But one troop of the 11th A.L.H. under Lieutenant A. R. Brierty, not noticing the signal to dismount, rode right through the Turkish line, to be virtually annihilated a few moments later. Continuing the advance on foot, the two regiments had penetrated but a few hundred yards beyond the line reached by the advanced troops of the 60th Division when they were brought to a halt by the Turkish machine-gun fire. There they remained all afternoon, often in considerable danger of being broken by local counter-attacks launched by the enemy.

The 5th Mounted Brigade had taken cover in the Wadi Barrata, east of and parallel to the railway, and in other tributaries of the Wadi esh Sheria further east. Br.-General Fitzgerald, recognizing the urgency of pushing on and at the same time the hopelessness of pressing the attack frontally, sent a message to divisional headquarters asking for leave to work round to the right flank of the 4th L.H. Brigade and

---

[1] Whether or not it would still have been possible to have ordered the Australian Division to cross at the same point as the A. & N.Z., without undue waste of time, is a difficult problem. The distance between the crossing-places of the two divisions was rather under two miles. It is, however, probable that, even crossing where it did, the Australian Division could have struck off east of the Wadi Barrata and thus passed through the gap.

thus make use of the gap found by the A. & N.Z. Mounted Division in the morning, if it still existed. But the reply was slow in coming, and it was not till 4.45 p.m. that he received permission to do so. The 3rd L.H. Brigade, which had watered so far away as Kharm—12 miles to the southwest—in the morning, was also crossing the Wadi esh Sheria, but was not up on the Yeomen's flank when the 5th Mounted Brigade advanced, cantering in lines of squadrons, at 5.20 p.m. There appeared to be no enemy in front, but the movement was too late. The short Palestine twilight died away, leaving the troops in pitch darkness.[1] The Gloucester Yeomanry in the van lost direction and was fired on by British infantry to the west. There appeared to be no object in remaining out for the night on broken and unknown ground, so the brigade was brought back, with much difficulty and after losing its way several times, to the Wadi Barrata. The 3rd L.H. Brigade, having the railway line as guide, pushed forward till it made touch with the 2nd L.H. Brigade of the A. & N.Z. Mounted Division at 7.30 p.m.

Meanwhile Major-General Shea had learned that the 4th L.H. Brigade was held up and had ordered the 179th Brigade to clear the enemy from its path. Two battalions, the 2/14th and 2/15th London, moved up, crossed the Wadi esh Sheria at 5 p.m., and, though the Turks had now had time to dig themselves in, drove them out with the bayonet just as darkness fell, suffering only 24 casualties in their charge. Finally a line was taken up with left on the Sheria–Huj road, 4½ miles north of the Wadi esh Sheria. The 4th L.H. Brigade was then withdrawn south of the wadi and came into corps reserve.

The day had been bitterly disappointing, and the chances of capturing prisoners and guns had been greatly diminished by the delays at Tell esh Sheria. Once again the difficulties of water supply were becoming pressing. The horses near Tell esh Sheria could be watered during the night, but there was no water for those of the A. & N.Z. Mounted Division, of which the 2nd L.H. Brigade's had been in many cases without a drink since they left Beersheba; nor for those of the 3rd L.H. Brigade, which had last watered early in the morning at Kharm.

---

[1] The hour of sunset was 4.47 p.m. The moon, just past the last quarter, did not rise till 12.12 a.m. on the 8th November.

## THE DESERT MOUNTED CORPS ON THE 8TH NOVEMBER. THE AFFAIR OF HUJ.

At 1 a.m. on the 8th General Chauvel issued orders for the resumption of the advance with the object of outflanking the enemy. The A. & N.Z. Mounted Division was to move on the Wadi Jemmame, in which there was known to be water, and afterwards on Bureir, a large village 4 miles N.N.E. of Huj. It was to endeavour to keep in advance of the Australian Mounted Division, directed on Huj, so as to outflank opposition. The 60th Division was to be prepared to march on Huj at 7 a.m.

*1917.
8 Nov.
Maps 2, 4.
Sketch 7.*

On the front of the A. & N.Z. Mounted Division the 1st A.L.H. advanced at 5.45 a.m. on Tell en Nejile, the 3rd A.L.H. remaining at Ameidat to guard the right flank. On the left the 5th and 7th A.L.H. of the 2nd L.H. Brigade advanced on Kh. Jemmame. The 7th Mounted Brigade, which had been put at Major-General Chaytor's disposal, reached his divisional headquarters at 9 a.m., and as the leading brigades were meeting with stiff opposition, was ordered up between them. It had had better fortune than any other of the troops under his command; for it had been able to water its horses in the Wadi esh Sheria before moving up.

From 9 a.m. onwards long columns of the enemy, with guns and transport, could be seen moving northward through Kh. el Kofkha towards Jemmame and on neighbouring tracks. It was a sight such as cavalrymen in all ages have longed for, such as would have fired the blood of a Le Marchant or a Scarlett. But the day was to prove the vast transformation in warfare made by the machine gun. The retreating Turks had strong flank guards provided with artillery, but it was not the guns which held off the Australian regiments. Again and again throughout the course of the day staunch machine gunners prevented them from breaking through wearied-out and demoralized columns.

Presently the advance was met by a more than passive defence. After the evacuation of Gaza, the Turkish *53rd Division* had been ordered to move across the front through Huj to stop the break-through of the British mounted troops, which it had been anticipated would have been made twenty-four hours earlier. After its long march and its pounding at Gaza it now acted with remarkable energy.[1] The leading squadrons of the 2nd L.H. Brigade were driven in, and the advance temporarily brought to a standstill. The *53rd Division* then continued its march across the British front towards the railway, and next attacked the 7th Mounted Brigade, on the right of the 2nd. Again the advanced squadrons were driven in, but two determined Turkish attacks were beaten off, with the aid of quick and accurate shooting by the Essex Battery R.H.A. The brigade had every man and every machine gun in line,[2] and its ammunition was running short. However, threatened by the advance of the 1st L.H. Brigade on the right, the Turks, having accomplished their purpose and allowed the retreating columns of the *16th* and *26th Divisions* to get clear, fell back on the Wadi el Hesi.

The 1st A.L.H. on the extreme right had captured Tell en Nejile Station without difficulty. The 3rd A.L.H., relieved at 1 p.m. from its position on the right flank, advanced very rapidly north-westwards as soon as Turkish resistance in that direction had ceased, and captured Kh. Jemmame at 3.45 p.m. This was one of the most important watering-places behind the Turkish front, and by good fortune its wells, cisterns, and a pump were all intact. The heights beyond the Wadi Jemmame were cleared by the 2nd L.H. Brigade, which drove off an enemy counter-attack, and the troops of the A. & N.Z. Mounted Division were enabled to water their horses. Those of the 1st L.H. Brigade had been without a drink in most cases for over fifty hours, but the 2nd had found a small supply at Tell en Nejile. The 2nd L.H. Machine-Gun Squadron, which had seen such hard fighting at Tell el Khuweilfe, and the other two squadrons left in that area rejoined at 4.30 p.m.

Meanwhile Major-General Hodgson ordered his two brigades to advance, 3rd L.H. Brigade with its right on Kh. el Kofkha, 5th Mounted Brigade with its left on Huj. The 4th L.H. Brigade was returned to his command early in

---

[1] It is convenient to describe this force as the *53rd Division*; actually it was made up of some of the fittest troops of the Gaza garrison. "Sinai" (Kress), i, p. 48.

[2] It will be remembered that the brigade consisted of two regiments only. On this occasion one squadron and two troops Sherwood Rangers had not returned from escorting prisoners of war, so the brigade consisted of little more than four squadrons and a machine-gun squadron.

## Sketch 7

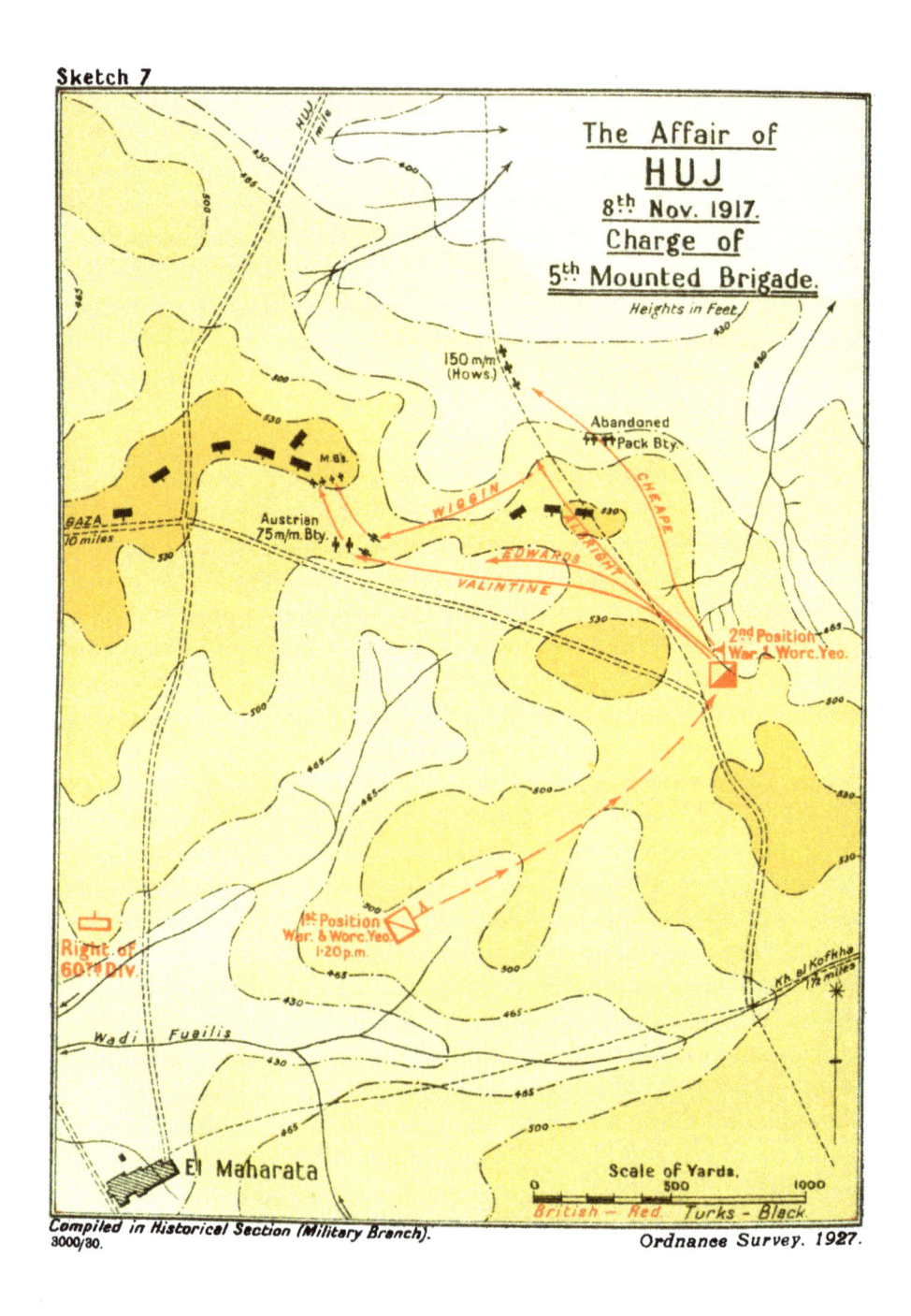

### The Affair of HUJ
### 8th Nov. 1917.
### Charge of 5th Mounted Brigade.

*Heights in Feet*

150 m/m (Hows.)

Abandoned Pack Bty.

GAZA 10 miles

Austrian 75 m/m Bty.

WIGGIN
CHEAPE
ALBRIGHT
EDWARDS
VALINTINE

2nd Position War. & Worc. Yeo.

1st Position War. & Worc. Yeo. 1·20 p.m.

Right of 60th Div.

Kh. el Kofkha 1¾ miles

Wadi Fueilis

El Maharata

Scale of Yards.
0    500    1000

British — Red.    Turks — Black.

Compiled in Historical Section (Military Branch).
3000/30.

Ordnance Survey. 1927.

## ADVANCE OF 60TH DIVISION

the day, except for the 4th A.L.H., which remained in corps reserve. It was known that the troops of the XXI Corps were advancing rapidly north and north-east from Gaza, and at 1 p.m., Major-General Hodgson, on General Chauvel's orders, directed this brigade to despatch a regiment towards Beit Hanun, make touch with the Imperial Service Cavalry Brigade, and carry orders to its commander to make a great effort to cut across the heads of the retreating Turkish columns. Covering twelve miles in an hour and a half, the 12th A.L.H. found the Imperial Service Brigade near Beit Hanun, engaged with the enemy on the Wadi el Hesi near Tumra; but the Turks were already out of the net.

1917.
8 Nov.

On the right of the Australian Mounted Division the 3rd L.H. Brigade pressed forward. Held up momentarily near the village of Kh. el Kofkha, it was able to continue its advance as soon as the Notts Battery had unlimbered and come into action to support it. The village was occupied before midday, and the brigade pushed on towards the Wadi Jemmame, capturing several guns after shooting down the teams. The 5th Mounted Brigade advanced on its left, on the right of the 179th Brigade, advanced guard to the 60th Division, which moved in two columns, 2/15th London followed by 2/13th on the right, 2/14th followed by 2/16 on the left. The 179th Brigade occupied the ridge east of Kh. Zuheilika without much opposition, moved swiftly into the valley of the Wadi Fuailis beyond, and found the Turks holding the village of El Maharata [1] and the heights to north of it. The leading battalions advanced under considerable shell fire, drove the enemy out of the village, and captured the spur above it, the 2/14th turning the enemy's right flank, while the 2/15th attacked frontally. After a short pause for reorganization, the advance was resumed.

Major-General Shea, who was close to his leading troops, took advantage of this pause to drive forward in an armed Ford car to make a personal reconnaissance. After going a short distance he saw a long, straggling column of the enemy moving from west to east some three miles ahead, and a

---

[1] Neither this village nor Kh. el Kofkha were marked on the maps in use at the period. In the case of the former, the name even did not appear, the site being marked Kh. Muntaret el Baghl. Khirbet means ruin, so that it is to be presumed that new villages had been built on the sites of the old ones since 1878, the date of the Conder-Kitchener survey.

flank guard with artillery hastily taking up a position to the right front. Immediately afterwards he caught sight of some British cavalry on the right. It appeared to him that here was a golden opportunity for the mounted troops to break through the flank guard and crush the column beyond —an opportunity which time did not allow his own infantry to seize. He drove across the front of the 179th Brigade, met Lieut.-Colonel H. A. Gray-Cheape, commanding the Warwickshire Yeomanry of the 5th Mounted Brigade, and ordered him to charge the Turkish covering force. Lieut.-Colonel Cheape was set an extremely difficult task. The 5th Mounted Brigade was on a wide front, its attached battery was some distance behind, its machine-gun squadron had also been outpaced, while the Gloucester Hussars, in brigade reserve, could not possibly be brought up in time, since instant action was called for. Lieut.-Colonel Cheape sent back word to Br.-General P. J. V. Kelly, commanding the brigade,[1] that he was about to attempt mounted action, then collected all the detachments of his own regiment and of the Worcestershire Yeomanry from his right on which he could lay hands—a squadron and a half of each—and led them forward.[2]

The enemy was established on a slight ridge about half-way between Maharata and Huj. To his front, that is to south and south-west, he had a clear field of view and fire, but on his left flank the ridge curved southward, and a slight, undulating spur, almost equal in height to his own position, ran down toward the valley of the Wadi Fuailis. Taking advantage of the folds in this ground, Lieut.-Colonel Cheape led his force in a north-easterly direction. The dust raised by his advance warned the Turks of his approach, and as he came momentarily into view they opened fire to their threatened flank; but the

---

[1] Br.-General Kelly had succeeded Br.-General Fitzgerald in command of the 5th Mounted Brigade that morning. On arriving at its bivouac he found that the Warwick and Worcester Yeomanry had already moved forward, and that the Gloucester Hussars, " B " Battery H.A.C., and the machine-gun squadron (less two guns which had accompanied the leading regiments) were still watering.

[2] Lieut.-Colonel H. J. Williams, commanding the Worcester Yeomanry, had just ridden eastward to request the 3rd L.H. Brigade on the right to co-operate in an advance on Huj, and the troops of the regiment led forward by Lieut.-Colonel Cheape were commanded by Major W. H. Wiggin.

# THE CHARGE OF HUJ

Yeomanry rode into the cover of a knoll upon the ridge without suffering much loss. It was now seen that on the Turkish left was a body of infantry about two hundred strong, covering a battery of 150-mm. howitzers, in the centre a battery of 75-mm. guns and four machine guns in action, while a large body of infantry was further along the ridge to the west.

1917.
8 Nov.

Though hidden from the field battery, the Yeomanry were now under rifle fire from the infantry on the Turkish left, many of whom were standing up to aim. Lieut.-Colonel Cheape therefore ordered a squadron of the Worcestershire Yeomanry under Major M. C. Albright to charge this body.[1] Directly this attack was launched he ordered a squadron of the Warwickshire under Captain R. Valintine, with two troops of the Worcestershire under 2/Lieutenant J. W. Edwards slightly echeloned to the right, to charge the 75-mm. battery. He himself kept the two remaining troops of the Warwickshire in support.

Major Albright's squadron formed column of half squadrons and dashed straight at the Turkish infantry, which broke to avoid the shock, and streamed away northward in flight, though not before many had been killed with the sword. The Yeomanry, whose blood was up, would have pursued and captured the 150-mm. battery in rear of the position, but were stopped by Major W. H. Wiggin, who, seeing the desperate situation of the detachment which had charged the field battery, rallied the Worcestershire squadron and galloped up to its assistance. The howitzer battery and also an abandoned camel pack battery were taken by Lieut.-Colonel Cheape, who led his two troops of the Warwickshire round the eastern edge of the ridge.

Captain Valintine's squadron also formed column of half squadrons, and with Lieutenant Edwards's two troops on its right bore left-handed and galloped for the guns. The ground dipped, then rose again, between his starting-point and the position of the battery, and nearly half a mile had to

---

[1] This action is extremely difficult to reconstruct owing to the very heavy casualties which occurred and to the fact that Lieut.-Colonel Cheape was drowned in 1918. There is some doubt as to whether Major Albright actually received an order to charge. Major Wiggin's recollection is that " he went straight on to attack this lot immediately he realized the position, " and without waiting for further orders either from me or from Lieut.-" Colonel Cheape."

be covered under the continuous fire of the machine guns before the charge could be driven home. Moreover, the Austrian artillerymen, taken thus in flank, showed great gallantry. Two of the four guns were swung round to face the oncoming horsemen, and, with fuses set at zero, fired point-blank at them until the last moment, so that the final shot passed through a horse that was almost on the gun's muzzle. Despite their losses the Yeomen never checked their speed. Shouting, they burst through the battery position, sabreing and riding down the gunners, and dashed on, though reduced now to a mere handful, to attack the machine guns. About these raged a furious struggle.

It was at this moment, when perhaps twenty mounted men were confronting several hundred Turks, that Major Wiggin led up Major Albright's squadron of the Worcestershire which he had rallied. It passed through the Austrian battery only a few seconds after the Warwickshire squadron, swung right, and captured the machine guns. The Turkish infantry, to whom the spectacle of the second squadron thundering up in a cloud of dust doubtless gave the impression of a far greater reinforcement, broke and fled northward in panic. Within five minutes the subsection of the machine-gun squadron came up and turned its own and the captured Turkish machine guns on to the flying enemy with great effect. Long-range fire was also opened upon the Turkish column seen by Major-General Shea; but pursuit with the handful of mounted men remaining was out of the question. Nor, apparently, were the Australians of the 3rd Light Horse Brigade near enough to take it up. Only about seventy prisoners were taken, but a large number of Turks were killed. Men unhorsed and those outpaced in the charge were brought up by Major A. C. Watson, Warwickshire Yeomanry, and the position gained was consolidated The 60th Division in the course of the afternoon established itself 3 miles north-west of Huj.

This was the first time the sword had been used in this theatre, with the exception of the charge of the Dorset Yeomanry at Agagiya in the Western Desert against the forces of the Senussi, and for sheer bravery the episode remains unmatched. Unlike the charge at Maghar, which was to follow it within a few days, it is not fruitful of lessons in cavalry tactics, though the skilful use of ground by

## VALUE OF SHOCK TACTICS

Lieut.-Colonel Cheape is well worthy of note. At Maghar artillery and machine guns will be found co-operating to perfection with a mounted attack. Here the charge lacked fire support of any kind, and in consequence suffered very heavily. Of 162 men who took part in the action—of whom perhaps 120 actually charged—70 were killed or wounded, and about one hundred horses were lost. All the leaders, Major Albright, Captain Valintine (who died of his wounds almost immediately afterwards), and Lieutenant Edwards, were killed. Had the Turkish infantry had a tithe of the resolution of the Austrian gunners, who fought like lions, the attacking force would have been annihilated. On the other hand, great risks are permissible in the pursuit of an enemy showing signs of demoralization, and in this case the little British force accomplished what it had been set to do ; that is, it cleared the way for an attack on the flank of the main Turkish column, though unfortunately no troops could be assembled quickly enough to take that opportunity. The charge itself must ever remain a monument to extreme resolution and to that spirit of self-sacrifice which is the only beauty redeeming ugly war.[1]

1917.
8 Nov.

In view of the success of the attack and of others which followed, it may be pointed out that the British command, before the arrival of Sir Edmund Allenby, had contemplated withdrawing the swords from the Yeomanry regiments to lighten the burdens of their horses, on the ground that the *arme blanche* was little likely ever to be used. The day had doubly proved its value in this theatre, directly and indirectly, for the Australian troops, compelled to make dismounted attacks, had, in the judgment of some of their own commanders, lost several opportunities of capturing large numbers of prisoners.

---

[1] Lieut. W. B. Mercer, who was in the leading line of Captain Valintine's squadron, and the only officer not hit, has given the following account of the charge :
"Machine guns and rifles opened on us the moment we topped the "rise behind which we had formed up. I remember thinking that the "sound of the crackling bullets was just like a hailstorm on an iron-roofed "building, so you may guess what the fusilade was. . . . A whole heap "of men and horses went down twenty or thirty yards from the muzzles "of the guns. The squadron broke into a few scattered horsemen at the "guns and then seemed to melt away completely. For a time I, at any "rate, had the impression that I was the only man left alive. I was "amazed to discover we were the victors."

Huj was occupied without difficulty, but the enemy had here destroyed the water supplies. From midnight onwards the 3rd L.H. Brigade began sending horses over to Jemmame to water, but these had to take their turn with the horses of the A. & N.Z. Mounted Division, and the proportion of horses which got a drink was not large. The position was now very serious, as the 3rd Brigade had not watered since the previous day, and the greater part of the 5th Brigade not since the night of the 6th. Not horses only, but men were suffering severely from thirst. Nor were all these sufferings and exertions largely rewarded, for 23 guns and some four hundred prisoners made but a poor haul.

### THE DESERT MOUNTED CORPS ON THE 9TH NOVEMBER— THE ADVANCE TO THE MEDITERRANEAN SHORE.

Maps 1, 2.

On the morning of the 8th, while the pursuit of the Turks by the mounted troops was still proceeding on parallel lines, while the XXI Corps was preparing to turn the enemy out of the Wadi el Hesi line, and consequently Sir Edmund Allenby could still hope that the retreating garrison of Gaza would be destroyed, he had ordered the Yeomanry Mounted Division to rejoin the Desert Mounted Corps as quickly as possible.[1] The reinforcement was urgently needed. The six mounted brigades now under General Chauvel's orders were already very wearied, and the 60th Division could help him no more. The Commander-in-Chief had decided to press the advance of the XXI Corps along the coast with all the resources at his disposal, and it was necessary for General Chetwode to return to General Bulfin the transport he had borrowed for the Beersheba and Sheria operations.

---

[1] Barrow's Detachment.
O.A. 741.   8th Nov.
You will move north-west as soon as possible with Yeomanry Mounted Division on Nejile. Right of Anzac Mtd. Division at present about Kh. Umm Kelqa in H.35. Your division to assist in Descorps operations against eastern flank of enemy rear guard, and to prevent its escape by pushing on to Bureir. You will come under command of Descorps as soon as you get communication with them during your movement. Camel Brigade will be withdrawn to Beersheba as soon as possible, watered, and replenished with supplies, ready to rejoin Descorps. Instructions regarding 53rd Division and N.Z.M.R. Bde. sent XX Corps. Report if your division watered in Khuweilfe area and when moving. Addressed Barrow's Detachment, repeated XX Corps and Descorps.
G.H.Q.   12.40 p.m.

In these circumstances it was impossible to supply the 60th Division further north than Huj, and in that neighbourhood it was to remain.

1917.
7 Nov.

Major-General Barrow had, it will be remembered, taken over command of the covering force in the hills when the Desert Mounted Corps began its attempt to break through at Tell esh Sheria on the morning of the 7th. The troops at his disposal consisted of the Yeomanry Mounted Division, the New Zealand Brigade, the Camel Brigade, part of the 2nd Australian Machine-gun Squadron, the 53rd Division, and the light armoured car batteries. The rôle of his force was to form a defensive flank on the line then occupied to the troops operating north of Tell esh Sheria, and to take "every opportunity of punishing the enemy."

The 53rd Division was preparing yet another attack, with the object of taking the remainder of the Khuweilfe heights. This was, however, cancelled by G.H.Q., and at 2.20 p.m. Major-General Mott reported that columns of the enemy could be seen moving north from his front, probably with the intention of passing round the Camel Brigade at Ras en Naqb and gaining the Hebron road. He asked if cavalry could be spared to advance through the Camel Brigade and cut them off.

Major-General Mott, not being for the moment in telephonic communication with his own commander, Major-General Barrow, sent his message through the XX Corps. Though neither the Yeomanry Mounted nor the 53rd Division was under General Chetwode's orders, he thought himself justified in intervening and pointing out that big things were afoot at Tell esh Sheria and that it was inadvisable to move the Yeomanry Mounted Division across the front, further from the scene of action on which it might shortly be required to play a part. Nothing was done that afternoon, but at night Major-General Barrow decided that the opportunity was too good to be lost, and that, without too far committing his mounted troops, it might be possible to cut off the Turkish forces still on the front of the 53rd Division and to capture any guns and transport not yet withdrawn. He therefore ordered the Yeomanry Mounted Division to be concentrated at dawn and to advance in a north-easterly direction. A copy of these orders he sent to G.H.Q. They were received soon after 11 p.m., and no comment was made upon them, so that he was able to assume that his project met with the Commander-in-Chief's approval.

1917.
8 Nov.

But at 5 a.m. on the 8th Sir Edmund Allenby received a message from General Chauvel, pointing out how jaded his horses were becoming after their great marches on inadequate water and suggesting that some of Major-General Barrow's fresh troops should be sent to him. G.H.Q., as we have seen, did not send the order for the Yeomanry Mounted Division to move to Nejile till 12.40 p.m., and it took nearly an hour to reach Major-General Barrow. By that time the leading brigade of the division was about three miles north of Bir Abu Khuff, having captured 31 prisoners and 200 camels, and the enemy had broken off contact, though the mountain artillery of his rear guard was shelling the advance. As a consequence, the division was unable to get further than Tell esh Sheria that night, where it watered and bivouacked.

Before returning to record the events of the 9th November on the front of the Desert Mounted Corps, a word must be added to describe the position in which the XX Corps, to the command of which both the 53rd and 60th Divisions now returned, found itself. Called upon to send back the transport borrowed from the XXI Corps, General Chetwode was for the time being immobilized. The 60th Division remained at Huj, one brigade being sent to guard the water at Jemmame. The 10th Division, after clearing the battlefield, concentrated at Kharm, where it could be fed directly from the railway. The 74th moved to Abu Irquaiyiq, on the Turkish railway, also within easy reach of Kharm. The 53rd Division remained at Khuweilfe with the XX Corps Cavalry Regiment and for a short time the New Zealand Brigade under its orders to watch the Hebron road; and later, when the enemy had definitely withdrawn north of Hebron, withdrew closer to Beersheba. Opportunity was taken, while the troops were resting, to equip the 10th, 53rd, and 74th Divisions with winter clothing in place of the drill which they had been wearing, to their great advantage when they were next called upon to come into action, in the winter of the Judæan Hills. The 60th Division had no such good fortune.

General Chauvel's instructions from G.H.Q., received by aeroplane on the 8th, were to push on towards Majdal, a large village near the coast and 13 miles north-east of Gaza, so as to co-operate with the XXI Corps, the advanced guard of which had a bridgehead north of the Wadi el Hesi at the mouth. He ordered the A. & N.Z. Mounted Division to close up to its left and advance on Bureir, 4 miles north of Huj, with the high ground north-west of Huleikat, another 2 miles north, as its second objective. The Yeomanry Mounted Division was to move on Simsim, 2 miles W.S.W. of Bureir. The Australian Mounted Division was to water its horses and be prepared to advance when that had been done.

1917.
9 Nov.

By no means the whole of this programme could be carried out. The Yeomanry Division had, as has been stated, gone to Tell esh Sheria on the night of the 8th, and did not reach Huj till the afternoon of the 9th. It was ordered to bivouac there, water again, so far as that was possible, and resume the advance next day. The Australian Division found the task of watering at Jemmame very slow. Patrols pushed out as far as Najd, west of the Huj railway, and Simsim, found only a few small wells, very deep, and with primitive lifting apparatus. A small proportion of the horses were watered here, but the great bulk at Jemmame, and the work was not completed till after sunset. The 4th L.H. Brigade covered an enormous tract of country in its search for water. The 12th A.L.H. marched in the afternoon to Faluja, 8 miles north-east of its starting-point at Bureir.

So it came about that the A. & N.Z. Division was the only one prepared to advance on the 9th. It moved off at 6 a.m., 2nd L.H. Brigade on right, 1st on left, 7th Mounted Brigade in reserve. Bureir was occupied at 8.15 by the 2nd L.H. Brigade, which met with no opposition, but for some long-range shrapnel fire. By 10 a.m. the high ground north of Huleikat (the former headquarters of the Turkish *Eighth Army*) was in the hands of the 2nd L.H. Brigade. In the village bread still hot from the field-ovens was found, and the Australians gnawed hunks of it as they rode on. The litter of wagons and stores upon the road and the complete exhaustion of the stragglers reeling along at the tail of the retreat gave Br.-General Ryrie a notion of the confusion ahead, and he ordered the advance to be pressed boldly towards Qauqaba, 2¼ miles N.N.E. of Huleikat. Here the 7th A.L.H. dashed into a crawling column of transport and took the whole convoy of nearly four hundred men and over one hundred wagons. The column was a horrible spectacle, for the wretched animals—ponies, bullocks, and donkeys—were in many cases in a dying condition and the men in little better case.

At Qauqaba the brigade halted for about three hours, while the transport came up and a certain amount of rations were issued, then marched on northward toward the main Ramle road at Es Suafir el Gharbiye. Suddenly the scouts espied another big transport column, protected by a party of infantry, moving along this road. The 5th A.L.H. with two squadrons of the 7th advanced in pursuit and came up with the end of the column near Suafir, but had to urge their weary horses on at a canter for another three miles before they got to its head—just in time, for it was now close to Qastine, which was strongly held by the enemy. Three hundred and fifty prisoners and 110 wagons were captured here. The Turkish artillery to the north shelled friend and foe alike. Meanwhile the remaining squadron of the 7th had been in action on the right, a mile north-east of Ebdis, with a large party of the enemy, and had had some difficulty in holding its own. After darkness fell a body of Turks approached with fixed bayonets. The Australians greeted them with shouts of "Surrender!" in Turkish, and to their astonishment were obeyed. Br.-General Ryrie had sent a message to the squadrons near Qastine to withdraw to Suafir and hold that village for the night. As the 7th A.L.H. rode back in the darkness it captured a number more from this party, 234 prisoners being added to the brigade's haul, which now considerably exceeded its own strength. Meanwhile the 1st L.H. Brigade on the left, moving *via* Bureir and Ejje, entered Majdal, already occupied by a mounted party of the 52nd Division, at 12.50. Watering some of its horses here and at Hamame a little further north, the brigade pushed on to within about three miles of Sdud, the ancient Ashdod, where it bivouacked. It had left behind a squadron at Majdal to hand over prisoners and the invaluable water supply to the advancing infantry of the XXI Corps.

It had been a remarkable drive. From its starting-point to the area of its bivouac the 1st L.H. Brigade had advanced 16 miles as the crow flies, and many of its squadrons must have covered a distance half as great again. Everywhere they had found roads and tracks bestrewn with the debris of a defeated army. But the Turkish main forces had escaped the pincers. Those captured on this date were either the weaklings always to be found straggling at the tail of a big retreat or else bodies of transport in which the galled and starving beasts could respond no longer to the flogging of their drivers. Nevertheless, had the supply of water permitted the Australian Division to take a hand in the pursuit, perhaps even had the Yeomanry Division not been employed the previous morning in following the Turks north of Beersheba, greater loss might have been inflicted on the enemy.

1917.
9 Nov.

The Turkish prisoners were suffering from thirst even more keenly than their captors, and it was only with great difficulty that they could be supplied during the night. There was danger in the situation; for the Turks were in a filthy condition, including a great proportion of sick who had been unable to keep up with their fellows, and dysentery particularly was rife among them. The 7th Mounted Brigade's diary records that no food or forage whatever reached it. A certain amount of tibben and some food for the men were, however, found in the villages and requisitioned for the troops.

The Capture of the Wadi el Hesi Defences by the XXI Corps, 7th–8th November.

It may appear that there has been undue delay in returning to the fortunes of the XXI Corps, but it has seemed appropriate to follow those of the Desert Mounted Corps in its great drive across Southern Palestine until its head was almost at the shore and it had established touch with General Bulfin's advancing infantry. The record of the mounted troops has been brought up to a moment sixty hours ahead of that of the XXI Corps, which was left at the end of Chapter IV preparing to advance along the coast in the early hours of the 7th November. It will be recalled that its object was to prevent the retreating Turks from consolidating their position north of the Wadi el Hesi and that speed was therefore urgently necessary.

7 Nov.
Map 2.

Long before he had news of the evacuation of Gaza

General Bulfin guessed what had happened, and sent about 2.30 a.m. for the commanders of the sole cavalry at his disposal—Br.-General C. R. Harbord, commanding the Imperial Service Cavalry Brigade, and Lieut.-Colonel G. G. M. Tyrrell, commanding the composite regiment of Corps cavalry. He ordered the Corps Cavalry Regiment to advance at dawn, gain touch with the enemy, cross the Wadi el Hesi if possible, and report to the 52nd Division. The Imperial Service Cavalry Brigade he ordered to move on Deir Sneid and Beit Hanun, harrying the enemy by all means in its power. The brigade was, however, in the act of moving from Tell el Jemmi, far up the Wadi Ghazze, to a position north of the wadi's mouth in the dunes. It had some eight miles to cover before it reached this spot, known as "Regent's Park," where it watered, and then another five miles to Gaza, and consequently did not reach the town until nearly noon.

The Corps Cavalry Regiment reached a point on the beach due west of Beit Lahi, a small village in the sand-dunes 3¼ miles north-east of Gaza, whence it despatched patrols towards Hill 226 (Rijal el Arbain) between the shore and the village, and drove the few Turks there established back into Beit Lahi. The patrols were then fired on from the village, but two troops quickly worked round it from the south and took it, with 27 prisoners. At noon the regiment received orders to despatch a squadron to come under the orders of the 52nd Division.

The Imperial Service Cavalry Brigade emerged from the streets of Gaza at 1 p.m., and at once the Mysore Lancers was fired on from a strong position on the ridge a mile and a half south-west of Beit Hanun. On evacuating Gaza the Turks had split up its garrison into three detachments, of which one had, as related, moved east and come in contact with the troops of the Desert Mounted Corps, one had been withdrawn to the line of the Wadi el Hesi, and the third had taken up this rear-guard position at Beit Hanun. As no progress could be made against it, the Hyderabad and later the Mysore Lancers were ordered to move through Jebaliye, make touch with the Corps Cavalry Regiment at Beit Lahi, and threaten the enemy's flank. As a result of this movement the Hyderabad Lancers, advancing at 3 p.m., were able to occupy the ridge west of Beit Hanun at Sheikh Munam, but the village itself was stoutly defended by a

Sketch 8.

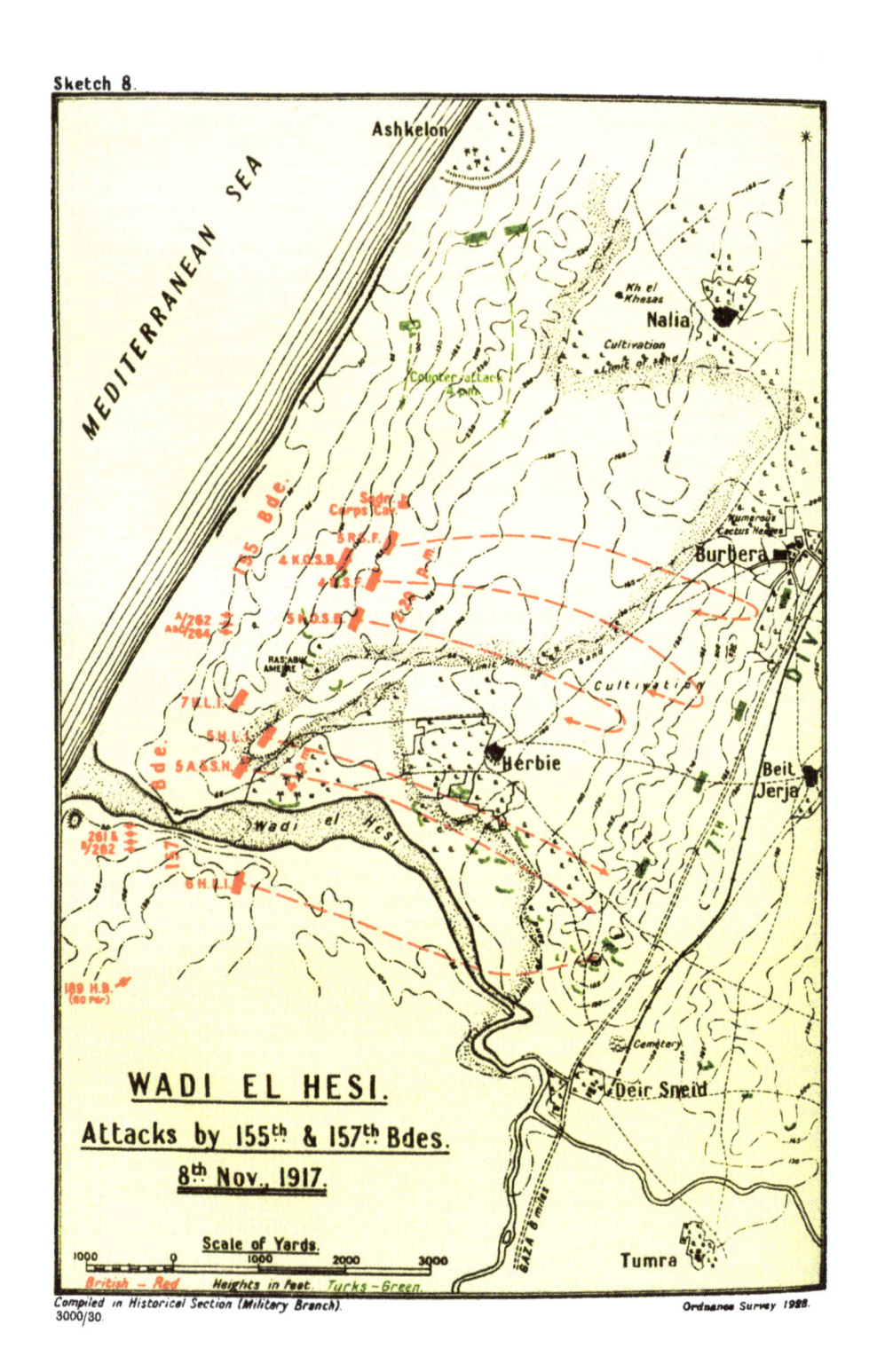

# WADI EL HESI.
## Attacks by 155th & 157th Bdes.
### 8th Nov., 1917.

number of machine-gun detachments and could not be taken before nightfall. The brigade was then withdrawn north of Beit Lahi to bivouac. The horses had been severely tried by the soft sand, and no water had been found for them.

1917.
7 Nov.

The Wadi el Hesi, the sources of which are in the Judæan Hills, runs to the sea roughly parallel to the Wadi Ghazze, its mouth being 12 miles N.N.E. of that of the latter and 7 miles N.N.E. of Gaza itself. It is the last of the big water-courses along the coast described as a "wadi" and not dignified by the title of "nahr," which means a perennial stream, but it holds some water at all seasons, almost everywhere just below the surface and at many places in large pools. On either side of its mouth the sand dunes run from three to four miles inland, but within this area there is on the right or northern bank the small village of Herbie with groves and cultivation extending to within a mile of the beach. Three or four miles north of the wadi the sand-dune area narrows for a short distance, where a spit of good soil runs towards the sea, and there are several villages quite close to the shore. It was on the northern bank of the wadi, both in the dunes and amid the cultivation, that the Turks had begun the construction of their second line of defence. This consisted merely of a series of short lengths of trench, and the position, though fairly strong by nature, was not nearly so formidable as that along the Gaza–Beersheba road, because the dunes gave considerable cover to troops attacking from the south.

Sketch 8.

As has been stated, the task of crossing the Wadi el Hesi near the mouth and consolidating a position on the right bank was entrusted to the 157th Brigade, to which were attached a squadron of the Corps Cavalry Regiment, the 264th Brigade R.F.A. (to the wheels of which the pedrails used in the Sinai Desert had once more been fitted), and the 413th Field Company R.E.

The 157th Brigade advanced along the shore below the cliffs, which gave complete cover, its left files marching at the water's edge. At about noon observers on the higher ground saw a great column of smoke go up from the neighbourhood of Beit Hanun, then heard a tremendous roar. This was obviously the explosion of munitions at Turkish railhead and betokened that the enemy had withdrawn all he could behind the Wadi el Hesi and was destroying the remainder. When a mile and a half short of the Wadi el Hesi, the advanced guard, the 6/H.L.I., turned away from the shore in a north-easterly direction and took up a position on the south bank of the wadi some fifteen hundred yards inland. The 5/H.L.I., followed by the 7th, had orders to push forward across the wadi and advance due eastward to the attack on Ras Abu Ameire, a high dune defended by several trenches. Should it meet with serious opposition, Br.-General Hamilton Moore gave orders that the 7/H.L.I. should continue along the shore till level with Ras Abu Ameire, then turn eastward, deploy, and attack on its left. The cavalry squadron had reported that the enemy appeared to be holding the position in some strength.

As it proved, the Turkish detachment at Ras Abu Ameire was neither strong nor with much stomach for a fight. The advance of the 5/H.L.I. did not begin till darkness had fallen, yet by 7 p.m. Colonel F. L. Morrison reported that it had its objective. But the map in use was uncontoured, and it was found that the crest had not been reached and was still occupied by the enemy. The true objective was captured at 8.20 p.m., with one machine gun and a few rifles, but no prisoners. The great merit of the operation lay not in the quality of the opposition it had overcome but in the speed with which it had been set on foot and in the advance over unreconnoitred ground in pitch darkness. Water was found in the Wadi el Hesi near the mouth, and a plentiful supply developed by the 413th Field Company R.E.

1917.
8 Nov.

The 155th Brigade had moved along the beach in support of the 157th, and bivouacked for the night south of the Wadi el Hesi near the mouth. At 5.30 a.m. on the 8th Br.-General Pollok-M'Call rode back to divisional headquarters and received from Major-General J. Hill verbal orders to capture "Sausage Ridge," which ran from south of the village of Burbera almost to the right bank of the Wadi el Hesi and 3½ miles inland. He was instructed to avoid the low ground about Herbie and attack from the ridge to the north-west of that village, which runs up from Ras Abu Ameire. The 264th Brigade R.F.A.[1] was put at his disposal. The Navy had also been asked to assist by the XXI Corps, and monitors were to support him from off the mouth of the Wadi el Hesi, but of this he had not been informed.

[1] Consisting temporarily of A/ and C/264, with A/262 attached.

Br.-General Hamilton Moore was informed that the rôle of the 157th Brigade was defensive and that the 155th Brigade was moving up to attack Sausage Ridge from his left.  He therefore decided to extend his flank further north along the Ras Abu Ameire Ridge, the bottom end of which he had captured the previous night, in order to provide the 155th Brigade with a good covered position upon which to deploy.  The northern part of the ridge was still held by the enemy, and unless it were taken the 155th Brigade would be forced to deploy under fire.  The 7/H.L.I. was ordered to clear the ridge, and did so to a distance of several hundred yards in face of stiff opposition.  The work was completed by the 5/K.O.S.B., the leading battalion of the 155th Brigade, by 10.30 a.m.  When, however, Br.-General Pollok-M'Call came to reconnoitre the position which he was to attack he found that his task was more formidable than had appeared from the map or from the other information supplied to him.  Sausage Ridge was further from Ras Abu Ameire—its northern end about a thousand yards further—than appeared on the map, and also extended further north. It was, moreover, considerably higher than he had been led to expect, well over two hundred feet at certain points, with a glacis on the western face.  He reported to Major-General Hill that the operation was exceedingly difficult and also very dangerous, as he would be exposing his left flank in the course of his advance to attack from the north, the enemy being reported to be in some strength at Ashkelon.  However, time being the one vital factor, General Bulfin, who had come up to Major-General Hill's headquarters, decided that the attack must be carried out as ordered.

By 12.30 p.m. the 155th Brigade was formed up on the Ras Abu Ameire Ridge, its right three-quarters of a mile north-east of that point, on a frontage of 1,200 yards; 5/K.O.S.B. on the right, 4/R.S.F. in the centre, 5/R.S.F. on the left, 4/K.O.S.B. in reserve.  The attached squadron of the Corps Cavalry Regiment covered the left flank.  The attack was launched at 2.20 p.m., and from the first was met by heavy shelling.  The enemy's guns were not easily located by the 264th Brigade R.F.A., and naturally still less so by the monitors, but he appeared to have four field batteries, two field howitzers, a 150-mm. howitzer and two 100-mm. high-velocity guns.

1917.
8 Nov.

From the beginning there was serious anxiety as to the left flank. Even before the advance began Lieut.-Colonel J. B. Cook, commanding the 5/R.S.F. on the left of the line, had noticed a squadron of Turkish cavalry moving southwards from the direction of Ashkelon,[1] the men leading their horses. There were also some groups of Turks in the dunes, one of them with a machine gun, which completely enfiladed the advance. One company was detailed to drive this party off the little ridge which it was holding, and succeeded in its task. This company afterwards entered the gardens west of Burbera and got within a few hundred yards of two abandoned enemy batteries. But as a result of anxiety with regard to Ashkelon and of the movement to drive off the flanking party, the battalion approached the line of its objective about a thousand yards too far to the left, so that a gap appeared between it and the 4/R.S.F. Before that gap could be filled, about 4.30 p.m., counter-attacks were launched both from the front and the direction of Ashkelon, the latter estimated at a strength of two battalions, supported by mountain howitzers and machine guns. It fell to a single company of the 5/R.S.F. to hold off the Ashkelon attack, giving ground gradually, until the left flank of the brigade had been withdrawn to the Ras Abu Ameire Ridge, from which it had originally advanced. The right was compelled to withdraw in conformity with this retirement, and the whole brigade fell back to a position slightly south of that from which it had launched the attack. It had suffered 285 casualties, and had not only failed in its endeavour, but had risked something like a disaster, for the avoidance of which it had chiefly to thank the coolness and steady courage of the company of the 5/R.S.F. under Major R. W. Paton, which had protected its flank and covered its retirement. The enemy had been within a quarter of a mile of the little detachment covering the guns—six platoons of the 4/K.O.S.B. and brigade headquarters.

Just before the whole of the Ras Abu Ameire Ridge had been occupied by the 155th Brigade preparatory to the advance, the 157th Brigade had been warned to be prepared to support the attack with one battalion, but at 1.30 p.m., it was ordered to attack with its whole strength on the right

---

[1] A tiny village upon the site of the ancient Ascalon.

## ATTACK ON SAUSAGE RIDGE 135

of the 155th brigade, Major-General Hill having taken into account Br.-General Pollok-M'Call's message as to the difficulty of his task. This left Br.-General Hamilton Moore unable to protect the northern flank of the 155th Brigade, as he had promised Br.-General Pollok-M'Call. He sent him a message that he was withdrawing the battalion, but it apparently did not reach him. It took him some time to collect his own battalions, which were considerably scattered, one being some distance south of the Wadi el Hesi, protecting the artillery of the 52nd Division.

1917. 8 Nov.

While his battalions were marching into positions of deployment, Br.-General Hamilton Moore collected his battalion commanders on the Ras Abu Ameire Ridge and gave them their orders personally. The brigade was to advance as quickly as possible on the right of the 155th Brigade (the attack of which had now been launched) through Herbie, and to capture the southern edge of Sausage Ridge, overlooking the railway to Beit Hanun. The 5/Argyll & Sutherland Highlanders and 5/H.L.I. were to extend along the southern end of the Ras Abu Ameire Ridge and advance frontally on the objective, while the 6/H.L.I., which was south of the Wadi el Hesi, was to carry out a turning movement, crossing the wadi south-west of Sausage Ridge. It was 4 p.m. before the attack could be launched, and there remained only about another hour of daylight in which to advance three miles.

There was no opposition from the Turkish infantry till the troops had emerged from the gardens of Herbie and covered three-quarters of the distance between the village and their objective. Then, just as dusk began to fall, heavy rifle and machine-gun fire was opened by the Turks, which caused considerable casualties. The Argylls and 5/H.L.I. advanced steadily in deepening darkness, and about 6 p.m. their leading wave reached the foot of the hill, charged straight up the slope, and temporarily established itself on the crest. Here, however, it was met by very heavy machine-gun and minenwerfer fire, while here and there, in darkness now so deep that it was hard to distinguish friend from foe, small bodies of British and Turks came to close quarters and fought furiously with bomb and bayonet. A few minutes later a Turkish battalion counter-attacked and drove the Scotsmen off the ridge.

Four times the two battalions rallied and attacked the ridge, four times they were driven off it. The Turks fought desperately, as was proved by the fact that a large proportion of the British dead found next morning had been killed with the bayonet. The enemy was also well supplied with hand grenades and trench mortars, and it was believed that there had been a bombing school east of Sausage Ridge. On the side of the Argylls and H.L.I. courage and pertinacity were as notable. "There were cases," Br.-General Hamilton Moore wrote in his report, "of companies and platoons coming "back without officers or N.C.O's., and of privates forming "themselves up and going forward to the attack without "officers or N.C.O's leading them. All ranks in the leading "waves who survived took part in all four attacks."

Heavy loss had been suffered, particularly in the ranks of the 5/H.L.I. The brigadier therefore ordered the line to stand fast, till he could pass his reserve, the 7/H.L.I. through that battalion and withdraw it into support. The delay gave time for the turning movement of the 6/H.L.I. to make itself felt. This battalion had been forced to move slowly over the heavy sand so as to maintain formation and connection in the gathering darkness and to ensure that it arrived complete at the point where it had to change direction left. But the enemy was unprepared for this attack in flank, which was completely successful. As the 6/H.L.I. reached the south-western edge of Sausage Ridge it met groups of the other battalions which had been driven down to the foot, and took them on with it. Then the whole line again advanced and at 8.50 p.m. carried the position with the bayonet. Br.-General Hamilton Moore made a personal reconnaissance and found that some opposition was still coming from certain higher features of the ridge about two hundred yards away. He sent forward strong officers' patrols which drove the Turkish riflemen off this higher ground, the position being finally cleared at 3.30 a.m. on the 9th.

In this very hard-fought action the losses of the 157th Brigade amounted to over four hundred.[1] Of 18 officers of the 5/H.L.I. who took part in the attack only six were

|  | Killed. | Wounded. | Missing. |
|---|---|---|---|
| [1] Officers | 3 | 19 | — |
| Other Ranks | 41 | 269 | 85 |

unwounded. Only about a dozen prisoners were taken, but 1917. this was partly owing to the fact that the men's blood was 8 Nov. roused by seeing wounded comrades bayoneted on the ground by the Turks. The result of the fighting was to render it finally impossible for the Turks to establish themselves upon the line of the Wadi el Hesi. It would appear, however, that they had previously abandoned hope of doing so; for after the repulse of the 155th Brigade's attack a force of about a thousand was seen to form up and march away north.

The Imperial Service Cavalry Brigade had been ordered Map 2. to advance eastwards, make touch with the Australian Mounted Division, and if possible cut off the Turkish troops remaining in the Atawine and Tank trenches on the Gaza–Beersheba road. The brigade left its bivouac at 2.45 a.m. on the 8th November, the two squadrons of the Corps Cavalry Regiment leading, and advanced on Beit Hanun. The advanced guard was checked by machine-gun fire from this village, and an indecisive action at long range followed. Shortly after noon, however, the enemy began to retreat north-eastward up the road to Bureir. The Corps Cavalry galloped across the ridge east of Beit Hanun and brought its Hotchkiss guns into action against the retiring column, to which it caused considerable loss. The team of one 150-mm. howitzer was shot down, and the gun subsequently captured. At 3 p.m. the Imperial Service Brigade met the 12th A.L.H. a mile east of Beit Hanun, but the combined forces were not strong enough to interfere seriously with the Turkish rear guard. In the course of the day the brigade had captured, in addition to the gun, 23 prisoners, a great quantity of ammunition, and the pumping machinery at Beit Hanun intact. These pumps had been converted by the German engineers to use gas made from charcoal and could not be worked until they were reconverted. The horses were therefore withdrawn to Jebaliye to water.

Before midnight G.H.Q. issued instructions that the XXI Corps was to employ a second division as soon as transport could be provided, and that the two were to advance to the line Julis–Hamame, 20 miles north-east of Gaza, to support the mounted troops. The 75th Division was ordered 9 Nov. to be ready to move, and its front at Sheikh Abbas was taken over by part of the Composite Force. On the 9th November there was, however, little movement by the XXI Corps. The arrival of the transport borrowed by the XX Corps had to be awaited, and above all the return of the 75th Divisional Train. This arrived at Sheikh Nebhan during the morning, but had to rest there till the following day. All the transport in process of transfer from the XX to the XXI Corps had long marches, as when it set out the enemy was still holding portions of his trenches on the Gaza–Beersheba road, and a detour had to be made lest the columns should come under fire. One brigade group of the 75th Division, the 232nd Brigade, with the South African Brigade Field Artillery, 495th Field Company R.E., and two sections of a field ambulance, did advance to Beit Hanun. Here it was found that the water supply was not yet sufficiently organized for the group to be supplied at short notice, so the troops moved on to Deir Sneid.

On the front of the 52nd Division the 156th Brigade, which had advanced to the line of the Wadi el Hesi the previous night, was ordered to send out two infantry patrols in support of the squadron of Corps Cavalry to reconnoitre Ashkelon. The squadron was unable to move, neither men nor horses having had water for thirty-six hours. It was an improvised mounted party of nine grooms and signal orderlies from the 156th Brigade headquarters, led by Lieutenant T. McClelland, which reached the mounds marking the site of that historic town, found the place unoccupied, boldly pushed on to Majdal, and handed that large village and its stores over to the troops of the A. & N.Z. Mounted Division. The Turks had fallen back after their beating of the previous night, and patrols reported Beit Jerja, Burbera, and Huleikat all clear of the enemy.

In the last three days the great material and moral effect of aircraft boldly handled against a retreating enemy had been notably exemplified. On the 7th November, when the precipitate movement northward of Turkish columns had first been seen by observers, a period of extreme activity began for the Royal Flying Corps. Hitherto it had been engaged chiefly in strategical reconnaissance carried out by the 40th (Army) Wing, while the 5th (Corps) Wing had carried out artillery registration and tactical photography prior to and during the attacks on Beersheba, Gaza, and Tell esh Sheria. Now, however, specialization was for the

Sketch 9.

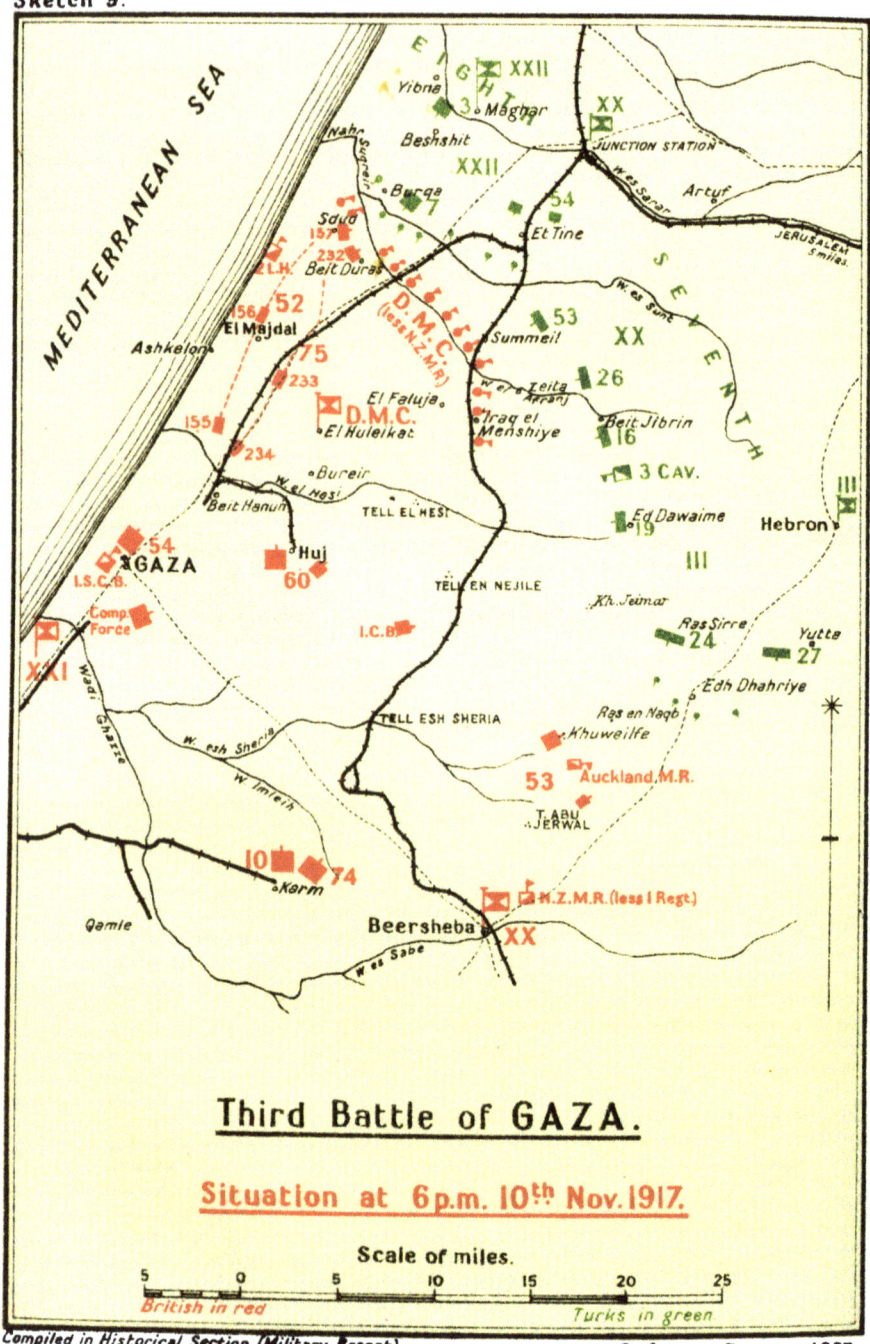

Third Battle of GAZA.

Situation at 6 p.m. 10th Nov. 1917.

Scale of miles.

British in red    Turks in green

Compiled in Historical Section (Military Branch).
3000/30.
Ordnance Survey, 1927.

moment abandoned, and all available machines engaged 1917.
upon a series of bombing and machine-gun attacks upon the 9 Nov.
retiring columns. Raids upon the aerodromes at 'Iraq el
Menshiye on the 8th and Et Tine on the 9th, resulted in the
destruction of at least nine enemy machines, the charred
remains of which were found later by the advancing troops.[1]
Railway stations, troops on the march, transport, were
continually attacked with the bomb and the machine gun.
The enemy made determined attempts to challenge the new
British superiority in the air by employing formations of
from two to four aircraft, but on almost every occasion his
machines were either driven down or repulsed, while only
on two occasions were British aeroplanes so damaged as to
be obliged to abandon the work they had in hand After
this attempt the German airmen, doubtless handicapped by
loss of material from bombing attacks and by the rapidity of
the British advance, showed no activity till the 24th
November, by which date some reorganization seems to have
been achieved.

\* \* \* \* \*

The pursuit had now been transferred to the coast plain. Sketch 9.
The next objective was " Junction Station " on the Wadi es
Sarar, where the railway to Beersheba joined the Jerusalem–
Jaffa line (of which the portion from Jaffa to Lydda had been
picked up by the enemy early in the war). The capture of
Junction Station, which was less than twenty miles north-
east of Majdal, would have the effect of splitting the Turkish
forces in two, cutting off the *Seventh Army* from the main
railway, and leaving it dependent on the Nablus–Jerusalem
road for supplies, except for such as could be brought
to Jerusalem from over the Jordan. Sir Edmund Allenby
had transferred the weight of his attack to the front of the
Turkish *Eighth Army* in the coast plain, and was for the
moment neglecting the *Seventh* in the hills. Knowing the
character of his opponent, he could not doubt that Falkenhayn would attempt a diversion against the British right
flank in order to ease the pressure on Kress's *Eighth Army*
and permit it to establish itself upon the line of the Wadi es
Sarar. There were actually signs that a counter-attack of
this nature was impending, but they left the Commander-

---

[1] For the extraordinary moral effect of the raid on Et Tine, see Note at end of Chapter.

in-Chief quite unperturbed, and in no way interfered with his plans. He knew that the enemy forces in the hills were weak in numbers, disorganized, and short of transport, and therefore felt that he had little to fear from them. His sole precaution was to order the Camel Brigade to move from Beersheba to Tell Abu Dilakh on the railway north of Sheria, where it would be in a convenient position to support his flank in case of need. General Chetwode also warned the 60th Division at Jemmame that it might be called upon to intervene and take the enemy in flank if he attempted to advance against Tell en Nejile, and the 179th Brigade was moved to that point on the 13th.

In one respect the enemy's situation had improved. The pursuit was no longer on parallel lines, and the Turkish forces, as a result of the delays at Sheria, of the shortage of water, and, it must be added, of their own remarkable exertions and stout defence of excellently chosen rear-guard positions, were clear of the net in which it had been designed to take them. They had lost very heavily in prisoners, transport, guns and stores, but they had been able to form a new front, even though it might be very unstable. Yet, so great was the disorganization of the *Eighth Army* that, if the two infantry divisions now being brought forward could really come to grips with it, there might be opportunity to rout it, perhaps even to destroy it, especially as the British were now entering more fertile and better watered country than that between Gaza and Majdal. How far that could be achieved would depend partly upon the resolution of the leadership on either side, but also to a great extent upon how fortune distributed her favours. In any case the course before the British Commander-in-Chief was clear: to urge his troops forward with all possible expedition upon Junction Station.

NOTE.

THE TURKISH MOVEMENTS FROM THE 7TH TO THE 9TH NOVEMBER.

The attack of the 60th Division at Tell esh Sheria in the early hours of the 7th November was planned as a surprise, for which reason artillery was not employed in the early stages, and it succeeded in completely surprising the enemy, according to the report of Mohammed Arif, Chief of the Staff of the *XX Corps*. On hearing that British cavalry (the A. & N.Z. Mounted Division) had broken through and reached Kh. Umm Ameidat, the commander of the *Seventh Army*, Fevzi Pasha, put the *19th Division*, previously under the *III Corps*, under the *XX* and ordered it to be prepared to withdraw. About 1.30 p.m. Falkenhayn sent an order to Colonel Ali Fuad, commanding the *XX Corps*, to withdraw astride the railway, keeping his right a mile east of it. But this was an impossibility, since the A. & N.Z. Mounted Division was in fact occupying the area through which he was directed to retire. On the morning of the 8th November the *XX Corps* was completely lost, but was discovered in the afternoon well west of the railway, with a large gap between it and the forces in the hills, which had also withdrawn, to the neighbourhood of Dawaime. Its retreat was only made possible by the action of the *53rd Division* marching up from the south-west, which, as has been explained, checked the advance of the British mounted troops.

To turn now to the right flank on the coast, the troops defeated by the British 52nd Division and turned out of the line of the Wadi el Hesi consisted of the *7th Division*, the *3rd Division* having been sent east of the railway to Beit Hanun and opposed to the Imperial Service Cavalry Brigade, which it held in check. After the *7th Division* had been driven from Ras Abu Ameire, it took up a position along Sausage Ridge facing the sea, repulsed the attack of the 155th Brigade, but was itself overwhelmed by the attack of the 157th Brigade after nightfall on the 8th November. Refet Bey, commanding the *XXII Corps*, wished to counter-attack and attempt to drive the British back across the Wadi el Hesi, but Kress saw no prospect of success in such an operation, and ordered a retirement, withdrawing his own headquarters to Et Tine.[1]

It was at this point that the celebrated panic among the retreating enemy broke out. Hitherto there had been disorganization, but, generally speaking, extraordinary doggedness in the ranks of the enemy. Yet many of the troops were near breaking-point. It was in rear, as so often happens in a retreat, that the panic began. It may be described in the words of Kress ("Sinai," i, p. 51) :—

"On the afternoon of the 9th November there broke out a panic at "Et Tine, the main ammunition depot and railhead behind the *Eighth* "*Army* front, among the large number of troops there assembled, transport "columns and trains, mechanical transport, aircraft personnel. This did "more to break the heart of the *Eighth Army* and to diminish its fighting "strength than all the hard fighting that had gone before. Several "bombing attacks by powerful enemy flying formations had caused "explosions in the big dump of munitions at Et Tine, had cut all tele-"graphic and telephonic communication, and created wild excitement, "when suddenly news spread that hostile cavalry had broken through the "main Turkish line and was moving against the headquarters of the "*Eighth Army* at Et Tine.

"Although this rumour was false and fantastic, yet it caused such "agitation that many formations began to retreat without orders and "broke into flight. A great number of officers and men could not be "stopped till they had reached Jerusalem or Damascus. Baggage and "supply columns, in particular, having lost touch with their troops and "headquarters staffs owing to the numerous changes in location of the "latter in the course of the battle, fell into indescribable confusion. The "results of the panic were especially fatal, because not only was all tele-"graphic and telephonic communication destroyed, but almost all the "horses of Army headquarters were stampeded, so that it was left unable "to send out orders to the troops. Thanks to the devotion and energy of a "number of German and Turkish officers, order was in a measure restored "the following day. But on the evening of the 9th the rumour spread in "Jerusalem that the English had broken through our line and captured "the headquarters of the *Eighth Army*. As may easily be imagined, this "rumour caused considerable agitation in the city."

---

[1] Turkish "*Yilderim*," Part 3, Chap. V.

# CHAPTER VII.

PREPARATIONS FOR THE ATTACK ON JUNCTION STATION.

(Maps 1, 2, 9; Sketch 9.)

## THE OPERATIONS OF THE 10TH NOVEMBER.

Maps 1, 2.
Sketch 9.
WHEN it had been found impossible to cut off the enemy retreating from Gaza, operations developed into a pursuit, of which the first object was to prevent him from establishing himself upon the main watercourses of the Philistine Plain, the Nahr Suqreir and the Nahr Rubin. And from the 9th November the problem of the pursuit became, in the words of the Commander-in-Chief's despatch, " one of supply " rather than manœuvre." This situation made the administrative responsibility of the corps very great, since supply from railhead forward was under its control—a departure from the current Field Service Regulations.[1] The 75th Divisional Train had rejoined on the 9th, and that of the 52nd Division, which had not been lent to the XX Corps, was available, while lorries and tractors of the XXI Corps Heavy Artillery were also used for supply. The companies of the Camel Transport Corps employed by the XX Corps in its operations had not yet reached the coast area. Two joined the XXI Corps on the 11th, one on the 12th, and one on the 13th; but even then their value was diminished by their fatigues of the past fortnight. The roads were bad, the belt of sand on the shore impassable for wheels without pedrails,

---

[1] " The supply columns (M.T.) are L. of C. units under the orders of " the I.G.C. . . . The sphere of command and responsibility of both I.G.C. " and commander of L. of C. Defences will usually extend to and include " the rendezvous." (F.S.R. Part II, 1913, p. 85.)

It will be recalled that the functions of the Inspector-General of Communications had been absorbed by G.H.Q. in October 1916 (Vol. i, p. 244). Therefore, instead of L. of C. supply columns being sent forward from railhead, as contemplated in Field Service Regulations, to connect with divisional trains, supply columns under corps control were sent back for supplies—the necessary transport being allotted to the corps by G.H.Q.

and the soil east of that belt as far as the Wadi el Hesi light and friable. North of the wadi, however, there were large stretches of rich dark cotton soil over which transport could often move off the roads in dry weather, though these areas became sloughs when the rains began. Major-General Walter Campbell, Deputy Quartermaster-General of the Force, had previously made arrangements to land supplies at the mouth of the Wadi el Hesi under the protection of the Navy. Unloading was begun on the 11th, Commander G. Gregory, R.N., taking responsibility for starting it, and thus allowing the XXI Corps to advance on the enemy's heels. From that date onwards also a certain number of sheep were requisitioned, so that some units had the luxury of an issue of fresh mutton, and a fair amount of forage was found locally.

1917
10 Nov.

Supply was never to become an easy matter till the front had once again become more or less stabilized the following month, but there were prospects of an early improvement, and if for the moment affairs were at their worst it seemed that all would be comparatively well, so far as rations were concerned, when the next two or three anxious days were over. The situation regarding water was far more serious. Wells there were now, generally several in every village, but they were often very deep, and many had been damaged by the Turks. In some cases even such primitive tackle as existed had been removed by the enemy, and the only way of drawing water was to lower the little service canvas buckets on a length of telephone wire—a painfully slow method when all the horses of a mounted brigade were waiting to drink.

In these circumstances Major-General Chaytor was forced to report to General Chauvel on the morning of the 10th that the A. & N.Z. Mounted Division, after its great drive on the previous day, was ridden out, and that it positively must halt till its horses had drunk their fill. They had reached a stage very near to collapse. Major-General Chaytor had some eight hundred prisoners for whom to provide water, while the villagers had been kept away from the wells for twenty-four hours and were clamouring to take their turn at them. There was therefore only one movement of importance that day on the division's front. The 1st L.H. Brigade, finding that the enemy had evacuated

Sdud, pushed on through it and won a bridgehead over the Nahr Suqreir at Jisr Sdud.

Maps 2, 9. Sketch 9.

The Australian Mounted Division, on the other hand, had employed the 9th in watering, and had moved off before midnight for Tell el Hesi. It reached this point at 4.30 a.m., and halted till dawn. There were some pools in the wadi, which was very fortunate, for a second drink given to horses within a few hours increases their endurance considerably. By 10.30 a.m. the 3rd L.H. Brigade had occupied 'Iraq el Menshiye on the railway and the 4th Faluja, 2 miles to the north-west. It appeared that the enemy was digging in on a line from Summeil, 4 miles north of 'Iraq el Menshiye, to Zeita, 3 miles north-east. Unfortunately the 3rd and 4th Brigades did not establish touch with one another till the fall of darkness made impossible a projected attack on Summeil. The division held at night an outpost line over 8 miles long, running northward from 'Iraq el Menshiye, then westward north of Hatte to Beit Affe, where the 4th L.H. Brigade had found touch with the A. & N.Z. Mounted Division. The Yeomanry Mounted Division, having watered at Tell en Nejile, advanced in rear of the Australian Mounted Division. It was ordered at night to move westward to Majdal and relieve the tired Anzacs.

The orders received by General Bulfin overnight from G.H.Q. were to establish two divisions on a line from Es Suafir el Gharbiye to Sdud. He ordered the 75th Division to despatch one brigade group to Suafir el Gharbiye and the 52nd one to Sdud. The Imperial Service Cavalry Brigade had to be withdrawn to a ration dump near Gaza, as it could no longer be supplied.

It was the 157th Brigade of the 52nd Division, with " B " Battery 262nd Brigade R.F.A. and the 413th Field Company R.E., which was ordered by Major-General Hill to occupy Sdud, and it had an eventful day. A *Khamsin* was blowing in the faces of the troops, making the temperature extraordinarily high for the season and trying them so severely that 82 men of one battalion fell out in the course of a thirteen miles' march. The road past Burbera, Majdal, and Hamame was littered with the wreckage of the retreating enemy : men shot down by the machine guns of the Australians the day before, broken-down wagons, dead and dying animals. On the brigade struggled till as it approached

Sdud, where it had hoped to pass the night, it was seen that 1917.
the place was under fire. Br.-General Hamilton Moore rode 10 Nov.
forward and met Br.-General Cox, commanding the 1st L.H.
Brigade, who informed him that Sdud had been captured,
but that the Turks were established on the ridge 3 miles to
the east, preventing the Australians watering their horses
at some cisterns east of the Wadi el Mejma. He at once
decided to attack and capture the ridge, so as to win the water
and also protect the right of the 1st L.H. Brigade. He rode
back and hurried forward his battery, which began to shell
the Turkish position while yet there was light. By this time
his leading battalion had reached Sdud, where it was informed that instead of going into quarters it had in front of it
a march of another three miles, to be followed by an attack.

Weary as the troops were, they responded with such
alacrity to the call that by 4.25 p.m. packs had been piled,
hasty instructions given, and the brigade was ready to
advance eastward from the southern outskirts of Sdud.
There was, however, only another quarter of an hour before
sunset, and by the time half the distance had been covered
it was dark. Compass bearing had been taken, and the
advance continued, met as it approached the position by
machine-gun fire, in addition to that of artillery, which it
had to face from the first. When within a hundred yards of
the Turkish position, located by the flash of machine guns
and rifles, the 5/Argyll & Sutherland Highlanders on the
right, the 7/H.L.I. on the left charged and took the trench,
with three machine guns. It was then discovered that small
bodies of the enemy were still in position further along the
ridge, and a second advance was made to drive them off it.
The Turks fought hard. They had a number of rockets
which they dropped down-wind, so they fell behind the
trenches which the British troops were digging, and then
raked the working-parties with machine-gun fire. Several
of these guns had been sited by daylight to sweep the ridge
with grazing fire. Br.-General Hamilton Moore brought
up his Stokes mortars, which considerably quietened the
machine guns. At midnight a counter-attack was launched
against the 7/H.L.I., which left its trenches and threw the
enemy back with the bayonet. It was found that the
Turkish position consisted in fact of two parallel ridges, with
a gulley between. The first was captured, and a footing

obtained on the second, but it was impossible to clear the enemy from the latter before dawn. However, he had had enough of close fighting, and was gone before daylight when another British attack was about to commence. The troops holding the position were the remains of the hard-fighting *3rd Division*, which had already met the British with varying fortune at Qatiya, Romani, Rafah and the three Battles of Gaza. Its infantry now numbered between a thousand and twelve hundred, but it had begun this fight with twelve machine guns. The casualties of the 157th Brigade were 98, the 5/A. & S.H. being much the heaviest sufferers. This was the second successful attack carried out by this brigade within the space of forty-eight hours, after dark and against unreconnoitred positions. The fashion in which the leading battalions maintained direction and touch with one another during the approach was as notable as their resolution when they came to close quarters.

THE 11TH AND 12TH NOVEMBER—THE TURKISH COUNTER-ATTACK AT BARQUSYA AND THE CAPTURE OF BURQA.

The 11th November was a day of preparation. Sir Edmund Allenby had come to the decision that his advance on Junction Station could most easily be made from the south-west, by turning the enemy's right on the coast. East of the railway the rough foothills of the Shephelah made progress more difficult than in the plain, while there was less water and supply was a harder task. He had instructed General Bulfin to close his two divisions up upon their advanced guards, of which that of the 75th was at Suafir el Gharbiye, where it had relieved the 2nd L.H. Brigade, and that of the 52nd on the ridge north-east of Beit Duras which it had just captured. He had allowed General Chauvel to move the Yeomanry Mounted Division westward to the coast, thus relegating the Australian Mounted Division on the right flank to the rôle of a covering force. He still thought that there was a probability of a Turkish counter-stroke against his right, but was confident that Major-General Hodgson would be able to withstand it. He was, in fact, taking a risk rather greater than he contemplated; for his intelligence service had for the moment lost touch with the Turkish forces upon the greater part of the front and he

## CONCENTRATION OF XXI CORPS 147

was unaware until the enemy actually attacked that there 1917.
were three Turkish divisions, the *53rd, 26th* and *16th*, between 11 Nov.
the railway and Beit Jibrin, 6 miles east of it, all more or less
reorganized and all within striking reach of his right. On
the 11th the R.F.C., which had bombed Junction Station
the previous afternoon, reported considerable numbers of
troops in that neighbourhood; but the movement of transport seemed to be mainly northward. Yet Sir Edmund
Allenby's bold policy was to pay him well; for his concentration westward enabled him to break the Turkish right and
capture Junction Station without serious loss, while his
reliance upon the steadiness of the Australian Mounted
Division was amply justified.

This division was ordered by General Chauvel to carry
out vigorous patrolling in order to mask the concentration
taking place nearer the coast. Summeil, a mile north of the
previous night's outpost line, was found to have been
evacuated by the enemy, and the ridge upon which it stood
was occupied by the 3rd L.H. Brigade. Barqusya, 2 miles
to the north-east, was apparently held in strength by the
Turks. During the day as many horses as possible were
watered, the outposts being held by mounted men, while
those dismounted were grouped at points from which they
could be swiftly moved up in the event of a Turkish attack.
The outpost line, nearly twelve miles long, ran from 3 miles
south of 'Iraq el Menshiye, through that village, through
Summeil, then turned westward across the railway to
Jelediye, south-west of which the flank was in touch with
the 75th Division.

The two infantry divisions closed up in accordance with
orders. By nightfall the 75th Division had its 233rd Brigade
half way between Julis, 5 miles south of Sdud, and Suafir
el Gharbiye, with outposts covering Suafir esh Sherqiye and
Suafir esh Shemaliye; [1] the 232nd Brigade 2 miles east of
Beit Duras with outposts in touch with those of the 233rd
and of the 52nd Division on its left; the 234th Brigade
at Ejje, 10 miles S.S.W. of Sdud. On the front of the 52nd
Division the 156th Brigade had taken over the ridge northeast of Beit Duras captured by the 157th the previous day;

---

[1] These somewhat complicated names mean simply Western, Eastern
and Northern Sapphire respectively. See "Place-names, Palestine and
Syria."

the latter had moved to rest at Sdud; and the 155th had advanced to Majdal. By the exertions of the Royal Engineers just, but only just enough water was obtained for men and horses. On the left of the infantry the 1st L.H. Brigade held the line from Sdud to the sea, while the 2nd L.H. and 7th Mounted Brigades were watering and resting near the shore at Hamame.

The 1st L.H. Brigade had, it will be remembered, won a narrow bridgehead across the Nahr Suqreir north of Sdud on the 10th.[1] This was of value, because that perennial stream was a considerable obstacle, but it was necessary to enlarge it. The 2nd A.L.H. found it impossible to debouch owing to the enemy's shell fire, so rode 2½ miles north-westward across the dunes and effected a crossing near the shore, driving off the small bodies of the enemy holding the high ground beyond the river, linked up with the detachment of the regiment already on the right bank, and by nightfall enlarged the bridgehead to a depth of a mile and a half.

The Yeomanry Mounted Division accomplished a considerable march in the course of its movement to the left flank. First of all the 6th and 8th Mounted Brigades had to be sent to Tell el Hesi to water; then the division marched to Faluja, to which its rations had been sent, then it set off westward and arrived at Majdal in rear of the A. & N.Z. Mounted Division between 6 and 7 p.m. The 6th Brigade had covered at least twenty miles. But a much greater march was made by the New Zealand Brigade, which was ordered on this date to rejoin its division at Hamame. It left Beersheba at 4.30 p.m., halted to rest and water at Kh. Jemmame in the early hours of the 12th, and reached Hamame at 11 p.m.; thus covering a distance of 52 miles in 18½ hours. The total distance covered by the Auckland Regiment was over sixty miles, because it was near Tell el Khuweilfe with the 53rd Division when the order to march was received. The Camel Brigade reached Julis during the afternoon of the 11th, and returned to the command of the Desert Mounted Corps.

On the 12th November a minor but still important operation was to be carried out by the 52nd Division in preparation for the general advance upon Junction Station. It was to drive the enemy from his position north of the Nahr

---

[1] See p. 144.

Suqreir between the villages of Burqa and Yazur, which are on the right bank 3 miles apart, while the Yeomanry Mounted Division was to relieve the 1st L.H. Brigade, cover the infantry's left flank, and extend the gains across the Nahr Suqreir from the Jaffa road to the sea.

1917.
12 Nov.

The Australian Mounted Division was ordered to assist this attack by pressing the enemy on its front as strongly as possible. It appeared at first that the Turks had retired altogether from the front of this division. On the right a squadron of the 9th A.L.H. rode unmolested through Barqusya, where the inhabitants related that a large body of the enemy had passed through their village the previous day, retreating northward. One troop pressed on and occupied Tell es Safi, 2 miles to the north-east : a village on a hill-top with a cluster of poor huts approached by precipitous paths, which yet has double claim to the respect inspired by vast age and great events ; for it is probably the Blanchegarde of Fulke of Anjou and Coeur-de-Lion, and possibly also the Gath of the Philistines. The 5th Mounted Brigade found Balin unoccupied, and the Gloucester Yeomanry took up a position north of the village, two squadrons east of the railway and one west of it. West of the Beersheba railway the 4th L.H. Brigade sent out a squadron of the 11th A.L.H. which crossed the Huj branch of that railway at Qastine without coming in contact with the enemy.

Suddenly it became clear that the counter-attack which the division had been warned to expect was impending. Three miles east of Qastine was the important station of Et Tine, where the Huj line branched off from that leading to Beersheba. Here and further north along the railway trains were observed from which troops were issuing. On the 11th A.L.H. squadron's quitting Qastine, the enemy occupied the place in strength. Then at midday three separate columns of all arms were seen advancing in the direction of Tell es Safi from north and north-east. Ten minutes later the H.A.C. battery opened fire on the advancing Turks, but was hopelessly outnumbered and outranged by the enemy's artillery. The 5th Mounted Brigade rushed up its two other regiments, which were both far below establishment since the charge at Huj,[1] to the

---

[1] One squadron of the Warwickshire Yeomanry, left at Khuweilfe, had not yet rejoined.

support of the Gloucester Yeomanry; the Worcesters taking up a position on the right on the ridge north-east of Balin, and the Warwicks moving up behind the squadron west of the railway. On the right of the 5th Brigade the 9th A.L.H. quickly withdrew its troop from Tell es Safi, which was then occupied by the enemy, and took up a position north of Barqusya; the 4th L.H. Brigade occupied the high ground from a point north-west of Summeil towards Jelediye, on the left of the 5th Mounted Brigade but considerably in rear of it. The 8th A.L.H. was ordered to support the 5th Mounted Brigade, but, seeing that the enemy was advancing in greatly superior numbers against its own brigade at Barqusya also, it sent two squadrons to its support, leaving only one to assist the Yeomanry, which had to bear the brunt of the attack.

The advance was well supported by artillery, and it was calculated that some five thousand Turks were engaged. This figure is now known to be pretty accurate, for four weak divisions, *54th* west of the railway, the *53rd* and *26th*, with the *16th* in support, east of it, took part. Just after the launching of the attack two large cars were seen to drive swiftly into Tell es Safi, and several officers, one of whom was thought from his great height to be Marshal von Falkenhayn himself, got out and watched the fight through their glasses.[1] The advance was temporarily checked by the British fire, but the leading waves were seen to be reinforced, and soon came on again. In face of heavy machine-gun, Hotchkiss and rifle fire the Turks showed great determination, but moved very slowly. An observer in the 4th L.H. Brigade reported that they were obviously good and well-disciplined troops, but very tired. Many of them had, in fact, made long marches—the *16th Division* having moved up from Beit Jibrin during the night—and the men were hardly conscious of their surroundings till they were fired on. Then their extraordinary physical toughness enabled them to respond to the call made upon them, but, fortunately for the Yeomen, there was no dash in their attack.[2]

---

[1] This party actually consisted of Lieut.-Colonel Hussein Husni, Sub-chief of the Staff, another staff officer, and possibly Colonel Ali Fuad, commanding the *XX Corps*. (Turkish " *Yilderim*," Part 4, Chap. III.)

[2] There is an unusual, and to the historian a very welcome, similarity in the accounts of this action from both sides, even as regards the fatigue of the enemy and his determination in spite of it. Lieut.-Colonel Hussein

A single troop of the Gloucester Yeomanry, in a position which formed a sharp salient north of Balin, was forced to withdraw, after several of the enemy had been shot down within ten yards of its line. This gave the enemy the highest point on the ridge and enabled him to enfilade the rest of the position, and a retirement had to be made to the next ridge, about half a mile further south, the brigade being now approximately in line with the 3rd L.H. Brigade at Barqusya. The Gloucesters managed by great exertions to evacuate their dressing station in Balin, some of the wounded being carried out on horseback at a gallop, but it was touch and go, with a margin to be reckoned by seconds.[1] Scarcely had the new position been taken up when the enemy appeared on that just vacated, and shortly afterwards his artillery and machine guns were concentrated on a little "sugar-loaf" knoll on the right, held by the Worcester Yeomanry. It was clear that this position could not be held in face of greatly superior numbers and fire power, so a further withdrawal of the whole line of the 5th Mounted and 3rd L.H. Brigades was made to north of Summeil, where it was continued by the 4th L.H. Brigade in a north-westerly direction. This brigade had been heavily attacked, the enemy penetrating to within a hundred yards of its position on the left, held by the 4th A.L.H., but being repulsed by machine-gun and rifle fire. It was now dark, and at 6 p.m. the attack

1917.
12 Nov.

---

Husni (Turkish "*Yilderim*" Part 4, Chap. III), thus describes the attack of the *53rd Division* on Balin :—
 "Another line of skirmishers came along some hundreds of metres
" behind the first, being the leading company of the advanced guard. It
" was composed of about fifteen rifles and four machine guns. They too
" seemed very tired and sleepy. From their gait it was evident that the
" men had difficulty in getting along. But the noise of firing which broke
" out in front of these men, so faithful to their duty, enlivened their
" enthusiasm, and their sleepy eyes opened once more as they turned
" towards the enemy. I do not exaggerate ; perhaps, indeed, I do not
" give them their full due. . . .
 "Further to our left the *26th Division* was advancing, and the
" enemy guns distributed their fire on both formations. Now the artillery
" of the *53rd Division* came into action, and a minor combat ensued. The
" villagers [of Tell es Safi] came out and watched from the hill crests.
" Our guns quickly got the range and increased their fire, and the enemy
" horse battery was at once silenced. The *54th Division* south of Et Tine
" attacked the weak enemy forces on its front with infantry supported
" by artillery fire, and began to gain ground."
 [1] It is interesting to note that the medical personnel had practised evacuating wounded men on horseback, those old "V.C." exercises which seemed out of place in modern war.

died down, the weary enemy digging himself in upon the line which he had gained through Balin and Barqusya. Never had dusk been more welcome, for there were now no reserves behind the position, though on the extreme left flank the 75th Division's right at Es Suafir esh Sherqiye was prepared to support the 4th L.H. Brigade. The line taken up for the night ran from 'Iraq el Menshiye to Summeil (3rd. L.H. Brigade), thence westward to north of Ipseir (5th Mounted Brigade), and on to the right of the infantry at Suafir esh Sharqiye (4th L.H. Brigade).

As a result of this action the British had been driven back a maximum depth of 4 miles, upon ground which had for the moment no considerable tactical significance. Their casualties were very light, about fifty, of which the great majority were suffered by the 5th Mounted Brigade, but there had been dangerous moments, and an ugly situation had been averted only by the coolness and steadiness of the troops, especially, perhaps, the machine-gun squadron of the Yeomanry and the 4th A.L.H. This steadiness had availed them more than they knew at the moment; for they were then unaware that the Turkish *3rd Cavalry* and *19th Divisions* had advanced during the night to Beit Jibrin or that the former was actually deployed for an advance on 'Iraq el Menshiye. Had this force marched simultaneously with the attack from the north and north-east the situation of the Australian Mounted Division would have been indeed precarious. But it waited in hopes that the British, after throwing in all their reserves to resist the *XX Corps* would fall an easier prey to a flanking attack, and waited too long.

Meanwhile an operation, which was carried out in preparation for the general advance on the following day, but also had the effect of relieving the Australian Mounted Division of any further anxiety, had taken place on the front of the XXI Corps. A necessary preliminary to the advance on Junction Station from the south-west was to secure the remainder of the left bank of the Nahr Suqreir and drive off the enemy holding the village of Burqa. This task was set to the 156th Brigade (Br.-General A. H. Leggett) of the 52nd Division.

The Turkish rear-guard position ran from Burqa to Hill 220, known during the operation as " Brown Hill," a little over a mile east of the village. The advance on Burqa began at 11 a.m. from the neighbourhood of Sdud, 7/Royal Scots leading, 8/Scottish Rifles in echelon on its left, and was carried out in artillery formation up to within a few hundred yards of the cactus hedges about the village. Then, covered by the fire of a battery of the 264th Brigade R.F.A., the two battalions quickly secured a lodgment in the enemy's first line, but a long-drawn and bitter fight ensued before they were able to capture the two further Turkish positions on the ridge beyond. The last was taken with the bayonet as darkness fell. On this occasion the enemy attempted no counter-attack, but he fought with grim determination and inflicted over two hundred casualties on the two battalions. Two officers and 54 other ranks, one field gun, five machine guns and a great quantity of ammunition were captured.

The 4/Royal Scots had an even stiffer task against Brown Hill, though it had powerful artillery support, as in addition to two batteries of the 264th Brigade R.F.A., the South African Field Artillery Brigade of the 75th Division was able to cover its advance. Brown Hill, steep-sided and topped by a large cairn, was a commanding position, with a long field of fire over the plain south of the Nahr Suqreir. It also enabled the enemy to direct with great accuracy the fire of several howitzers in action behind it. The Royal Scots, already weak, suffered heavy casualties,[1] and their advance was very slow. But they went doggedly forward, and at 4 p.m. captured the hill by a most gallant charge. The battalion was, however, reduced to a handful by the time it reached the crest, it had only one company officer left, and it was unable to withstand the counter-attack immediately launched by the enemy. Twenty minutes after taking its objective it had been driven off it again, after a fierce struggle at close quarters.

At 1 p.m. Br.-General H. J. Huddleston, commanding the 232nd Brigade, had ridden up to visit a section of the South African Artillery Brigade west of Butani esh Sherqiye, a little over a mile south of Brown Hill. These guns were in action against the Turkish artillery, and were covered by two companies of the 2/3rd Gurkhas. Seeing that the attack of the Royal Scots was making slow progress, he telephoned to Major-General P. C. Palin, commanding the

---

[1] The battalion had had over 250 casualties in the attack on the Gaza defences, and had not yet received many reinforcements.

75th Division, for permission to support it, and was told to do so. Before he could take action the Royal Scots had captured Brown Hill and lost it again to the counter-attack. He thereupon ordered the 2/3rd Gurkhas to attack the hill, while the 2/5th Hampshire occupied the ridge east of it. The Gurkhas were received with a burst of cheering by the remnant of Royal Scots, now not much over a hundred strong, who prepared to join in the attack. It was now growing dark, and the artillery was no longer able to give much assistance, owing to the difficulty of distinguishing friend from foe. The hill was nevertheless quickly retaken by a dashing bayonet charge, and two Lewis guns lost by the Royal Scots recovered. The enemy then fell back under cover of darkness.

In this afternoon's heavy fighting the casualties were high, over four hundred in the 156th Brigade, of which the 4/Royal Scots suffered more than half.[1] The 2/3rd Gurkhas had 50 casualties. The Turkish *7th Division*, which opposed the advance must have suffered still more heavily, for, in addition to 56 prisoners being taken, 170 dead were found upon the field.

Disregarding the enemy threat to his right, Sir Edmund Allenby had now effected his concentration in the plain. He was prepared to launch on the morrow the general attack which resulted in the capture of Junction Station and once more divided the forces of the enemy into two separate halves.

NOTE.

TURKISH MOVEMENTS FROM 10TH TO 12TH NOVEMBER.

Lieut.-Colonel Hussein Husni (Turkish " *Yilderim* " part 4, chap. I.) gives an interesting account of the critical decision faced by the Turkish command on the 9th November. The *Eighth Army* was, according to all reports, breaking up. Thousands of men in panic-stricken mobs had made their way to Junction Station, Ramle and El'Affule. The *Seventh Army*, on the other hand, though weary and weak in numbers, was, as a result of the slackening of British pressure on its front, far less disorganized. In

---

[1] The casualties of the 156th Brigade were as follows:—

|  | Killed. | Wounded. | Missing. |
|---|---|---|---|
| Officers | 4 | 13 | – |
| Other Ranks | 88 | 309 | 6 |

To this total of 420 must be added 53 in the 75th Division, making, with the few in the 52nd Divisional Artillery and 13 in the 1st L.H. Brigade, nearly 500.

Sketch 10

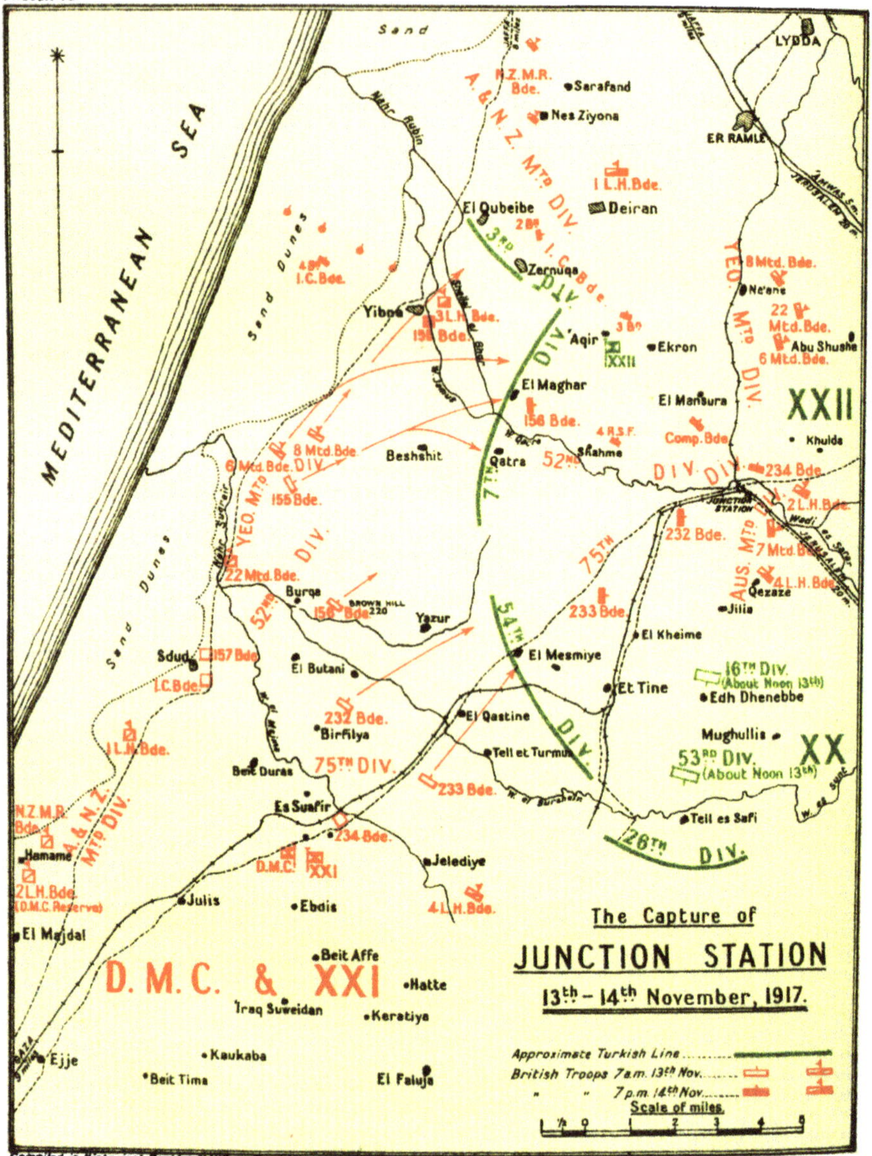


Compiled in Historical Section (Military Branch).
3000/30

Ordnance Survey. 1937

these circumstances there were divided counsels in *Yilderim* headquarters. Hussein Husni desired an immediate withdrawal to a line south of Jaffa and Jerusalem. With shortage of transport and equipment, with discipline bad and the fatigue of the troops very serious and hourly increasing, it seemed to him " useless to attempt a war of movement against the superior " forces of the British until the arrival of fresh troops." The Chief of the Staff, Oberst von Dommes, shared his opinion, but had fallen sick through overwork. And yet, while they urged this course upon the Marshal, one and all had a sort of mystic faith in his genius, and hoped, against their better judgment, that he would be able to strike a heavy blow at the British right flank, and thus save the *Eighth Army*.

Hussein Husni describes a long walk with Falkenhayn in the gardens of the German Hospice on the Mount of Olives, in which he frankly gave his opinion that a counter-attack was hopeless in the circumstances. Falkenhayn made the typical retort that, as the Turkish troops were too weak in numbers to organize and hold once more a line of resistance of such great length as would be required, he was in favour of an aggressive movement. The counter-attack was planned for the 11th November, but had to be postponed until the following day.

On the 10th November Hussein Husni states that 10,000 men were stopped and reorganized at Ramle, formed into units of 200 each, and put under the command of officers present. " With this semblance of order " achieved, I then found out every man's unit, formed groups according " to divisions, and inspected them in the evening. We were getting on ! " All these groups were to be sent to their divisions early in the morning."

By the morning of the 11th November the *Eighth Army* had the *7th Division* from Burqa to Yazur and the *54th* on its left to approximately the railway. The *3rd Division* was in reserve. The *XX Corps*, or " Ali Fuad Group," which constantly fluctuated between the *Eighth* and *Seventh Armies*, had the *53rd Division* on its right in touch with the left of the *54th*, and the *26th* and *16th Divisions* thence on a line to south of Beit Jibrin. The *3rd Cavalry* and *19th Divisions* carried on the line to Ed Dawaime.

Various contradictory orders as to the counter-attack were issued by *Yilderim*, the *Seventh Army* and the *XX Corps*, but their gist was that the *XX Corps*, with the *53rd* and *26th Divisions* in first line and the *16th* support, should attack the British right flank about Barqusya in a south-westerly direction. The *54th Division* was to co-operate west of the railway. A group consisting of the *3rd Cavalry* and *19th* [1] *Divisions* was to advance to Beit Jibrin and simultaneously attack in the direction of 'Iraq el Menshiye. The result of the counter-attack has already been fully described. Falkenhayn intended that it should be continued on the morrow. But as a result of the defeat suffered by the Turkish *7th Division* at the hands of the British at Burqa and Brown Hill, he was forced to withdraw the *16th Division* and attached *57th Regiment*, temporarily known as the " Hergott Group " from the German officer of that name who was put in command of it, and place it behind the *Eighth Army*. This left Ali Fuad without sufficient resources to continue the counter-attack on the following day.

---

[1] The *19th Division* had at this date at least one regiment of the *16th* under its orders, while the *16th Division* had attached to it the *57th Regiment* of the *19th Division*, which had recently reached Junction Station and had not yet been in action.

# CHAPTER VIII.

### THE CAPTURE OF JUNCTION STATION.
(Maps 2, 9; Sketches 10, 11.)

### THE PLAN OF ATTACK.

Maps 2, 9.    SIR EDMUND ALLENBY met Generals Bulfin and Chauvel at
Sketch 10.    the latter's advanced headquarters near Julis at noon on the 12th November and gave them his final instructions for the morrow's attack.[1] No intelligence service, however good—and that of the E.E.F. in Palestine was highly efficient—can hope to keep in close touch with the dispositions of a disorganized and hastily retreating enemy. Falkenhayn had frequently in the past few days been unable to locate his own formations at any given moment; still less had it been possible for Sir Edmund Allenby to trace them all. By the night of the 12th, however, the general line of the enemy and the general dispositions of his troops were becoming clear to the British command, though several divisions were still unlocated. The Turks were hastily consolidating a line of defence to cover Junction Station. This position faced south-west, with right on El Qubeibe, 5 miles from the sea, and left at Beit Jibrin. To hold this front the enemy had not more than 15,000 rifles and sabres. In the Philistine Plain, where the British Commander-in-Chief designed to attack him, his defences had no great natural strength, except for one narrow, steep-sided ridge, on which stood the village of Maghar, 6 miles W.N.W. of Wadi Sarar or Junction Station. In the words of Sir Edmund Allenby's Despatch, the enemy's present dispositions " had been dictated to him " by the rapidity of our movement along the coast, and the " determination with which his rear guards on this flank " had been pressed." The capture of the line of the Nahr Suqreir had brought the left of the British line far in advance

---
[1] General Bulfin had already made his plans to attack north-eastward, of which the Commander-in-Chief approved.

of its right, and left it admirably disposed for the turning of the Turkish right flank.

The difficulties of supply which had hitherto beset the XXI Corps were now to a great extent mastered. The transport brought over from the XX Corps had settled down to work and got to grips with its new task, though rations were almost always late in delivery. The roads were for the time being just good enough for the employment of a column of 22 lorries sent up by G.H.Q. on the 12th, to refill the 52nd Division's dump at Sdud from the corps dump established at Deir Sneid. This latter dump was kept filled both by road from the south and by camel columns from the mouth of the Wadi el Hesi, where stores and artillery ammunition were being landed from the sea.[1] There was a fair amount of water in the villages, and the horses of the mounted troops were for the most part better supplied with it than they had been at any time since the beginning of the offensive.

Junction Station was the immediate goal, but Sir Edmund Allenby's eyes were fixed upon another more distant and, politically if not strategically, far more important. The railway junction taken, he would have reached the latitude of Jerusalem and would be close to the two roads from Jaffa to that city, of which the southern, through Ramle, was the best in Palestine. He then intended to strike eastward, mount at this point the Judæan Hills, and capture Jerusalem, though he had not yet decided upon an immediate advance. The Holy City had a certain military value, but its capture was chiefly desired by the Government for moral effect. On the 11th November the Commander-in-Chief had received from Whitehall a telegram which, though it was somewhat vague in form, suggested a limitation of his activities. He was reminded that he might be called upon ere long to despatch some of his divisions to France, and warned that he must be careful, while doing all he could to weaken the enemy's offensive power, not to be drawn into the occupation of positions difficult to defend. He did not, however, feel that there was anything in this message to cause him to reconsider his project, and shortly afterwards another telegram from the C.I.G.S. informed him

---

[1] Ammunition, petrol and oil were dragged by caterpillars, on hastily made wooden sleighs, across the heavy sand to Deir Sneid, beyond which they could be transported by lorries.

that the War Cabinet had no wish to interfere with his plans for securing Jerusalem. He replied briefly that he quite understood the policy required of him and would go forward with his programme without committing himself too deeply.

The main attack of the 13th November was to be carried out by the XXI Corps, the right flank of which was to be protected by the Australian Mounted Division, while the remainder of the Desert Mounted Corps operated on the left. General Bulfin's orders were issued on the afternoon of the 12th.[1] The attack was to be launched at 8 a.m. after an hour's bombardment and to be carried out by the 75th Division on the right and the 52nd Division on the left. The 75th was to advance astride the Gaza–Junction Station road and attack the line Tell et Turmus–El Qastine–Yazur, and as soon as that was reached to seize Mesmiye. The 52nd was to advance to a line from the western outskirts of Yazur to Beshshit, $4\frac{1}{2}$ miles north-east of Burqa, and then eastward to the capture of Qatra. A pause was to be made upon the line of Mesmiye and Qatra to enable the artillery to move forward and fresh troops to be pushed through to the final objective of Junction Station and Mansura, $2\frac{1}{4}$ miles N.N.W. of the station. No time-table was drawn up for the attack, except, as has been stated, that the bombardment was to begin at 7 a.m. and the advance of the infantry an hour later. It will be convenient to describe first the operations of the 75th Division; then those of the 52nd Division and the mounted troops on the left of the XXI Corps together, because these two last were far more closely connected than were those of the two infantry divisions; and finally those of the right flank guard, the Australian Mounted Division.

THE ACTION OF EL MAGHAR AND OCCUPATION OF JUNCTION STATION.[2]

(7 a.m. 13th November to 9 a.m. 14th November.)

There had been some anxiety regarding the weather. The wet season had given warning of its approach by

---

[1] XXI Corps Order No. 12 is given in Appendix 14, Desert Mounted Corps Order No. 7 in Appendix 15.
[2] According to the Report of the Battles Nomenclature Committee, the Third Battle of Gaza continued until the 7th November. The action of Maghar, 13th November, " with subsequent Occupation of Junction

another thunder-storm, with heavy rain, on the night of the 11th, and it was obvious that the dark cotton soil on which the infantry was now operating would not require many hours of such a downpour to turn it into a morass. However, the 12th had been fine, so that the roads had dried a good deal, and now the 13th dawned with a clear sky. As the sun rose, the rolling plain, with villages for the most part set on the low hill-tops, surrounded by trees and cultivated enclosures which gave them, at least from a distance, a picturesque air, appeared pleasant enough. In the pastures sheep were grazing, and during the early stages of the advance there were no signs of the enemy or that a fateful battle was about to open. In the distance, on the right hand, the wall of the Judæan Hills stood out with a clarity unusual even in this land of good light and long views, the spurs and valleys being distinctly visible even to the troops on the left flank. There were no serious obstacles confronting the advance except the villages themselves, but they were for the most part surrounded by groves and orchards bounded by hedges of prickly pear or cactus and were almost all natural centres of resistance. Fortresses some of them were in very ancient times; for Yibna, under the name of Jamnia, saw fighting in the days of the Maccabees, and under that of Ibelin, in those of the Crusaders; and Qatra was held by the Syrians against Simon Maccabæus and captured by him.

1917.
13 Nov.

On the front of the 75th Division the 233rd Brigade on the right and 232nd Brigade on the left were to capture Tell et Turmus, Qastine, and Yazur as the first phase, Mesmiye el Gharbiye being the subsequent objective of the 233rd. One field artillery brigade was to support each infantry brigade, while the third was kept under the hand of Major-General Palin, but was to cover the whole front from a position near Butani esh Sherqiye. The heavy artillery at the disposal of the corps consisted only of the 189th Heavy

---

"Station, 14th November," is a separate incident. This more or less accords with the Turkish system of nomenclature. To the E.E.F., however, the Action of Maghar meant and will always mean the attack on the Qatra-Maghar line by the 155th Brigade and Yeomanry Mounted Division, and this is looked upon as the chief tactical incident of the "Capture of Junction Station." While the official title is set at the head of this section, on the maps and sketches and in the tabular record (Appendix 1), the more general usage is followed.

Battery and 380th Siege Battery—all that could as yet be brought forward—and one section of each had been put under the orders of each division. The 75th Division's two sections of heavy artillery were to be employed in the bombardment of Yazur. The second phase was to consist of the advance of the same two infantry brigades to a line from the point where the Gaza–Junction Station road crossed the Wadi el Mukheizin, 2¾ miles north-east of Mesmiye el Gharbiye, to the Mesmiye–Shahme track. In the third phase, which was to have the support of all the artillery at the division's disposal, the 234th Brigade was to pass through the 233rd and capture Junction Station.

The 233rd Brigade (Br.-General the Hon E. M. Colston) occupied Tell et Turmus and Qastine without opposition from the Turkish infantry, though it met with fairly heavy artillery fire; and the 232nd (Br.-General H. J. Huddleston) reached the line Qastine–Yazur, being also subjected to considerable shelling. Then the 5/Somerset Light Infantry and 4/Wiltshire of the 233rd Brigade advanced on Mesmiye el Gharbiye in artillery formation, sections in single file. The troops came under shrapnel and long-range machine-gun fire from the right, which was uncovered until the 4th L.H. Brigade advanced in the afternoon. The Somerset on the exposed flank showed great steadiness and maintained its direction perfectly throughout this trying ordeal. A pause was made where the Gaza railway crossed the line of advance, but, finding that the far side of the embankment was being swept by machine-gun fire from the right, the troops pushed on again. Mesmiye el Gharbiye was reached by noon, but parties of the enemy maintained themselves both in the village and among the cactus hedges about it. After a determined counter-attack had been repulsed by the Somerset, finely supported by the South African Field Artillery Brigade, the main body of the Turkish rear guard fell back to a slight ridge a mile to the north-east. The portion of this ridge between the Junction Station road and El Kheime was off the actual objective allotted to the brigade, but the machine guns on it were sweeping the ground directly north of Mesmiye el Gharbiye. Br.-General Colston decided at 2.15 p.m. that he must drive the enemy from his flank before attempting to begin the second phase. He entrusted the attack to the senior officer at Mesmiye el Gharbiye,

Lieut.-Colonel A. Armstrong, commanding the 4/Wiltshire, and put at his disposal two companies 5/Somerset and two sections of the 230th Machine-Gun Company.[1] He then ordered the 3/3rd Gurkhas to move up to Mesmiye el Gharbiye, and while the attack was in progress this battalion cleared the place of snipers. The Wiltshire, its right flank covered by the two Somerset companies, advanced at 4 p.m. under heavy fire and quickly secured the high ground.

1917. 13 Nov.

The preparations for this local operation had delayed the 233rd Brigade, which had now fallen behind the 232nd. The latter also experienced difficulty in taking the high ground north of Mesmiye el Gharbiye—a continuation of the ridge which had checked the 233rd. A considerable gap had appeared between the two brigades. The 5/Devon of the 232nd was brought up to fill this, and advancing in conjunction with the Wiltshire, drove the enemy off the ridge, capturing three machine guns. The remainder of the line then pressed forward until held up by fire from the gardens south of Qatra, to the attack upon which by the 52nd Division we shall presently turn. As darkness fell the troops began to dig themselves in.

Meanwhile the 234th Brigade was moving up with a company of the 58th Rifles as right flank guard. This company, under Captain R. B. Kitson, advanced considerably further to the right than had the leading troops, and approaching Mesmiye esh Sherqiye from the south-west came up against an entrenched position on the railway line. As Captain Kitson and the only other British officer with the company were killed, it is not quite certain what induced him to attack this frontally; but it seems from the reports of Indian officers that he saw large numbers of the enemy north of the line about to attack the right flank of the 233rd Brigade and gallantly determined to attack himself in order to check them. His company was met by a storm of machine-gun fire, and suffered 72 casualties, but its self-sacrifice achieved its purpose. At this moment the 11th A.L.H. came up on the right. Two troops galloped into a position which turned the enemy's flank, and a frontal attack covered by machine-gun fire drove the Turks off

---

[1] The machine-gun companies of the 75th Division did not bear the same numbers as the brigades to which they were attached. They were numbered 229, 230, and 231.

the ridge, enabling Mesmiye esh Sherqiye to be occupied soon afterwards.

Though it was now nearly night and the second phase had not been completed, Major-General Palin, having heard of the capture of Qatra by the 52nd Division, decided to attempt to carry out the third, and sent an order to the 234th Brigade (Br.-General F. J. Anley) to advance on Junction Station.[1] Two battalions of this brigade were now at or near Mesmiye el Gharbiye, the other two with brigade headquarters at Qastine. It took the brigade some time to concentrate at Mesmiye el Gharbiye and refill water-bottles, but the advanced guard, the 123rd Outram's Rifles, moved out at 10.25 p.m., directly after Br.-General Anley's conference was over. The brigadier felt himself handicapped in advancing to an objective so far behind the enemy's present line by his lack of knowledge of the country surrounding the station, and decided, in view of the wording of his order—to " make for " it—that he would try to capture it by surprise before daylight, but if surprise was impossible would not attack in the darkness. He also decided to go through the 233rd Brigade on the main road rather than the 232nd in the broken country on the left. His instructions to Lieut.-Colonel G. R. Cassels, commanding the 123rd Rifles, were to halt when he reached a suitable point about a mile and a half short of the station and send out a platoon with a demolition party to cut the railway to the north. He bade him not wait for this party, which marched with the main body of the brigade at 11.30 p.m.

1917.
14 Nov.

The advanced guard marched steadily forward, meeting with no opposition, and about 1.30 a.m. on the 14th reached the road junction W.S.W. of the station, whence Lieut.-Colonel Cassels sent back a message asking for the demolition party. While he was awaiting it a Turkish transport column came down the Et Tine road and blundered straight into the battalion. There was a scuffle in the darkness, and a number of prisoners were captured by the advanced guard. Lieut.-Colonel Cassels then decided to move closer to the station, of which he could plainly see the lights, and was

---

[1] G. 84    13th.
52nd Division in Qatra and Maghar.  234th Brigade is to push through the 232nd Brigade and make for Railway Junction.
5.5 p.m.                                              75th Division.

about to do so at 2.30 a.m. when the brigadier came up and informed him that he was sending forward the demolition party without delay.  Immediately afterwards a body of Turks three or four hundred strong attacked from the right, charging determinedly with shouts of " Allah ! Allah ! " The battalion faced right, and there was confused fighting, in which brigade headquarters just behind was involved, before the enemy was driven off with considerable loss. Br.-General Anley thereupon concluding that there was no hope of surprising the station, decided to await daylight, and ordered the column to take up a position capable of all-round defence.  The struggle with the enemy had one unfortunate result : the sudden burst of fire caused the pack-horse carrying the demolition party's explosives to bolt, and it could not be found for a long time.  The party was late in consequence and, meeting with bodies of the enemy along the railway line as day was breaking, was forced to return without carrying out its task.  One, or according to some reports two, trains left the station between 6 and 7 a.m., and some prisoners afterwards affirmed that Kress von Kressenstein thus escaped.

Major-General Palin did not hear of the skirmish or that the 234th Brigade was halted until 6.15 a.m.  At the same time he was informed by Br.-General Colston that there were at Mesmiye two cars of the 12th Light Armoured Car Battery which had orders to report to the Australian Mounted Division at dawn.  He sent a message that they should instead join the 234th Brigade.  At its headquarters they were ordered by Major G. M. Glynton, G.S.O.2. of the division, who had been sent forward to obtain information, to advance on the station.  They drove straight down the road, passing two platoons of the 123rd Rifles which had now been sent forward, and at 8.25 a.m. came into action near the station against a party of Turks just quitting it, shooting down a number and driving the rest in wild confusion up the Ramle road.  The platoons of the 123rd Rifles found the station abandoned, and the remainder of the 234th Brigade was by Major-General Palin's orders moved up shortly afterwards.

In the fighting of the 13th and early hours of the 14th November the 75th Division had captured 297 prisoners, though there seems no doubt that a far bigger haul, as well as the trains, were lost by the 234th Brigade's inaction in the morning. The division's own casualties were 506.[1]

Junction Station proved to be a prize worth fighting for. Most valuable of all, perhaps, was its steam pumping plant, which, thanks to the rapid attack of the armoured cars, had not been destroyed. The station was, in fact, the first point since the advance began at which water was found in unlimited quantity and easy of access. Next in value came the rolling stock, there being two engines and sixty trucks in the station, which were to be of great service also. Great quantities of food were also found—grain, flour, tibben, and even live sheep. There was a military hospital complete and in working order, the doctors and attendants having remained behind to look after the wounded and sick who could not be moved. There were machine-shops for the upkeep of the rolling stock, huge dumps of timber, petrol and grease. All was well organized, and the place bristled with notice-boards and finger-posts. It was clear that the station had been entirely under German control. This control had, however, evidently broken down in the past week, for everything was now filthy, and rotting carcases lay about.

**1917.**
**13 Nov.**

The operations of the 52nd Division were to be divided into two phases. The 155th Brigade Group [2] was to capture Beshshit and then advance against the village of Qatra. That taken, it was to push north and capture Maghar.[3]

---

[1]
|  | Killed. | Wounded. | Missing. |
| --- | --- | --- | --- |
| Officers . . | 3 | 19 | — |
| Other Ranks . | 60 | 395 | 29 |

[2] 155th Brigade, divisional cavalry squadron (less 2 troops), 261st Brigade R.F.A., 410th Field Company R.E. (less 2 sections), 1 section 3rd Lowland Field Ambulance.

[3] There is some little difficulty in ascertaining the precise orders on which the troops of the 52nd Division acted, because the records are scanty owing to the prolonged fighting in which it was subsequently engaged. The formal operation order directed the 156th Brigade to attack Qatra and the 155th to attack Beshshit, the latter then pushing on to Maghar. This order was, however, issued before the heavy engagement of the 156th at Burqa and Brown Hill. In consequence of its fatigue and losses, Qatra was included in the objective of the 155th by a wire which reached Br.-General Pollok-M'Call at 2.40 a.m. on the 13th, the 156th being merely given the task of linking the 155th with the 75th Division. Again, the orders of the XXI Corps did not include Maghar in the objective of the 52nd Division, but Major-General Hill's orders directed the 155th Brigade to capture that village, which was certainly an objective better suited to infantry than cavalry.

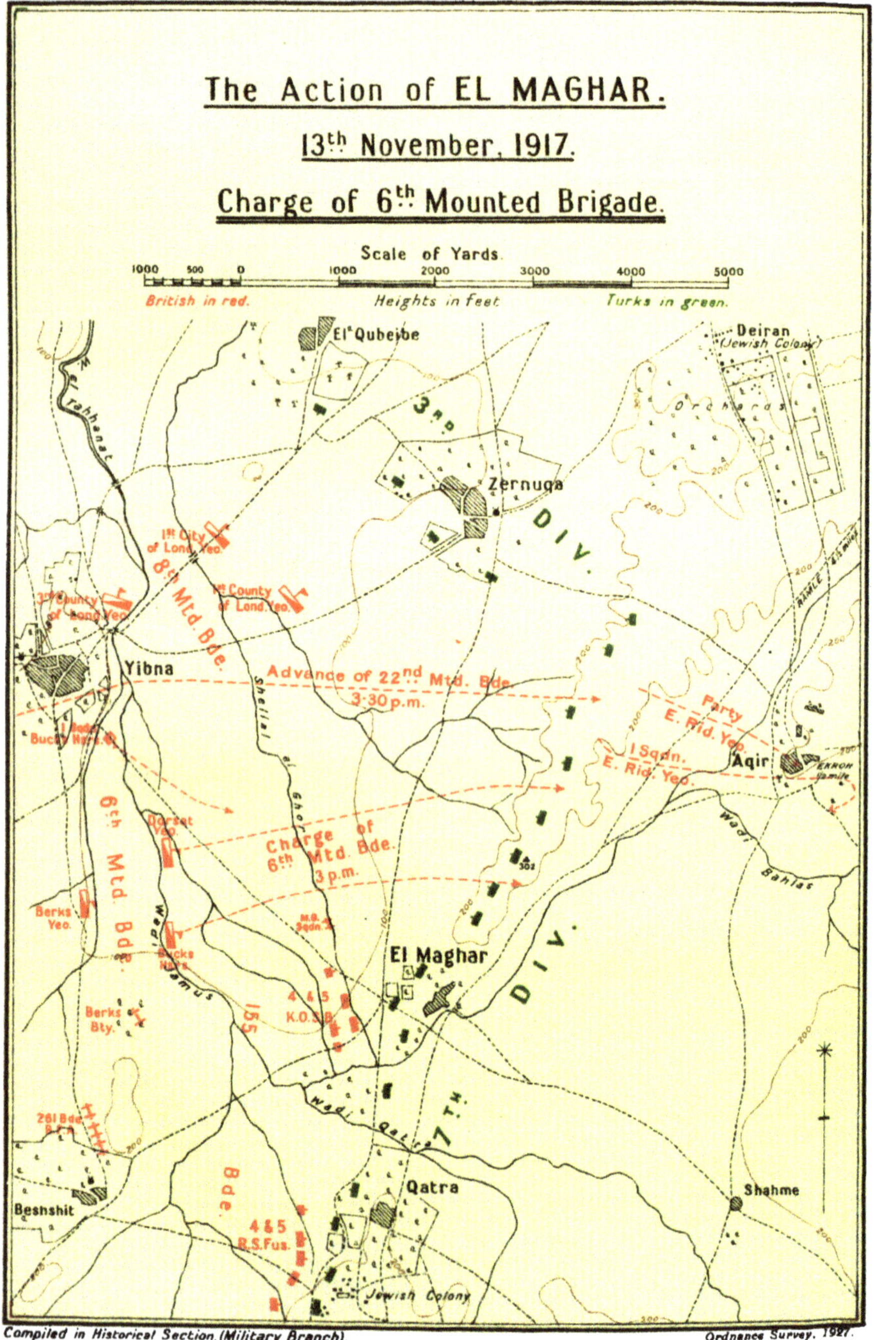

The 156th Brigade Group was to fill the gap between its right and the left of the 75th Division. On the left the Yeomanry Mounted Division was attacking the town of Yibna, and the 157th Brigade was ordered to take it over when captured. The second phase was to consist of the advance of the 155th Brigade on Mansura and the railway line east of that village. In addition to the divisional artillery—one artillery brigade being attached to each infantry brigade—and the heavy artillery, of which details have been given, " B " Battery IX Mountain Brigade was available to support the advance. The troops were to march as light as possible, carrying one day's ration on the mobile scale in addition to the iron ration, but dumping their packs. Beshshit was occupied with little opposition by the 5/Royal Scots Fusiliers. Br.-General Pollok-M'Call then went forward to reconnoitre the ground to the east and observed that the Turks were reinforcing Qatra and Maghar. Having been informed before he started by Major-General Hill that the 155th Brigade was to attack both villages at once, he ordered the 5/Royal Scots Fusiliers to advance against Qatra, and the 4/K.O.S.B., with the 5/K.O.S.B. slightly echeloned to its left rear, to attack Maghar. There was as yet no sign of the Yeomanry Mounted Division on the left flank.

1917.
13 Nov.

The two villages were divided by the Wadi Qatra, Sketch 11. which broke through the ridge in a slight depression. This ridge was of no great height but fairly steep, especially just north-east of Maghar. Both villages were covered by a maze of gardens, and south of Qatra there was a small Jewish settlement with several hundred acres of enclosed orchards still further south. Between Beshshit and the ridge lay a flat, shallow valley, in which the only cover consisted of the beds of the Wadi Jamus and its tributaries. Altogether the position was a very formidable one, and it could be seen that it was fairly strongly held. In fact from Qubeibe or thereabouts to Qatra all that remained of the much-battered Turkish *3rd* and *7th Divisions* was in line; perhaps 3,000 rifles at most, but with the bulk of this number concentrated at Qatra and from Maghar to about a mile to the north-east.

Between 11 and 11.30 a.m. the two leading battalions, advancing under shrapnel and machine-gun fire, reached the shelter of the wadis opposite their objectives, from which they were about six hundred yards distant. Just before this the enemy attempted a counter-attack from Qatra, but was quickly driven back again to his defences. Both battalions were now under cover, but both were held up by heavy fire from the gardens ahead and were unable to make further progress. The 5/K.O.S.B. was ordered up to support the 4th, and two companies of the 4/Royal Scots Fusiliers attempted a flanking attack on the right against Qatra, but only succeeded in prolonging the right of their 5th Battalion. An attempt was also made to work up the Wadi Qatra, between the two villages, but was frustrated by machine-gun fire. Still no progress was made, and about 1 p.m. Major-General Hill saw Br.-General Pollok-M'Call and arranged for a quarter of an hour's intense bombardment of Qatra and Maghar at 3.30 p.m., by all the artillery available; that is, one section 60-pdrs., the 261st Brigade R.F.A., and " B " Battery IX Mountain Brigade (directed against Maghar), and the 264th Brigade R.F.A. (directed against Qatra). He then went back to find the headquarters of the Yeomanry Mounted Division, which was 3 miles south-west of Yibna, saw Major-General Barrow at about 2.30 p.m., and asked for support on his left against the Maghar ridge. The urging was, however, not required. The Bucks Yeomanry of the 6th Mounted Brigade was already concentrated in the Wadi Jamus on the left of the two battalions attacking Maghar, and at the time of the conversation between the two divisional commanders the brigade was preparing to charge the Maghar ridge.

Major-General Barrow's second objective was from 'Aqir to Yibna, and he had been directed to advance subsequently on Ramle. The Camel Brigade was put under his command, and, as the splitting up of the troops of the Desert Mounted Corps necessitated its headquarters remaining far in rear during the battle,[1] he was authorized to issue orders to the A. & N.Z. Mounted Division in emergency. This division was to be prepared to follow the Yeomanry and exploit any success gained.

The Yeomanry Mounted Division had, it will be recalled, moved across to the neighbourhood of Majdal

---

[1] Advanced headquarters was established in the morning just south-west of Es Suafir el Gharbiye, 11 miles S.S.W. of Yibna, the first objective of the Yeomanry Mounted Division.

during the night of the 11th. During the fighting at Burqa on the 12th it had moved up in rear of the A. & N.Z. Mounted Division on the coast. It appears to have received no more than a summary of the orders of the Desert Mounted Corps until nearly 1 a.m. on the morning of the 13th. Major-General Barrow's orders, issued at 7 p.m. on the 12th, gave as the second objective a line from 'Aqir to a bridgehead over the Wadi Jamus east of Yibna, but made no mention of co-operation with the infantry because he had not been informed that this was expected of him.[1]

At 10.30 a.m. a squadron of the 3rd County of London Yeomanry, 8th Mounted Brigade, galloped up to Yibna. A small body of Turks which had been covering the place withdrew at its approach, but there was still machine-gun fire from within this large village. With the co-operation of a squadron of the Bucks Hussars, 6th Mounted Brigade, it was cleared an hour later. Major-General Barrow issued an order to the 6th Mounted Brigade to move on Maghar and to the Camel Brigade to attack the villages of Qubeibe and Zernuqa. The 22nd Mounted Brigade was to advance

---

[1] The staff of the Desert Mounted Corps had despatched the orders (Corps Order No. 7) to Major-General Chaytor's headquarters, anticipating that the Yeomanry Mounted Division would relieve the A. & N.Z. Mounted Division that afternoon. The G.S.O. 3 of the Yeomanry Division, Captain H. C. H. Robertson, who was sent to get the orders, had some difficulty in finding A.& N.Z. headquarters, where he arrived between 7 and 7.30 p.m. Lieut.-Colonel J. G. Browne, G.S.O.1. of the Anzacs, gave him a copy, but asked him to wait while arrangements were made for co-operation between the Yeomanry and 52nd Divisions on the morrow, stating that he could help in this matter as he had telephone communication with the 52nd Division. Meanwhile a thunderstorm had burst; a telegraph post was struck by lightning, and this communication cut. Captain Robertson waited till after 11 p.m., while efforts were made to get through on the telephone, then declared that he must ride with the orders to Major-General Barrow. The night was dark and heavy rain was falling. He rode into a maze of trenches, round which he had to make a detour, and did not reach his headquarters, then arriving at Sdud, until between 12.30 and 1 a.m. on the 13th. Thus it came about that Major-General Barrow's orders issued at 7 p.m. the previous evening, which were those acted upon by the brigades on the morning of the 13th, did not completely reflect those issued by the corps, and above all did not contain the important sentence: " Desert Mounted Corps will co-operate by vigorous action in advance of "the flanks of the infantry." Major-General Barrow states that he met General Chauvel next morning on the high ground near Sdud, and was given verbal instructions to " drive back any Turkish rear guards who " might oppose me and endeavour to reach Ramle." He had no notion that the 52nd Division was likely to meet with opposition which it would be unable to break down without his assistance.

168 THE CAPTURE OF JUNCTION STATION

on 'Aqir after the capture of these villages. As the Camel Brigade was not up in time—having only reached Sdud at 5.30 that morning—the 8th Mounted Brigade (Br.-General C. S. Rome) was directed to take over its task, and despatched a regiment against each village. Both regiments were held up north-east of Yibna by heavy machine-gun fire.

Meanwhile the Bucks Hussars, less the squadron co-operating with the 8th Mounted Brigade, had established itself in the Wadi Jamus. The Berks Battery R.H.A. unlimbered in the cover of a little group of trees west of the wadi and came into action against Maghar at a range of 3,000 yards. Lieut.-Colonel the Hon F. H. Cripps, commanding the Bucks Hussars, sent forward Lieutenant C. H. Perkins to reconnoitre the Wadi Shellal el Ghor. He cantered up and down under a hail of machine-gun fire which, in the words of an eye-witness, " followed him as the spot-" light follows a dancer on the stage," seeming to bear a charmed life, and returned in safety to report that there was good cover for the machine-gun squadron to support the attack. Br.-General C.A.C. Godwin had joined Lieut.-Colonel Cripps in the Wadi Jamus after ordering the Dorset Yeomanry to dash forward in small bodies and take up a position on the left of the Bucks. The Berkshire Yeomanry was in support, about half a mile in rear.

Br.-General Godwin now gave his orders personally to the commanding officers in the Wadi Jamus. The Bucks and Dorset Yeomanry were to advance simultaneously in column of squadrons, extending to five paces, the Bucks directed on the ridge about a thousand yards north of Maghar; the Berks Yeomanry to push forward to the Wadi Jamus as soon as the Bucks Hussars quitted it.[1] The machine-gun squadron, except for one subsection which went forward with each of the leading regiments, was massed in the Wadi Shellal el Ghor to the right of the line of advance, and was able to support the attack until the charge closely approached the ridge.

At 3 p.m. the two regiments scrambled up the steep eastern bank of the Wadi Jamus, the third squadron of the

---

[1] The reason for not bringing up the third regiment until the charge of the Bucks and Dorset had begun was that the bed of the wadi was wide enough only for a single rank of horses.

THE QATRA—MAGHAR POSITION.

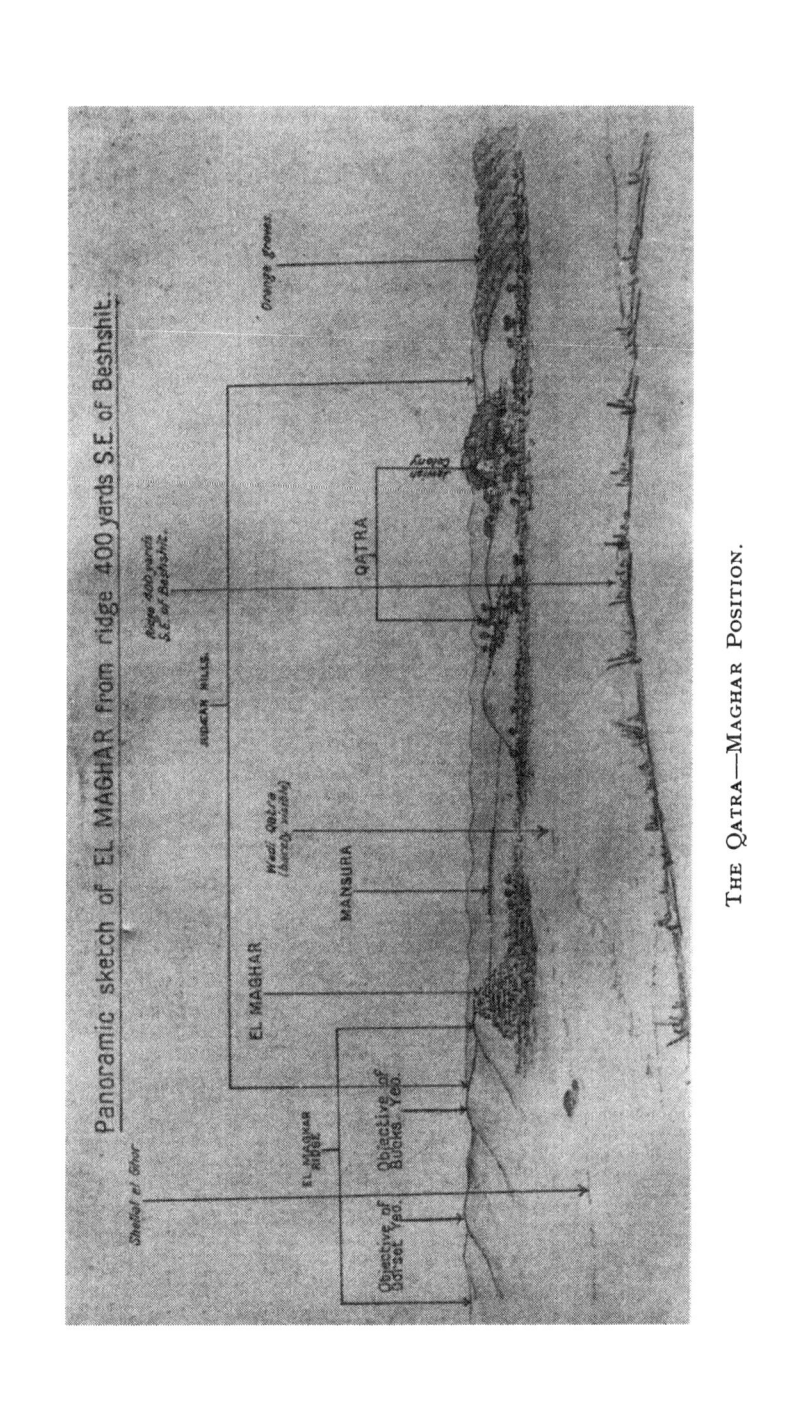

## THE CHARGE OF MAGHAR

Bucks crossing the Dorset's front to rejoin its regiment. They had 4,000 yards to cover and began their advance at the trot, at once drawing some Turkish artillery fire. After trotting a little over a mile, at the end of which they came under heavy but for the most part plunging machine-gun fire, the pace was quickened to a gallop, and the two regiments swept up the hill. The Dorset squadron on the extreme left, which had farthest to go and the horses of which were blown when they reached the ridge, dismounted and advanced to the crest on foot. In front of the Bucks a fox went away between the two lines and was greeted by many view halloas, perhaps taking some minds back for a fraction of time too small to measure to the pleasant Vale of Aylesbury at home.

1917. 13 Nov.

As the charge reached the summit the Turks fled. A number, however, seeing the weakness of the opposition—for the two regiments had lost very heavily, especially in horses, on the top of the ridge—took up positions on the flanks of the attack and opened fire. The arrival of the supporting squadrons and the Hotchkiss sections, which had most fortunately been ordered to ride in the charge, decided the issue. Several hundred prisoners were taken, with two field guns and twelve machine guns, some of which were turned against the retreating Turks and the village, to prevent a counter-attack from its direction. For Maghar itself still held out, and the Berks Yeomanry, which had been brought up by Br.-General Godwin, was ordered to clear it.

Meanwhile Br.-General Pollok-M'Call had made his way forward to the wadi in which was the firing line of the two battalions of Borderers, to reorganize them for their final assault. In the interval a party of about one hundred men of the 4th, advancing in extended order under heavy machine-gun fire, had contrived to reach a shallow wadi 150 yards in advance of this line. When he saw the Yeomanry crossing the plain on his left and realized that it was drawing much of the Turkish fire from his own front, the brigadier decided to wait no longer, but to seize this brief opportunity. Picking up a rifle, he ran out into the open and signalled to the Borderers to follow him. They dashed across the five or six hundred yards of open ground which separated them from the gardens, and by the time the Yeomanry reached the crest beyond Maghar, had hacked for themselves gaps in the hedges and were closing in on the village. Here and there small bodies of the enemy continued to resist stoutly, but for the most part the defenders fled, and after some wild shooting the Borderers captured Maghar, meeting the Berks Yeomanry in its northern skirts and taking four hundred more prisoners.

Opposite Qatra the Scots Fusiliers, under the command of Lieut.-Colonel J. B. Cook of the 5th Battalion, waited for the preliminary bombardment to be carried out according to plan, and then at 3.45 p.m. advanced to the assault. Here the Turkish infantry began to stream back, but the machine gunners for the most part held their ground to the last, inflicting serious losses. Many of them were shot down at point-blank range. By 4 p.m. Qatra was in the hands of the attackers, with four hundred prisoners more.

This remarkable day was not to terminate without another dramatic incident. The 22nd Mounted Brigade (Br.-General F. A. B. Fryer), which was just south of Yibna, was directed to advance on the left of the 6th Mounted Brigade. The leading regiment, the East Riding Yeomanry, was ordered to secure the Maghar Ridge, but apparently received no instructions to push on subsequently to 'Aqir. The brigade went forward at a canter in extended order about half an hour after the 6th had begun its advance, so that the leading squadrons were just crossing the Wadi Jamus when they saw the Dorsets getting up to the crest of the Maghar Ridge. When the East Ridings in their turn reached the crest an extraordinary spectacle met their eyes. The whole steep eastern slope was covered with the running figures of many hundreds of Turks converging on 'Aqir, which lay in full view below. Beyond it were the red roofs of a village of European type, which was not marked on the map in use.

Major J. F. M. Robinson, commanding " A " Squadron East Riding Yeomanry, being unable to find his commanding officer, conferred with two other squadron leaders (one of his own regiment and one of the Staffordshire Yeomanry), and decided to attempt to seize 'Aqir, while the other two cut off flying Turks to the north and north-east. He had only half his squadron at hand and had to leave the bulk of it on the position which he had been ordered to hold, so was

## GALLANT ACTION OF REFET BEY

1917.
13 Nov.

followed only by fifteen men, who scrambled and slid in single file down a water-course, spread out on the lower ground, and raced for 'Aqir, cutting down a number of fugitives as they rode. The little party passed through the village, driving the Turks out of it, and dismounted behind a ridge on the far side, where they used their rifles with great effect against a column retiring across their front at a distance of a thousand yards. Major Robinson set up a helio, but could get no answer to his calls, and finally, as he realized that the bulk of the brigade had not quitted the Maghar Ridge, withdrew. A second squadron of the regiment had moved down on his right and passed south of 'Aqir, but suddenly came under heavy fire and was brought to a halt. What had happened was that Refet Bey, the commander of the Turkish *XXII Corps*, seeing as he thought the whole front broken and the Army in danger of annihilation, had collected his corps headquarters in a wadi near his command post at Ekron or New 'Aqir—the European village of which mention has been made—waited till the squadron was close upon him, and opened fire upon it just as the sun set.[1]

The officers commanding the East Riding and Staffordshire Yeomanry had in the meantime decided, in the absence of orders from brigade headquarters, that as the light was rapidly failing and Ekron appeared to be strongly held by the enemy, it would be impossible to drive him out that night. Shortly afterwards an order arrived from Br.-General Fryer that the brigade would hold the ridge for the night.

As a result of the combined attack of the 6th Mounted

---

[1] " The enemy cavalry which penetrated the front north of El Maghar " immediately turned towards 'Aqir. The sun was about to set. The " corps commander at 'Aqir realized the situation and with all the officers " and men of corps headquarters, mustering about a company, took up a " position south and west of [? New] 'Aqir. The enemy cavalry advanced " rapidly. At a suitable range a heavy fire was opened upon them and " they were thrown into confusion. They continued to advance, however, " until the effect of the fire caused them to hesitate, and finally to halt. " Thus this strong force of cavalry failed to pass a line of skirmishers and " retired. This episode saved the *XXII Corps*." (Turkish " *Yilderim*," Part 4, Chap. III.)

The Turkish account may be exaggerated, because it was not a strong force of cavalry which Refet Bey brought to a halt, but he could doubtless see that there was a strong force just behind on the Maghar Ridge. Major Robinson states that his party saw the Turkish corps commander, mounted on a white horse, riding up and down to organize his defence, and repeatedly fired upon him without success.

## 172 THE CAPTURE OF JUNCTION STATION

and 155th Brigades, the Turkish *XXII Corps* was shattered. Over a thousand prisoners were taken, and over four hundred of the enemy found dead upon the field, though the gardens of Qatra and Maghar were never thoroughly searched. The British also suffered serious loss, the casualties amounting to 616. Of these the losses of the 155th Brigade were 486, the two battalions of the Borderers at Maghar having suffered more than those of the Scots Fusiliers at Qatra. Yet, taking into consideration the strength of the position, these casualties cannot be considered excessive.[1]

The action must always rank as a notable example of the successful employment of all arms on a small scale. Its conduct was as bold and skilful as its execution was gallant. The enterprise of Lieut.-Colonel Cripps in advancing swiftly to the Wadi Jamus and thence despatching officers' patrols, which after a reconnaissance under heavy fire found cover for the machine guns in the Wadi Shellal el Ghor ; the co-ordination by Br.-General Godwin of these machine guns and the Berks Battery in support of the mounted assault ; Br.-General Pollok-M'Call's instant apprehension of the opportunity before him when he caught sight of the Yeomanry advancing, and the inspiration of his personal leadership ; all these factors make the attack well worth study. Yet none of them would have availed had these officers not been in command of troops imbued with the offensive spirit, confident of success, and ready to sacrifice themselves to attain it.[2]

---

[1] The casualties by brigades are as follows :—

6TH MOUNTED BRIGADE.

|  | Killed. | Wounded. | Missing. |
|---|---|---|---|
| Officers . . | 1 | 6 | — |
| Other Ranks . | 15 | 108 | — |

155TH BRIGADE.

| Officers . . | 5 | 19 | — |
|---|---|---|---|
| Other ranks . | 79 | 373 | 10 |

The 6th Mounted Brigade had 265 casualties to horses.

[2] It must be added that this account, though written with the help of all information now available, fails to clear up a controversial point. On the Yeomanry side it is stated that the Berks took Maghar on foot, no infantry being in the village till after it was taken. On that of the infantry it is declared that the Scottish Borderers captured the village, and the Yeomanry collected the prisoners. It is for this reason that no precise figures are given for the prisoners captured on the ridge and in the village respectively.

## AN OPPORTUNITY LOST

Yet it would appear that a still heavier blow might have been dealt the enemy had the 22nd Mounted Brigade been pushed forward to 'Aqir. It must be remembered that, though the capture of Junction Station has already been recorded, the troops of the 75th Division were at this time not far north of Mesmiye el Gharbiye. A mounted brigade at 'Aqir would have been astride one of the two roads along which the enemy could retreat to Ramle (the Mesmiye–'Aqir–Ramle road), and within striking distance of the other (the Junction Station–Ne'ane–Ramle road) and the railway itself. The 6th Mounted Brigade after its very heavy loss in horses was hardly in a position to pursue, and had, moreover, first to see that Maghar was secured; but there seems no doubt from Major Robinson's testimony that if two regiments of the 22nd had pressed forward there was little to stop them. In the words of the Turkish historian, the Turkish *Eighth Army* was threatened by " irretrievable " disaster." 'Aqir was not actually occupied until 6 a.m. on the 14th, by which time the bulk of the Turks retreating from Junction Station had passed northwards to Ramle.

On the left the Middlesex Yeomanry of the 8th Brigade entered Zernuqa at 9 p.m. The Camel Brigade was now concentrated at Yibna. As the Yeomanry Mounted Division had swung right-handed, the A. & N.Z. Mounted Division had moved up on its left, pushing forward the 1st L.H. Brigade and the newly joined New Zealand Brigade to watch the country between Yibna and the sea.

The 156th and 157th Brigades of the 52nd Division were by nightfall disposed as follows:—the 156th Brigade, less two battalions, was between Qatra and the 75th Division. These two battalions were at Beshshit, where were also headquarters and two battalions of the 157th Brigade. The two remaining battalions of the 157th were at Yibna.

On the front of the Australian Mounted Division the enemy had been found on the morning of the 13th to be holding Barqusya in strength, but there was no sign of a renewal of his counter-offensive. The Turk had, indeed, shot his bolt, and the necessity of defending Junction Station, while it was being cleared as far as possible of its huge accumulation of stores, prevented him from following up the slight advantage he had gained against the British right flank. He was, however, strong enough to hold his

1917.
13 Nov.

Map 9.
Sketch 10.

ground against the Australian Mounted Division, which made no general progress all day save when a way was cleared for it by the advance of the infantry. The 5th Mounted Brigade had had many casualties to its horses in the fighting of the last few days, and the remainder were suffering seriously for want of water. Major-General Hodgson therefore asked General Chauvel to relieve this brigade by the 7th, which was in corps reserve. His request was granted, and the 5th Brigade moved back during the afternoon to Hatte for water and rest. At 11.30 the 4th L.H. Brigade was ordered to advance and cover the right of the 75th Division; its timely assistance at Mesmiye esh Sherqiye has already been mentioned. In the afternoon the 7th Mounted Brigade was brought up on its right, and by dusk the outposts of the two brigades ran from the right of the infantry, on the main road a mile and a half north-east of Mesmiye, to south-east of Tell et Turmus, a front of nearly four miles facing east. The 3rd L.H. Brigade was further south, at Jelediye, watching the right flank. Here, however, there was no danger, for the enemy began to withdraw from his position at Barqusya before nightfall as a result of events upon other parts of the battle-front.

During the night the enemy also evacuated Et Tine, the junction of the railway lines which had supplied the two flanks of the old Turkish Gaza–Beersheba front, and it was entered by the 4th L.H. Brigade at 6.30 a.m. on the 14th. Considerable booty was captured at the station. The brigade was ordered to water here, while the 7th Mounted Brigade pushed on to support the right of the 234th Brigade in its advance on Junction Station. The 7th Mounted Brigade marched up the railway, passing through Et Tine at 7 a.m. The Field Squadron Australian Engineers of the division, with an escort from the 7th Mounted Brigade, was ordered to advance rapidly and destroy the railway bridge half a mile north of Junction Station. Too literally interpreting its orders, it did so after the station was in British hands and there were actually posts on the railway north of the bridge.

## OPERATIONS FROM THE 14TH TO THE 16TH NOVEMBER.

The 14th November was employed in carrying out the portion of the programme which had not been completed by daybreak. The enemy was in full retreat, the *Eighth Army* to the line Jaffa–Lydda, with a detachment covering Ramle and another Latron, the junction of the Jaffa-Jerusalem road with that from Junction Station; the *XX Corps* of the *Seventh Army* falling back eastward to a position astride the Junction Station–Latron road near Khulda. As a consequence there was no serious fighting on this date except in the case of the New Zealand Brigade, which was heavily engaged at Nes Ziyona.

On the front of the Australian Mounted Division troops of the 4th L.H. Brigade entered Qezaze, 2 miles S.S.E. of Junction Station, at midday, the 7th Mounted Brigade on its left then being half a mile south-east of the station. The 2nd L.H. Brigade (A. & N.Z. Mounted Division), the horses of which were fairly fresh, had been ordered to move across the front and come under the orders of the Australian Mounted Division. This division had now attached to it no less than five brigades: the 2nd, 3rd, and 4th L.H. Brigades, the 5th and 7th Mounted Brigades, in addition to two cars of the 12th L.A.M. Battery. It came temporarily under the orders of General Bulfin, owing to the great distance from General Chauvel's headquarters at Suafir el Gharbiye of its advanced troops.

Neither the 75th nor 52nd Divisions came in contact with the enemy. The 233rd Brigade marched north to a position south of Mansura, which it reached after nightfall, while the 234th consolidated the ground north of Junction Station and hauled out the engines to preserve them from Turkish shell fire. On the front of the 52nd Division a composite brigade, formed of the four battalions in Beshshit, with almost all the artillery at the disposal of the division, and detachments of cavalry, engineers and medical services, was put under the orders of Br.-General Hamilton Moore, who was ordered to occupy Mansura. The enemy quickly evacuated the place, which was occupied at 10.30 a.m., and the Composite Brigade then took up a position with the village as its centre, facing north and east.

On the left of the 52nd Division the Yeomanry Mounted

Division continued its advance. After the occupation of 'Aqir the 22nd Mounted Brigade marched on the railway, where it picked up 72 prisoners. The East Riding Yeomanry seized Ne'ane at 10 a.m. The whole division then moved across the railway, finding itself at once on much rougher and more hilly ground than that on which the recent action had been fought, and took up a position facing the village of Abu Shushe, 4 miles north-east of Junction Station, in touch with the Composite Brigade.

The A. & N.Z. Mounted Division had now two brigades only at its disposal: the 1st L.H. and N.Z.M.R. Major-General Chaytor ordered the 1st Brigade to advance through Zernuqa and reconnoitre towards Ramle, the New Zealanders to march through Qubeibe upon the Jewish colonies to the north along the Wadi Hanein. Zernuqa and Qubeibe were taken over by the 2nd Battalion Camel Brigade after the horse had passed through, while the 3rd Battalion covered 'Aqir; a detachment of the 4th Battalion at Major-General Chaytor's disposal watched his left in the dunes.

At 9.50 a.m. the 1st L.H. Brigade occupied the village of Rehovoth or Deiran, south-west of Ramle, a fine Jewish colony, the widely separated buildings of which covered some three hundred acres and were surrounded by vineyards, orange groves, and gardens. Great was the astonishment of the troops as its excellent red-tiled houses, its synagogue, wine-presses, and factory, came in view; for its site on their map was marked only by the words "Khirbet Deiran," or the ruins of Deiran, and there had not been a house upon it when Conder and Kitchener surveyed Palestine. This was one of the largest of the colonies founded by wealthy Jews for their people in the latter part of the nineteenth century. Jewish colonies were henceforth to be met with in numbers in the rich plain. The main body of the Yeomanry Mounted Division were at this moment watering in the little one, Ekron or New 'Aqir, east of the old Arab village of 'Aqir; the New Zealanders were about to have fighting for two more: Nes Ziyona or Wadi Hanein, a comparatively small but well-built village, and Rishon le Ziyon, north of it, a large and important settlement. These settlements, and the warm welcome received from their inhabitants, were to represent to the troops the pleasantest aspect of the operations in the Philistine Plain. Even fair-sized Arab towns like Majdal and Yibna made to them 1917. no such appeal as the Jewish villages, in which they found 14 Nov. dwellings and a mode of existence resembling those of their own distant countries. It was not merely that they were able to purchase here many comforts, including wine of very fair quality, which they could not procure from the natives; the chief comfort was the discovery of a civilization entirely unsuspected and a social life recalling that which they knew but for the most part had not seen for over two years; and even though little English was spoken by the colonists the British and Australian soldiers at once felt themselves at home. The Jews for their part were delighted to be rid of the Turks. They had suffered a good deal at their hands, but generally speaking had not been actively ill-treated.

West of the villages of Sarafand el Harab and Nes Ziyona the Turks were found to be holding a strong position.[1] The Canterbury Regiment on the right was held up by the enemy in the orange groves of Nes Ziyona and took all the afternoon to expel him from the villages. West of the Wadi Hanein the Wellington and Auckland Regiments at first advanced quicker over the more open but hillocky country, their left on the edge of the dunes. The Somerset Battery supported the attack from north of Qubeibe. The Turkish position was in form of an inverted " L," one arm pointing in the direction of the Wellington Regiment, the other at right angles to the line of advance of the two regiments. By 1.30 p.m. the projecting arm had been rolled up by the successive rushes of the Wellington Regiment, and the Turks had been driven back from their main position on the ridge south of the groves of Rishon le Ziyon.

Meanwhile considerable bodies of Turks were seen moving on Rishon le Ziyon from the east. At 2.30 p.m. a counter-attack was launched against the Wellingtons and beaten off by their machine-gun fire. Next a Turkish battery was run forward under cover of the trees and opened fire at a range of 1,200 yards. Another counter-attack, two or three hundred strong, was launched against the Aucklands, the Turks approaching in places to within fifteen yards and making use of hand-grenades. The enemy's machine

---

[1] The action which followed was known to the Force as that of 'Ayun ('Uyun) Qara from the Arabic name of Rishon le Ziyon.

guns were handled with skill and boldness. One of them, which was causing heavy loss, was seized by a troop of the Wellingtons, which galloped up to the foot of the knoll from which it was firing, dismounted, and charged on foot. At 4.15 p.m. a squadron of the same regiment carried out a bayonet charge against the enemy who had established himself close to its line, and hurled him back. Soon afterwards the Turks desisted from their efforts and fell back beyond Rishon le Ziyon, leaving behind them five machine guns, two Lewis guns, and about one hundred and fifty dead. Their strength was estimated to have been 1,500, with a great number of machine guns—some of them with prismatic sights—and automatic rifles. In truth it would appear that the bulk of the much-depleted *3rd Division* was engaged against the New Zealanders.[1] The casualties of the latter numbered 175.[2]

After midnight on the 14th November General Chauvel issued orders to the Yeomanry and A. & N.Z. Mounted Divisions to continue the advance on Ramle and Lydda in accordance with the plan previously decided upon. The Camel Brigade, less a detachment from the 3rd and 4th Battalions, which was to watch the coast west of the A. & N.Z. Mounted Division, was attached to the Yeomanry Mounted Division. Major-General Barrow had already, at 8.10 p.m on the 14th, issued orders for the capture of the Abu Shushe Ridge, towards which Br.-General Godwin had advanced with the Berkshire Yeomanry that afternoon and which he had found to be strongly held. Major-General Barrow was not minded to leave this dominating position, which rose boldly out of the plain, a sort of natural outpost of the Judæan Hills, on his right flank as he moved on Ramle. It was, however, a difficult objective to set to cavalry, for it could be seen through glasses to be rough-faced and studded with great boulders. Near the northern end was the village of Abu Shushe ; a mile and a quarter to the south-west and on the lower slopes the smaller village of Sidun. The ground between the railway and the ridge rose gradually, but was

---

[1] " Hostile cavalry followed up the *3rd Division* along the coast, " pressing it still further back." (Turkish " *Yilderim*," Part 4, Chap. IV.)

[2]

|  | Killed. | Wounded. |
|---|---|---|
| Officers . . . | 3 | 11 |
| Other Ranks . . | 29 | 132 |

## CAPTURE OF ABU SHUSHE RIDGE

undulating and afforded fair cover. The 6th Mounted Brigade was to advance against the ridge from the west and the 22nd from the north-west. The 3rd Battalion Camel Brigade was to co-operate from a position on the railway and to fill any gap that might appear between the two brigades. The divisional commander directed that the attack should be carried out " as far as possible mounted," in accordance with the principle which he always maintained that, whether or not a mounted attack could be pushed home, the best way to cross the fire-swept zone was at a gallop.

1917. 15 Nov.

Br.-General Godwin, who had reconnoitred the position at daybreak, ordered the Berks Battery into action against the southern part of the ridge, and the Berkshire Yeomanry (less one squadron) to move forward against the highest point upon it. Directly this attack—which was to be made dismounted—was checked, the Bucks Yeomanry was to advance mounted on the right against the lower southern slopes.

Lieut.-Colonel the Hon. F. H. Cripps, whose regiment had suffered heavily in the charge at Maghar, was now in command of two composite squadrons of his own Bucks Hussars and one of Berkshire Yeomanry. The Berks squadron he pushed forward dismounted with six machine guns, to bring covering fire to bear on the ridge. Then he led forward the Bucks squadrons at a gallop and took up a position on the right of the machine guns, about a thousand yards north-west of Sidun, in dead ground. Seeing that the enemy was strong in machine guns on his right flank, he signalled for support, whereupon Br.-General Godwin ordered his reserve regiment, the Dorset Yeomanry, to advance on the right of the Bucks. The Berks Battery R.H.A. moved forward from the railway to support the attack. The 22nd Mounted Brigade, supported by the Leicester Battery, had meanwhile begun its advance on Abu Shushe from the north-west, the 8th Mounted Brigade covering its left flank.

The leading squadron of the Dorsets charged straight through the village of Sidun and on toward the higher ground beyond it. The led horses of the Bucks, which had been withdrawn a little for safety, were galloped up, and the regiment joined in the charge. Swinging left-handed, it made for the highest point of the ridge, a thousand yards south of Abu Shushe. Scrambling through the rocks, the horses, though slipping often, yet for the most part kept their feet. The Berks Yeomanry, after the enemy on its front had fallen back, mounted and followed the Dorsets on to the ridge. The final attack on the crest had to be made dismounted, but the Turks were now thoroughly shaken and made no great resistance. Three hundred and fifty were captured, and at least as many killed with the sword or by fire. The 22nd Mounted Brigade, coming up dismounted on the left, found the northern part of the ridge evacuated, but the fire of the Staffordshire Yeomanry inflicted heavy loss upon the flying enemy. The Berks Battery moved swiftly up to Sidun after it was taken and shelled the Turks retiring from the ridge and also a large column seen behind, which was thrown into confusion. In the evening the Camel Brigade took over the ridge from the Yeomanry.

The difficulty of Camel Corps supporting mounted troops in an action of this nature was proved by the fact that the 3rd Battalion Camel Brigade had advanced only a mile from the railway when the attack was delivered. On the other hand the Berks Yeomanry and the 22nd Mounted Brigade, though likewise attacking dismounted, were able to canter forward two miles. The value of Hotchkiss sections accompanying the regiments in a mounted attack was again clearly proved. They came into action directly the crest was reached, and the Bucks Hussars counted over a hundred Turks killed by their fire in a gully.

This was the second successful mounted action in the course of three days, and another good example of the co-operation of artillery and machine guns with cavalry. It was even more daring than that of Maghar owing to the rocky ground, but the effect of that action had been to make the Turks less ready to face a cavalry charge; consequently their shooting was wild, and casualties very low. Those of the 6th Mounted Brigade were 37; one officer only was killed, Major the Hon. Neil Primrose,[1] who had been until recently Under-Secretary of State for Foreign Affairs.

---

[1] Major Primrose's cousin, Major Evelyn de Rothschild, second-in-command of the Bucks Yeomanry, died soon afterwards in hospital of wounds received at Maghar; two members of the Rothschild family thus being killed as the force entered the area of the Jewish colonies, which that family had played the chief part in founding.

On the right of the Yeomanry Division the Australian Mounted Division, directed on 'Amwas, made little progress in very rough country. Observing the success of the charge above described, Br.-General J. T. Wigan, commanding the 7th Mounted Brigade, ordered the South Notts Hussars to cut off the enemy's retreat along the Jerusalem road. The regiment was, however, held up by machine guns on the southern flank of the ridge, which had not been affected by the charge, and was withdrawn by Br.-General Wigan, though not before it had found some good targets for its Hotchkiss guns. After the successful attack of the Yeomanry Mounted Division the 234th Brigade of the 75th Division advanced east of the railway and took up a position between it and the Jerusalem road near Khulda.

1917.
15 Nov.

In the plain on the left the A. & N.Z. Mounted Division met with little or no opposition, the Turks having drawn off from its front after their severe handling by the New Zealand Brigade the previous day. The 2nd A.L.H. of the 1st Brigade and the Inverness Battery entered Ramle—a squalid little town, without the historical associations of many of the villages in its neighbourhood—at 11 a.m. The 1st A.L.H. then advanced quickly up the road towards Lydda, caught up a retreating Turkish column which was too weary and demoralized to offer any resistance, and captured nearly three hundred prisoners. The much more interesting town of Lydda—interesting to Englishmen, if for no other reason than because of its association with their patron saint; for it is the reputed scene of his martyrdom and contains a tomb said to be his—was then occupied without resistance. Major-General Chaytor, observing that the enemy was in full retreat, referred back to corps headquarters the order previously received to cut the railway a mile north of Lydda. He was bidden, by what appears to have been an error of judgment, to carry out the order, and this was done in the course of the night by a demolition party of the A. & N.Z. Field Squadron. The New Zealand Brigade moved up through Rishon le Ziyon to the Jaffa–Lydda road.

The general result of these operations had been to split in two the Turkish forces. The *Eighth Army* of Kress, consisting now of the *3rd, 7th, 16th,* and *54th Divisions,* was still in the coast area and upon the main line of railway communication. Fevzi's *Seventh Army* had been driven into the Judæan Hills, and its only railway was that to Jerusalem, which ended there. Its supplies had therefore to be brought by road from Nablus to Jerusalem, a distance of 40 miles, though a certain quantity came from the Hejaz Railway at 'Amman by way of the indifferent road through Jericho, 60 miles in length.

NOTE.

TURKISH MOVEMENTS FROM 13TH TO 15TH NOVEMBER.

It is not easy to reconstruct the chain of command on the Turkish side at this moment, though the dispositions of the troops are clear enough. It appears that the *Eighth Army* (Kress) had under its command the *XXII Corps* (*3rd* and *7th Divisions*) and, directly, the *16th* and *54th Divisions*. The *XX Corps* (*26th* and *53rd Divisions*) had been receiving its orders direct from *Yilderim*, but it strictly formed part of the *Seventh Army* (Fevzi), which thus consisted of three groups : *XX Corps* east of the Beersheba Railway ; *3rd Cavalry* and *19th Divisions* about Beit Jibrin ; *III Corps* (*24th* and *27th Divisions*) on the Hebron road.

As already stated, the *16th Division* and attached *57th Regiment*, known temporarily as the *Hergott Group*, had been withdrawn by Falkenhayn from the *XX Corps* to serve as a reserve to the *Eighth Army* on the evening of the 12th November, thus making it impossible for the *XX Corps* to continue its counter-attack against the Australian Mounted Division.[1] The *16th Division* consisted of only two regiments mustering 600 rifles apiece, but the *57th Regiment* (which actually belonged to the *19th Division*) was fresh and strong, its two battalions probably mustering another 1,200 rifles. As soon as the British drove the troops of the *54th Division* out of Mesmiye, Kress decided to employ the *Hergott Group* to carry out a counter-attack,[2] but according to the Turkish historian, who comments severely upon the "tiredness and demoralization of Army headquarters," it was unable to find the group.[3] Finally the *Hergott Group* was withdrawn to Ramle without being engaged on the 13th. The troops defeated at Maghar consisted of the *XXII Corps* (*3rd* and *7th Divisions*), which was on the line Zernuqa, Maghar, Qatra. On the events of this day Hussein Husni comments shrewdly :—

"Unfortunately there was a lack of good communication between the "*Seventh Army*, *XX Corps*, and *Beit Jibrin Group* (*3rd Cavalry* and *19th* "*Divisions*), and advantage could not be taken of the ever-changing "situation. Wireless stations and telephone detachments could not give "assistance owing to the retreat and the continual movement. On the "12th and 13th we were on exterior lines. The chief virtue of forces "acting on exterior lines is their ability to converge on a given point, but "such forces must act without hesitation and with rapidity, as the enemy "on interior lines can beat in detail separated forces which are out of reach "of each other."

---

[1] See p. 155.
[2] It is curious that Falkenhayn, whose reports were as a rule candid, telegraphed to Constantinople that night that Mesmiye was recovered by a counter-attack.
[3] Turkish "*Yilderim*," Part 4, Chap. III.

# ENVER PASHA AT JERUSALEM

On the evening of the 13th Falkenhayn issued orders for both Armies to withdraw " to a more favourable line." The *Eighth Army* was to withdraw to the line Jaffa-Lydda, maintaining a group to keep touch with the *Seventh Army* in the " Barriye hills." [1] The *Seventh Army* was to take up a position astride the Junction Station-'Amwas road about Khulda with its *XX Corps (26th* and *53rd Divisions*), the *19th Division* to block the road leading from Beit Jibrin to Bethlehem, while the *3rd Cavalry Division* maintained touch between it and the *III Corps*—now a mere shell—astride the Hebron road.

That evening Enver Pasha visited Falkenhayn at Jerusalem, and, according to Hussein Husni, at dinner the Vice-Generalissimo was " more " gay and more optimistic than usual." Enver and Falkenhayn discussed the question of the defence of Jerusalem, and decided that it must not entail a siege ; in other words, that the garrison must not be allowed to be shut up in it if the troops on the flanks of the city were driven back.

With regard to the capture of Junction Station on the morning of the 14th November, Hussein Husni states that he had made all arrangements for the destruction of the buildings and sidings two days before, but that the station commander and engineer officer abandoned their posts.

By the 15th November the Armies had completed their retreat, the *Eighth* being on the line Jaffa-Yehudiye-Jimzu,[2] the *Seventh* in touch with its left near Jimzu and holding a very extended line to Yutta, south of Hebron. No mention is made in the Turkish account of the capture of the Abu Shushe ridge, which appears to have been defended by the *54th Division*, but the *XX Corps* astride the Junction Station-'Amwas road is described as having repulsed three attacks. In fact the only movement against it remotely resembling an attack was the advance of the South Notts Hussars on Khulda. Otherwise the operations of the Australian Mounted Division were in the nature of a reconnaissance in force.

---

[1] Barriye, on the Jaffa-Jerusalem road, is itself not on very high ground, and the reference is doubtless to the Abu Shushe ridge, the village of Abu Shushe being $2\frac{1}{4}$ miles south of Barriye.

[2] Yehudiye, 8 miles E.S.E. of Jaffa ; Jimzu, 3 miles south-east of Lydda.

# CHAPTER IX.

## THE ADVANCE INTO THE JUDÆAN HILLS AND BATTLE OF NABI SAMWEIL.

(Maps 1, 2, 10, 12; Sketches A, 12, 13, 20; Diagram I).

### THE PLANS AND THE COUNTRY.

**1917.**
**16 Nov.**
**Maps 1, 2.**

A SHORT pause was now necessary to prepare for the advance into the Judæan Hills, during which no operations took place but for the occupation of Jaffa and a reconnaissance towards 'Amwas, on the Jerusalem–Jaffa road, on the 16th November. The march of the New Zealand Brigade on Jaffa met with no opposition except from a few snipers, and the troops rode light-heartedly, plucking oranges from the trees as they passed through the groves. The Wellington Regiment entered the town about 10 a.m., to be warmly welcomed by the remaining inhabitants—about 8,000 out of a normal population thrice as big. Jaffa, one of the oldest towns in the world, does not ill deserve its name, which means "Beauty." On this occasion it had escaped the destruction which had been its fate so often in former wars, and contained abundance of wine and fruit. The Yeomanry Mounted Division had meanwhile found 'Amwas strongly held.

The loss of Junction Station, and the necessity of opposing the British advance in the plain on the one hand and of defending Jerusalem on the other, had split the Turkish forces in two. On the right the *Eighth Army* had retired to the line of the Nahr el 'Auja, which enters the sea 4 miles N.N.E. of Jaffa; on the left the *Seventh Army* had been forced into the hills. It was Sir Edmund Allenby's intention to contain the *Eighth Army* in the plain, follow the *Seventh Army* eastward into the hills before it could reorganize, and capture Jerusalem.

With regard to supply the situation was now easier so far as the troops in the Philistine Plain were concerned, but great difficulties were ahead when transport in the hill

PALESTINE. THE LIE OF THE LAND

Diagram I

country came to be considered. On the 17th November 1917. the landing place was shifted 17 miles north, from the mouth of the Wadi el Hesi to that of the Nahr Suqreir. It was thus possible on the following day to move the main supply depot of the XXI Corps from Deir Sneid to Yibna, an advance of over 20 miles, and to employ a whole company of the Camel Transport Corps in moving stores to that point from the new landing place. Within the next few days, however, heavy rains damaged the Gaza–Junction Station road, and at the same time bad weather temporarily put an end to the landing of stores at the mouth of the Nahr Suqreir.

The time was now approaching when the Turkish railway from Junction Station to Beit Hanun was to be of great value. It had been repaired as the advance up the Philistine Plain progressed, in the hope that rolling stock would be captured, but only one derailed engine and a few trucks came into the hands of the British until Junction Station was occupied. By the 20th November this line was working up to Junction Station, the invaluable but very worn engines and the trucks there taken being used. Four new engines arrived from Egypt on the 24th, and on the 1st December seven trains, each carrying about one hundred tons, ran to Junction Station. On the 5th the line was opened to Ramle and Lydda. The British standard-gauge railway had meanwhile advanced slowly across the difficult dune-country about Gaza to Deir Sneid, three Railway Construction Companies R.E., with Egyptian Labour Corps, being at work on it. It reached Deir Sneid on the 27th November, thus freeing a number of lorries hitherto required to fill the gap between the two lines, and a reloading station was laid out for the swift transfer of supplies from one gauge to the other. It had been necessary to cease work on the doubling of the railway in Sinai in order to make preparations for the offensive against the Gaza–Beersheba position. On the 1st November this work was resumed, but at first with only a small construction party, the great bulk of the labour, skilled and unskilled, being required further forward.

Though these details of railway progress have been here recorded, it must be borne in mind that at the moment when the advance into the hills began the British railway was practically no further forward than at the opening of the Third Battle of Gaza and that the Turkish railway had not been taken into use. The necessity for a swift pursuit therefore increased the already hard problem of maintaining a force in the Judæan highlands.

Map 1.
Diagram I.
The physical features of Palestine are extraordinary. So strong was their influence upon this campaign, as upon the innumerable campaigns of the past, that they require detailed description. From west to east there are four distinct topographical provinces: the plain skirting the Mediterranean, the hill country which rises out of it, the great trough of the Jordan Valley and the Dead Sea, known to the Arabs as " El Ghor," and the high plateau beyond the Ghor. The coast plain (known as the Plain of the Philistines to approximately the Nahr el 'Auja and as the Plain of Sharon further north) is some ten miles wide and from one to three hundred feet in height. It is covered with soil which, light on the uplands, is rich and dark in the valleys, though along the shore the sand has encroached seriously upon it and is yearly encroaching further. It is virtually without stone fit for road-making. The hill range consists of a saddle-shaped block of limestone, rising to a regular crest, in general just under 3,000 feet high, then dropping to far below sea-level. On the western flank of this range the foot-hills are in parts separated from it by shallow valleys running north and south, so that they appear to be a distinct lower ridge outlying the higher, and justify the bestowal upon them of a separate name—the Shephelah. On its eastern flank the range sinks to the Ghor, one of the most curious features of the earth's surface. This is a rift forming a gigantic trench, the bottom of which is by far the lowest ground not covered by water in the world. At the Jordan's mouth the floor of this rift is more than 1,200 feet below sea-level. In the Dead Sea itself a sounding of over 1,300 feet has been taken, making its bottom about 2,600 feet below sea-level and 6,000 feet below Hebron, 20 miles to the west. East of the Ghor the Plateau of Moab rises steeply to a height about equal to that of the spine of the Judæan Hills. All these features are contained within a strip of land scarcely more than fifty miles in breadth from the sea at Jaffa to the top of the plateau near Es Salt.

The history of the Jewish Kingdom or Kingdoms of

Palestine was moulded by the configuration of the country. The Jews could not, except at rare intervals, occupy the coast plain, but the hills were their salvation. In them they were preserved while army after army swept up and down the plain, the great high-road to Egypt, all the more important because the coast is almost without harbours. The Philistines were superior to them in weapons, but, while Egyptians and Assyrians ravaged the cities of the Philistines and finally extinguished them, the Jews remained. They might be conquered in turn by Philistine, Assyrian, Babylonian, Persian, Macedonian; but their state survived until the methodical, road-making Roman brought it to an end.

At the latitude of Lydda the foot-hills of the Shephelah begin 12 miles from the sea. Eastward thence the country changes swiftly in character. The fertile plain, covered with orange groves, vineyards, ploughland, and pasture, gives place to a series of spurs running east and west, often barren and boulder-strewn, in places of naked rock, separated by steep-sided, narrow valleys. Many of the hills are artificially terraced. There is occasionally cultivation on their flanks, the soil being held in place against the winter rains by stone walls, while the bottoms of the larger wadis are often fertile, yielding crops of olives and barley. In general, however, it is a hard, stony country, in which a man must toil to earn his bread, and after the months of summer sun almost a wilderness. To-day it is apparently more thinly cultivated than in old times, though the western slope, which has the heavier rainfall and the slower drainage, is more fruitful and supports more inhabitants than the eastern. The hills lack the majesty which great height bestows, but have a wild and strange beauty that is impressive enough—their strangeness being rather increased by the regularity of their shape and their rounded, dome-like tops. The chief towns are close to the watershed: Hebron, Bethlehem, and Jerusalem being just east of it, Ram Allah just west.

One fair road ran from north to south of the hill country, through Nablus, Jerusalem, and Hebron to Beersheba, keeping close to the crest-line. The only good road running eastward from the plain at this date was that from Jaffa through Ramle and Qaryet el 'Inab to Jerusalem. It entered the hills by the Vale of Ajalon near 'Amwas, 9 miles south-east of Ramle, and 2 miles further on ran through a celebrated and easily defensible pass known as the Bab el Wad. The Jaffa – Lydda – Beit Liqya – Jerusalem road further north was of fair quality in the plain, but in the hills degenerated into little more than a bridle-path.

The water supply in the plain is in general good when time is available to develop it ; that is to say, water is always found at sea-level, though it varies in salinity, being bad about Gaza, improving gradually to northward, and becoming quite sweet at Jaffa. In the populated districts there are many wells, some of them very ancient. Where the orange was cultivated there were, even before the war, wells in the nature of bore-holes, of unlimited capacity. In the hills the situation is quite different. Here there are occasional springs, but when these are lacking the villagers save the water of the rainy season in large rock-cisterns, lined with plaster and shaped like ginger-jars. During the rains, of course, the hills are seamed with swift-flowing streams.

The Commander-in-Chief had decided to cut the Nablus road at Ram Allah and Bire, 8 miles north of Jerusalem, thus avoiding any risk of damage to the Holy City. His original intention was to hold the line he had gained in the Philistine Plain with the XXI Corps and one mounted division, while the remainder of the Desert Mounted Corps, to be supported by a division of the XX Corps, moved eastward into the hills. The other divisions of the XX Corps (less the 53rd on the Hebron Road) were to be brought up as soon as possible. Orders to this effect were actually issued on the 16th November. Major-General Walter Campbell, the Deputy Quartermaster-General, informed him, however, that he could not maintain more than one additional infantry division until the Turkish railway was working ; so the project was abandoned. The difficulty of ammunition supply remained ; for that was dependent rather upon the amount of fighting than upon the number of mouths to be fed. The third division of the XXI Corps, the 54th, now had its leading brigade north of Yibna. Sir Edmund Allenby therefore decided to hold the front in the plain with this division and the A. & N.Z. Mounted Division, while the Australian, Yeomanry, 52nd and 75th Divisions carried out the operation in the hills. The two mounted divisions were ordered to begin their advance on the 18th, the first task of

Sketch 12.

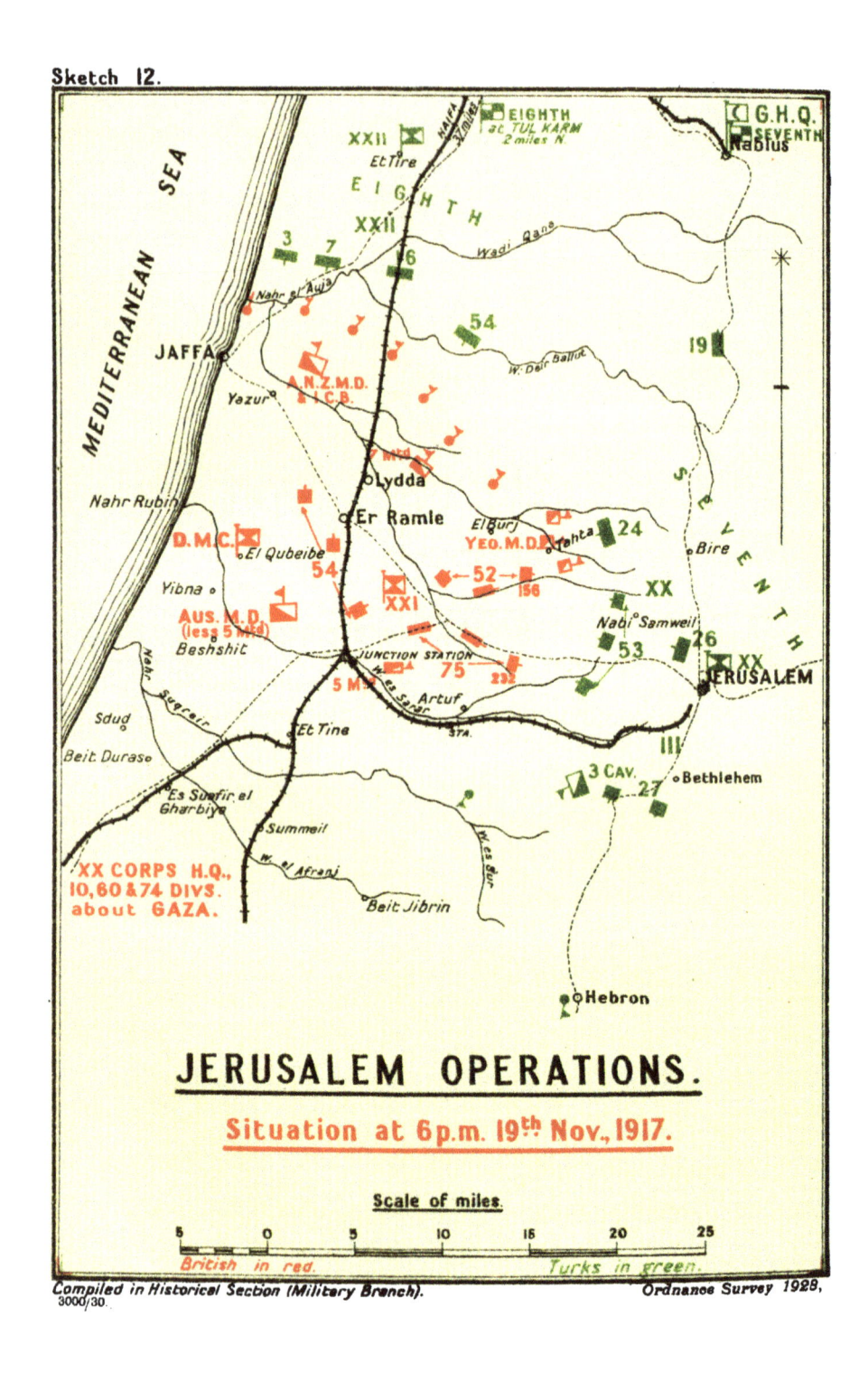

# JERUSALEM OPERATIONS.

Situation at 6 p.m. 19th Nov., 1917.

Scale of miles.

British in red.   Turks in green.

Compiled in Historical Section (Military Branch).   Ordnance Survey 1928.

THE ADVANCE INTO THE HILLS    189

the Australian Division being the capture of 'Amwas, in order to secure the heights on either side of the Jaffa-Jerusalem road. However, at a conference held by Sir Edmund Allenby on the 18th at XXI Corps headquarters at El Qastine it was decided that the advance up the main road should be carried out on the following day by the 75th Division, and the attack of the Australians was cancelled. Not receiving the order of recall, the 9th A.L.H. carried out a remarkable turning movement up the Wadi es Selman, north of 'Amwas, and reached the village of Yalo, 2 miles east of it. It was probably as a result of this bold advance that the 75th Division found 'Amwas evacuated the following day.

1917.
18 Nov.

Though the infantry was to take over the task originally allotted to the Australian Mounted Division, the Yeomanry Mounted Division's advance was not cancelled. Its orders were to move straight on Ram Allah by way of Beit 'Ur et Tahta, the Lower Bethoron of the Bible, a hill village 7 miles north-east of 'Amwas. The advanced guard of the 8th Mounted Brigade, the 3rd County of London Yeomanry, struggled forward to within two miles of Beit 'Ur et Tahta by an abominable road, and the 22nd Mounted Brigade reached Shilta. Nearly all wheeled transport and the Leicester Battery had to be sent back to Ramle, the Hong Kong Mountain Battery being attached to the division instead of the horse artillery.

Meanwhile on the coast patrols of the A. & N.Z. Mounted Division, to which the 7th Mounted Brigade was now attached, found the crossings of the perennial Nahr el 'Auja strongly held by the enemy.

THE FIRST STAGE OF THE ADVANCE, 19TH–20TH NOVEMBER.

General Bulfin's orders assigned to the 75th Division the one metalled road. It was to seize 'Amwas by noon on the 19th and then advance to Qaryet el 'Inab, 7 miles E.S.E. of Amwas. Meanwhile the 52nd Division was to advance by the Lydda–Jerusalem road to Beit Liqya, 5 miles north-east of 'Amwas.[1] On the following day it was General Bulfin's intention to get " astride the Jerusalem–Bire road,

19 Nov.
Maps 2, 10.
Sketches
A, 12.

---

[1] XXI Corps Order No. 14 is given in Appendix 16.

" in the neighbourhood of Bire, and cut off the troops " retreating from Jerusalem." Reports from the air of columns moving north in the direction of Nablus had given the impression that the enemy was evacuating Jerusalem. This was a complete, though natural, error. Falkenhayn was, in fact, merely moving the *III Corps*, hitherto on his left flank, north of Jerusalem to hold the Nablus road, while the *XX Corps* was to fall back and undertake the defence of the city itself. The reason for this move was mainly personal. Falkenhayn did not desire that the defence should be conducted by the young corps commander who had suffered disaster at Beersheba. He hoped that Ali Fuad, who had shown ability in the retreat, would put up a more vigorous resistance—a hope which was not destined to be fulfilled.[1]

The 75th Division's right was to be covered by the 5th Mounted Brigade of the Australian Mounted Division. It had also at its disposal " B " Battery IX British Mountain Artillery Brigade, the 12th Light Armoured Motor Battery, and a squadron of the Hyderabad Lancers. The mountain battery, however, which was transferred from the 52nd Division and moved under the escort of the cavalry squadron, did not arrive in time to take part in the first day's operations. A thousand camels of " A " Company Camel Transport Corps had been handed over to the division, but these too were not available on the 19th to replace the wagons of the train. It was not known whether the hills at 'Amwas were held, but Major-General Palin did not expect strong resistance until the defile of the Bab el Wad, two miles further down the road, was reached. He ordered the 232nd Brigade, with the South African Field Artillery Brigade attached, to occupy the hills at 'Amwas by 8.50 a.m., and thenceforward act as advanced guard through the defile. To this brigade he attached the 58th Vaughan's Rifles, from the 234th Brigade.

The 232nd Brigade left Abu Shushe at 7.30 a.m. and occupied 'Amwas without opposition. At 11 the 58th Rifles began crowning the heights of the Bab el Wad. The enemy was in no great strength, but small parties dug in upon the hills had to be dislodged. The Indian troops, highly

---

[1] See Note at end of Chapter.

## DIFFICULTIES OF THE ADVANCE 191

skilled in operations of this type, completely outmanœuvred the Turks, turning every successive position occupied by them with great speed. After the narrowest portion of the defile had been passed the leading battalion was reinforced by two companies of the 5/Devonshire on the right of the road and by the 2/3rd Gurkhas on the left. All movement off the road was, however, very difficult, and the enemy had to be driven off successive commanding ridges. A rainstorm made the ground slippery and dense black clouds brought early darkness, so that no advance was possible after 5 p.m., by which time the foremost piquet was within half a mile of the village of Saris, 6 miles south-east of 'Amwas. The head of the division had thus advanced 10 miles since morning. The whole brigade bivouacked astride the road, under fire from enemy snipers. The night was cold, with heavy rain, and the troops in their summer clothing suffered severely.

1917.
19 Nov.

The 52nd Division had a difficult task, and the 156th and 157th Brigades had been deprived of much-needed rest by being ordered to strike camp at Ramle on the afternoon of the 18th and move to Lydda. As a fact, the track from Ramle to Jimzu on the Lydda-Jerusalem road, was afterwards found to be quite passable for wheels, so that their march was unnecessary. Jimzu, 3 miles, and Berfiliya, 6 miles south-east of Lydda, were found to be unoccupied, the head of the 156th Brigade reaching the latter village at noon.

Now began the most difficult part of the march, though no resistance was encountered. The road was a mere track marked by usage, in places soft, in others solid rock, often strewn with boulders which had rolled down from the hills above. The head of the 156th Brigade, with the benefit of daylight, reached Beit Liqya at 4 p.m., taking four hours to cover seven miles. After a reconnaissance of the road the C.R.A., Br.-General E.C. Massy, ordered the 264th Brigade R.F.A. to make an attempt to reach Beit Liqya, with eight-horse teams and only three wagons per subsection. It struggled forward and, by dint of constant man-handling, arrived at 6 p.m., not without breaking several wheels by the way. A great deal of delay was caused by the transport of the Yeomanry Mounted Division blocking the road in front.

The 157th Brigade, following the 156th, had the worst

ordeal. It reached Berfilya about 3 p.m. There the 261st Brigade R.F.A. was ordered to pull out of the column owing to the state of the road. In doing so several guns were stuck in exceptionally bad ground, and the advance of the infantry was held up until 5.15 p.m., just before the fall of darkness. Half an hour later it was pitch dark and rain began to fall in sheets. The road was now, if it can be said to have existed at all, over long stretches undiscoverable. The few limbered wagons brought forward had to be divided and man-handled. The camels slipped in the wet, cut their feet on the rocks, in some cases broke legs, in others fell into ravines. Many of the men had their boots so torn that they had to take them off and bind their puttees round their feet. The head of the brigade reached Beit Liqya at 9.45 p.m., but the transport was not all in until 1 a.m. on the 20th. As the 157th Brigade was under orders to capture Beit Duqqu, 3½ miles to the east, by 8 a.m. that morning, it was obliged to be on the move again by 5 a.m. It was therefore useless to attempt to draw blankets from the transport for the troops, who had to pass the night in their torn drill jackets and shorts.

The Yeomanry Mounted Division, having crossed the front of the 52nd, was now on the left flank of the advance. Major-General Barrow ordered the 8th Mounted Brigade to move on Beitunye, 3 miles south-west of Bire, and the 22nd on 'Ain 'Arik, on the track from Beit 'Ur et Tahta to Ram Allah and Bire. These troops were thus called upon to advance across one of the roughest and bleakest areas of the Judæan Hills. The 8th Brigade passed through Beit 'Ur et Tahta, but was soon afterwards held up in the Wadi es Sunt, which runs through a deep valley north-east of the village, and spent the night there halted in the rain. The 22nd Mounted Brigade also made slow progress, partly owing to the time taken in crowning the precipitous heights on either side of its line of march, but still more owing to the nature of the track. The column had to move in single file, and was nearly six miles long. Little opposition from the enemy was met with, but every time a horse foundered as a result of lack of water and of fatigue during the previous week, every time a camel escaped his miseries by deliberately (as it appeared) dying in his tracks, a halt had to be made while the carcass was dragged off the path. The brigade eventually bivouacked just west of its objective, the village 1917. of 'Ain 'Arik. Rations could be brought by the train no 19 Nov. farther than 'Annabe, about 12 miles as the crow flies west of 'Ain 'Arik, and had to be fetched thence by units with pack-animals, in hastily-made canvas sacks, or at best with half limbers. Several regiments got none that night, and the most fortunate received them very late.

The sudden break in the weather, though not unexpected—for the early rains were actually rather overdue—had vastly increased the difficulties of a task already hard. The roads in the hills, even before the rain fell, were worse than had appeared from the reports of agents, and the Palestine Exploration Fund map was all too flattering to them. Already the three divisions were in trouble with their transport; troops and animals alike were fatigued, though all the worst lay ahead. Neither the camels nor their Egyptian drivers were suited to rugged country of this nature or to the climate. The Egyptians had proved themselves efficient, tireless, and cheerful in the plain; but the rocks, the cold, and the rain bewildered and terrified them. There were instances of extraordinary devotion to duty in their ranks, but in many cases their spirits were broken by their miseries and it was hard to prevent them seating themselves by the roadside in the belief that only death would deliver them. Nor was it only in the hills that the rains affected the troops. In the plains the bottoms fell out of the roads by which their supplies were moved, and a few days later the flooding of the Wadi Ghazze temporarily cut the broad-gauge railway line.

On the 20th November the 75th and Yeomanry Mounted 20 Nov. Divisions were to converge on Bire, the 52nd Division keeping connection between them. General Bulfin's orders to the 75th were " to reach Bire at all costs as early as " possible, leaving strong detachments at Qaryet el 'Inab " and Qalandye." The 52nd he directed to send one infantry brigade, if possible with artillery, to Beit Duqqu, 3¾ miles N.N.E. of Qaryet el 'Inab. The 75th Division moved on again along the Jaffa–Jerusalem road, the 232nd Brigade still leading. Progress was slow, but by about 11 a.m. it appeared that resistance at Saris was weakening. The 2/4th Somerset Light Infantry, supported by the fire of the 12th Light Armoured Motor Battery, then carried out an attack and captured the village, suffering only 11 casualties and taking 30 prisoners. The 3/3rd Gurkhas, which had been sent up from the 233rd Brigade to support this attack but had arrived too late, was at once despatched by Br.-General Huddleston to seize the high ground beyond Saris on the other side of the road. This advance was carried out with rapidity and dash, the Gurkhas taking the ridge at small cost with 45 prisoners. The brigadier rode forward to the position and gave orders for the advance to be continued to Qaryet el 'Inab, 2 miles E.N.E. of Saris. At this moment, when he was about to attack with his own exhausted troops, he received from the 233rd Brigade two more battalions, which Br.-General Colston had sent forward on his own initiative. These were the 5/Somerset and 4/Wiltshire; with them and the 2/3rd Gurkhas of his own brigade he launched an attack at 3.30 p.m., supported by the motor battery, on the last high crest (Hill 2486), which covered 'Inab. As the 5/Somerset reached his position, overlooking the valley between him and his objective, rain began to fall and the hills were veiled in mist. Realizing how good was the opportunity, he ordered that battalion and the Gurkhas to attack at once, pushing on the Wiltshire to support them as soon as it arrived. The troops were able to get close up to the ridge unseen, and then charged with the bayonet. The Turks broke and at once evacuated the village, one of the largest in the area. To General Bulfin, standing in the road near Saris, the first news of the success came when, above the rattle of musketry and the boom of the Turkish artillery, there were heard the shrill cheers of the Gurkhas and the deep-throated roar of the British troops, followed by regimental bugle-calls. Soon after 5 p.m., as dusk was falling, the whole of the division moved forward to Qaryet el 'Inab and its neighbourhood. The troops ate their iron rations that night—a great proportion of them in the welcome shelter of the big monastery and of a sanatorium, the less fortunate bivouacked under miserable conditions of wet and cold. No supplies arrived till noon on the 21st owing to the congestion of the narrow road.

On the front of the 52nd Division the 157th Brigade moved off for Beit Duqqu at 5 a.m. on the 20th, while the 155th Brigade was ordered to join the 156th at Beit Liqya. A single section of the 264th Brigade R.F.A. was ordered to

The Jaffa–Jerusalem Road in the Hills of Judah.

[Australian Official Photograph.

accompany the 157th Brigade, but got no farther than two miles east of Beit Liqya, where the road became quite impassable. Native guides were procured by Br.-General Hamilton Moore, but they appeared to have a very hazy knowledge of the way and informed him erroneously that there were no Turks in Beit Duqqu or its neighbourhood. The brigade crawled forward in a long column, for the troops were often forced to move in single file. After daylight the brigadier carried out a reconnaissance with his commanding officers and decided that three battalions should advance along the old Roman Road to Beit 'Anan, a mile and a half south-west of Beit Duqqu, while the 7/H.L.I. should move on Beit Duqqu by the track following the Wadi Selman, known as the "Ancient Road."

1917. 20 Nov.

On approaching Beit 'Anan the leading battalion, the 5/H.L.I., was ordered to crown the heights to protect the advance of the brigade. Meanwhile the 7/H.L.I. found its track so ancient that one company lost it in broad daylight and turned right-handed down the bed of the Wadi Qeiqabe, an affluent of the Wadi Selman. This mistake had a fortunate result, for the company appeared north of Beit 'Anan, just as the attack from the west was meeting with stubborn resistance. The Turks then abandoned the village, falling back to the commanding heights beyond. The 6/H.L.I. was now ordered to assist the 7th Battalion in the attack on Beit Duqqu. This village was captured at 10.30 a.m., though, visual signalling being impossible in the rain, the news did not reach Br.-General Hamilton Moore by messenger till two hours later.

By 1 p.m. most of the enemy had been pushed off the ridge south-east of Beit 'Anan, but one party clung to a strong position in a walled enclosure. The brigadier, whose troops were now exhausted, decided that a direct attack on this post would entail unnecessary loss, while he could easily work round its flanks in the morning. In fact the Turks fell back after dark. Prisoners stated that there had been 700 men holding the Beit Duqqu position, and that they had had serious losses. The casualties of the 157th Brigade were less than fifty. The division endured another cold and wet night, and its rations were very late in arriving.[1] That

---
[1] The refilling point was Qubab, 7 miles south-east of Ramle. On this date 500 camels loaded with iron rations were put at the division's disposal.

afternoon the 412th Field Company R.E. began work on improving the Roman Road east of Beit Liqya, aided by parties of infantry from the 156th Brigade.

The Yeomanry Mounted Division further north continued its attempt to reach Bire. As the 22nd Mounted Brigade was held up in front of 'Ain 'Arik in very rugged country, Major-General Barrow ordered the 6th Brigade, followed by the 8th, to move through Beit 'Ur el Foqa (Upper Bethoron), a mile and three-quarters E.S.E. of Beit Ur et Tahta, on Beitunye, 3¼ miles further east. East of Foqa rises a steep ridge, known as the "Zeitun Ridge" (from the shrine of a sheikh of that name at its western end), which was to see heavy fighting on several occasions during the next two months. It is narrow from north to south, but nearly two miles long from west to east, fairly flat on the top but with steep sides, rising nearly 1,100 feet in three-quarters of a mile. The advance from Beit 'Ur et Tahta, where the 6th Brigade had bivouacked the previous night, was not contested until the Dorset Yeomanry in the van descended at 11.30 a.m. from the hills on which Foqa stands and found the enemy holding the western rim of the Zeitun Ridge above. The Berks Yeomanry, moving up on the left, succeeded in working its way on to the edge of the ridge near Kh. er Ras, but no further progress was made. The Berks lay out all night on the ridge, facing the enemy at close quarters, in torrents of rain, their horses in the deep valley below. Meanwhile the 22nd Brigade, meeting with little opposition, struggled into 'Ain 'Arik, leading its horses, the head of the column reaching the village at 2 p.m. and the tail not till about 10 p.m Two squadrons of the Stafford Yeomanry, pushing on towards Ram Allah, established themselves on a hill known as El Muntar, a mile north of Beitunye.

Thus the night of the 20th November, by which time General Bulfin had hoped to be astride the Nablus road at Bire, found him far short of his goal. It is true that the most advanced of the mounted troops, the Stafford Yeomanry on El Muntar, were only 2½ miles from Bire, but the nearest infantry at Beit Duqqu were 6 miles from it. Moreover, it was now pretty certain that the enemy meant to defend Jerusalem after all. Only small rear-guard detachments had yet been encountered, and the great difficulty found in dislodging them from positions so admirably suited to their tactics augured ill for the moment obviously drawing nigh when the Turks should be met with in strength.

1917.
21 Nov.

### THE CAPTURE OF NABI SAMWEIL.
#### 21ST-22ND NOVEMBER.

General Bulfin ordered the 75th Division to move directly on Bire on the 21st, and the 52nd to stand fast. This advance by the 75th Division involved quitting the metalled Jaffa-Jerusalem road and following the track which turned off it at Qaryet el 'Inab and ran *via* Biddu, 3 miles north-east of 'Inab, to El Jib. To move field guns by this track was out of the question. The Yeomanry Mounted Division was advancing on Bire by way of Beitunye. Major-General Palin ordered the 234th Brigade (less 58th Rifles) with the squadron of Hyderabad Lancers to act as advanced guard, the main body being composed of the 233rd Brigade. Both brigades were put under the command of Br.-General Colston. The 232nd Brigade was ordered to detail two battalions, each four hundred rifles strong after all unfit men had been left at 'Inab, as escort to the first-line transport of the 233rd and 234th Brigades, which was to march in their rear. This transport was now entirely composed of camels, the limbered wagons being left at 'Inab with the artillery and details, covered by the 232nd Brigade (less 5/Devonshire and 2/3rd Gurkhas, detailed for escort duty), with the 58th Rifles still attached. Although Sir Edmund Allenby was determined to have no fighting near Jerusalem, the 232nd Brigade was ordered to make a demonstration along the main road to divert the attention of the enemy. This it carried out successfully, driving a party of Turks out of Qastal, 2½ miles E.S.E. of 'Inab and only 4 miles west of the suburbs of Jerusalem.

Maps 2, 10.
Sketches A, 13.

The enemy bombarded 'Inab at dawn and caused some loss, one shell wounding four British officers of the 3/3rd Gurkhas. At 10.30 a.m. the column moved forward on Biddu. Little opposition was encountered, but the roughness of the track and the steepness of the gradients made the advance slow. The camels in rear had to move in single file. The vanguard, the 2/4th Dorset, cleared the enemy out of Biddu without difficulty and pushed on to occupy the high ground just east of the village, and Beit Surik to the south. The troops east of Biddu now came under fire from the famous hill of Nabi Samweil, a mile to the east: assumed to be the Mizpah of the Bible, and venerated by Christians, Jews, and Mohammedans alike as the resting-place of the Prophet Samuel, above whose traditional tomb there is a mosque. Obviously the advance north-eastward could not continue while the enemy held this dominating hill, the summit of which is four or five hundred feet above the plateau to north of it, on the flank. Br.-General Colston ordered Br.-General C. A. H. Maclean, commanding the advanced guard, to capture it, sending up the 2/4th Hampshire (less a company left to garrison Beit Surik) and the 3/3rd Gurkhas to assist him. Br.-General Maclean ordered the Dorsetshire to hold the positions it had gained, and directed Lieut.-Colonel G. R. Cassels, commanding the 123rd Rifles, to attack the hill with his own battalion and the 4/D.C.L.I., supported by the 231st Machine Gun Company. Darkness was at hand, so Lieut.-Colonel Cassels—weak as he was [1]—did not await the arrival of the two battalions from the 233rd Brigade, which came up a few minutes after the advance began and were sent forward in support of it.

The attack was launched at 5.15 p.m. along the lower northern slopes of the spur running eastward from Biddu, the two battalions each on a frontage of 400 yards, the left marching on the mosque. They had over a mile to cover, and were under machine-gun fire all the way, but the failing light was friendly. They reached the mosque and the summit of the hill, capturing 42 prisoners and 2 machine guns, their own losses being only 36. The Turks must have had very much greater casualties, for a formed body moving off south was fired into in the darkness at a range of little over a hundred yards by the Lewis guns of the leading platoons of the D.C.L.I. A defensive line was then established beyond the mosque, on the outskirts of a tiny native hamlet.

The 5th Mounted Brigade, which had been held up by the congestion of the road at 'Amwas on the 20th and only reached 'Inab on the afternoon of the 21st, was unable to

---

[1] In addition to the wastage caused by sickness, battle casualties, and detachments left behind in the Gaza area, some 400 men, being Mohammedans, had been withdrawn from the 123rd Rifles and were being retained at 'Inab to guard the Holy Places in Jerusalem when captured. Neither battalion had 250 rifles in this attack.

## THE YEOMANRY IN DIFFICULTIES   199

fulfil its mission of covering the right flank. This was undertaken by two of the three battalions left at 'Inab in the morning, the 58th Rifles occupying Soba, a mile and three-quarters south-east of 'Inab, with a long piquet-line on the hills to the south-east, and the 2/4th Somerset Light Infantry making similar dispositions at Qastal, on the main road. It must be added that the 10th A.L.H. had been attached to the 5th Mounted Brigade in place of the Gloucester Hussars in order that the Australian forces should be represented in the capture of Jerusalem.

1917.
21 Nov.

The 52nd Division had carried out a small demonstration to aid the 75th. One company of the 6/H.L.I. with machine guns advanced on Beit Izza, whereupon a body of Turks promptly evacuated the place.

Major-General Barrow, grimly determined to carry out the orders he had received, unpromising though his prospects seemed, directed the 6th Mounted Brigade to resume its attack on Beitunye and the 22nd to move on Ram Allah. The Berks Yeomanry of the 6th Brigade attempted to move eastward from the positions which it had gained overnight, while the Dorsets attacked Beitunye from the south. The Bucks Hussars, at first in support, was ordered to capture a hillock on the Zeitun Ridge (Point 2709). The top was reached, but the Turks were found established upon it behind a stone breastwork. Br.-General Rome, commanding the 8th Brigade, moved up the City of London and 3rd County of London Yeomanry to the close support of the 6th Brigade. The City of London began a dismounted attack up the narrow valley on the right of the Bucks, but that regiment, now hard pressed on the high ground, called urgently for reinforcements. Three squadrons from the City of London and 3rd County of London were sent up in succession to its support. The horses of practically two brigades were now massed below the hill. The Turks strove continually to reach this tempting target, but the sides of the ravine were too steep and deep for their shrapnel to do any harm.

Meanwhile the East Riding Yeomanry of the 22nd Brigade, supported by a section of the Hong Kong Battery, had moved forward on Ram Allah. The fire of two Turkish batteries installed upon the matchless observatory of the Ram Allah spur and shooting over open sights, and the extreme exhaustion of the troops, who were suffering severely from exposure and short rations, soon brought this advance also to a halt. At 12.45 p.m. the Lincoln Yeomanry was ordered to assist the 6th Brigade by attacking Beitunye from the north, but was unable to get within 800 yards of the village. The three very weak brigades were, in fact, now opposed by the whole of the Turkish *3rd Cavalry Division* and about half the *24th Division*.

About 2 p.m. reinforcements were seen arriving on the plateau of Beitunye, and half an hour later the Turks began a strong outflanking movement on the right of the Dorsets, who were compelled to fall back. This retirement necessitated that of the Bucks, which fell back to the position occupied by the Berks. Major-General Barrow, recognizing that his troops were in a precarious situation, decided to retire to Beit 'Ur el Foqa, and withdraw the 22nd Brigade to Beit 'Ur et Tahta, the 8th Brigade covering the retirement. That of the East Riding Yeomanry, the most advanced regiment, took nine hours, during the first five of which horses were led. The 3rd County of London Yeomanry, rear guard of the 8th Brigade, did not reach Foqa till 5.30 a.m. on the 22nd. Very fortunately the enemy did not attempt a pursuit. The casualties of the day's fighting were 196, while 108 horses were killed or foundered.

The difficulties of this abortive but doggedly-conducted operation can scarcely be exaggerated. The ground, rocky, boulder-strewn, often precipitous, slippery from the rain, would have been hard enough to advance across had there been no enemy, and there was actually an enemy superior in numbers and infinitely superior in artillery.[1] The

---

[1] Of the Hong Kong and Singapore Battery (of camel screw-guns with Indian personnel), an eye-witness writes :—" The section attached " to the 22nd Brigade by sheer determination got their little gun as far " forward as El Muntar [a mile north of Beitunye and a mile and a half " from Ram Allah, from which, as recorded, the Turkish batteries were " firing over open sights]. Their camels' feet were bleeding, and as they " progressed by the narrow wadi beds it was not an uncommon sight to " see them practically lifting their animals laden with ammunition over " high boulders and rock which obstructed the path. They started " dauntless and remained undaunted. . . . Even when they were actually " in action, each time they fired their gun a cloud of black smoke gave " away their position, and they were replied to by batteries which they " could not reach with shells that came over them like coveys of partridges. " . . . Yet, despite the fact that on account of range they could really do " little damage, they continued to invite destruction all through the " afternoon."

LOOKING WESTWARD FROM RAM ALLAH.

## FALKENHAYN'S STRATEGY

division after its numerous actions in the plains had a fighting strength of about 1,200; in many cases squadrons in the firing line, without horse-holders, had less than twenty rifles in addition to the Hotchkiss sections. There had been little communication between the 6th and 22nd Brigades, as the latter's wireless aerial was broken and cloud made the use of the helio impossible. Messages had to be carried by officers' patrols, at great risk, as the enemy was between the two brigades. Both men and horses were half starved—the East Riding Yeomanry, for example, had in 60 hours one half day's rations and some figs, which, with a little tibben for the horses, were procured in the hamlet of 'Ain 'Arik on the production of some gold sovereigns by Br.-General Fryer. Five hundred camels had been handed over by the XXI Corps in exchange for the G.S. wagons of the divisional train, but they did not reach Tahta till the night of the 22nd. They were thenceforward kept there to work between that point and the front line, supplies being brought up from 'Annabe to Tahta by the 1st Echelons.

Bad weather had greatly hindered aerial reconnaissance, but it had now become clear that, at least upon the Yeomanry Division's front, the advance had come up against the line upon which the enemy meant to fight in order to defend the Nablus road and Jerusalem. For the first time his strategy was apparent. He had left small rear guards to delay the advance into the hills, preferring to withdraw the bulk of the *Seventh Army* from contact with the British in order to reorganize it and employ it upon the construction of defences already begun. The morrow was to prove that the 75th Division also was close up to his defensive position.

General Bulfin ordered this division to continue on the 22nd the advance necessarily interrupted the previous day by the capture of Nabi Samweil. He also ordered Major-General Hill to despatch a brigade of the 52nd Division from Beit Liqya to take over the hill during the day; but the 75th Division was obliged to leave that morning four battalions to hold it, in addition to keeping the 2/4th Dorset on the high ground east of Biddu. As it was considered necessary to leave three battalions on the Jaffa–Jerusalem road, Br.-General Colston had available only four battalions, the 4/Wiltshire and 5/Somerset of his own brigade and the

5/Devonshire and 2/3rd Gurkhas of the 232nd, the cavalry squadron, and the 230th Machine-Gun Company.

A necessary first step was the capture of El Jib, the Gibeon of Scripture, the famous rallying-point of Israel. North of Nabi Samweil is a plain, unusually flat for this neighbourhood, from which rises a pear-shaped hill, low but steep-faced, terraced along the flanks, with the little village of El Jib at its northern end. As often in this very broken country, an attack on one position involved the preliminary capture of another scarcely less formidable. The advanced guard [1] was forced to move west and north of Biddu to avoid the enemy's shell fire, and speedily became involved with small parties of the enemy on the high ground east of Beit Izza. Its commander, Lieut.-Colonel A. Armstrong, 4/Wiltshire, decided that he must first capture this position and then move on El Jib from the west. This he found himself unable to do without artillery support—no batteries having yet been able to move north of 'Inab. All that could be attained was the occupation of the tail of the spur east of Beit Izza by two companies of the Wiltshire. Leaving these companies in their position, he withdrew at dusk to the valley north-west of Biddu.

Not only was the advance of the 75th Division thus held up, but it came near to losing Nabi Samweil. Here the 3/3rd Gurkhas had now been brought up on the left of the 4/D.C.L.I. at the mosque, the 123rd Rifles was in its original position on the right, and the 2/4th Hampshire in close support.

At 7.45 a.m. the Turks began to bombard Nabi Samweil from east, south, and later from the north, a battery northwest of El Jib taking the position in enfilade. The first infantry attack came mainly up the valley in which lies the village of Beit Iksa, and was completely broken up by the fire of the 123rd Rifles and 4/D.C.L.I. As it faded away a body of Turks on the left attempted to rush the trenches of the 3/3rd Gurkhas, but was beaten off by its fire. The second onslaught was better organized, coming all along the front, but chiefly from east and north-east, out of the Wadi Beit Hannina. This was stronger and pushed with greater

---

[1] One squadron Hyderabad Lancers, 5/Somerset, 4/Wilts, one section 230th Machine-Gun Company.

## COUNTER-ATTACK ON NABI SAMWEIL 203

resolution. On the right the Turks climbed the terraces under cover of the bombardment and rushed the crest when it had ceased, but were driven off it by the counter-attack of two companies of the 123rd Rifles. On the rest of the front they were brought to a halt, except for a moment on the extreme left, where the left company of the Gurkhas was driven back, but re-established its position with the aid of a company of the Hampshire. After continuous bombardment another attack was launched about 2 p.m. On the front of the 123rd Rifles the Turks again reached the top of the ridge, but again were hurled back from it by a counter-attack. On that of the D.C.L.I. they were repulsed, though they established themselves close to the British line behind walls and boulders. A party which reached the spur running towards Biddu was driven off it by the 2/4th Dorset.

1917.
22 Nov.

At the mosque itself, now held by the Gurkhas, there was bitter close fighting. Two guns of the 231st Machine-Gun Company mounted in the minaret caused the enemy heavy losses, but one was quickly put out of action by a shell. The building was a land-mark for miles, and the enemy had its range exactly. The roof was partly blown in, big stones falling among the numerous wounded inside, who were then carried down to a crypt below. The shrine of the Prophet, which was supported by four ancient and massive silver lanterns, was smashed to pieces by a direct hit. At 3.30 p.m. the bombardment increased in violence, and the Turkish infantry attacked immediately afterwards in greater strength. Fresh ammunition had been brought up through the barrage by a party of the D.C.L.I. under Captain C. Kendall, the remainder of the Hampshire had been placed in position on either side of the mosque, and this attack was repulsed.

After a short lull there was yet another assault, and the mosque was soon almost completely surrounded. The remaining machine gun took up a position in the court-yard, and did good service till it was put out of action by Turkish bombers. It was then replaced by the last remaining Lewis gun of the Gurkhas. The court-yard gate having been left open, Lieut.-Colonel G. K. Channer went to close it, and met a German officer just entering at the head of his men. He bayoneted the leader and managed to close the gate amid a shower of bombs. Then, leaving the building held by a handful of wounded men, he led out the remainder by the back gate. The Gurkhas charged with bayonet and *kukri* and after fierce close fighting drove the Turks down to a terrace below the mosque, where they killed every man within reach by hurling boulders down upon them. The respite was, however, short, and it seems possible that the position, and certainly the mosque, would have been lost within the next hour but for the timely assistance which now arrived.

The 156th Brigade had moved out of Beit Liqya at 7 a.m., with orders to relieve the troops of the 75th Division at Nabi Samweil, marching without transport and leaving all unfit men behind. Following the very bad road through Beit 'Anan and Qubeibe, it halted near Biddu for a short time just before two o'clock. Then two battalions, the 7th and 8th Scottish Rifles, were sent forward under the command of Lieut.-Colonel J. M. Findlay of the 8th, to Nabi Samweil, where it could be seen that a battle was in progress. Advancing by companies in artillery formation, they suffered little loss from shell fire, and reached a covered position 200 yards from the mosque. Here Lieut.-Colonel J. G. P. Romanes, commanding the 7/Scottish Rifles, learnt the situation from Br.-General Maclean. Lieut.-Colonel Findlay had meanwhile ordered the 7th Battalion to push on to the mosque. Companies moved up on either side of it, and the reserve company charged in the darkness a body of the enemy on the western side. The Turks fell back into cover, leaving a number of dead on the ground. It was now possible to carry out the relief, the 8/Scottish Rifles taking over the right of the line and the 7th the left  The latter battalion had further heavy close fighting after the troops of the 75th Division had been withdrawn.

The losses of the four battalions holding Nabi Samweil were 567, of which the Gurkhas suffered 216. It must be remembered that they were already very weak, owing to sickness, guards left on depots, and parties withdrawn for guard duty after the expected capture of Jerusalem, so that these losses represented about 50 per cent. of their total fighting strength. The 3/3rd Gurkhas had one Indian officer and sixteen riflemen unwounded. When to these are added the losses of the two Scottish battalions, of the Dorsetshire, of the Wiltshire and 5/Somerset north of Beit Izza, and of other units, the total of the day's fighting is over seven hundred and fifty.[1]

1917.
22 Nov.

The Yeomanry Division, after its fight of the previous day and long retirement through the night, was in no case to give any assistance by pressing the enemy on its front. The 8th Brigade held Beit 'Ur el Foqa, with a squadron of the City of London Yeomanry on the western edge of the Zeitun Ridge. The wounded of this division, without tents or bivouacs, suffered terribly from the weather.

THE ATTACKS ON EL JIB, 23RD–24TH NOVEMBER.

Freed now of its responsibility for guarding Nabi Samweil, which had been taken over by the 156th Brigade, the 75th Division was ordered to make yet another attempt to continue its advance. The attack on El Jib was again entrusted to Br.-General Colston. Two of his battalions had lost heavily on Nabi Samweil the previous day, the 3/3rd Gurkhas having been reduced to a handful, while the 4/Wiltshire still had two companies out east of Beit Izza. The 2/3rd Gurkhas of the 232nd Brigade, one of the two battalions escorting the transport, was put at his disposal. He ordered the attack on El Jib to be carried out by the 5/Somerset, while the 2/3rd Gurkhas was to follow and later move up on the right of the leading battalion in order to capture Bir Nebala, a thousand yards east of El Jib. The only artillery support on which he could rely was that of B/IX Mountain Battery,[2] though one or two batteries of the divisional artillery fired a few rounds on El Jib at extreme range from their positions near 'Inab.

23 Nov.

Biddu lies in a fold of the hills and is hidden from both Nabi Samweil and El Jib. Just east of it, however, the ground is smoothed out into the plain previously mentioned, sometimes known as the " Plain of Gibeon." After leaving the protection of the valley the attack had two thousand yards of this open ground to cross, dominated by the northern slopes of the Nabi Samweil ridge to the south, El

---

[1]
|  | Killed. | Wounded. | Missing. |
| --- | --- | --- | --- |
| Officers. . . | 6 | 23 | 1 |
| Other Ranks. . | 92 | 539 | 91 |

[2] This battery had only three guns in action, and they were worn and consequently inaccurate; so that, gallantly as they were handled, they were not of great service.

Jib to the north-east, and the high ground east of Beit Izza to the north-west. The attack was conducted with great gallantry. Directly the extended lines of the Somerset emerged they came under machine-gun fire from these three points, and also under shrapnel and high explosive. The battalion went steadily forward, despite its losses, and actually reached the foot of El Jib. A few men even succeeded in scrambling up the terraces, carrying three Lewis guns with them, and in entering the village, but they were all killed or captured. The remainder of the battalion was pinned to the ground The 2/3rd Gurkhas had no fairer fortune. Going forward with equal steadiness, it reached the Wadi 'Amir, 700 yards south-west of El Jib, but found itself unable either to advance or retire from the cover which this gulley afforded, so heavy was the machine-gun fire. The 5/Devon was then put at Br.-General Colston's disposal and ordered to attack El Jib from the west, where the terraces appeared to be somewhat less steep. All forward movement on the part of other troops having now ceased, this battalion became the target of the Turkish guns, but the little columns in wide artillery formation suffered very small loss until within a mile of the village and abreast of the Turks on the Nabi Samweil ridge, when they came under enfilade machine-gun fire at a range of about 1,500 yards. The battalion then deployed and steadily continued its advance. As the fire grew hotter, the companies raced for a slight valley at the foot of the terraced hill of El Jib. Here they found good cover, but could make no further advance. Many of the imperturbable Westcountrymen, ignoring their dangerous situation, went to sleep in the afternoon sunshine.

It was clear now to Br.-General Colston that no more progress could be made, and he reported the fact to Major-General Palin. Nor was it possible to withdraw until dusk had fallen, and even then it was a matter of great difficulty to bring in the numerous wounded, while most of the dead had to be left where they had fallen. The casualties in this gallant failure amounted to 372 in the three attacking battalions, while the losses of the whole division in the course of the day were 480.[1] Those of the 5/Somerset were 162.

|  | Killed. | Wounded. | Missing. |
|---|---|---|---|
| [1] Officers | 3 | 16 | — |
| Other Ranks | 46 | 387 | 28 |

Sketch 13.

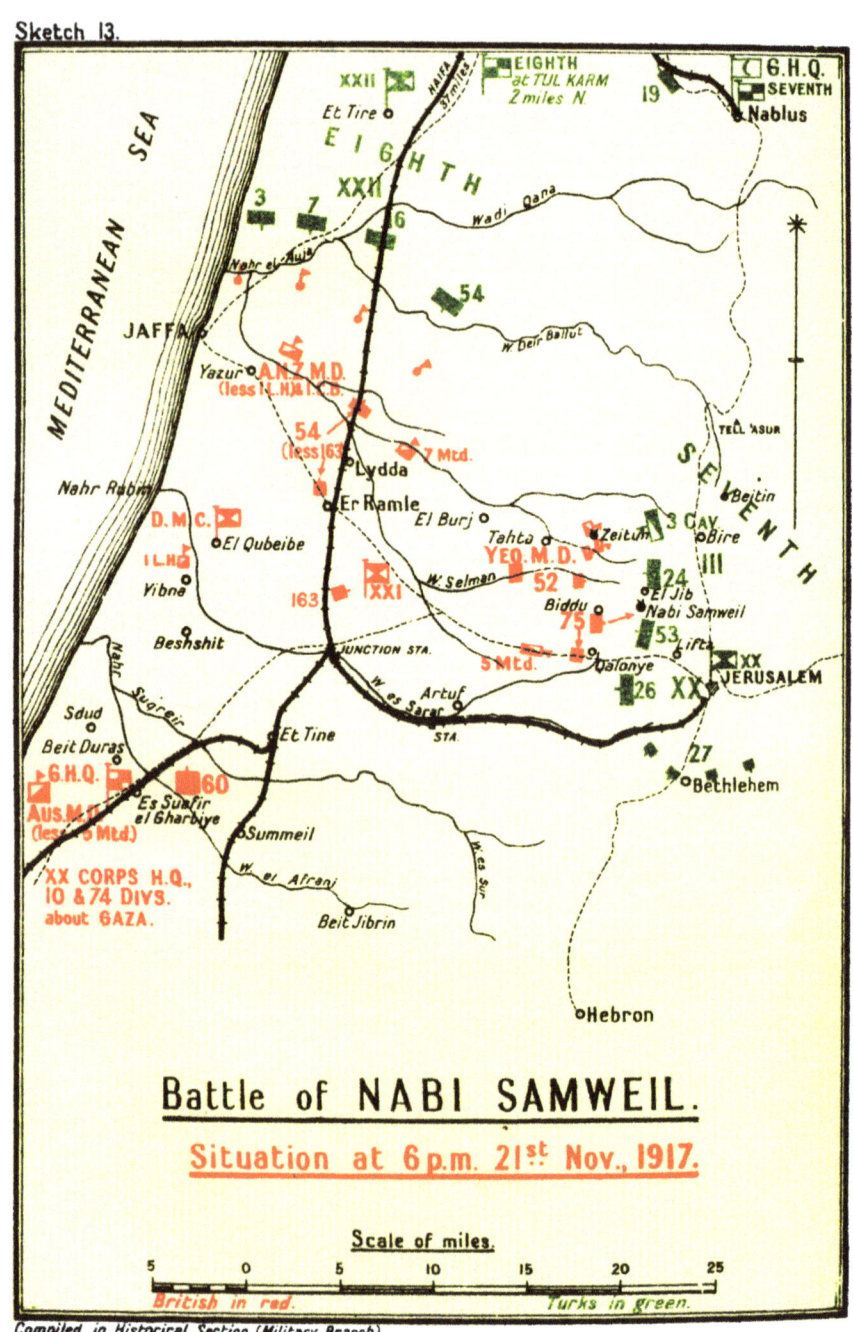

## Battle of NABI SAMWEIL.
### Situation at 6 p.m. 21st Nov., 1917.

Scale of miles.

British in red.   Turks in green.

Compiled in Historical Section (Military Branch).
3000/30.

Ordnance Survey 1928.

The result proved that it was not advisable to attack El Jib 1917. until the high ground north-east of Beit Izza was captured. 23 Nov. But even had that been taken the capture of El Jib would have been all but impossible so long as the northern slopes of the Nabi Samweil ridge on the other flank were in the hands of the enemy; for it seems to have been machine-gun fire from this quarter which caused the heaviest losses.

At 3.40 p.m. the 155th Brigade of the 52nd Division arrived at Beit Izza. One section each of A/262nd, B/262nd, A/264th, C/261st, and C/264th Batteries of the 52nd Divisional Artillery, each with ten-horse teams, moved up to Biddu via Beit 'Anan and Qubeibe, under the command of the 264th Brigade R.F.A. Starting at 8.30 a.m., the leading section was in action against El Jib by 3 p.m., but by that time the failure of the attack was certain. General Bulfin, in congratulating Br.-General E. C. Massy, the C.R.A., described the march as "a magnificent feat." The track from Qaryet et 'Inab to Biddu, on the 75th Division's front, was cleared by the Royal Engineers of this division, the 412th Field Company of the 52nd, detachments of Outram's Rifles from 'Inab, and four hundred men of the 1st Battalion British West Indies Regiment, which had been put at the disposal of the XXI Corps by G.H.Q. In some cases the old track was abandoned and a new one made round the lower terraces of the hills. The road was practicable by 9.30 p.m. and C/XXXVII (Howitzer) Battery moved to Biddu at night, the ammunition being carried on camels. The lack of a pioneer battalion was very seriously felt.[1]

On this date the Yeomanry Mounted Division again remained on the defensive. It was transferred from the command of the Desert Mounted Corps to that of the XXI, thus bringing the whole force in the hills under the orders of General Bulfin, an arrangement which was overdue. On the previous day the responsibility of the Desert Mounted Corps had extended from Beitunye to the mouth of the Nahr el 'Auja, a distance of 27 miles. Major-General Barrow obtained from General Bulfin leave to send back to Ramle

---

[1] No Territorial divisions had originally pioneer battalions, and none had been allotted to those in Palestine or to the two divisions, the 74th and 75th, formed in the country. Thus only two divisions, the 10th and 60th, newly arrived from another theatre, had them. The 75th had only two field companies R.E.

## 208 THE BATTLE OF NABI SAMWEIL

1917.
24 Nov.

and Lydda all his horses, except a few kept for the machine guns and for pack transport, as the shortage of water and the difficulty of bringing up forage made it useless to attempt to keep the division mounted. Since the 20th regimental commanders had been representing that the horses were an encumbrance, lessening rather than increasing mobility.

On the 24th November was made the final attempt to take El Jib and advance to the Nablus road at Bire. In view of the fatigue and losses of the 75th Division this attack was to be carried out by the 52nd. As a diversion and to induce the enemy to believe that the British advance along the coast was to be resumed, Sir Edmund Allenby had ordered the Desert Mounted Corps to carry out an attack across the Nahr el 'Auja, while the Yeomanry Mounted Division was ordered by General Bulfin to demonstrate against Beitunye.[1] To enable the 52nd Division to employ its full infantry strength the 234th Brigade of the 75th Division was to relieve the 156th Brigade at Nabi Samweil and Beit Surik. The 179th Brigade of the 60th Division, which had reached Junction Station on the 22nd, was to relieve the battalions of the 75th Division at Qaryet el 'Inab and on the Jerusalem road, and these troops were then to move forward to Biddu.

For the first time a fair amount of artillery was available: the six 18-pdrs. and four 4·5-inch howitzers of the 52nd Divisional Artillery mentioned above, C/XXXVII Battery of the 75th Divisional Artillery, and B/IX Mountain Battery. The sections of the 52nd Divisional Artillery were in position in a little cup south-east of Biddu, C/XXXVII south-west of the village, and the mountain battery on the Biddu–El Jib road, south-east of Beit Izza. One section 189th Heavy Battery was on the Jaffa–Jerusalem road near Beit Naqquba.

Major-General Hill had before him the object lesson of the 75th Division's failure to take El Jib the previous day, largely due to enfilade fire from the slopes behind Nabi Samweil. He therefore decided that simultaneously with the main attack on El Jib from the south-west by the 155th Brigade the 156th Brigade should advance and capture the

---

[1] Lieut.-Colonel the Hon. G. G. Wilson, East Riding Yeomanry, who was in command of this demonstration, found and destroyed some wounded horses of the 6th Mounted Brigade which had had no water since the 18th.

whole of the ridge, then cross the Wadi Beit Hannina and take the village of Bir Nebala, a mile and a quarter north-east of the mosque and half a mile east of El Jib. After the capture of El Jib the 155th Brigade was to advance on Qalandye, a mile and a half north-east of El Jib, while the 157th Brigade moved south of Bir Nebala and marched on Er Ram, a village on a hill-top east of the Nablus road and 2½ miles E.N.E. of Bir Nebala. The attacks of the 155th and 156th Brigades were to be launched at 12.5 p.m., all the artillery except the mountain battery supporting that of the 156th. It was arranged that the R.F.C. should bomb Bir Nebala.

The 155th Brigade advanced in artillery formation across the rising plateau previously described: 5/R.Scots Fusiliers on the right, 5/K.O.S.B. on the left, 4/K.O.S.B. in support. To avoid the steepest approach to El Jib, Br.-General Pollok-M'Call had ordered the right to be directed upon a walled garden a thousand yards west of the village. On this the attack was to pivot, the left swinging up to attack El Jib from the north-west. There was some Turkish artillery fire and a good deal of machine-gun fire both from the left and about El Jib, but on the Nabi Samweil ridge the enemy was fully occupied by the attack of the 156th Brigade, and no such fire as the 75th Division had experienced from that quarter on the previous day is reported. The excellent protective colouring in this gray, stony country of khaki drill long exposed to weather is also mentioned in one of the reports, and the attack appears to have suffered very few casualties in the early stages.

At 1.15 p.m. the leading wave of the 5/Scots Fusiliers reached the garden, but from that moment the attack was held up by heavy machine-gun fire from front and left flank. The commanding officers of both the leading battalions were hit, Lieut.-Colonel J. B. Cook, 5/Scots Fusiliers, being killed, and Lieut.-Colonel A. Kearsey, 5/K.O.S.B., wounded. Major-General Hill then directed Br.-General Pollok-M'Call to launch a new attack at 4 p.m., which would have the support of all the artillery available. This attack was actually launched and was making some progress, when a verbal order to stand fast was received from divisional headquarters.

To explain this order we must turn to the fortunes of

the 156th Brigade on the Nabi Samweil ridge. Br.-General Leggett's prospects were not good, first, because of the difficulty of deploying from Nabi Samweil owing to the maze of walled gardens in front of the mosque, held by the enemy with numerous machine guns and trench mortars; secondly, because the Turkish artillery about Lifta, Er Ram and Ram Allah could shell the advance frontally, in enfilade, and in reverse. He ordered the 7/Royal Scots, supported by the 4/Royal Scots, to deploy on either side of the mosque and move north-eastward, clearing the enclosures and cluster of native houses, and, on reaching the north-eastern end of the hill, dig in and assist by fire the advance of the 7/Scottish Rifles. This battalion was to move parallel with the 155th Brigade between Nabi Samweil and the Roman Road and to capture Bir Nebala as soon as El Jib fell. The 8/Scottish Rifles was to hold the position on Nabi Samweil. The machine-gun companies of the 155th and 156th Brigades were both placed on the most commanding points of Nabi Samweil to cover the advance of the two brigades, and Br.-General Leggett had also two Stokes mortars to support his own infantry.

The attack of the 7/Royal Scots was met by a storm of fire, and close fighting began almost at once. Little or no progress was made—not two hundred yards at the most favourable point. The enemy was able to reinforce his line by way of a gulley on the eastern side and throw some three hundred men into the enclosure north-east of the mosque. The 7/Scottish Rifles was meanwhile unable to carry out its mission against Bir Nebala.

Br.-General Leggett decided to make another desperate attempt to clear the enclosures, arranging that the 234th Brigade should relieve the 8/Scottish Rifles in the defences so that he should have his whole strength available. At 2.25 p.m., however, he received an order from the 52nd Division to advance no further, but to support the 155th Brigade to the best of his ability with machine-gun fire.

Meanwhile the 157th Brigade had marched up from Beit 'Anan and Beit Duqqu, and at 10.30 a.m. was half a mile south-west of Beit Izza. Here Br.-General Hamilton Moore made a reconnaissance with his commanding officers. He decided that it was impossible to advance as he had been ordered between El Jib and Nabi Samweil and south of Bir

## FAILURE OF THE ATTACK

Nebala, and indeed it is clear that to have done so, until he had been assured that both hills were in British hands, would have been sheer madness. His only possible line of advance upon Er Ram appeared to be along the valley south of Nabi Samweil and thence along the eastern side of the hill. If the Turks held Beit Iksa to the south and Beit Hannina to the east in strength, he would again be marching across their front, but at least there was here a chance and by the other route none.

1917.
24 Nov.

The matter was soon settled. Every attempt to advance along the eastern slope of the Nabi Samweil ridge was met by what he described as a " terrific cross-fire from " machine guns and rifles," and he finally decided that the operation was impossible. It was now 2 p.m., that is, two hours after the start of the 156th Brigade's attack. He could not get touch with its headquarters, but as the British artillery fire had shifted from the Nabi Samweil ridge it seemed possible that there would now be room for him to advance along the western slope between the crest-line and the 156th Brigade, and that the Turks in Bir Nebala would have their attention fully occupied. Leaving the 5/Argyll & Sutherland Highlanders on the eastern side of the ridge to protect his right, he diverted the rest of the column to the western slope. Here at 2.45 p.m. its head came up against the troops of the 156th Brigade, and he learnt from Br.-General Leggett that the attack of that brigade had failed. At 4.10 p.m. he received a telephone message from Major-General Hill ordering him to abandon his advance on Er Ram and instead to assist the 155th Brigade in its attack on El Jib. The 157th Brigade moved down into the valley west of Nabi Samweil, but immediately afterwards the order came to stand fast.

The 52nd Division, with more battalions and considerably greater artillery support, had failed as completely as the 75th the previous day, the casualties of the 156th Brigade amounting to 256 out of a rifle strength of about 1,400 and the total casualties of the division being 630.[1] Major-General Hill reported to the commander of the XXI Corps that the task was quite beyond the means at his disposal and that a

|  | Killed. | Wounded. | Missing. |
|---|---|---|---|
| [1] Officers . . | 5 | 25 | — |
| Other Ranks . | 91 | 492 | 17 |

renewed attack must fail unless made upon a broader front and with more artillery support.[1] General Bulfin, with heavy heart, had to admit that he was right. The Commander-in-Chief, who had on the 21st established a small advanced headquarters at Es Suafir el Gharbiye, 5 miles south-west of Junction Station, and had been up to visit the front, was now convinced that he had to meet a reorganized Turkish army upon a strong position, which could not be taken without deliberate preparation. At 7.50 p.m. G.H.Q. telegraphed the following message :—

"XXI Corps' attack on enemy's position Beitunye–
"El Jib–Lifta will be discontinued till arrival of fresh
"troops. Report exact line on which you consolidate.
"Chief congratulates you and all under your command on
"the unflinching determination which has led to great
"successes under the most adverse circumstances."

These congratulations were well deserved. Though the swift advance to cut the Nablus road had failed in its latter stages, it had indeed been, taken as a whole, a substantial success. In the capture of Nabi Samweil there had been an element of luck because, without previous intention of attacking it in the dusk, the leading troops of the 75th Division had found themselves face to face with it as daylight was fading.[2] Its defence had been a brilliant feat of arms. The attacks on El Jib had been resolutely carried out. The whole advance by the three divisions against an ever-

---

[1] XXI Corps.
G.H.420.      24th.

Regret failure to carry out mission to-day. Summary day's information would show enemy holds practically continuous line strongly from south of Iksa to Beitunye with large number of machine guns. Enemy shows no disposition to break and a different morale to that experienced last three weeks. He has much more artillery at his disposal than we have managed to get forward. Further attack in this sector by one division will in my opinion fail unless supported by simultaneous attacks by other formations on north and south. All hostile artillery both from north and south has been concentrated on this sector to-day.

6 p.m.      52nd Division.

[2] Officers were of opinion that the column fired on by the 4/D.C.L.I. after the capture of the mosque was either a reinforcement or a night garrison moving up. In either case it is clear that the mosque position was weakly held. But in war what is called "luck" is often the reward of a quick and bold decision. Had Lieut.-Colonel Cassels waited for the arrival of the supporting battalions before launching his attack, he would have encountered that reinforcing column in position and would have had a very different reception.

SITUATION IN THE PLAIN 213

stiffening defence had been characterized by boldness, 1917. determination, and a spirit which triumphed over hunger, Nov. cold, wet, and sickness amid harsh and stony hills.

### CONTEMPORARY EVENTS IN THE PLAIN, 19TH–25TH NOVEMBER.

On the 19th November the Desert Mounted Corps line Maps 1, 2. in the Shephelah and the plain ran from Nalin (7 miles east of Lydda through El Yehudiye (5 miles north of Lydda), Tell Abu Zeitun, on the left bank of the Nahr el 'Auja, and thence along the river to the sea, the 7th Mounted Brigade being east of the railway and the remainder of the front being held by the A. & N.Z. Mounted Division with the Camel Brigade attached. This big front, in length 18 miles as the crow flies, was held by posts about half a mile apart with mounted patrols to keep them in touch. On the night of the 20th the 54th Division, less one brigade, was put at the disposal of the Desert Mounted Corps and took over the centre of the line, relieving the 7th Mounted Brigade on the night of the 22nd and extending its right to Nalin. It was on the 20th that the captured Turkish railway was first put into working order between Beit Hanun and Junction Station, thus greatly lessening the difficulties of supply,[1] and on this date the 60th Division arrived in the Majdal area. It reached Junction Station on the 22nd. The Australian Mounted Division, less the 5th Mounted Brigade attached to the XXI Corps, was withdrawn to Majdal where it could be fed directly from the railway, in order that a proportion of its camel transport might be handed over to the Yeomanry Mounted Division in the hills. G.H.Q. issued orders on the 23rd for the 74th Division to move up to Gaza from Deir el Balah, and to begin its advance to Junction Station on the 25th.

The line had been very quiet in the plain and the foot-hills. Refugees were returning to Jaffa, and shops were re-opening. The enemy did not shell the town, in which some of the most valuable property was owned by Germans and Turks, or the wealthy little German colony of Sarona north-east of it.

As previously stated, the Desert Mounted Corps had

---
[1] See p. 185.

## 214 THE BATTLE OF NABI SAMWEIL

1917.
24 Nov.
Map 12.
Sketch 20.

been ordered to seize a bridgehead across the Nahr el 'Auja on the 24th November to induce the enemy to believe that the advance was to be continued along the coast. The A. & N.Z. Mounted Division's plans for this operation had to be made very swiftly. General Chauvel's orders to establish a bridgehead and seize Muwannis, a village half a mile north of the river and a mile and a half from the sea, were not issued to Major-General Chaytor until 12.15 a.m. on the 24th November; the latter's orders, after having been approved by the corps, were issued at 10 a.m., and the advance took place at 1 p.m. The division had been given a call upon the 189th Heavy Battery (less one section) and 380th Siege Battery attached to the 54th Division,[1] and any of its divisional artillery which that division could spare. The heavy artillery could not be brought up in time, but the 270th Brigade R.F.A. (less one battery) of the 54th Division was temporarily transferred to the A. & N.Z. Mounted Division. The 1st L.H. Brigade with the Inverness Battery attached had been withdrawn to rest at Sdud, so that the division had only two other batteries at its disposal. The Inverness Battery was ordered to march to Jaffa on the 25th in case it should be needed.

The main operation was to be carried out by the New Zealand Brigade, which was to be relieved on the banks of the 'Auja by the 161st Brigade, 54th Division, less two battalions, the latter brigade having been put under the orders of the A. & N.Z. Mounted Division. The New Zealanders were to cross the bar at the river's mouth, turn east, clear the right bank for two miles, and attack Muwannis from the west. On the right the 2nd L.H. Brigade (less the 6th A.L.H. attached to the 54th Division at Lydda) was to demonstrate against Mulebbis. At the last moment it was decided that the battalions of the 161st Brigade, the 4th and 6th Essex, should also cross, at the mill at Jerishe, S.S.E. of Muwannis. These battalions only received orders to co-operate while their relief of the New Zealanders was in progress during the morning of the 24th.

---

[1] It will be recalled that one section of each of these batteries had been attached to the 52nd and 75th Divisions respectively at the capture of Junction Station (see p. 159). On the advance into the Judæan Hills beginning they had been transferred to the 54th Division, one section of the 189th being sent up to the XXI Corps as recorded on p. 208.

# A DIVERSION AND ITS FATE 215

The little operation [1] was conducted without a hitch **1917.** and took the enemy completely by surprise. The Canter- **24 Nov.** bury Regiment crossed the bar at a gallop, the Turkish post defending the crossing taking to flight. Despatching a squadron northward to cover the approach to the bar, the regiment wheeled right-handed and occupied Muwannis before 2 p.m. The Wellington Regiment, which had followed the Canterbury across the bar, took Kh. Hadra, a mile and a quarter E.N.E. of Muwannis, at 3.30, and with the support of the 3rd Light Armoured Motor Battery captured Hadra bridge. A company of the 4/Essex crossed at Jerishe and moved into Muwannis. The captures included 29 prisoners of the *31st Regiment, 3rd Division*, a machine gun and a Lewis gun, while the British suffered no casualties whatever. At night a position was organized, two companies 4/Essex digging themselves in north of Hadra, and two and a half companies of the 6/Essex at Muwannis. Two squadrons of the Auckland Regiment patrolled in front of the infantry position at Hadra, one of the Wellington at Muwannis, and a squadron of the Canterbury held the ford at the mouth of the 'Auja, the remainder of the New Zealand Brigade being south of the river. The A. & N.Z. Field Squadron threw across a pontoon bridge at Jerishe.

The Turks quickly gave proof that they did not intend **25 Nov.** to permit the establishment of a bridgehead. At 4.15 a.m. on the 25th November the outpost squadron of the Auckland Regiment north of Kh. Hadra perceived the enemy concentrating to the north-east, and a few minutes later the Turks began their advance, shelling Kh. Hadra heavily. The Canterbury Regiment was ordered to cross the bar at the mouth of the 'Auja and advance against the right flank of the attacking column, but before this move took effect the position had to be abandoned. The Wellington Regiment was ordered to move up towards Jerishe and to be ready to cross to support the position at Hadra. It came under heavy shell fire some distance south of Jerishe and took cover while awaiting orders, but at 9.50 was withdrawn as it was now too late for it to intervene. The two companies of

---

[1] It has not appeared necessary to prepare a separate map or sketch for this attack or the counter-attack of the following day. They can be followed on Map 12 and Sketch 20, " The Passage of the Nahr el 'Auja," which relate to the more important operations of a month later.

the 4/Essex, whose trenches were too shallow to give adequate cover from artillery fire, fell back at 8.15 a.m., with the Auckland squadrons, and both managed to cross under fire, several wounded being brought over by strong swimmers. The New Zealand machine guns inflicted considerable loss on the advancing enemy, and his pursuit was checked by the fire of the Somerset Battery; otherwise the situation of the troops on the right bank would have been very ugly.

At 9.30 a.m. a strong body of the enemy attacked Muwannis, which had to be hastily evacuated. The companies of the 6/Essex were withdrawn, and crossed by the pontoon bridge at Jerishe and by the mill weir. Then the mounted troops withdrew by the bar at the mouth of the 'Auja, covered by a squadron of the Canterbury Regiment under Major H. C. Hurst and several guns of the machine-gun squadron. Major Hurst's squadron retired mounted from one fire position to the next, and was able to cross mounted. In this case also the artillery did good service in checking the Turkish pursuit, particularly the Somerset Battery, the commander of which, Major M. Clowes, remained on the right bank observing for his battery until the last moment, and had to swim across.[1]

The enemy made no attempt to follow up his success, and by the time the two remaining battalions of the 161st Brigade had moved up from Sarona any danger there may have been of his obtaining a footing south of the 'Auja was over. The casualties of the New Zealand Brigade in the action were 54; those of the 161st Brigade 120, which included a number of men drowned in attempting to swim the river, and, as is known from Turkish reports, 45 captured by the enemy. The attack was carried out by parts of the *3rd* and *7th Divisions* and its losses were nearly thrice as great as those of the British.[2]

The defects of the operation are sufficiently obvious. A weak force was hastily pushed across a river forty feet in breadth and set to hold a position of insufficient depth with the river at its back, with every prospect that the enemy would make a strenuous effort to regain the bank. The 270th Brigade R.F.A. was moved back into bivouac after the crossing, and arrived on the scene of action the following

---

[1] "New Zealand Official History," p. 163.
[2] See Note at end of Chapter.

Sketch 14.

# TURKISH COUNTER-OFFENSIVE.

Situation at 6 p.m. 28th Nov. 1917.

Scale of miles.

British in red.     Turks in green.

Compiled in Historical Section (Military Branch).     Ordnance Survey 1928.

day too late to be of much service, the whole artillery defence thus resting upon a single horse-artillery battery.

NOTE.

### TURKISH MOVEMENTS FROM THE 16TH TO THE 25TH NOVEMBER.

At midnight on the 14th November Falkenhayn issued orders for a general withdrawal. The *Eighth Army* was to retire behind the Nahr el 'Auja. On the *Seventh Army* front the *III Corps* was to withdraw north of Jerusalem by the 18th, with rear guards at Bethlehem, which were to maintain their position until the *XX Corps* had retired. The last-named was to fall back on Jerusalem and take over the defences, on which work had begun. Its commander, Colonel Ali Fuad, did not like this task, but Falkenhayn promoted him to the rank of major-general, which apparently assisted to overcome his reluctance. The Marshal withdrew his own headquarters from Jerusalem to Nablus on the 19th. He had also intended to withdraw the *19th* and *24th Divisions* to that town, but the latter, moving up the Nablus road, was compelled to face west to meet the advance of the British. By the 20th the troops for the defence of Jerusalem had taken up their positions: at Bethlehem *27th Division* (probably only a few hundred rifles); from the railway to some distance north of the Jaffa road *XX Corps* (*26th* and *53rd Divisions*); about Bire *III Corps* (*3rd Cavalry* and *24th Divisions*).

The Turkish attack of the 25th which threw the British south of the Nahr el 'Auja was carried out by Falkenhayn's orders by the *XXII Corps* with parts of the *3rd* and *7th Divisions*. Forty-five prisoners, all belonging to the 4/Essex, were captured. The casualties were comparatively heavy, amounting to 437, including 86 killed.

The *19th Division* made an extraordinary march. It appears to have moved from Jerusalem north to Nablus, west to Tul Karm, then south to Abud, 10 miles north-east of Lydda, and must have covered over one hundred miles between the 18th and 25th, to find itself in the end less than 20 miles north-west of Jerusalem.

# CHAPTER X.

## THE TURKISH COUNTER-ATTACKS IN DEFENCE OF JERUSALEM.[1]

(Maps 2, 10; Sketches A, 14, 15, 16, 17.)

### THE ATTACKS OF THE 27TH NOVEMBER.

Maps 2, 10. Sketches A, 14.

IN war, as in sport, there comes sometimes a moment when—to borrow a phrase from the jargon of the latter—the attacker is forced to "take a breather." War is not sport, and the military commander can give new impetus to an attack which has run down by relieving his tired troops. But in either case the moment is critical, for it provides the quick-thinking and resolute defender with a chance to turn to the offensive.

This moment had now come. The British Commander-in-Chief had been forced to order the relief of the weary and weakened divisions of the XXI Corps by the fresher ones of the XX Corps in order to complete the operations for the capture of Jerusalem. A pause was unavoidable, and Marshal von Falkenhayn did not neglect his opportunity. Fortunately the fact that all his divisions had been heavily engaged, while many had lost a high proportion of their strength and had been severely shaken, lessened the risk to which the British were exposed by being compelled to allow the enemy a moment's respite.

The 60th Division had moved up one brigade group (the 179th) to Qaryet el 'Inab on the 24th November, taking over the front at Soba and Qastal from the 75th Division.[2]

---

[1] The Report of the "Battles Nomenclature Committee" fixes the Battle of Nabi Samweil as lasting from the 17th to the 24th November. The next action, according to the Report, is the Capture of Jerusalem, 7th to 9th December. This chapter is concerned with events which come in the Report under the general heading of "Jerusalem Operations." The fighting between the 27th November and 3rd December, which was hard enough and critical enough to be remembered as a separate battle, has here been recorded under the heading "The Turkish Counter-Attacks in Defence of Jerusalem."

[2] See p. 213.

The remainder of the 60th Division advanced to 'Inab on the night of the 25th, and in the early hours of the 26th the 180th Brigade relieved the 156th Brigade of the 52nd Division between Beit Surik and Nabi Samweil, the Scots brigade moving back to bivouac near Beit 'Anan.

1917.
25 Nov.

On the 25th Sir Edmund Allenby issued his orders for the relief of the XXI Corps by the XX, of which the 60th Division was now in line, the 74th on the march to Majdal in the Philistine Plain and the 10th preparing to advance northward from Deir Sneid—the two latter being about four and five days' march respectively from the front. The line in the hills, less that held by the Yeomanry Mounted Division, was to be taken over by one division of the XX Corps. The XXI Corps was to leave one of its divisions in reserve to this part of the front and send the other back to Junction Station. General Bulfin thereupon issued orders for the relief of the 52nd Division by the 60th to be completed by dawn on the 28th. The 75th Division was to move back into the plain. For the time being the Yeomanry Mounted Division was to remain in its present position, but was later to be relieved by the Australian Mounted Division; while the 5th Mounted Brigade was to concentrate about 'Artuf, north of the Jerusalem railway and south-east of 'Amwas.

The dispositions of the XXI Corps on the morning of the 27th November were, then, as follows:—on the right the 179th Brigade of the 60th Division held the line astride the Jaffa road, through Soba and Qastal, its left a mile and a half south-east of Beit Surik. On its left was the 180th Brigade, under the orders of the 52nd Division, its line curving sharply eastward from near Beit Surik to take in the mosque at Nabi Samweil. From north-west of Nabi Samweil to beyond Beit Izza was the 157th Brigade. Then came the exhausted and depleted Yeomanry Division, mustering about eight hundred rifles, the 8th Brigade on the right covering Beit Duqqu and Et Tire, the 6th in the centre covering Beit 'Ur el Foqa, the 22nd on the left facing almost north between Foqa and Tahta. By great exertions the Leicester Battery had been brought up to cover the Foqa position and the Berks Battery to Tahta. From Tahta to the nearest post of the 54th Division west of Shilta was a distance of 5 miles. This gap, in rough and trackless country, had not hitherto had much significance, while the

27 Nov.

Turkish forces defending Jerusalem had been separated from those in the plain; yet it seems doubtful if G.H.Q. realized how wide it was, for the situation map of the 26th shows a continuous line of posts across the hills. Falkenhayn, having transferred the *19th Division* from the *Seventh Army* to the left flank of the *Eighth*, was now in a position to advance into the gap,[1] but this fact was unknown to the British Intelligence.

The first activity of the Turks was shown at 2.30 a.m. on the 27th, when several parties penetrated between the 179th and 180th Brigades and attacked the flank posts of each. The enemy was quickly driven out, and all was quiet until noon, when Nabi Samweil was bombarded for three hours. At 3 p.m. there came an infantry attack of which the main weight fell upon the 2/19th London of the 180th Brigade just west of the mosque. This was broken up chiefly by the fire of rifles and Lewis guns, but Stokes mortars and in some cases hand grenades were employed to drive away parties of the enemy hiding behind boulders and stone walls close to the British line. After 6 p.m. the artillery fire slackened, and it was found possible to relieve the last brigade of the 52nd Division, the 157th, by the 181st. All three brigades of the 60th Division were now in line from Soba to north-west of Beit Izza, and Major-General Shea assumed command of this front. The 52nd Divisional Artillery had not yet been relieved.

On the thinly held line of the Yeomanry Mounted Division the attack was more serious. There were advanced posts of this division at " City Hill " a thousand yards east of Et Tire, and at Sheikh Abu ez Zeitun, a mile and a quarter east of Foqa: the former held by a troop of the City of London Yeomanry, 8th Mounted Brigade; the latter by 3 officers and 60 men of the Berks Yeomanry, 6th Mounted Brigade. To the Zeitun Ridge from Foqa was a climb of two hours. Major-General Barrow was somewhat uneasy for this post, but its maintenance seemed to him a necessity; for should the Turks establish artillery on the ridge—and the approach from their side was far less difficult—the position at Foqa, and even perhaps Tahta, would become almost untenable. At 2 p.m. both posts were attacked, City Hill

---

[1] See p. 217.

Sketch 15.

by about three hundred Turks, Zeitun by about six hundred, each party supported by artillery.  1917. 27 Nov.

The troop at City Hill fell back after being heavily shelled and losing its commander. A second troop was then sent forward and temporarily re-occupied the hill, but was soon forced to withdraw to "Signal Hill," half a mile to the north-west. This position was reinforced by two squadrons of the 1st County of London Yeomanry, who built stone sangars. Meanwhile at Zeitun the garrison held out gallantly all day, beating off repeated attacks. Though a few reinforcements reached it during the afternoon its strength by nightfall had fallen to one officer and 26 men. It was reinforced at night by about fifty officers and men of the Bucks and Berks.[1]

Hard as it had been, and was like to be on the morrow, to withstand the Turkish attack from the east, Major-General Barrow was still more concerned regarding the gap on his left. He had been told that the 7th Mounted Brigade was to move up on the following day to his support, and now telegraphed to the Desert Mounted Corps requesting that the brigade should march through the night. It moved back during the 27th from Rishon le Ziyon to Deiran, left Deiran at 9.30 p.m., and accomplished a fine march in the darkness over an abominable track. The XXI Corps also sent an order to the 52nd Division that a battalion of the 155th Brigade, which was near Beit Sira, should move up before dawn to El Burj, a mile south of Shilta, to cover the gap.

In the Philistine Plain the enemy struck at Wilhelma, Sketch 15. the prosperous little German colony just west of the railway, his attack falling mainly upon the 162nd Brigade of the 54th Division. When day broke it was discovered that the Turks had moved forward in strength and were holding a line between Rantye, north of Wilhelma, and the railway. Their first attack, however, was to the south-east, against the 10/London at Deir Tureif, and was beaten off without difficulty at 10 a.m. A smaller attack against the 5/Bedfordshire at Beit Nebala also failed. The fall of Bald Hill on the left flank (which will presently be described) exposed the front of the 4/Northampton, which had three companies in line between Wilhelma Station and El Yehudiye, to the

---

[1] These attacks were carried out by the *24th Division*, the *3rd Cavalry Division* supporting it by fire.

enemy's observation, and his artillery fire increased considerably. Soon after midday a heavy attack was launched, mainly against the station, which was lost, but recovered by a counter-attack. Meanwhile the enemy was building up a strong firing line in the Wadi Rantye, south of the village of that name, while about twenty guns were shelling Wilhelma and B/272 Battery in the Wadi Qureika close behind. In answer to this threat Lieut.-Colonel J. Brown, who had just been literally blown out of a window in Wilhelma from which he was observing the battle, but had not been seriously hurt, was forced to move his reserve company into the gap between Wilhelma and the station. At 5 p.m. an attack was launched against Wilhelma, covered by the fire of small groups which had worked their way forward, and was pressed with some resolution until the Turks were within four hundred yards of the British line. There they could be seen, with bayonets fixed, preparing for a final assault, but for the moment unable to make headway against the hail of machine-gun and Lewis-gun fire and that of B/272. In all some 2,000 infantry appeared to be engaged. Though the Turks had been so far held by the steadiness of the 4/Northampton, Lieut.-Colonel Brown decided that if he let them remain so close to his position he would be overwhelmed in the darkness. He therefore sent instructions to his two flanking companies at the station and El Yehudiye each to leave one platoon to hold these positions and with the remaining three counter-attack the enemy on either flank. This bold policy was successful. The flanks of the attacking force gave way, and finally the whole force withdrew to Rantye. The situation of the Northampton had been critical, for any withdrawal would have been most dangerous in view of the fact that the main line of communication with the hills, the Jaffa-Jerusalem road, was so close to the front. The battalion's losses were 93. One Lewis-gun post in a very exposed position was found to have only one man alive when visited after dusk; but he was even then loath to leave, declaring that he had never had such targets before and would probably never see their like again.[1]

---

[1] This attack was carried out by the *16th Division* under the eyes of the Army commander, Kress von Kressenstein, and resulted in " serious "casualties." This is not surprising owing to the Northampton's good field of fire and to the fact that B/272 Battery fired 800 rounds at infantry in

Sketch 16.

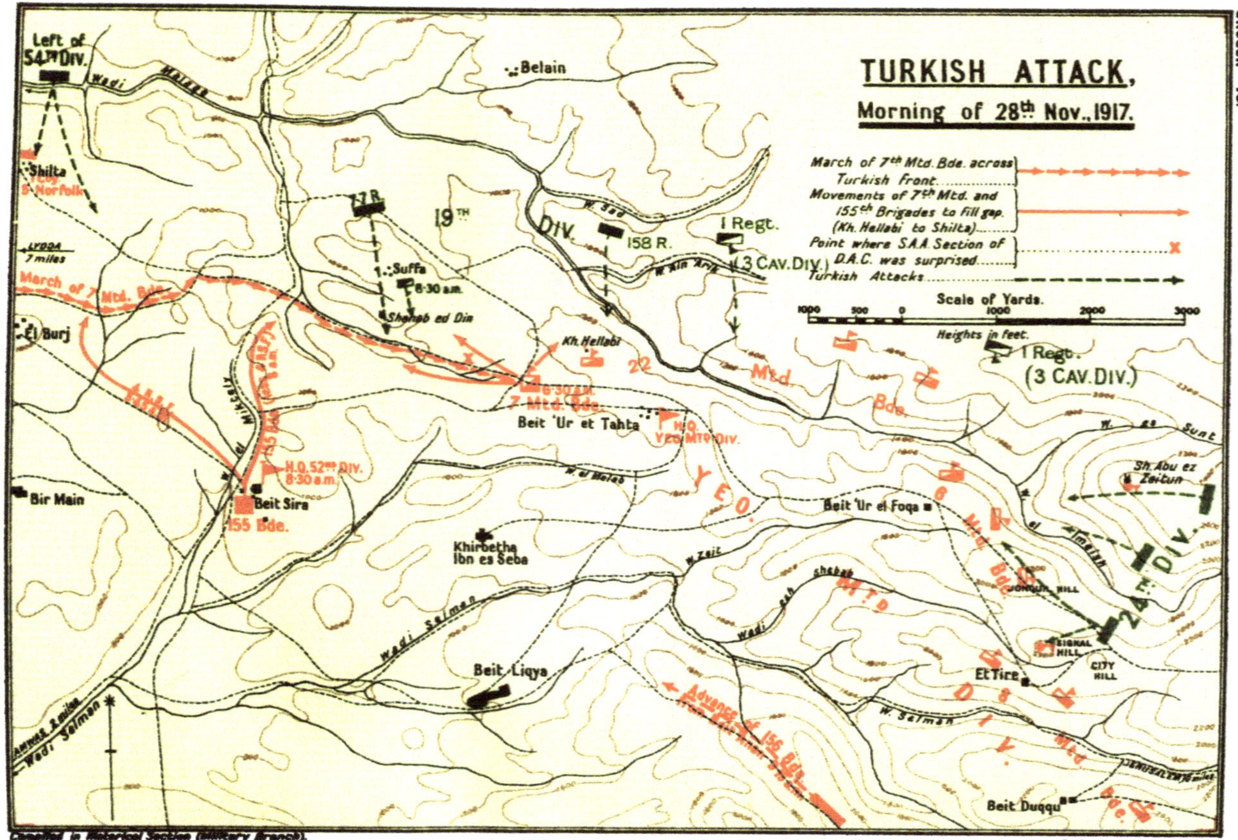


Compiled in Historical Section (Military Branch).
3000/30.

Ordnance Survey 1928.

# LOSS OF BALD HILL

On the left of the 54th Division one company of the 4th Battalion Camel Brigade at Bald Hill, south of Mulebbis, was attacked at 8.30 a.m. by a party 400 strong. The company was driven back 500 yards, and other posts in the neighbourhood were then forced to withdraw. Major-General Chaytor ordered Bald Hill to be recaptured, but, the difficulty of the operation having been represented to him, he decided that the denial of the hillock to the enemy by artillery fire would suffice. The other posts were retaken by the Camel Battalion with the bayonet at dusk.[1]

One cause of the enemy's failure was that he had withdrawn from contact with the British in the neighbourhood of Rantye and Mulebbis after his successful counter-stroke of the 26th, and had had a long and exhausting approach-march—especially in the case of the *20th Division*. Except against the 4/Northampton his blow had been struck more or less in the air. But nothing can excuse his lack of determination in allowing each flank to be turned by three platoons.

1917.
27 Nov.

## THE ATTACKS OF THE 28TH NOVEMBER.

So far the Turkish attacks had met with small success. The enemy's main effort had been reserved for the morrow, but by that time the British had a better chance of parrying it. The 155th Brigade had, as stated, been ordered to send up a battalion to the left of the Yeomanry, and the 4/R. Scots Fusiliers moved off from Beit Sira before 6 a.m. towards El Burj, 2 miles to the north-west. The 7th Mounted Brigade had been marching through the night to Tahta, and at 8.30 the Desert Mounted Corps ordered the 4th L.H. Brigade of the Australian Mounted Division to move to Berfilya, 2 miles west of El Burj. The division, less the 5th Mounted Brigade, had been resting at Majdal until the 27th. On that

28 Nov.
Maps 2, 10.
Sketches A, 14, 16.

---

the open at an average range of 3,700 yards. The other batteries of the 272nd Brigade R.F.A. were also in action, but at long range. Owing to the length of the front held by the brigade and the flatness of the ground behind Wilhelma, the bulk of the artillery had to be stationed at such distance from the line that it could be moved in case of need. Once action was joined these batteries were prevented from advancing by the Turkish fire.

[1] This Turkish attack was carried out by troops of the newly-arrived *20th Division*, which had just marched down from Tul Karm. (See Note at end of Chapter.)

day the 4th L.H. Brigade marched to Deiran, and was followed at night by the divisional troops and 3rd L.H. Brigade, which reached Deiran at 7 a.m. on the 28th.[1] The 4th L.H. Brigade set out at once for Berfilya, but while on the march received orders to move straight on to Beit 'Ur et Tahta.

The march of the 7th Mounted Brigade is an extraordinary example of what may occur in war when lack of imagination causes each side to disregard the possible moves of the other. The brigade turned off the Lydda–Jerusalem road west of El Burj on to the track leading to Tahta. Thence for over four miles it moved across the gap in the British front and, though neither side was aware of the other's presence, across the rifle muzzles of the *19th Division*, which was prepared to attack at dawn. The cavalry squadron of that division must have been in Suffa, 3 furlongs north of the track, before the long British column had passed it. By 4.45 a.m. the head of the brigade was halted in the valley three-quarters of a mile west of Tahta. The regiments began to off-saddle after their march and set about preparing a breakfast not destined to be eaten.

The situation of the 22nd Mounted Brigade was at this moment as follows:—the East Riding and Stafford Yeomanry, under the command of Lieut.-Colonel the Hon. Guy Wilson of the East Riding, were holding the high ground N.N.W. of Foqa to cover the left of the 6th Mounted Brigade and had come under the orders of Br.-General Godwin. The Lincoln Yeomanry was at Kh. Hellabi, north-west of Tahta; so that, in addition to the great five-mile gap on the left of the brigade, there was one of a mile and a half between its two right-hand regiments and that on its left.

Br.-General Wigan rode on to see Major-General Barrow at Tahta, who instructed him to reinforce the 22nd Mounted Brigade. He returned just as day was breaking and was in the act of preparing his orders when there came a sudden burst of fire from the hill above and a line of Turkish infantry was seen advancing. A squadron of the Sherwood Rangers

---

[1] The move of the 4th L.H. Brigade was unconnected with the Turkish attacks and simply preparatory to the relief of the Yeomanry Mounted Division by the Australian. The night march of the rest of the division, on the other hand, was ordered by General Chauvel when he heard how hard pressed the Yeomanry Division had been that morning.

was at once sent up to the left of the Lincoln Yeomanry at Kh. Hellabi and brought this advance to a halt. Br.-General Wigan next sent two squadrons of the Notts Hussars to hold the western end of the Hellabi spur. Soon afterwards Turkish patrols were seen moving down from the high ground just east of Shehab ed Din, a hill crowned by a sheikh's tomb a mile and a quarter west of Kh. Hellabi. A few of the enemy were actually crossing the valley in rear of the brigade and beginning to ascend the heights on the south side. The remaining two squadrons of the Sherwoods with two machine guns were sent to occupy the high ground on the north side and cover that end of the valley. Immediately afterwards the enemy attacked the Lincoln Yeomanry in great strength and momentarily forced it back, but was then checked by the enfilade fire of the Sherwood squadron. The South Notts Hussars carried out a counter-attack, the Lincoln Yeomanry gallantly rallied, and after bitter hand-to-hand fighting the Turks were driven back. For a few minutes they had been firing point-blank down into the valley and had wounded a number of horses.

1917.
28 Nov.

Every man of the 7th Mounted Brigade, but for one horse-holder to every twelve horses, had by now been hurried into the line. Br.-General Wigan, while placing a machine gun in position on a knoll at the western end of the Hellabi spur, had been wounded by a bullet, and Lieut.-Colonel C. A. Calvert, South Notts Hussars, had taken over the command of the brigade. By 9 a.m. the enemy in front was being firmly held but was working round the brigade's flank west of Suffa and Shehab ed Din, where he was opposed only by a car of the 2nd Light Armoured Motor Battery, sent up by General Chauvel. A small party of the Sherwood Rangers under Lieutenant J. C. H. Harter captured the tomb of Shehab ed Din, but was soon afterwards driven out by overwhelming numbers after its gallant commander had been killed. However, the 4/R. Scots Fusiliers was now near El Burj, and further help was forthcoming. At 8 a.m. Br.-General Pollok-M'Call had been ordered to despatch another battalion of the 155th Brigade in the direction of Suffa, but on receiving news of the dangerous situation in that quarter he had set forth with all three battalions. At 9.30 he began an attack on Suffa from the south, with the 4/K.O.S.B., covered by the fire of ten machine guns, while companies of the 5/Scots Fusiliers and 5/K.O.S.B. attempted to turn the Turkish position from the south-west. The attack failed, but by 11 a.m. the ridge on the south side of the valley was occupied, so that the enemy was prevented from advancing further and taking the 7th Mounted Brigade in rear. While this fighting was in progress Br.-General Pollok-M'Call received an urgent appeal from the Yeomanry Division, and at once despatched two companies of the 5/K.O.S.B., his last reserve, to Tahta. The leading company moved up to the Hellabi ridge to the assistance of the 22nd Brigade. Early in the afternoon the enemy got some mountain howitzers into action, and, owing to the scanty numbers of the horse-holders, the valley was soon filled with loose horses, many of them wounded, dashing madly about. The S.A.A. Section of the Yeomanry D.A.C. was caught by a burst of shell fire and had most of its horses killed.

From the east pressure on the 6th Brigade had continued all night. In the morning the garrison of the Zeitun post was shelled out of the tomb and suffered heavy loss. Br.-General Godwin decided to withdraw it to avoid its annihilation, and with great difficulty it crossed the valley. The remnants of the Berks and Bucks, now numbering 120 rifles, were disposed to cover Foqa, on which a strong attack was launched at 2 p.m. The detachment held out stubbornly, but two hours later the Dorsets holding "Jonquil Hill" to the south-east were driven back. About thirty men reached the right of the Berks and Bucks line south of Foqa; the remainder, hard-pressed by the enemy, fell back down the Wadi Zeit, when suddenly the way was barred to the pursuing Turks by the fire of Australian troops. It was the head of the 4th L.H. Brigade. Once again reinforcement had arrived at the most desperate moment

The 4th L.H. Brigade had moved by the same route as the 7th Mounted Brigade till on reaching the neighbourhood of El Burj it had found the road blocked by fire. It then moved up south of El Burj, and Br.-General Grant reported at about 5 p.m. to Major-General Barrow, who placed the brigade south of Tahta in support to the 6th Brigade. The 11th A.L.H. was pushed forward with two machine guns to hold the Wadi Zeit, south-west of Foqa. All horses save a few officers''chargers and packs—180 in all—were sent back to the plains.

On the Yeomanry Division's right the 8th Brigade had held its ground stoutly until the loss of Jonquil Hill exposed its left.  Br.-General Rome then withdrew the 1st County of London from Signal Hill to Beit Duqqu.  The troop of the City of London at Et Tire was almost surrounded, but managed likewise to withdraw to Beit Duqqu.  At 5.30 p.m. Major-General Barrow had a consultation on the telephone with Br.-General Godwin, who informed him that the garrison of Foqa was ready to fight to the last but that there was every prospect that it would be overwhelmed and annihilated.  The divisional commander thereupon ordered the evacuation of the village.  This was covered by fifty rifles of the Bucks Hussars, and the line withdrawn to east and south-east of Tahta, where the 22nd Brigade joined hands with the 6th.  The withdrawal and organization of the new position were made easier by a curious phenomenon, impressive in that historic setting.  There was virtually no darkness that night.  The rocks shone fiery red in the light of the sinking sun, yet threw deep shadows on the same side from that of the rising moon.  The signalling lamps of the 22nd Mounted Brigade had been destroyed by shell fire, but the East Riding Yeomanry was able to keep touch with its brigade headquarters by helio on the moon.  It seemed that once again the sun stood still in the Vale of Ajalon.

The 156th Brigade had also been brought up from Beit 'Anan, and arrived at Beit Liqya at 11.30 a.m.  At 1 p.m. the 4/Royal Scots and one section of the machine-gun company moved up west of El Burj to obtain touch with the 54th Division.  It was now attached to the 155th Brigade and extended its left, while the 156th took over part of the 155th's front.  At night the line from the left of the 60th Division ran as follows:—8th Mounted Brigade, Beit Duqqu; 6th and 22nd Mounted Brigades with two companies 5/K.O.S.B., Tahta; 7th Mounted Brigade (under the orders of the Yeomanry Division), Hellabi Ridge; 156th Brigade (less 4/Royal Scots), on a front of 3,000 yards along the ridge south of the Wadi el Qible to north of Beit Sira; 155th Brigade, from its left to the neighbourhood of Shilta.  The 4th L.H. Brigade was south of Tahta, covering a dangerous point; for there was no touch between the 8th and 6th Mounted Brigades.  A valuable artillery reinforcement had arrived, the 268th Brigade R.F.A. of the 74th Divisional Artillery, which, leaving Latron at 2 p.m., came into action south of Beit Sira after dusk in time to render assistance at Tahta. In the midst of the battle the XX Corps had taken over command from the XXI at noon.

The line was hard pressed after dusk, and the 7th Mounted Brigade repulsed one very fierce bombing attack. And hardly was the original gap closed when a new one appeared on the extreme left.

In the morning a company of the 5/Norfolk, 163rd Brigade, had been sent to occupy Shilta, a thousand yards east of the brigade's right post, this being the only measure possible to the 54th Division, owing to the length of its front, to diminish the gap. At 6.50 p.m. the enemy closed on Shilta unobserved and rushed the position. The company held on to the skirts of the village for three hours, making two counter-attacks. The only surviving officer then decided to fall back half a mile W.S.W. to avoid being surrounded. When this news reached the 155th Brigade two companies of the 4/Royal Scots moved up to a ridge between Berfilya and Shilta, where they found touch with the 163rd Brigade. Once again a dangerous breach was plugged.

In the plain the enemy did not renew his attacks, and the only event of any importance on this date was a raid by a detachment of the 5/Essex, 161st Brigade, attached to the A. & N.Z. Mounted Division, on an enemy post south of Kh. Hadra, which resulted in the capture of eight prisoners and a machine gun.[1]

The enemy had little to show for his excellently conceived surprise advance against the gap in the British front. His failure to gain a great success lay partly in the fact that he was, like the British, fighting in the dark. Falkenhayn may have been accurately informed of the British dispositions, but his *19th Division*, on which his scheme mainly depended, had made long marches over unknown and difficult country, with indifferent maps, and was unaware of the golden opportunity within its grasp. By the evening it was firmly held. But there was another cause: the initiative displayed by the commanders of the 7th Mounted and

---

[1] The enemy lost altogether 23 men in this raid. Turkish "*Yilderim*," Part 4, Chap. IV.

# TURN OF THE TIDE

155th Brigades and the stubborn defence of all the troops engaged.[1]

### THE FIGHTING FROM THE 29TH NOVEMBER TO THE 3RD DECEMBER.

By dawn on the 29th November the situation on the XX Corps front was generally assured. The 231st Brigade of the 74th Division had, after marching for twelve hours out of the preceding eighteen, arrived at Beit 'Anan; a second field artillery brigade, the 264th, was moving up to Beit Liqya. The 10th Division was on the move to Junction Station. The 3rd L.H. Brigade of the Australian Mounted Division was about to set out for Berfilya. The 5th Mounted Brigade was ordered to rejoin its division, leaving the 10th A.L.H. under the orders of the 60th Division. The Turks, considerably inferior in numbers, had had on the morning of the 28th superiority at a vital point. They had not succeeded in breaching the line, and now their superiority was gone. They persisted in their attacks on the 29th, but without success.

1917.
29 Nov.

The enemy began shelling Nabi Samweil at 9 a.m., the mosque, which had already lost its minaret, gradually crumbling away under the bombardment. At 1.30 p.m. the fire was intensified and the enemy, who was always able to reinforce his front line amid the houses and stone walls of the native village unobserved, tried to rush the position. The 2/20th London met the attack by fire of Stokes mortars, Lewis guns, and rifles, and with a shower of bombs. The Turks drew off, rallied and advanced again, then took to flight. A second attack at 5 p.m. gained no ground, though one post of the London battalion had only two survivors out of a platoon.

The enemy occupied Foqa after its evacuation but did not seriously press his attack from that direction. North of Tahta, however, there was bitter fighting. Here the 7/Scottish Rifles, the last reserve of the 156th Brigade, had been brought up into line during the night and was thenceforward continually in action till about 10 a.m. The 7th Mounted Brigade and the 155th Brigade were likewise

---

[1] The attack from the Turkish point of view is described in Note at end of Chapter.

heavily engaged, but resolutely maintained their positions. One shell fell in the 7th Brigade's headquarters, killing the brigade-major, Captain W. O. Bell-Irving, and stunning Lieut.-Colonel Calvert, who, however, remained at his post. The 157th Brigade of the 52nd Division handed over Beit 'Anan to the 231st Brigade of the 74th and marched up to cover the Lydda–Jerusalem road at Beit Liqya. The 231st Brigade began relieving the 8th and 6th Mounted Brigades up to the Wadi Zeit, while the 157th took over from the 7th and 22nd Mounted to half way between Kh. Hellabi and Shehab ed Din. Here the Turks launched yet another attack during the night, but were completely repulsed. The 3rd L.H. Brigade relieved the 155th at El Burj.

On the front of the Desert Mounted Corps the enemy renewed his attacks, but they were on this date less serious. A body 350 strong attacked Deir Tureif, west of Beit Nebala, at 3 p.m., but was driven off. Then, at 6.30 p.m., after a short bombardment, the enemy occupied a hillock north of Nebala. The 5/Bedford promptly carried out a successful counter-attack. At 10 p.m. a company of the 4th Battalion Camel Brigade raided Bald Hill, covered by the fire of " B " Battery H.A.C. and the Inverness Battery, and brought in the bivouac-sheets and ammunition which the battalion had been forced to abandon when it lost the position two days earlier. While the raid was in progress a body of Turks boldly advanced and drove in the right outpost of the 2nd L.H. Brigade, on the left of the Camel Brigade, south-west of Bald Hill. Elated by this success the Turks pressed in upon the outposts all along the 2nd Brigade's front. Repulsed by the Australian fire, they began to dig themselves in, very unwisely as it proved. For dawn discovered them in an untenable position, overlooked by one Australian post and enfiladed by others on either flank. Unable either to advance or retreat, a party consisting of three officers and 147 rank and file, with four light machine guns, surrendered to the 7th A.L.H.

To return to the front in the hills, the events of the morning of the 30th were even more extraordinary, and the fighting more confused, than on the 28th. It has been stated that the 231st Brigade began relieving the 8th and 6th Brigades of the Yeomanry Mounted Division on the 29th. One battalion, the 10/Shropshire Light Infantry,

Sketch 17.

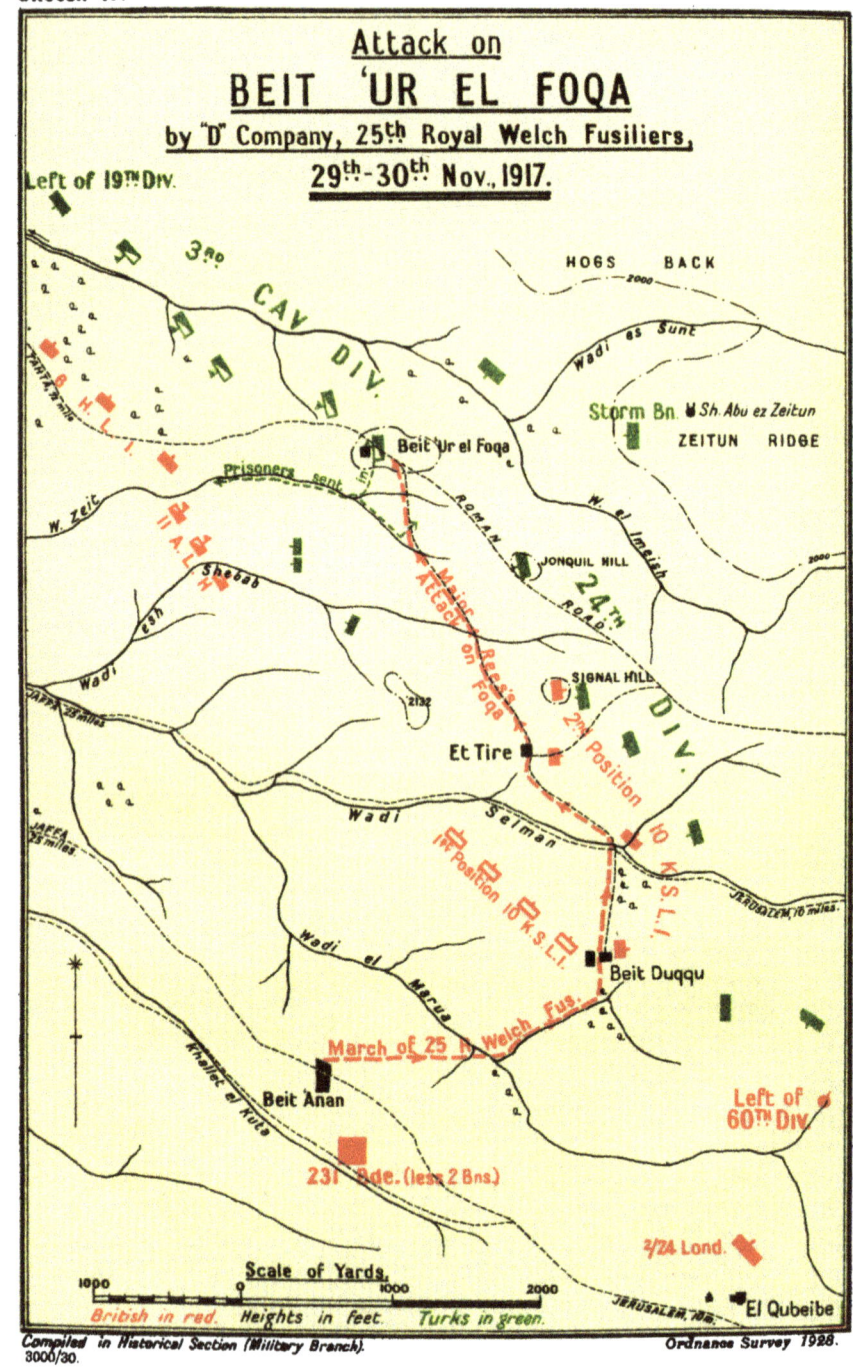

A CONFUSED RELIEF 231

began by taking over a line between Beit Duqqu and the "Ancient Road" south-west of Et Tire. The brigade was ordered by the 52nd Division, to the command of which it had passed, to take over the whole front between Beit Duqqu and the Wadi Zeit—a front held by the scanty remnants of the 8th Mounted Brigade of which no one at that moment seems to have known the exact dispositions. The 52nd Division's order to the 231st Brigade has not been preserved : this is unfortunate, as it might have explained the misunderstandings which followed. It appears that the brigade was ordered to take over Foqa if still in British hands, the staff of the 52nd Division being unaware that it had been evacuated on the night of the 28th.[1] At 6.20 p.m. the 231st Brigade issued orders for the 25/Royal Welch Fusiliers to relieve the 6th Mounted Brigade and " take up a " position from the Wadi Zeit inclusive about Q.5c. [*i.e.* " about 400 yards south-west of Foqa and in advance of " any post then held by the 6th Brigade] to Point 1750 in " Q.12d. inclusive [*i.e.* a quarter of a mile N.N.W. of Et Tire " and at least a thousand yards in front of the line held, if " such can be said to have existed—as a fact it seems certain " that there was a wide gap south of the Wadi Zeit without " a post of the 6th Brigade in it]." To heighten the difficulty, no hill existed where Point 1750 is marked on the old survey, and it in fact represented Point 2297, known to the Yeomanry Division as Signal Hill and lost by it on the 28th.[2] In the same order the 10/Shropshire, which had already taken up a line from Beit Duqqu to the " Ancient Road " south-west of Et Tire, was ordered to swing its left forward and " prolong the right of the 25th Bn. R.W.F. from Point " 1750 exclusive to Beit Duqqu."

1917.
29 Nov.
Sketch 17.

This order, it will be seen, was not only based on a defective map but enjoined the " relief " of a line actually not in British hands. Even then the difficulties of the executants did not end. There were also, it appears, personal instructions

---

[1] The following entry in the War Diary of the 52nd Division, dated the 29th, is apparently a summary of an order issued to the 231st Brigade :—
" 12.10 p.m. 231st Brigade will relieve Yeomanry Division in the line
" Beit Duqqu–Foqa, their left being prolonged by 157th Brigade, who will
" take over the defence of Tahta from Wadi Zeit to right of 156th Brigade.
" If Foqa is held by the cavalry 231st Brigade will send forward one
" battalion to relieve and hold that place. . . ."
[2] See p. 227.

given to Lieut.-Colonel Lord Kensington, commanding the 25/Welch Fusiliers, when he called at brigade headquarters, to be prepared to take up a line from " Point 1750 " to Foqa, and only to rest the left of his battalion on the Wadi Zeit if he failed to occupy the village. These instructions were obviously based upon the 52nd Division's order, of which a summary has been quoted.

The 25/Welch Fusiliers was at Beit 'Anan. It could only reach the position assigned it by way of Beit Duqqu and Et Tire, and Et Tire at least was *known* to be in possession of the enemy. Lord Kensington arranged with Lieut.-Colonel H. Heywood-Lonsdale, commanding the 10/Shropshire, that the latter, swinging forward his left as ordered, should seize the village before the 25/Welch Fusiliers arrived. Two companies accomplished this task with little opposition by 10 p.m. on the 29th. The 25/Welch Fusiliers, however, delayed by the roughness of the country, did not reach Et Tire until 2 a.m. on the 30th. As soon as it arrived one of its companies, with one of the 10/Shropshire, attacked and took Signal Hill, killing a number of Turks and capturing a machine gun. Another company of the 25/Welch Fusiliers, commanded by Major J. G. Rees, was ordered to advance north-west on Foqa.

Major Rees pushed forward up the rough track as swiftly as possible in order to reach Foqa before daylight. His Lewis-gun sections could not keep up with him, and he arrived south-east of Foqa without them, the strength of his company being then about eighty.

The track from Et Tire to Foqa runs into the Roman road just east of the latter village, and it was therefore from the east that Major Rees approached. He had warned his advanced guard that it would find Foqa held by " Scotsmen " or Turks, probably the latter." It found the enemy in great strength, standing to with arms piled, while the morning meal was being cooked over camp fires. Hesitation meant annihilation, and Major Rees instantly ordered the interpreter to summon the enemy to surrender. Several machine guns opened fire, but within a few moments about 450 Turks laid down their arms. Major Rees ordered them to be formed up under their own officers and marched off down the Wadi Zeit under an escort. The head of the column took the wrong path and moved south by the route

Sketch 18.

## Capture of JERUSALEM.

Situation at 6 p.m. 7th Dec., 1917.

Scale of miles.

British in red. Turks in green.

Compiled in Historical Section (Military Branch).
3000/30.
Ordnance Survey 1928.

followed by the company in its attack. Fired on by the enemy from east and south-east, a number of the prisoners broke away and escaped. Then the 11th A.L.H. astride the Wadi Zeit became aware of these strange and unexpected operations in front of its line. The commanding officer, Lieut.-Colonel J. W. Parsons, quickly realized the situation, and his covering fire enabled the little escort to bring in the remainder of its prisoners, numbering 8 officers and 298 other ranks.

1917.
30 Nov.

Major Rees had now only 60 men to hold Foqa, which was strongly attacked. He beat off the enemy until at 8.30 a.m. on the 30th he found himself almost surrounded, then broke out by the way he had come and with the remnant of his company succeeded in joining the support company of the 10/Shropshire covering Et Tire and facing Signal Hill.[1] The Turks next turned their attention to that point. At 2.30 p.m. a party 400 strong drove the detachment from Signal Hill, and was thence enabled to render Et Tire untenable and force the 10/Shropshire to fall back to its original line. Several Lewis guns and a number of prisoners fell into the hands of the enemy.

As soon as the situation was known, which was not until Major Rees reported at brigade headquarters at 5 p.m., the 74th Division (which had meanwhile taken over its 231st Brigade from the 52nd Division) issued orders for the 229th Brigade to make good the line from the Wadi Zeit to " Hill " 1750 " (Signal Hill), while the 231st pushed forward a fresh battalion on the left of the 10/Shropshire to recapture Et Tire. This attack could not be carried out until daylight on the 1st December. The 24/Welch retook Et Tire without difficulty, but found that the right of the 229th Brigade was not on Signal Hill (the so-called " Hill 1750 "), but on Hill 2132 half a mile west of it.[2] The brigade was asked to rectify the error, but intense machine-gun fire prevented any advance. In these circumstances it was impossible to hold

1 Dec.

---

[1] Foqa was recaptured by the Storm Company of the *50th Division*, one of the formations which had been broken up. (See p. 24.) Turkish " *Yilderim,*" Part 4, Chap. IV.

[2] Lieut.-Colonel J. Younger, commanding the 14/Black Watch of this brigade, had despatched six platoons during the night of the 30th to occupy Signal Hill and had received a report that the detachment had reached its destination. Going to his right flank at dawn he discovered the error.

Et Tire, and the 24/Welch took up a line west of it, in touch with the 10/Shropshire on the "Ancient Road" and with the right of the 229th Brigade at Hill 2132. In all this confused fighting the 231st Brigade had 251 casualties,[1] but it captured 8 officers and 300 other ranks, in addition to inflicting considerable loss on the enemy.

Maps 2, 10.
Sketch 16.
On the night of the 30th November the 4th L.H. Brigade, having been relieved by the 74th Division at Tahta and in the Wadi Zeit, had relieved the left of the 156th Brigade east of El Burj. The 3rd and 4th L.H. Brigades were now in line side by side, with the 7th Mounted Brigade in support, awaiting relief by the 5th Mounted Brigade, which had now reached Qaryet el 'Inab. Major-General Hodgson took over command of the front from north of Beit Sira to south-west of Shilta.

About 1 a.m. on the 1st December the Turks renewed their attacks, both at Tahta against the 157th Brigade and north-east of El Burj against the 3rd L.H. Brigade. At Tahta they succeeded after two fruitless attempts in driving the right company of the 5/H.L.I., which had lost half its strength, off two hundred yards of the ridge in front of the village. Br.-General Hamilton Moore forbade an immediate counter-attack and ordered the rocky ground to be first thoroughly searched by Stokes mortars. At 4.30 a.m. a company of the 5/Argyll & Sutherland Highlanders and the company of the H.L.I. reoccupied the position with little difficulty.

The other Turkish attack penetrated the line of the 8th A.L.H. north-east of El Burj, but four separate onslaughts with stick bombs were driven back by a squadron under Major A. Crawford on a rocky hill. A squadron of the Gloucester Hussars, still attached to the 3rd L.H. Brigade,[2] was rushed up to fill gaps in the line, and the Hong Kong Battery came into action. Next a company of the 4/Royal Scots Fusiliers from Beit Sira, led by Lieut.-Colonel N. G. Stewart-Richardson with a small party of bombers, arrived on the scene just as the Turks were launching a new assault. A bombing party under 2nd Lieutenant S. H. P. Boughey

---

[1]

|  | Killed. | Wounded. | Missing. |
|---|---|---|---|
| Officers | 3 | 11 | 1 |
| Other Ranks | 38 | 152 | 46 |

[2] See p. 199.

## ANOTHER ATTACK ON FOQA

attacked the enemy bombers engaging Major Crawford's squadron and after a fierce struggle forced them back. The Turks continued to attack with desperate bravery, but another company of the 4/Scots Fusiliers came up, and the enemy, galled by the steady fire of the 3rd L.H. Brigade and assailed by a shower of bombs from the Fusiliers, fell back to cover. The Scotsmen, infuriated at losing their hard-earned rest, vented their rage upon the enemy, pursuing him without respite.[1] Boughey outran his men and forced twenty-five Turks to surrender. A moment later he was shot dead. He received the posthumous reward of the Victoria Cross.

1917.
1 Dec.

Australians, Scotsmen, and Yeomen held their position till dawn, when it was found that the attacking force was at their mercy, since its retreat was barred by a barrage laid down by the machine guns of the 3rd L.H. Brigade. Six officers and 106 other ranks surrendered, while over one hundred dead were found upon the ground. The prisoners belonged to the *Storm Battalion* of the *19th Division*. They had proved themselves troops of high quality, and were far better equipped than most Turkish troops at this period, wearing shrapnel helmets and carrying 1917 Mausers.[2] The battalion, 600 strong, was almost annihilated.

On the morning of the 3rd December a last attempt was made by the 74th Division to recover Beit 'Ur el Foqa. This attack was carried out by the 16/Devonshire, 229th Brigade, and launched from the head of the Wadi Zeit at 1 a.m. At 3.30 the village was captured with 17 prisoners and three machine guns. But heavy counter-attacks were launched before consolidation could be carried out, and the battalion was galled by machine-gun fire from the neighbouring ridges. Bombing and hand-to-hand fighting continued all the morning. The 74th Division was, in fact, learning over again the lesson which had been impressed upon Major-General Barrow when he had had time to study the ground,

3 Dec.

---

[1] The story goes that one was heard to cry, as he threw bomb after bomb : " They mairched us a hunder miles ! (Tak' that, ya . . . !) An' " we've been in five fechts ! (Anither yin, ya . . . !) And they said we " wur relieved ! (Tak' that, ya . . . !) And we're oot oor beds anither nicht ! (Swalla that, ya . . . !) " " The Fifty-Second (Lowland) " Division," p. 471.

[2] It appears from Turkish " *Yilderim*," Part 4, Chap. IV, that the left of the *54th Division* also took part in the attack.

## 236  THE TURKISH COUNTER-ATTACKS

that Foqa was untenable while the Zeitun Ridge, Jonquil Hill, and the hills to the north were in the enemy's hands. Soon after noon Lieut.-Colonel A. C. Mardon obtained permission to withdraw through Tahta. The losses were heavy, numbering 286, and included three company commanders.[1]

It was obvious that local attacks of this nature were not worth their cost, and General Chetwode, who had now had time to reconnoitre the front, ordered them to stop. The Turks had been defeated and fought to a standstill; he had now all the fresh troops of his own corps up—the 10th Division having relieved the 52nd—and could afford to mature his preparations for the capture of Jerusalem.

### NOTE.

#### THE BATTLE FROM THE TURKISH SIDE.

Falkenhayn's aim was now to take pressure off the *Seventh Army* and delay an attack on Jerusalem until the reinforcements which he was expecting had arrived. These consisted of the *20th Division*, which was to join the *Eighth Army ;* the *1st Division*, the *Caucasus Cavalry Brigade*, the *Asia Corps*, and from east of Jordan the *7th Cavalry Regiment*[2] and *150th Regiment*, destined to support the *Seventh Army*. The *20th Division*, as we have seen, was in action on the 27th November. The leading battalion of the *Asia Corps* was expected at Nablus on the 12th December, and the *70th Regiment* of the *1st Division* at Jenin about the same date. The troops from over Jordan began to arrive in Jerusalem on the 1st December.

The *19th Division* was placed under the orders of the *Eighth Army* for good reason, though its attack was intended to assist the *Seventh*. The Marshal feared that if he handed it over to Fevzi Pasha the latter would draw it closer to his own front, whereas he wished to make a divergent attack against the British left and the gap at Suffa. The plan was brilliantly conceived, but it failed to take into account the fatigue of this very fine division after its long marches. " On the 1st December," writes Colonel Hussein Husni, " our attack gave out and was stopped " before positions which Falkenhayn could not penetrate."[3]

Yet the Marshal did not despair. He was quite convinced that the British would never reach the Nablus road at Bire. He " fixed his "attention on the daily change of the enemy's dispositions," confident that Jerusalem could not be taken until the British shifted their attack further south and drove the *XX Corps* from its position south of Nabi Samweil. Sir Philip Chetwode, we shall see, was of the same opinion. It was the Marshal's misfortune that, while his *III Corps*, not thought worthy of defending Jerusalem, had defended the Nablus road with courage and devotion, his *XX Corps*, selected for the greater task, was to fail abjectly when put to the test.

---

[1]
|  | Killed. | Wounded. | Missing. |
|---|---|---|---|
| Officers . . | 3 | 9 | 2 |
| Other Ranks . | 49 | 132 | 91 |

[2] See p. 12, f.n.
[3] Turkish " *Yilderim*," Part 4, Chap. IV.

# CHAPTER XI.

## THE CAPTURE OF JERUSALEM.

(Maps 1, 2, 11; Sketches A, 18, 18A, 19; Diagram II.)

THE PLAN OF ATTACK AND ADVANCE OF MOTT'S DETACHMENT.

THE advance on Ram Allah had been made in order to capture the Holy City without bringing it into the immediate zone of operations and risking damage to sites held sacred by men of three religions. That advance had failed to reach its objective. On coming up into the hills General Chetwode had decided that, despite this risk, it would be necessary to shift his right further south so as to have full value from the Jaffa–Jerusalem road, which had hitherto been on the British right flank and of little use for artillery and supply. The road was now doubly valuable because the Turkish railway had been restored as far north as Ramle, to which supply trains were run on the 5th December; thus for the first time since the opening of the offensive it was possible to discharge stores directly from the rail on to a good road. The line from Junction Station to Jerusalem was also taken into use on the 3rd December as far as 'Artuf, a distance of 8 miles. Progress in restoring this line was very slow owing to the number of bridges destroyed by the enemy, which in the narrow gorges could only be rebuilt one after another, and through traffic to Jerusalem was not established until the 27th January.

Maps 2, 11. Sketches A, 18.

At a conference at Qaryet el 'Inab on the 3rd General Chetwode outlined his plan to his divisional commanders. This was, in brief, to extend his right to 'Ain Karim, south of the Jaffa–Jerusalem road, and advance north-eastward from the line 'Ain Karim–Biddu with the 60th and 74th Divisions, skirting the western suburbs of Jerusalem; while the 53rd Division, now returned to his command, advanced up the Hebron road from the neighbourhood of Edh Dhahriye to cover the right flank of the attack and threaten Jerusalem from the south. The preliminary moves were to begin on the 4th, and that night the 10th Division, on the left of the 74th, extended its right, taking over the front up to Beit Duqqu.

1917.
1 Dec.

On the morning of 1st December G.H.Q. issued instructions to "Mott's Detachment" which consisted of the 53rd Division, the XX Corps Cavalry, the 91st Heavy Battery, and the 11th Light Armoured Motor Battery, to be prepared to move to the Seil el Dilbe, 5 miles south-west of Hebron, leaving one brigade to guard the Hebron road between Dhahriye and Beersheba. An extraordinary little exploit by two cars of the 7th Light Car Patrol proved that the enemy had not only withdrawn from Hebron, as was known, but even so far north as Bethlehem was merely watching the country by means of patrols. Captain W. A. Mulliner, A.P.M. of the Australian Mounted Division, had learnt from an informer that a notorious enemy agent was at a place called "Khalil Rakhman," which he took to be near Hebron, but was in fact Hebron itself.[1] On the afternoon of the 30th November he set off from Junction Station with two Ford cars, commanded by Lieutenant W. P. McKenzie, for Beit Nettif, 11 miles south-east. Darkness caught them on a bad track west of that village, and they were forced to halt for the night at Zahariye. Here they were hospitably entertained at the house of the Greek Patriarch of Jerusalem and informed that the track south-east of Beit Nettif, which they had intended to follow, was impassable. Rather than abandon their mission they recklessly determined to reach the Hebron road by way of El Khudr, south-west of Bethlehem, having been told that there were no Turks actually in the village.

In Beit Nettif next morning they had news that there were after all Turkish patrols at El Khudr, but even this did not dismay them. Driving down into the village, which lies in a valley, they suddenly caught sight of a body of infantry encamped on the slope above. Either the Turks took them for friends, or they were too astounded to fire. In El Khudr itself they were fired on by a cavalry patrol of six, but shot down five of the men and all six horses. A second patrol

---

[1] The Arabic name for Hebron is El Khalil.

# JERUSALEM.

Sketch 18A.

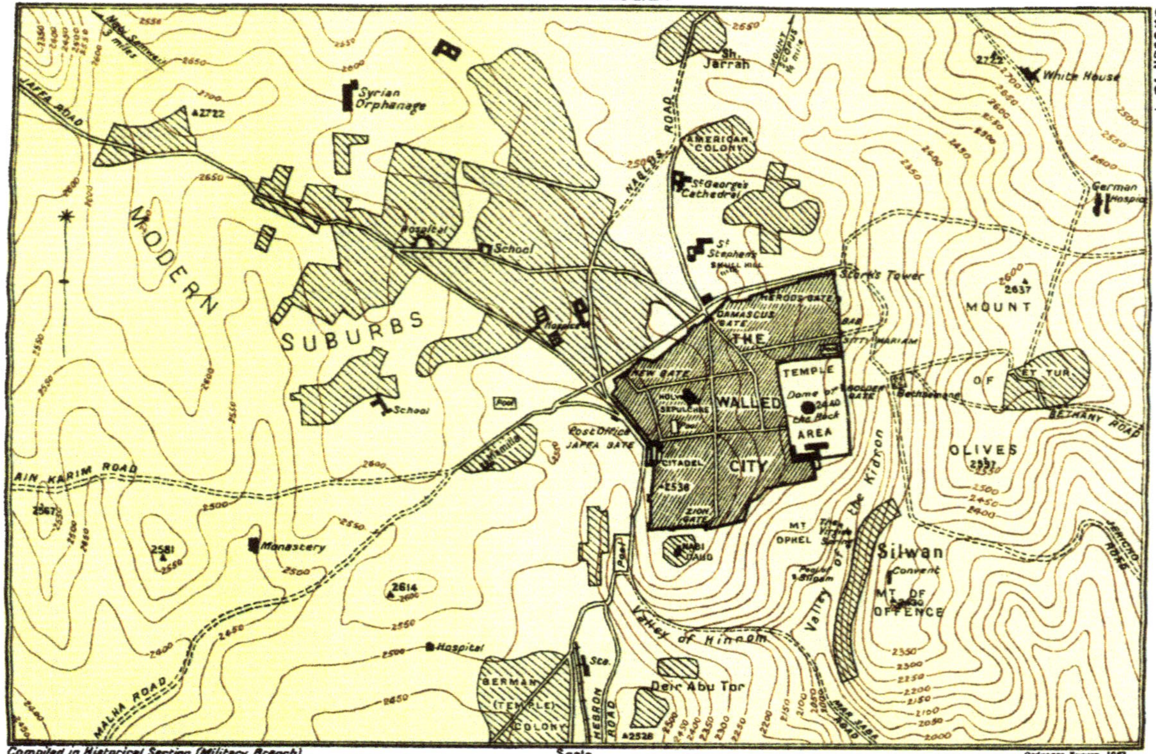


Compiled in Historical Section (Military Branch).
3000/30.

Scale.
0 ¼ ½ ¾ 1 MILE
Contours at 50 Feet V.I.

Ordnance Survey, 1927

## ADVANCE OF MOTT'S DETACHMENT 239

on the Hebron road was scattered, and Hebron reached at 1 p.m. Here there was a Turkish hospital in charge of a medical officer, but there were no combatant troops in the place. The spy had escaped. The road south of Hebron had been damaged by the enemy, but the townspeople, who welcomed the party enthusiastically, sent out a working party and repaired it sufficiently for the cars to pass. That afternoon they drove through the astonished outposts of Mott's Detachment near Dhahriye, reaching Beersheba at 8 p.m.[1]

1917.
1 Dec.

On the 4th December Mott's Detachment advanced to the Dilbe valley.[2] Its only telegraphic communication with the XX Corps was through Beersheba, Gaza, and Advanced G.H.Q.; so on that morning General Chetwode sent his instructions to Major-General Mott by aeroplane. The advance of the detachment was to be as rapid as possible, and it was to be on the line Sur Bahir–Sherafat (that is, astride the Hebron road 3 miles south of Jerusalem) by the morning of the 8th December, the day on which the main attack was to be carried out. Major-General Mott sent back a message by the aeroplane suggesting that he should on the following day move forward and cover Hebron to establish north of the town a refilling point whence he could be supplied during his advance by his camel train.[3] General Chetwode

4 Dec.

---

[1] It must be added that, leaving one car behind for repairs, Captain Mulliner and Lieutenant McKenzie rejoined the Australian Mounted Division in the other on the 2nd December, *via* Gaza, Majdal, and Qatra, having covered 210 miles. Their drive is extraordinary enough to merit record, but, as often happens with remarkable exploits, a myth has grown up about it. It is not the fact that after hearing of the cars' passage through the Turkish lines G.H.Q. issued hasty and indignant orders to Mott's Detachment to advance. As has been stated, G.H.Q., which was aware that there were no Turkish troops south of Hebron, had already warned Major-General Mott to be prepared to advance to the Dilbe valley, and no further instructions were sent to him immediately on receipt of Lieutenant McKenzie's news. The information obtained was, however, valuable, for it showed that no resistance was likely to be met with until the neighbourhood of Bethlehem was reached, and also that the road, except at one point, was in fair condition.

[2] The Seil el Dilbe is not marked on Map 2. It crosses the Hebron road 4½ miles south-west of the town.

[3] The difficulty of supplying Mott's Detachment was great. Supplies were unloaded from the railway at Kharm and carried by caterpillar tractors to Bir Abu Irqaiyiq. Thence they were transported in trucks drawn by mules on the Turkish railway to Beersheba. The divisional train and motor lorries conveyed them, after the advance on Jerusalem had begun, to a dump 3 miles north of Hebron, where they were loaded on to camels.

1917.
5 Dec.

telegraphed his agreement, and on the 5th December the 7/Cheshire established an outpost line north of the town.

On the 5th December General Chetwode issued his orders.[1] It was his intention to attack the enemy positions west of Jerusalem from 'Ain Karim to Nabi Samweil on the 8th December. The main operation was to be carried out by the 60th and 74th Divisions, the boundary between the two being in the first instance the Jaffa–Jerusalem road. After the capture of the Turkish redoubts and trenches the left of the attack was to pivot on Nabi Samweil, the right swinging up so that the advance continued in a north-easterly direction, the boundary between the divisions being now the Wadi Beit Hannina. The final objective was a line astride the Nablus road from Ras et Tawil, $3\frac{1}{4}$ miles north of Jerusalem, through Beit Hannina to Nabi Samweil, that is, facing due north.

The attack was to be made in four stages. In the first the two divisions were to capture the works from north-west of Malha to south of Nabi Samweil. In the second the 60th Division alone was to advance, to a line from the suburbs of Jerusalem on the Jaffa road to the village of Lifta. In the third the swing of the whole line on its pivot at Nabi Samweil was to begin, continuing until the 60th Division's right was on the Nablus road just north of the city. In the last stage the 60th Division was to advance to a line astride the Nablus road at Shafat, 2 miles north of Jerusalem, thence pushing forward detachments to take the high ground at Ras et Tawil; the 74th was to link up with it, occupying Beit Hannina if it appeared to be of value. Special instructions attached for Mott's Detachment laid down that, if the resistance of the enemy were so strong that the line Sur Bahir–Sherafat could not be reached, the 60th Division would be ordered to detach troops to advance eastward towards the Hebron road to assist the detachment. In the more likely case of the detachment's being able to reach its objective, it was thenceforward to co-operate with the main attack by pushing forward one brigade to Malha, north of the railway, to make touch with the 60th Division, while the other moved east of Jerusalem and seized a position covering the Jericho road.

---

[1] XX Corps Order No. 17 is given in Appendix 17.

## PREPARATIONS FOR ATTACK 241

The only heavy artillery available to support the attack, in addition to the 91st Heavy Battery with Mott's Detachment, was the XCVI Heavy Group, which, with the exception of one 60-pdr. battery, was allotted to the 60th Division.

1917.
5 Dec.

On the morning of the 5th December patrols of the 10th Division and Australian Mounted Division discovered that the enemy had withdrawn somewhat during the night. The divisions were instructed to take every opportunity of improving their positions by seizing points of tactical value, but not to become involved in fighting. By midday on the 6th Kh. Hellabi, Suffa, and Shilta were reoccupied. At night the 231st Brigade of the 74th Division relieved the 60th Division at Beit Izza, Nabi Samweil, and Beit Surik, in order to allow the latter to concentrate for the attack. A minor bombing attack on the mosque at Nabi Samweil was repulsed before the relief took place.

6 Dec.

The 7th December passed quietly. The weather was very bad, though this was not wholly a disadvantage, as rain and mist screened the movements of the troops. The men were, however, chilled and wet to the skin. General Chetwode on this date issued to his divisions a rough outline of his future plans. As soon as possible after the objective had been reached the advance was to be continued to secure ground sufficiently far north of Bire and Ram Allah to cover the water supply there. Probably one brigade group of the 53rd Division, the 60th Division, and part of the 74th Division would advance on a narrow front astride the Nablus road, while the 10th Division, hitherto stationary, advanced eastward from Tahta.

7 Dec.

Special instructions were issued regarding the sanctity of the Dome of the Rock and the Church of the Holy Sepulchre within the walls of Jerusalem, and the Garden of Gethsemane and David's Tomb outside them. Warning was sent to Major-General Mott that the Church of the Nativity in Bethlehem and Rachel's Tomb north of the town were likewise to be respected at all costs.

During the night of the 5th December Major-General Mott's advanced guard moved three miles north of Hebron to get a good start for the the next day's march. It had instructions not to delay for tactical reconnaissance but to push straight forward till fired on. Thus only could the detachment hope to be up in time, the distance to the line

5 Dec.

## 242  THE CAPTURE OF JERUSALEM

Sur Bahir–Sherafat being 17 miles as the crow flies and perhaps half as far again by a road with many windings and sharp bends on the hills.

**1917.
6 Dec.**
On the morning of the 6th the advanced guard went forward as soon as it was light enough to see, and, meeting no resistance, gained by noon a strong position 2½ miles north of the Seil el Arrub and some ten miles north of Hebron. During the afternoon the whole detachment closed up to the water which this stream afforded. No further advance appeared possible that day, as the nearest water supply was at Solomon's Pools, about six miles along the winding road. Orders were issued for an advanced guard to push forward at 6.30 a.m. on the morrow in two horns, the 4/Cheshire on the right of the road, the 7/Cheshire on the left, directed against Ras esh Sherife, south-west of Solomon's Pools.

**7 Dec.**
Before daylight failed enemy cavalry had been seen at Sherife, which dominated the road. However, the 7/Cheshire made good the southern end of the ridge by 7 a.m. on the 7th, and after C/265 Battery had fired a few ranging shots the enemy was seen to evacuate his position. Well-sited sangars were found on the hill, which would have given a good deal of trouble had it been defended. The detachment was now on the very spine of the Judæan Hills, Ras esh Sherife being considerably higher than Nabi Samweil, and from the summit Jerusalem could be clearly seen. Shortly afterwards, however, the heights were veiled in cloud and mist, rain began to fall, and it became impossible to see more than two or three hundred yards ahead. At 3 p.m. the advanced guard met with opposition at Solomon's Pools and had a sharp engagement before capturing the ridge which covered them. Major-General Mott went forward to the pools to find out if a further advance were possible. He decided that, as he had come up against the Turkish position defending Bethlehem [1] and could not locate the enemy's artillery or machine guns, and as his transport was held up

---

[1] The defences of Jerusalem on the southern side were actually north of Bethlehem, as will appear from Map 11. The trenches between Malha and Sur Bahir, and also those north of Jerusalem between the Wadi Abeide and Tell el Ful, have been taken from a comparatively small-scale Turkish map, and can only be considered approximate in shape and position. The front-line defences from Malha to Nabi Samweil are from a British map, and may be considered exact.

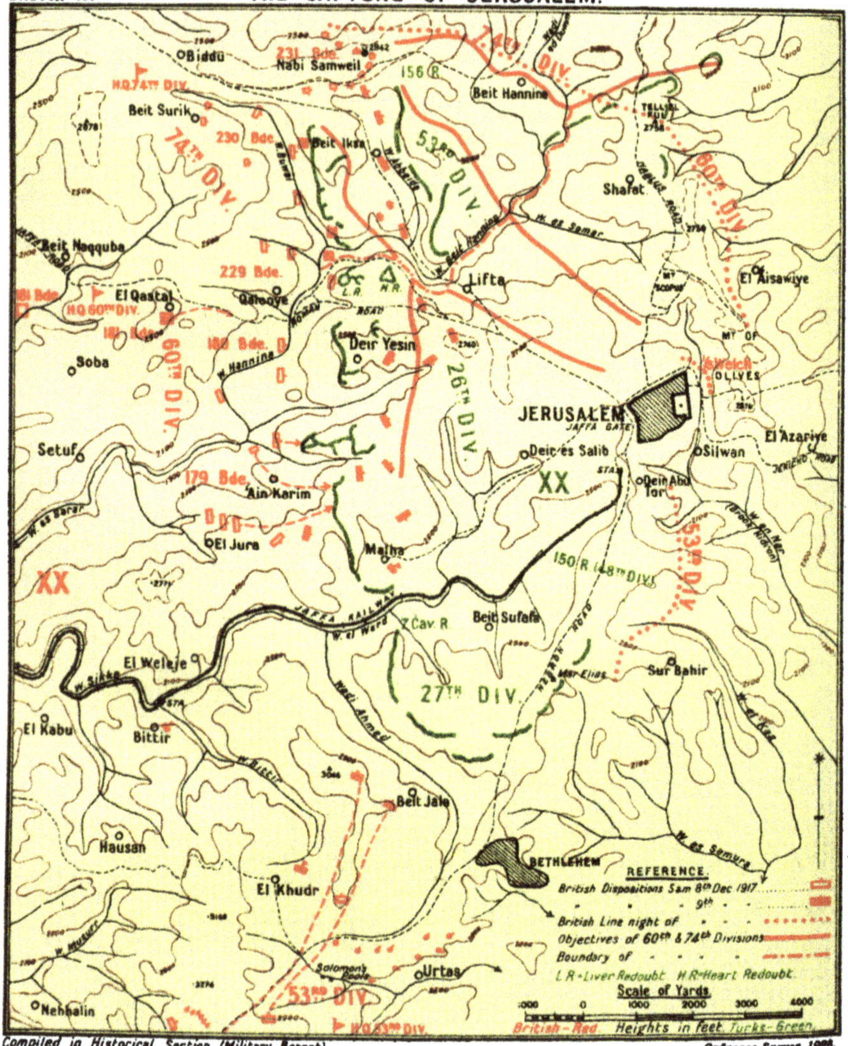

## GENERAL MOTT'S DIFFICULTIES

by the state of the road, he must wait until the following morning. He had hitherto been in advance of his time-table, and it was a stroke of bad fortune that the weather should now have held him up only 4 miles from the objective which he should have reached by dawn on the 8th. At 10.30 p.m. he was able to report to the XX Corps that the Beit Nettif and Et Tine road which runs from the Hebron road at Burak had been cleared as far as El Khudr, and that two troops of the 10th A.L.H. had made touch with his left. General Chetwode telegraphed that the advance must be continued on the 8th, regardless of weather. The troops passed a wretched night in cold, driving rain. Whole teams of gunhorses came down together on the slippery road, to kick and flounder in the darkness and block the struggling traffic. Camels fell with their legs splayed outwards, split at the quarters, and had to be bundled off the road after their loads had been taken off. Several of their Egyptian drivers died from exposure.

*1917. 7 Dec.*

### THE CAPTURE OF JERUSALEM. THE OPERATIONS OF THE 8TH DECEMBER.

The results of the attack carried out by the XX Corps on the 8th December may be shortly summarized before the operations are described in detail. The 60th and 74th Divisions attacked the Turkish works on a front of 4½ miles from south-east of 'Ain Karim to south of Nabi Samweil. The first objective, including the defences east of 'Ain Karim, the village of Deir Yesin and its redoubts, the "Heart" and "Liver Redoubts" covering the Jaffa–Jerusalem road, and the trenches west of the Beit Iksa, was for the most part captured by 7 a.m. Owing to Mott's Detachment being delayed it appeared that the 60th Division's right flank would be in considerable danger if it attempted to continue the advance, which was therefore brought to an end. The 74th Division took Beit Iksa at 11 a.m., but on its front any further advance was checked by the enemy's fire. The corps commander went to the 60th Division's headquarters west of Qastal, and after consultation with Major-General Shea decided to postpone the remainder of the operation until the following day. His reasons were, first, that the 53rd Division was far short of its objective, not having reached

*8 Dec. Maps 1, 11. Sketches 18A, 19.*

Beit Jala, 2 miles south of Sherafat, until the afternoon; secondly, that there was great difficulty in moving forward artillery to support the main attack; and, thirdly, that the troops were already fatigued by the long and difficult approach marches, in cold and wet, which had in most cases preceded their attack on the Turkish works.

*60th Division.* The operation to be carried out by the 179th Brigade, on the 60th Division's right, was of peculiar difficulty. The village of 'Ain Karim and the high ground south of it, in front of the main defences, were known to be held by the enemy, and these had to be captured before the general attack all along the front took place.[1] Rain continued all night. The brigade, which had concentrated about Soba, nearly three miles north-west of 'Ain Karim, during the afternoon of the 7th, was to advance in two columns. The preliminary operation was entrusted to the advanced guard of the right column, consisting of the 2/13th London, with a section of the 521st Field Company R.E. and a company of the 12/Loyal Regiment (Pioneers). The main body consisted of the 10th Mountain Battery, the 2/14th and 2/15th London, and the 2/23rd London from the 181st Brigade; the left column of B/IX Mountain Howitzer Battery and the 2/16th London.

On the left the 180th Brigade was to move down from Qastal and deploy in the Wadi Hannina south of Qalonye at 3.30 a.m.

The capture of the first objective was to be carried out by surprise, without artillery support. As soon as this was completed the field artillery, which was divided into three groups, was to advance gradually through Qalonye, one group being left in action in its old position until the other two were established in the new. The XCVI Heavy Artillery Group was to engage all active enemy batteries on the front of both divisions.

The right column of the 179th Brigade crossed the Wadi es Sarar near Setuf, the advanced guard moving off at 5.15 p.m. on the 7th in order to give the sappers and pioneers some time to improve the route. The column followed the wadi to the point where a small affluent from the village of El Jura entered it, moving thence E.S.E. to a white tower

---

[1] 60th Division Order No. 60 is given in Appendix 18.

above the Russian Colony of 'Ain Karim. This route had been previously reconnoitred; and the 2/13th London, led by Captain E. R. Kisch, reached its destination without hitch, despite the intense darkness,[1] deploying along a stone wall running south-east from the tower. The left column had an easier route, but the approach to the Turkish work on its front from the Wadi es Sarar was precipitous.

1917.
8 Dec.

The task of the advanced guard to the right column was to seize the heights south of 'Ain Karim with two companies, while one company cleared the Russian colony. At 2 a.m. both parties began their advance, and though both met with stubborn resistance the heights were secured by 3.30 a.m. and the colony soon afterwards. The companies on the heights had to meet a succession of counter-attacks which were driven off with the aid of the fourth company, hastily moved up; but the situation of the battalion was for some time dangerous.

At 4.50 a.m. the head of the main body reached the tower, and a company of the 2/15th London was at once sent forward to support the 2/13th on the high ground. Then, at 5.15 the 2/14th London, with two companies in line and two in support, began its attack on the Turkish trench east and south-east of 'Ain Karim. Two machine guns which held up the advance were put out of action, Corporal C. W. Train creeping round a wall and attacking the detachments with rifle grenades, while Corporal F. S. Thornhill supported him by bombing them from the front.[2] Lewis guns were pushed forward to enfilade the trenches, which were then hastily evacuated by the enemy. Having captured them, the battalion pushed on to the higher ground a thousand yards beyond, where it found touch with the 2/16th London at 7.25 a.m.

The left column deployed south of the Wadi es Sarar at 2.30 a.m. and at 3.30 one company of the 2/16th London cleared the village of 'Ain Karim. At 4.15 a.m. the remainder of the battalion attacked the redoubt north of the

---

[1] The commanding officer, Lieut.-Colonel C. M. Mackenzie, had reconnoitred the ground by daylight, on one occasion creeping to within a few hundred yards of the tower. Captain Kisch had spent the four previous nights on reconnaissance, and had made small landmarks, which Turkish patrols were unlikely to notice, to guide himself along the route chosen.

[2] Corporal Train was awarded the Victoria Cross, Corporal Thornhill the Distinguished Conduct Medal.

'Ain Karim–Jerusalem road. The garrison of the front trench was completely surprised and the whole of the work was quickly captured, the first objective being reached at 6.30. It had previously been noted that a Turkish battery was in action behind this ridge, and one company had been detailed to push forward and engage it at once. The battery was caught by Lewis-gun fire as it was limbering up. One gun escaped, after one horse had been killed and cut loose, but the remaining three and the ammunition wagons were taken. The battalion was at the moment isolated, being ahead both of the right column of its own brigade and of the 180th Brigade on its left, and had to face a counter-attack. It held its ground until the 2/14th London came up on its right at 7.25 a.m.

So the line remained until afternoon, when the 2/23rd London was sent up to the heights south of 'Ain Karim to relieve the 2/13th, which moved forward to cover the right flank and took up a position overlooking Malha. This village was occupied by a squadron of the 10th A.L.H. There was no sign of the 53rd Division, and it was clear that were a further advance to be attempted in daylight it would be taken in enfilade and would have poor prospects of success. Br.-General Edwards intended to begin the second stage at 5 p.m., supported by the mountain batteries if they could be brought forward by that hour, but this was, as has been related, cancelled by order of the XX Corps. The brigade had suffered only 277 casualties,[1] while its captures were 12 officers and 230 other ranks, three 77-mm. guns, 4 ammunition wagons, and 12 machine guns.

The 180th Brigade attacked with three battalions in line: 2/19th London the southern portion of the Deir Yesin redoubt, 2/17th the northern, 2/18th the Liver and Heart Redoubts. The Wadi Hannina south of the Jaffa road is broad, covered with olive trees, and rather less steep-sided than north of the road. The movement to the line of deployment down the terraced hillside was, however, difficult. The accuracy with which it was carried out was due to repeated reconnaissances, rendered possible by the sluggishness of the Turks at night. When that was accom-

|  | *Killed.* | *Wounded.* | *Missing.* |
|---|---|---|---|
| [1] Officers . . | 3 | 8 | — |
| Other Ranks . | 54 | 211 | 1 |

plished the brigade had to face the most elaborate defences on the front. All went with amazing speed in the centre and on the left, the garrison of the first-line trenches being completely surprised. Red flares, signals that the front line had been captured, were seen at 5.40 a.m. on the left and 5.55 in the centre. The 2/19th London was, however, held up by machine-gun fire, thus exposing the right of the 2/17th, and did not capture the trenches south-west of Deir Yesin till 7.5. It then pushed on rapidly through the village. On the left the 2/18th London had captured the second great work, the Heart Redoubt, one hour earlier. It then advanced south of its boundary line, the Jaffa–Jerusalem road. The leading platoon saw an enemy column, about two hundred strong, which had apparently retired down the Wadi 'Abbeide from the village of Beit Iksa as a result of the 74th Division's attack, and surprised it by a burst of fire from Lewis guns and rifles. The column was almost destroyed, and of the survivors 5 officers and 50 other ranks surrendered to the 2/18th London.

All attempts to continue the advance were now held up by heavy machine-gun fire from the hill of Kh. el Buqeia, south of the village of Lifta. At 1.15 p.m. Br.-General C. F. Watson went forward to meet Lieut.-Colonel H. J. Dear, commanding the 2/17th London, and decided that this height, which dominated the present position, must be captured. Two howitzer batteries, C/301 and C/302, had now moved forward through Qalonye and were available to support this attack. One company of the 2/20th London was brought up to the right of the 2/17th. The assault was launched at 3.15 p.m., all four battalions taking part in it: a frontal attack being carried out by the 2/19th, the company of the 2/20th working round the right flank of the position, two companies of the 2/17th and a company and a half of the 2/18th round the left. The operation was carried out with great dash, under the eyes of Generals Chetwode and Shea, and the ridge taken at the bayonet's point. General Chetwode had previously come to his decision that no further advance, but for this local improvement of the position, should be made till the following morning. The ground gained was therefore consolidated so far as its rocky nature permitted, the right flank being refused, since the brigade was considerably further forward than the 179th on its right. The 181st Brigade in reserve moved forward two miles, bivouacking south of Qastal.

*74th Division.* The attack of the 74th Division was to be carried out by the 229th Brigade (less two battalions in support to the 10th Division) on the right, and the 230th Brigade (less one battalion in the Beit Surik defences) on the left. The 231st Brigade in the Nabi Samweil defences (less two battalions in the neighbourhood of Beit Izza) was to assist the advance by flanking fire. The first objective was the system of trenches north of the Jerusalem–Jaffa road and west of the village of Beit Iksa. The divisional artillery was prepared to support the attack from south of Biddu and west of Beit Surik, but, as with the 60th Division, the capture of the first objective was to be achieved by surprise. Field batteries and the attached Hong Kong Mountain Battery were subsequently to move forward along the Biddu–Beit Iksa road. In the result, only two groups (six batteries) of the three into which the divisional artillery was divided ever came into action, the third group being prevented from firing a round by bad visibility.

The 229th Brigade (Br.-General R. Hoare) had a narrow frontage, and the attack was carried out by one battalion, the 12/R. Scots Fusiliers, supported by the 12/Somerset Light Infantry. There seems no doubt that the enemy on its front was fast asleep; for hardly a shot was fired as the leading battalion, after descending into the bed of the Wadi Buwai, a tributary of the Wadi Hannina, scaled the steep ascent on the farther side. There was a fight for a few minutes in the trenches, but they were swiftly taken, with 104 prisoners and a machine gun.

Major-General Girdwood had suggested to Br.-General M'Neill that the two attacking battalions of the 230th Brigade should advance to their positions of assembly in the Wadi Buwai over the top of the hill west of its gorge as the Scots Fusiliers had done. The brigadier, however, feared that the descent of this slope, higher and steeper on his front than on that of the 229th Brigade, would cause so much noise that the enemy would inevitably be warned, and he obtained permission for them to move along the wadi from south of Biddu in single file. This arrangement was successful in effecting a silent approach. The darkness of the night and the roughness of the wadi's bed made the advance so slow that, though it began at 12.30 and even the leading battalion had only about three miles to go, the 10/Buffs and 12/Norfolk did not begin their climb out of the wadi on to the Beit Iksa ridge till nearly 5 a.m. They had to face the steepest hillside on the whole front of attack, solid rock covered with loose boulders; and its ascent took them about forty minutes, so that they were twenty-five minutes late in launching their assault, which should have been made at 5.15. As a consequence they did not reap the full advantage of the general surprise, and met with fairly heavy machine-gun fire. During the climb the Buffs converged slightly on the Norfolk, with the consequence that the enemy was able to work a small body of men round their right flank. The Turkish counter-attack was, however, half-hearted and was easily beaten off. The Buffs then brought their left shoulders up and advanced directly on the Turkish trench, which was taken with little further trouble, 25 prisoners being captured.

At 7.30 a.m. the two battalions advanced on Beit Iksa, and now for the first time had serious difficulty from the cross-fire of machine guns on Nabi Samweil on the left flank and the El Burj ridge in front. The Nabi Samweil guns must have been served by stout-hearted men, for some of them fired from positions in the enclosures within fifty yards of the line held by the 231st Brigade. Nabi Samweil, now a filthy shambles, littered with the bodies of men and animals, some of them over a fortnight old, was continuing to fulfil the important rôle it had played in all the earlier fighting in this area; for the 230th Brigade also had the majority of its machine guns and its Stokes mortars in action on the hill to cover its advance. About 11 a.m. the outskirts of Beit Iksa were reached, but here the advance was for some time held up. One company of the 15/Suffolk was brought up from support and placed on the left of the 12/Norfolk. The artillery had been bombarding El Burj since 7.30, but it was the fire from the left flank rather than from that point which was causing trouble. The village of Beit Iksa was occupied during the afternoon, but it was decided to postpone the advance across the deep gully separating it from El Burj till the morrow. The brigade's casualties numbered 181.

The troops of both divisions who had taken part in the attack passed an unpleasant night. Owing to the nature of the country which they had to traverse, they had advanced without greatcoats or packs, and the waterproof sheets which they carried rolled on their shoulders were their only protection. For water they had in most cases to be content with a half-bottleful saved from the morning, while, as all the convoys had broken down owing to the slippery state of the tracks, rations had not arrived when the troops left their bivouac, so that they had to rely upon their iron ration till the following morning.

*Mott's Detachment.* Mott's Detachment, it will be recalled, had possession of Solomon's Pools south of Bethlehem on the night of the 7th.[1] Soon after daybreak on the 8th the atmosphere cleared sufficiently to permit observation of the ground north and north-west of Bethlehem, but this period of good visibility was very short. The enemy's guns in and around Bethlehem at once began to shell the road-junction at Burak very accurately. The difficulty in communicating with the XX Corps—helio not being available owing to the absence of sun—was now seriously felt; for Major-General Mott, in face of the instructions he had received regarding the sanctity of Bethlehem, was unwilling to take the responsibility of engaging this artillery without reference to General Chetwode. A wireless message was sent off at 8.40, but not received till 11.40, and then in a mutilated form. The reply empowering him to engage the Turkish artillery does not appear ever to have reached Major-General Mott.

Meanwhile General Chetwode, who had no mounted troops but the 10th A.L.H. to cover his right flank, was becoming concerned for it, and indeed for the success of the whole operation. He sent Major-General Mott two urgent messages at 9 and 9.30.[2] In the first he called for a report of progress and pointed out the importance of pushing on, as the 60th and 74th Divisions had taken their first objective. The second was even more emphatic :—" Report your posi-
" tion. Report situation on your front. Push your attack."

At 11.37 Major-General Mott telegraphed in reply that he had ordered an attack on the high ground about Beit Jala, which should start about noon. According to the divisional war diary, this order had been issued seven minutes earlier, at 11.30, but there is no record of its receipt by the 160th

---

[1] See p. 242.
[2] The first was received at 9.33, the second at 10.12.

## MOTT'S DETACHMENT DELAYED

Brigade.¹ That morning at dawn there had been two battalions only north of the road junction at Burak: the 4/Welch covering Solomon's Pools and the 7/Cheshire east of El Khudr. Major-General Mott did not desire that these two battalions should leave their positions, so fresh troops had to be moved up to capture the hills at Beit Jala. These were the 2/4th Queen's and 2/10th Middlesex of the 160th Brigade (Br.-General V. L. N. Pearson) which had been brought up during the night close to Solomon's Pools. The Queen's had received an order at 6 a.m. to advance to a position behind the outpost line of the 7/Cheshire, and both this battalion and the 2/10th Middlesex had some difficulty in passing the road junction, the enemy's shelling being so accurate that this had to be carried out by rushes in small parties. The two battalions received no order to capture the hills at Beit Jala till 4 p.m.² When they did advance they met with no opposition whatever, and occupied the position before darkness fell.

1917.
8 Dec.

Major-General Mott telegraphed to General Chetwode at 6.15 p.m. that the advance had taken place, that the enemy had been reported leaving Bethlehem during the afternoon, and that artillery fire from east and north of the town had ceased soon after mid-day He added that he hoped to occupy Beit Sufafa, 2 miles north-east of Beit Jala, by 9 a.m. next day, unless seriously delayed by fog. General Chetwode replied that if the enemy had retired he must quicken his advance by keeping as many troops as possible on the main road. On reaching the line Sur Bahir–Beit Sufafa he was to carry out the programme of the 8th, that is, to move one brigade east of Jerusalem and one south-west of the city. As soon as a message was received by XX Corps giving the hour at which he was prepared to move north of that line, orders would be sent to the 60th Division to advance simultaneously.

---

¹ Major-General Mott states that he had previously seen Br.-General Pearson and pointed out to him his objective, the Beit Jala heights.
² The authority for this statement is the War Diary of the Queen's. The other records of the division for this date are meagre, owing to the conditions in which they were written.

## The Surrender of Jerusalem.

1917.
9 Dec.
Map 11.
Sketches A, 19.
Diagram II.

The surrender of Jerusalem on the 9th December was one of the most dramatic incidents of the war. At a moment when a resumption of fighting and, indeed, a stouter resistance than that of the previous day were to be expected, it was found that the enemy had vanished. It seems that something like panic had spread among several Turkish units after the loss of their works, and that the commander of the *XX Corps*, despairing of rallying the troops for a further defence of Jerusalem, ordered the evacuation of the city. By dawn, therefore, the British found themselves with no enemy in front of them and Jerusalem at their mercy. An element of comedy was added by the Mayor's attempts to hand over the keys to a number of chance-met individuals and his difficulty in persuading any one to accept them.

The first to encounter the Mayor and his party appear to have been Privates H. E. Church and R. W. J. Andrews, mess cooks of the 2/20th London, who had lost their way during the night and wandered about in search of water till they reached the suburbs about 5 a.m. Here they met a crowd of civilians who informed them that the city desired to surrender. Not feeling themselves to be equal to the occasion, they returned to their battalion. The next British soldiers to meet the party—which was now displaying a flag of truce—were Sergeants F. G. Hurcomb and J. Sedgewick, 2/19th London, on outpost duty, who likewise professed themselves unable to accept the surrender. The third meeting was with two officers of the 60th Divisional Artillery, Majors W. Beck and F. R. Barry, who were carrying out a reconnaissance near Lifta. They promised to telephone back news of the surrender, and returned to their batteries to do so. The most fruitful meeting was with the commander of the 303rd Brigade R.F.A.

This brigade had been posted near Qastal, on the Jaffa–Jerusalem road, and had during the night got orders to move forward as many guns as possible across the Wadi Hannina. The weary, fine-drawn horses stumbled and slipped among the wet rocks before reaching the road, but by dawn all three batteries were close to Qalonye. The brigade commander, Lieut.-Colonel H. Bayley, rode forward with his three battery commanders to reconnoitre. Beyond Qalonye they took

Diagram II

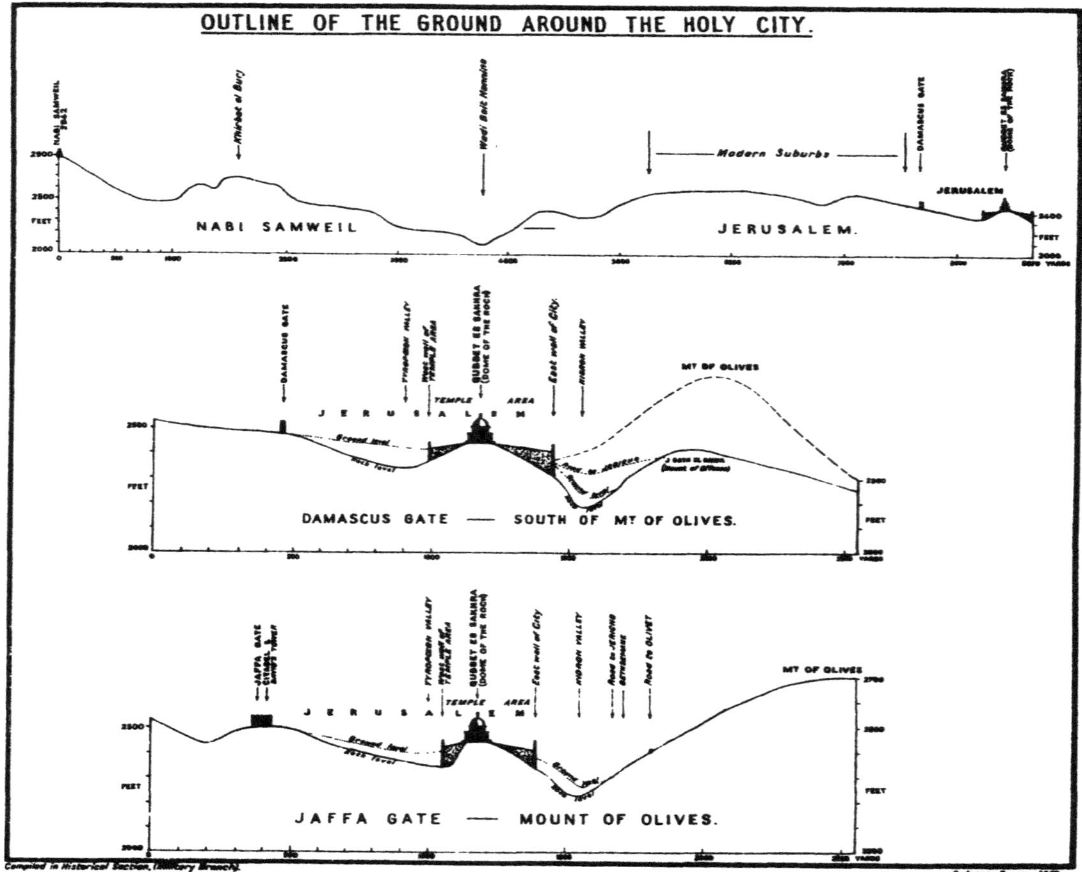


Compiled in Historical Section, (Military Branch).

Ordnance Survey, 1927

3000/30.

the Roman road up the hill. This would, it was evident, involve a gruelling pull for the horses, but the newer branch passing near Lifta seemed too exposed. The rain had ceased and a clear day was dawning. It was Sunday.

Having reached the junction of the two branches and seen no signs of the enemy, Lieut.-Colonel Bayley concluded that it would be safe to bring up his guns by the Lifta road. He sent back his battery commanders to do so, directing them to rejoin him as soon as they had seen their batteries on the move. One of them, Captain R. Armitage, returned within a few minutes, and the two officers walked forward, followed by their horse-holders. Among the first houses of the suburbs, which now came into view, they saw a group of people, and in their midst a white flag displayed.

Lieut.-Colonel Bayley at once sent back Captain Armitage to bring up a couple of armed gunners, so that he was now alone but for his orderly. A man from the group in front whom he beckoned forward told him in French that the Turks were gone and that the Mayor of the City was with the white flag. Walking up to the group, he was introduced to an Arab gentleman in European clothes, who greeted him with the declaration, in English :—" I am the Mayor of " Jerusalem, and I desire to surrender the City to the British " General."

After questioning the Mayor and learning that the enemy had indeed evacuated Jerusalem, Lieut.-Colonel Bayley sent back his second battery commander, Major F. G. Price, who had now returned, to telegraph to Major-General Shea a message to that effect.[1] He was then rejoined by the third battery commander, Major E. M. D. H. Cooke, whom he directed to ride down the Jaffa road with his orderly and an Arab policeman and take over the Post Office. He remained some time in conversation with the Mayor, who gave him all the information he could, and then decided to ride on and see if all was well with Major Cooke. At this moment he was joined by Br.-General C. F. Watson, commanding the 180th Brigade, who had seen his message.

Major Cooke had meanwhile reached the Post Office,

---

[1] Priority 60th Division.
Jerusalem has surrendered. Colonel Bayley, R.F.A., is now with the Mayor awaiting any General Officer to take over the City.
Major Price, R.F.A. 8.55 a.m.

discovered that all the telegraph wires were cut, assembled the officials, and had the building locked up. As time went by without British troops appearing and a small party of Turkish stragglers actually passed the Post Office, the officials had grown nervous, and were much relieved when Br.-General Watson and Lieut.-Colonel Bayley, with an escort of ten gunners, arrived upon the scene. They rode amidst the plaudits of the crowd to the Jaffa Gate, and walked through the gap beside it made for the German Emperor's entrance. Inside the walls there was no disturbance of any sort; in fact, they were greeted by some American ladies, overjoyed at their arrival. Br.-General Watson put a guard of one officer and one gunner on the gate until two companies of the 2/17th London, which he had sent for, should arrive. Actually, however, the first formed body of troops upon the scene was the Westminster Dragoons, advanced guard to the 53rd Division, which came up the Station Road from Bethlehem. Then Major-General Shea, who had been ordered by General Chetwode to take over the city, arrived in a car and formally accepted the surrender of Jerusalem in the name of Sir Edmund Allenby. He established his headquarters at the English Ophthalmic Hospital of St. John on the Jaffa Road.

Since midnight, it was learned, the Turks had been streaming through the suburbs, moving either north along the road to Nablus or east along that to Jericho. By a fitting coincidence the morning which saw their sullen departure was the festival of the Hanukah, commemorating the recapture of the Temple from the Seleucids by Judas Maccabæus in 165 B.C. The haste of their flight saved many of the principal Christian and Jewish citizens, who had been ordered to leave with their families and walk—for all vehicles had been seized by the enemy—to Nablus. The inhabitants received Major-General Shea with wild enthusiasm. There was a little looting by the populace, mainly from sheer exuberance of spirits, which promptly ceased on the arrival of troops of the 53rd and 60th Divisions.

Thus fell Jerusalem, which is recorded in its lengthy annals to have been thirty-four times captured by, or retaken from, an invader. Among those who have entered it as conquerors after storm, siege, or surrender without fighting, are some bearing famous names in religious and secular history, as David, Nebuchadnezzar, Alexander, Antiochus the Great, Judas Maccabæus, Pompey, Herod, Titus, Omar, Godfrey of Bouillon, Saladin. It is known to fame for over three thousand years, though tradition puts the Jebusite city stormed by David about 1000 B.C. on Mount Zion, outside the present walls. These walls are not ancient (as we reckon antiquity when we have to do with Jerusalem), but for the most part they stand upon the foundations of ancient fortifications and their stones can often be identified as having been used in the walls of Herod or of the Crusaders. To the hasty or thoughtless visitor the city is disappointing. The walls themselves are stately and some of the gates dignified, especially the Damascus Gate; the Dome of the Rock is magnificent. But everywhere, especially outside the walls, he sees what is modern, trivial, or unworthy of its setting; much also that is ancient enough, but has had ascribed to it age greater than is its due and associations which obviously date from the Middle Ages or even later. Nevertheless, study or the aid of a scholarly guide will enable him to summon up on their actual sites scenes from the city's wonderful history. The most sacred of all sites, Golgotha, will probably always be a matter of dispute, because the line of the "city wall" without which it lay is uncertain; but the foreground of the view from the Mount of Olives must be almost what it was two thousand years ago; the Dome of the Rock stands upon the site of the Temples of Solomon, Nehemiah, and Herod; Hezekiah's subterranean conduit to the Pool of Siloam is as authentic as any work ascribed to an age so distant can be; and all about are genuine vestiges of a mighty past. Within the walled city the narrow streets, sometimes covered in, sometimes broken by flights of steps, follow very much the same courses as when they were trodden by the occupying Crusaders.

The western and northern suburbs are modern, and contain many churches, hospitals, schools, Jewish colonies, and along the Jaffa road shops. It was the suburbs alone which were now occupied by the British, who placed guards over the gates of " Old Jerusalem " and allowed no troops to pass through until the Commander-in-Chief had made his formal entry.

Later on, when the safety of Jerusalem was assured, it was constantly visited during the intervals of active operations by the troops, to whom a number of chaplains, deeply instructed in its history, acted as guides. Its capture made an extraordinary impression upon all men's minds. Lieut.-Colonel Bayley writes of the companies of the 60th Division marching down the Jaffa road on the 9th December :—" I " have seen troops under many different circumstances, but " never have I seen more joyful faces than had those Lon-" doners." These men were under no illusion that the war was over or that the capture of the Holy City was more than a stage in it. Undoubtedly they were affected by the spell of the place. When the days of sight-seeing came, parties followed their guides from point to point with reverence and eager curiosity. Half-forgotten lessons of childhood were recalled and given new significance by association with their scenes, in and about a city which had been very familiar by name, indeed, but almost as a site of legend, as " in the Bible," and not quite belonging to this world.

### The Advance of the 9th December.

Between 8 and 9 a.m. messages had reached XX Corps headquarters that patrols of the 179th Brigade, moving up the road from 'Ain Karim, had found no enemy on their front up to the Jaffa road ; and that those of the 231st Brigade reported a withdrawal on the brigade's left. Having likewise learnt that the leading troops of the 53rd Division had reached the line Sur Bahir–Beit Sufafa at 8.30 a.m.. General Chetwode ordered the 60th and 74th Divisions to resume their advance to the objectives of the previous day, while the 53rd Division was also ordered to carry out its original programme. The advance began at 10.30 a.m., though the 181st Brigade, which had orders to pass through the 179th at 'Ain Karim, was able to move forward only one battalion, the 2/24th London, at 10.45, the main body following three-quarters of an hour later. This brigade had prior to the attack handed over most of its machine-gun and Lewis-gun mules to the 179th in exchange for camels, in order to increase the latter brigade's mobility. As a result, the 181st had great difficulty in moving ; nor was there time for its mules to be returned to it before it passed through the 179th. Heavy rain began to fall about midday, to add to the hardships of the troops and the obstacles even to pack transport caused by the inundation of the country.

1917.
9 Dec.

The Turks were still holding the ridge (Mount Scopus) north of the city along which runs the Nablus road, and as the leading battalion of the 181st Brigade debouched from the network of streets between Lifta and Jerusalem about 1.45 p.m. it came under machine-gun fire from this high ground, the 2/21st and 2/24th London having some sharp fighting before the enemy was driven back from the neighbourhood of Sheikh Jarrah. Over seventy Turkish dead were found upon the position and ten prisoners taken, the casualties of the 181st Brigade being 43. On the left the 180th occupied Shafat on the Nablus road at 1.30 p.m.; and half an hour later Tell el Ful, which dominates all the country round, was taken by the 2/20th London, touch being made there with the 74th Division. So far there had been no more than rear-guard actions, but now heavy fire was opened on Tell el Ful from the hills south of it and east of Shafat. An attack was quickly organized and carried out frontally by a company of the 2/17th London, and against the enemy's right flank by the 2/20th with two machine guns. By 4 p.m. the Turks were dislodged, and soon afterwards the 2/20th was able to establish outposts facing north-east along the whole of the original fourth objective.

The 74th Division met with opposition from a few snipers only, the ground proving the most formidable obstacle to its advance. The 229th Brigade (the two remaining battalions of which rejoined that morning from their position in support to the 10th Division) reached without fighting a line from Tell el Ful to the Wadi ed Dumm, and the 230th Brigade thence, north of Beit Hannina, to the neighbourhood of Nabi Samweil. The 231st Brigade, thus relieved at Nabi Samweil, took over from the 10th Division as far as the Wadi esh Shebab, so that the front of that division should be closed up in case of a counter-attack from the north; but this move, owing to the roughness of the country was not completed until the early hours of the 10th December.

On the 53rd Division's front the 159th Brigade was ordered to move at dawn, and at 5.30 a.m. the advanced guard, consisting of two squadrons of the Corps Cavalry Regiment (Westminster Dragoons), the 5/Welch, a section of the 91st Heavy Battery, the 436th Field Company R.E. (less one

## 258  THE CAPTURE OF JERUSALEM

section), the brigade machine-gun company, and 30 cyclists, marched past Solomon's Pools. A few Turkish stragglers were found in Bethlehem, but no resistance was encountered. The ancient monastery of Mar Elias, 2 miles north of Bethlehem, was reached at 8 a.m., and at 8.45 the advanced guard was at the walls of Jerusalem. It then marched past the Jaffa Gate and through the suburbs past the Damascus Gate, amidst a wildly excited populace, and took up a position at the north-east corner of the city. Large numbers of Turks were still on the road running north and south across the Mount of Olives, and there was some machine-gun fire from that direction. At 2.20 p.m. the 5/Welch, which had meanwhile been visited by the brigade commander, Br.-General N.E. Money, received orders to advance down the Jericho road and if possible seize El 'Azariye (Bethany) for the sake of its water, and was informed that the 4/Welch was being despatched to outflank the enemy's left on the Mount of Olives. Unfortunately the latter battalion was ordered, without preliminary reconnaissance, to advance across country from the Hebron to the Jericho road instead of following the leading battalion through the city. This was a sheer impossibility; for between the two roads lay the valleys of the Hinnom and the famous Brook Kidron, or Wadi en Nar, and not even a pack-mule could cross these steep-sided gorges. The 4/Welch, however, found touch with the 4/Cheshire, which had pushed out companies from Mar Elias to positions west and north of Sur Bahir. Br.-General Money intended to make an attack on the Mount of Olives at 4.15 p.m., but this was postponed until the following morning. Long columns of troops and transport were observed by the R.F.C. retreating by the Nablus and Jericho roads. A hundred bombs were dropped upon them, most of which were within effective distance and about twenty direct hits.

1917.
10 Dec.

Preparations had been made for an advance by the 60th and 74th Divisions north of Jerusalem on the 10th, but General Chetwode decided that, owing to the necessity of clearing the country immediately east of the city and the great transport difficulties which he had to face, this must be postponed. The day, therefore, passed quietly except on the front of the 53rd Division. The 60th Division relieved the 74th as far as the Wadi Beit Hannina. The 159th

Brigade found the Mount of Olives clear of the enemy and by evening had advanced to the western outskirts of Bethany. It was ordered to occupy both this village and Abu Dis to the south-east, and was established in both by daybreak on the 11th.

1917. 10 Dec.

The 10th A.L.H. despatched two squadrons from Jerusalem to Shafat, from which point they carried out two bold and deep reconnaissances. One advanced straight up the Nablus road and reached the outskirts of Er Ram, 2 miles north, beating off an attack by about fifty Turkish infantry. The other despatched troops eastward towards 'Anata and north-eastward towards Hizme, both of which came under artillery fire. It appeared that the enemy held a line through these villages, that is, facing the Nablus road and some two miles east of it, in considerable strength.

There was little fighting on the 11th. The 30th Brigade of the 10th Division found the high ground north of the Wadi esh Shebab and south of Beit 'Ur el Foqa unoccupied, and took possession of it. On the 12th the 53rd Division advanced about a mile beyond Bethany, capturing 39 prisoners. All along the front of the XX Corps on the general line Sur Bahir–Bethany–Tell el Ful–Beit Izza–Et Tire–Beit 'Ur et Tahta–Suffa, there was now a lull; the Turks were breathless after their defeat and hasty withdrawal, the British not yet ready for the effort which would be needed to win more elbow-room about Jerusalem. For the moment the fighting was at an end.

12 Dec.

Sir Edmund Allenby's Entry into Jerusalem.

The Commander-in-Chief entered Jerusalem by the Jaffa Gate at noon on the 11th December. Guards representative of the troops in Palestine were drawn up at the gate: outside a British guard of fifty all ranks, including English, Scottish, Irish, and Welsh troops, on the right of the gate, and an Australian and New Zealand guard on the left; inside a French guard of 20 all ranks on the right of the gate and an Italian guard of the same number on the left. These guards, both inside and outside, were drawn up facing one another, their inner flanks resting on the wall. Sir Edmund Allenby drove up the Jaffa road, lined by the 180th Brigade, left his car and entered the gate on foot, preceded by two

11 Dec.

aides-de-camp, Captain W. L. Naper and Lieutenant R. H. Andrew, and followed by two staff officers, Lieut.-Colonel Lord Dalmeny, his Military Secretary, and Lieut.-Colonel A. P. Wavell, Liaison Officer with the War Office. On his right and left were the officers commanding the French and Italian Contingents, Colonel P. de Piépape and Lieut.-Colonel F. d'Agostino, each followed by a staff officer. Then came M. Picot, the French High Commissioner, Br.-General G. F. Clayton, Political Officer, with Major T. E. Lawrence as staff officer, and Lieut.-Colonel W. H. Deedes, G.S.O.1 Intelligence; flanked by the French and Italian Military Attachés, Commandants R. de Saint-Quentin and Caccia. The Chief and Deputy Chief of the General Staff, Major-General L. J. Bols and Br.-General G. P. Dawnay, followed, and then the commander of the XX Corps, Lieut.-General Sir Philip Chetwode, and his staff officer, Br.-General W. H. Bartholomew. The four guards fell in behind the procession in column of fours.

The Military Governor of Jerusalem, Br.-General W. M. Borton, met the Commander-in-Chief at the gate and conducted him to the steps of the Citadel, where the notables of the City met him. The guards then formed up facing the steps, and a proclamation was read to the citizens in English, French, Arabic, Hebrew, Greek, Russian, and Italian. Its terms, which had been decided upon by the British Government and telegraphed to Sir Edmund Allenby three weeks before, were as follows:—

" To the inhabitants of Jerusalem the Blessed and the
" people dwelling in its vicinity.
" The defeat inflicted upon the Turks by the troops
" under my command has resulted in the occupation of your
" city by my forces. I therefore here and now proclaim
" it to be under martial law, under which form of administra-
" tion it will remain so long as military considerations make
" it necessary.
" However, lest any of you should be alarmed by reason
" of your experience at the hands of the enemy who has
" retired, I hereby inform you that it is my desire that every
" person should pursue his lawful business without fear of
" interruption. Furthermore, since your city is regarded
" with affection by adherents of three of the great religions
" of mankind, and its soil has been consecrated by the prayers

"and pilgrimages of multitudes of devout people of these
"three religions for many centuries, therefore do I make
"known to you that every sacred building, monument, Holy
"spot, shrine, traditional site, endowment, pious bequest, or
"customary place of prayer, of whatsoever form of the three
"religions, will be maintained and protected according to the
"existing customs and beliefs of those to whose faiths they
"are sacred."

1917.
11 Dec.

This proclamation was also posted on the walls. After the chief inhabitants of the city had been presented to the Commander-in-Chief, he passed out again through the Jaffa Gate.

The whole ceremony was simple and dignified. The onlookers were obviously content with the turn of events, but there was no exuberant enthusiasm. No flags were flown.

Guards had already been placed over the Holy Places, and the Haram esh Sherif, enclosing the site of the Temple, on which now stands the mosque known as the "Dome of "the Rock"—or, erroneously, as the "Mosque of Omar"— was put under Moslem control, a cordon of Indian Mohammedan officers and men being established round it. The hereditary custodians of the *Wakf* at the gates of the Holy Sepulchre were requested to take up their accustomed duties, in remembrance of the magnanimity of Khalif Omar.[1]

\* \* \* \* \*

The surrender of Jerusalem marks a definite period in the Palestine campaign, a fact which the Commander-in-Chief emphasized by addressing his first despatch to the Secretary of State immediately afterwards. The result was

---

[1] A *Wakf* is a fund formed from the enormous religious or charitable bequests made by pious Moslems. In many Moslem countries there is a department of the State charged either with the direct administration or the control of the trustees of the various *Wakfs*. Omar captured Jerusalem from the Byzantine Roman Empire in A.D. 637. He entered the Church of the Holy Sepulchre and was requested to say a prayer in the Sepulchre. He replied that if he did so others of his religion would have the right to pray there also, and that the place would become a mosque, which Christians might not enter. He therefore preferred to pray at the door, and appointed guardians to ensure that the church and the rights of Christians in it should be preserved.

The retention of the Moslem door-keepers had been suggested to the Prime Minister by Sir Mark Sykes, the Government's political representative with the E.E.F., and was undoubtedly a well-inspired political courtesy.

thus epitomized in a Special Order of the Day issued by him on the 15th December :—

"In forty days many strong Turkish positions have been captured, and the Force has advanced some sixty miles on a front of thirty miles."

The enemy had been heavily defeated, only the nature of the country saving his forces from complete destruction. Over twelve thousand prisoners and more than one hundred guns had been taken, and the Turkish casualties for the period were approximately 25,000, almost half as many again as the British, which were about 18,000.[1] Jerusalem had been captured without damage to a single sacred building.

The opening of the campaign had been marked by a brilliant flanking operation, resulting first in the capture of an outlying fortress-town on the enemy's extreme left and then in the rolling up of the left of his main position. Thereafter supply, and particularly that of water, had been the factor governing the extent of the advance. When the XXI Corps, after the evacuation of Gaza, moved up the coast plain, the XX Corps became immobilized, the bulk of the transport having to be transferred from the right flank to the left. The problem of water had been particularly difficult during the pursuit of the beaten enemy by the mounted troops. Had the Desert Mounted Corps been directed further to the east, the opposition of Turkish rear guards would have been to a great extent avoided and the pursuit would have been on parallel lines, but the supply of water east of Jemmame was even worse than that on the route followed.

---

[1] The British casualties, as reported weekly to Whitehall, from the week ending the 3rd November to the week ending the 15th December, were 18,928, made up as follows :—

|  | Killed. | Wounded. | Missing. |
|---|---|---|---|
| Officers | 203 | 807 | 32 |
| Other Ranks | 2,306 | 13,891 | 1,689 |

It is known that of the wounded about 99 officers and 278 other ranks remained at duty. Of these casualties, 16,862 were suffered by British troops, 1,138 by Australian and New Zealand, 928 by Indian.

The Turkish figures supplied by the Historical Section of the Turkish General Staff are from 31st October to 31st December, and amount to 28,443, made up as follows :—

|  | Killed. | Wounded. | Missing. |
|---|---|---|---|
| Officers | 181 | 394 | 464 |
| Other Ranks | 3,387 | 9,021 | 14,996 |

## SUPPLY AND TRANSPORT

After the capture of Junction Station a great effort had been made to isolate Jerusalem by cutting the Nablus road at Bire by means of the rapid advance into the hills of one mounted and two infantry divisions. The attempt had failed, despite the gallantry and pertinacity of the troops employed, owing to the extreme difficulty of the country and the facilities for defence which it afforded. But it had accomplished much in winning the passes and capturing the dominating position of Nabi Samweil. Had the British waited until they were in a position to maintain in the hills a force of the strength of that which eventually took Jerusalem, they would have found their way barred by almost impregnable defences. Then it was decided to bring up fresh troops and direct the attack closer to Jerusalem, while still taking all precautions possible against damage being done to the city. This plan enabled full use to be made of the Jaffa road and also permitted the co-operation of the detachment moving up the Hebron road. When the final attack took place fortune favoured the British, for after their front-line defences had been captured by surprise, the resistance of the Turks collapsed, partly through the error or weakness of the corps commander concerned, partly owing to the gradual decay of morale resulting from continuous defeat, partly because of the threat to their line of supply and communications constituted by the British occupation of Nabi Samweil.

The fighting troops had been well seconded by the services of supply. Though rations were late on many occasions, it was as a result of good organization and unremitting labour that they were delivered at all. A particularly heavy burden had fallen upon the Camel Transport Corps, in which men and beasts alike had shown great powers of endurance in weather such as they had never before experienced. An additional means of transport, which was to prove very valuable, had just been brought into action. With notable forethought the organization of donkey transport companies, in anticipation of a winter in the Judæan Hills, had been commenced in September. By the early days of December No. 1 D.T.C., with an establishment of 2,000 donkeys, was ready ; a thousand were handed over to the 74th Division on the 8th and five hundred to the 60th four days later. The donkey is the ideal transport animal for the hills, as is proved by the fact that it is universally used by the villagers. Extraordinarily hardy and tireless, contemptuous of shell-fire, a small eater, it was to be a very good friend to the troops in the hills for the rest of the campaign. A second company was moved up early in the New Year and two more formed later.[1]

The medical services had also performed admirable work under heavy strain, above all the field ambulances of the divisions. Until the capture of Jerusalem the nearest casualty clearing station was at Junction Station—and for Mott's Detachment at Kharm, reached *via* Beersheba—but the difficulties were eased when it was possible to instal one in the city itself, so that the wounded could have a comfortable break in their journey down the line.

The capture of Jerusalem followed upon the Italian reverse at Caporetto, the collapse of Russia, the elimination of Rumania from the war, and the German counter-offensive at Cambrai. Coming at such a black moment, it had a heartening moral effect. The circumstances in which it was achieved, while incidents such as the bombardment of Rheims Cathedral and the destruction of the University of Louvain were still bitterly remembered, did high honour to British arms.

---

[1] Some officers have criticized the statement that these donkeys were valuable. Their first objection is that they were far inferior to even the smallest pack-mules. This is probably self-evident, but then pack-mules were not available for the work they did. The second criticism is that, not being hill-bred and accustomed to wet weather, but mostly the little white asses of the Delta, they died in great numbers from exposure. It is true that the mortality was high in December, during which 233 from No. 1 Company died. That, however, was largely due to over-work and lack of food. The total casualties from exposure in the year 1918, during which four companies were employed, were two donkeys.

## CHAPTER XII.

### THE BATTLE OF JAFFA AND THE DEFENCE OF JERUSALEM.

(Maps 1, 2, 12, 13; Sketches A, 20, 21.)

#### THE PASSAGE OF THE NAHR EL 'AUJA.

THE British had now won both Palestine's capital and its second town. But Jerusalem and Jaffa were still within easy range of Turkish artillery, and the proximity of the enemy's forces exposed them to some slight risk of recapture by surprise attacks. It was therefore imperative to push back the Turks on either flank of the British front as soon as possible. Formal orders to this effect were issued by G.H.Q. on the 18th December, but corps plans for the two operations had already been drawn up and accepted by Sir Edmund Allenby. The XXI Corps had actually begun a minor preliminary operation a week earlier.

There had been no action of importance in the plain and foot-hills since the events described in Chapter X but for a determined attack on the morning of the 1st December upon the 2/4th Hampshire of the 233rd Brigade, which had then just entered the line east of Lydda under the orders of the 54th Division. A strong party of Turks crawled up the slope at Sheikh Gharbawi, west of the village of Midie, and under cover of overhead machine-gun fire assaulted the two companies holding this position. The post was reinforced by a company of the 3/3rd Gurkhas, and after heavy fighting the Turks were driven back.

On the 7th December General Bulfin took over command from General Chauvel, the A. & N.Z. Mounted Division remaining in the forward area until the 52nd and 75th Divisions were established in the line. By the 11th the front of the XXI Corps was held by the 75th Division on the right, east of the railway, the 54th Division in the centre, astride it, and the 52nd Division on the coast. The 75th Division's line, from south of Midie to south-east of Beit Nebala, was held by the 232nd Brigade, with the 58th Rifles attached, covered by the South African F.A. Brigade and one battery XXXVII Brigade. Soon after dawn, as the first step in the preliminary operation, the 2/5th Hampshire occupied Midie, encountering no opposition. The 2/3rd Gurkhas then pushed forward patrols towards Budrus, 2 miles N.N.W. of Midie, and after a Turkish counter-attack had been beaten off by artillery fire, captured the village about noon.

While the attack of the 232nd Brigade was in progress the enemy bombarded Kh. Zeifizfiye, a few hundred yards north-west of Beit Nebala, on the right flank of the 54th Division, with four batteries. This hill was held by a company of the 4/Norfolk. At 9 a.m. an attack at least a battalion strong was launched against it, and about thirty of the enemy succeeded in entering the trench on the summit. An immediate counter-attack by the 4/Norfolk restored the position, and the enemy was caught in flank during his withdrawal by machine guns at Nebala and Deir Tureif. Over fifty Turkish dead were afterwards found on the field, while the casualties of the 163rd Brigade were 55.

1917.
15 Dec.

The object of the 232nd Brigade's advance had been to secure gun positions within effective range of Kh. Ibanne, north-east of Beit Nebala, a ridge which dominated all the plain about Lydda, and to enable the 75th Division to co-operate with the 54th in an operation to capture the line Ibanne–Et Tire. The XXI Corps was now well provided with heavy artillery, two heavy artillery groups with 22 more heavy guns and howitzers and a sound-ranging section having arrived from the Gaza area by the 13th. The advance was carried out on the 15th, when the 75th Division attacked the Turkish positions from the village of Qibye,[1] a mile north-east of Budrus, to Ibanne, and the 54th from thence to Et Tire. The C. Heavy Artillery Group of two 60-pdr. and one 6-inch howitzer batteries co-operated, first by counter-battery work, then by the bombardment of any positions with which it was called on by the infantry to deal. As a preliminary the 2/3rd Gurkhas of the 232nd Brigade,

---

[1] Kibbia on Map 2. Kh. Ibanne is Point 903 on the Ibanne Ridge on Map 19.

supported by the South African F.A. Brigade, attacked the Qibye ridge, south of the village, at 6 a.m., and took it without great difficulty, afterwards capturing the village itself. The main attack on Kh. Ibanne, launched at 8 a.m., was carried out by the 2/5th Hampshire on the right and 58th Rifles on the left. So swiftly did these battalions advance over the broken ground and up the steep hillside that the Turks early withdrew their machine guns to avoid losing them, and the casualties amounted only to 18. Fifteen prisoners and a machine gun were captured. The 163rd Brigade of the 54th Division likewise reached its objective, but suffered much more severely. Though they nowhere awaited the final onset, the Turks kept up heavy machine-gun fire, and mainly from this cause over one hundred and fifty casualties were suffered by the brigade. Now the way was cleared for an attempt to advance the line nearer the shore by crossing the Nahr el 'Auja.

1917. 15 Dec.

The river was a formidable obstacle, forty to fifty feet in width [1] and ten feet in depth, with banks generally soft and muddy in this wet season. The northern bank commanded the lower and much flatter ground to the south. The village of Sheikh Muwannis, which had been occupied by the British in November and lost to a counter-attack on the 25th, was in a particularly dominating position, with a view all the way to Jaffa ; while Kh. Hadra looked down on to the river almost to the sea. Since the November fighting the enemy had entrenched the high ground on the right bank, and also established works on the left covering the villages of Fajja and Mulebbis, at Hadra Bridge, and at Jerishe. The bar at the mouth was now the only place where the river could be crossed without military bridges or boats, as the bridge at Hadra and the mill dam at Jerishe, which had played a part in the November operations, had been destroyed.

Maps 2, 12. Sketch 20.

General Bulfin's plan was to carry out a twenty-four hours' bombardment of the Turkish trenches and batteries and then attempt the passage of the 'Auja by night. Time pressed, for the river was daily swelling with the rains and the south bank becoming more and more marshy. Twelve pontoons, with twelve Weldon trestles, were demanded by

---

[1] In several published accounts the 'Auja is described as being forty *yards* in width. At Hadra it is, in fact, little over forty feet, but at its mouth about forty yards.

telegram from Egypt on the 7th December, arrived at Jaffa on the 16th, and were handed over to the 52nd Division the following day.[1] Meanwhile, under the instructions of the C.R.E., Lieut.-Colonel L. Fortescue-Wells, a number of "coracles" were made, consisting of a wooden framework over which a standard canvas tank sheet was lashed. These were to be used in the first instance as rafts, and afterwards linked up and covered with decking to form bridges to take infantry and pack mules. Two infantry barrel pier bridges were also prepared, differing only from the types laid down in works on military engineering in that the local wine-casks were larger than the standard pattern. This work was carried out by the 413th Field Company R.E., with the carpenters and joiners of the other companies attached. Local timber was used, a number of sheds at Jaffa having to be demolished to provide it. Light orange boxes such as are to be seen at Covent Garden were also used. The supply of material was, indeed, not the least of the difficulties to be faced. Major-General Walter Campbell, the D.Q.M.G. of the Force, was anxious to assist the XXI Corps by establishing a new landing-place at Jaffa and laying down a light railway from the shore, but Rear-Admiral Jackson found himself unable to give naval protection here while stores were still being landed at the mouth of the Nahr Suqreir. As a consequence, only one consignment of R. E. stores arrived by sea, in a single trawler, on the 15th December.

The commander of the 52nd Division, Major-General Hill, liked the prospect before his troops less, the more he contemplated it. There was no lack of cover from view for his preparations, for between Jaffa and the 'Auja were hundreds of acres of orange, lemon, and eucalyptus groves; but any attempt to launch bridges would be met by the fire of machine guns in most advantageous positions. On the 14th December he suggested to General Bulfin that the 52nd Division should attempt a surprise crossing by night, without warning the enemy by a heavy bombardment. General Bulfin gave his permission, as the scheme appeared to him to be promising, but directed that in the event of its failure the previous plan should come into force and the bombardment should begin the following morning. The arrangements for

---

[1] Pontoons had been left behind by the field companies R.E. when the advance across Sinai began. They had not hitherto been required.

## PLAN FOR THE CROSSING

the actual passage of the river remained unaltered. Strong covering forces were to be conveyed across by means of the rafts and light bridges, and, bridgeheads having been established, the pontoon bridges were to be thrown for the passage of the remainder of the troops, including the artillery. The night of the 20th December was chosen for the crossing, previous to which the 54th Division was to extend its left to the neighbourhood of Hadra Bridge, and the defences of the 52nd Division were to be taken over by the 1st L.H. Brigade and Auckland Mounted Rifles.

1917.
20 Dec.

Reconnaissances of the right bank would have been well nigh impossible had the Turkish patrolling been efficient, but several were carried out by swimmers or by officers' parties in small boats. On the night of the 14th Lieut.-Colonel J. Anderson, commanding the 6/H.L.I., and Lieutenant C. H. Hills of the same battalion swam out to sea from the British post on the shore, crossed the mouth of the river, and landed behind the Turkish lines. They ascertained the position of the ford, that the depth of water in it was about three feet, and that no obstacles had been placed below the surface. Still undetected by the Turkish sentries, they made their way out to the surf again and swam back.

As a result of these reconnaissances it was decided that the 156th Brigade should force a passage below Muwannis and seize that village;[1] that the 157th should cross by the bar and take Tell er Ruqti, a sandhill 2 miles north ; and that the 155th should subsequently cross above Muwannis and turn right-handed to secure Kh. Hadra. The crossing was to be carried out in silence by the infantry and with only normal artillery fire, while the remainder of the operation was to be covered by a bombardment, in order to take advantage of the British superiority in artillery, which was particularly great in heavy guns and siege howitzers. Batteries were gradually brought forward into concealed positions ; till by the morning of the 20th December the 100th and 102nd Heavy Artillery Groups, consisting of four 60-pdr., one 6-inch howitzer, and one (two-gun) 6-inch gun batteries, for counter-battery work, and a bombardment group of two 6-inch howitzer batteries were in readiness to support the attack and the subsequent operations of the 54th Division. The

---

[1] The orders of the 52nd Division are given in Appendix 19.

only artillery fire in the first stage of the attack was to be a slow bombardment of the enemy's positions by the divisional artillery, accompanied by bursts of machine-gun fire, with the object of lessening the activity of the Turkish patrols. So that the enemy might suspect nothing unusual, a similar programme of firing was carried out on several previous nights.

The first covering party was to be thrown across halfway between the sea and the point where the Nahr el Baride enters the Nahr el 'Auja. One battalion of the 157th Brigade was then to cross by the rafts and move north-westward against the works covering the bar at the river's mouth. A battalion of the 156th Brigade was to follow and attack a group of buildings known as " Slag Heap Farm " three-quarters of a mile west of Muwannis. These battalions were, if possible, to capture their objectives simultaneously. Thereafter there was a good deal of elasticity in the scheme. The subsequent moves were to take place during the remaining hours of darkness. If they could not be carried out then a renewed attack was to be undertaken after twenty-four hours' bombardment in accordance with General Bulfin's original plan. But it was hoped that the enemy would be unable to appreciate the situation quickly enough to launch a strong counter-attack before dawn and that, if the initial crossing were successful, it would be possible for the remainder of the division to cross that night.

Two further battalions of the 156th were next to follow by the same crossing-place, and another just west of it, employing the bridges if ready : one to capture the village of Muwannis, the other to roll up from the west the trenches south of it. At the hour of this assault two battalions of the 155th Brigade were to cross by bridges thrown half-way between Jerishe and Hadra Bridge to assault Kh. Hadra, and the remainder of the 157th Brigade was to pass along the bar, capture the second-line defences on the shoreward flank, and advance on Tell er Ruqti.

On the 20th it blew cold out of the north-west with sheets of rain, which, while it increased the difficulties of the bridging, was ideal weather for a night attack. In the afternoon, however, it cleared, and during the night there was hardly a cloud in the sky to veil the stars and a half-moon. One company of the 7/Scottish Rifles, 156th

Brigade, furnished the covering party for the construction of the two bridges at the first crossing-places.[1] " Zero " was at 8 p.m., and by that hour four rafts were in the water. The party was across by 8.35. Then the 412th Field Company R.E. set to work to construct the bridges by linking up the rafts. Three-quarters of the first was completed, when trouble arose through the canvas being holed and making water. Fresh rafts had to be brought up, the carrying parties floundering in mud to their knees. Towing parties of fifteen to twenty men across on single rafts was a very slow process, and Br.-General Leggett obtained permission to postpone the attack from 10.30 to 11 p.m. By that hour there were across, in addition to the covering party, one company 7/Scottish Rifles, the 7/H.L.I. of the 157th Brigade, the 4/Royal Scots, and one company 7/Royal Scots. No further delay was possible, and the artillery, which had been carrying out a slow bombardment of Slag Heap Farm and the trenches west of it, was about to lift. The company of the 7/Scottish Rifles therefore advanced on the big orange grove east of the crossing, took post on its western side to prevent the attacking troops being enfiladed as they advanced from the crossing-places, and subsequently formed a dump of fifty boxes of ammunition and five hundred bombs in the building at its north-west corner. The 7/H.L.I. turned north-westward and, despatching one company against the rifle-pits covering the ford, advanced with its main strength against the defences behind them. The Turkish guard at the ford over the bar was completely surprised, two officers in a boat and eighteen men in a dug-out being actually found asleep. In the trenches in rear 4 officers and 62 men, with three machine guns, were captured.[2]

Meanwhile the 4/R. Scots, with a section of the 156th Machine-Gun Company and one Stokes mortar, had attacked Slag Heap Farm, and captured it without serious difficulty. By midnight the first of the footbridges was completed and the whole of the 156th Brigade was on the right bank. The 7/R. Scots and 8/Scottish Rifles then advanced in a north-easterly direction, marching in fours covered by a small advanced guard. After the two battalions had moved

---

[1] Marked C.1. and C.2. on Map 12.
[2] Marked Z. 13a. and b. on Map 12.

side by side for three-quarters of a mile the 8/Scottish Rifles turned eastward and captured the trenches south of Muwannis very swiftly. The 7/R. Scots marched straight on to Muwannis, which was captured after some fighting among the houses. About fifty prisoners were taken, including the commander of the *1/31st Battalion*.

Meanwhile a lamp signal that the passage of the bar could be made had been given by the 7/H.L.I. The 413th Field Company R.E. had prepared a guide-rope, but when the sappers advanced to drive in stakes for it, the marks set at the water's edge could not be found, so much had the river deepened and widened even since the previous night. Lieut.-Colonel J. Anderson, whose battalion was to be first to cross, was the only man who really knew the position of the bar, his companion in his exploit on the 14th being in hospital. He at once stripped and entered the water, swimming about until he found the ford, now four feet below water; the engineers were then able to drive in stakes. Without waiting for the completion of the guide-rope Lieut.-Colonel Anderson then ordered the 6/H.L.I. to begin crossing in fours, with arms linked. The Turkish artillery had opened fire, and the battalion suffered thirty casualties in crossing. It was over by 1.35 a.m. and was followed by the 5/Argyll and Sutherland Highlanders. The advance on Tell er Ruqti then began. The intermediate trenches (Z. 7a. and Z. 8a.) were captured by 2.45 a.m., several officers being taken in night clothes; the trenches covering the hill were rushed with the bayonet, and Tell er Ruqti itself taken without further opposition at 3.30.

To cover the crossing of the 155th Brigade in the bend of the river half-way between Hadra bridge and Jerishe, a building known as "Pink House" on the left bank had been seized on the 18th, and two machine guns installed in its upper storey, which commanded the Turkish trenches about the bridge at six hundred yards' range. While the crossing was in progress a demonstration was carried out by a platoon of the 5/K.O.S.B., which advanced over the boggy ground east of the bridge and opened fire on the enemy positions north of the river, drawing considerable fire. Two companies of the 5/K.O.S.B. crossed by rafts to cover the construction of the bridge by the 410th Field Company R.E. But here also there were serious delays, largely owing to the weight which heavy rain and mud had added to the rafts.[1]

1917.
21 Dec.

Br.-General Pollok-M'Call therefore ordered the 4th and 5th Royal Scots Fusiliers to be towed across on the rafts already in the water, without waiting for the bridge. This process was not completed until 3.30 a.m., by which time the enemy had begun to shell the crossing. The artillery programme was therefore postponed, but the barrage came down at exactly the right moment as the 5/R. Scots Fusiliers advanced on Kh. Hadra. There was little resistance from the trenches, and the battalion pressed on up the hill. The 4/R. Scots Fusiliers then sent forward companies which occupied " Woodside Farm " and " White Hill," north-east of Kh. Hadra. The two battalions had only a dozen casualties between them, while they took 131 prisoners and two machine guns.

At 5 a.m. a company of the 5/K.O.S.B. from Pink House attacked the trench covering Hadra Bridge under a barrage of Stokes-mortar fire. Here for the first time there was bitter hand-to-hand fighting. Twelve Turks were captured, a number killed, and about a score, over-weighted by the bombs they carried, drowned in the 'Auja. The company crossed by the remains of the broken bridge, took the works on the right bank, and established a bridgehead.

The attack had, then, been a complete success at every point. About daybreak pontoon bridges were thrown at Jerishe and near the river's mouth, but prior to this two field batteries had managed to cross by the bar. The 412th Field Company had assembled a barrel bridge in the Nahr el Baride and floated it down into the 'Auja, but the sodden state of the banks prevented its completion until the morning of the 22nd. The 410th Field Company repaired the stone bridge at Hadra.

The passage of the 'Auja has always been regarded as one of the most remarkable feats of the Palestine Campaign. A great achievement it was, but its chief merits were its boldness—justifiable against troops known to be sluggish and slack in outpost work and already shaken by defeat—its

---

[1] There was no lack of labour to carry the rafts forward, the 4/K.O.S.B. being largely available for this task, but they weighed more than the number of men who could get a grip on them could carry, except at a very slow pace.

planning, the skill of the engineers, the promptitude with which unexpected difficulties in the bridging of the river were met; finally, the combined discipline and dash of the infantry which carried out the operation without a shot being fired before daylight and won the works on the right bank with the bayonet. The hazard was great, for had the enemy defended his strong positions with vigour the conditions under which the crossing was carried out would have been very unfavourable to the attackers. So far as fighting went the 52nd Division had actually not to face any such resistance as it had overcome in its succession of dourly-contested brigade actions between Gaza and Maghar or in the Judæan Hills. Its casualties were, in fact, only 102.

The establishment of the general line Qibye–Rantye–Fajja–Mulebbis–Tell el Mukhmar–Sheikh Balluta–Jlil, the objective set to the XXI Corps by G.H.Q., was to be carried out on the 22nd December. As a preliminary the 162nd Brigade of the 54th Division was to capture Yafa Hill, half-way between Mulebbis and Yehudiye, and Bald Hill, a mile north-west of Yafa Hill, during the night of the 21st. Yafa Hill was an outpost position, and was easily captured by a company of the 5/Bedfordshire. Bald Hill was now in the enemy's main line and strongly fortified. Its defences, however, faced south-west, and Major-General Hare therefore directed that the attack should be carried out from the south-east. On the night of the 20th a hill 350 yards east of it, from which fire could be brought to bear on its trenches, was occupied, apparently without attracting the enemy's attention. The attack, carried out by the 11/London, was preceded by a bombardment of five minutes by three batteries, during which the enemy put down a barrage along the south-western flank of the hill and manned his defences to meet an attack in that quarter. The charge of the 11/London came as a surprise, and the position was captured with small loss. Within the next two hours the Turks made three determined counter-attacks across the open, which were beaten off by machine-gun and rifle fire, and also launched several bombing attacks up communication trenches. One attack by Turkish bombers was repelled single-handed by Lce-Corporal J. A. Christie, who went forward fifty yards beyond the British line and drove them back with bombs, afterwards scattering another party which

# THE GENERAL ADVANCE

had entered a communication trench and barred his return. Lce-Corporal Christie was awarded the Victoria Cross.

**1917. 22 Dec.**

At dawn on the 22nd it was seen that the enemy's guns and transport were everywhere moving northward, and when the general advance began at 8 a.m. there was no serious resistance. The 162nd Brigade quickly secured a line from a mile north-east of Et Tire, through Wilhelma Station, to Fajja, the 161st Brigade prolonging the line thence to the 'Auja at Ferrikhiye.

On the coast likewise the 52nd Division had no great difficulty in completing its operations. H.M.S. *Grafton*, flying the flag of Rear-Admiral T. Jackson, accompanied by monitors *M. 29*, *M.31* and *M.32*, and the destroyers *Lapwing* and *Lizard*, appeared off the coast north of the 'Auja and shelled parties of the retreating enemy, while British aeroplanes dropped bombs on them, causing them to flee headlong northward as fast as they could move through the mud. This mud prevented any serious pursuit by the Auckland Regiment, attached to the 52nd Division. At 9 a.m. the division, with all three brigades in line, moved forward in artillery formation, followed by the artillery. The latter was obliged to use eight-horse teams, so that only four guns or three howitzers per battery could take part in the advance. The line Ferrikhiye–Jlil was reached without opposition. General Bulfin himself rode up to Jlil early in the afternoon and directed the 157th Brigade to push forward to Arsuf, over two miles further north, and occupy the high ground in its neighbourhood. On the rest of the front the positions already attained were satisfactory and were consolidated. Thus, as the result of the successful passage of the 'Auja in the preliminary move, the objects of the whole operation had been attained, and at very small cost. Jaffa was put out of range of Turkish artillery, unless the enemy should employ a high-velocity gun of large calibre, and the British had a very favourable line.

### PREPARATIONS OF THE XX CORPS.

The Jaffa flank being secured, it remained only to free Jerusalem from hostile pressure. On the 14th December General Chetwode outlined to his divisional commanders his plan, based upon the instructions he had received from Sir

**Maps 2, 13. Sketch A.**

Edmund Allenby. The corps was to advance to a line from Beitin (Bethel), 2 miles north-east of Bire, to Deir Ibzia, 6 miles west of Bire. He proposed to carry this out by means of an attack northward astride the Nablus road by the 53rd and 60th Divisions, an attack from the south-west on the Zeitun Ridge by the 74th Division in the centre, and an attack almost due eastward by the 10th Division on the left. Major-General Longley put forward a scheme for advancing by way of the formidable Kereina and Deir Ibzia spurs, north-east of Beit 'Ur et Tahta. This was adopted by the corps commander, who thought so well of it that he placed at Major-General Longley's disposal a brigade of the 74th Division, to advance eastward along the Zeitun Ridge. The force moving north along the Nablus road under the direct control of corps headquarters was to be known as the " Right Attack "; that moving east from Et Tire and Beit 'Ur et Tahta under the command of Major-General Longley as the " Left Attack."

At least ten days of hard work were needed on roads and water supply before the offensive could take place. This was begun under the direction of Br.-General R. L. Waller, Chief Engineer of the XX Corps, immediately after the capture of Jerusalem. The Royal Engineers of the 53rd Division had for their chief task the repair and maintenance of the Hebron road, and were obliged to leave a detachment as far back as Beersheba. The ancient aqueduct from Solomon's Pools, the main supply of Jerusalem, had to be repaired, and a new pumping engine installed. The 60th Division was mainly responsible for the Jaffa road, on which natives hired from a contractor were employed, and also developed the water supply at Qalonye. The 74th Division remade the track from Qaryet el 'Inab to Biddu, three battalions working for several nights under the engineers. This track, which had been impassable for wheeled traffic when first the 75th Division moved up it in November, was by the 26th December completely though roughly metalled. The almost indistinguishable bridle-path from Biddu running past Nabi Samweil to Beit Hannina was also made fit to carry wheels. Most important of all, the tracks required by the Left Attack to bring up ammunition for the big part it had to play in the offensive were vastly improved by the 10th Division, which had had much experience of

Sketch 20.

# Passage of the NAHR EL 'AUJA.
## 20th & 21st Dec. 1917.

British in red.    Turks in green.

Compiled in Historical Section (Military Branch).    Ordnance Survey 1928.

## GENERAL CHETWODE'S PLAN

such work in Macedonia. These tracks ran from various points on the Lydda–Jerusalem road up the parallel valleys and were the 10th Division's only supply routes. The roadmaking on this flank quite transformed the situation, for it enabled a force of all arms with wheeled transport to be maintained in country through which hitherto pack transport had moved only with great difficulty.

During the night of the 16th the 53rd Division seized the high ground east of Abu Dis, a mile south-east of Bethany, the 160th Brigade taking 117 prisoners and three machine guns at a cost of 26 casualties. By the morning of the 21st the 53rd Division relieved the 60th up to the Wadi el Khulf, east of Shafat on the Nablus road, the 60th extended its left to take in Nabi Samweil, and the 231st Brigade of the 74th took over from the 10th up to Beit 'Ur et Tahta.

The Commander-in-Chief had given his approval to General Chetwode's scheme and to the dates on which he proposed to carry it out—a preliminary advance by the Right Attack to a line astride the Nablus road through Kefar Akab and Ra-fat on the 23rd; the advance of the Left Attack along the Zeitun, Kereina, and Deir Ibzia spurs on the 24th; the final advance of the 60th Division to cover Bire and Ram Allah on the 25th. If, however, the weather was bad, the attack would be postponed; and the weather was unpromising. Sir Edmund Allenby insisted upon the need for holding the final objective, once consolidated, with the minimum force that safety would allow, because his difficulties of supply could not be lightened until the standard-gauge railway reached Ramle and the Jaffa–Jerusalem line had been repaired up to Jerusalem.

On the 21st December the 160th Brigade carried out another minor operation to improve its position north of the Jericho road, where it was overlooked by the enemy. At 5 a.m. three companies of the 2/4th Queen's captured a Turkish post, and a company of the 2/10th Middlesex, passing through, took Ras ez Zamby, 3 miles north-east of Jerusalem. The enemy fell back to "White Hill," the next prominent height, which was at once attacked by a company of the Queen's and one of the Middlesex. Fierce close fighting with bomb, bayonet, and clubbed rifles followed; but the position was captured and two counter-attacks beaten off in the afternoon. The brigade had over one hundred casualties, with a high proportion of killed, but captured 35 Turks and six machine guns. At night the 231st Brigade occupied the village of Beit 'Ur el Foqa, which had been frequently entered by patrols of the 10th Division when holding this part of the line.

The weather was now very bad indeed, so wet that the advance was postponed. It was still hoped to begin it on the 24th, and the 60th Division was ordered to occupy Kh. 'Adase, a hill between Bir Nebala and the Nablus road, by dawn on the 23rd. The 2/18th London of the 180th Brigade met with an unexpectedly stout resistance, failed after several gallant attempts to carry the summit, and was eventually withdrawn to its original line.

All was ready by the 24th, but on that date there was a downpour which continued throughout Christmas Day. The roads on which so much labour had been expended were again almost impassable: six inches deep in mud where soil and metal had not been washed off them by the hill streams in spate, with the solid rock exposed where this had happened. The advance was again postponed.

Meanwhile the situation had changed dramatically. It had been discovered that the enemy was about to make a desperate attempt to recover Jerusalem. By decoding wireless messages, by the examination of prisoners, by agents' reports, Falkenhayn's scheme was pieced together. The main attack, by the hard-fighting *19th Division*, was to come astride the Nablus road and extend some distance west, though how far was not quite clear, while subsidiary attacks were to be made by the Turkish *XX Corps* north-east, east, and south-east of Jerusalem. There was some conflict of evidence as to the date.

General Chetwode at once decided that the plan for the offensive which he had drawn up was excellently designed to meet this emergency. Not more than one new division, the *1st*, could have been brought up to reinforce the enemy. Let the attack come; he did not fear it. But, as soon as the Turks were thoroughly committed to it, he would launch the Left Attack along the three parallel spurs due eastward. He held a last conference with his divisional commanders on the 24th at Jerusalem, and was visited that afternoon by Sir Edmund Allenby, who gave approval to his design. Christmas Day passed quietly. For the troops, so near the scene of the event which Christians celebrate by festivity, it was one of misery. The pack-mules and donkeys struggled through the mud with the essential supplies, but the only luxury to add to the dinner—for most, of biscuits and cheese —consisted of Jaffa oranges. Turkeys and plum puddings were held up by the floods in the plain, and could hardly have been cooked in the rain-swept valleys if they had been brought up. On the 26th the weather improved, and fresh information received made it almost certain that the enemy would attack the following day.

1917.
Dec.

### THE TURKISH ATTACK.

The enemy's attack astride the Nablus road began shortly after 1.30 a.m. on the 27th December. Immediately north of Jerusalem the country is very broken, and the road winds fantastically. Thenceforward up to the point where the Wadi ed Dumm crosses it, 4 miles north of the city, is a fairly smooth-topped ridge, and the road, following the watershed, is comparatively straight. Here troops could, though with some difficulty, deploy and act in open formations, and here, therefore, the main attack fell on the 179th Brigade of the 60th Division. The first hint of what was coming was given when a post of the 2/13th London on the main road half a mile in front of the line fell back before midnight to report that it had been in contact with the enemy. Then at 1.45 a.m. an outpost company of the 2/16th London was driven off Kh. Ras et Tawil, east of the road. Soon afterwards a general attack developed. Rushing forward and hurling bombs, which now as almost always they used with effect, the Turks put out of action two machine guns on the right of the 2/13th London and made a lodgment in its position, only to be driven out a few minutes later with the bayonet. Everywhere else on the brigade's front their resolute attacks were repulsed by rifle and machine-gun fire, aided by the barrage, which came down very quickly after red rockets had been fired. The enemy then apparently made a slight withdrawal to reorganize.

27 Dec.

A bombardment with field artillery and 150-mm. howitzers followed, particularly heavy on Tell el Ful, just east of the Nablus road, and on the Kh. 'Adase ridge [1] to the north-east. A strong and determined attack on this ridge was repulsed at 3.30. At 5.30 another assault in greater numbers succeeded in occupying the 2/16th London's line, and the enemy reached the lower slopes of Tell el Ful. Had he captured that dominating height with its view over all the country except the valley bottoms right down to Jerusalem, the situation would have been ugly; but that he never did. From the high ground which he had gained, however, he galled the 2/13th London on the left of the 2/16th, and its line was withdrawn a couple of hundred yards at 9 a.m. A company of the 2/15th was sent in platoon by platoon to strengthen the line. Another company, attached to the 2/16th, counter-attacked the enemy's right flank, but though it temporarily dislodged him from the British line it was forced to withdraw after suffering heavy casualties. Two cars of the 3rd Light Armoured Motor Battery, which had just arrived from the Philistine Plain, gave valuable assistance. One of them, however, backing under shell fire, left the road and, becoming bogged, was put out of action by the Turkish artillery.

For some hours there was a respite, but just before 1 p.m. the enemy launched another attack on the 2/13th London from behind the ridge north-east of Beit Hannina. Lieut.-Colonel C. M. Mackenzie, commanding the battalion, had prudently withdrawn into support the company of the 2/15th after the previous attack had died down, and now had it available to reinforce his line at the threatened point. His own battalion which had evacuated its front-line sangars on a forward slope, now counter-attacked across the top of the ridge, with the company of the 2/15th on its right. The Turks did not await the onset; they streamed back, many being shot down as they fled.

Meanwhile the 181st Brigade had also been attacked. At 2.30 a.m. a determined assault was made upon the advanced position of the 2/24th London on the ridge between the Wadi ed Dumm and Wadi Beit Hannina. It was immediately repulsed, but during the next four hours three further attacks were launched in greater numbers, covered

---

[1] It will be noted that there are two points of this name in close proximity, on either side of the Nablus road. That now referred to is the one east of the road.

by artillery fire and by enfilade machine-gun fire, the guns being skilfully placed on both flanks at Kh. 'Adase and Bir Nebala. In each case the Turks were beaten off, but the position became untenable, and the line was withdrawn to the less exposed southern flank of the ridge. By 6 p.m. all activity on the enemy's part on the whole front of the division had ceased. Soon afterwards patrols of the 2/16th London discovered that he had withdrawn from the Kh. 'Adase spur, though he still held Ras et Tawil.

1917.
27 Dec.

Thus the main Turkish attack, conducted with resolution by the enemy's best troops, had almost wholly failed. Nowhere had dangerous progress been made, nowhere had the reserve battalions of the 60th Division's two front-line brigades been seriously involved. As for the 180th Brigade, which was in Jerusalem, with the 2/20th London in the Wadi Beit Hannina, only one other battalion had left its billets. The steadiness of the defence had been admirable, but the Turks had obviously lacked the weight of numbers necessary to success. Their attacks had been on isolated portions of the line, skilfully enough chosen, but even then they had been unable to mass sufficient strength against them.[1]

The attacks on the 53rd Division were directed against its outposts only, but led to hard fighting. This division was holding a long line covering Jerusalem from north-east, east, and south-east, with its left flank on the Wadi 'Anata. On its left, between the Wadis 'Anata and Ruabe, was the fresh 158th Brigade, which had hitherto been stationed between Beersheba and Hebron and had just relieved the 159th, the latter being withdrawn to Jerusalem. On the 158th Brigade's front the Turks contented themselves with demonstrations, and during the afternoon it was ordered to extend its right to the Jericho road in relief of the 160th, which was harder pressed. At dawn the Turks attacked White Hill and Ras ez Zamby, captured from them on the 21st. Ras ez Zamby was lost, but retaken by a company of the 2/10th Middlesex; and though the 2/4th Queen's withdrew from White Hill, its machine guns prevented the enemy from reoccupying it in force. On the extreme southern flank, $4\frac{1}{2}$ miles south of Ras ez Zamby and about

---

[1] The Turkish dispositions and an estimate of their numbers are given in Note at end of Chapter.

the same distance east of Bethlehem, was another company of the Middlesex in an exposed position at Deir Ibn Obeid, where there was an ancient monastery. This post was attacked by a Turkish cavalry regiment, which rode in to within half a mile of it and then attacked dismounted. The Corps Cavalry Regiment's efforts to relieve the garrison were unsuccessful, and the enemy gradually worked round to north and south of the hill, while continuing his pressure from the east. Major-General Mott was concerned for the safety of the post, but was informed by General Chetwode that, though it might be withdrawn if necessary, no troops were to be moved down from Jerusalem to Bethlehem to reinforce it. At 6 p.m. the enemy brought forward two mountain guns and attempted to breach the walls of the monastery, but the stout old masonry was hardly scarred by the little shells. For a time it appeared impossible to extricate the company, but it succeeded in withdrawing next morning under cover of supports to north of Sur Bahir. The 160th Brigade had suffered nearly three hundred casualties, but had lost no ground of any value. Even White Hill was found to be held only by an outpost screen of the enemy and was reoccupied by the 158th Brigade during the night.

### The Left Attack.

So certain had General Chetwode been over-night that the Turkish counter-offensive astride the Nablus road would be launched on the 27th December that he had given definite orders to Major-General Longley to carry out his attack that morning. During the night of the 26th, therefore, the troops of the Left Attack had taken up their positions of deployment.

The country in which the British had here to operate is as rough and broken as any in the Judæan Hills, west of the watershed, though not comparable in wildness and barrenness to that lying to the east. The wadis, in very deep beds, run almost due west, and between them are parallel ridges, rising in some cases 800 feet in 800 yards. Rugged and craggy as are these ridges, movement along them from west to east was easier than in the boulder-strewn bottoms of the gorges, while they gave command which the valleys did not afford. Major-General Longley had therefore, as we

Sketch 21.

## Defence of JERUSALEM.

Situation at 6 p.m. 30th Dec. 1917.

Scale of miles.

British in red   Turks in green.

Compiled in Historical Section (Military Branch)
Ordnance Survey 1928.

have seen, suggested to the corps commander that his attack 1917. should take the form of an advance along three of them: 27 Dec. the Zeitun ridge, between the Wadi el Imeish and Wadi es Sunt; the Kereina ridge, crowned by a 2,200-foot hill known as the " Hog's Back," between the Wadi es Sunt and Wadi 'Ain 'Arik; and the Deir Ibzia ridge, between the Wadi 'Ain 'Arik and Wadi Sad. For this purpose the attack was to be made in three groups: the Right Group consisting of the 229th Brigade (74th Division); the Centre Group of the 31st Brigade; the Left Group of the 29th and 30th Brigades, both under the command of Br.-General R. S. Vandeleur, commanding the 29th. The Left Group was made strongest, because, though it would have the shortest distance to go, it would be obliged to throw out a defensive flank to northward as it moved.

The advance was to be carried out in two phases. In the first the Right Group was to capture the eastern end of the Zeitun ridge and the Centre the Kereina ridge up to Kh. el Hafy, just west of the village of 'Ain 'Arik, while the Left advanced between the Wadis Sad and 'Ain 'Arik and formed a long defensive flank facing northward. In the second phase the final objective was from the high ground beyond the village of Beitunye to the hill of Abu el 'Ainein, half-way between 'Ain 'Arik and 'Ain Kanie, the Left Group now having a flank of about five miles to cover. After the opening of the attack two battalions of the 231st Brigade were to concentrate at Beit 'Ur et Tahta and come under Major-General Longley's orders as a reserve.

The attack was to be strongly supported by artillery. Five four-gun batteries of the 74th Divisional Artillery [1] were to cover the Right Group; the LXVIII Brigade R.F.A. the Centre Group; whilst the LXVII Brigade R.F.A. divided its support between the two. The Left Group was to have that of the 263rd Brigade, B/IX and 10th Mountain Batteries, while the artillery of the Australian Mounted Division would also be able to assist it. The XCVI Heavy Artillery Group was to be employed mainly

---

[1] This group was under the command of Lieut.-Colonel W. Kinnear, and consisted of A/117, C/117 and A/44 near Beit Izza, C/268 between Biddu and Qubeibe, and a battery made up from sections of A/117 and B/117 at Biddu. These batteries, owing to difficulties of supply and the need for employing extra horses to draw them, were all at four-gun strength.

for the neutralization of the enemy's artillery, though if batteries could be spared it might be called upon to give direct support to the infantry. The success of the operation depended to a great extent upon the rapidity of the artillery's advance. It was decided, in view of the difficulty of the country, to concentrate upon a single track up the Kereina ridge for the artillery, though rougher tracks had to be made across the other ridges for supply.

By 5 a.m. the 229th Brigade or Right Group was deployed in the Wadi el Imeish to attack the Zeitun ridge. At 7.50 it began its long and stiff climb up the south-western slope of the hill, on a front of two battalions, each with two companies extended in line. Well covered by the supporting artillery, the troops moved at great speed considering that in some places men had to pull their comrades up, and by 9.20 Kh. er Ras was in their hands. The attack was now ahead of that of the Centre Group, and exposed to constant shelling and machine-gun fire. The main line therefore halted, though patrols pushed boldly forward along the ridge. The general advance to the eastern ridge did not begin until 5.45 p.m. The 12/R. Scots Fusiliers on the right reached its objective without difficulty. On the left, however, the 14/Black Watch met with stout opposition at Kh. Bir esh Shafa, west of Beitunye. On this prominent hill the enemy was established in two tiers of stone sangars above a sheer cliff eight feet high, and a hot engagement followed before it was cleared at the point of the bayonet.

The Centre Group, consisting of the 31st Brigade, advanced from the Wadi es Sunt at 6.45 a.m. and by 8.30 the 6/R. Inniskilling Fusiliers on the left had captured Kereina Peak. A halt was made until Deir Ibzia had been occupied by the Left Group, and then at 11.30 two companies of the 5/R. Inniskilling Fusiliers attacked the Hog's Back, which while it remained in Turkish hands prevented any advance of the artillery along the road under construction. The hill was captured about 1 p.m., while the 6/R. Inniskillings established itself at Kh. el Hafy to the north. Then the 5/R. Irish Fusiliers passed through the 5/R. Inniskillings and pushed forward along the ridge until level with the 229th Brigade. In the fighting on the Kereina ridge, Private James Duffy, a stretcher-bearer of the 6/R. Inniskillings, won the Victoria Cross for conspicuous bravery in bringing in and attending to the injuries of two wounded men under heavy fire.

1917.
27 Dec.

On the front of the Left Group patrols were sent forward at 5.45 a.m., and the general advance began at 6. The 1/Leinster moved up the Deir Ibzia ridge, the 5/Connaught Rangers up that north of the Wadi Sad in order to establish itself on the high ground south of the village of Kefar Nama. It was then Br.-General Vandeleur's intention that the 6/Leinster should move up the Wadi Sad to capture the prominent knoll of Shabuny under cover of the fire of the 1/Leinster on its right and 5/Connaught Rangers on its left. The 6/R. Irish Rifles had the task of forming a defensive flank from the left of the Connaught Rangers to the right of the Australian Mounted Division north-east of Suffa. The 7/R. Dublin Fusiliers from the 30th Brigade was concentrated in reserve at the junction of the Wadis Sad and Sunt; the remainder of the 30th Brigade in the valley east of Suffa.

At the beginning of the advance little resistance was met. Thereafter several machine guns on the wooded ridges west of Kefar Nama gave considerable trouble, and the Turks made a small and fruitless counter-attack against the 1/Leinster. Artillery co-operation with this battalion was most successful, but the forward observing officers with the Connaught Rangers and Irish Rifles were for some time hampered by shortage of telephone wire. For about half an hour the advance came to a halt, but then the accurate fire of the 263rd Brigade R.F.A. notably diminished the activity of the enemy's machine guns on the Deir Ibzia ridge. By 11 a.m. the 1/Leinster had reached its objective. The two leading companies of the Connaught Rangers being held up, with a deep valley separating them from the enemy on the far hill, Lieut.-Colonel V. M. B. Scully ordered them to sweep the opposite crest and the face of the hill, where the enemy was hidden behind boulders, with machine-gun and rifle fire. At the same time he instructed them to begin putting up sangars, as if they were consolidating the position. Meanwhile he brought forward his two remaining companies, and at 11 a.m. launched them to the attack across the gorge, covering fire from the machine guns, Lewis guns, and rifles of the other companies being kept up till the last possible moment. The assault evidently surprised the enemy, who streamed away in disorder. Patrols from both the 1/Leinster and the Connaught Rangers found Shabuny unoccupied, so that the 6/Leinster was able to take over the hill without having to fight for it. The whole objective of the first phase was now securely in the hands of the Left Attack. On the right the 231st Brigade of the 74th Division had seized Kh. ed Dreiheime, east of Et Tire village, after stiff fighting that morning, in order to prevent the Right Group from being enfiladed during its advance across the Zeitun ridge. On the left patrols of the Australian Mounted Division had found the villages of Deir el Kuddis and Khirbetha Ibn Harith unoccupied. Hard work by the Royal Engineers and the Pioneer Battalion (5/R. Irish) of the 10th Division made it possible to push forward some of the artillery after dark.

### The General Attack of the XX Corps.

Before dusk came down General Chetwode had the comfortable assurance that his plan had been entirely successful. On the right the enemy's counter-offensive had been defeated. On the other flank the British attack had reached its first objective without heavy loss. The morrow would complete the discomfiture of the Turks. For the moment he hesitated whether or not to accomplish this with Major-General Longley's force alone, thus driving the enemy off the Nablus road by an attack from the west. That scheme had its attraction; could it have been carried out with the necessary speed the Turks would doubtless have been hard put to it to escape disaster. But the extreme difficulty of the country in which the 10th Division was moving had to be taken into account. The night's reflection decided the corps commander that the 60th Division, with the Nablus road at its disposal, must take part in the operation; and at 9.40 a.m. he ordered it to advance, its right flank covered by the 53rd, in accordance with the orders issued before the Turkish attack. At 10.40 he sent a message to Major-General Longley that the Left Attack should take its second objective as soon as possible, and also instructed Major-General Girdwood to advance with his left flank on Beitunye.

During the morning the 60th Division recovered the outpost positions lost by it on the previous day, the 179th Brigade retaking Ras et Tawil with 36 prisoners and two machine guns. On the left the 181st Brigade occupied Bir

Nebala and El Jib, almost without a shot fired. At 1.20 p.m. 1917.
Major-General Shea issued orders for the 180th Brigade to 28 Dec.
pass through the 179th, and advance with the 181st on the
villages of Er Ram, Qalandye, and Ra-fat, which lay in a
line almost at right angles to the Nablus road, about a mile
and a half north of that now held. At Er Ram only did the
Turks make a stand, and a ten minutes' concentration of
artillery expelled them from this, one of the strongest positions near the Nablus road. Exhausted by his fruitless
assaults of the previous day, the enemy had little heart left
in him, even for a rear-guard action. The 230th Brigade of
the 74th Division had no greater difficulty in taking Kh. el
Jufeir, a mile and a half south-west of Ra-fat, and linking up
its right with the 60th Division at that point.

To protect the right flank of the 60th Division Major-
General Mott at 11.15 a.m. ordered the 158th Brigade to
capture Ras Arqub es Suffa, north-east of Ras ez Zamby, and
the village of 'Anata, 3 miles north-east of Jerusalem. At
3.15 the divisional artillery began an intense bombardment
of these two points, and the attack was launched a quarter
of an hour later. The 7/Welch Fusiliers was held up by
machine-gun fire, but a further bombardment enabled it
to occupy Ras Arqub es Suffa after dusk. The 1/Hereford,
sending forward two companies, one on either side of the
village, each extended on a platoon frontage, captured 'Anata
at 4 p.m., thus effectually covering the right of the 60th
Division.

The Left Attack met with rather more resistance, though
its greatest difficulties were caused by the roughness of
the country. The Right Group attacked Beitunye. The
14/Black Watch was effectively covered by an overhead
machine-gun barrage as well as artillery fire, the XCVI
Heavy Artillery Group having accomplished a remarkable
feat in getting a battery up to Foqa. At Beitunye the
stiffest fighting of the day took place in the streets. One
small party of the enemy barricaded itself into a house, and
would not surrender till bombed through the windows. In
all 70 prisoners and seven machine guns were taken.

The Centre Group, advancing on Kefar Shiyan, east of
the village of 'Ain 'Arik, had only to meet the machine-gun
fire of rear guards, which were dispersed by the supporting
artillery. After capturing Kefar Shiyan, El Muntar a mile

to the south-east was occupied, and afterwards handed over to the Right Group. The 6/R. Inniskillings established a strong position on Knot Hill, due east of Kefar Shiyan and north of El Muntar.

On the front of the Left Group the 29th Brigade had, it will be remembered, captured the ridge north of the Wadi Sad from Shabuny westward. It was now the task of the 30th Brigade (Br.-General F. A. Greer) to move up the Wadi 'Ain 'Arik behind the 29th and attack the hills north and north-east of 'Ain 'Arik. These hills were found to be strongly held when approached by patrols at dawn. The movement of the brigade up the wadi was very slow, but directly artillery opened fire and the advance began the Turks were seen almost everywhere withdrawing from their foremost positions. By 4.30 p.m. the objective was captured by the 1/R. Irish and 6/R. Munster Fusiliers, the right of the 30th Brigade being in touch with the left of the 31st 800 yards north of Kefar Shiyan and the line running thence north to Kh. Rubin, then west to the junction with the 29th Brigade north of Deir Ibzia. The Australian Mounted Division on the left had established itself on the line north of Khirbetha Ibn Harith and Deir el Kuddis to which its patrols had advanced the previous day.

1917.
29 Dec.

General Chetwode ordered the 60th and 74th Divisions to continue their advance northwards on the 29th, the right flank of the attack being again covered by the 53rd Division. The 60th Division at first met with very slight opposition, but the 180th Brigade was held up for some time facing Shab Sala, a precipitous hill a mile south of Bire. The 181st Brigade west of the Nablus road advanced a little further, but at noon was also brought to a halt within a couple of hundred yards of the Bire–Ram Allah road. It was now necessary to await the movement forward of the artillery, as the 180th Brigade had to advance down a bare slope, cross a gully at the bottom, and scale the steep flank of Shab Sala on the other side. The attack was carried out by the 2/19th and 2/20th London, covered by the fire of the 302nd Brigade R.F.A. and twelve machine guns, four of them belonging to the 53rd Division. The Turks resisted stoutly, but Shab Sala was captured with 20 prisoners at 3.30 p.m. The bombardment of Bire began at 4.15, and the village was captured with 42 prisoners by the 181st Brigade.

## CAPTURE OF RAM ALLAH

The artillery of the 60th Division and certain guns of the 10th, 1917. which by extraordinary exertions had been brought up within 29 Dec. range of the Nablus road, shelled a dense column of the enemy retreating northward. About 9.30 p.m. the whole line of the two brigades went forward. On the front of the 180th the advance lasted all night, Beitin, 2 miles north-east of Bire, being taken at 4 a.m. on the 30th. There was little further opposition, but this night march by compass was in itself a fine achievement, for it was made across a series of steep and rocky ravines, and the troops had to carry their Lewis guns and ammunition. Though the moon was almost full the sky was overcast. To cover the 60th Division's flank the 158th Brigade of the 53rd captured Kh. Almit, a mile north-east of 'Anata, during the night of the 28th, while the 159th Brigade took possession of Hizme at 8 a.m. next morning. Then as the 60th Division moved forward, the 159th Brigade moved up battalions in succession to fill the gap created by its advance, finally having its left near Burqa, 2½ miles S.S.E. of Beitin and at least 4 miles north of the position held the previous day.

On the front of the 74th Division the 230th Brigade captured Ram Allah at 9.15 a.m. on the 29th, but, attempting to occupy Kh. el Burj to the northward met with determined resistance. As the 181st Brigade on the right was held up, thus exposing the advance to fire from the east, there was little more progress during daylight. When the 60th Division captured Bire and moved northward after the fall of darkness the 230th Brigade also resumed its advance and took Kh. el Burj soon after midnight. In the Latin Church at Ram Allah about one hundred sick and wounded Turks were found in a dreadful state of filth and exhaustion; almost starving and not having had their wounds dressed for five days. Among them were eight British wounded.

The 229th Brigade, originally the Right Group of the Left Attack, had now returned to the command of Major-General Girdwood. It was not required to make a further advance on the 29th, being already almost level with the corps right and in a good position at Knot Hill and El Muntar. Nor was the 10th Division, on a line through Kh. Rubin, Janiya, and Ras Kerkur, called upon for another effort. On the 30th the 60th Division advanced its line slightly on the Nablus road. Then General Chetwode ordered the attack to cease.

Sketch 21.    Thus, after almost continuous fighting throughout November and December, the year ended with a cessation of the British pressure. So far as attack from the north was concerned, Jerusalem was safe. The Turkish attempt to retake it had not merely failed—it had actually facilitated Sir Edmund Allenby's plans; for, exhausting itself against the steady British defence astride the Nablus road, it had been unable to withstand the counter-attack on that front after the advance of Major-General Longley's columns had bored into its flank. Falkenhayn's scheme had played into General Chetwode's hands. It would seem that his intelligence service must have failed him in not reporting the great improvement in communications which the British had effected since the Yeomanry Mounted Division, largely owing to the lack of artillery support, of ammunition, food, and water, had been unable to advance eastward across the ridges now faced by the 10th Division. Nor can he have, it must appear, anticipated the wonderful work of the Royal Engineers, pioneers, and infantry of the 10th Division, under the direction of its C.R.E., Lieut.-Colonel E. M. S. Charles, after the attack had been launched. He thought his right flank secured by the difficulties of the country, and was almost justified in believing that a British advance was impracticable.

General Chetwode, by coolly awaiting the attack on his right and setting his left in motion, had taken advantage of his opportunity. The Royal Flying Corps had contributed to the enemy's demoralization. On the 27th, the day of the attack, it had scattered Turkish troops and transport near Qalandye, and throughout the three following days it dropped bombs and used its machine guns against columns on the Nablus road. Yet once again the highlands and the wintry weather had saved the enemy from the full consequences of his defeat. He left about a thousand dead upon the field, but lost no artillery and only 558 prisoners. The losses of the XX Corps were in the neighbourhood of a thousand.[1]

---

[1] The casualties of the whole Force for the week ending the 29th December were 1,360. The casualties for the fortnight ending on that

## NOTE.

### THE BATTLE FROM THE TURKISH SIDE.

In his report to Germany regarding the Passage of the Nahr el 'Auja Falkenhayn correctly estimated Sir Edmund Allenby's intention to safeguard Jaffa as a base for disembarkation. He added that the British gained "an easy and unhoped for success owing to the complete negligence "of the protective troops of the *XXII Corps* in this zone." He at first contemplated a counter-attack to throw the British back across the river, but abandoned it because it would have rendered his projected attack on the Nablus road impossible.

The objectives set to the Turkish divisions for the first day's attack in the Jerusalem counter-offensive were Tell el Ful for the *53rd Division*, Beit Hannina and Nabi Samweil for the *19th Division*, Beit Izza and Beit Duqqu for the *24th* and *1st Divisions*. It can only be surmised that the two last-named divisions were to start later than the *53rd* and *19th*, for they were themselves attacked before they began their advance. Falkenhayn attributed his lack of success, first, to the stubborn defence of the British, who were, he recognized, forewarned, and secondly, to the failure of his *1st Division*, which had been hastily brought up and met the full weight of the British 10th Division's attack.

There were in action against the British XX Corps, from (Turkish) right to left, the *3rd Cavalry Division*, the *1st*, *24th*, *19th*, *53rd*, *26th Divisions*, and *7th Cavalry Regiment*,[1] which attacked Deir Ibn Obeid. The *27th Division*, which had not been of any value as a fighting formation since the capture of Beersheba, seems to have been broken up by this date; at least it makes no further appearance in reports or on maps. The *61st Regiment* of the *20th Division* was also on the *Seventh Army* front. The enemy strength is difficult to calculate. We know that the ration strength of the *XX Corps* was 12,300 on the 6th December, and that of the *III Corps* 10,000.[2] The *1st Division* and the presumably strong *61st Regiment* had arrived since then, raising the ration strength to perhaps 30,000. At most, allowing for some drafts from the depot regiments, which seem to have disappeared for the moment, the fighting strength of the *Seventh Army* cannot have exceeded 20,000. As that of the British XX Corps was 33,000, it will appear that the counter-offensive was a desperate venture.

date, which include those of the Battle of Jaffa and the Defence of Jerusalem, were as follows :—

|  | Killed. | Wounded. | Missing. |
|---|---|---|---|
| Officers | 31 | 87 | 3 |
| Other ranks | 297 | 1,348 | 124 |

A total of 1,890.

[1] This regiment, from east of Jordan (see p. 12, f.n.) never rejoined the *3rd Cavalry Division*, and later returned to Moab, where it became part of the newly-arrived *Caucasus Cavalry Brigade*.

[2] From the note-book of the Director of Supplies of the *XX Corps*. This elderly officer, immaculately dressed in civilian clothes and carrying a gold-headed cane, gave himself up to the 60th Division after the capture of Jerusalem. He announced that he was the only Arab on Ali Fuad's staff, and, being consequently unpopular, had hidden himself when the Turks left.

## CHAPTER XIII.

PROBLEMS OF THE FUTURE.

(Maps 1, 2, 23.)

TRANSPORT AND POLICY.

1917.
Dec.
Maps 1, 2.
EVIL as had been the effect of the torrential rains in the hills, they wrought destruction yet worse in the Philistine Plain, into which the streams poured foaming down the gullies of the Shephelah, overflowing a thousand watercourses great and small, and flooding big tracts of the low-lying country. Even where the flood-water did not lie the soil was turned to the consistency of glue, and from every bit of rising ground runnels descended to cut trenches in the dirt roads. The British broad-gauge line and the captured Turkish railway were both repeatedly broken by the earth being washed away from under the sleepers; so that during the last week of the year fresh construction had to be stopped, and all labour employed in repairing the track and the culverts. The British railway, which had been laid beside the Turkish from Deir Sneid to Ejje, S.S.E. of Majdal, had from thence been directed on Ramle. It passed through Sdud, 17 miles south-west of Ramle, and here railhead had been established by Christmas Day. The great depot at Sdud was on this date an island in a brown sea. The extraordinary difficulties of supply were increased by the fact that the landing of stores at the mouth of the Nahr Suqreir was at the same time made impossible by tempestuous seas.

Christmas Day was, in fact, the climax to a period of nightmare for the services of supply, on the eve of the battle in defence of Jerusalem. The railways were cut or submerged at many points. A train on the Turkish line was derailed the previous night near Et Tine. At sea there was a gale. It was temporarily impossible owing to the floods

## THE GOVERNMENT'S DEMANDS

to transfer grain to the forward depots of the XX and XXI Corps at Latron and Ramle; consequently all animals had to be put on half rations. Indeed, the camel convoys had the greatest difficulty in making their way forward from Sdud for many days to come. In some cases beasts which had slipped and fallen could not be got to their feet again and were actually drowned. Fortunately, there were at these forward depots nearly three days' reserve rations for the infantry divisions, while the bulk of the cavalry had already been withdrawn to railhead or its neighbourhood.

1917. Dec.

However, that was the worst, for the weather improved just as the situation was becoming critical. By the 27th wind and sea had abated enough for a ship to discharge 300 tons of supplies at the Nahr Suqreir, and that evening large convoys of camels struggled through to Ramle. Even then supply to the troops in forward areas was slow and precarious.

As soon as the floods to some extent subsided in early January, the construction of the broad-gauge line was resumed, and by the end of the month it reached Bir Salem, 2 miles west of Ramle. At the same time the railway in Sinai was doubled as far as El 'Arish, some 25 miles beyond Bir el Mazar, the double-track railhead of October. On the 28th January the Turkish railway was restored from Junction Station to Jerusalem. Though there were many stoppages still owing to floods, there was never again a risk of the advanced depots running short. Supply by sea also was improved when the Navy agreed to afford protection both at the Nahr Suqreir and at Jaffa. Half the boats and personnel were transferred to Jaffa, and throughout the month of January the two landing-places were used about equally.

1918. Jan. Map 23.

It was on the eve of this crisis, which he had to a great extent foreseen, that Sir Edmund Allenby was called upon by the Government to exploit his success. Immediately after the capture of Jerusalem he was informed that another division, the 7th Indian, would arrive from Mesopotamia, and was asked to outline his plans. He replied on the 14th December that, having experienced the results of the comparatively slight amount of rain which had fallen hitherto, he realized how serious a handicap the wet season would prove once it really set in. Not until January was

1917. Dec.

over could he hope that the country would be suitable for campaigning, and even then he would have to depend largely on the progress of his railway.  After establishing the XXI Corps beyond the Nahr el 'Auja, he proposed to advance his right to the Wadi el 'Auja, which runs into the Jordan 10 miles north of the Dead Sea.  Next, during the remainder of the wet season, while the railway was being pushed on, he would operate against the Hejaz Railway, as he was informed that there were still 20,000 Turks south of 'Amman.  Then he hoped gradually to advance his left to Tul Karm, covering railway construction and preparing for a major offensive with naval co-operation.

This was by no means sufficient to please the Government, least of all the Prime Minister, who was now, after the carnage of the Battle of Ypres, more than ever set upon a policy of " knocking out the props " by operations in the Near and Middle East against Germany's allies.  Mr. Lloyd George desired that Turkey should at a blow be eliminated from the war.  That would, he considered, be effected by an advance to Aleppo which would cut Turkish communications with Mesopotamia ; but, if the project were beyond the means available, he wished at least to see the whole of Palestine occupied.  The C.I.G.S. therefore asked Sir Edmund Allenby what force he would require for each of these alternative policies, Palestine being considered as " embracing the whole country between Dan and Beer-"sheba."

The War Cabinet's Scriptural northern objective puzzled the Commander-in-Chief, but he replied that " understanding Dan to be about Baniyas, i.e. half-way " between Nazareth and Damascus,"[1] he expected to be able to place a force of his present strength north of the line Nazareth–Haifa by June or July, provided that the enemy did not oppose him with a fighting strength of more than 60,000 and that he met with no extraordinary difficulties in railway construction.

Regarding the alternative scheme, he pointed out that to advance against Aleppo from the Nazareth–Haifa line meant moving against Damascus and Beirut, a front served

---

[1] Dan, the northern frontier-town of the Israelites, apparently stood on the hill known as Tell el Kadi, just west of Baniyas, which is 11 miles N.N.E. of Lake Hule and 29 miles east of Tyre.

CONFLICT OF OPINION 295

by a broad-gauge railway, with good lateral communications 1917.
and apparently ideal ground for defence. If that front Dec.
were strongly held, he would require at least sixteen divisions in addition to his mounted corps, but doubted if he
could supply such a force, even with his railway doubled
and making allowance for sea transport. Aleppo was 350
miles off, and his single-track railway was now advancing
at the rate of about half a mile a day. He still thought
that the plan which he had outlined in his telegram of the
14th was the best, and that it was advisable to deal
with the Turkish forces on the Medina railway before
continuing his advance northward. Further pressed, he 1918.
insisted that it was essential at the moment to consolidate Jan.
on his present line,[1] secure his eastern flank as far as the
Jordan, and dislodge the Jericho garrison. He was, in
fact, already making arrangements to carry out the first
part of his plan.

In reading the pages which follow it must ever be
borne in mind that it was the British Government's assumption that the shock which Turkey would suffer as the result
of a British advance to Aleppo, following upon a series of
great blows, would drive her out of the war, and that the
defection of Bulgaria would probably follow. How far
either of these assumptions was justified it is not easy to
decide. Turkey had suffered vast losses in battle and yet
vaster from sickness and disease. She was known to be
weary of a war into which she had been drawn by a handful
of adventurers. Terms would be far easier to make now
that Russia had forfeited all right to have her claims
heard. Yet military opinion was far from assured either
that the objective could be rapidly attained or that, if
attained, the result would be the elimination of Turkey.
Sir W. Robertson, in a memorandum to the War Cabinet 1917.
on the 26th December, stated that in the opinion of the Dec.
General Staff it would be a grave risk to increase British
commitments in a secondary theatre at a moment when
all the omens pointed to a German offensive on the Western
Front. As for the political aspect, he wrote :—
" It would seem to be very difficult for Turkey to shake
" off the German grip—even if she wished to do so. The

[1] This message was sent on the 4th January, that is, after the Passage
of the Nahr el 'Auja and the advance beyond Bire on the Nablus road.

"Turkish General Staff and War Office are largely in the hands of Germans; Turkish armies and minor units are commanded by German officers; German machine-gun units and artillery are to be found in all Turkish theatres; Germany is the source of Turkish munition supplies; and several thousand German and Austrian troops are in Constantinople, which is at the mercy of German warships, the *Goeben* and *Breslau*, anchored in the Golden Horn."

It appears that the crux of this statement lies in the parenthesis "even if she wished to do so." If Turkey were eager to surrender, then the weight of the German grip might prove an added inducement or, at all events, cause her to continue the struggle only half-heartedly and under protest. That, despite her losses and defeats, she was on the eve of such a collapse was by no means certain to all observers. Lieut.-Colonel A. P. Wavell, liaison officer between the War Office and the E.E.F., who had seen the Turkish prisoners, spoken with British commanders regarding the quality of the resistance they had had to meet, and had at his disposal all information in the hands of the British Intelligence in Egypt and at the War Office, stated in a memorandum drawn up at the request of the British Representative on the Supreme War Council at Versailles that the prospects of a rapid advance through Palestine and a complete defeat of the Turks were not so favourable as the Government seemed to suppose. Possibly, discovering to his astonishment that there was at Versailles no conception of the difficulties of an advance to Damascus and Aleppo, he deliberately laid stress on the obstacles and causes of probable delay as a corrective to roseate optimism. On the immediate question under discussion he wrote:—

"As far as can be judged from the morale and attitude of the Turks in Palestine, there seems no good reason to believe that another defeat or even the occupation of Damascus and Aleppo would cause them to rise against their German masters and conclude a separate peace."

The reader may make his own decision between these points of view, if he can; but he will more probably conclude that the question cannot be isolated and therefore cannot be answered. At least let him beware of finding

## VISIT OF GENERAL SMUTS

too close an analogy between the proposals for a great 1917
British offensive in the early months of 1918 and the Dec.
offensive which actually took place in September of that
year. By that time all the weakening influences which the
exponents of a "knock-out blow" now detected at work
in Turkey had without doubt made great progress, while
the hopes of a victorious ending to the war on the Western
Front, which had buoyed up Turkish spirits from March
to August, had been destroyed. Rulers, nation, troops,
had suffered much in spirit, and the two last in body,
during those deceptively quiet months. It is not suggested
that Sir Edmund Allenby could not have routed the
Turkish Armies in the spring, but it is not so certain that
the rout would then have induced Turkey to make peace.

However, valid or not, the assumption was that upon
which the British Government were inclined to act. At
the end of December the Prime Minister requested the
Permanent Military Advisers of the Supreme War Council
at Versailles to "report on the military and strategical
"position" in the Turkish theatre. The correspondence
that ensued recalls scenes from a Greek drama. Versailles
(or, it may be said, the British Representative, for the
French were luke-warm) the Protagonist, announced
its plans and aspirations; the War Office, as Chorus,
criticized: the one optimistic, the other rather pessimistic.
The general conclusion of the Supreme War Council was
that Turkey was the weakest point in the hostile coalition
and should be the object of attack. Offensive action in
Palestine and Mesopotamia, with a subsidiary offensive in
Macedonia, was suggested; a new attempt to force the
Dardanelles, or, in default of that, a landing at Alexandretta,
was considered. The final decision, embodied in a Joint
Note of the Military Representatives on the 21st January
1918, was to stand on the defensive in France, Italy, and
the Balkans, and to "undertake a decisive offensive against
"Turkey with a view to the annihilation of the Turkish
"armies and the collapse of Turkish resistance."

Early in February the British Government sent out to 1918
Egypt Lieut.-General J. C. Smuts to consult with Sir Feb.
Edmund Allenby, Rear-Admiral Jackson, and Major-
General W. Gillman, Chief of the Staff of the Mesopotamian
Expeditionary Force, as to the best methods of co-ordinating

British efforts in the Middle East and of employing British resources for the elimination of Turkey from the war. General Smuts's mission had the merit of bringing the discussions down from the somewhat fanciful realms in which they had hitherto revolved to the solid earth of reality. After the consultations had taken place, he telegraphed home his views on the 15th February. He began by stating that neither force was strong enough for offensive action to be continued upon both the Syrian and Mesopotamian fronts. One of the two, therefore, should in future act on the defensive and hand over reinforcements to the other. The Mesopotamian Force was the further from Aleppo; its requirements for railway construction would be the greater; and its right flank would be in danger should it advance beyond Mosul. It should therefore assume a defensive rôle. Of its six infantry divisions,[1] two, including the 13th British Division, and one cavalry brigade should be transferred to Palestine. Sir Edmund Allenby would then have ten infantry divisions, an Indian cavalry division which it was proposed to send out from France, the cavalry brigade from Mesopotamia, and his own three mounted divisions. With this force he was prepared to undertake an offensive as vigorous as the progress of his railway would permit.

His plans would be to begin with those which he had already outlined: first, an advance to the Jordan and thereafter the demolition of the Hejaz Railway, to isolate the Turkish forces from Ma'an to Medina; secondly, an advance towards the line Haifa–Tiberias. The standard-gauge railway would be pushed forward as rapidly as possible along the coast, directed first on Haifa, and thereafter possibly on Beirut. The main body would advance with this railway, developing en route ports such as Haifa, Tyre, and Beirut for supplies. The line across the Plain of Esdraelon, from Haifa to Der'a, where it joined the Hejaz Railway, would be used by a smaller column, which would move on Damascus by this route and occupy the Hauran in conjunction with Arabs and Druses. Vast quantities of rails would be required: 388 miles to carry a double track

---

[1] The 7th Indian Division had arrived in Egypt at the beginning of January and is therefore not included in the six.

to Haifa and a single track thence to Beirut, 261 miles if 1918. the line were doubled no further than Rafah, which might Feb. suffice if the fullest value were got from sea transport. Much additional labour, including two Canadian railway battalions, would be needed. The supply of coal, at present 6,000 tons a month, would have to be greatly increased.

It is unnecessary to enter more fully into the details of the additional transport which would have been required had the scheme been carried out. It received the Government's approval but almost immediately afterwards collapsed owing to the needs of the Western theatre. It is of interest to compare it with that put into force in the autumn, to which it bears a slight resemblance. It was sound, but stiff and mechanical, and it made transport master instead of servant. By reflection during the summer Sir Edmund Allenby so transformed it that it achieved in less than a fortnight what its original would have taken many months to perform.

ADMINISTRATIVE AND POLITICAL PROBLEMS.

The period of Sir John Maxwell's command, when administration was on a peace basis, and even that of Sir Archibald Murray's, with his Army still on the fringe of Egyptian territory and his headquarters in Cairo, were now far behind. These generals were commanders in Egypt engaged with an enemy at the gates; Sir Edmund Allenby was commanding a force, based on Egypt, indeed, but carrying out a campaign, which might have a very distant objective, in a foreign country. He was in the field with his Army, too far away and too preoccupied to control internal administration or co-ordinate the work of the existing sub-commands. He therefore asked for leave to appoint a major-general to command in Egypt, with brigadier-generals for two sub-commands: (i) Delta and Western Force, absorbing the Southern Canal Section and including the detachments at Tor and Abu Zenima in southern Sinai; (ii) Alexandria District, which would include the garrisons along the coast as far as Sollum. He also proposed to amalgamate the Headquarters Lines of Communication Defences and Headquarters Inspector Lines of Communication. The War Office agreed with these suggestions. Br.-General H. D. Watson, who had commanded the Composite Force at the Third Battle of Gaza, was appointed to command in Egypt with the rank of major-general, the old title of Force in Egypt, which had disappeared when Sir J. Maxwell returned to England, being revived.

In the previous volume the situation in Egypt at the end of Sir A. Murray's period of command was discussed at some length. It may be said that thenceforward there was no abrupt or notable change in it, but that a gradual deterioration in British-Egyptian relations set in. War is a jealous mistress, prone to look upon liberty as a rival in the affections of those who woo her. The irritants described [1]—of which the continued burden of martial law, the military demands for labour, animals, and supplies were the most serious—were material rather than moral, and so could not be checked by Sir Reginald Wingate's tact and long experience of Egyptian affairs. It was inevitable that they should increase with the passage of time and the growing urgency of the Army's needs, until by the end of the war they had produced open sores. Then, indeed, they resulted in lamentable disorders; but while hostilities with Turkey were in progress they never embarrassed the Commander-in-Chief or hampered his activities.

With regard to Palestine, Sir Edmund Allenby asked for a major-general as chief administrator of occupied territory—which at present corresponded roughly with the Turkish *Sanjak* of Jerusalem—and for the division of the country now in his hands into four districts, Jerusalem, Jaffa, Majdal, and Beersheba, each under a military governor. To these requests also the War Office assented. The Chief Political Officer, Br.-General G. F. Clayton, carried out the duties of Chief Administrator until the 16th April, when he was succeeded by Major-General Sir A. W. Money. The most important and difficult district, that of Jerusalem, was placed under Colonel Ronald Storrs, a former Egyptian official, who was notably successful in cooling the religious animosities which have long been the curse of the city. This is not the place to speak

---

[1] See Vol. I, pp. 364–7.

at length of the remarkable administrative work carried out during spring and summer in Southern Palestine by Br.-General Clayton, Major-General Money, and their subordinates. Suffice it to record that all the usual departments of civilized government, which on the flight of the Turkish officials had broken down, were gradually reestablished and the finances of the country restored to order; postal services were organized; the schools reopened. To assist the trade of the occupied territory and bring Egyptian currency into circulation, Major-General Campbell employed trains returning to Egypt, which would otherwise have been empty, for the carriage of products of Palestine to the Egyptian market. In March 1918 taxes were again collected, and it was found possible to provide for the payment of the dues appropriated to the service of the Ottoman Public Debt, in accordance with international arrangements.

The most urgent problem confronting the Administration of the Occupied Territory was the rehabilitation of agriculture, on which not only the bulk of the revenue but also the general welfare of the country chiefly depended. During the progress of the war cultivation had entirely ceased in many areas. The majority of the male population had been conscribed; stocks of grain had been almost entirely depleted; and all live-stock requisitioned to provide for the needs of the Turkish Army. At the same time the people were without current money to replenish these stocks; prices were abnormally high; the usual sources of supply cut off, and communications restricted. These difficulties were met by the importation of live-stock and seed grain, which were supplied to the cultivators on the deferred payment system; and later on these measures were supplemented by an agricultural loan of £500,000 obtained on easy terms from the Army bankers.

It was during these months of war that were laid the foundations of the sound and stable administration in Palestine which for over ten years went forward steadily and quietly, with turmoil and uncertainty among neighbours on all sides. The unhappy events of 1929 are, it is to be hoped, but a temporary interruption of its progress.

# CHAPTER XIV.

THE CAPTURE OF JERICHO AND ACTIONS OF TELL 'ASUR.

(Maps, 1, 2, 14, 15; Sketches A, 22, 23.)

### THE CAPTURE OF JERICHO.

Maps 1, 2.
Sketch 22.
AFTER the successful operations north of Jerusalem and Jaffa Sir Edmund Allenby, on the 29th December, issued to his corps commanders an outline of his intentions regarding future dispositions. He had decided to withdraw the Desert Mounted Corps for rest to Deir el Balah,[1] leaving one of its divisions to hold the front between the XX and XXI Corps. He contemplated that there would be a gap of about six miles between the inner flanks of the two corps, but this was eventually reduced to three by the XX Corps extending its left to Deir el Kuddis, 8¼ miles east of Lydda. To patrol this gap he considered that one mounted brigade would suffice; the remainder of the division to which it belonged would be stationed near Yibna till the railway reached Ramle, when it would be moved up to railhead. General Chauvel selected the Australian Mounted Division for this task, as it already knew the country, but, in view of its weariness, decided that it should be relieved at an early date by the A. & N.Z. Mounted Division. On the front of the XX Corps General Chetwode arranged to withdraw the 74th Division into reserve in the Biddu area.

As has been stated, the Commander-in-Chief considered

---

[1] The casualties of the Desert Mounted Corps had not been high except in the Yeomanry brigades, but the men were in need of rest. It was, however, for the horses, debilitated by their long marches without water, that repose was most urgent. The shortage of remounts was serious, and the only hope of maintaining the corps was to restore the horses to fitness. For this purpose it was necessary to withdraw them to dry lines and put them back on to ample rations, which could be transported to Deir el Balah by rail or water with comparative ease.

Sketch 22.

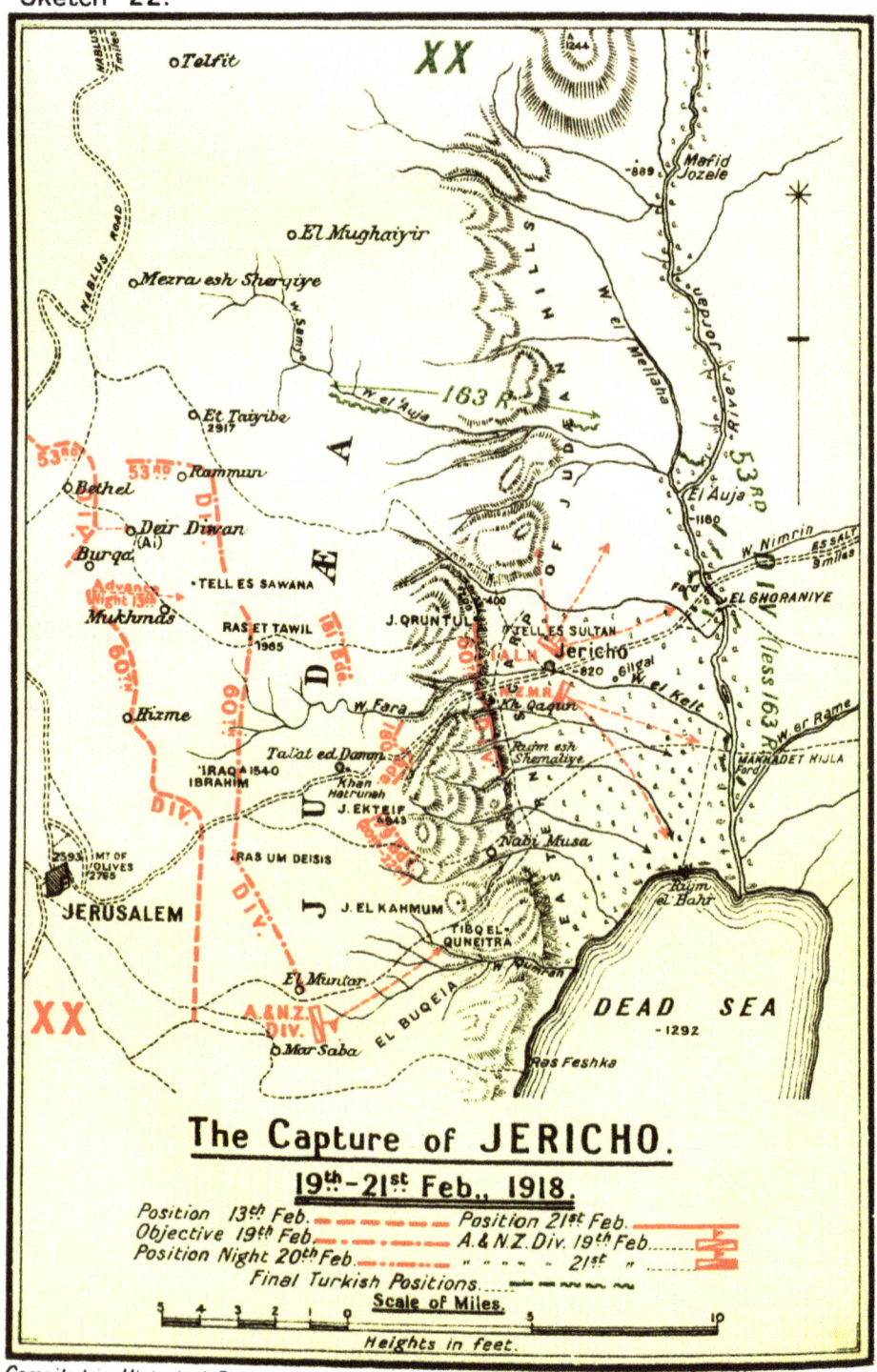

## The Capture of JERICHO.
### 19th–21st Feb., 1918.

Position 13th Feb.
Objective 19th Feb.
Position Night 20th Feb.
Position 21st Feb.
A. & N.Z. Div. 19th Feb.
" " 21st "
Final Turkish Positions.

Scale of Miles.
Heights in feet.

Compiled in Historical Section (Military Branch).
Ordnance Survey, 1928.

that no further progress northward was possible for the time being, until the railway had been advanced and the roads improved to permit the accumulation of supplies and stores in the forward area. Meanwhile he proposed to remove any threat to his right flank by driving the enemy across the Jordan and securing the crossings. Their possession would also prevent enemy raids into the country west of the Dead Sea, and provide a starting-place for operations against the Hejaz Railway.

By the beginning of February, as is recorded in the last chapter, the railway situation had considerably improved. There had also been progress in road-making in the hills. A great lateral line of communication north of the Jaffa–Jerusalem road had been begun by the complete reconstruction of the track running north from 'Amwas through Beit Sira. This work had been done under the orders of the Chief Engineer of the XX Corps, Br.-General R. L. Waller, mainly by Egyptian labour and that of other units put at his disposal by G.H.Q. From it there turned off eastward a metalled road up the Wadi Sad to 'Ain 'Arik (" Irish Road ") made by the 10th Division, with a subsequent continuation (" 'Ain 'Arik Road ") to Bire on the Jerusalem–Nablus road. Short spurs were made northward from Irish Road for supply, but the C.R.E. of the 10th Division, Lieut.-Colonel E. M. S. Charles, discovered by reconnaissance that they could not be extended far enough to enable the road to be used as a main line of supply in the event of a further advance. In January, therefore, a new 18-foot metalled road (" Great North Road ") was made by the 10th Division, following the track from Beit Sira to Khirbetha Ibn Harith and thence along the Wadi en Neda to Abu Shukheidin (" South Circular Road "), subsequently to be extended to Bir ez Zeit and further north during the March operations. A spur taken off from Nabi Eyub (" Job's Well ") to Beit Ello was to prove of great importance for artillery in this fighting.

Communications were now sufficiently good for General Chetwode to consider the occupation of Jericho and the driving of the enemy east of Jordan. On the 9th February he sent G.H.Q. an outline of his plan, to be put into effect as soon as the weather, at that date very bad, should permit. He had already been informed that one or two brigades of the A. & N.Z. Mounted Division would be put at his disposal, and now asked for two, with the headquarters of the division. In consequence, the 1st L.H. and New Zealand Brigades marched from Rishon le Ziyon, reaching Bethlehem on the 17th and 18th February.

Prior to the main operation the 60th Division was to advance its line to Mukhmas (the Biblical Michmash), 8 miles N.N.E. of Jerusalem. Then the division, to which a mounted regiment would be attached, was to advance to a line 6 miles east of Jerusalem, through El Muntar, 'Iraq Ibrahim and Ras et Tawil, while the 53rd Division on its left covered its flank by capturing the high ground about Rammun, 3 miles north of Mukhmas. The right flank of the 60th Division would be covered by the A. & N.Z. Mounted Division.

The second step was to consist of the advance of the 60th Division in three brigade columns, each with a 60-pdr. or 6-inch battery, a field artillery brigade, and a field company R.E. attached: the right to Jebil Ekteif south of the main Jericho road, the centre to Tal'at ed Damm on that road, the left along the " Ancient Road " running east from Mukhmas, to a point which would be decided on later. Finally, when Major-General Shea considered that they were in a position to do so, the three columns were to advance to the edge of the ridge overlooking Jericho and the Jordan Valley. Meanwhile the A. & N.Z. Mounted Division, operating on the right, was if possible to cut off the enemy retreating from Jericho and drive the remainder east of Jordan; to cover Jericho while it was examined by the intelligence and political officers; and to detach squadrons to seize any boats and stores at Rujm el Bahr, the Dead Sea port 5½ miles south-east of Jericho.

The country on the eastern side of the Judæan watershed is far bleaker and more barren than that on the western. The main wadis run in deep-cut gorges from west to east, that of the Wadi Kelt in particular being famed for the wild beauty of its winding, steep-walled bed. Movement between one valley and the next is often quite impossible for men carrying arms and equipment; indeed it may fairly be said that there is in a military sense no communication from north to south, while that from west to east is hindered by minor gullies at right angles to the greater. For a few miles, as one "goes down from Jeru-"salem," one sees gallant efforts to win something from this hard soil, and in March little patches of barley appear in the valley bottoms. But further on comes what is fittingly called "The Wilderness." All that this land supports is sheep and goats. These graze in large flocks, intermingled in a fashion which recalls the Scriptural phrase, the adventurous seeking sweet morsels on ledges not a foot wide with a drop of hundreds of feet below. Watching each flock is perhaps a single Arab boy, solacing himself and his charges with the music of a Pandean pipe; otherwise hardly a soul is met with. One encounters even to this day more human beings on the "Way of the Pilgrims" about Bir el Abd in Sinai than on this road. Before the war tourists on their way to Jericho were often enough robbed by brigands; and tradition has identified Khan Hatrurah, below the hill of Tal'at ed Damm, with the parable of the Good Samaritan. In spring wild flowers, especially anemones, tulips, poppies, and cyclamen, soften the general harshness, but when the troops first advanced eastward from Jerusalem these were only just beginning to bloom. Yet, whether seen at its most cheerless or at its pleasantest, there can be few countries in the world where hills of insignificant height give so strong an impression of savage and melancholy grandeur.

Between Jerusalem and the top of the scarp above the Jordan Valley there is a fall of over 2,000 feet in twelve miles, but the descent is not continuous, and several ridges afforded the enemy good defensive positions, notably between Ras um Deisis and 'Iraq Ibrahim, astride the Jericho road. Sir Edmund Allenby believed that the advance might be faced by 5,000 rifles of the XX Corps; later information from prisoners and from a monk, who entered the British lines after the first stage of the operation, reduced this estimate to 3,000. From the scarp it was not intended that the infantry should at this stage descend, unless called upon to succour the cavalry in the plain below. The drop to this plain is almost sheer; due west of Jericho, for example, there is a cliff 600 feet in height, the top being 200 feet above sea-level, the floor of the valley 400 feet below it. All through the summer the Jordan Valley is suffocatingly hot and breathless, burnt dry by a pitiless sun. By mid-February, however, at which time the troops first looked down upon it, it is just reaching its short-lived best. There is then pleasant greenery about Jericho, where the ground is cultivated, and among the trees and scrub through which the muddy Jordan winds its way; so that, at least from the vantage of the escarpment, with the dark background of the Hills of Moab and on the right the smooth blue waters of the Dead Sea to set off the view, it is a fair enough sight. In Roman times Jericho, or its near neighbourhood, was a winter resort, and it is at this season a welcome place of refuge from the biting winds of the hills; but before May is out it becomes a very inferno.

1918.
14 Feb.

On the 14th February the preliminary advance was carried out, the 60th Division occupying Mukhmas, while the 53rd captured the village of Deir Diwan on its left flank.

19 Feb.

The first objective of the 60th Division was to be attained by 6 a.m. on the 19th February, with the exception of 'Iraq Ibrahim and Ras et Tawil, which were to be subjected at dawn to a bombardment before they were assaulted. The attack was to be carried out by the 179th Brigade (to which the Wellington Mounted Rifles was attached) on the right, the 180th in the centre, and the 181st on the left. The position was held by no more than rear guards and was easily taken, the only serious fighting being at "Splash Hill," on the extreme left flank north of Ras et Tawil. This was defended by 300 Turks, and the 2/23rd London of the 181st Brigade suffered some fifty casualties before capturing it with 25 prisoners and two machine guns. Ras et Tawil itself was soon afterwards abandoned by the enemy. The 60th Division then made a slight advance in its centre, so as to lessen the considerable distance to be covered next day to the second objective, the flanks standing fast. In the course of this movement the 2/20th London had a difficult task in capturing the high ground to the north-east of 'Iraq Ibrahim, being forced to move to the attack along a narrow ridge on the south bank of the Wadi Fara and suffering 66 casualties. On the right the Wellington Regiment, after leading its horses in single file through a gorge on the track from Bethlehem to the Greek monastery of Mar Saba, debouched on to the plateau of El Buqeia,

## DIFFICULTIES OF THE ADVANCE 307

cupped in hills west of the Dead Sea, and found the enemy 1918. entrenched astride the Mar Saba-Jericho road, south of Nabi Musa, the traditional tomb of Moses. The remainder of the A. & N.Z. Mounted Division moved down from Bethlehem to assemble at El Muntar, on the infantry's right. On the left the 160th Brigade of the 53rd Division captured Rammun (where a company of the 2/10th Middlesex had some hard fighting) and the heights south of it, thus effectively covering the 60th Division's flank.

On the 20th the three columns had in each case a long and difficult approach march. The 2/13th London, 179th Brigade, found itself faced by a sheer drop of over twenty feet in the wadi which it was following. At first Lieut.-Colonel C. M. Mackenzie tried the experiment of lowering men down by ropes made from their putties, but found this method hopelessly slow. Then, having sent back a report of his predicament to brigade headquarters, he sent his leading companies across the intervening ridges into parallel wadis on either side and ordered them to push forward as rapidly as possible. Despite all their efforts, they were late for the attack on Jebel Ekteif, so two companies of the 2/16th, which had followed an easier route, were ordered to take their place in support of the 2/15th. The advanced Turkish trenches were captured by 8.15 a.m.; then the two companies of the 2/16th and one of the 2/13th managed to make their way up into the firing line, and the summit of the hill was carried at 11.25. In the centre the 180th Brigade Group was comparatively well served by the Jerusalem-Jericho road, so that both infantry and artillery were prepared for the attack at an early hour. Tal'at ed Damm was captured by the 2/18th and 2/19th London after an hour's bombardment in which the 10th Heavy Battery and one 6-inch howitzer of the 383rd Siege Battery took part. On the left the progress of the 181st Brigade was slow, being disputed by small rear guards which showed skill in manœuvre. By the evening the brigade had covered only 2½ miles and was about half-way between Ras et Tawil and Jebel Qruntul. No further advance was possible before morning light. The 231st Brigade of the 74th Division was now concentrated in the 181st Brigade's former position as reserve.

On the right of the 60th Division the A. & N.Z.

*19 Feb.*

*20 Feb.*

Mounted Division had advanced from El Muntar at 3.30 a.m., the New Zealand Brigade leading. This brigade picked up the Wellington Regiment, now returned to its command, and carried out a dismounted attack on the Turkish position from Tibq el Quneitra to Jebel el Kahmum, astride the Mar Saba–Jericho track. Opposition was stout at first, but the capture of Jebel Ekteif by the infantry caused the Turks to fall back towards Nabi Musa, and both hills were occupied soon after 2 p.m. The advance to Nabi Musa, where the enemy held a strong position, was very difficult, and eventually Major-General Chaytor decided to postpone it until next morning. Meanwhile, learning that a patrol had found the path down the Wadi Qumran to the Dead Sea unguarded, he ordered the 1st L.H. Brigade to move down into the plain, so that the position at Nabi Musa should be taken in rear.

1918.
21 Feb.

When the advance was continued on the 21st it was found that the enemy had fallen back all along the front, doubtless in part influenced by the 1st L.H. Brigade's threat to his communications. The infantry moved up to the top of the cliffs overlooking the Jordan Valley, from Nabi Musa to Jebel Qruntul, the traditional Mount of Temptation. The 1st L.H. Brigade rode straight on Jericho. Br.-General Cox was disappointed in his hopes of cutting off the enemy retreating from the hills, nor did he find any stores at Jericho, which was entered at 8 a.m. The little town, which is not on the sites bearing its name mentioned in either the Old or New Testament, was a scene of abominable filth, and a number of Turks suffering from typhus were found in it. A squadron of the Wellington Regiment rode out to Rujm el Bahr on the Dead Sea, but had nothing to show for its march, for the enemy had removed the grain transported to this place and either sunk the boats or drawn them up the Jordan.[1]

---

[1] It was afterwards discovered that there were a number of boats on the shore a mile and a half east of the river's mouth, and a remarkable attempt to secure these with the aid of a hydroplane was made by the R.F.C. The machine was brought down by lorries to a point south of Jericho, thence carried down to the shore, and launched on the 1st March. Off Rujm el Bahr the rudder-yoke came adrift, and the machine drifted southward and was beached. It was then determined by Captain J. A. D. Dempsey to convert the floats into two boats, each to carry four men, with improvised paddles. On the night of the 2nd the boats were

## END OF THE OPERATION

The mounted troops were ordered to cover Jericho during the night, while search was made by special intelligence officers for the spies who were known to haunt it. The only Turkish troops west of the Jordan between the Dead Sea and the Wadi el 'Auja now appeared to be a detachment holding a strong bridgehead at Ghoraniye on the main Jerusalem–Jericho–Es Salt road, and a smaller detachment covering the ford at Makhadet Hijla, the traditional scene of Christ's baptism. The enemy's camps could be seen east of the river.

1918. 21 Feb.

The operation had thus been successfully accomplished. On the 22nd the 60th Division's main line was withdrawn to Jebel Ekteif–Tal'at ed Damm–Ras et Tawil, outposts being left on the cliffs above the valley. The mounted troops marched back to Bethlehem on their way to the coast, the Auckland Rifles remaining encamped west of Jericho under the orders of Major-General Shea. The captures amounted to 144 prisoners and eight machine guns, the casualties to 510.[1] It was agreed by all the troops who took part in the advance that the country over which it had been made was the most difficult yet encountered. In these circumstances the work of the Royal Flying Corps had been even more valuable than usual. It had completely dominated the enemy and broken up all his formations in the air. From it early information of his dispositions and of his successive retirements had always been obtained. Owing to the comparatively small number of troops engaged, the problem of supply had been easier than in any operation hitherto carried out. A supply depot was formed at Bethany, from which camel convoys worked to Tal'at ed Damm or even Jericho. Good water was found at Nabi Musa and an ample supply in the plain, so that the large water convoys collected in case of need by Br.-General C. W. Pearless, D.A. & Q.M.G. XX Corps, were not required.

22 Feb.

---

[1] launched. They actually reached the east shore of the Dead Sea, but were carried by the current 5 miles south of their objective, and had to return next day without accomplishing their mission.

|  | Killed. | Wounded. | Missing. |
|---|---|---|---|
| Officers | 5 | 22 | — |
| Other Ranks | 75 | 404 | 4 |

## THE ACTION OF TELL 'ASUR—OPERATIONS OF THE XX CORPS.

Maps 2, 14.
Sketch A.

The advance to the edge of the escarpment above the Jordan Valley had made the British right flank secure, but had not won a frontage wide enough to allow operations to be carried out east of Jordan. For this Sir Edmund Allenby considered it necessary to advance his right to the line of the Wadi el 'Auja. He discussed with the corps commanders his plans at a conference on the 26th February. In a telegram to the War Office he stated that, after he had reached the Wadi el 'Auja, he hoped to force the passage of the Jordan about the 21st March, then capture Es Salt and destroy the Hejaz Railway at 'Amman. Leaving a detachment near Es Salt to prevent repairs and encourage the Arabs, he would next prepare for a general advance on Nablus and Tul Karm, which he hoped to begin by the 12th April. In order to deny to the enemy the use of the tracks leading to the lower Jordan Valley he proposed to combine the extension of his line to the Wadi el 'Auja with an advance astride the Nablus road, which in turn necessitated the advance of the XXI Corps' right flank.

It was at the moment when his attack was being launched that Sir Edmund Allenby learnt of a recent event which was to have a profound effect upon the remaining course of the campaign. On the 1st March Falkenhayn was succeeded by General der Kavallerie (Marshal in the Turkish Army) Liman von Sanders, Chief of the German Military Mission and recently commander of the Turkish *Fifth Army* in Western Anatolia.[1] Falkenhayn had been in command for five months, and already it was apparent that *Yilderim* was a failure. A German staff, however able, unfamiliar with the Turks and their methods, conversing with their senior officers as a rule in French, handing over its orders to translators before they were issued, could not make the best of a situation already discouraging. Jemal Pasha had returned to Europe, so that at least the irritation of his passive resistance had been removed, but

---

[1] The first intimation of the change came from refugees on the 9th March. A few days later there was found in a prisoner's diary the entry, " Liman Pasha has arrived."

Falkenhayn had still had to face opposition in many quarters. The new commander made it a condition of his acceptance of the post that he should take with him the Turkish General Kiazim Bey as Chief of the Staff, and other Turkish officers, so as to make his staff predominantly Turkish; also that the *Sixth Army* in Mesopotamia, the operations of which had been directed by *Yilderim*, should be separated from the command.

1918. March.

For the moment the change was to the enemy's advantage. Liman, if without Falkenhayn's great strategic ability, was the best type of Prussian officer, and brought with him the inestimable prestige of his defence of Gallipoli, whereas Falkenhayn's broader fame was shadowy to the Turkish soldier. Though high-tempered and unable to work with the Turks with as little friction as Kress, Liman knew them better and could obtain better results from them than Falkenhayn. It was not until the last stage of the campaign that the lack of the greater military science and foresight, which she had thrown away when she demanded of Germany that Falkenhayn should be recalled, was fatal to Turkey. Liman was above all, in a phrase to which the war gave birth, " a good trench fighter." It was his policy, as it had always been, to keep the front closed up, which meant that in Palestine, with the scanty resources at his disposal, he had hardly ever a reserve worth mentioning, and that what he had was stationed very far forward.[1] The policy paid, and paid for over six months, but only because circumstances robbed his opponent of the means to attack in strength. Disaster to the Turkish Armies might well have come about in the spring of 1918

---

[1] It is true that at Gallipoli, before the British landing, Liman had left only outposts along the coast and kept his main force in reserve to be employed where necessary. But after the landing he refused to allow a foot of ground to be abandoned, even when it was pointed out to him that a slight withdrawal on the southern front of the Peninsula would afford better positions and some protection from the fire of the British warships.

After the above appreciation had been written from a study of the orders and reports of the two commanders, a Turkish officer who had served both at Gallipoli and in Palestine stated to the writer:—" The "policy of Falkenhayn was defence by manœuvre; that of Liman defence " by resistance in trenches. Falkenhayn never fully realized how difficult " manœuvre was to troops short of transport on bad roads; Liman never " realized that ground in Palestine had not the value it had had at " Gallipoli."

instead of the autumn, had it not been for the transference of the greater part of Sir Edmund Allenby's British battalions to France. To contrast the events of Falkenhayn's command with those of Liman's without taking this fact into consideration is unreasonable, though it is perhaps natural that the latter has himself complacently done so.

Another change of which the British were also aware had taken place some weeks earlier. Kress von Kressenstein had been superseded in the command of the *Eighth Army* by the Turkish General Jevad Pasha. His departure was undoubtedly a severe loss, but it appears that he had forfeited the confidence of senior Turkish officers as a result of his dispositions at the Third Battle of Gaza and his failure to anticipate that the main British attack would come on the Turkish left.

The final objectives of the XX Corps were Kh. el Beiyudat and Abu Tulul, in the Jordan Valley, north of the Wadi el 'Auja; and, further west, astride the Nablus road, the road running from Mughaiyir through Sinjil and Jiljliya (Gilgal) to 'Abwein. Simultaneously the XXI Corps was to advance its right to Deir Ballut and Majdal Yaba, the latter being $4\frac{1}{2}$ miles north of its present front line at Et Tire. Certain preliminary operations were to be carried out by both corps, chiefly in order to obtain better gun positions and more suitable areas of deployment for the main operation. On the night of the 2nd March the 53rd Division advanced its line slightly on a front of over three miles, from north-west of Rammun to south-west of Bir ez Zeit, which is west of the Nablus road; while the 10th Division continued this movement to Beit Ello, 5 miles west of Bir ez Zeit. The 231st Brigade was at this time on the left of the 53rd Division and under its orders, the other brigades being engaged on road work and bivouacked in the 'Amwas area. Major-General Girdwood now took over command of the 231st Brigade, while the other two began their march to Lake Balua, north of Bire, in preparation for the coming attack. On the night of the 6th the 53rd Division made a further advance, meeting with but slight opposition and occupying the village of Taiyibe. The artillery was then brought up to give the infantry close support. This involved the hasty preparation of a track to take wheels from Rammun to Taiyibe.

# ADVANCE IN JORDAN VALLEY 313

The opening of Jerusalem Station and the improvement of the roads eased the difficulties of supply, though these were still to prove great enough in the final stage of transporting food and ammunition to the troops in the firing line. The 53rd and 60th Divisions and the mounted troops on the right flank were supplied from Jerusalem, lorries working to "Junction Dump," east of Tal'at ed Damm, for the 60th Division and to Ram Allah for the 53rd. The depot for the 10th and 74th Divisions was Latron, lorries working to Deir Ibzia and Khirbetha Ibn Harith on the front of the 10th Division, and to Ram Allah on that of the 74th. Convoys of camels and donkeys assisted the divisional transport to carry supplies from lorry-head; while special water-convoys, with *fanatis* ready filled, were held in reserve by corps headquarters.

1918.
8 March.

The main advance of the XX Corps began during the night of the 8th March and was carried out by the 53rd Division (1st L.H. Brigade attached), 74th Division (one light armoured motor battery attached), and 10th Division. The heavy artillery, under the orders of Br.-General P. de S. Burney, commanding XX Corps Heavy Artillery, consisted of the XCVI and XCVII Heavy Artillery Groups of seven siege and heavy batteries.[1] The 181st Brigade Group of the 60th Division took part in the action on the first day only, its object being to secure the line of the Wadi el 'Auja in and just above the Jordan Valley and guard against an attack on the open right flank of the 53rd Division. The brigade group [2] consisted of a force of all arms and was commanded by Lieut.-Colonel H. S. Streatfeild, 2/23rd London, Br.-General Da Costa being on leave.

The enemy had shown no signs of activity in the Jordan Valley. He had abandoned the ford at Makhadet Hijla and blown up the bridge at Ghoraniye, though he still held here a post on the right bank.[3] He also held

---
[1] The following batteries were allotted to the direct support of divisions:—383rd Siege and one section 91st Heavy Battery to the 53rd Division, 334th Siege and one section 91st Heavy Battery to the 74th Division, 195th Heavy Battery to the 10th Division.

[2] 181st Infantry Brigade and Light Trench-mortar Battery, Auckland Mounted Rifles (less one squadron), 302nd Brigade R.F.A. (less one battery), one section 522nd Field Company R.E., 2/6th London Field Ambulance.

[3] The reason for this inactivity will be found in the Note at the end of the Chapter. Liman had ordered the *XX Corps* to recross the Jordan

positions north of the 'Auja, but took no steps to prevent its reconnaissance by the British. The wadi, swollen by recent rains, was found to be nearly twenty yards wide, and near the bank three feet in depth, but the bed was of gravel, and it was a matter of no great difficulty to cross.

On the evening of the 8th March the brigade concentrated at Tell es Sultan, and after dark marched northward to its positions of deployment, south of the Wadi el 'Auja.

1918.
9 March.

In the plain the 2/22nd and 2/21st London crossed the wadi before 5 a.m., but the 2/24th in the hills on the left was held up at that hour by precipitous gorges, which it was impossible to pass before morning light. As this battalion was to attack Abu Tulul from the west, while the other two advanced on Kh. el Beiyudat, a short postponement of the attack was necessary.

The attack on Abu Tulul was launched at 8.15 after half-an-hour's bombardment, but the 2/24th London was at once pinned to the ground by machine-gun fire. At noon the hill was again bombarded, and the attack resumed. One company of the 2/24th established itself on the southeastern slope of the hill, but the attack from the west was still held up. The 2/23rd London was therefore ordered forward by Lieut.-Colonel Streatfeild to reinforce the company of the 2/24th, and an attack from this direction at 2.30 p.m. was successful. The brigade now had its right battalion astride the Wadi el 'Auja, with a company watching the 'Auja ford where it entered the Jordan, while its left lay in the hills about a mile north of the wadi. There was a gap of nearly five miles between its left and the right of the 53rd Division, patrolled only by a squadron of the Auckland Regiment, but in this country, rocky and tangled even beyond the average of "The Wilderness," there was no risk of anything more than a small local counter-attack.

The 53rd Division's main objective was the hill of Tell 'Asur, the highest point of Judæa north of Jerusalem, which was to be captured by the 158th Brigade on the left. The division had without doubt the most difficult country

---

during the nights of the 3rd and 4th (or possibly the 4th and 5th) March, leaving only a small detachment in the bridgehead. East of Jordan there were now only small detachments guarding the railway under the orders of the *VIII Corps*.

Sketch 23.

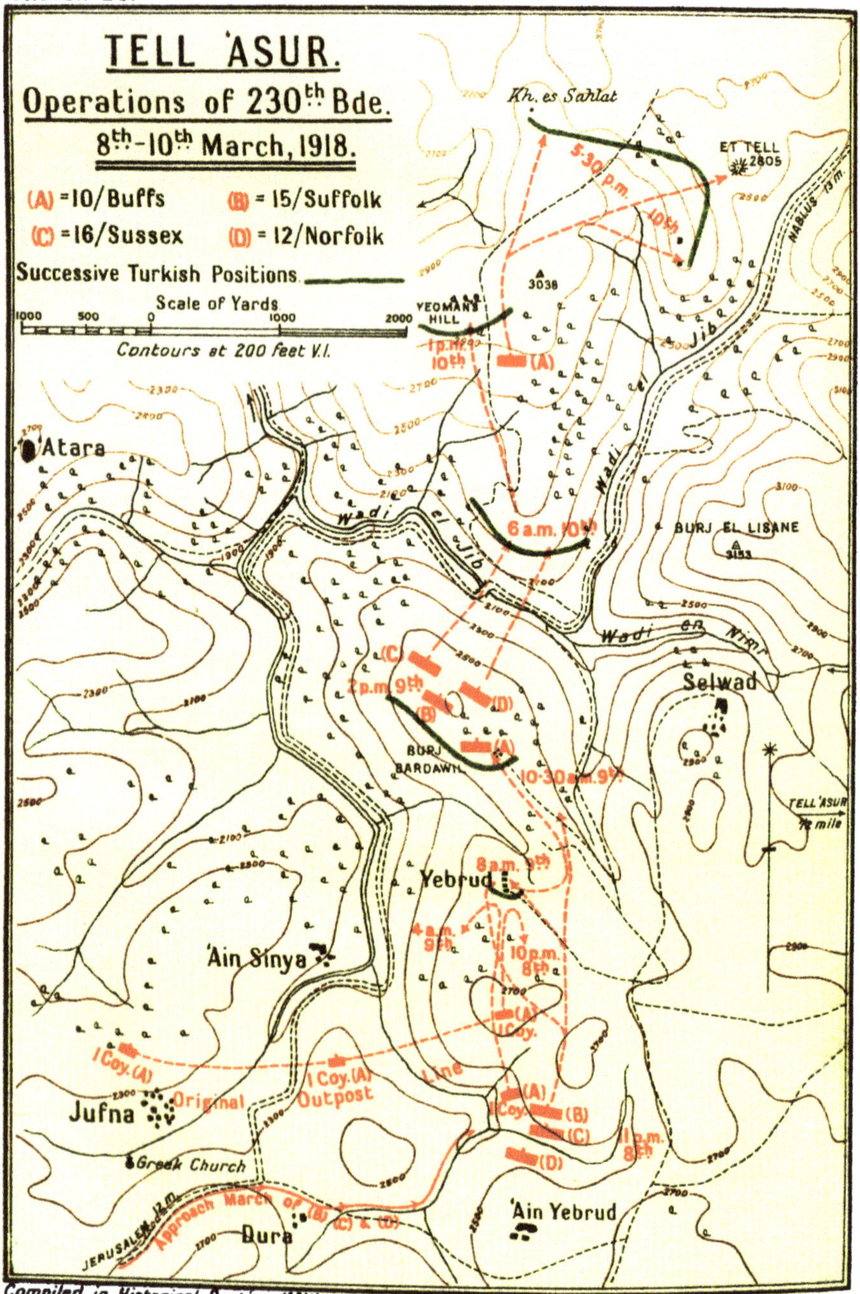


Compiled in Historical Section (Military Branch).
3000/30.

Ordnance Survey 1928.

## CAPTURE OF TELL 'ASUR 315

of the whole advance to traverse; so steep were many of 1918.
the gorges and ridges that men could cross them only by 9 March.
their fellows lying down and lowering or hoisting them up
on their shoulders. The artillery support was powerful, as
a brigade and one battery of the 60th Divisional Artillery,
a battery of the newly-arrived 7th Divisional Artillery, and
the 10th Mountain Battery were put at Major-General
Mott's disposal. After a heavy bombardment, in which
the 91st Heavy Battery took part, Tell 'Asur was captured
by the 5/R. Welch Fusiliers about 9.30 a.m., but the Hereford of the same brigade after capturing Chipp Hill to the
north-east, was driven off it. Nor were the Turks prepared
to lose Tell 'Asur without a struggle. They quickly counterattacked to regain this wonderful observation post, from
which the view extends northward to the hills of Galilee,
with white-capped Hermon, 90 miles away, in the background; eastward and south-eastward to Gilead, Moab,
and almost the whole of the Dead Sea; southward, over
the Mount of Olives, to the heights of Hebron; westward
to the Mediterranean shore from south of Jaffa to north of
Cæsarea. They regained the summit, but were driven off
it by the 6/R. Welch Fusiliers, which had been moved up
in relief of the 5th. In the next four hours the enemy
launched four most determined but fruitless attacks. The
158th Brigade had not succeeded in retaking Chipp Hill
when Major-General Mott learnt from Major-General
Girdwood that the 74th Division would continue its advance
to its objective as soon as it was dark, and gave orders to
his own brigades to do likewise.

The 74th Division's attack was to be made astride the
Nablus road, the 231st Brigade on the right being directed
on Mezra esh Sherqiye, just east of the road and a mile
and a half N.N.W. of Tell 'Asur. Vigorous patrolling had
been carried out during the last few nights, and it was
known that, though Tell 'Asur and the village of Selwad
to the north-west were strongly held, the Turkish outposts
in front of these positions might be disregarded. Accordingly the 10/Shropshire moved out from its outpost line at
2 a.m., and deployed nearly 1,500 yards further north,
quite close to the trenches covering Selwad, two hours
later. The trenches were carried in the first rush, 28
prisoners being taken. So swift had been the advance,

which was accomplished without artillery support, that the brigade was now out of touch with the troops on either flank—Tell 'Asur not having yet been taken—and was, moreover, faced by the steep descent to the Wadi en Nimr, the only paths across which were swept by machine-gun fire from Burj el Lisane to the north. To advance down this slope was found quite impossible while daylight lasted.

Sketch 23. The operations of the 230th Brigade (Br.-General W. J. Bowker) merit a more detailed description than any other portion of the attack, because they illustrate so well the difficulties of a night advance in hill country—difficulties, however, which were more than compensated for by the advantage of surprise and the screen of darkness. The 10/Buffs, holding the outpost line astride the Nablus road with its left near the village of Jufna, had been ordered to capture Yebrud, east of the Nablus road, before midnight. The 15/Suffolk, 16/Sussex and 12/Norfolk were then to leave the Nablus road at Dura and assemble at the junction of wadis north of 'Ain Yebrud, the first-named battalion in front line. They were then to advance east of Yebrud, their left protected by the 10/Buffs, and capture from the south-east the dominating height of Burj Bardawil, a fortress of crusading times.[1] Yebrud had been reconnoitred on the night of the 7th and found to be occupied only by a few snipers, so that it was thought that a company would suffice to clear it. But the Turks unmasked several machine guns the presence of which had not been suspected, and the company was beaten off. Lieut.-Colonel Lord Sackville then ordered a second company up to its assistance, but it was 4 a.m. before the reinforcement was ready to attack.

The other battalions had meanwhile made their way painfully forward to the position of assembly, halted there, and boiled tea before their long day's work. The 15/Suffolk had begun its advance in file to a position of deployment on the hill above when Lieut.-Colonel F. W. Jarvis learnt

---

[1] It is a curious fact that in a land covered with relics and teeming with traditions of the Crusaders only two of their place-names should have survived, and these very close together. One is Burj Bardawil (" Baldwin's Tower "), the other Sinjil (" Saint-Gilles ") 3¼ miles to the north-west. The Sabkhet el Bardawil (" Baldwin's Lake ") in Sinai likewise owes its name to the Latin Kingdom of Jerusalem.

## PROGRESS OF 74TH DIVISION

that the second company of the Buffs had also failed to capture Yebrud. He decided that he must take a hand, in order to bring the enemy's resistance to an end as quickly as possible. He sent a message to the two leading companies under Captain G. P. Barker to move up east of Burj Bardawil, while the remainder of the battalion turned westward to attack Yebrud. When these two latter companies crossed the front of the 16/Sussex, Lieut.-Colonel H. I. Powell-Edwards halted that battalion until he had ascertained the situation, and then directed two of his companies to attack Yebrud from the west. The village was eventually captured at 8 a.m.

1918.
9 March.

While the two commanding officers and the brigade major, Major I. Buxton, were reorganizing the 15/Suffolk and 16/Sussex, the artillery supporting the 230th Brigade was ordered to carry out a bombardment of Burj Bardawil from its position east of Jufna [1] at a range of 4,000 yards. Captain Barker had meanwhile begun his attack on Burj Bardawil, without waiting for the rest of the battalion, and a message by flag failed to reach him in time. Directly the barrage fell on the hill he realized the situation and at once gave an order to withdraw, having only one man hit by the British fire. The general advance was then continued, and the hill captured without further trouble at 10.30 a.m. The next objective was "Yeoman's Hill," 2 miles to the north, but it was found impossible to cross the cavernous gorge of the Wadi el Jib, with the enemy holding the opposite side. Br.-General Bowker obtained permission from Major-General Girdwood to await dusk before attempting to do so.

The 10th Division was operating in two groups, the right consisting of the 30th and 31st Brigades, less a battalion of each in divisional reserve, and the left of the 29th Brigade. The former, known as the "Right Attack," was supported by the LXVII and LXVIII Brigades R.F.A.; the latter, known as the "Left Attack," by the 263rd Brigade R.F.A.; while the 195th Heavy Battery was employed on counter-battery and bombardment. The first objective of the Right Attack was the high ground between

Maps 2, 14.

---
[1] The "Left Group," under the command of Lieut.-Colonel F. G. T. Deshon, consisted of five batteries, A/XLIV, B/XLIV, B/117, C/117, and the 527th Battery from the 7th Indian Divisional Artillery.

the villages of 'Atara and 'Ajul, commanding the crossings of the Wadi el Jib; that of the Left Attack from the Wadi el Jib at Deir es Sudan to Nabi Salih. The advance was delayed by dense fog, and the troops did not quit their positions of deployment till 6.30 a.m. Then, however, the attack was carried out with great speed. On the front of the 31st Brigade on the right the 2/R. Irish Fusiliers captured Sheikh Kalrawani, a hill south-west of 'Atara, enabling the 5/R. Irish Fusiliers to take that village by 9.30 a.m. The 30th Brigade came under heavy shell fire south of 'Ajul, but the 1/R. Irish occupied the village by 12.30 p.m. The Left Attack did not meet with serious resistance. By 11 a.m. the 1/Leinster had occupied Umm Suffa; by 4 p.m. its patrols had reached Deir es Sudan. The 5/Connaught Rangers was in occupation of Nabi Salih. The artillery, in order to support the attack on the second day's objectives north of the Wadi el Jib, had to retrace its steps down the Beit Ello–Nabi Eyub road, march east to Bir ez Zeit, and then westward towards Umm Suffa, thus covering nearly twenty miles in order to move about three miles to the north-east. The last eight miles were on a track which that morning had scarcely existed, wonderful work in improving it being accomplished by the Royal Engineers and 5/Royal Irish (Pioneers).

During the night the advance was continued on the whole front of the corps except for the 60th Division on the extreme right and the Left Attack of the 10th Division on the extreme left. The 158th Brigade of the 53rd Division quickly secured a footing on Chipp Hill, and though neither from this point nor from Tell 'Asur was it found possible to make further progress, the 6/R. Welch Fusiliers (relieved on Tell 'Asur by the 5th) was ordered by Br.-General Vernon to advance from Cairn Hill between the two, and had established itself on Tinto Hill, a mile to the north, by dawn. Patrols of the 159th Brigade entered the village of Kufr Maliq at 2 p.m. on the 10th after crossing several veritable crevasses.

On the right of the 74th Division the 231st Brigade found the crossing of the Wadi en Nimr possible as soon as night had screened the troops from the machine guns on Burj el Lisane. The 10/Shropshire and 24/Welch deployed in the bottom of the Wadi at 8.30 p.m. and commenced

## 230TH BRIGADE'S BRILLIANT WORK

their long climb up the wall of the Lisane Ridge. The position was carried at 3 a.m. on the 10th. The enemy launched three successive counter-attacks with bomb and bayonet, all of which were beaten off after hard close fighting. During the first and heaviest Private H. Whitfield of the Shropshire charged single-handed a Lewis gun, bayoneted the men working it, and turned it against the enemy. By an extraordinary coincidence this gun belonged to his regiment and had been lost at Et Tire.[1] For this action and the subsequent destruction of a hostile bombing section on his company's flank Private Whitfield was awarded the Victoria Cross.

*1918.
10 March.*

On the left the 230th Brigade had an equally severe task in descending to the Nablus road and the Wadi el Jib and climbing the other side of the gorge. Reconnaissances carried out before daylight failed had shown that both sides were terraced, but extremely steep, with little foothold. At the bottom the road appeared as a mere white ribbon. Lieut.-Colonel H. I. Powell-Edwards, 16/Sussex, was directed to co-ordinate the advance, to be carried out by his own battalion and the 12/Norfolk in first line, with the 15/Suffolk in support. He decided that each of the leading battalions should move with one company in extended skirmishing formation, the remainder following in lines of platoons in fours. When, however, the descent began this formation was found to be impossible to maintain. Frequently there was only one spot where men could drop from one terrace to the next, and the attempt to keep the line led to dangerous crowding. The enemy was sweeping the face of the hill with fire, so far without success, but a single burst on a crowded terrace might at any moment cause heavy casualties. The troops were therefore halted, and made the rest of their way down in file. They reached the road with little loss, finding the bridge across the Wadi el Jib intact. Then began a climb even more difficult than the descent. The enemy fired until the last moment, but the grim determination of the attackers shook his resolution, and the top of the cliff was won just before dawn. The 10/Buffs then advanced and captured Kh. es Sahlat and Et Tell, south of the village of

*9 March.
Sketch 23.*

---

[1] See p. 233.

## THE ACTIONS OF TELL 'ASUR

Sinjil. The whole of this operation had been carried out without artillery support, it being impossible for the guns to support the infantry in the crossing of the Wadi el Jib in the darkness, while they had not moved forward within range of Kh. es Sahlat by the time the Buffs attacked.

*Maps 2, 14.* Though the Right Attack of the 10th Division had captured the objectives set to it for the day, it was decided that it should occupy during the night two hills on the right bank of the Wadi el Jib, south and south-west of the village of Jiljliya, as they dominated the positions it had reached on the left bank.[1] Detachments of the 5/R. Irish Fusiliers of the 31st Brigade and the 1/R. Irish of the 30th made the attempt. They succeeded in crossing the wadi, after a descent in which they had had to jump or lower each other from one terrace to another in the darkness. The northern bank proved even steeper, some of the terraces being twenty feet apart with sheer walls of rock dividing them. In such cases the men could only grope till they came on clefts which they might scramble up in single file.

*1918. 10 March.* For all their efforts dawn found them on the lower slopes of the hills. In the morning the attempt was resumed, under cover of a bombardment. The 5/R. Irish Fusiliers, supported by two companies of the 5/R. Inniskillings, captured the hill south of Jiljliya,[2] but the men of the 1/R. Irish were held up by machine-gun fire and bombs dropped on their heads from the ledges above, and suffered over a hundred casualties. The 6/R. Irish Rifles of the 29th Brigade captured Sheikh Redwan, south-west of 'Arura, at 7.30 a.m., but could not take the village itself in face of half a dozen machine guns handled with great skill and boldness by a German officer. The enemy was evidently determined to stand on the northern bank of the Wadi el

---

[1] These hills are indicated on the uncontoured Map 14, which illustrates this action, by the detachments shown on their lower slopes on the morning of the 10th March. They were afterwards named " Richill " and " Clonmell Hill," and can be seen on Map 19, which also shows the steepness of the wadi's banks.

[2] Lieut.-Colonel A. W. S. Paterson, commanding the 5/Inniskillings, writes of his own climb out of the wadi :—" We then realized what an " amazing achievement these men had carried out. This hill was a " straight climb of 1,100 feet. It consisted of ledges of rock varying from " one to twenty feet sheer. It took me two hours' hard climbing with " only a haversack and glasses, yet these men had fought their way up " carrying all the impedimenta of war."

Jib, and it was extremely difficult to put his machine guns out of action. Major-General Longley gave orders for a new bombardment to be carried out at 3 p.m., followed by a general attack. The 5/Connaught Rangers at Nabi Salih on the open left flank had to meet a determined counter-attack in the morning and a less serious one at dusk. They beat off both and captured two Germans, proving that the German *702nd Battalion* had taken part in the operation.

1918.
10 March

During the night of the 10th March the 53rd Division attempted to cross the Wadi el Kola, a tributary of the Wadi el 'Auja, but found it too precipitous except on the left flank, where a passage had already been made by the 6/R. Welch Fusiliers. Here the 160th Brigade, which was commanded by Lieut.-Colonel H. M. Lawrence as Br.-General Pearson was on leave, had relieved the 158th. Fighting its way steadily forward over broken ground, the brigade reached the hills north-west of Kh. Abu Fala, its final objective, though it was unable to enter the village. The 159th Brigade remained south of the Wadi el Kola throughout the hours of daylight on the 11th, but contrived to cross at dusk. It then speedily completed its task, and by dawn on the 12th all the objectives of the division, except Kh. 'Amuriye, a hill on the extreme left, were captured. The 74th Division was compelled to pause till the exhausted men of the 230th Brigade were fed. Their rations for the 10th had not arrived till the small hours of the 11th, and when they did come up it was necessary to cut ramps for the mules and donkeys to climb the hillside from the Nablus road. At noon the Buffs and Norfolk took the high ground south of Sinjil, and patrols moved down into this large village. It was, however, found that the line laid down as the final objective, from Turmus 'Aya to Sinjil, was low and overlooked on all sides, so the heights just south of it were consolidated. The 231st Brigade on the right had been unable to advance past Kh. 'Amuriye. Early on the morning of the 12th General Chetwode came up with Major-General Girdwood and decided to hold the front then in possession of the 53rd and 74th Divisions, from Kufr Maliq to south-west of Sinjil. The 10th Division, though its attack at 3 p.m. had made little progress, had taken its objectives after dusk, and was on the line Jilj-liya–'Abwein–'Arura–Deir es Sudan–north of Nabi Salih.

11 March.

12 March.

Between the 53rd and 60th Divisions the 1st A.L.H. had taken up a line of posts.

The operation was now at an end, and had been successful everywhere except at one or two points of small importance. The depth of the advance in the centre was 5 miles, the frontage over 14 miles, exclusive of the operation of the 181st Brigade on the first day. Yet the cost had been high in proportion to the apparent strength of the Turks, the casualties amounting to over 1,300,[1] while only 169 prisoners were taken. With few exceptions the enemy's resistance had never been really stout, but time after time a few boldly-handled machine guns had been sufficient to hold up resolute attacks. It was only by waiting for dark and then pushing on regardless of the nature of the country —on the assumption that loss from broken limbs would be less than that from aimed bullets [2]—that any advance at all had been possible in several instances. The Royal Flying Corps had done all that was in its power to assist, but had not been so serviceable as in the advance to Jericho owing to persistent fog and low-hanging cloud. Each successive position had had to be most carefully reconnoitred by the infantry, not so much to discover the best point to attack as to find a possible way of approach. Frequently several hours had then been needed to place the troops in positions of assembly. Excellent work had been accomplished by the engineers of all the divisions concerned in the swift clearing of tracks for the guns, but even then the infantry had been frequently beyond range of the artillery's support. The first stage of the evacuation of the wounded, particularly those of the 53rd and 74th Divisions, who had to be brought from the advanced dressing-stations in the hills to a casualty clearing station at Ram Allah before they could be placed in the corps ambulance cars, had also been very difficult. The country ahead was no more favourable than that just conquered; it therefore became clear that in any general advance to be attempted later, operations in the hills north of Jerusalem would have to be subsidiary to those in the plains.

[1]

|  | Killed. | Wounded. | Missing. |
|---|---|---|---|
| Officers | 13 | 81 | 3 |
| Other Ranks | 168 | 975 | 73 |

[2] Broken legs, broken arms, and sprains were fairly numerous in both the 53rd and 74th Divisions.

## ATTACK OF XXI CORPS

### The Operations of the XXI Corps.

The attack of the XXI Corps to bring its right into Maps 2, 15. line with that of the XX (though a considerable gap was to separate the two) was carried out without any of the difficulties which had attended the operations astride the Nablus road. It is of interest to compare the two, for the vastly greater exertions and loss of the XX Corps were by no means due only to the hill country in which it was engaged. The XXI Corps had another great advantage in good positions for supporting artillery.

The advance was to be carried out by the 75th Division and the right of the 54th. The final objective was a line north of the Wadi Deir Ballut, one of the greatest of the watercourses, known in its upper stretches as the Wadi el Jib, and as the Wadi Abu Lejja where it enters the Nahr el 'Auja north of Mulebbis. On the 6th March the 75th Division's right was at Shuqba, half way between the Wadi es Sarar and the Wadi Deir Ballut, so that at its greatest point the advance to be undertaken was one of 4½ miles. On the 7th the right was swung up to 'Abud, 2½ miles north-east of Shuqba, in order to bring it directly opposite to the ultimate objective and approximately level with the 10th Division, and also to enable routes for artillery and supplies to be made. The Turks retired rapidly, the only opposition coming from a few snipers. On the night of the 8th the 54th Division advanced its line slightly west of the railway.

It will be recalled that after the passage of the Nahr el 'Auja the left flank of the XXI Corps on the coast had reached El Haram, near the site of the ancient Arsuf,[1] 2 miles north of Jlil, the front running thence south-east to cross the Nahr el 'Auja near Fajja and the railway between Rantye and Et Tire. It was therefore possible to support an advance east of the railway by heavy artillery firing north-east or even due east, and thus taking the Turkish positions in enfilade. Moreover, since the Turkish infantry was neither close at hand nor aggressive, the batteries could be placed almost in front line. The heavy artillery at the disposal of the corps, under the command of

---

[1] See p. 275.

Br.-General O. C. Williamson Oswald, consisted of nine heavy and siege batteries. With the exception of one section 134th Siege Battery (6-in. howitzers) under the orders of the 75th Division, it was divided into three groups: a Right and a Left Counter-Battery Group and a Bombardment Group.[1] The section of 6-inch howitzers at the 75th Division's disposal was equipped with caterpillar-draught and moved up to Qibye after the advance of the right flank already described. It was to be employed for the bombardment of strong points that could not be reached by the Bombardment Group, of which all but one section was west of the railway. The field artillery of the two divisions was to move forward by batteries as the infantry advanced. On the right of the 75th Division the 172nd Brigade R.F.A. had been moved up to the neighbourhood of 'Abud after the preliminary advance on that flank, a road having been constructed from Shuqba to that village by the 495th Field Company Royal Engineers and 10th Q.V.O. Sappers and Miners, assisted by parties of infantry.

The attack[2] was carried out by the 232nd and 234th Brigades of the 75th Division and the 162nd Brigade of the 54th, the boundary between the two divisions being a line drawn north-eastward from Et Tire. At 4 a.m. on the 12th March patrols of the 232nd Brigade occupied the high ground south of El Lubban and in the neighbourhood of Rantis, bringing up a machine-gun section to Rantis to support the main advance. This began on the front of the 232nd Brigade at 5 a.m. By 7 a.m. El Lubban was captured by the 5/Devon, and at the same hour the 234th Brigade began its attack. In general the method of moving forward the artillery was for one section to follow

---

[1] Right Counter-Battery Group (C Heavy Artillery Group: Lieut.-Colonel W. H. Moore), 15th and 181st Heavy Batteries, one section 43rd Siege Battery (6-in. gun); Left Counter-Battery Group (102nd Heavy Artillery Group: Lieut.-Colonel F. P. Hutchinson), 189th and 202nd Heavy Batteries, 380th Siege Battery, one section each 43rd and 304th Siege Batteries; Bombardment Group (XCV Heavy Artillery Group: Lieut.-Colonel A. H. Moberley), 209th Siege Battery, one section each 134th and 304th Siege Batteries. (All batteries of the Corps Heavy Artillery are shown, with their arcs of fire, on Map 15, except one section 189th Heavy Battery, which was on the coast south of El Haram, and the section of the 304th Siege Battery in the Left Counter-Battery Group, which was north of the Nahr el 'Auja and just off the map.)

[2] Map 15, illustrating this attack, is not contoured, but the terrain can be studied on Map 19.

## CAPTURE OF BANAT BARR

close behind the infantry, leaving the rest of the battery in action, and, as soon as the leading section was able to open fire, for the other four guns to join it. The only serious resistance met with by the 75th Division was on the final objective at Banat Barr and Deir Ballut, north of the Wadi Deir Ballut. In the razor-backed ridge of Banat Barr there were several caves, one of which ran through it from north to south. The 2/3rd Gurkhas was held up for some time in front of it by machine-gun fire, but a small detachment worked its way round the right shoulder of the hill. The attack was then pressed home, and the defenders, issuing from the northern exits of the cavern, were cut off, over sixty prisoners being taken. On the front of the 234th Brigade Deir Ballut was taken by the 4/D.C.L.I. about 2 p.m., that battalion being greatly assisted by a company of the 2/4th Dorset, which had scaled the ridge first on its left. At the same hour the Dorset was twice counter-attacked on the ridge west of the village. The Turks were beaten off and fell back to a line of sangars 500 yards north-west of Deir Ballut, to be driven out with the bayonet by the Dorset at 4.15 p.m. This attack was very effectively supported by the South African Field Artillery Brigade, which had now moved forward to its second position.

The 162nd Brigade, carrying out the attack on the 54th Division's right flank, was not holding the line. The other two brigades of the 54th Division pushed forward parties during the night of the 11th to cover its assembly and the positions of batteries which were actually placed in the wide No Man's Land, the whole of the 270th Brigade R.F.A. and two sections of heavy artillery at Qule, east of the railway, "A" and "B" Batteries 272nd Brigade R.F.A. at Nabi Tari, west of it. A bombardment of the Muzeir'a ridge by the heavy artillery and the artillery of the 54th Division began at 6 a.m., and at 7.45 the infantry advanced to the attack. By 11 a.m. the enemy had evacuated all ground south of the Wadi Deir Ballut. A final bombardment of Majdal Yaba began at noon, and a quarter of an hour later the village was captured. Forty prisoners were taken, while the casualties of the brigade amounted only to 15.

The whole operation is an interesting example of an

*1918.*
*12 March.*

attack by infantry in small numbers—only three brigades on a front of about seven miles—but strongly supported by artillery with good observation from the ground and from the air, against a position held mainly by machine guns. It was based upon the known British preponderance in both field and heavy artillery; had there been anything approaching equality the British field batteries would not have been able to move forward as they did, and the infantry could only have taken the position at vastly increased cost. As it was, the casualties of the two divisions were only 104. The Turks must have suffered at least twice as heavily, for 112 prisoners were taken and about 40 dead found on the ground. The line won was most favourable, with excellent covered positions for artillery, and was to be, with but slight exception, the front for the whole of the summer. On the 13th March the Corps Cavalry Regiment moved to 'Abud to establish a strong point on the right flank and patrol the gap of $3\frac{1}{2}$ miles between the right of the 75th Division and the left of the 10th near Nabi Salih.

### NOTE.

The Actions of Tell 'Asur are known to the Turks as the Battle of Turmus 'Aya. The direction of the Turkish defence was the first duty of the new Commander-in-Chief, who certainly acted with great promptitude. Exactly what were Falkenhayn's intentions during the last days of his command it is difficult to divine, but it seems clear that he had made preparations to hold his front with reduced strength and withdraw as many troops as possible into reserve. So far back as the 29th December he had announced in a message to Germany that he would probably withdraw the *Eighth Army* on the coast behind the Nahr Iskanderune, which he considered a more favourable position than that at present occupied. He had already sent back all except the Operations Section of his Staff from Nazareth to Damascus, and seems to have contemplated withdrawing there himself. With prophetic insight he remarked: "The "Staff has already had to clear out once at the very last moment, from "the Mount of Olives; that must not happen again. The work of the "Staff must be carried out in a careful and orderly manner, without "undue excitement." [1] He had also decided to transfer the headquarters of the *Seventh Army* from Nablus to 'Amman, and that of the *Eighth Army*, which was to have command of all troops west of the Jordan, from Tul Karm to Nablus.

Liman at once cancelled all these orders, and sent telegrams to recall the Staff to Nazareth. He then hurried down to Nablus and ordered Jevad Pasha, the commander of the *Eighth Army*, to return to his old headquarters at Tul Karm. He also issued orders for the *XX Corps*,

---

[1] German "*Yilderim*," p. 158.

## Sketch 24.

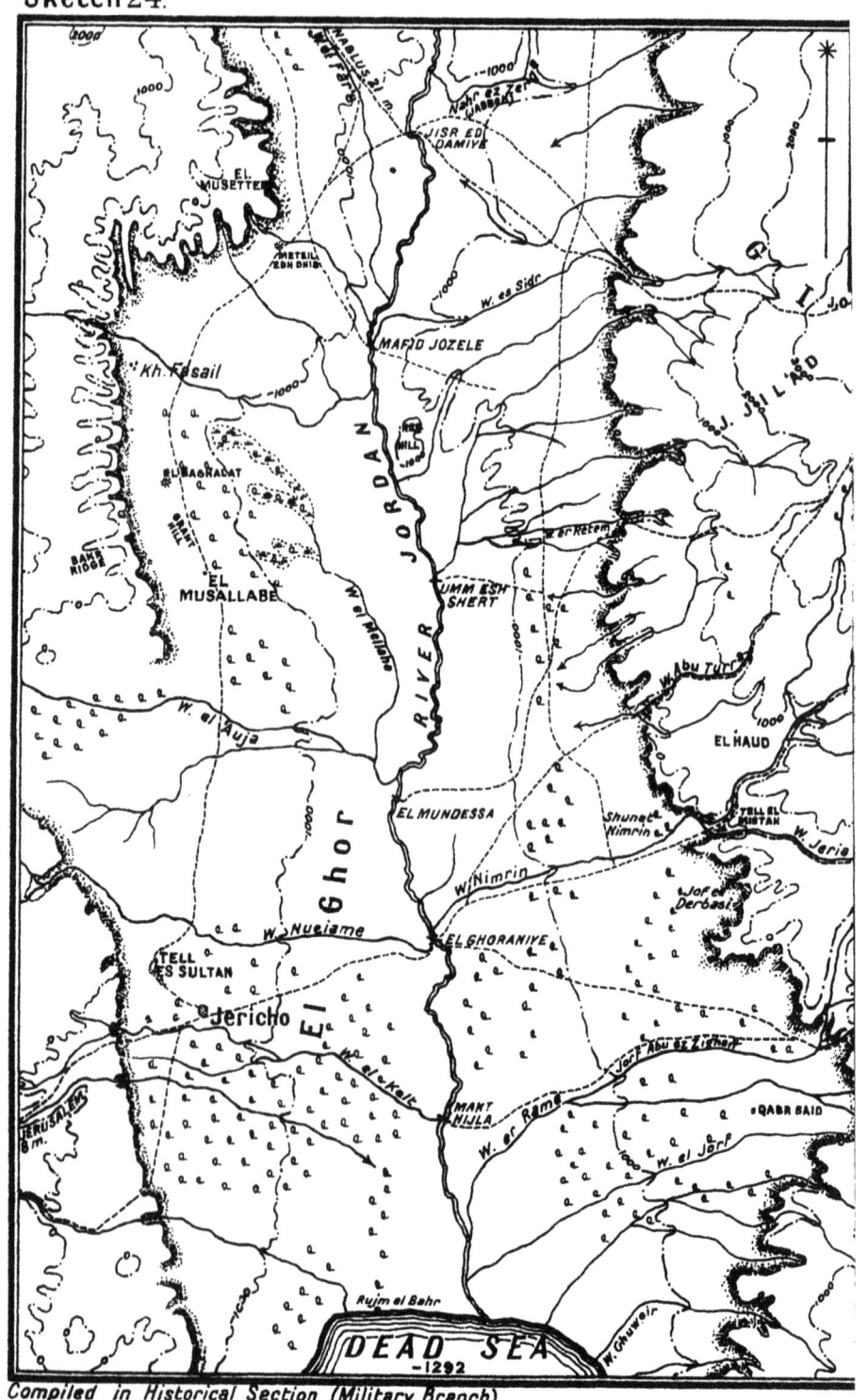

# Theatre of Operations in TRANS-JORDAN.

(First Trans-Jordan Raid, 21st March – 2nd April; Second Trans-Jordan Raid, 30th April – 4th May; & Operations of Chaytor's Force 20th–29th September, 1918.).

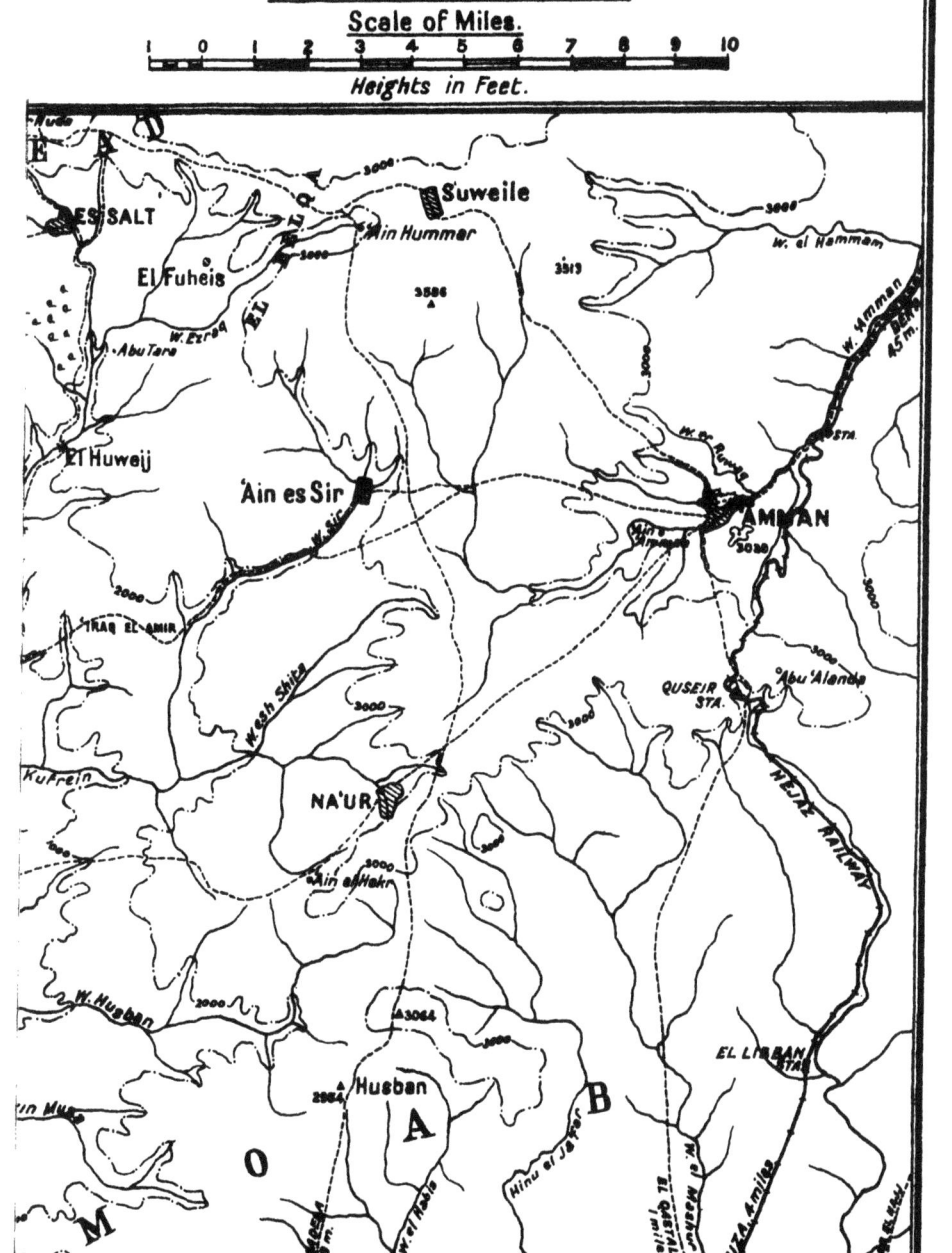

Scale of Miles.

Heights in Feet.

Ordnance Survey 1929.

which had retreated across the Jordan after the British occupation of Jericho, to recross the river and take up a position on the right of the *III Corps*, which was astride the Nablus road. The British were aware that the *53rd Division* had returned, but not that the *26th* also was there to take part in the battle. A new division, the *11th*, had arrived at Damascus from Northern Syria (having been previously on the Caucasus front), and was ordered to hasten down to Nablus.

Liman professes himself to have been satisfied with the result of the action. The *24th Division*, he states, bore the brunt of the attack—it was opposed to the 74th Division and perhaps the right of the 10th—and suffered severely. It was afterwards relieved by the *11th Division* and withdrawn to rest.

In the last week of December 1917 Ahmed Jemal Pasha *Biyuk*, "Commander of Syria and Western Arabia," went to Constantinople, ostensibly on leave, but never to return. The whole of his area was then transferred to Falkenhayn's command, which now included the defence of the Syrian coast. Falkenhayn then decided to resuscitate the old *Fourth Army* under the command of Mohammed Jemal Pasha *Kuchuk*, at Damascus.

## CHAPTER XV.

THE PASSAGE OF THE JORDAN AND THE RAID ON 'AMMAN.

(Map 16 ; Sketches 24, 25.)

### THE PASSAGE OF THE JORDAN.

Map 16.
Sketch 24.
IT has been shown that it was Sir Edmund Allenby's intention, after gaining a front broad enough for the purpose in the valley of the Jordan, to force the passage of the river and destroy the Hejaz Railway at 'Amman. One of the chief reasons which had led him to his determination was the success gained during the winter by his Arab allies in the country south-east and east of the Dead Sea. The progress of the Emir Feisal's forces since the capture of 'Aqaba will be recorded later in some detail, but it is necessary to summarize their achievements at this point. After the establishment of a new base at 'Aqaba the Arabs had extended their raiding of the railway northward from Tebuk. They had established a small trained force, partly of infantry, partly mounted on mules and camels, in the Wadi 'Araba, the prolongation of the Ghor south of the Dead Sea, threatening not only Ma'an but the Hishe Forest and the corn country to north-west from which the Turks drew wood for the railway and grain. A Turkish attack in the Petra region, north-west of Ma'an, in October 1917, gained some slight success, but had no effect in checking the raids. At the end of the year the Arabs advanced south-east of the Dead Sea, took Shobek, took Tafila, 45 miles north of Ma'an, and in January annihilated a Turkish detachment sent to recover the place. This roused Falkenhayn to concentrate a force, including a German battalion, at Qatrani, on the railway half way between Ma'an and 'Amman, which drove them back to Shobek in early March. The moment was therefore ripe for a British invasion of Trans-Jordan. The bulk of the

## FEATURES OF TRANS-JORDAN

Tafila expeditionary force, drawn from the 'Amman area, could not yet have returned, so that strong resistance to the first dash into Moab was not to be anticipated. On the other hand, should that force be drawn northward by the attack on 'Amman, the Emir Feisal might be enabled to capture Ma'an itself, the biggest and most important station between Der'a and Medina. There was also prospect of establishing touch for the first time between the Arabs and the E.E.F.

1918. March.

From the Jordan Valley the ground rises, gently at first, then very abruptly, to a mighty limestone plateau rather higher than the Judæan range. The final ascent is almost everywhere steep and difficult, though generally not comparable to that of the cliff-like ridge above Jericho. Once atop the plateau, the conditions are from the military point of view far more favourable than those in the highlands on the other side of the river. There are some sharp hills and two or three big gorges between Es Salt and 'Amman, but in general the surface is fairly level, though, much of it being ploughland, boggy after rains. The deployment of troops on one side or other of the Jericho–Es Salt–'Amman road, sometimes on both, is possible. In March the country is green and pleasant, with numerous streams to sparkle in the sunlight and patches of dwarf lupins covering whole acres with a sheen of turquoise, with orchards in blossom at Es Salt and Suweile. The midday sun is hot when the sky is cloudless, but winds are chilly and the nights often bitterly cold.

From the ford at Ghoraniye runs the ancient road to 'Amman, which had been metalled by the Turks to a couple of miles beyond Es Salt but was ill tended. It enters the hills at Shunet Nimrin and winds north-eastward along the flank of the Wadi Shu'eib, through Es Salt, 15 miles north-east of Ghoraniye, through Suweile, then south-east to 'Amman. Es Salt stands 4,000 feet above the Jordan and 2,700 above sea-level, a dark-hued, picturesque town upon a hillside, with a number of large, solid old houses. Its population before the war was 10,000, about half Christians. Suweile is merely a big, straggling village. 'Amman, the Rabbath Ammon of the Ammonites and the Philadelphia of the Decapolis, lies cupped in hills. It has fine Roman ruins, including a famous amphitheatre

## 330  THE PASSAGE OF THE JORDAN

and a citadel on a hill covering the approaches from north and west—a strong position even in the day of artillery. Here, at Suweile, and in neighbouring villages were colonies of Circassians, a virile race which the Turks were wont to plant in regions where they desired to keep unruly subjects quiet. The Hejaz Railway followed the Wadi 'Amman east of the town, the important station with its turn-table and sidings being two miles away. But the most vulnerable point in the line was south of the station, where the railway crossed a ten-arched viaduct and passed through a tunnel 462 feet long.

All the other routes across the plateau were mere bridle-paths. There was one from Makhadet Hijla, an ancient ford 3½ miles south of Ghoraniye, running fairly directly to 'Amman through the village of Na'ur. Another left the main road at Tell el Mistah in the foothills and ran through 'Ain es Sir to 'Amman. North of the main road was another track from Ghoraniye along the Wadi Abu Turra to Es Salt, which was joined 3 miles south-west of the town by yet another from Umm esh Shert, a ford 8 miles north of Ghoraniye.[1] One lateral communication connected these routes: an ancient track from 'Ain Hummar, east of Es Salt, which ran due south to Madeba, thence through Tafila and Shobek to 'Aqaba. The so-called fords where the routes cross the Jordan are almost breast-deep even in summer and at this season did not deserve the name.

The garrison of 'Amman was believed to consist of part of the *150th Regiment (48th Division)* which was also distributed in posts along the railway for many miles north and south. One battalion of this regiment, one of the *159th*, and some Circassian irregular cavalry were between Es Salt and Ghoraniye, with posts watching the Jordan. The British were unaware that a very formidable unit of the Tafila force, particularly strong in machine guns, the German *703rd Battalion*, had returned. It arrived in the foot-hills on the 'Amman road on the 21st March. Even

---

[1] In the accounts of this operation and of the second raid into Trans-Jordan the routes will for convenience be described as the " main road," the " Na'ur track," the " 'Ain es Sir track," the " Wadi Abu Turra " track," and the " Umm esh Shert track." In reports and orders of this period the Wadi Abu Turra is described as Wadi Arseniyat, owing to a defective map.

with this reinforcement there cannot have been more than about fifteen hundred rifles, in addition to the irregulars, between 'Amman and the river when its passage was forced.

1918.
March.

The operation was to be carried out under the orders of the XX Corps, and was entrusted to Major-General Shea, commanding the 60th Division. "Shea's Force," as the column was called, consisted of the A. & N.Z. Mounted Division, the 60th Division, the Imperial Camel Brigade, the 10th Heavy Battery, the IX British Mountain Artillery Brigade, the Light Armoured Car Brigade, the 13th Pontoon Park, and the Desert Corps Bridging Train. Major-General Shea was instructed to force the passage of the Jordan on the night of the 19th March. He was then to occupy Es Salt with his infantry and push his cavalry on to 'Amman to destroy the railway. His attention was particularly directed to the viaduct, a bridge " believed to exist between " the viaduct and the tunnel,"[1] bridges between 'Amman and El Libban Station, the tunnel itself, and a masonry bridge to the north. When this task was accomplished he would probably be instructed to withdraw west of Jordan, leaving a strong detachment at Es Salt and mounted troops to protect its communications.[2]

The supply problem before Br.-General C. W. Pearless, D.A. & Q.M.G. of the XX Corps, was not easy, but at least it was not complicated by lack of water as the Sheria operations had been, for there was known to be plenty on the plateau. The force was to be based for supplies on the Jerusalem railway, from which lorries were to work to Jericho, and afterwards to the Jordan, a road journey of nearly thirty miles. Thence the train transport of the formations was to carry the supplies to Shunet Nimrin on the main road. The A. & N.Z. Mounted Division was to have three camel echelons, each of 550 camels, one to work between Shunet Nimrin and Es Salt, the other two to carry each one day's supplies forward to 'Amman. The 60th Division was to have two camel echelons, each of 805 camels, each to carry one day's supplies and to work between

---

[1] This passage was based on defective information. There was no bridge between the viaduct and tunnel, but there were bridges north of them and close to the station. The map issued for the operation was very inaccurate.

[2] The instructions issued by General Chetwode to Shea's Force are given in Appendix 20.

## 332  THE PASSAGE OF THE JORDAN

Shunet Nimrin and Es Salt. Ample reserves were provided, as five days' supplies were collected at " Junction Dump," east of Tal'at ed Damm, where a reserve of camels was also maintained under the hand of the corps.

As the date of the raid approached the expected improvement of the weather did not come. The rains were unusually heavy for March; the Jordan was very full and swift, though it had ceased to overflow its banks. The operation was postponed for two days, during which there was a slight change for the better. Repeated reconnaissances of the crossings were made by both cavalry and infantry.

1918.
21 March.

On the night of the 21st the troops were concentrated in readiness. The A. & N.Z. Mounted Division was at Tal'at ed Damm in the hills, or between that point and the edge of the scarp; the Camel Brigade was also arriving there, after a long march from Bethlehem; the 60th Division was in or north of the Wadi Nueiame, which enters the Jordan at Ghoraniye, with one battalion in the Wadi Kelt, which enters the river $3\frac{1}{2}$ miles further south at Makhadet Hijla. The 53rd Division had taken over the defence of the Wadi el 'Auja. Major-General Shea had decided to throw bridges at both Ghoraniye and Hijla : a cavalry steel pontoon bridge at the latter, and three bridges—a standard pontoon, a barrel pier, and a foot-bridge—at Ghoraniye. The 180th Brigade was to force both crossings and then advance to secure a position in the foot-hills astride the 'Amman road. The 179th Brigade was to follow and move up on the Wadi Abu Turra track on the left of the 180th, while the 181st remained at Ghoraniye in reserve. The mounted troops were to cross at Hijla, the 1st L.H. Brigade moving with and protecting the left flank of the infantry. The remainder of the division, detaching a regiment of the New Zealand Brigade to act under the orders of the 180th Brigade, was to advance on 'Amman by the Na'ur and 'Ain es Sir tracks, followed by the Camel Brigade. Feints were to be made against other fords south of Hijla and north of Ghoraniye, and a party of 3 officers and 42 men was to cross the north end of the Dead Sea in three motor-boats and assist the 180th Brigade in clearing the left bank of the Jordan at Hijla.

The night was fine. The British aircraft had had good

## A BRIDGE THROWN AT HIJLA

observation all day, but had seen little or no movement till about 3 p.m., when some hundreds of enemy infantry approached Ghoraniye and two squadrons of cavalry moved on Hijla. The 2/18th London was thereupon ordered down to Hijla to reinforce the 2/19th, which was to make the passage at this point. It was approaching the crossing-place at midnight, just as a party of the 2/19th was stripping for its difficult task of getting a rope across the swollen river.

1918.
21 March.

On the stroke of midnight the 2/17th London at Ghoraniye launched several boats and small rafts. So swift was the current that they were all either swept back to the bank or borne downstream. After a quarter of an hour's fruitless work a party of swimmers tried its fortune, but the current carried the men away, to regain their own bank with difficulty some way down. The enemy was alert, and his small posts had opened fire. It was an unpromising start.

22 March.

The 2/19th London had greater success at Hijla. A party of nine picked swimmers under 2nd Lieutenant G. E. Jones and several Australian engineers crossed with a line at 12.30 a.m., and pulled over a raft with six men. There was no opposition but from some musketry fire. Thenceforward until morning the ferrying across of the battalion was continued in quiet, though after daybreak fire was resumed.

Br.-General Watson, commanding the 180th Brigade, had meanwhile decided to give up the attempt at Ghoraniye and concentrate all his efforts on Hijla. He ordered the 2/20th London to march down to that point and subsequently directed the 2/17th to follow, leaving only the 519th and 521st Field Companies R.E. at Ghoraniye.

By 7.45 a.m. on the 22nd the whole of the 2/19th London was across, and the 2/18th was ordered to follow. But by 8.10 the field squadron of the A. & N.Z. Mounted Division had completed the cavalry pontoon bridge, with the assistance of which the 2/18th was across before 10. An attempt was made to clear the thick scrub beyond the bank, but was checked by the enemy's fire. The remaining battalions of the 180th Brigade reached the right bank at Hijla at about 1.30 p.m., both fatigued after a sleepless night and a long march, having moved *via* Jericho. General

Chetwode, accompanied by H.R.H. the Duke of Connaught, who was paying a visit to the Palestine theatre, then arrived to compliment the brigade on the crossing. The corps commander agreed with Major-General Shea that a further attack in daylight would entail heavy loss. Br.-General Watson was therefore authorized to rest his troops, most of whom had had little sleep for 48 hours, and resume the attempt to advance at midnight. In the interval the mountain batteries succeeded to a great extent in silencing the enemy machine guns. The 181st Brigade, which had unfortunately had no opportunity of reconnoitring the river bank, was ordered by Major-General Shea to move down to Ghoraniye and make a new attempt to cross, simultaneously with the advance of the 180th.

**1918.**
**23 March.**
The whole of the 180th Brigade was brought across for the attack at midnight, which met with little opposition. By 2.30 a.m. on the 23rd a line had been established astride the Na'ur track at an average distance of a thousand yards from the river. Once again, however, all efforts to cross at Ghoraniye failed. It now appeared that the quickest means of securing this crossing—the best from the point of view of bridging and because it was on the main road—was by attack from Hijla.

At 4 a.m. the Auckland Mounted Rifles, the regiment attached to the 180th Brigade, was ordered to cross at Hijla and clear the left bank to Ghoraniye. It was over by 7.30 and pushed out troop patrols east and north. One troop was charged by an enemy squadron and its commander killed in a hand-to-hand duel with a Turkish officer, but the weight of the New Zealand horses told, and the Turks were driven off, leaving 20 dead on the ground and 7 prisoners. The New Zealanders rode straight at every Turkish post they encountered, and suffered no check till they reached the main road. Here they were temporarily driven back by machine-gun fire, but by noon they were at Ghoraniye, having captured 68 prisoners and four machine guns. The river had now dropped slightly, so that before they reached the opposite bank swimmers of the 2/24th London, 181st Brigade, had at last succeeded in crossing. The infantry foot-bridge was thrown by 4.30 p.m., by which hour the 2/21st London had crossed on rafts, the pontoon and barrel bridges by 9.30. Another pontoon

Pontoon Bridge over the Jordan at Ghoraniye, March 1918.

[Imperial War Museum Photograph.]

## THE ADVANCE BEGINS

bridge was put across at Hijla, so that at the day's end there were altogether five bridges over the Jordan. 1918. 23 March. The situation at 10 p.m. was that at Ghoraniye the 181st Brigade and its transport had crossed; at Hijla the 179th Brigade had crossed and extended the line of the 180th to Ghoraniye; the A. & N.Z. Division had two regiments (the Auckland and 2nd A.L.H.) across, the remainder being ready to cross at Hijla. During the morning the little motor-boat party (of the 2/24th London), of which nothing had been heard, had reported to the 2/19th London. It had successfully crossed the Dead Sea, but had been forced to lie in hiding all through the 22nd, and was not at first aware that the right of the 180th Brigade had moved up to within a mile of its position.

The Jordan had been crossed with slight loss, almost all in the 180th Brigade;[1] the Turks had been caught napping. All was now ready for the advance on Es Salt. But, through no fault of the troops, there had been a delay of twenty-four hours, which by giving the enemy time to take measures for the defence of 'Amman seriously prejudiced the success of the enterprise.

THE CAPTURE OF ES SALT AND FIRST ATTACKS ON
'AMMAN.

During the night of the 23rd and morning of the 24th the A. & N.Z. Mounted Division crossed at Hijla. The 303rd Brigade R.F.A. crossed by the pontoon bridge at Ghoraniye to support the 60th Division. At 5.30 a.m. Major-General Shea issued orders for the advance to be carried out in accordance with the original plan, except that the 181st Brigade was to take the place of the 180th, the latter becoming divisional reserve. 24 March.

The advance began at 8.30 a.m., 181st Brigade on right, 179th on left, each with two battalions in line. The opposition was not serious, the shooting of the few Turkish guns in action being wild. The 2/14th London captured 3 officers and 33 men of the German *703rd Battalion* on the

---

[1] The following were the casualties of the 180th Brigade:—

| | *Killed.* | *Wounded.* | *Missing.* |
|---|---|---|---|
| Officers | 1 | 3 | — |
| Other Ranks | 25 | 55 | 1 |

slope of El Haud, a cone-shaped hill north of the road and 6 miles east of the Jordan. At Tell el Mistah, further south, a most formidable position standing square against the road, which runs straight up to it and then turns abruptly away to pass it by, the 2/22nd London shot down the detachment and horses of a battery and captured three guns. The 181st, with a squadron of the Wellington Regiment attached, then pushed on up the road to secure the bridge across the Wadi Shu'eib at Huweij, 4 miles south of Es Salt, but was about the same distance short of its objective when darkness fell and a halt was ordered.

The A. & N.Z. Mounted Division was split into three. Divisional headquarters with the 2nd L.H. Brigade and the Camel Brigade advanced on 'Amman by the Na'ur track; the New Zealand Brigade, picking up the Auckland Regiment, turned off the main road at Shunet Nimrin along the 'Ain es Sir track; the 1st L.H. Brigade moved up the Jordan Valley and took up a position, with its left on the river about Umm esh Shert, to cover the flank of the advance, and despatched the 3rd A.L.H. up the Umm esh Shert track towards Es Salt.

Another unfortunate delay now occurred. It had been reported that the Na'ur track was fit for wheels; the 2nd L.H. Brigade had therefore moved along it accompanied by half-limbers with ammunition and tools. It had not made much progress before Br.-General Ryrie was compelled to order the wheeled vehicles to be sent back to Shunet Nimrin and the ammunition, as well as the large amount of explosives carried, to be transferred to camels. The march was resumed at 9.30 p.m. and continued all through the night, the head of the column reaching 'Ain el Hekr, south-west of Na'ur, at 4.30 a.m. on the 25th. The Camel Brigade which followed had a most distressing march, in single file, the men leading—often dragging—their camels all the way; and the whole column was not in until 7.30 p.m. The New Zealand Brigade, likewise forced to send back its wagons, bivouacked by the roadside on the night of the 24th and by 1.30 p.m. on the 25th was concentrated at the cross-roads beyond 'Ain es Sir to await the head of the main column from Na'ur. Heavy rain and sleet throughout the 25th made the routes muddy and slippery. The camels which fell often broke their

1918.
25 March.

## OCCUPATION OF ES SALT 337

legs and had to be shot where they lay; their Egyptian drivers had their thin clothes caked with mud, were chilled to the bone, and in several cases died of exposure. But the Australians and New Zealanders, who had the skill of old campaigners in making the best of whatsoever conditions they encountered, tore scrub from the hillsides, hacked telegraph poles into short lengths with their bayonets, and contrived in the wet to light fires to warm themselves and boil their tea.

*1918.
25 March.*

The 181st Brigade, much hampered by the condition of the road, covered only eight or nine miles on the 25th, though the sole opposition came from a few snipers, and at 4.15 p.m. halted a mile short of Es Salt. The 179th Brigade advanced slowly along the Wadi Abu Turra track, piqueting the heights. During a halt a message reached it from Major-General Shea that it was needless to continue this process, as reports from the air showed no signs of opposition on its route. The brigade therefore pushed straight on and at the junction of the Wadi Abu Turra and Umm esh Shert tracks, 4 miles from Es Salt, met the 3rd A.L.H. of the 1st L.H. Brigade. Br.-General E. T. Humphreys ordered the Australian regiment to take Es Salt that evening. The leading squadron, meeting with no resistance, entered the town at 6 p.m., the head of the 179th Brigade arriving two hours later.

During the night of the 25th the main A. & N.Z. column advanced through Na'ur, still in rain and mud, meeting the New Zealand Brigade at the 'Ain es Sir cross roads next morning. Leaving there the New Zealanders and the Camel Brigade, the animals of the latter in a state of exhaustion, Major-General Chaytor advanced with the 2nd L.H. Brigade a mile and a half north along the 'Ain Hummar track. An enemy column was observed on the main Es Salt–'Amman road, and Major A. J. Bolingbroke, commanding the 5th A.L.H., was instructed to capture it. Advancing with two squadrons, he quickly drove off the enemy and took 19 motor lorries, 4 cars, and a number of carts, with 12 prisoners; but the vehicles were stuck in the mud and could not be moved. Major-General Chaytor had orders to push on to 'Amman at once, but decided that this was impossible, as men and horses were fatigued after three consecutive night marches and the camels quite unfit

*26 March.*

to move. The sun had at last appeared, giving the troops a chance to dry their sodden clothing. He reported to Major-General Shea (who had moved his headquarters forward from Ghoraniye to Shunet Nimrin) that he could not continue the advance till the following morning. He gave orders, however, for two raids against the railway to be carried out that night, north and south of 'Amman. That to the south, made by a detachment of the New Zealand Brigade, was successful, a section of the line 7 miles south of 'Amman being blown up. The northern party, from the 2nd L.H. Brigade, encountered enemy cavalry in superior strength and was driven off without fulfilling its mission.

The infantry also was forced to halt on the 26th. In the course of the day 49 unwounded prisoners were collected in Es Salt, and 90 sick and wounded, including a British soldier, were found in the hospital. The 181st Brigade was ordered to form a flying column of two battalions of infantry, three mountain batteries, and the Wellington squadron, to march on 'Amman on the 27th in support of the mounted troops. The 179th Brigade, less the 2/15th London left at Es Salt, was ordered to move back to the Huweij bridge, where it could more easily be fed. The 180th Brigade had advanced to Shunet Nimrin in the foot-hills and was at work on the main road.

1918.
27 March.

The A. & N.Z. Mounted Division and Camel Brigade marched at 9 a.m. on the 27th. The country was still wet and boggy after the rain, and progress was slow. By 10.30 a.m. the head of the New Zealand Brigade had reached 'Ain 'Amman, a mile south-west of the town, while that of the 2nd L.H. Brigade on the left was within three miles of 'Amman Station. Major-General Chaytor at once issued orders for an attack. The New Zealand Brigade, advancing with its right on the railway, was to capture the dominating position of Hill 3039, south of the town ; the Camel Brigade, having despatched one battalion (the 4th) with a demolition party to Quseir Station, 3½ miles south of 'Amman, was to attack the town from the west ; the 2nd L.H. Brigade was to attack from the north-west.

The attack of the Camel Brigade was to be carried out by the 2nd Battalion, supported by the 1st, less two companies,[1] under cover of the Hong Kong Mountain Battery,

---
[1] These two companies had remained in the Jordan Valley.

'AMMAN FROM THE SOUTH-WEST.  [*R.A F. Photograph*, 1929.

## FIRST ATTACK ON 'AMMAN

the only guns brought forward. The task was a difficult one. The track into 'Amman from 'Ain es Sir runs along the crest of a bare, open ridge, on either flank of which the ground falls steeply to the bed of a wadi. These wadis converge at 'Amman behind a hill covering the approach to the town from the west. This hill was held, and the brigade was likewise exposed to machine-gun fire from both flanks, against which it had no cover. The attack was pressed to within 600 yards of the hill, when it became exposed to fire so heavy that no further progress was possible. The New Zealanders and Light Horse on either flank were also held up, and were unable to clear the enemy from his positions on Hill 3039 south of the town and the Citadel to the north, from which the Camel Brigade was being enfiladed. The enemy had posted his machine guns cleverly, at varying heights on the hills about 'Amman, and kept up fire on all approaches. A squadron of the Wellington Regiment, working round 'Amman from the south, perceived a train coming up and galloped to cut it off, but became bogged within three hundred yards of the line. With a whistle of triumph the train ran on into 'Amman. It was afterwards discovered that when the train reached the breach previously made by the New Zealanders the Turks clamped the rails together with logs of wood and enabled it to cross. The 4th Battalion of the Camel Brigade also reached the railway near Quseir soon afterwards and destroyed culverts for a distance of three miles along its course. On the other flank a squadron of the 5th A.L.H. escorted a party of the New Zealand Engineers to a bridge five miles north-east of 'Amman, and blew a breach of 25 feet in it. The town was therefore for the moment isolated. The casualties for the day were 26 killed and 183 wounded, while 54 prisoners were taken.

The flying column of the 181st Brigade, which left Es Salt at 5 a.m., was delayed by a tribal brawl. As the advanced guard approached Suweile the place was being attacked by two or three hundred Christians from El Fuheis, and a score of deaths had already resulted from the fighting. The Wellington squadron, with some difficulty and no little risk, drove back the Christians a few hundred yards, and a parley was held. The Christians had long been oppressed by the Circassians; they were almost starving, and complained that some of their people were detained in Suweile. Br.-General Da Costa ordered the release of the prisoners and forced the Circassians to hand over a supply of grain. He then put a company of the 2/21st London into Suweile, and continued his march, bivouacking two miles south-east of the village, after covering only about twelve miles. It must be added, however, that in no case would the column have been in time to take part in that day's attack, especially as the road beyond Es Salt was in a far worse state than its first section owing to lack of metal. Br.-General Da Costa was ordered to push on towards 'Amman before dawn.

In the Jordan Valley the 1st L.H. Brigade, the flank guard engaged in keeping open the corridor through which all supplies passed, had improved its position by a slight advance in face of fire from small bodies of the enemy north of Umm esh Shert. On the morning of the 27th a squadron of the 2nd A.L.H. established itself a mile north of Umm esh Shert on the lower slope of a ridge afterwards known as "Red Hill," but at night was driven back again on the ford. It was evident that the enemy had brought troops over from the right bank, but for the time being he made no serious attempt to dislodge the flank guard in the valley.

**1918.
28 March.** In front of 'Amman the morning of the 28th passed fairly quietly. The British line ran from the railway near Quseir, across the 'Ain es Sir track a mile west of 'Amman, to a mile north-west of the town. One Turkish attack on the right was driven off. About 9.30 Br.-General Da Costa rode forward to meet Major-General Chaytor and report the arrival of his column. Though he had not been definitely placed under the latter's command he was naturally prepared to take his orders. Having seen something of the ground, he urged that the attack should be carried out after dusk, as it seemed to him that an advance across the open ground separating him from the enemy's defences, with inadequate artillery support, had small chance of success in daylight. Major-General Chaytor replied that it was imperative to capture 'Amman by nightfall and ordered the attack to begin at 1 p.m. The two infantry battalions were to advance on the left (north) side of the main road, supported by the three batteries of the IX

Mountain Artillery Brigade, which were also to shell Hill 3039 to support the attack of the New Zealand Brigade from the south. Between the New Zealanders and the infantry the Camel Brigade (less the 4th Battalion, still on the extreme right under the orders of the New Zealand Brigade) was to renew its attack of the previous day. The 2nd L.H. Brigade was to cover the left flank of the infantry, while one regiment advanced on the latter's right flank to link it up with the Camel Brigade.

1918. 28 March.

The attack had little success. Just before it began the New Zealand Brigade was counter-attacked, and though it drove off the enemy it made practically no progress against Hill 3039. The Camel Brigade advanced to within 250 yards of the enemy's trenches, but was then held up by heavy machine-gun fire. The two infantry battalions (2/21st and 2/23rd London) covered the first thousand yards without great difficulty, but then passed over the brow of the crest, out of sight of the supporting artillery, and more and more exposed to machine guns in front and on the flanks and to artillery fire. On their left the 6th and 7th A.L.H., advancing dismounted, were counter-attacked and forced to give ground. The two battalions were eventually held up on a line facing south-east towards 'Amman and about 700 yards from it. On their left the 2nd L.H. Brigade was echeloned back more than a mile, and the enemy was making constant attempts to work round that flank.

Meanwhile Br.-General Da Costa had learnt from Major-General Shea that the 179th Brigade had been ordered to take over the defence of Es Salt, and that one of his own battalions, the 2/22nd London, together with the 2/17th and 2/18th of the 180th Brigade, were moving up to his support. He was asked by Major-General Chaytor whether he preferred to renew the attack with his two battalions or await these reinforcements. He replied that owing to the fatigue of the 2/21st and 2/23rd it would be advisable to wait, but again suggested that as the approach to the enemy's position was so exposed the attack should be made at night. This would also give the three new battalions some opportunity for rest. The two from the 180th Brigade had actually worked all the morning of the 28th on the 'Ain es Sir track and then had a march of from twelve to fifteen miles on this abominable route before they joined him. Major-General Chaytor agreed, and issued orders for the attack to take place at 2 a.m. on the 30th.

1918.
29 March.

In the course of the 29th the communications were seriously threatened. The enemy had brought across the Jordan troops which had advanced from Jisr ed Damiye, 16 miles north of Ghoraniye, occupied Kufr Huda, north of Es Salt, and driven in patrols of the 3rd A.L.H. In the Jordan Valley the squadron of the 2nd A.L.H. re-established itself on the lower end of the Red Hill ridge, but Br.-General Cox considered that it was imperative to get a better grip on that formidable position. The 1st A.L.H therefore pushed a thousand yards further up the ridge. The Umm esh Shert crossing was now effectively covered and horses could be watered in the Jordan without molestation. It was evident, however, that the enemy's strength had increased in the valley, and the 2/20th London, in reserve at Shunet Nimrin, was moved up to support the Australians. No serious attack followed at either point, but at both it looked as though one was brewing. At Shunet Nimrin thirteen German aeroplanes carried out a bombing attack, killing 116 and wounding 59 camels, and causing 39 casualties to troops and to Egyptians of the Camel Transport Corps. To add to the British difficulties, the transport of supplies was interfered with by a further rise in the Jordan, and, though the river was now falling again, only one bridge, with long causeways at either end, was open on this date, the approaches to the others being too boggy even for camels.

During the morning of the 29th enemy reinforcements were seen arriving in 'Amman from the north, having evidently detrained north of the bridge broken by the New Zealanders. But Major-General Chaytor did not give up hope of success. The three battalions brought up would to some extent counterbalance the fresh arrivals of the enemy, and he was expecting one more battery, the Somerset. This by great exertions was got forward to support the 2nd L.H. Brigade, but did not come into action until 9 a.m. when the fate of the attack was practically sealed. He had also been informed by Major-General Shea that, according to intercepted wireless messages, there was a proba-

Sketch 25.

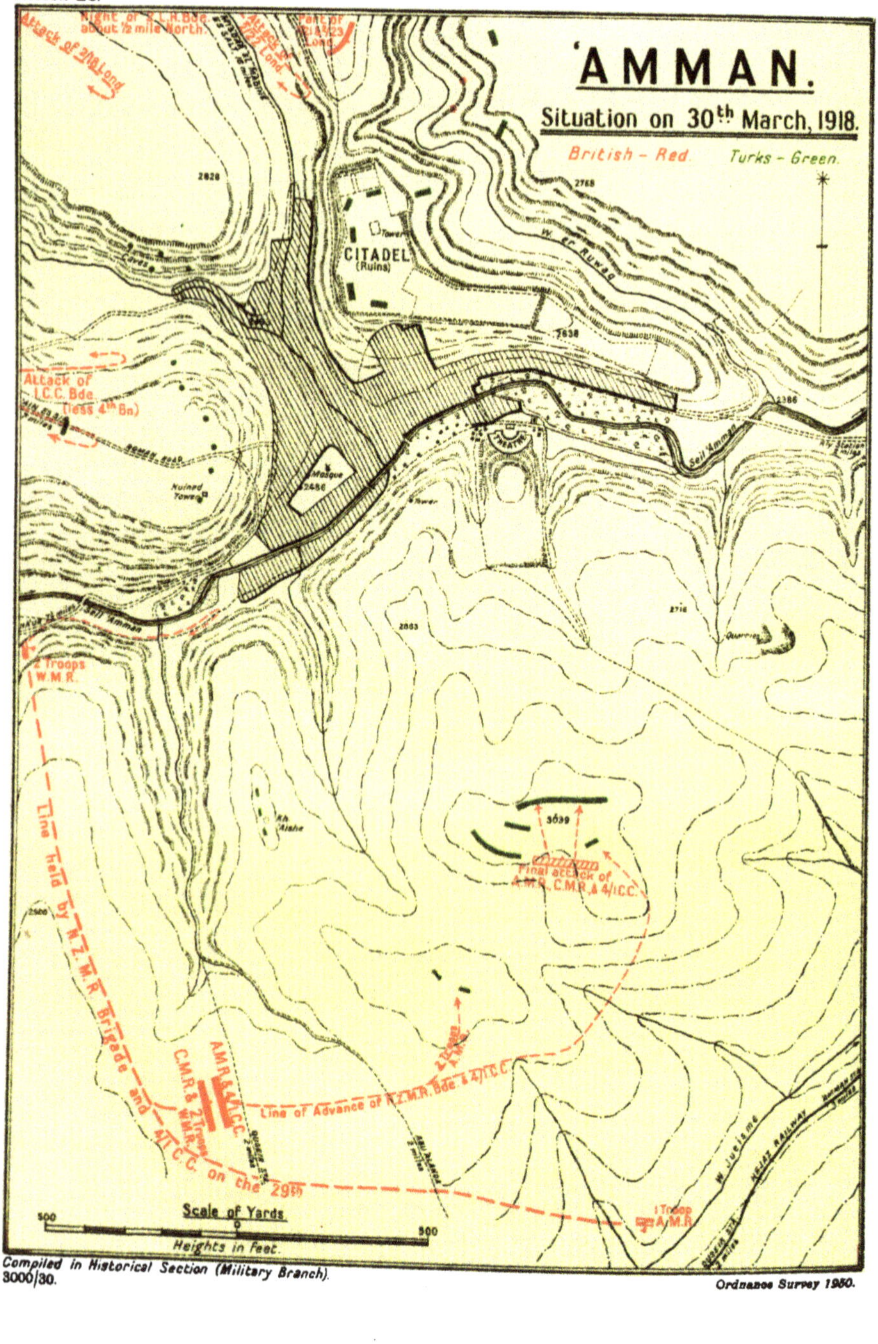


Compiled in Historical Section (Military Branch).
3000/30.

Ordnance Survey 1930.

## THIRD ATTACK ON 'AMMAN 343

bility that the enemy would evacuate 'Amman;[1] while he had the good news that two large bodies of friendly Arabs had volunteered to watch the demolitions and prevent repairs on the railway north and south of the town.

1918.
30 March.

### THE LAST ATTACK AND THE WITHDRAWAL.

As the troops took up their positions for the attack rain once more began to fall heavily. The objectives set by Major-General Chaytor were as follows :—the New Zealand Brigade and 4th Battalion Camel Brigade were to capture Hill 3039 ; the Camel Brigade less the 4th Battalion was to advance directly on 'Amman astride the 'Ain es Sir track. On the front of the 181st Brigade the 2/18th London on the right, less two companies attached to the Camel Brigade, was to attack the Citadel, while the 2/22nd London was to cross the main road where it bends southward to enter 'Amman and advance north of the Citadel to the Seil 'Amman at the eastern end of the town. North of the main road the 2/21st and 2/23rd London were to hold the ground gained the previous day at all costs ; the enemy's increasing strength on that flank made it unlikely that they would be able to accomplish more than this. The 2/17th London was held in brigade reserve, with one company as a reserve in Major-General Chaytor's hands. On the extreme left the 2nd L.H. Brigade, now weak in numbers and exhausted, was to make as great a demonstration as it could.

Sketch 25.

The attack of the New Zealand Brigade and 4th Camel Battalion was skilfully planned by Br.-General Meldrum. Avoiding the southern works on the hill, the leading wave, consisting of the Camel Battalion and the Auckland Regiment, passed round them to the east and attacked the main position. The foremost trenches were seized by a sudden rush with the bayonet, the garrison being killed except for 23 prisoners taken, and five machine guns were captured. Fire then burst out from another line of trenches

---

[1] The Turkish Historical Section denies that there was ever any intention of so doing. It appears, however, that Jemal Pasha, ordered down from Damascus by Liman to take command, held a conference at which the question was discussed. Liman states that on the 30th he was asked whether the place should be abandoned and ordered it to be held to the last.

300 yards in rear, which was charged by the second wave, consisting of the Canterbury and Wellington Regiments. These trenches were also captured with 14 more prisoners and another machine gun; several more machine guns were taken in the outlying works isolated by this assault. The southern wing of the attack had fully carried out its rôle.

The Camel Brigade attacked in two waves, the first consisting of four companies of its 1st and 2nd Battalions, the second of the two companies of the 2/18th London attached. One line of Turkish trenches was captured, with 28 prisoners, but machine-gun fire from the Citadel hill prevented any further advance.

The Citadel was, in fact, the key to the western defences, and while it was in the hands of the enemy and he had machine guns upon it there was little chance of a general success. The attack upon it by the 2/18th London broke down without getting within a thousand yards of it. This not only checked the Camel Brigade on the right, but seriously endangered the 2/22nd London on the left. This battalion had made considerably greater progress in a brilliant and dashing attack, and had captured 80 prisoners, but found its flank completely exposed and was forced to take up a defensive position astride the main road. Here it was soon afterwards subjected to a fierce counter-attack, and beat it off, taking another 50 prisoners and two machine guns.

Dawn showed that the success of the attack had been but limited, except on the front of the New Zealand Brigade. Moreover the Turks now turned to the offensive with vigour, particularly on the left flank. Again and again they advanced against a hill a mile north of 'Amman, held by four weak companies of the 2/21st and 2/23rd London. After hand-to-hand fighting they got a footing on it, but a prompt counter-attack with the bayonet drove them off, and they left 20 prisoners in the hands of the Londoners. Yet again they returned to the attack, led by a German company, and this time established themselves firmly upon it, the British taking up a position on the next ridge. On the right a counter-attack against the New Zealand Brigade was beaten off with the aid of captured machine guns. A second followed, and, an unauthorized order to retire having been passed along the line, a withdrawal began. The Turks then reached the ridge, but were immediately swept off it by a bayonet charge. Soon afterwards two troops of the Wellington Regiment, holding the left of the original line of that morning, worked their way along the Seil 'Amman into the town, but were fired on from the houses and driven out again. Thereafter the enemy kept Hill 3039 under heavy artillery fire, while on the British side the ammunition of the mountain batteries was beginning to run short.

1918.<br>30 March.

At 2 p.m. a last attempt on the Citadel was made. Major-General Chaytor sent up the one company of the 2/17th London which constituted his sole reserve to support the two companies of the 2/18th. A bombardment was carried out with all available artillery and the attack made some progress, but was soon held up by machine-gun fire.

It was evident that the exhausted troops could do no more. On receiving news of the failure, Major-General Shea asked Major-General Chaytor whether he thought there was any chance of taking 'Amman that night, and on being told that there was little or none, instructed him to break off the action. Major-General Shea had previously told the Commander-in-Chief that he would take 'Amman if given time to get up more troops, but that losses would be heavy and that unless the capture of the place was essential he advised a retirement. At 5.45 p.m. the XX Corps directed Shea's Force to withdraw across the Jordan, leaving an outpost at Ghoraniye.

Orders were issued for a general retirement during the night, the 2nd L.H. Brigade moving by Es Salt, the remainder of the force by 'Ain es Sir. The withdrawal of the New Zealand Brigade and 4th Camel Battalion on Hill 3039 was perhaps the most difficult feature of the operation. It was accomplished with great skill and coolness immediately after dusk, the wounded being carried in blankets to the dressing-station a mile and a half away. On the infantry front the 2/17th London covered the withdrawal of the other four battalions, with the 2/24th London, which had arrived meanwhile from Es Salt. All wounded were brought in and as many dead as possible buried. The withdrawal to the line from which the last attack had been launched was completed by 3 a.m. on the 31st.

31 March.

346    THE RAID ON 'AMMAN

At 4.30 a.m. the Camel Brigade began its march back to 'Ain es Sir, which it reached at 7.15 a.m. This track, especially after the passage of the camels, was too boggy for the infantry to follow, and Major-General Chaytor ordered the 181st Brigade to make a big detour, marching along the main road as far as Suweile and then down to 'Ain es Sir. It arrived at this village before nightfall, finding there the New Zealand Brigade, which was henceforward to act as rear guard. The enemy had advanced from 'Amman with caution and had not seriously troubled the retirement.[1]

The 181st Brigade still had in front of it the worst part of its march. It was burdened by a large camel train and a number of wounded, while the route as far as Shunet Nimrin was execrable. At 10 p.m. on the 31st the camels were sent forward, and to give them time to get clear the brigade remained at 'Ain es Sir till 2 a.m. on the 1st April. Then, in bitter cold and rain, the weary march was resumed, covered by the New Zealand Brigade, while battalions took up rear-guard positions in turn. As the New Zealanders quitted 'Ain es Sir they were attacked by the enemy, who had continued to advance during the long halt, and while the last squadron of the Wellington Regiment was riding out of the village into the gorge of the Wadi Sir it was fired on at close range by a party of Circassians from a mill. The mill was promptly stormed and its occupants were killed, but the squadron suffered 18 casualties, its commander, Major C. Sommerville, being mortally wounded. The 181st Brigade was not concentrated at Shunet Nimrin till 5.30 a.m. on the 2nd, by which time the 179th Brigade had also withdrawn from Es Salt and reached the Jordan Valley without incident.

1918.
1 April.

The retirement was conducted in very bad weather and amid the most depressing circumstances. The raid had been the Army's first failure since the Second Battle of Gaza a year before, and the troops were bitterly disappointed. The tracks, especially the road from Es Salt, were thronged with wailing refugees, mostly Christians but with a fair number of Mohammedans among them, who had shown such obvious delight at the arrival of the British

[1] " Having no cavalry but for a few patrols," writes Liman, " the Turks could follow but could not pursue."

## CAUSES OF THE FAILURE 347

that they dared not await the returning Turks. The wounded suffered terribly on their camel *cacolets* or on the backs of horses On the greasy roads the camels often slipped and fell with their burdens; sometimes in narrow passages the *cacolets* struck the rocks bordering the paths. For once the Jordan Valley was welcome. As the troops moved down, the sun came out and they descended the flower-carpeted slopes, sheltered from the east wind, into an ever-increasing heat bath. The change was violent, from sleet, and at Suweile actually snow, to a high summer temperature, but for the moment was very pleasant. The withdrawal of the whole force, less the 180th Brigade, across the Jordan was completed by the evening of the 2nd. The brigade was relieved next day in the bridgehead by the 1st L.H. Brigade and a regiment of the 2nd.

*The 1918. 2 April.*

\* \* \* \* \* \*

The main objects of the raid had not been achieved. The 'Amman viaduct had not been reached, and what damage had been done to the railway was easily reparable. The Turks had almost certainly suffered more heavily than the British, for they had lost 986 prisoners, including 61 Germans, and four guns, while the total British casualties were 1,348.[1] Morally, however, the attack did a good deal to restore the confidence of the Turkish troops. It was their first success after a series of heavy reverses. Their new Commander-in-Chief had likewise begun happily.

The causes of the failure are plain enough. In the first place the delay of twenty-four hours in the passage of the Jordan was most serious. Then the weather was exceptionally bad for March, which in Trans-Jordan is often cold but rarely so wet as this year. The wet not only exhausted the troops, but prevented the advance to 'Amman of the field artillery of the 60th Division, which might have had a decisive result. Two of the field artillery brigades as well as the XVIII Brigade R.H.A. crossed the Jordan, but

[1]

|  | Killed. | Wounded. | Missing. |
|---|---|---|---|
| Officers | 19 | 70 | 4 |
| Other Ranks | 196 | 940 | 119 |

This was one of the rare actions in which the loss of the mounted troops was greater than that of the infantry, the casualties of the A. & N.Z. Mounted Division and Camel Brigade amounting to more than half the total.

only the Somerset Battery reached the neighbourhood of 'Amman and only two batteries of the 60th Divisional Artillery that of Es Salt, though the teams were increased to eight horses. The light armoured cars were helpless, and even the Fords did not get far beyond Es Salt. The Turkish defence was most dogged and the behaviour of the German battalion, in action from first to last, particularly admirable. The inspiration of its steadiness and the personal leadership of its officers seem to have acted as a tonic to the heterogeneous collection of units which made up the garrison. As the fight went on, too, the enemy was continually strengthened from the north, and it is not surprising that the Arabs who volunteered to watch the broken bridge were swept away. So completely did the Turks restore the situation on the line to northward that wounded were actually evacuated by it on the 29th, being presumably carried across the broken bridge. The British troops all fought well enough to deserve success, but, labouring under every possible disadvantage except that of inferiority in numbers, could not command it.

NOTE.

THE BATTLE, FROM GERMAN AND TURKISH SOURCES.

It would appear that none of the Tafila Expeditionary Force, which consisted of the bulk of the garrison of 'Amman, had returned when the passage of the Jordan took place except the German *703rd Battalion*, which had then just reached Shunet Nimrin. The battalion had attached to it its cavalry troop, artillery section, and the *Asia Corps* Machine-Gun Company. A battalion of "Mule-mounted Infantry," which also took part in the expedition, arrived at Es Salt during the retirement to 'Amman.

The passage of the Jordan was opposed by only about a thousand rifles and six guns, with a few squadrons of cavalry. According to Turkish reports the garrison of 'Amman on the 27th March consisted of 1,841 rifles, 34 machine guns, and 8 guns. With the Germans added, the force would be about 2,150 rifles, 70 machine guns, and 10 guns. It is not possible to ascertain the exact number of reinforcements which reached 'Amman during the course of the action. Liman, on hearing that the British had crossed the Jordan, ordered all available troops on the railway and in Damascus to be sent down. They appear to have been for the most part single battalions, or even drafts. The German battalion, for example, received a reinforcement of 2 officers and 70 men, of which only 4 men were infantry. At a rough estimate, the enemy received 2,000 reinforcements up to the 30th, and considerably more thereafter. Jemal *Kuchuk*, Commander of the *Fourth Army*, arrived in 'Amman on the 28th and took over command of the defence.

Liman also ordered the *Seventh Army* to despatch over Jordan a force to harass the British communications, under the command of

# A GERMAN OFFICER'S VERDICT

Essad Bey, commanding the *3rd Cavalry Division*. Unfortunately for him the bulk of this division, which still constituted his best troops, was in line on the *Eighth Army* front, so that the force under Essad Bey consisted of a few squadrons only, together with the *145th Regiment, 46th Division*.[1] It numbered about 1,800 rifles and sabres. It was this force, which crossed at Jisr ed Damiye, that threatened the 1st L.H. Brigade in the Jordan Valley and occupied the heights at Kufr Huda, north of Es Salt.

The German battalion commander, Hauptmann Grassman, writes in his account of the fight at 'Amman regarding the final British attack:—
" Why the enemy did not follow up the success he gained during the night " it is hard to explain. His entry into the town and from thence an " advance against the rear of our positions could not have been prevented."

---

[1] Colonel Hussein Husni, formerly Sub-chief of the Staff to Falkenhayn, was now in command of this division, and unfortunately from now onwards we are without his able and careful record of operations.

## CHAPTER XVI.

OPERATIONS BETWEEN THE FIRST AND SECOND TRANS-JORDAN RAIDS.

(Maps 1, 2, 17; Sketches 24, 26.)

THE ACTION OF BERUKIN.[1]

Maps 1, 2. ON the 21st March, the day on which Shea's Force was concentrated for the raid into Trans-Jordan, the long-gathering storm broke in France, and the great German offensive swept across the British positions on both sides of the Somme. The effect on Palestine was instantaneous. The War Office had already, in view of the growing strength of the enemy on the Western Front, decided to incorporate Indian troops in the formations of the E.E.F., excepting only the Australian and New Zealand Contingents. Each Yeomanry Brigade was in future to consist of one British and two Indian regiments, while nineteen Indian battalions were to replace the same number of British in the infantry divisions. The success of the German attack in France made greater changes imperative. Two days after it was launched, on the 23rd March, Sir Edmund Allenby was ordered to relieve one of his British divisions by the 7th Indian Division and to hold the former ready for embarkation at short notice. The relief was complete on the 1st April, when the 7th Indian Division (Major-General Sir V. B. Fane) took over the left or coast sector of the XXI Corps from the 52nd. This division sailed early in April, its headquarters quitting Egypt on the 11th.

Sir Edmund Allenby had informed the War Office that, after capturing Es Salt and destroying the Hejaz Railway at 'Amman, he hoped to resume his advance on Nablus and Tul Karm in April. By the beginning of April his raid had

---

[1] There is no official name for this action in the Report of the Battles Nomenclature Committee. The above title has been chosen because it is that employed in Turkish reports.

## SITUATION ON THE COAST 351

failed to do serious damage to the railway, and he had 1918. evacuated Es Salt; the 52nd Division had entrained for April. Egypt; the 74th Division was under orders to go; and he was only too well aware that further heavy demands would be made upon him within the next few weeks. Nevertheless, he decided to go forward with an attack already projected, to be carried out by the XXI Corps—an operation which, if the greatest possible measure of success were attained, would carry him to Tul Karm, where were the headquarters and railhead of the Turkish *Eighth Army*.

As a result of the operations following the passage of Map 17. the Nahr el 'Auja and those east of the railway on the 12th March, the line attained by the XXI Corps ran from north of Arsuf on the coast in a south-easterly direction to the railway, then along the north bank of the Wadi Deir Ballut. In the coast sector was a broad No Man's Land— as much as 3,000 yards at one point. The Turkish defences between the railway and the sea were the strongest, with the exception of those covering Jerusalem, that had been faced since the enemy had been ejected from Gaza. In the plain the enemy had no position of natural strength, as he had in the hills; and he had worked hard to secure his front artificially, especially since the arrival of Liman, who had urged on the construction of a formidable trench system. In rear, at a distance of from four to eight thousand yards behind the front line, ran the perennial Nahr el Faliq, which in the wet season forms for four miles inland a series of marshes and large pools.[1] There is one track along the coast, crossing the river near its mouth, and 3 miles further inland an indifferent passage at Kh. ez Zerqiye. The next road northward runs through the village of Et Tire, 7 miles inland, to Tul Karm. If, therefore, a very swift advance to Et Tire could be made, while

---

[1] These marshes are a serious obstacle enough after the rains, but a very exaggerated idea of them was entertained by the British, who had to rely on guide-books and the reports of agents, as well as air reconnaissances, for their information. It was believed in September, after the summer's drought, that they might form a difficult barrier for the cavalry, but it was found when they were reached that they were almost dry. The glinting of the sun on mud—of no great depth—had given the impression from the air of standing water, and (so strong is the effect of imagination) an officer of the R.A.F. declared to General Bulfin, who was somewhat sceptical regarding the amount of water, that he had seen the surface broken into little waves by a high wind.

## THE ACTION OF BERUKIN

the two crossings of the Nahr el Faliq were barred by fire from the sea, the attackers might fairly hope for a big haul of prisoners and booty, especially guns, from the area south of the marshes. Et Tire was nowhere nearer than 7 miles to the British front line; the only hope, therefore, of reaching it quickly enough was suddenly to open a wide breach in the enemy's defences through which mounted troops could be passed.

The Turks had now, for the first time, regularized the organization of the *Eighth Army*, which had hitherto had under its orders one corps and a group of divisions. The front was now divided between the *XXII Corps* (Refet Bey: *19th* and *20th Divisions*) on the right, and the *Asia Corps* (Colonel von Frankenberg: *7th, 16th*, and *46th Divisions*, with the German troops, less the *703rd Battalion*). The boundary between the two groups was the railway; the left boundary of the Army was at Qurawa Ibn Zeid, south-east of Berukin, or almost precisely the same as the right boundary of the British XXI Corps. The Turks had strengthened their artillery on this front since the March fighting, but it was still very weak by comparison with the British.[1]

The plans of the XXI Corps may be considered in less detail than if the operation had been carried through to its conclusion, but they are of interest from their similarity, on a very small scale both as to numbers and objectives, to those of the great final offensive, five months later.[2] The first phase was to be the capture by the 75th Division on the right of the village of Berukin, "Mogg Ridge," and Sheikh Subi, one and two miles respectively north-west of Berukin; the village of Ra-fat and the hill of 'Arara, north-east of it.[3] Next the 7th Indian Division, on the

---

[1] The artillery on the front of the Turkish *Eighth Army* was estimated by Br.-General H. Simpson Baikie, Br.-General R.A. XXI Corps, to be 4 mountain guns, 48 75-mm. or 77-mm. guns, 12 105-mm. howitzers, 11 100-mm. guns, 10 150-mm. howitzers. Against this the British XXI Corps had approximately 12 mountain guns or howitzers, 84 18-pdrs., 36 4·5-inch howitzers, 12 60-pdrs., 16 6-inch howitzers, 2 6-inch guns.
[2] XXI Corps Letter S.G.113 is given in Appendix 21.
[3] After the operations of the 12th March the 75th Division's flank had been at the hill of Banat Barr. It had since extended its line east of the great bend in the Wadi Deir Ballut, where the 58th Rifles had captured the village of Deir Ghussane; west of the bend it had slightly

## PLAN OF ATTACK

corps left, was to advance its line 2,000 yards on a front of about five miles in the wide No Man's Land and prepare gun positions from which the enemy's position from Tabsor, 4 miles from the coast, to Jaljulye, on the railway, could be bombarded. The 159th Brigade Group, lent by the XX Corps for the operation, having come in on the right of the 75th Division and taken over a portion of the ground won by it, the main advance by the 75th and 54th Divisions to a line north of the Wadi Qana with the left flank facing westward towards Qalqilye and Jaljulye was to follow. Finally, the 54th Division was to sweep westward along the Turkish defences, rolling them up and capturing Jaljulye, Byar 'Adas, and Tabsor in the first line, Qalqilye and Kufr Saba in the second.

1918.
9 April.

The breach would thus be open. The Australian Mounted Division, originally assembled among the vineyards in rear, would have moved into it at Hable as soon as Qalqilye and Jaljulye were taken. It was next to advance with all possible speed through Qalqilye on Et Tire. Its principal mission was to close the enemy's line of retreat; but if any considerable portion of the enemy's forces between the railway and the sea had already fallen back through Et Tire, it was to carry out a vigorous pursuit, though not north of Tul Karm. Warships lying off the mouth of the Nahr el Faliq were to endeavour to close the crossings over the marshes by fire. The importance of capturing as many guns as possible was particularly impressed by General Bulfin on Major-General Hodgson. It was an ambitious scheme which depended entirely upon the speedy success of the initial attacks, but it had the advantage that if these fell short of expectation the whole operation could be broken off without committing any troops but those of the 75th Division.

The preliminary attack of the 75th Division began at 5.10 a.m. on the 9th April. On this occasion the artillery at the division's disposal, which included the VIII Mountain Artillery Brigade and one section 134th Siege Battery, was put under the command of the infantry brigade commanders. The first stage of the assault was carried out by all three infantry brigades in line: the 232nd Brigade

---

advanced its front on either side of the village of Deir Ballut, the line now being 500 yards south of El Kufr and 1,000 yards south of Ra-fat.

## THE ACTION OF BERUKIN

on the right against Berukin and El Kufr, the 233rd in the centre against Ra-fat, while the 234th Brigade [1] was to capture "Three Bushes Hill" and the ridge between it and Ra-fat, in order to protect the 233rd's left. The objective was swiftly captured all along the front, except on that of the 232nd Brigade. On this brigade's left the 2/3rd Gurkhas seized El Kufr; but on the right the 2/4th Somerset, descending into and climbing out of the great gorge of the Wadi Deir Ballut,[2] came under heavy fire not only from "Tin Hat Hill," its objective, but also from Kufr 'Ain Hill on its right flank. The latter hill was to have been captured by the 10th Division, but was not occupied until dusk and proved a thorn in the side of the 232nd Brigade. By 9.45 Tin Hat Hill was in the hands of the Somerset, but the battalion had encountered opposition so strong that Br.-General Huddleston sent forward the 5/Devon to attack Berukin. Three companies advanced up the Wadi el Mutwy, leaving it at the bend south of the village and then rushing across the open, while one company covered their advance from Tin Hat Hill. Berukin was captured at 4 p.m.

This delay had thrown the attack out of gear, as neither the left of the 232nd Brigade nor the 233rd could advance to their second objective until Berukin was secured. Meanwhile the enemy had recovered from his surprise. On the front of the 234th Brigade he launched two counter-attacks before 10.30 a.m. against the 2/4th Dorset on Three Bushes Hill, and though the line was maintained the Turks established themselves just short of the crest. Eventually Major-General Palin decided that he could not complete the operation that day and that the advance to Mogg Ridge, Sheikh Subi, and 'Arara—between two and three thousand yards north of the first objective—must be postponed till the morrow. The 5/Devon in Berukin was heavily attacked, and fighting with bomb and bayonet amid the houses lasted all night. A company of the 2/4th Somerset, coming up at dawn, found a desperate struggle in progress and the enemy holding more than half the

---

[1] The brigade was under the command of Lieut.-Colonel G. R. Cassels, Br.-General Maclean being in hospital.
[2] The lie of the ground, not shown on Map 17, which illustrates the action, can be studied on the layered Map 19.

village; but he was finally ejected. On other parts of the front also there were counter-attacks, and all night there was constant roar of artillery, rattle of musketry, and glare of rocket signals. The constant calls for support by the infantry caused heavy expenditure of ammunition, particularly shrapnel, so that the supply at the gun-pits could only with difficulty be replenished in time.

1918.
10 April.

The advance was resumed at 6 a.m. on the 10th. The 2/3rd Gurkhas of the 232nd Brigade reached the western edge of Mogg Ridge, but there was confused and fluctuating fighting on this hill all day. In the centre the attack on Sheikh Subi broke down, the 3/3rd Gurkhas being unable to secure the whole of the preliminary objective, the high ground to the south-west on the south bank of the Wadi Lehham.[1] The 2/4th Hampshire attempted to go through but was brought to a halt by machine-gun fire and a barrage of high-explosive. Further west the 5/Somerset got a footing on 'Arara by 9.30 a.m. After a twenty minutes' bombardment in the afternoon the 2/3rd Gurkhas, assisted by companies of the 2/4th Hampshire and 58th Rifles (attached to the 233rd Brigade)[2] secured almost the whole of Mogg Ridge, but a counter-attack, launched under cover of a trench-mortar bombardment and carried out with great determination by German troops, drove them right off it. In this fierce fighting Rifleman Karanbahadur Khan, 2/3rd Gurkhas, won the Victoria Cross for a succession of deeds of extraordinary gallantry. In the attack his Lewis-gun section engaged a Turkish machine gun at close range. The No. 1 of the gun having been shot, Rifleman Karanbahadur pushed his body off the gun and took his place; then, under a shower of bombs, he fired a burst which destroyed the Turkish machine-gun detachment. He next switched his fire on to the bombers and silenced them. When the battalion fell back he covered the withdrawal by fire until the enemy was close upon him.

---

[1] This high ground is shown as "Gurkha Hill" on Map 19. The Gurkhas captured the whole of it but for a redoubt on its extreme western edge, which defied all their efforts.

[2] The 75th Division had at this time 13 infantry battalions, the 2/4th Devonshire having joined the 234th Brigade in December. The 58th Rifles had been for some time detached from the 234th to the 232nd Brigade. For this operation it was attached to the 233rd Brigade, but was put at Br.-General Huddleston's disposal by Br.-General Colston.

For a time the situation looked ugly, as the troops had suffered heavily and were seriously shaken. Two battalions of the 159th Brigade (53rd Division), which were on their way to take over the right of the 232nd Brigade at Berukin, were temporarily moved to El Kufr. But the Germans were checked by the fire of small groups of the Gurkhas, including battalion headquarters under Major W. L. Dundas, and then caught by a heavy-artillery barrage which appeared to inflict considerable loss upon them and certainly prevented them from following up their success. The front therefore remained almost unchanged except that the 5/Somerset was withdrawn from its exposed position at 'Arara, which it was impossible to consolidate under fire. On the extreme left the 123rd Rifles had relieved the 2/4th Dorset and cleared the crest of Three Bushes Hill by a most gallant charge. During the night the enemy launched a determined counter-attack and again drove the line back to the position previously occupied. The enemy's attempt to take the whole hill was beaten off by the quick and accurate barrage of the South African Field Artillery Brigade, which ranged on the flashes of the Turkish rifles, and by the timely arrival of three companies of the Dorset.

1918.
11 April.

Such was the situation on the 11th, when, after two days' bitter fighting, the 75th Division was still short of its first day's objective, hard enough put to it to hold what it had got, fatigued, and depleted in numbers. The Chief of the General Staff, Major-General Bols, visited the headquarters of the division with General Bulfin, the latter afterwards reconnoitring the front. It was clear that the enemy was prepared to dispute every foot of the ground and that the operation would prove extremely costly, while even if the 75th Division took its second objective it would be in poor case for carrying out the rolling up of the Tabsor defences. It had to meet several more counter-attacks on this date. It was decided to postpone the final stages of the operation for several days, but on the 15th Sir Edmund Allenby authorized General Bulfin to cancel them. On the 21st Three Bushes Hill was evacuated: Berukin, El Kufr, and Ra-fat—the last-named forming an acute salient in the line—being retained and consolidated.

The failure was due in part to the fact that the enemy was on this occasion thoroughly on the alert, but it takes

Sketch 26.

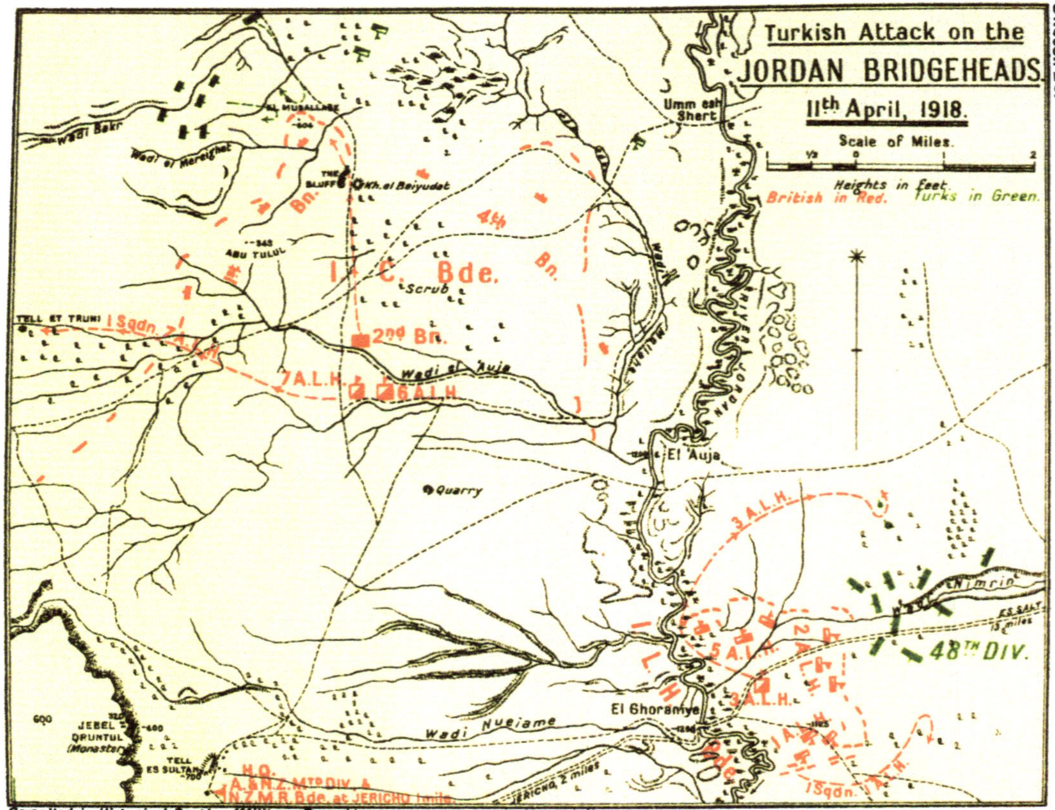


Compiled in Historical Section (Military Branch).
8000/30.

Ordnance Survey 1929.

more than that to explain why his defence was so much more vigorous on this occasion than in any recent fighting west of Jordan. Undoubtedly the methods of the new Commander-in-Chief served him well, for the Turkish soldier is always at his best when set down upon a position and bidden to hold it at all costs. It is also certain that marked maps and orders, imprudently carried in the attack, were captured on the first day, showing the enemy the magnitude of the British scheme and the importance of defeating it. Again, the enemy had excellent artillery observation from the high ground about Furqa, and could see down the ravines, the general run of which was from north-east to south-west. It appears, indeed, that to ensure the success of the operation it would have been necessary for the 10th Division simultaneously to have attacked this high ground. But the most important factor of all seems to have been the defence and determination in counter-offensive of the two German battalions, with their numerous machine guns and trench mortars, and the support of their own artillery. Undoubtedly the three German batteries had remained silent in their positions before the attack and escaped the notice of the counter-battery staff. The 75th Division had suffered 1,500 casualties.[1] Only 27 prisoners, including 9 Germans, were captured, but about two hundred dead were buried. The enemy losses were probably about seven hundred.[2]

---

[1] The casualties in the 232nd and 233rd Brigades, with the artillery and other arms, were as follows :—

|  | Killed. | Wounded. | Missing. |
|---|---|---|---|
| Officers | 13 | 46 | 6 |
| Other Ranks | 96 | 792 | 131 |

The total casualties of the 234th Brigade, which are not in all cases given by categories, were 414, making a total for the division of 1,498. The 123rd Rifles suffered very heavily at Three Bushes Hill, that battalion's losses amounting to 237.

[2] Liman states that the brunt of the attack fell on the German battalions of *Pasha II* and on the *16th Division;* it may therefore be presumed that these formations suffered most heavily. The only formation for which we have an exact casualty list is the *46th Division*, which is given by Colonel Hussein Husni, then in command of the division. His losses were 9 officers and 193 other ranks.

358    ATTACKS ON JORDAN BRIDGEHEADS

THE TURKISH ATTACK ON THE JORDAN BRIDGEHEADS.

Sketch 26.

Before the action in the neighbourhood of Berukin had died down the enemy severely tested the British positions in the Jordan Valley. After the withdrawal across the river of Shea's Force, Major-General Chaytor had taken over command here on the 3rd April, with the A. & N.Z. Mounted Division and Camel Brigade under his orders. On the northern front of the XX Corps the 74th Division, destined for France like the 52nd, was relieved by two brigades of the 53rd Division. All remained quiet in the valley for several days, while the troops got a foretaste of its summer conditions. The enemy was seen to be building up a strong position astride the Es Salt road to prevent another advance into Moab. His patrols on occasion moved down from the hills, but did not closely approach the bridgehead. British aeroplanes were active in reconnaissance, and on the 4th bombed 'Amman Station, hitting a train.

Major-General Chaytor's force was divided into two groups: one to defend the Ghoraniye bridgehead from the east, the other to defend the position north of the Wadi el 'Auja (also in the nature of a bridgehead) from the north. The Ghoraniye group, under the command of Br.-General Cox, consisted of the 1st L.H. Brigade and the 5th A.L.H. from the 2nd L.H. Brigade, supported by an artillery group consisting of a section 10th Heavy Battery, and the Ayrshire, Inverness, and Somerset Batteries. The 'Auja group, under the command of Br.-General Smith, consisted of the Camel Brigade, with the 2nd L.H. Brigade less one regiment in support; one section 10th Heavy Battery, the 301st Brigade R.F.A. (60th Divisional Artillery) and a captured 77-mm. gun. The New Zealand Brigade, in reserve, was bivouacked near Jericho. The positions were well sited and within a few days fairly well wired, though the 'Auja defences had as yet no great depth and there seems to have been less hard work expended on them than on those at Ghoraniye. Between them, from the left of the bridgehead to the right of the Camel Brigade's position at the mouth of the 'Auja, the ground about the Jordan's banks was still swampy.

On the night of the 10th April at about 10 p.m., there

## THE GHORANIYE ATTACK

was a sudden burst of fire from the Wadi Nimrin, a stream 1918. which cut the Ghoraniye bridgehead into two halves.[1] 11 April. Then silence fell, and a quiet night followed; nor did patrols which moved out before dawn at first encounter any enemy. At 4 a.m., however, came the sound of heavy shelling from north of the 'Auja, and twenty minutes later a patrol of the 2nd A.L.H. reported that it was in contact with the enemy on the south bank of the Wadi Nimrin. Then a body of about a hundred Turks was seen advancing on both sides of the wadi.

It was thought at first that this betokened no more than a reconnaissance, but as the light improved wave after wave of the enemy was seen on a frontage of 600 yards astride the wadi. Favoured by the dim light and the nature of the ground—just broken enough to afford good cover, while without serious obstacles—the first wave of the attack got to within a hundred yards of the wire, but was there held up, completely dominated by the fire of the Australians, particularly of the 2nd A.L.H. in the centre of the bridgehead. The Turks also suffered from gun fire, the British artillery observers on a knoll beside the Wadi Nimrin and on the high ground just west of the bridge having an admirable view. On several occasions bodies of reinforcements attempted to move forward, but were always broken up by the British artillery fire as they emerged from the scrub some 1,500 yards in front of the position. The Turks who had advanced beyond the cover of the scrub were pinned down, unable either to advance or retreat. However, they brought into action a number of machine guns, which kept up an accurate fire on the Australian trenches. A fire fight followed.

At 12.30 p.m. Br.-General Cox ordered his reserve regiment, the 3rd A.L.H., to move out mounted on the left, sweep round the right flank of the enemy, still on his original frontage, and strike the Wadi Nimrin behind him. At the same time a squadron of the 1st A.L.H. on the right of the bridgehead was ordered to endeavour to envelop the left flank of the attacking force. This squadron was quickly held up, but the 3rd A.L.H. made good progress at first and captured a dozen prisoners. Then it also came under

---
[1] The Turks had intended to carry out a night attack, but mismanaged the affair and were late. See Note at end of Chapter.

heavy fire, suffered considerable casualties among its horses, and was ordered to withdraw at 2.20 p.m. The Turks had now entrenched themselves in depth along the Wadi Nimrin, so that there was no chance of enveloping them. After dusk there were some signs of activity among the enemy, and a renewed attack was anticipated. However, fighting patrols sent out at 3 a.m. on the 12th found that he had gone back to his old position at Shunet Nimrin. His attack had been a complete and apparently a costly failure.

North of the Wadi el 'Auja the chief feature of the position held by the Camel Brigade was the hill of Musallabe, jutting out from the Judæan foot-hills into the valley. It was sharply defined, the ground falling away steeply on its eastern side,[1] and was of great importance in the defence of the Ghoraniye bridgehead and its communications against attack from the north. It formed an acute salient in the British line.

The Turks in this case made no attempt to effect a surprise. They bombarded the position for an hour, some forty shells a minute falling, chiefly on and about Musallabe. At 5.30 a.m. a heavy attack was launched against the hill from east and north, but was repulsed by the 1st Battalion of the Camel Brigade. The enemy, however, finding such cover as he could, remained all day at close quarters, continually sweeping Musallabe with machine-gun fire. A company of the 2nd Battalion was moved up to reinforce the 1st. Foiled in his frontal attack the enemy attempted to work round the left of the position, but was checked by a squadron of the 7th A.L.H., which moved out from the defences to Tell et Truni, on the upper reaches of the 'Auja. The remainder of the 2nd Battalion of the Camel Brigade was now brought up into line.

At 3 p.m. the Turks were seen massing in the Wadis Bakr and Mereighat, the latter of which entered the British position just south of Musallabe. An hour later the bombardment was renewed, and there followed another attack. This time the Turks established themselves here and there

---

[1] Heights in the Jordan Valley are indicated by decreasing instead of increasing numerals, with a minus sign, because all the ground is below sea-level. Musallabe is −604 feet, the ground 2,000 yards east of it −1,000 feet.

## THE MUSALLABE ATTACK

on the crest, but were driven down into the wadis by bombs. Here also the enemy withdrew after his failure under cover of darkness.

1918.
11 April.

These two abortive actions, undoubtedly undertaken in order to prevent another raid into Moab and to shorten the Turkish front, cost the attackers four or five times the losses of the defenders. Three officers and 135 other ranks were captured, and a large number of dead were afterwards buried.[1] The British losses were exactly one hundred, and there was about the same number of casualties among horses and camels. The Turks were evidently taken by surprise at finding strong wire in front of the Ghoraniye bridgehead, and, though this was much the heavier and the more determined of the two attacks, they caused little anxiety to the defence at this point. At Musallabe their threat was sharper because the defensive work was not so forward, and they were only prevented from taking that invaluable hill by the coolness and steadiness of the Camel Corps. Yet even here the attack did not seriously disquiet Major-General Chaytor, as is proved by the fact that he did not order the New Zealand Brigade to quit its bivouac.

### A Demonstration over Jordan.

From the 11th April to the end of the month the Arab forces were engaged in continuous operations against the Hejaz Railway in the neighbourhood of Ma'an. The fighting, which resulted in the destruction of all the stations and long sections of the line from Ma'an southward to Mudauwara, a distance of 70 miles, reached its climax on the 17th.[2] To assist and coincide with this attack Sir Edmund Allenby decided to make a demonstration in force in the Jordan Valley, with the object of inducing the enemy to believe that a new advance on 'Amman was about to take place, and thus preventing the despatch of any Turkish reinforcements towards Ma'an. The operation was entrusted to Major-General Chaytor, who had at his disposal, in addition to his own division, the 180th Brigade, the 10th Heavy Battery, and the 383rd Siege Battery. The

Sketch 24.

---

[1] The Historical Section of the Turkish General Staff gives the casualties as 472, which is far less than the British estimate.
[2] See Chapter XVIII.

## 362  ATTACKS ON JORDAN BRIDGEHEADS

1918.
18 April.

20th Indian Brigade [1] (Br.-General E. R. B. Murray), less two battalions, was detailed to hold the bridgehead defences while the A. & N.Z. Mounted Division was in action. On the 18th the heavy artillery was to open fire from west of the river on the enemy's position at Shunet Nimrin, while the 180th Brigade marched in daylight to a bivouac a mile west of Ghoraniye. During the night the A. & N.Z. Mounted Division would cross the Jordan and take up positions to cover the artillery, which would carry out a heavy bombardment, while demonstrations were made against the enemy's flanks by the mounted troops. Major-General Chaytor was instructed by General Chetwode not to become committed to a general engagement but, should the enemy retire, to follow him up. In no case, however, was Es Salt to be entered again.

The operation was duly carried out, but, far from retiring, the Turks opened so hot a fire that none of the mounted detachments sent forward to probe their position were able to approach the foot-hills. At 6.30 p.m. orders were issued for withdrawal. The demonstration may have prevented the despatch of troops southward, if this was ever intended, but unfortunately it put the enemy on the alert against another raid; and he was very watchful when Sir Edmund Allenby decided a few days later to translate his threat into action.

NOTE.

THE ACTIONS OF BERUKIN AND THE BRIDGEHEADS, FROM GERMAN AND TURKISH SOURCES.

The enemy forces which opposed the attack of the 75th Division were the *16th Division*, the left flank of which was west of Ra-fat, the German *Pasha II*, which had a sector to itself extending from Ra-fat to about El Kufr;[2] and the *46th Division*. Liman writes :—" El Kufr and " Berukin were the centres of the fighting, which was very violent. "Generally speaking the attack was repulsed, and in spite of heavy

---

[1] This brigade, which was never included in a division of the E.E.F., now consisted of the three Imperial Service Indian battalions which had been in the theatre since 1914 (see Vol. I, p. 15) and the 110th Mahratta Light Infantry. It had been on the Lines of Communication since forming part of the Composite Force at the Third Battle of Gaza, but was henceforth to be employed in the Jordan Valley throughout the summer.

[2] According to one German witness, it was under the orders of the *16th Division*.

# A GERMAN VIEW OF BERUKIN

" casualties the ground gained by the British was of no importance. The
" brunt of the attack was borne by the *Asia Corps* [1] and the *16th Division*."
  A full and interesting account of the action is given by a German
battery commander, Hauptmann Simon-Eberhard, who describes it in
detail.[2] His howitzer battery had been ordered to move up from the
coast on the 3rd, and had only been about three days in position when
the attack was launched. It was confidently expected; and the information given by him confirms the impression of British staff officers that
there was altogether too much talk in advance regarding this operation.
He himself fought his battery from Sheikh Subi, and records that the
Indian troops crowded together, offering easy targets, but admits that
the position was very favourable for defence. He is uncomplimentary to
the British airmen, declaring that though they were continually less than
1,500 feet over his guns they never apparently saw their flash, for he was
not fired on. He fired 734 rounds on the first day, having to replenish
ammunition from Et Tire, 16 miles away. The situation was desperate
on the 10th, for, he declares, had 'Arara been consolidated by the British,
the whole position would have become untenable. He seems to think
that the British would have broken through on this date had their attacks
all been simultaneous. As it was, the artillery was able to break up each
in turn. His final comment is of great interest:—" There is no doubt
" that if the attack had been made with more brigades and more powerful
" artillery support, and had fallen on Turkish troops only, the catastrophic
" break-through would have taken place in April."
  The Turkish attack on the Jordan bridgeheads is not mentioned by
Liman. The Historical Section of the Turkish General Staff states that
it was believed that the British forces in the Jordan Valley were weak
and there was a favourable opportunity to prevent any further raid into
Moab. The attack at Ghoraniye was carried out by the *48th Division*,
consisting of six battalions, and another formation of four battalions and
four squadrons of cavalry; that at Musallabe by three battalions and
four squadrons. The force east of the Jordan moved so slowly that it
had to postpone its attack until the morning instead of carrying it out
at night as it had been ordered to do.

---

[1] Here Liman refers not to the German headquarters, which was now
practically a corps staff, but to the troops. It seems best to reserve this
title for the headquarters and describe the troops as *Pasha II*.
[2] " Mit dem Asien Korps zur Palästinafront," pp. 89 *et seq*.

## CHAPTER XVII.

THE SECOND RAID INTO TRANS-JORDAN.

(Map 18; Sketch 24.)

PREPARATIONS FOR THE RAID.

IN Moab the time of the harvest was drawing near. Sir Edmund Allenby desired to deny to the Turks the valuable store of barley and wheat which would presently be reaped. He had therefore decided " to seize the first opportunity " to cut off and destroy the enemy's force at Shunet Nimrin, " and, if successful, to hold Es Salt till the Arabs could " advance and relieve my troops." [1] Down at Ma'an the activity of the Emir Feisal's Arabs continued, and tribesmen who had offered him their allegiance had temporarily occupied the railway between Qatrani, near the southern end of the Dead Sea, and 'Amman.

The E.E.F. was in the midst of its reorganization.[2] The 74th Division was to sail for France at the end of April; the Yeomanry Mounted Division was to exchange Yeomanry for Indian cavalry regiments, and had moved back at the beginning of the month to Deir el Balah for the purpose. The Commander-in-Chief would have preferred to carry out the raid in mid May, when this division would have been ready to take part in it. Meanwhile, however, envoys from the powerful tribe of the Beni Sakr, of which there was an encampment at Madeba, only 19 miles south-east of Ghoraniye, came in and declared that their people would co-operate in an advance east of Jordan if it were made before the 4th May; after that date they would be compelled, owing to lack of supplies, to disperse to various distant camping-grounds. Sir Edmund Allenby thereupon decided to begin the operation on the 30th April.

---

[1] Despatch, 18th September 1918.  [2] See Chapter XIX.

## SIR E. ALLENBY'S DESIGNS

He was, unfortunately, deceived regarding the help of the Beni Sakr. The envoys who promised it could in fact bind only a sub-tribe, and of this the greater part was already engaged in attacks on the railway further south.

1918. April.

The Commander-in-Chief had two other objects in view. He knew now that, owing to the reorganization of his force and the substitution of Indian troops—in part untried—for his British veterans, he was debarred from a major offensive till after the summer. But he looked far ahead. He was already turning over in his mind plans for a decisive attack when he had power to carry it out; and the experience of the fighting since the capture of Jerusalem led him to perceive the advantages of striking when that time came in the Plain of Sharon. All the more reason then that the enemy should be induced to concentrate his attention on the opposite flank and be made fearful of an attack on the railway directed against the vital focal point of Der'a. Again, if the British could establish themselves firmly on the plateau east of Jordan, it would be necessary to keep only a small number of troops exposed to the torrid heat of the Jordan Valley during the summer.

The operations were to be carried out by the Desert Mounted Corps, General Chauvel taking over command in the Jordan Valley from General Chetwode. The troops were to consist of the A. & N.Z. and Australian Mounted Divisions, the 60th Division (less the 181st Brigade, which was in reserve on the XX Corps front), and the 20th Indian Brigade. There were also available from the mounted troops in process of reorganization two Indian regiments under the staff of the Imperial Service Cavalry Brigade and two Yeomanry regiments under that of the 6th Mounted Brigade.[1]

Of a total fighting strength east of Jordan of from six to eight thousand, the bulk of the enemy lay astride the main road in the foot-hills, where a position some 6,000 yards

---

[1] The regiments in the Imperial Service Cavalry Brigade were the Mysore and Hyderabad Lancers; those in the 6th Mounted Brigade the Dorset Yeomanry and Middlesex Yeomanry (from the 8th Mounted Brigade). It must be added that the 5th Mounted Brigade, Australian Mounted Division, had attached to it in place of the Warwick Yeomanry the Sherwood Rangers, late 7th Mounted Brigade. The Stafford Yeomanry, 22nd Mounted Brigade, was attached to the Imperial Camel Brigade west of Jordan.

long was held by the motley collection of troops now known as the *VIII Corps* under Colonel Ali Fuad Bey.[1] Es Salt was held by a few companies only; 'Amman by two or three battalions. The essence of General Chauvel's plan was the envelopment of the right flank of the Turkish main position by the infantry, while the Australian Mounted Division pushed swiftly northward up the valley east of the river, dropped detachments to prevent Turkish reinforcements crossing from the west bank, and moved on Es Salt by the tracks approaching it from west and northwest. The defence of Es Salt from the north having been secured and a detachment moved out towards Suweile to cover it from the east, a force was then to be despatched down the main road towards Shunet Nimrin to take in rear the Turkish troops opposed to the infantry. The previous raid had proved that this road was the only one fit for wheeled transport.[2] The arrival of the Australian Mounted Division at Es Salt would sever the enemy's main communication and force him to employ for supply—and, if it so fell out, for retreat—the 'Ain es Sir track, which had proved only just passable for mounted troops a month earlier. And this track, together with that through Na'ur, the Arabs at Madeba had promised to bar. The enemy could again bring reinforcements from his Lines of Communication and the depots in Damascus by the Hejaz Railway to 'Amman, but, so short of troops was he and so slowly did the railway work, that no great increase of strength was anticipated from this source. He would also undoubtedly again attempt to reinforce his front from west of Jordan by way of Jisr ed Damiye, perhaps also at Umm esh Shert, or Mafid Jozele, between the two. To prevent this was the task of the Australian Mounted Division's detachment which was to be left in the valley. As an additional measure to deny to him the Umm esh Shert crossing, the Camel Brigade west of the river was to throw forward its right flank and establish a post to command

---

[1] Formerly Chief of the Staff to Jemal Pasha *Biyuk* and before the war Military Attaché in Paris; not to be confused with Major-General Ali Fuad Pasha, commanding the *XX Corps*.
[2] The Turks would seem to have improved the 'Ain es Sir track behind their position; they certainly used it to supply their troops at Shunet Nimrin. In any case the change in the weather made it and all the other tracks better.

SUPPLY AND TRANSPORT 367

the right bank at a point where the Jordan bends sharply 1918.
westward, 2 miles north-west of Umm esh Shert. April.
The number of troops engaged, particularly of mounted
troops, was far greater than in the previous raid, and the
supply problem therefore more difficult. Horses, camels
and mules might be expected to find ample grazing, so that
only the grain ration need be carried. The men would be
limited to a "mobile ration" of meat, biscuit, and tea.
The arrangements for supply made by Br.-General E. F.
Trew, D.A. & Q.M.G. Desert Mounted Corps, were generally
similar to those of the March operation. There was to be
a supply depot in the Jordan Valley about half way between
Jericho and Ghoraniye, to be filled by lorry from the
Jerusalem railhead. The 60th Division was to be maintained by wheeled train and first-line transport. The four
and a half heavy-burden camel companies for the mounted
troops, consisting of 5,400 camels, were to move east of
Jordan, supplies being taken across to them from the
depot by the wheeled trains of the two divisions and
improvised trains for the other mounted brigades. This
arrangement broke down owing to the inability of the
60th Division to capture the enemy's position at Shunet
Nimrin, and camel convoys took supplies over the river
from the depot for the troops distant from the bridgehead.

THE SECOND ACTION OF ES SALT—30TH APRIL.

By the morning of the 29th April the 60th Division 1918.
was concentrated in the bridgehead, the 180th Brigade 29 April.
south, the 179th Brigade north, of the Wadi Nimrin. The Sketch 24.
artillery allotted to Major-General Shea consisted of the
91st Heavy Battery, his own 301st and 302nd Brigades
R.F.A., and the IX Mountain Artillery Brigade, less one
battery with the Australian Mounted Division. One regiment of the New Zealand Brigade was to cover the right
flank of the 60th Division and one squadron of the 2nd
L.H. Brigade its left. The 2nd L.H. Brigade moved that
night down the left bank of the Jordan from Ghoraniye
to Makhadet Hijla to cover the construction of a bridge
at that point by the Corps Bridging Train. From Hijla a
subsidiary operation was to be carried out by a force of

all arms [1] under the command of Lieut.-Colonel G. M. M. Onslow, 7th A.L.H., against the flanking works of the enemy at Qabr Said and Qabr Mujahid, about 7 miles south-east of Ghoraniye.

The Australian Mounted Division, to which were attached the 1st L.H. Brigade, Hong Kong Mountain Battery, and 12th Light Armoured Motor Battery, was allotted the Ghoraniye crossing from 10 p.m. on the 29th to 2.30 a.m. on the 30th, and was to be prepared to advance northward, east of Jordan, by 4 a.m.

The Camel Brigade, with the Staffordshire Yeomanry, the 383rd Siege Battery and the XVIII Brigade R.H.A. attached, held the 'Auja bridgehead west of Jordan, and was to be prepared to advance its right at 4 a.m. to cover the approaches to Umm esh Shert from the west.

The A. & N.Z. Mounted Division, thus reduced to two brigades, each less one regiment, and without artillery,[2] was held in reserve to Major-General Shea. After the capture of the main Turkish position it was General Chauvel's intention that it should advance and hold the Madeba–'Ain Hummar track from the 'Ain es Sir cross-roads to 'Ain Hummar, supported by a proportion of the 60th Divisional Artillery. The corps reserve consisted of the 20th Indian Brigade (less Patiala Infantry), which was to improve the approaches to Ghoraniye under the direction of the C.R.E. 60th Division and be prepared to occupy the bridgehead if necessary; and the 6th Mounted and Imperial Service Cavalry Brigades, which did not reach Jericho till the evening of the 29th.

Demonstrations were carried out on this date by the XX Corps west of Jordan, and the 10th Division occupied the village of Mezra, north-west of 'Arura.

After dark on the 29th the Australian Mounted Division moved out from its camp, leaving lights burning, and

---

[1] 7th A.L.H., one squadron Hyderabad Lancers, Patiala Infantry, XX Brigade R.H.A. (less one battery).

[2] That is to say, the 1st L.H. Brigade was attached to the Australian Mounted Division, one regiment 2nd L.H. Brigade (7th A.L.H.) was engaged under the orders of the 60th Division in the operation against Qabr Said and Qabr Mujahid, one regiment New Zealand Brigade was covering the right of the 60th Division. The divisional artillery (XX Brigade R.H.A.) was also engaged in the Qabr Said operation, less one battery, which was attached to the 6th Mounted Brigade.

## FIRST ATTACK OF 60TH DIVISION 369

emerged from the bridgehead by the Abu Turra track at 4 a.m. on the 30th. Major-General Hodgson's orders from General Chauvel were to advance as rapidly as possible northwards east of the Jordan, to place one mounted brigade, supported by at least two R.H.A. batteries, astride the track from Jisr ed Damiye to Es Salt, facing north-west,[1] and with the remainder of his force move on Es Salt from west and north-west: Major-General Hodgson directed the 4th L.H. Brigade (Br.-General W. Grant) to carry out the duty of flank guard in the valley. This brigade was to be followed by the 3rd L.H. (Br.-General L. C. Wilson), which, after assisting the 4th if necessary to establish itself in its position, was to ride hard for Es Salt up the Damiye track. The 5th Mounted Brigade (Br.-General P. J. V. Kelly) was to turn off on reaching the Umm esh Shert track and also make for Es Salt, and the 1st L.H. Brigade was to follow by the same route.

1918.
30 April.

The first objective of the 60th Division's main attack was on the right (180th Brigade) from Ma'qqer ed Derbasi to Tell Buleibil, two hills rising from the plain south and north respectively of the Wadi Nimrin; and on the left (179th Brigade) the dominating height of El Haud. The second stage of the operation was to be carried out by the 180th Brigade alone, the brigade swinging up its left until it secured a line from Tell Buleibil to El Haud. Ma'qqer ed Derbasi and Tell Buleibil were both flat-topped plateaux running westward from the hill range, each with steep western faces, and each commanded by a ridge at its eastern end.

By 2.15 a.m. the leading battalions were deployed opposite their first objectives, at a distance of between five and seven hundred yards from them. On the right of the 180th Brigade the 2/19th London, advancing south of the Wadi Nimrin, had by 3 a.m. reached the wall of Ma'qqer ed Derbasi. Most gallant efforts were made to reach the summit by the only approaches, two narrow paths swept by machine-gun fire. Three attempts before dawn failed.

[1] "Australian Official History," p. 601, states that "Chauvel "resolved to seize the Damiye crossing and deny it to the enemy." It is important to note, in view of what followed, that Major-General Hodgson's written orders did not enjoin him to seize the crossing, but only to establish himself astride the track leading from it.
Desert Mounted Corps Order No. 16 is given in Appendix 22.

On one occasion two officers and a small party of men made their way up, but were counter-attacked on the top, and only one officer, severely wounded, managed to return. Renewed attempts at 7.30 and at 8.30 a.m. were likewise unsuccessful, though the second was preceded by a heavy bombardment of the position. North of the wadi the 2/20th London had rather better fortune. It met with little opposition till it reached the first crest, where a line of sangars and trenches was cleared with the bayonet. A Turkish counter-attack momentarily checked the advance, but was completely routed by the reserve company, 40 Turks being killed and about one hundred prisoners taken. The advance was then resumed, but the battalion was now suffering from oblique machine-gun fire from the adjoining heights, particularly Ma'qqer ed Derbasi. At 8 a.m., after repeated efforts to get forward had been made, the enemy forced a slight withdrawal by means of a single mountain gun which enfiladed the line at point-blank range. Br.-General Watson decided not to court further loss by pushing on this isolated battalion, but to resume the attack next morning. During the afternoon he replaced the 2/19th by the 2/17th and the 2/20th by the 2/18th London, keeping the relieved battalions in close support.

On the front of the 179th Brigade the 2/14th London was to attack El Haud and the 2/16th the high ground north of the hill, while the 2/13th followed a thousand yards in rear. The 2/15th was in divisional reserve at Ghoraniye. Directly the leading battalions emerged from the cover of the scrub seven hundred yards from the foot-hills they were seen in the moonlight and met by machine-gun fire. The 2/14th fought its way five hundred yards up the slope, despite determined resistance from the enemy's advanced troops in sangars and trenches, and took 118 prisoners. It was galled by fire from a spur on its left, on the south bank of the Wadi Abu Turra, but a swift attack by the 2/16th carried this strong position, taking 73 prisoners and three machine guns. Then progress came to an end. Communication with the artillery over the bullet-swept ground was extremely difficult, and delayed messages resulted in lack of support at critical moments. There was also shortage of small arms ammunition; for though each man carried a spare bandolier, this supply was largely needed to

## CAVALRY'S DASH UP THE VALLEY 371

refill machine-gun belts and Lewis-gun drums. Three 1918.
limber loads were rushed up under fire to the 2/16th London 30 April.
during the morning and restored the situation till more
could be sent up after dark. On the front of this brigade
also the attack was postponed until the following morning,
the 2/15th London being returned to the command of
Br.-General Humphreys for the purpose.

The containing attack by Lieut.-Colonel Onslow's
detachment was launched at the same hour as the main
operation, and at first met with little resistance. The
7th A.L.H. occupied Qabr Said before 3 a.m., and the
Patiala Infantry Qabr Mujahid at 5.35. The latter was
shortly afterwards evacuated, since the enemy shelled it
so accurately as to make its retention impossible without
heavy loss. This the commander of the detachment had
been ordered to avoid.

While the infantry was finding the Turkish main
position so formidable, the Australian Mounted Division
was swiftly carrying out its less arduous mission. From
the clay mounds near the Jordan's left bank to the foot-hills
there are for a considerable distance north of the Wadi
Nimrin no serious obstacles to the movement of mounted
troops. Beyond the banks, clothed with semi-tropical trees
and bushes, the ground is level over a breadth of three miles
or more, and the wadis which cut through it are of no great
account. Above Umm esh Shert the valley is narrowed by
hills on either flank, whereof one named Red Hill dominates
the plain and was to have an important part in the coming
battle. Pushing rapidly forward, the 4th L.H. Brigade
overran the Turkish Cossack posts extended across the
valley from Umm esh Shert, the sole link between the
Turkish *VIII Corps* at Shunet Nimrin and the forces west
of Jordan. The bulk of the enemy cavalry fell back on
Mafid Jozele, 4½ miles north of Umm esh Shert, to hold the
ford there.

Coming under ragged fire from Red Hill, the Australians quickened their pace. Screened in the white clouds
of their own dust, ever increasing speed until they were
moving at a hand-gallop, broadening their front till they
covered well nigh the whole width of the valley, they
pressed on northward. The pace, the dust, the shock to
the enemy's nerves of this inruption, all contributed to

make the casualty list very low. The head of the brigade reached the Damiye track, 15 miles north of its starting-point at Ghoraniye, at 5.30 a.m. Patrols pushed forward and at 8 a.m. reached the Nahr ez Zerqa, or River Jabbok, finding its water clean and easily approached. A squadron of the 11th A.L.H. then advanced on the Damiye bridge, but was met by machine-gun fire and reported that it was unable to get within 2,000 yards of the Jordan. Lieut.-Colonel P. J. Bailey, commanding the 11th A.L.H., reinforced it, but a squadron of Turkish cavalry, followed by infantry, advanced boldly across the bridge to the attack, and the Australians withdrew about a mile eastward. This was quite consistent with the orders issued to the division, but it gave the enemy opportunity not only to make the crossing secure but also to pass troops over it in his own good time, especially as the bridge was no longer under observation from the ground. In rear the 1st A.L.H. of the 1st L.H. Brigade had occupied Umm esh Shert; the enemy cavalry at Red Hill then retired to the right bank, apparently by a ford, and the position was seized by a squadron of the regiment. The enemy was in greatly superior strength on the right bank, and an attempt to approach the Jordan between Red Hill and Mafid Jozele was frustrated by machine-gun fire. West of the river the Camel Brigade also was checked a mile north-west of Umm esh Shert.

Br.-General Grant was uneasy as to his position. There was nothing to prevent the enemy from passing troops across at Jisr ed Damiye; while the Turks also held Mafid Jozele, where it was now discovered they had a pontoon bridge. Between Grant's left and the squadron of the 1st A.L.H. at Red Hill there was a gap of four miles. He explained his difficulties to General Chauvel, who came up to see him in the afternoon.[1] The corps commander, under whose direct orders he had now been placed, directed him to withdraw from the Jabbok but to continue covering the Damiye track where it entered the hills. Br.-General Grant asked for at least another regiment to enable him to hold Red Hill and keep connection with that *point d'appui*, thus protecting his line of retreat. General Chauvel replied that

---

[1] The hour is not recorded, but it was apparently about 4 p.m.

## 3RD L.H. BRIGADE ON THE PLATEAU 373

he could spare no more troops. He had already allowed 1918.
the 1st L.H. Brigade to move towards Es Salt, merely 30 April.
ordering it to leave the squadron at Red Hill with four
machine guns under Br.-General Grant's orders, and had
even withdrawn the 2nd L.H. Brigade from Major-General
Shea's command, placed it under that of Major-General
Hodgson, and ordered it to follow the 1st. The 6th Mounted
Brigade, he states in his report, he did not then feel himself
justified in withdrawing from the west bank of the Jordan,
doubtless because he thought there was some risk of the
enemy attacking at Musallabe instead of on the eastern side
of the valley. After General Chauvel had returned to his
headquarters Br.-General Grant received a telegram from
Br.-General Howard-Vyse, B.G.G.S. of the corps, directing
him to dispose his batteries so that he could be certain
of being able to withdraw them if necessary. But he
apparently felt that, with the force at his disposal, he
could not protect them in the plain and at the same time
keep his troops astride the Damiye track. They therefore
remained among the low hills on the eastern side of the
valley.

Meanwhile the 3rd L.H. Brigade on the Damiye track
and the 5th Mounted Brigade on the Umm esh Shert track
had scrambled up on to the plateau. An observer in the
plain noted that the 3rd L.H. Brigade took three hours to
pass a point upon which he had fixed his eyes. Five miles
W.N.W. of Es Salt the Damiye track forks, both branches
leading to the town, but the northern over very broken
ground past Kufr Huda, or Jebel Osha, the traditional tomb
of the Prophet Hosea. The brigade took the right-hand
track. A Turkish cavalry outpost was soon afterwards
surprised, but the supporting troop escaped to give the
alarm. The brigade was now on the great range of Jebel
Jil'ad, and perceived the enemy above in some strength,
holding a number of sangars. Br.-General Wilson first sent
a squadron of the 9th A.L.H. dismounted against the
enemy's right flank on a detached hillock. This was
quickly seized, and from it enfilade fire was opened on the
main position. Then, under cover of fire from the Hong
Kong Battery, another dismounted attack was launched
frontally by the 9th and 10th A.L.H. After a brilliant
assault the enemy was driven from the position with a loss

of 28 prisoners. Br.-General Wilson had kept the 8th A.L.H. standing by its horses for a dash on the town directly the way was open; and, disregarding fire from isolated bodies of Turks in the hills, its final advance was carried out at a gallop. The other regiments remounted quickly and followed. The first troop entered Es Salt at 6.30 p.m. The troop leader, Lieutenant C. D. Foulkes-Taylor, forced a German officer who was rallying the Turks to surrender. Frequently using their bayonets as swords, the Australians soon ended all resistance, and pursued the remnant of the enemy down the 'Amman road. About two hundred prisoners were taken, a considerable amount of transport, and 28 new machine guns still in their packing-cases.

Br.-General Wilson had orders to seize the junction of the 'Amman and Madeba roads at 'Ain Hummar, and though the 5th Mounted Brigade had not yet arrived he sent forward two squadrons at 10 p.m. This detachment was, however, held up over a mile from the road junction by machine-gun fire.

The 5th Mounted Brigade had encountered a certain amount of resistance from small parties of Turks with machine guns, which had to be outflanked in turn—a long and arduous process—and it was twilight when the top of the plateau was reached. The brigade therefore bivouacked for the night. In ignorance that the 3rd L.H. Brigade was already in Es Salt Br.-General Kelly prepared to carry out a mounted attack on the town the following morning.

### THE TURKISH COUNTER-ATTACK IN THE VALLEY—
### 1ST MAY.

1918.
1 May.

The second attempt of the 60th Division against the main Turkish position can be described in a few words. The attack was launched at 5.30 a.m. after a bombardment of 75 minutes, the objectives of the two brigades being the same as on the previous day. The scrub, which did not extend to the foot of the hills, gave cover for approach, but then served the enemy as an aiming-mark. He concentrated his machine-gun fire on its edge and thus defeated effort after effort to cross the open ground. A rush by a company of the 2/18th London, which was attacking Tell Buleibil, captured two Turkish sangars and a few prisoners,

## LAUNCH OF THE COUNTER-ATTACK 375

but that was all the day's success. At 10.20 a.m., as a result of events further up the valley soon to be recorded, orders were issued for the attack to be resumed along the whole divisional front at 2 p.m., a regiment of the New Zealand Brigade being put under the orders of the 179th Brigade for the purpose of advancing up the Abu Turra track and turning El Haud from the north. The attack was later cancelled, and it was decided to carry it out under cover of darkness the following morning. The New Zealand regiment, the Leicester Battery, and the 11th Light Armoured Motor Battery were withdrawn from the division to support the left flank of the corps, now in a highly critical situation.

1918.
1 May.

On the evening of the 30th April General Chauvel, having learnt that there was a pontoon bridge at Mafid Jozele, had ordered the Camel Brigade to carry out an attack in the morning and attempt to destroy it, the squadron of the 1st A.L.H. on Red Hill being instructed to co-operate east of the river. The message did not reach the 4th L.H. Brigade till the morning, and then Br.-General Grant instructed the 11th A.L.H. to despatch another squadron to Red Hill to assist in the operation. It was 6 a.m. before this squadron set out. By this time considerable movement could be seen in the direction of the Jabbok, and it was evident that the enemy had brought large numbers of troops across at Jisr ed Damiye. Br.-General Grant had just decided on a further slight withdrawal, which would have left his right still covering the Damiye track where it entered the hills, when the blow fell.

Suddenly a body of the enemy emerged from the cover of the mud banks near the Jordan south of Jisr ed Damiye and advanced to the attack in open order upon a frontage of a thousand yards. At the same time another force consisting of cavalry deployed from the Jabbok and advanced against the British right flank, moving into the foot-hills with the evident intention of turning it.[1] The

---

[1] The first force was estimated by Br.-General Grant at 4,000 strong, the second at 1,500 strong. We know, in fact, that the main attack consisted of one Turkish infantry regiment, one storm battalion, two German companies (of which one was presently detached to join the cavalry on the left) and a German machine-gun company ; the secondary attack of the *3rd Cavalry Division* of two regiments, with one or two

enemy infantry swept rapidly across the plain, its right on the gap between the left of the 4th L.H. Brigade and Red Hill. The three British batteries found good targets, and for a short time checked the advance.

Two cars [1] of the 12th Light Armoured Motor Battery took up a position on the left flank. One stuck in a deep rut and was abandoned; the other did good service in covering the gap between the left and Red Hill, till it was forced to withdraw owing to casualties and shortage of ammunition. Here also the squadron of the 11th A.L.H., which had not yet reached Red Hill, came into action against the enemy's right flank.

At 10 a.m. a body of the enemy, which had apparently crossed at Mafid Jozele, attacked Red Hill and swept straight over it, the squadron of the 1st A.L.H. retiring hastily to avoid being surrounded. Next the attack was renewed on the British right. The flanking movement of the enemy caused the 4th A.L.H. to fall back, and this in turn forced the artillery to withdraw. The situation of the guns was now perilous, since, owing to the succession of rough ridges and gullies, they could not move southward without turning westward first, and on that side were penned in by the Turkish advance. " B " Battery H.A.C., the furthest out, had the fairest fortune. Retiring along the track following the edge of the foot-hills, it lost one gun, which was stuck in a wadi, but extricated the other three after great exertions.

Worse was to follow. By 11 a.m. the enemy had driven back the light horsemen till he was within 700 yards of the guns. " A " Battery H.A.C. and the Notts Battery R.H.A. could no longer retreat. The Turkish and German machine guns shot down the teams which were brought up to withdraw the limbers. The guns were served as long as possible ; then they were abandoned. They were the first British guns lost in the course of the whole campaign, and the last. At the same time about fifty limbered and G.S.

---

regiments of the *Caucasus Cavalry Brigade*. The fighting strength of the main attack cannot have exceeded 1,750, while independent Turkish and German accounts both put it lower. (See Note at end of Chapter.)

[1] The other two had had mechanical trouble and returned to Ghoraniye over night. After being repaired they returned to the line after the withdrawal of the 4th L.H. Brigade.

wagons, ambulances, and water-carts fell into the hands of the enemy.

1918.
1 May.

Seeing the enemy pressing down the centre of the valley, attacking Red Hill, and also striking at the right of the brigade's position, Lieut.-Colonel M. W. J. Bourchier, commanding the 4th A.L.H. on the right, and Lieut.-Colonel D. Cameron, commanding the 12th in the centre, had a hasty consultation and decided that withdrawal by the plain or across the low hills in which their regiments were posted was for them impossible. The 4th A.L.H., which was in the more difficult position, therefore moved well up on to the plateau, the 12th holding on as long as possible to give it a start. The 11th fell back due southward, and was the only one to save any wheeled transport—a water-cart and a limbered wagon. The retirement of the two regiments in the hills, and especially that of the 4th, was extremely arduous and hazardous owing to the series of deep gullies which had to be traversed. At one moment four camels which had come up with water toppled backwards owing to the steepness of the slope they were attempting to scale, fell three hundred feet, and were killed. During the first stage of the withdrawal the enemy pressed in boldly, once getting to within three hundred yards of the rear squadron of the 4th A.L.H. ; and only the steadiness of troops posted on the flank with Hotchkiss rifles saved the retreating column from being completely cut off. The men showed great gallantry in rescuing under fire wounded comrades who would otherwise have fallen into the hands of the enemy, carrying them in waterproof sheets up stony hills and across steep and rugged defiles.

On hearing of the attack launched against the flank guard but before he knew how all too successful it had been, General Chauvel at 10 a.m. issued an order placing the 4th L.H. Brigade under the command of Major-General Chaytor and putting also at his disposal a regiment of the 6th Mounted Brigade and the New Zealand Brigade less two regiments. At the same time he urged the 60th Division to press its attack.[1] Major-General Chaytor, while

---

[1] G.A.68. 1st.
60th Division will press the attack. 20th Indian Inf. Bde. and 1 Regt. N.Z.M.R. Bde. is placed at his disposal in addition to troops already under his command. Anzacs will take over command of front

these troops were moving up, himself motored forward to discover the situation. Meeting a linesman who told him where Br.-General Grant was, he took the man's horse and rode to find him. The brigadier was now holding the line of a wadi due east of Red Hill with the 11th A.L.H. ; the other two regiments could be seen moving southwards, leading their horses, over the broken ground on the lower slopes of the hills. It appeared to Major-General Chaytor that this position was unfavourable, particularly as there was a wide gully running into the hills just behind the right flank. He therefore decided to make a further withdrawal, to a line just north of the Umm esh Shert track. At 12.50 Br.-General Godwin, commanding the 6th Mounted Brigade, was ordered to hand over command of the Dorset Yeomanry and Mysore Lancers [1] to the officer commanding the Dorset, Lieut.-Colonel G. K. M. Mason, while he himself, with headquarters, the 17th Machine-Gun Squadron and the Berks Battery, followed the Middlesex Yeomanry over the Jordan and resumed command. The Dorset Yeomanry and Mysore Lancers (temporarily known as "Mason's Detachment") were ordered to be ready to cross at short notice if required.

The further withdrawal of the 4th L.H. Brigade was accomplished without incident, and about 2 p.m. the Middlesex Yeomanry came up on its left, taking up a line north of the Umm esh Shert track in the plain. This line was continued by the Auckland Regiment to the bank of the Jordan north of Umm esh Shert, and was covered by the Berks Battery and 17th Machine-Gun Squadron when they arrived. At 2.45 p.m. the Canterbury Regiment and

---

now held by 4th L.H. Bde. with object of protecting left flank of Corps from Jisr ed Damiye–Es Salt track inclusive to the river Jordan. 6th Mtd. Bde. will place one British Regt. at disposal of G.O.C. Anzacs to report at exit from bridgehead on track towards Wadi Arseniyat [Wadi Abu Turra] forthwith, moving at 4 miles per hour. Acknowledge. Addressed 60th Division, Aus. Div., Anzacs., 6th Mtd. Bde., 4th L.H. Bde., 20th Ind. Inf. Bde., repeated D.A. & Q.M.G., G.O.C.R.A., C.R.E., A.D.A.S.

Advanced Descorps, 10 a.m.

[1] Br.-General Harbord, commanding the Imperial Service Cavalry Brigade, had taken over the command of Onslow's Detachment and relieved the 7th A.L.H. by the Hyderabad Lancers, in order to allow the former to rejoin its brigade at Es Salt. He had left the Mysore Lancers under Br.-General Godwin's orders.

## SITUATION AT ES SALT

11th Light Armoured Motor Battery were withdrawn from the 60th Division to support the left. Fresh attacks by the enemy on the 4th L.H. Brigade were beaten off.

1918.
1 May.

The left flank of the corps had been secured, but at the expense of withdrawing troops sorely needed by the 60th Division. Moreover, the Damiye track, up which the 3rd L.H. Brigade had moved to the capture of Es Salt, had passed out of British hands and was being employed by the enemy; for the Turkish cavalry which had moved into the hills set off along it for Es Salt. The Abu Turra track was still commanded by the enemy, not yet driven from El Haud, so the sole exit for the force in the hills was the Umm esh Shert track, barely covered by Major-General Chaytor's line.

Quite ignorant of what was happening in the valley, the four brigades which had moved up into the hills, were carrying out their tasks. Br.-General Kelly, commanding the 5th Mounted Brigade, on learning at 4 a.m. that Es Salt had been captured, ordered the Gloucester Hussars to pass through the town and advance down the main road on the bridge at El Huweij, thus getting right behind the main Turkish position. At 8.40 the regiment reported that it was within half a mile of the bridge, but that further progress was impossible. At 11 Br.-General Kelly received an order from Major-General Hodgson, who had established his headquarters south-west of Es Salt, to attack vigorously down the road towards Shunet Nimrin, taking in rear the enemy opposed to the 60th Division. The remainder of the brigade had now come up behind the Gloucester Hussars, but after a personal reconnaissance of the Turkish position, which was on the top of a precipitous cliff, the brigadier sent back a report pointing out the extreme difficulty of his task and asking for further orders. While awaiting these he proceeded with the plan which to his mind was the only one possible: to take up a strong position astride the road and await the attempt of the Turks to force a way back for their guns. This he confidently expected would occur, as he understood that the attack of the 60th Division was meeting with success. At 3 p.m. he rode back to interview Major-General Hodgson, who, in view of his emphatic representation of the strength of the Turkish position, decided to postpone the attack until the following dawn and to employ the 2nd L.H. Brigade in addition to the 5th Mounted.

The 3rd L.H. Brigade had meanwhile taken up a position covering Es Salt from the east, distant about half a mile from the town. The 2nd L.H. Brigade, which had also arrived, had been ordered to move on the 'Ain Hummar cross roads, in which direction two squadrons of the 10th A.L.H. had advanced during the night. At 1 p.m. the 8th A.L.H. (3rd L.H. Brigade) with two guns of the Hong Kong Battery was also ordered to advance towards 'Ain Hummar, as the position covering the village was reported to be strongly held. The Turks, however, fell back at sight of the Australian reinforcements. The 1st L.H. Brigade was ordered to hold in strength the junction of the Umm esh Shert and Abu Turra tracks to prevent any escape northward of the Turks at Shunet Nimrin.

Not till 4.40 p.m. did Major-General Hodgson learn of the catastrophe in the Jordan Valley that morning, or that the Damiye track, unprotected by his present dispositions, was open to the enemy. The small reserves—two troops only—at Es Salt were rushed round to the north-western side to bar the advance of the enemy, already reported, along the Damiye track. The force at 'Ain Hummar was ordered to withdraw under cover of darkness: the detachment of the 3rd L.H. Brigade returning to its brigade for the defence of Es Salt, the 2nd L.H. Brigade getting touch with the 5th Mounted Brigade and assisting it in the attack on Huweij Bridge which, despite his somewhat precarious situation, Major-General Hodgson was not prepared to abandon. He was in any case precluded from doing so, since General Chauvel had ordered him to employ no more than a brigade to protect Es Salt and two brigades for the attack south-west, to co-operate with the renewed attack of the 60th Division.

DEADLOCK AND WITHDRAWAL—2ND-4TH MAY.

The capture of Ma'qqer ed Derbasi by the 60th Division having proved impossible by daylight, it was now decided to carry out an attack upon it by a battalion of the 180th Brigade at 2 a.m. At 6.30 the 179th Brigade was to resume the attack on El Haud, while the 180th co-operated

## 60TH DIVISION RENEWS ATTACK 381

by attacking Tell Buleibil. To replace the New Zealand 1918.
regiment withdrawn to protect the left flank of the corps, 2 May.
Major-General Shea had formed a detachment, under the
orders of Major S. A. Tooth, 6th A.L.H., consisting of his
squadron (which had been covering the 60th Division's left),[1]
two companies Patiala Infantry, and the 16th Mountain
Battery. "Tooth's Detachment" was to advance up the
Wadi Abu Turra and attack El Haud from the north-west.
The night attack on Ma'qqer ed Derbasi was to be made
without preliminary fire; the main attack to be preceded
by an artillery preparation of 50 minutes.

Ma'qqer ed Derbasi was to be assaulted simultaneously
from north and south, one and a half companies of the
2/17th London operating on each flank. The northern
detachment captured the line of sangars on top of the hill,
but was counter-attacked and compelled to withdraw, the
southern party having been held up before reaching the
crest. The enemy succeeded in working his way round the
right party's flank and captured some twenty men during
the retirement.

This failure compromised the main attack, which was,
however, proceeded with. As a preliminary move Tooth's
Detachment cleared a Turkish work on the bank of the
Wadi Abu Turra, due west of El Haud, at 5.15 a.m. The
advance made fair progress at first, but the 2/18th London
was soon held up by fire from Ma'qqer ed Derbasi, while
the 2/15th London was also brought to a halt. The lack of
success at Ma'qqer ed Derbasi had indeed a disastrous effect
on the fortunes of the day, for on the left of the 179th
Brigade the 2/13th London, in face of considerable fire,
made an advance of nearly a thousand yards and actually
established its flank well north of El Haud; while the
Patialas, leaving the Wadi Abu Turra, reached a hill a
thousand yards north-west of El Haud. The attack had
come within a little of turning the enemy's position,[2] but
once again, owing to the exposure of the troops to machine-
gun fire, it was decided to hold what was won and make
another attempt at night.

---
[1] See p. 367.
[2] Liman, who describes the attacks of the 30th April and 1st May on the main position as fruitless, states that the situation of the *VIII Corps* was serious on this date. The Turkish Historical Section also states that the right was in very grave danger.

It will be recalled that the infantry attack was to be assisted by the 2nd L.H. and 5th Mounted Brigades, which were to move down the main road against the rear of the enemy's position. Hardly had their advance begun when the enemy, about five hundred strong with a mountain battery—obviously the troops which had moved up the Damiye track from the Jordan—drove in the outposts of the 10th A.L.H. north-west of Es Salt. Before 10 a.m. an advance on the other flank from 'Amman began to make itself felt also. At 11.30 Major-General Hodgson sent a message to the 2nd L.H. and 5th Mounted Brigades that if the attack from the east developed in strength the 3rd Brigade at Es Salt would be unable to cope with it in addition to that from the west, and ordered the 2nd Brigade at once to despatch a regiment to Es Salt. Br.-Generals Ryrie and Kelly both informed the divisional commander that in view of the strength of the Turkish position they had little or no hope of reaching their objectives before dark. Major-General Hodgson replied that the attack must continue.

However, after further conversation with the two brigadiers, he telephoned to General Chauvel at 2.20 p.m. to recommend that, in consequence of the large numbers of the enemy now seen to be advancing along the 'Amman road, the attack by the 2nd and 5th Brigades should be broken off, so that those troops should be available in case of need at Es Salt. General Chauvel refused to hear of the abandonment of the attack, which, if successful, would have solved all the difficulties of the 60th Division; but he gave permission for another regiment of the 2nd Brigade to be withdrawn.[1] The 5th Mounted Brigade was thus left to carry out with three regiments an operation which to its commander had appeared impossible with five. The Worcester Yeomanry and Sherwood Rangers attempted to move in single file down the wadi east of and parallel to the Es Salt road; but, finding progress impossible, withdrew slightly, climbed up on to the east bank south of Abu Tara, and deployed. Half-way down the slope leading

---

[1] The third regiment, the 7th A.L.H., which had originally been, it will be remembered, on the right flank of the 60th Division in the Jordan Valley, had moved through Es Salt and reached its brigade headquarters at about this time.

## FAILURE OF ATTACK ON HUWEIJ 383

to the deep gorge of the Wadi Naheir, they came under 1918.
artillery fire and lost several officers. Lieut.-Colonel H. J. 1 May.
Williams, commanding the Worcester Yeomanry, decided
that the enemy's position on the far bank of the wadi was
too strong for the troops, exhausted by the heat, and broke
off the action on his own initiative.

The general situation of Major-General Hodgson's command at 5.30 p.m. was as follows :—the 5th Mounted Brigade remained in observation of the enemy on the main road, its outposts 3,000 yards north of Huweij Bridge ; the 2nd L.H. Brigade was engaged east of Es Salt with an enemy force estimated at 400 infantry, 200 cavalry, and four heavy guns, advancing from Suweile ; the 3rd L.H. Brigade was north-west of Es Salt, with a regiment covering the Damiye track ; the 1st L.H. Brigade (less the 1st A.L.H., which had been ordered to join the 2nd Brigade at Es Salt and was on the move) had its right two miles west of Es Salt and its left in touch with the troops under Major-General Chaytor's command, north of the Umm esh Shert track. The Turkish attack from the east was held without great difficulty, but that along the Damiye track was pressed boldly and vigorously. By nightfall there was close touch here between the contestants ; one attack at 8 p.m. got to within 20 yards of the right of the 3rd Brigade's line. All along that brigade's front there was intermittent fighting throughout the night, and in Es Salt could be heard the continual crash of bombs, with sudden heavy outbursts of musketry.

Major-General Hodgson's command in the hills had now come to the end of the three days' rations which it had carried with it, and no more was sent to it owing to an exaggerated account of the difficulties of the Umm esh Shert track having reached corps headquarters. However, neither men nor horses suffered severely. A little grain, raisins, and fresh meat were requisitioned in Es Salt, while there was excellent grazing for the horses, and never any shortage of water. A small pack column with ammunition reached Es Salt on the 2nd, and a supply of medical comforts for the wounded was dropped from an aeroplane.

Against the left flank in the Jordan Valley the enemy renewed his attempts with increased strength. The 4th L.H. Brigade had in front of its main line on the right two troops of the 11th A.L.H. and one of the 4th holding a small flat-topped hill known as "Table Top." This outpost was assaulted from both flanks at 3.45 p.m., and after repulsing the attackers twice with the bayonet was forced to withdraw. The loss of Table Top did not seriously endanger the position, but that of a good spring behind it was of some inconvenience. The dash, skill, and high discipline of the attacking troops—apparently the *Assault Battalion* of the *24th Division* and German companies — were such as the 4th Brigade had never before experienced.

The Canterbury Regiment was moved round from the left of the line in the Jordan Valley to behind the 4th Brigade and came under Br.-General Grant's orders; it was not, however, called upon to reinforce the firing line, as the enemy for the time being contented himself with this minor success.

Major-General Shea was now set one of the cruellest tasks which can fall to a commander : to launch an assault in the success of which he did not believe, for the sake of other troops. Having to make the best of a bad job, and coming to the conclusion that there was small prospect of further progress by the 60th Division till El Haud itself was captured, he resolved to make an attempt to seize this prominent hill by an attack under cover of darkness. This was to be carried out by the 179th Brigade, the 2/18th London of the 180th co-operating if possible by sending strong patrols along the Tell Buleibil spur toward the objective. Assistance by the 5th Mounted Brigade from north of Huweij Bridge having been proved to be out of the question, it was arranged that the 1st L.H. Brigade should send a detachment down the Wadi Abu Turra track from its junction with the Umm esh Shert track to attack El Haud from the north. The main attack on El Haud was to be carried out by the 2/13th London, the 2/16th protecting its right and two companies of the Patialas its left. The remainder of Tooth's Detachment was to work up the Wadi Abu Turra and endeavour to find touch with the 1st L.H. Brigade's detachment moving down it from the north-east.

Once again the task was found to be hopeless. Two companies of the 2/13th, beginning their advance at 2 a.m., had by 5.30 reached a hill a thousand yards north-west of

## CRITICAL SITUATION IN THE HILLS

El Haud. But they were unable to make any further progress, and were, in fact, forced to remain while daylight lasted lying flat on the summit under heavy machine-gun fire, and to withdraw from their exposed position under cover of darkness. A squadron of the 1st L.H. Brigade, moving down the Abu Turra track, almost gained touch with them, reaching a point about a thousand yards north of El Haud at 6 a.m.; but was soon afterwards compelled to fall back up the track. General Chauvel was at first inclined to renew these attacks, as he thought the Abu Turra track would be required for the retirement of Major-General Hodgson's troops. He altered his plans, however, when he learnt that Major-General Hodgson had decided to rely entirely upon the Umm esh Shert track for the extrication of his force. The 60th Division was now ordered to keep the enemy occupied during the afternoon by sudden bursts of artillery fire and feint attacks. The R.A.F. dropped 600 lbs. of bombs on 'Amman, reporting direct hits on the railway station.

Meanwhile the Commander-in-Chief had ordered up the 181st Brigade. It had arrived at Bethany from Ram Allah at midnight on the 2nd, had been brought down to the Jordan Valley in lorries, and during the morning of the 3rd was concentrated in the Wadi Nimrin east of Ghoraniye.

At Es Salt the enemy, while continuing his pressure against the 3rd L.H. Brigade covering the Damiye track, came to close quarters before dawn with the 2nd L.H. Brigade covering the road to 'Amman. The 5th Mounted Brigade was ordered to send a regiment into reserve southeast of the town. But the serious situation was relieved by a blunder on the part of the enemy and dashing work by the defenders. The Turks had closed in upon the position of two squadrons of the 8th A.L.H., which had been sent to the support of the 2nd L.H. Brigade, about the point where the 'Amman road turns sharply southward into Es Salt, and when light appeared the firing line was commanded in enfilade by the 5th A.L.H. on the right of the 8th. Major Y. H. Walker, commanding the left squadron of the 8th, despatched a troop to turn the enemy's flank, and at the same time carried out a frontal assault. The result was a brilliant success, 319 Turks surrendering and the attack from the east being broken up. That from the Damiye track met with more success, a post of the 10th A.L.H. (3rd L.H. Brigade) being driven off Kufr Huda. It was observed that a fresh column of Turkish infantry had arrived in this quarter.[1]

In the Jordan Valley the enemy renewed his attacks, a bombing assault on Black Hill, on the right of the line, getting to within 20 yards of the 4th L.H. Brigade's position at 4 a.m. The enemy was driven down the hill, and left a machine gun behind. Another vigorous attack after dusk was also beaten off. Officers and men knew that the fate of Major-General Hodgson's force in the hills depended upon their covering the Umm esh Shert track at Black Hill, and they were prepared to fight to the last for it. Weary, thirsty, longing for sleep, under the gloomy shadow of recent events, they were determined that the enemy should not advance another yard. The Turks, flushed by success and reinforced, thrust against them in vain. The loss of the spring behind Table Top was severely felt, the horses of the brigade having to be watered in the Jordan at long intervals. The Dorset Yeomanry was brought east of Jordan and placed in reserve to the 6th Mounted Brigade.

At 3 p.m. the Commander-in-Chief came down to confer with General Chauvel. He knew of the failure of the infantry attack and that Es Salt was pressed from both flanks, while he had had a somewhat exaggerated report regarding the loss of Kufr Huda.[2] He had learnt from the air that the troops facing Major-General Chaytor's force had been reinforced. It appeared to him that there was little to be gained and great risk in further resistance. He therefore empowered General Chauvel to issue orders for a general withdrawal. His first project, embodied in

---

[1] This was the *2nd Regiment, 24th Division*, which had crossed at Mafid Jozele on the night of the 30th while the remainder of the division was crossing at Damiye, had then been withdrawn, had recrossed at Damiye, and had been put under the command of the *3rd Cavalry Division* which was attacking Es Salt. See Note at end of Chapter.

[2] The post lost was not of great tactical importance, as the path covered by it was commanded by other posts. The news seems to have come by telephone in a form indicating the gravest danger to Es Salt, for Sir Edmund Allenby has annotated Major-General Hodgson's subsequent report :—" Then I got wrong information at Corps H.Q." The 10th A.L.H. was, in fact, hard pressed, but the enemy was unable to advance another yard.

## WITHDRAWAL FROM ES SALT 387

orders issued that night, was to hold a large bridgehead, 1918. from Makhadet Hijla to the line now occupied by the 3 May. 60th Division and thence to Umm esh Shert. In a letter despatched from G.H.Q. before midnight emphasis was laid upon the vital importance of holding the Umm esh Shert track until the withdrawal from Es Salt was complete.

At 5.15 p.m. Major-General Hodgson issued orders for the withdrawal of the force under his command, of which the first stage was to be covered by the 2nd L.H. Brigade in a rear-guard position south-west of Es Salt. The 1st L.H. Brigade was to piquet the heights covering the Umm esh Shert track all the way down from this position, while both the 2nd and 3rd Brigades were to leave small parties on tracks north and east of Es Salt to keep up intermittent firing until dawn.[1]

The withdrawal, awaited with so much anxiety, passed off more easily than might have been expected, its success being doubtless largely due to the sharp lesson learnt by the enemy on the 'Amman road the previous morning. By 2.20 a.m. on the 4th the evacuation of Es Salt was 4 May. complete. Thereupon the 2nd L.H. Brigade was ordered to withdraw all but the fighting troops of one regiment from its rear-guard position. Divisional headquarters moved to the junction of the Umm esh Shert and Abu Turra tracks, whence Major-General Hodgson was able to report at 6.10 a.m. that all camels, pack-animals, and prisoners had passed down. A column of donkeys with ammunition and biscuits—the first food yet received—reached Es Salt just as the order for retirement was issued. The column was therefore turned back, and the biscuits were dumped by the roadside for the troops to help themselves as they passed. The enemy made slight attacks against the screen left out by the 3rd L.H. Brigade, and was beaten off with the aid of Turkish bombs, of which there was great store in Es Salt. The 5th Mounted Brigade

---

[1] This order was based on telephonic instructions from General Chauvel. The only telegraphic message so far received by Major-General Hodgson enjoined him merely to " make arrangements for withdrawal to " position south-west of Es Salt . . . with view to further retirement " later." It is significant of how grave he considered his situation that he then telephoned to Br.-General Howard-Vyse asking, in the words of his war diary, whether he should " endeavour to withdraw entirely from " the mountains *if able to do so.*" He was told that this was General Chauvel's intention, and then issued the above order.

had the greatest difficulties, as it had to move by a bad bridle-path from the main road to the Umm esh Shert track, which Br.-General Kelly had fortunately found after long reconnaissance that morning. Beginning its retirement at 8.30 p.m., it did not reach Jebel Umm 'Awiya till 2.45 a.m., when it came under the command of Br.-General Cox, 1st L.H. Brigade, the Sherwood Rangers assisting that brigade to cover the final withdrawal under long-range machine-gun fire.

Two sections of the 519th Field Company R.E. (60th Division) had been despatched the previous evening to work on the Umm esh Shert track, and the passage of troops over it had actually rather improved it since the 5th Mounted Brigade had marched up it and been obliged to leave its camels behind. Yet the movement of the great column in the dark was very arduous. Hardest of all was the lot of the wounded, many of whom had now been three days in Es Salt. All rode who could sit horses, and several of the Australians with really terrible wounds insisted on being lifted to their saddles rather than trust themselves to the camel *cacolets*. Refugees from Es Salt encumbered the retreat. The troops were all extremely fatigued, and in some cases suffering from want of food. Nevertheless, the tail of the column reached the plain at 10.30 a.m.

At this moment there was some confusion, owing to insufficient warning having been given to the 4th L.H. Brigade that its right was about to be uncovered. The Turks followed up quickly, firing on the rear of the column, while German aeroplanes swooped down and used their machine guns against it. Br.-General Grant piqueted the hills with the handful of men he could spare, but these were at once driven in. Then the Canterbury Regiment, which had advanced to meet the retreating troops and was moving back with them, was ordered to turn about and take up a position on the 4th Brigade's right. Meanwhile Br.-General Godwin, commanding the 6th Mounted Brigade, saw from his command post what was happening, sent up a squadron of the Dorset Yeomanry, and brought the artillery (the Berks and Leicester Batteries and the three remaining guns of " B " Battery H.A.C.) into action against the enemy on the Umm esh Shert track. The 8th A.L.H. of the 3rd L.H. Brigade was later also sent back. The 1st and 3rd L.H.

# END OF THE RAID

Brigades with the 10th Mountain Battery were placed in reserve to Major-General Chaytor, while the 2nd L.H. and 5th Mounted Brigades marched straight through to the bridgehead.

1918.
4 May.

Sir Edmund Allenby had now decided that his projected large bridgehead would be too much commanded by the Turkish position at El Haud. In the evening, therefore, he issued orders that the original bridgehead at Ghoraniye should be maintained, but a second one created at El 'Auja, where a bridge was to be thrown. All troops other than those required to hold these bridgeheads were to be withdrawn west of the river.

After the withdrawal of the mounted troops, the 179th and 180th Brigades were also to move west of the Jordan, while the 181st held the Ghoraniye bridgehead. Major-General Chaytor was instructed to detail one regiment for the defence of the 'Auja crossing under the orders of Br.-General Smith, commanding the Camel Brigade. Meanwhile the engineers of the Desert Mounted Corps were to begin work on the defences of the new bridgehead at El 'Auja. The enemy made efforts all day to work round the right flank in the valley, but was firmly held, and Br.-General Grant was able to withdraw the troops by units from the left, beginning at 6.45 p.m., in good order. By midnight the withdrawal was complete and the operation was at an end.

The British casualties numbered 1,649.[1] In addition to the guns and transport lost in the Jordan Valley, some material of less importance was abandoned at Es Salt. The captures amounted to 44 Germans, 898 Turks, and 39 Bedouin. The Turkish casualties were therefore almost certainly higher than the British.

\* \* \* \* \*

From the moment when the 4th L.H. Brigade was driven back from the Damiye track the initiative may be said to have passed to the enemy; never afterwards, except possibly for a moment on the 2nd May when the

---
[1]

| | Killed. | Wounded. | Missing. |
|---|---|---|---|
| Officers | 16 | 84 | 3 |
| Other Ranks | 198 | 1,214 | 134 |

Of these casualties 1,116 (about two-thirds of the whole) were incurred by the 60th Division and attached Patiala Infantry.

O 2

179th Brigade was threatening to turn the Turkish right at El Haud, had a favourable outcome been probable. As in the First Battle of Gaza, a combination of mishaps or mistakes rather than any single great one appears to have brought about the failure. There were obviously three main causes: the driving in of the flank guard in the Jordan Valley (which, though the most dramatic and dangerous phase of the battle, had probably less effect upon the final result than the other two); the breakdown of the attack by the 5th Mounted Brigade against the rear of the main Turkish position; the fact that the 'Ain es Sir track had been made fit for wheels and that the Arabs did not attempt to close it.

With regard to the first there is still some conflict of opinion among experienced officers concerned as to what action the 4th L.H. Brigade should have taken. Had it been ordered to secure the Damiye crossing—or a position effectively covering it—at all costs on the first morning, it might have succeeded in doing so, in which case the enemy's counter-stroke from the crossing would have been prevented and Major-General Hodgson would have had no difficulty in holding Es Salt. This would have been costly, and losses would have been still heavier if a simultaneous attack had been made on Mafid Jozele. If the latter had not been attempted the enemy would still have had this crossing at his disposal, and strong flank protection at Red Hill would have been necessary. Again, had the 4th L.H. Brigade, admittedly in a dangerous situation and faultily disposed on the evening of the 30th April, been reinforced, the local disaster of the following morning would not have occurred; but the striking force would have been weakened. The third alternative would have been for the 4th L.H. Brigade to have withdrawn some distance down the centre of the valley as soon as the 3rd L.H. Brigade had reached the plateau. This would, of course, have left both the Damiye crossing and the Damiye track open to the enemy; but possibly a regiment might have been left to hold the track, to withdraw up it if the enemy advanced, and to dispute his progress towards Es Salt. At the worst this regiment could always have fallen back to the heights west of Es Salt and joined Major-General Hodgson—who would have been glad enough to see it—but it would have had a good

## A CONSIDERATION OF THE ACTION 391

prospect of preventing the Turks from reaching the plateau. On the whole, this last would seem to be the most promising of the three suggestions.

As affairs turned out, the British were more fortunate than they knew, for a whole Turkish regiment of the *24th Division* crossed at Mafid Jozele to take part in the counter-attack, but was straightway withdrawn and marched up to Jisr ed Damiye—and eventually to Es Salt—thus being completely wasted for over twenty-four hours.[1]

The attack of the 5th Mounted Brigade gave the enemy a serious fright, for he had few troops with which to meet it. Major-General Hodgson, reporting on this affair, stated that in his opinion, considering the strongly-worded orders received by the brigade, its reserves should have been pushed in to the last man. He added, however, that in view of the strength of the enemy's position and the fatigue of the attacking troops, it was probable that heavy casualties would have been incurred and no greater success achieved if the attack had been harder pressed. It is to be noted that Br.-General Ryrie, before his brigade was withdrawn, agreed with Br.-General Kelly that the capture of the Turkish position above the Huweij bridge was an impossibility.

Had the Arabs at Madeba cut the 'Ain es Sir track, as they had promised and as they could have done easily enough, the main body of the enemy at Shunet Nimrin would have received neither food nor ammunition, and its resistance must finally have collapsed. According to Turkish accounts they appear to have been bought off; at all events they broke camp and disappeared after action had been joined. Yet, though they might have decided the fate of the battle, the British could not fairly count upon their intervention even when they proffered it of their own accord; for the resolutions of the desert Bedouin are as shifting and unstable as their own sands.

Apart from the dashing and determined work in attack and defence of Br.-General Wilson's 3rd L.H. Brigade and the dogged resistance of the 4th L.H. Brigade after its initial reverse, the brightest aspect of the operation is the skill and coolness with which the troops under Major-

---

[1] See Note at end of Chapter.

General Hodgson's command extricated themselves from a most perilous situation. For the rest, the raid was to have in the months to come a very important effect : to concentrate the attention of the enemy command on the Jordan Valley, and thereby to assist materially the final British offensive.

NOTE.

THE BATTLE FROM GERMAN AND TURKISH SOURCES.

The general course of the battle from the enemy side is given by Liman, while the counter-attack in the Jordan Valley is described in great detail by the German officer who was in command of it.

Confident that the British would soon attempt a fresh raid into Trans-Jordan, Liman ordered the troops which had defended 'Amman (less the German battalion, which moved west of the river to rejoin the *Asia Corps*) to take up a position at Shunet Nimrin to defend the main road to Es Salt. These troops had mostly belonged to the *VIII Corps* on the Lines of Communication, and accordingly the formation was given that title. It was organized in two divisions, and some German and Austrian artillery was handed over to it. Germany's third reinforcement to the Palestine front, of which the infantry consisted of the *146th Regiment*, was now in process of arrival, and one company was attached to the *VIII Corps*. Headquarters of the *Fourth Army*, with Major von Papen of American notoriety as Chief of the Staff, was established at Es Salt. During April the whole of the *3rd Cavalry Division* and the *Caucasus Cavalry Brigade* were concentrated on the west bank of the Jordan near Mafid Jozele under the command of Colonel Essad Bey. The machine-gun detachment of *Pasha II* and the *German 205th Pioneer Company* were also put under his command.

" When first I looked for Essad Bey's camp in the Jordan Valley on " the Roman Road," writes Liman, " I had great difficulty in finding it. " It was extremely cleverly hidden. There was visible no collection of " buildings that looked like a camp. Isolated tents or huts made of " branches such as are constructed by the Bedouin were scattered about " in an irregular fashion, and not a horse was to be seen. On closer " inspection it was discovered that where no nullahs could be found for " them the stables had been sunk below ground-level. Each stable was " surrounded by a sloping hedge of branches, which also afforded pro- " tection from the sun. No aviator could recognize a cavalry camp or " even suspect its existence."

Liman then describes the beginning of the battle, mentioning that the advance of the British mounted troops to Es Salt was a " quite " exceptional " feat, but commenting on the fact that the detachment left in the Jordan Valley made no serious attempt to capture the Jisr ed Damiye crossing. It will be recalled that after the Actions of Tell 'Asur the *24th Division* had been relieved.[1] This division had therefore had seven weeks' rest, and had evidently been given serious training by its German commander Colonel Böhme. It was stationed in the villages of Telfit and Dome, east of the Nablus road, and some of its troops took part in opposing the First Trans-Jordan Raid, returning to Dome imme- diately afterwards. Here the whole division, at the moment consisting of the *2nd* and *143rd Regiments*, a storm battalion and a pioneer com-

---

[1] See p. 327.

# THE TURKISH SIDE

pany,[1] was concentrated on the 29th, having marched from Telfit in the night. This concentration was a piece of great good luck for the enemy, and was due to the fact that Liman had prepared another attack at Musallabe, to be carried out on the 1st or 2nd May. At 8.30 a.m. on the 30th Liman telephoned to the *Seventh Army*, ordering the division to be despatched at once to the Jordan, either to Mafid Jozele or Jisr ed Damiye according to the progress of events. It was then, in conjunction with Essad's cavalry, to cross the river and attack the enemy. Meanwhile the German *205th Pioneer Company* had prevented the British reaching the Mafid Jozele crossing, and a couple of companies of the newly-arrived German *146th Regiment* had repulsed the small detachment of the 4th L.H. Brigade which advanced on that at Jisr ed Damiye.

With Lieut.-Colonel von Falkenhausen, Chief of the Staff of the *Seventh Army*, Colonel Böhme worked out the following plan:—the cavalry was to cross at Jisr ed Damiye, followed by the *143rd Regiment* and the *Storm Battalion*; the *2nd Regiment* was to cross at Mafid Jozele and attack the British flank. All the German troops were put under Colonel Böhme's orders: the pioneers were to remain at Mafid Jozele, while the two companies of the *146th* and the machine-gun detachment crossed at Jisr ed Damiye. This really excellent plan was frustrated, to the good fortune of the British. At 1 a.m. on the 1st May came a telephonic order from the *Seventh Army* that the whole force should cross at Jisr ed Damiye. Colonel Böhme was in a quandary, for the *2nd Regiment* had made a most arduous march on the 30th, and was already on the east bank at Mafid Jozele. He decided to obey the order, withdrew the *2nd Regiment* across the river, set it to march to Jisr ed Damiye, and himself galloped to that point, where he found the force had crossed at 4 a.m.

Orders were then issued for the attack. The *3rd Cavalry Division* was to turn the enemy's right and afterwards march on Es Salt. The infantry was to attack in the valley. The Turkish *143rd Regiment* was disposed in first line, the *Storm Battalion* in second, one German company and a machine-gun company echeloned to the left rear, the other German company in reserve. The last-named was shortly afterwards handed over to Essad Bey. The horse-artillery battery of the *3rd Cavalry Division* was exchanged for a mountain battery and put under Colonel Böhme's orders. The advance was carried out " as though on the parade ground " —as indeed the Australians who saw it bear witness. Red Hill appears to have been captured by the German pioneers from Mafid Jozele. The rest of the action in the Jordan Valley need not be described, as Colonel Böhme's account [2] agrees with that given from the British side. It need only be added that the *2nd Regiment* when it crossed was put under Essad Bey's command and marched on Es Salt; and that during the following days the detachment under Colonel Böhme was reinforced by three Turkish battalions (of the *32nd*, *50th*, and *58th Regiments*) from over Jordan. Essad himself was wounded near Es Salt, and the German chroniclers suggest that the loss of this energetic officer had some effect on the fighting in that quarter.

For the rest of the battle Liman's account is the only one available. There were apparently only a few Turkish companies in Es Salt, protecting the headquarters of the *Fourth Army*; and Jemal was hard put to it to make his escape. Liman gave orders that all troops in course of transport and any others available should be sent by rail to 'Amman, and instructed Jemal to assemble them at Suweile for a subsequent advance on Es Salt.

---

[1] Its artillery was apparently in line.
[2] " Sinai," Böhme, ii, pp. 91–104.

Liman describes the 2nd May as a critical day. The right wing of the *VIII Corps* lost ground at El Haud, while its rear was threatened by the advance of the British cavalry down the main road from Es Salt. However, Jemal had now collected a considerable force, including a German howitzer battery, at Suweile, so that Es Salt was being attacked from east and north-west. On the 3rd the troops under Colonel Böhme were so exhausted that they were unable to carry out Liman's orders to capture the Umm esh Shert track in the valley and thus completely cut off the British forces in the hills.

It has been suggested that the enemy command committed an error of judgment in despatching the *3rd Cavalry Division* towards Es Salt, instead of using all the troops available to drive the British headlong down the Jordan Valley and thus isolate the town. To that it may be replied that but for the attack made by Essad Bey from the Damiye track Major-General Hodgson would have had the bulk of his troops available to force his way down the main road and take the *VIII Corps* in rear. There were two keys, not one only, to the situation, as Liman rightly divined : Es Salt itself, and the British flank guard in the Jordan Valley. The move which was most unhappy from the Turkish point of view was the withdrawal of the *2nd Regiment* from Mafid Jozele, where the admirably designed plan of Colonel Böhme and Lieut.-Colonel von Falkenhausen had placed it. The intervention of this regiment on the morning of the 1st might have had great results, considering how important a success was won without it. As it was the formation was practically wasted.

The Turkish Historical Section gives the casualties of the *VIII Corps* as 831, and states that "those of the troops which crossed at Jisr ed " Damiye were said to have been as much as 50 per cent." This appears to apply only to Colonel Böhme's detachment, which had a fighting strength of about 1,600, but it seems safe to conclude that the total casualties of the enemy exceeded 2,000.

# PLACE-NAMES—PALESTINE AND SYRIA.

**CONTENTS.**

1. Meanings of some place-names in PALESTINE and SYRIA.
2. Glossary of some terms found in components of place-names (Arab and Hebrew) on the maps of EGYPT, SINAI, PALESTINE, and SYRIA.
3. Comparative sizes (Palestine and England & Wales).
4. Some of the more important dates in the history of the HOLY LAND.

Note.—The lists of place-names and of components of place-names, mentioned above, have been compiled from the name-lists given in the "Survey of Western and of Eastern Palestine," issued by the Palestine Exploration Fund, as well as from "The Historical Geography of the Holy Land," by Sir George Adam Smith, and from numerous other books.

The names have been checked with those given in the lists issued by the Permanent Committee on Geographical Names, and the thanks of the Compilers are especially due to the Director-General of the Survey of Egypt for checking a list that was submitted to him.

## ABBREVIATIONS.

| | | | | |
|---|---|---|---|---|
| Ar. | = Arabic. | | abb. | = abbreviated. |
| Bib. | = Biblical. | | dim. | = diminutive. |
| Gr. | = Greek. | | fem. | = feminine. |
| Heb. | = Hebrew. | | masc. | = masculine. |
| Lat. | = Latin. | | pl. | = plural. |
| Pal. | = Palestine. | | pr. | = pronounced. |
| conv. | = conventional. | | prop. | = properly. |

# MEANINGS OF SOME PLACE-NAMES IN PALESTINE AND SYRIA.

| | |
|---|---|
| 'Adase, Khirbet | = The ruin of lentils. |
| Afranj, Wadi el | = Valley of the Franks. |
| 'Aneize, Jebel | = Mountain of the he-goat. |
| 'Aqaba | = Ascent, Pass. |
| 'Araba | = Desert. |
| Ariel | = The Lion of God. |
| 'Arish, Wadi el | = River of Egypt. |
| | |
| Bab el 'Amud | = Gate of the pillars (Damascus gate). |
| Bab es Silsile | = Gate of the chain. |
| Bahr el Kebir | = The Great Sea. |
| Bahret Lut | = Lot's Sea (Dead Sea). |
| Basse el Hindi | = Marsh of the Indian. |
| Bethany | = House of song. |
| Bethel (Ar. Beitin) | = House of God. |
| Bethesda | = House of mercy. |
| Bethlehem | = House of bread. |
| Bethphage | = House of figs. |
| Bethsaida | = House of fruits. |
| Beith Shean (Ar. Beisan) | = House of security and tranquillity. |
| Bir es Sabe (Beersheba) | = The meaning is uncertain. It may be the "Well of the Oath," or "the seven wells." But it is also possible that the "seven" in Bir es Sabe, "Well of seven," may be a Divine title, representing an aspect of the Moon-God and referring to one quarter, or the seven-day week (vide Hebron). |
| Butmet Halhul | = Prince's terebinth. |
| | |
| Cana | = Zeal. |
| Canaan | = Sunken or low land. |
| Capernaum (Heb. Kefar Nahum) | = Village of Nahum. |
| Carmel | = The garden or park. |
| | |
| Damascus (Ar. Dimishq, or Esh Sham) | = See Sham, Esh. |
| Deir, Ed | = The monastery. |
| Dothan | = The two wells. |

# PLACE-NAMES

| | |
|---|---|
| Ephraim (Ephrata) | = Fruitful. |
| Eyub, Bir | = Well of Job. |

| | |
|---|---|
| Gadara | = Surrounded or fenced. |
| Galilee | = The ring. (Galil=anything that rolls or is round.) |
| Gaza | = Gr. form of the Heb. 'Azzah (Fortress). |
| Ghor, El | = The depression or rift. |
| Gibeon | = Hill. |
| Gihon | = Gusher. |

| | |
|---|---|
| Haram Esh Sherif | = The Noble Sanctuary. |
| Har-Megeddon | = The Mountain of Megiddo. |
| Hauran | = Hollow. |
| Hebron | = The modern El Khalil, "the friend," an abbreviation of "Town of the friend of God" (the Mohammedan title for Abraham). But in Judges i, 10, it is stated that the name of Hebron was formerly "Qiryath-arba," which means "City of Four." In this case the "Four" like the "seven" in Bir es Sabe, may be a Divine title, representing an aspect of the Moon-God and referring to the four phases of the moon (vide Bir es Sabe). |
| Hejaz | = Barrier. |
| Hijla, Makhadet | = The ford of the partridge. |

| | |
|---|---|
| 'Iraq el Menshiye | = The cliff of the place of growth (possibly the site of ancient Gath). |
| 'Ir Hak-Kodesh | = The Holy City. |

| | |
|---|---|
| Jaffa (Heb. Yafo, Lat. Joppe (Conv. Joppa). | = The name is of doubtful meaning, but it is usually considered to signify " the beautiful." |
| Jemmal, Kufr | = Village of the camel-driver. |
| Jericho (Ar. Eriha) | = The city of palm-trees. |
| Jerusalem (Heb. Yĕrûshâlēm) | = City of peace ; place of safety. |
| (Ar. El Quds) | = The Holy Place. The Sanctuary. |
| Jeshimon | = Devastation (Wilderness of Judæa). |
| Jidda | = Grandmother. |
| Jil'ad, Jebel | = Mount Gilead. |
| Jisr Benat Yakub | = Bridge of the daughters of Jacob. |
| Jordan | = Swiftly descending, or down-comer. |

# PLACE-NAMES

| | |
|---|---|
| Kerak, El | = Corruption of Syriac Karko = Fortress. |
| Khalil, El | = (City of) the friend (of God) (vide Hebron). |
| Kidron | = Making sad. |
| | |
| Lajjun, El | = Arabic corruption of Latin Legio = The Legion. |
| Lebanon | = The White (mountain). |
| Leja, El | = The refuge; asylum. |
| Lisan, El | = The tongue. |
| Lut, Bahret | = Lot's Sea (Dead Sea). |
| | |
| Mahraqa, El | = The burning. |
| Mariam, 'Ain Sitti | = Fountain of Our Lady Mary. (The Virgin's Spring.) |
| Megeddon, Har- | = The mountain of Megiddo. |
| Muntar, El | = The watch-tower. |
| Muqaddas, El | = The Holy. |
| Muqatta', Nahr el (R. Kishon) | = River of the ford or shallow. |
| Mutesellim, Tell el | = The mound of the Governor. |
| | |
| Nabi Samweil, En | = The Prophet Samuel. |
| Nablus (Shechem) | = Corruption of Neapolis, the name given to it by Vespasian. |
| Nain | = Beauty. |
| Nar, Wadi en | = The fire wadi. |
| Nazareth | = Sanctified. |
| | |
| Ophel | = Lump; swelling. |
| | |
| Palestine | = Philistina. |
| Peræa | = (Land) on the other side of (Jordan). |
| | |
| Qatra | = A drop. (Possibly the site of Ekron.) |
| Qubbet es Sakhra | = Dome of the Rock. |
| Quds, El (Jerusalem) | = The Holy Place. |
| | |
| Rabbat | = Chief town; capital. |
| Rama | = Eminence. |

# PLACE-NAMES

| | |
|---|---|
| Salib, Deir es | = Monastery of the Cross. |
| Sha'ir, Wadi esh | = The vale of barley. |
| Sham, Esh | = The land-of-the-left-hand ; the north-west country, or Syria. |
| Sharon | = Smooth. |
| Shechem (Nablus) | = Back. |
| Sheikh Kudr | = St. George. |
| Shephelah | = The low-hills ; the low-lands. |
| Sheria, Wadi esh | = The valley of the watering-place. |
| Sherif (pl. Ashraf) | = A descendant in the male line from the Khalif Ali (656–661 A.D.), and his wife Fatima, daughter of the Prophet Mohammed. |
| Shomron (Heb.), (Samaria) | = Watch-tower. |
| Sion | = Fortress. |
| Syria (Ar. Suriya or Sham, Heb. Aram) | = See Sham, Esh. |
| Taiyibe, Et | = The good, sweet, or wholesome (water or land). |
| Tell es Safi (Blanche Garde) | = The shining mound. |
| Tire, Et | = The fortress. |
| Usdum, Jebel | = Salt Mountain. |
| 'Uyun Musa | = Springs of Moses. |
| Ye'or (Heb.) | = The Nile. |
| Zarqa, Nahr ez | = The Blue River. |

# GLOSSARY OF SOME TERMS FOUND IN COMPONENTS OF PLACE-NAMES (ARAB AND HEBREW) ON THE MAPS OF EGYPT, SINAI, PALESTINE, AND SYRIA.

| | |
|---|---|
| Abar (pl. of Bir) | = Wells. |
| 'Abarah | = Ferry, Crossing, Ford. |
| 'Abd | = Slave (Negro), Servitor. |
| Abel (Heb.) | = A meadow. |
| Abu | = Father (of) ; often=possessor (of). |
| Abyad (fem. Baida) | = White. |
| Ahmar (fem. Hamra) | = Red. |
| 'Ain (pl. 'Uyun) | = Spring. |
| Akbar | = Greater (from Kebir=great). |
| Akbar, El | = Greatest. |
| Akhdar (fem. Khadra) | = Green. |
| Akwam (pl. of Kom) | = Mounds. |
| 'Alam, 'Allem, 'Alim | = Cairn, Hill-summit, Monument, Prominence. |
| 'Alawi | = Height. |
| 'Araba | = Desert |
| Ard, El | = The earth. |
| Ard (h) | = Ground, Valley. |
| Ardi | = Earthen. |
| Areidj | = Sand-belt or barrier. |
| 'Arid | = Broad. |
| 'Arqub | = Rocky spur, Ridge. |
| Asfar (fem. Safra) | = Yellow. |
| Ashtum | = Strait. |
| Aswad (fem. Soda) | = Black. |
| 'Atshan | = Thirsty (of a wadi="without wells"). |
| 'Auja (masc, 'Awaj) | = Crooked. |
| Aulad (pl. of Walad) | = Children (of), Tribe. |
| Aulon (Gr.) | = Hollow. |
| Azraq (fem. Zarqa) | = Blue (in E. Desert of Egypt=dark). |
| | |
| Ba'al | = Lord. |
| Bab (pl. Biban) | = Gateway, door ; Strait. |
| Bahari | = North. |
| Bahr | = Sea, or large river. |
| Bahra-t, Bahret | = Low-lying ground, Marsh. |
| Baida (fem. of Abyad) | = White. |
| Balad | = Village, Town. |
| Ballut | = Tree (A species of oak). |
| Bar(r) | = Land, shore, bank. |
| Basse | = Marsh. |
| Basta | = Tower. |
| Batn | = Depression, hollow. |
| Beit (pl. Buyut), (Heb. Beith) | = House, tent, or dwelling. |
| Benet (pl. Benat) | = Daughter |
| Beni, Bani (pl. of Ibn) | = Sons (of) ; Tribe. |
| Bir (pl. Abar, Byar) | = Well, tank, rock-cistern. |

# GLOSSARY vii

| | |
|---|---|
| Birka-t, Birket | = Pool, lake, or pond. |
| Boghaz, Bughaz | = Strait, or Narrow Pass. |
| Borg, Burg, Burj (dim. Bureij) | = Tower, Watch-tower. |
| Buq'a-t (Heb. Bikah) | = Low ground with water. |
| Bustan | = Garden. |
| Buz | = Cape. |
| | |
| Chanaq | = Defile. |
| | |
| Dahr, Zahr | = Back ; Eminence ; Promontory. |
| Daiyiq | = Narrow. |
| Dan (Heb.) | = Judge. |
| Dar | = House. |
| Darb | = Road, or track. |
| Dawar, Duwwar | = House. |
| Deir (pl. Diyura) | = Monastery. |
| Dhahret | = Ridge, or spur. |
| Dirra-t | = Nipple. |
| Diwan | = A tribunal of revenue or of justice ; a council of state, etc. |
| | |
| El (Ar.) (Also Ed, Edh, En, Er, Es, Esh, Et, Eth, Ez) | = The. |
| El (Heb.) | = God. |
| 'Egiret, 'Ujra-t | = Knoll, or small hill. |
| 'Elwa-t | = Rising ground. |
| 'Eqeida-t, 'Aqida-t | = Sandhill. |
| 'Ezba-t, 'Ezbet | = Hamlet, village. |
| | |
| Farsh | = Plain. |
| Feik (pl. Fuleidj) | = Sand-dune forming large horse-shoe hollow in sand-bed. |
| Fisr (pl. Fizar) | = Pass ; defile. |
| Foqani | = Upper. |
| Ful (fem. Fula-t) | = Bean. |
| Fumm | = Mouth. |
| | |
| Gabr (pr. Qabr) | = Grave. |
| Gai (Heb.) | = Ravine ; a hollow ; a glen ; a valley without a winter brook. |
| Gara-t, Qaret | = Hill ; Bluff. |
| Garf, Jarf (pl. Jarfan) | = Bank of a watercourse ; Cliff. |
| Gebel (Egyptian Maps) | = Mountain. |
| Gedid, Jedid (fem. Jedida) | = New. |
| Gezira-t, Jeziret (pl. Gazair) | = Island ; Peninsula. |
| Ghadir | = Pool, Pond ; Temporary water-pan. |
| Gharbi, Gharbiye | = West. |
| Ghard (pl. Ghurud) | = A sand-dune. |
| Gharraqa-t | = Occasional water. |
| Ghor (dim. Ghuweir) | = Depression ; Valley. |
| Ghubba-t | = Gulf ; Bay. |

# GLOSSARY

| | |
|---|---|
| Gisr, Jisr | = Embankment; Causeway; Bridge. |
| Gor, Qor, Qur (pl. of Qarat) | = Hills. |
| Goz, Qoz (pl. Qowuz, Qizan) | = High sand-dune. |
| Gushalab | = Fat soil. |

| | |
|---|---|
| Hagar (prop. Hajar) | = A stone. |
| Haggag (pr. Haqqaq) | = A mountain range. |
| Hajara-t | = Stony plain. |
| Hajj (pl. Hajjaj) | = Pilgrim. |
| Halq | = A watercourse. |
| Hamad | = Hard barren desert. |
| Hamra (fem. of Ahmar) | = Red. |
| Haqfa | = A well. |
| Haraba-t | = Rock-cut water-cistern. |
| Harra-t | = Lava-flow; Volcanic debris. |
| Hatia-t | = Grazing ground; a plain surrounded by heights, and containing much vegetation. |
| Hazm, Hazam | = Rough elevated ground. |
| Hirsh | = Wood. |
| Hod | = Depression in sand, full of palms. |
| Hosn, Hisn | = Fortress. |

| | |
|---|---|
| Ibn (pl. Beni, Bani) | = Son (of). |
| 'Iraq | = Cliff. |

| | |
|---|---|
| Jarf, Garf (pl. Ajraf, Jarfan) | = Bank of a watercourse; Cliff. |
| Jebel, Gebel | = Mountain. |
| Jeziret, Gezira-t (pl. Gazair) | = Island; Peninsula. |
| Jisr, Gisr | = Embankment; Causeway; Bridge. |
| Jubb | = Deep hole; pit. |
| Juhr (dim. Juheir) | = Hole; burrow. |
| Jun | = Bay. |

| | |
|---|---|
| Kaa(r) | = Hollow where rain-water collects. |
| Kanan | = Ridge, or spur. |
| Karm (dim. Kareim) | = Artificial mound; Vineyard. |
| Kathib (pl. Kathaiib, Kutban) | = Moving sand-dune or sand-hill. |
| Kebir (fem. Kubra) | = Great, large. |
| Khabra-t | = Flooded area; hollow where rain-water collects. |
| Khadra (fem. of Akhdar) | = Green. |
| Khalig, Khalij | = Channel; watercourse; arm of the sea. |
| Khan | = Inn, Caravanserai. |
| Khartum | = Spur of a hill; sand-spit (lit. snout). |
| Khashm | = Snout; promontory. |
| Khirbet, Khirbetha | = Ruins. |
| Khor (pl. Kheiran) | = Ravine, generally dry. |
| Khubb (pl. Khubub) | = Low ground. |

# GLOSSARY

| | |
|---|---|
| Kidwa-t | = Small mound. |
| Kol, Kulet | = Small hill. |
| Kom (pl. Kiman, Akwam) | = Isolated hill ; mound. |
| Kufr (Ar.) (pl. Kufur), (Heb. Kefar) | = Village. |
| | |
| Leja | = Retreat ; refuge. |
| Lugga-t | = Open sea ; small bay. |
| | |
| Ma'abar | = Ford. |
| Ma'adiya-t (pl. Ma'adi) | = Ferry. |
| Mafraq | = Road-fork. |
| Maghara-t | = Cave, cavern. |
| Mahatta-t | = Station, or Halt. |
| Maidan, Meidan | = Open space ; plain. |
| Makhadet | = Ford. |
| Mallaha-t, Mellaha-t | = Salt-lake, or flat ; salt-pan. |
| Mandara-t (dim. Mineidra-t) | = Look-out place ; isolated hill ; watch-tower. |
| Maqta' | = Strait ; artificial channel. |
| Marj (pl. Murnuj) | = A meadow. |
| Marsa, Mersa | = Harbour ; anchorage. |
| Mashash (pl. Umshash) | = Well, water-hole. |
| Masrab | = Camel-road. |
| Mastaba-t | = Platform in front of a house, or in a garden. |
| Ma'tan, Ma'aten | = Place where beasts rest near a well. |
| Medina-t | = City. |
| Melek, Maliq (Bib. Moloch) | = King. |
| Mezra' | = Cultivated area. |
| Mina, Minet | = Harbour. |
| Minim | = Sorcerers (early Christians). |
| Minqar, Mongar | = Headland, bluff (lit. beak). |
| Mishor (Heb.) | = Plain, plateau, level. |
| Mitla' | = Rising ground, ascent. |
| Moiya-t | = Water (a little), watering-place. |
| Muqatta' | = Ford. |
| Mustawi | = Level. |
| | |
| Naba (dim. Nuweiba-t) | = Spring. |
| Nabi | = Prophet. |
| Nahal | = Watercourse ; a valley with a winter brook. |
| Nagb, Naqb, Neqb (pl. Nuqub) (dim. Enqeib) | = Mountain pass ; steep camel-track. |
| Nahr | = River. |
| Naqo (pl. Anqu) | = Depression where water collects. |
| Nefud | = Continuous area of deep sand. |
| Negeb (Heb.) | = Dry, parched land. |
| Nezle, Nezlet | = Hamlet, Settlement. |
| Niswet | = Mound marking old cistern ; Mark. |
| Nizwa | = A height. |
| Nuqra-t | = Low ground, Depression (cultivated). |

# GLOSSARY

| | |
|---|---|
| Olwet | = A height. |
| Ophel | = Lump, Swelling. |
| | |
| Qa' | = Plain. |
| Qabr, Gabr (pl. Qubur) | = Grave. |
| Qadi | = Judge. |
| Qadim (fem. Qadima) | = Old. |
| Qal'a-t | = Castle, Citadel. |
| Qalt (pl. Qalut) | = Artificial reservoir; natural rock-basin. |
| Qantara-t | = Bridge. |
| Qarya-t, Qaryet (dim. Qreiya-t) (Heb. Qiryath) | = Village; Ruins (in Egypt). |
| Qasab | = Reeds; Sugar-cane |
| Qasr, Qoseir (dim. Quseir) | = Fortress; Palace. |
| Qattar, Qattara-t | = Dripping well. |
| Qibli (fem. Qibliya) | = South. |
| Qubba-t, Qubbet (Qubeibe, dim.) | = Dome. |
| Quleib | = Unlined well. |
| Qurn | = Horn or peak. |
| | |
| Ramle | = Sandy plain. |
| Ras (dim. Ruweis) | = Headland, cape; top, summit; prominent hill. |
| Rayah | = Main canal. |
| Rayan | = Containing wells (lit. Not thirsty). |
| Resm | = Outline of ruins in the earth. |
| Rijm, Rujm | = Cairn, heap of stones. |
| Rod, Raud (pl. Riyad) | = Small valley. |
| | |
| Sabakha, Sabkhet | = Salt-lake, salt-marsh. |
| Safra (fem. of Asfar) | = Yellow. |
| Sahl | = Plain. |
| Sani (pl. Sawani), Saniya-t | = Deep well. |
| Sath | = Plateau. |
| Sawana-t | = Flinty plain; gravel mound. |
| Sebil | = Fountain. |
| Seil | = Torrent; Watercourse. |
| Sha'ib, Shu'eib (pl. Shuub) | = Small dry watercourse. |
| Shaluf, Shalufa-t | = Bluff. |
| Sharqi (fem. Sharqiya, Pal. Sherqiye) | = East. |
| Shatt | = River-bank, Landing-place; River. |
| Sheikh (abb. Sh.) | = Chief, Elder; Saint. |
| Shejeret, Shagara-t | = Tree. |
| Shellal | = Cataract, waterfall. |
| Sherm | = Creek, Harbour. |
| Sidi | = Master, Saint. |
| Sikka-t | = Road. |
| Siq | = Gorge. |
| Soda (fem. of Aswad) | = Black. |
| Suafir | = Sapphire. |
| Sughair (fem. Sughaiyira), Saghir | = Small. |

# GLOSSARY

| | |
|---|---|
| Tabia-t | = Fort. |
| Tahtani | = Lower. |
| Tal'a-t | = Ascent, rising ground. |
| Tantura | = Peak. |
| Tarbul | = Isolated hill. |
| Tariches (Gr.) | = Pickling places. |
| Tell (pl. Tulul, dim. Tuleil [Ar.]) (Heb. Tel) | = Mound (especially covering ruins). |
| Thamila-t (pl. Themail) | = Water-hole in wadi bed |
| Thelma-t | = Cleft ; Short cut. |
| Tuus | = High single dune or dunes. |

| | |
|---|---|
| 'Ubb | = Depression. |
| 'Ujra-t, 'Egiret | = Knoll, Small hill. |
| Um, Umm | = Mother (of). |
| Umshash (pl. of Mashash) | = Water-holes. |
| 'Uyun (pl. of 'Ain) | = Springs. |

| | |
|---|---|
| Wa'ar (Ar.), Trachon (Gr.) | = Rough, difficult, steep, or stony tract. |
| Wadi (pl. Widyan) | = Watercourse (normally dry). |
| Wah (pl. Wahat) | = Oasis. |
| Walad (pl. Aulad) | = Son. |
| Wely | = A saint. |

| | |
|---|---|
| Zarqa (fem. of Azraq) | = Blue. |
| Zawia-t, Zawiet | = Hamlet ; Senussi religious centre and school. |

## COMPASS POINTS.

| | |
|---|---|
| North | = Bahari, Shimal, (Pal. Shemaliye). |
| South | = Qibli, Qibliya, Ganub. |
| East | = Sharqi, Sharqiya, (Pal. Sherqiye). |
| West | = Gharbi, Gharbiye. |

## COLOURS.

| | |
|---|---|
| Blue | = Azraq (fem. Zarqa). |
| Black | = Aswad (fem. Soda). |
| Brown | = Asmar. |
| Green | = Akhdar (fem. Khadra). |
| Purple | = Argowani. |
| Red | = Ahmar (fem. Hamra). |
| White | = Abyad (fem. Baida). |
| Yellow | = Asfar (fem. Safra). |
| Colour | = Lon (pl. Alwan). |

# SOME OF THE MORE IMPORTANT DATES

B.C.

| | | |
|---|---|---|
| Earliest migration of Israel's ancestors from Harran to Canaan | Circa | B.C. 2,100 |
| Jacob tribes in Canaan; place-name Jacob-el mentioned by Thothmes III (XVIII Dynasty) who reigned | ,, | 1,501–1,447 |
| Oppression of Israelites in Egypt by Rameses II (XIX Dynasty) who reigned | ,, | 1,292–1,225 |
| Exodus of Israelites under Merenptah (XIX Dynasty) who reigned | ,, | 1,225–1,215 |
| Invasion of Canaan under Joshua | | Soon after 1,200 |

## THE UNITED KINGDOM.

| | | |
|---|---|---|
| Saul, anointed King | Circa | 1,020 |
| David, King | ,, | 1,000 |
| Solomon, King | ,, | 970 |
| The building of the Temple | ,, | 970 |
| Rehoboam becomes King | ,, | 935 |
| Disruption of the Kingdom | ,, | 933 |
| Shoshenk I of Egypt (XXII Dynasty) invaded Palestine | ,, | 930 |

## THE DIVIDED KINGDOM.

| | | |
|---|---|---|
| Northern Israel (Capital—Shechem, then Samaria) | ,, | 933–721 |
| Battle of Karkar | ,, | 854 |
| Judah (Capital Jerusalem) | ,, | 933–587 |
| Hezekiah (King of Judah) | ,, | 727–685 |
| Tiglath Pileser III of Assyria took Damascus | | 732 |
| Sargon captured Samaria after a three-years' siege | | 721 |
| Northern Israel falls | | 721 |
| Fall of Nineveh and rise of Babylon | | 612 |
| First Great Captivity of Jerusalem | | 597 |
| Second Great Captivity of Jerusalem | | 587 |
| Cyrus captures Babylon (Rise of Persia) | | 538 |
| Return of the Jews from exile | | 536 |
| The Temple rebuilt | | 515 |
| Alexander the Great in Syria | | 332 |
| Palestine conquered by Ptolemy, B.C. 312, and Egyptian domination | | 301–203 |
| The Maccabees | | 166–135 |
| John Hyrcanus | | 135–105 |
| Pompey enters Jerusalem (Roman Province of Syria) | | 63 |
| Herod the Great | | B.C. 37–4 A.D. |

# IN THE HISTORY OF THE HOLY LAND.

| | A.D. |
|---|---|
| Death of Herod the Great | 4 |
| The Kingdom divided between :— | |
| Archelaus, Herod Antipas, and Philip | 4 |
| Judæa under Roman procurator | 6 |
| Tiberius, Emperor of Rome | 14 |
| Pontius Pilate, Procurator of Judæa | 25 or 26 |
| Marcellus, Procurator of Judæa | 35 or 36 |
| Jewish rebellion against Rome | 66 |
| Siege of Jerusalem by Titus | 70 |
| Trajan forms Roman province of Arabia | 106 |
| Final overthrow of the Jews by Hadrian | 135 |
| Constantine the Great | 325–336 |
| Birth of Mohammed | 569 |
| El Hijra (The Flight) | 622 |
| Death of Mohammed | 632 |
| Moslem conquest of Syria | 634–638 |
| Invasion of Turks | 1,070–1,085 |
| First Crusade | 1,097 |
| Jerusalem stormed by the Crusaders, and Latin Kingdom of Jerusalem set up under Godfrey of Bouillon | 1,099 |
| Saladin's victory at the Horns of Hattin | 1,187 |
| Fall of Jerusalem | 1,187 |
| Third Crusade [Richard Cœur de Lion] | 1,191 |
| Latin Kingdom of Jerusalem finally lost | 1,291 |
| Napoleon in Syria | 1,799 |
| Invasion of Palestine and Syria by E.E.F. :— | |
| Gaza–Beersheba–Jerusalem | 1,917 |
| Jerusalem–Damascus–Aleppo | 1,918 |

## COMPARATIVE SIZES.

| PALESTINE. | | | ENGLAND AND WALES. | |
|---|---|---|---|---|
| *Miles.* | *Sq. miles.* | | *Miles.* | *Sq. miles.* |
| Length, 140 <br> Breadth, 25 to 80 } Approx. 6,040 | | | Max. Length, 425 <br> Max. Breadth 365 } Approx. 58,600 | |
| TRANS-JORDAN. <br> (Hermon–R. Arnon) ,, 3,800 | | | ENGLAND alone is  .. 50,800 | |
| JUDÆA with Shephelah and Plain } ,, 2,000 | | | DEVON .. .. .. 2,015 <br> NORTHUMBERLAND .. 2,015 <br> NORFOLK.. .. .. 2,017 | |
| JUDÆA apart from Shephelah and Plain (length 55 miles, breadth 25 miles, about half desert) } ,, 1,350 | | | ESSEX .. .. .. 1,413 | |
| SAMARIA .. .. .. 1,400 | | | KENT .. .. .. 1,515 | |
| GALILEE .. .. .. 1,600 | | | SOMERSET .. .. 1,659 | |